Consolidated B-32 Dominator

Consolidated B-32
Dominator

The Ultimate Look:

From Drawing Board to Scrapyard

William Wolf

Schiffer Military History
Atglen, PA

Published by Schiffer Publishing Ltd.
4880 Lower Valley Road
Atglen, PA 19310
Phone: (610) 593-1777
FAX: (610) 593-2002
E-mail: Info@schifferbooks.com.
Visit our web site at: www.schifferbooks.com
Please write for a free catalog.
This book may be purchased from the publisher.
Please include $3.95 postage.
Try your bookstore first.

In Europe, Schiffer books are distributed by:
Bushwood Books
6 Marksbury Avenue
Kew Gardens
Surrey TW9 4JF, England
Phone: 44 (0) 20 8392-8585
FAX: 44 (0) 20 8392-9876
E-mail: Info@bushwoodbooks.co.uk.
Visit our website at: www.bushwoodbooks.co.uk
Free postage in the UK. Europe: air mail at cost.
Try your bookstore first.

Contents

Acknowledgments

My lifelong hobby has been WWII aerial combat, and over the past 35 years I have collected over 15,000 books and magazines, along with hundreds of reels of microfilm on the subject. I probably have nearly every book written on WWII aviation, and complete collections of every aviation magazine published since 1939. Also included in my collection are many hundreds of aviation unit and pilots' histories, crew manuals, as well as aircraft technical, structural, and maintenance manuals. My microfilm collection includes vintage intelligence reports, USAF, USN, and USMC group and squadron histories, complete Japanese Monograph series, and U.S. Strategic Bombing Surveys, as well as USAF Historical Studies. Over the years I have been fortunate to meet many fighter aces, other pilots, and fellow aviation buffs who have shared stories, material, and photographs with me (I have over 5,000 photos of fighter aces alone). I have made many multi-day expeditions to various military libraries, museums, and photo depositories with my copy machine and camera, accumulating literally reams and reams of information and 1,000s of photographs. I also had a photo darkroom, where I developed 1,000s of rare photos from microfilm negatives. Over the past six years, in particular, I have made a concerted effort to utilize this information, and have had five books on World War II air combat published by Schiffer Publishing Ltd. (*see* book bibliography at the end of this book). Like my previous book on the B-29 that is the companion volume to this book, I have always intended to write a book on the B-32, and for many years I have collected material and photographs for this project.

Special thanks goes to R.T. "Lindy" LeVine and William "Bill" Chana, both of whom were flight engineers during XB-32 and production B-32 testing. Mr. LeVine initially sent me a volume of information, along with numerous photos and personal reflections. He also was sent overseas with the B-32, and provided a wealth of information and photos on that unknown phase of B-32 history. After I began my manuscript I had many questions that I posed to him, and his response was many handwritten pages of valuable information. Bill Chana was of great assistance, providing documents, photos, and access to his autobiography *Over the Wing*. Thanks also to David Dembeck, who took time from a busy teaching schedule to scan many photos from his collection, and photocopy information he had gathered over the years. To Raymond Stine, who sent a large number of photos he collected from Consolidated and the USAAF.

Scott Marchand, curator of the Pima Air & Space Museum, and Kate DeMeester, archivist of that museum, who were of invaluable help in aiding in photographing the museum's B-29 *Sentimental Journey*, and gathering and copying the B-29 aircraft and crew manuals for my B-29 book, were also of great help in gathering technical information and many photo-

Author's library

graphs of the B-32. Through them I was able to make this book into the detailed, ultimate book on the B-32.

A belated large thank you goes to Judy Endicott of the Albert F. Simpson Historical Research Center, Maxwell AFB, Alabama. Ms. Endicott was of great help during my 10 day expedition to that facility in the mid-1980s to collect photos, hardcopy, and microfilm on fighter aces and aircraft (especially fighter aircraft and the B-29 and B-32), and many other topics that I hope to write about in future projects. Thanks also go to the personnel at the Air Force Museum Archives at Wright-Patterson, Dayton, Ohio, and those at the Ferndale Photographic facility, Washington, DC, who aided me during my visits there. Thanks to the personnel at the USAF Archives for their help in procuring microfilm reports on the 312th BG, 386th BS, and testing the B-32.

Among the others to be acknowledged are: Robert Kirk for his insights on flying the B-32; Harold Johnson for providing information and photos on the post war Walnut Ridge aircraft disposal site; the docents at the Kingman Air Field Museum; Cal James; Norman Malayney; Michael Stowe of ACCIREPORTS; Mort Hans and the Cradle of Aviation Museum for information and photos of the Sperry Remote Gunnery System; and premier Consolidated test pilot Beryl Erickson for his insights.

The author wishes that every person who contributed to his collection over the past quarter century could be specifically mentioned. Over the years the origins of many of the 1,000s of photos I have copied or have been lent to copy, or have personally collected have become obscured. Most are from military and government sources, but many are from private individuals, and I apologize in advance if some of the photos are miscredited. Also, some of the photos are not of the best quality because of their age and sources—especially those copied from microfilm—but were used because of their importance to the book.

Again thanks go to my persevering wife, Nancy, who allows me to spend many hours researching and writing, and patiently (mostly) waits while I browse bookstores and visit air museums, in search of new material and photos. Also, I thank her because her car sits out in the hot Arizona sun as my WWII library luxuriates in the remodeled, air-conditioned three-car garage.

Foreword

Without a doubt author Dr. William Wolf takes WWII aviation history seriously. His earlier book on the Boeing B-29, his two books on the American fighter pilots and aircraft, and the American fighter-bomber in the ETO are examples of his thorough research and dedication that make these books the authoritative works on these subjects. In this book he relates the first *complete* story of the Army Air Force's WWII long-range B-32 heavy bomber that was designed and first built by Consolidated Aircraft in San Diego, CA, and then produced at the company's Fort Worth Texas Division. Thanks to Bill we are finally privileged to walk through the life of the little-known B-32 Dominator from its conception, birth, troubled youth, manhood, days as a warrior, and finally to the sad end of its life.

As a Convair Flight Test Engineer, I was introduced to the B-32 in mid-1942 and became closely involved in its development and testing.

Construction had begun on three XB-32 prototypes, and my assignment was to design and monitor the installation of flight test specific instrumentation for these three aircraft; a challenging assignment for a 20 year old. After 30 test flights in XB-32 No.1, I survived the ship's fatal accident on 10 May 1943. When I returned to flight status in September, I continued my flight testing role in XB-32s No. 2 and No. 3 until it was finally combat qualified.

The reader will find Dr. Wolf's book a fascinating and enlightening study on what was involved to develop a war time heavy bomber, and to phase it into combat at the close of WWII. The story of the trials and tribulations of the B-32's labored development should also be read by young people now entering the world of aerospace, where opportunities are unlimited, and future aircraft and spacecraft development will be the result of their visions and goals.

William F. Chana
President Emeritus
San Diego Aerospace Museum

Preface

During the last year of the war in the Pacific the Boeing B-29 Very Heavy Bomber (VHB) flew for the 20th Air Force, devastating 65 major Japanese cities, destroying 178 square miles of industrial urban areas, killing 330,000, and wounding 476,000 Japanese civilians. The direct civilian casualties caused in the concentrated 10 month B-29 bombing attacks were more than Japanese military forces suffered in three and half years of war. The American media deservedly hyped the B-29 as equal to its nickname, "Superfortress." But lost in the success of the B-29 was the story of the B-32 Dominator, another very heavy bomber that was designed as a backup to the B-29. The B-32 was a very small, and largely unsuccessful part of the hugely successful Consolidated-Vultee aircraft empire, which had designed and manufactured the renowned PBY Catalina flying boat and the prolific B-24 Liberator.

Over the years the B-32 has been described only in a small number of magazine articles and in a booklet, which have generally given a superficial and incomplete record, maligning the bomber as a mediocre design besieged with developmental problems and a lackluster combat record. The intent of this book is to be the definitive description and appraisal of this neglected bomber's development, testing, manufacture, and combat experience using company design and production information, flight and test evaluations, previously unexplored Consolidated-Vultee Erection and Maintenance Manuals, Flight Manuals, personal narratives and combat narratives, and reports from microfilm of original material.

Part One

Reuben Fleet, Consolidated Aircraft, and the B-32 Project

1

The Story of Reuben Fleet
and the Consolidated Aircraft Company

Few aircraft company presidents were as hands on as Reuben Fleet, and the development of his company's legendary PBY Catalina and B-24 Liberator can be traced directly through him. In August 1933 Fleet's contemporary, Bill Boeing, retired at only 51 years old, when his company was on the verge of finally emerging from financial limbo, and within several years of developing the company's signature B-17 and B-29 bombers. The development of the B-32 lays in the chronicle of Reuben Fleet and his management of the Consolidated Aircraft Company.

Reuben Fleet: The Early Years

On 6 March 1887 David and Lillian Fleet became the parents of Reuben Hollis Fleet in Montesano, Washington Territory. Young Reuben's father was elected as the county auditor and city clerk, and became a successful, but heavily leveraged, property owner due to the railway boom in the area. Unfortunately, the financial panic of 1893 that bankrupted one-third of all American railways also bankrupted the Fleets. While Reuben attended school in Montesano his father worked to recoup the family's fortunes by taking jobs as a civil engineer in Alaska's gold fields, and then returned to Montesano to form a successful abstract company. At 15 Reuben was accepted to Virginia Military Institute, where his father and his uncle Fred had graduated, but he was waylaid to the prestigious Culver Academy in northern Indiana by Uncle Fred, who was the superintendent there. In 1906 Fleet graduated second in his Culver class, and instead of continuing his college education he returned to Montesano to become a high school teacher. Soon his father talked Reuben into resigning his teaching position to join him in the abstract business. As a proviso to taking the job the young Fleet requested that he would also be allowed to sell real estate on the side, and soon he prospered in this undertaking. During this time a romance developed with Elisabeth Girten, whom he married in April 1908, and they would have two children over the next several years. Fleet joined the National Guard in nearby Aberdeen, where he was commissioned as a second lieutenant, and after several years rose to the rank of captain. In 1911 the Washington National Guard was activated and dispatched to the Mexican border, near Tijuana, to prevent labor agitators from reentering the country. During his stay in the area Fleet became captivated with San Diego, and nearly a quarter of a century later he would set up his aircraft business there. Over the next several years, on his return to Washington Fleet be-

came increasingly successful in real estate, particularly by speculating in timber property.

Fleet Catches and Pursues the Flying Bug

In 1914 Fleet had read of the flying exploits of barnstormer Terah Maroney, who was piloting flying boats out of Lake Washington, near Seattle. He soon took his first airplane ride with Maroney and became hooked on aviation. It is interesting to note that fellow lumberman Bill Boeing also took his first flight with Maroney that same year, and also became an aviation enthusiast, so much so he left the lumber business, and would soon form the Boeing Airplane Company. After this initial flight Fleet flew at every opportunity with a Tacoma seaplane operator.

In 1914 both Reuben Fleet and Bill Boeing took their first airplane flights with barnstormer Terah Maroney, who was piloting flying boats out of Lake Washington, near Seattle, and soon both young lumbermen became hooked on aviation. (National Archives)

Fleet in the Service of His Country

In 1916 Congress had appropriated $13 million for the Army Signal Corps Aviation Section, and in 1917 it set forth a provision to select one aviator from the National Guard of each state to qualify for a limited number of training positions. At the time the War Department prohibited married men with children from learning to fly. Fleet and one other officer, a bachelor, were the last of 83 Washington Guardsmen to survive the three day physical and mental examination for the pilot training position. The Adjutant General chose the bachelor, but the persistent Fleet persuaded the AG to submit applications for two Washington representatives. Only 11 National Guardsmen were chosen from the entire country, and Washington had two. In the spring of 1917, at the age of 30 Fleet closed his Montesano business and left for the Army's pilot training school in San Diego. Fleet reported on 5 April 1917, and the following day America declared war. Fleet received his wings as part of the sixth 1917 J.M.A. (Junior Military Aviator) Class, and was assigned to the 18th Aero Squadron as the commanding officer of the 260-man unit, which trained in the Curtiss JN-4-A Jenny. In early 1918 the now Major Fleet was sent to Signal Corps HQ in Washington, DC, to serve under Col. Henry "Hap" Arnold, who had just been selected as the Executive Officer of the recently formed Air Division. Fleet was assigned to be the assistant executive officer to Lt.Col. Byron Jones, the chief of training. Between July 1917 and June 1918 Fleet and Jones established 34 primary and six advanced training schools for the more than 38,000 cadets who had volunteered for the rapidly expanding Signal Corps. After initial training in America, the combat training of American flying personnel was conducted in England and France. From 15 May to 12 August 1918, in addition to his training duties, Fleet was appointed by Col. Arnold as the Officer-in-Charge of the newly formed Aerial Mail Service, under the Post Office Department. After a commendable Air Mail stint Fleet was assigned as temporary Officer-in-Charge of Flying and Commandant of Cadets at the newly opened facility at Mather Field, Sacramento, CA, where he spent two months. Fleet was then assigned on temporary duty to test foreign military aircraft at Dayton, and after assisting in the testing of 33 aircraft Fleet was anxious to be transferred to England to observe the renowned Royal Flying Corps Special Flying School at Gosport. Fleet arrived in England less than a month before the Armistice was signed, but managed to attend and graduate from this advanced training school, and was back in America just before Christmas 1918.

Fleet in the Postwar Air Service

After the war Maj.Gen. Charles Menoher, Chief of the Air Service, requested that the talented Fleet be granted any position he desired in the postwar Air Service. After observing the RAF Gosport facility and being involved in American air training, Fleet was convinced he could design a training aircraft better and safer than the British Arvo 504, or the U.S. Curtiss JN-4-A Jenny. To accomplish this undertaking, Fleet asked to be assigned to the Engineering Division at McCook Field, Dayton, OH, where Fleet's friend, Col. Thurman McBane, had been recently appointed as the commanding officer. McCook was in a war-to-peacetime transition, with civilian contractors and top personnel leaving. The Air Service contracted with companies throughout the U.S. for new designs, and Fleet's job at McCook was to act as a liaison with contractors, drawing up contracts and managing business negotiations. Between 1919 and 1922 McCook engineers designed and built 27 aircraft of various types and, in addition, the fledgling American aircraft industry also submitted many new designs. In

1920 the struggling Boeing Airplane Company was the low bidder for an Army contract for 200 Thomas-Morse designed MB-3 biplane pursuit aircraft. Ironically, Reuben Fleet was the contracting officer who signed the order that would keep his future competitor in business. While at McCook Fleet was able to continue his active flying, and soon after his arrival he and Capt. Earl White set an American long distance and speed record, flying a DeHavilland DH-9 to Hazlehurst Field, Long Island—over 664 miles in 4 hours and 33 minutes. Fleet also could not resist testing several of the aircraft he had personally contracted, rationalizing that he had to fly the aircraft himself in order to intelligently decide on its merits. Military life took its toll on the workaholic Fleet, as the long hours, constant moving, and absences led to his divorce from Elisabeth. By 1922 Fleet still had not accomplished his goal of developing his superior training aircraft, and the limitations and bureaucracy of a military career caused him to resign from the Air Service on 30 November.

Fleet Enters Civilian Aviation

It was not long before the talented 35-year-old Fleet was offered positions with three civilian companies. Boeing Airplane Company offered him a position as a Vice President and General Manager, and Curtiss Aeroplane and Motor Company President Clement Keys offered him a position as his personal aviation advisor. However, Fleet accepted a position with the pioneering Gallaudet Aircraft Corporation, which was highly respected in the industry due to its innovative founder, Edson Gallaudet, a former Yale Physics professor. The company was created in 1910 in Norwich, CT, and over the years created experimental aircraft with radical propulsion designs that, while revolutionary, were not viable at the time, and the company was chronically in financial difficulties until America entered the First World War. In May 1917 potential military orders prompted the company to open a large new factory in East Greenwich, RI. The firm received the anticipated contracts, but by 1922 it was having technical problems with its three Air Service contracts, and the impractical Professor Gallaudet left the company in acute financial straits. Fleet knew of the company's problems through his Air Service contract dealings, so when new company President Kelly Robinson and Wall Street multi-millionaire Harry Payne Whitney asked him to join Gallaudet as a company Vice President and General Manager he took the position. Fleet had ulterior motives in his decision, as he knew that besides Whitney there were many other leading Wall Street investors associated with the company whom he thought he could cultivate. Fleet's first step was to implement a financial analysis, and found the company had lost $3 million and was worth less than a $100,000. To forestall bankruptcy Fleet terminated Gallaudet's problem contracts and assumed a contract to modify 50 DeHavilland DH-4 aircraft.

Fleet saw that Gallaudet had no promising designs, and looked to the General Motors subsidiary, Dayton-Wright Airplane Company, as an opportunity to build his envisioned trainer. Like Gallaudet, Dayton-Wright was having postwar problems, as several of its commercial and private aircraft designs were failures, and the company was under a corruption investigation for the issue of production contracts during the war. The situation was so serious that GM wished to disband the company and use its factories for automobile production. In mid-April 1923 Fleet made GM an offer to purchase its aircraft designs, good will, drawings, tools, design rights, and patents. The company had built the TW-3 (Training, Watercooled) advanced trainer powered by the 180 horsepower water-cooled Wright Model E engine (a license-built Hispano-Suiza V-8). The seats and dual controls of the trainer were placed side-by-side so that there was continual communication and joint observation between the student and instructor. This system was a version of the RAF Gosport system that Fleet had observed during the war. The TW-3 had mainly non-wood design features, using commercial carbon steel tubing for fuselage structure, tail surface framework, struts, and landing gear components. Also the upper and lower wings of the biplane were interchangeable, as were tail surface members. Fleet saw the TW-3 as a future replacement for the Curtiss JN-4-A Jenny trainer, which was to be withdrawn from service. Wright's other contracts included the PS-1 Army pursuit version of the R.B. Racer monoplane, and the "Amphibian," which was the Navy W-A observation float biplane. As part of the Dayton-Wright deal Fleet wanted TW-3 designer Col. Virginius E. Clark and his small engineering staff to be included in order for them to improve its design to keep it competitive, and also to adapt it for the commercial market. The eccentric and unconventional, but brilliant Clark was a 1907 Naval Academy graduate who transferred to the Army in 1913, where he learned to fly. He then attended the Massachusetts Institute of Technology, and was its first recipient of a degree in aeronautical engineering. He had been the Army's Chief Aeronautical Engineer at McCook while Fleet was there, and left the Air Service in 1920 to become Dayton-Wright's Chief Engineer. In the negotiations GM wanted the Gallaudet Company to purchase the entire Dayton-Wright Company; not only the designs, drawings, tools, rights, and patents, but also its contracts and buildings.

Fleet Creates the Consolidated Aircraft Company

Fleet did not want to take over the Dayton-Wright PS-1 and Amphibian contracts, which he thought were losing propositions, and Gallaudet could not afford Dayton-Wright's buildings. He only wanted the TW-3 and its drawings, tools, and patents, as he felt Gallaudet could profitably build 20 to 25 TW-3s. Fleet recognized that Gallaudet, with its $3.5 million debt and past financial record, was in no position to meet GM's offer, and he made a personal proposal to the Gallaudet Company, hopefully receiving backing from Gallaudet's Wall Street investors that he had cultivated. Fleet wished only to acquire the TW-3, its drawings, tools, and patents, along with the services of Col. Clark from GM. He proposed to organize a new company, lease Gallaudet facilities, fulfill its contracts, and then terminate that company. Fleet offered Gallaudet a 40% stake in his new company, to

TW-3 The first aircraft that Fleet built was the TW-3 Camel advanced trainer at the Gallaudet factory in Rhode Island. Fleet saw the TW-3 as a replacement for the Curtiss JN-4-A Jenny, which had been withdrawn from service. (USAAF)

pay rent from 10% of his profits, to divide his salary 50-50 between Gallaudet and the new company, to split overhead, and to work out an agreement with the 400 Gallaudet workers to finish existing contracts while building the TW-3s. Gallaudet's Wall Street investors balked at joining Fleet, and on 29 May 1923 Fleet formed the Consolidated Aircraft Corporation without them. Fleet had a good relationship with Gallaudet President Kelly Robinson, who realized the financial importance of associating with Fleet, and an agreement was signed to lease the East Greenwich, RI, facility, and for the employment of it labor force. The lease was to expire at the end of 1923, or until Consolidated completed its anticipated government contract for the TW-3 training aircraft (the lease was contingent on Consolidated receiving the order). For the proposed venture to be consummated two major issues had to be resolved, starting with bankrolling the venture. The new company had an authorized capital of $60,000 (600 shares at $100 each). Fleet had $15,000 to invest, and he received $10,000 from his sister Lillian and her lumberman husband, Edward (Ned) Bishop, back in Montesano. Thus, to meet the GM offer Fleet was able to put up a $25,000 consideration. The final obstacle was hurdled when the Air Service signed a $200,000 contract with Fleet for 20 TW-3s and spare parts equal to three aircraft. This order came only two weeks before the Army's fiscal year production allotment would have reverted back to the Treasury Department. On 10 June Consolidated signed a contract with Dayton-Wright, for which it received a TW-3, manufacturing equipment and tools, and its design and production rights, as well as the services of Col. Clark. Fleet also received an unofficial agreement from GM that it would assign Dayton-Wright aviation patents to Consolidated.

As his first step Fleet moved the TW-3 project and Col. Clark from Dayton-Wright's Ohio factory to the Gallaudet factory in Rhode Island. As soon as the first TW-3 trainers came off the production line Fleet wished to stimulate sales by demonstrating them to the Army and Navy, and Fleet flew them back to Dayton and McCook Field for demonstration flights. By the end of the year Consolidated had delivered 20 TW-3s to the Army at Brooks Field in San Antonio, TX. To get feedback on the trainer Fleet, Gallaudet Factory Manager George Newman, and Col. Clark flew to Brooks Field. The Army instructors told them that they did not like the side-by-side seating arrangement, as they couldn't see the ground on the opposite side of the aircraft during the critical landing procedure. As a remedy Fleet narrowed the fuselage, and placed the instructor/student seating in tandem; this version of the TW-3 was dubbed the "Camel," because of the hump between the two cockpits. The large radiator and cowl of the in-line water-cooled Hisso Vee engine made forward visibility difficult. The solution was to remove the top of the cowl and deduct $50 from the cost of future trainers that were manufactured without cowl tops. The large radiator core presented a more difficult resolution. The costly radiator was an intricate 12-sided core built from hexagonal brass tubing that had to be laboriously fitted and dip-soldered. Fleet developed a successful rectangular radiator core placed below the propeller so the pilot could see over it.

Consolidated Produces the First Primary Trainer

In May 1924 the Army announced an official competition for its new PT (Primary Trainer) classification to replace the discontinued Jenny. Fleet had a contender ready in the tandem Camel, which Consolidated had redesignated as the PT-1 "Trusty." In a fly off on 10 June 1924 against such companies as Fokker, Thomas-Morse, Vought, Cox-Klemin, and Huff-Daland, Consolidated was awarded an initial contract for $500,000 for 50

PT-1 In mid-1924, when the Army announced an official competition for a new primary trainer to replace the discontinued Jenny, Fleet had a contender ready in the tandem Camel that Consolidated had redesignated as the PT-1 Trusty. Within a year the Army had approved an additional 150 trainers to be contracted at 50 trainers initially, and then 50 more in two months, followed by 50 more in another two months. (USAAF)

Navy NY-1 After receiving the PT-1 orders Fleet then won the Navy's best trainer and low bid competition against 14 other companies. The first order was for 16 model NY-1 trainers, nicknamed the Husky. Soon the Navy ordered 40 more, followed by 10 more, all with spares. (USN)

of its trainers, which were destined to remain America's primary trainer for many years. The PT-1 trainer can be best described as a very unattractive, but very functional and rugged aircraft that was the ideal for its intended job.

In May 1924 Fleet resigned as General Manager of Gallaudet, and began to look for a new factory to build the 50 PT-1s. Labor was a problem in the East, as to operate the 450 man Gallaudet plant workers had to be imported from New York and Boston. After investigating a number of locations Fleet settled on Buffalo, NY, as it had a large trained labor pool, and had been the home to the Curtiss Aeroplane and Motor Company. The modern, government-built wartime Curtiss plant had been purchased by the American Radiator Company, which leased it to Consolidated in September 1924 under a 10 year "accordion" lease that allowed Consolidated to expand or contract the leased square footage as dictated by the different demands of its various contracts. Fleet shipped Consolidated's equipment and records by rail from the Rhode Island plant, and soon PT-1 production began. Within a year the Army had approved an additional 150 trainers to be contracted at 50 trainers initially, and then 50 more in two months, followed by 50 more in another two months. Fleet then won the Navy's best trainer and low bid competition against 14 other companies. The first order was for 16 model NY-1 (N=Navy, Y=Consolidated) trainers, nicknamed the "Husky." Soon the Navy ordered 40 more, followed by 10 more, all with spares. The Navy decided to use the air-cooled 200 horsepower Wright J-4 nine-cylinder engine in the NY-1, while the Army continued with the water-cooled Hisso Vee engine. The NY series could be operated from either wheels or floats, but the most obvious feature was a fully rounded and much larger rudder, which was necessary to compensate for the increased length of the seaplane versions. The Consolidated Airplane Company had $213,975 in sales during its first year, and in 1925 passed $593,000; they then did over a million dollars over each of the next two years. It was America's leading training aircraft producer, selling 326 trainers; 260 to the Army, and 66 to the Navy. Through volume purchasing and an efficient production line Consolidated had managed to reduce the cost per unit to both the Army and Navy and boost its bottom line. However, the Army accused Fleet of making excessive profits from the PT-1 contracts. Maj.Gen. Mason Patrick seemed to have a particular axe to grind with the company, and insisted it return $300,000 (in the form of 50 free aircraft) of the

$800,000 in profits it had made in its first four years of business. Fleet confronted Patrick personally, and soon saw he had no alternative but to save face by selling 50 aircraft to the Army for $1 each! At Patrick's urging the Navy also received 13 NY-1s at $1 each. The result of this excess profits penalty was that Consolidated was unable to pay stockholder's dividends for nine and a half years, and Patrick's decision would be the first step in Fleet's disillusionment in doing business with the military and government.

Fleet realized that the Army would soon require that the Hisso Vee be replaced with a radial engine in the PT-3. Over the years the peculiar and gifted Col. V.E. Clark had regularly submitted his resignation from the company, often over petty squabbles with Fleet. In June 1927 Clark submitted his seventh resignation; unfortunately, it was during the development of the PT-3, and in the middle of the Patrick excess profit refund debate. Fleet had put up with Clark's unconventional actions, and had originally demanded his services from Dayton-Wright, despite Clark's being drummed out of the service in 1920 for "conduct unbecoming an officer and gentleman," which included a court martial and civil action for 40 counts of bigamy! The last straw for Fleet was Clark's contention that

PT-3 In 1927 Fleet realized that the Army would soon require that the Hisso Vee of the PT-1 be replaced with a radial engine. In response Consolidated produced 310 of the new PT-3 Husky trainers in 1928, and Fleet sold 865 of these trainers in seven years. (USAAF)

NY-2 The Navy version of the PT-3 was the NY-2, which is shown here as the floatplane version. Lt. James Doolittle flew the NY-2 in the first completely hooded "blind" flight on 24 September 1929 at Mitchell Field, LI, for which he was awarded the 1930 Harmon Trophy. (USN)

Consolidated actually owed the Army more than the $300,000 in excess profits! Fleet accepted Clark's resignation, and Consolidated was nevertheless able to produce 310 of the new PT-3 "Husky" trainers in 1928, 177 to the Army and 133 as NY-2s to the Navy. Lt. James Doolittle flew the NY-2 in the first completely hooded "blind" flight on 24 September 1929 at Mitchell Field, LI, for which he was awarded the 1930 Harmon Trophy.

In late 1926 the Army issued specifications for a new advanced trainer, and Consolidated responded with the XO-17 "Courier," which was a streamlined, modified PT-3/NY-2. The XO-17 was entered in a competition at McCook Field on 4 April 1927. Through the good showing of the trainer and Fleet's powerful sales pitch, emphasizing his company's strong position in the training aircraft field, Consolidated was contracted to deliver 28 O-17s in 1928. In 1929 Consolidated's primary trainer sales continued to be strong, as the Army purchased 73 PT-3s, and the Navy purchased 60 NY-2s and 25 NY-1s. In 1930 Navy sales slumped to 20 NY-2s and one NY-1, and sales to the Army diminished substantially. After selling 865 trainers in seven years as the largest volume manufacturer of aircraft in the U.S., the Consolidated Aircraft Company era of manufacturing the best and safest training aircraft in the world was at an end.

Consolidated Enters the Large Aircraft Market

In late 1926 the Army issued a requirement for a twin-engine night bomber. Fleet foresaw that the market for his PT-3 and NY-2 trainers would diminish, and decided to enter the multi-engine bomber competition. As an initial step the savvy Fleet opened an office in Dayton to be close to the Army's new Wright Field engineering and testing facility, and to his old base and contacts at McCook Field. Previously Fleet had optioned a parcel of land adjacent to the Army Wright Field facility for a new Consolidated design and research center, but was forced to abandon the idea by Brig.Gen. William Gillmore, Wright Field Commander, who cited that it gave Consolidated an unfair advantage. In March 1927 Fleet retained three design engineers from McCook Field when he hired Isaac Maclin "Mac" Laddon, who had previously headed the heavy aircraft Design Branch 2; he then added Bernard Sheahan from Design Branch 3 and Roy Miller, a structural engineer. These men formed the basis of the new Consolidated bomber design team that began work on the Model 11 night bomber.

In April 1927 Fleet wished to associate with a designer and builder of large aircraft, and contacted Igor Sikorsky, head of the Sikorsky Manufacturing Company of Long Island, NY, who developed the all-metal, 100

feet wingspan, S-35 trimotor, biwing seaplane. The S-35 had impressed the Air Corps during flights at Bolling Field, Washington, in early 1926. Later that year, French World War I fighter ace Rene Fonck, whose 75 victories ranked second after top World War ace von Richthofen's 80, had selected the Sikorsky plane for his attempt to be the first to fly from New York to Paris non-stop. Fonck's 20 September 1926 flight met disaster on takeoff, as a landing gear failed, and the overloaded plane crashed and burned off the end of the runway. Fonck and his co-pilot managed to escape, but two crewmen in the rear fuselage perished. The next year Fonck returned to America with new funding to again attempt the first trans-Atlantic flight, and chose Sikorsky's new S-37 design, which was similar to the S-25, but was powered by twin engines. When Charles Lindbergh flew solo across the Atlantic on 20-21 May 1927 in his Ryan monoplane, *Spirit of St. Louis*, Fonck canceled his plans, and his S-37, *Ville de Paris*, reverted back to Sikorsky, and would become the *Southern Star* that flew South America routes for American International Airways of Argentina.

The Fleet discussed the conversion of the S-37 design with Sikorsky as an entrant for the Army's bomber competition, but Sikorsky's facilities limited his company to the production of only the prototype. The two men struck a deal that if the Consolidated-Sikorsky team won the competition, Consolidated would manufacture all the bombers, but all design responsibilities were to be Sikorsky's, with Consolidated's Mac Laddon and Roy Miller to direct armament installation and supervise structural stress analysis. However, due to Sikorsky's poor financial position, major investors

In March 1927 Fleet hired Isaac Maclin "Mac" Laddon, who had previously headed the heavy aircraft Design Branch 2 at McCook Field. Laddon would become Fleet's chief designer, and would be responsible for the renowned PBY Catalina flying boat. (Consolidated via Pima)

refused to allow Sikorsky and his head engineer, Michael Gluhareff, to further develop the design and correct any faults. Consolidated would buy the prototype for $50,000, which also included a license to build aircraft on a royalty basis when (if) the government awarded the contract. Consolidated was to be the primary contractor, and would furnish engines and instruments, but Consolidated would subcontract 30% of the airframe work back to Sikorsky. The bomber was named the Consolidated-Sikorsky Guardian, and was powered by two Pratt & Whitney 525 horsepower Hornet engines, with their fuel tanks located in the nacelle behind the engine. Once the prototype was completed, Fleet employed Lt. Leigh Wade, a friend from his McCook days, as the company's test pilot. Initial tests were conducted at Roosevelt Field, Long Island, and it soon was apparent that the bomber was grossly underpowered, and its performance was mediocre at best. At the Dayton competition that was won by the Curtiss B-2 Condor, the Consolidated-Sikorsky Guardian placed a poor third, an inauspicious entry for Fleet in the bomber market.

Consolidated Designs and Builds Flying Boats

The Navy's early patrol flying boats had been biplanes, but by the late 1920s the Navy was interested in developing a large all-metal (except for fabric covered wings) monoplane with a 100 foot wingspan powered by radial engines with an operational range of 2,000 miles (the approximate distance between California and Hawaii), and a cruising speed of 110mph. Navy patrol planes had been exclusively designed by Navy designers, or by the Naval Aircraft Factory, and the hull design was furnished by Capt. Holden Richardson of the Navy's Bureau of Aeronautics, who was the world's leading expert on flying boat hulls. However, the Navy decided to open the new design to outside competition, but using Richardson's hull design. After the S-37 debacle Fleet moved Laddon, Miller, and the Consolidated design group back to the Buffalo home office to begin a new undertaking; the design and manufacture of flying boats, a domain in which Consolidated would become a world leader and purveyor through the end of World War II. While employed by the Air Service at McCook Field Mac Laddon and Bernard Sheahan moonlighted in Laddon's basement, and with Boeing engineer Louis Marsh had designed the Boeing PB-1 biplane flying boat. At Buffalo Laddon and Miller and Buffalo factory engineer Joseph Gwinn were given a 30-man engineering and drafting team that, on 28 February 1928, won the Navy design competition. A $150,000 contract was let to build a prototype that was designated as the XPY-1, the first e**X**perimental **P**atrol aircraft built by **C**onsolidated (Y was Consolidated's letter designator, because Curtiss had previously used the C designator). The smoozing Fleet decided to name the prototype the Admiral, after Rear Admiral W.A. Moffett, who was instrumental in administering the competition and drawing up the contracts. The XPY-1 was a five-man reconnaissance patrol plane powered by two 425 horsepower Wasp engines mounted on struts between the hull and wing. Laddon also patented a design for a third engine that was to be mounted on the wing center section. Fleet, ever the far-sighted and perpetual businessman, had the aircraft provisionally designed with a 60 foot cabin so it could be converted into a 32 passenger airliner. In March the Consolidated Company began work on the XPY-1 prototype. The company was inexperienced in producing what would be America's largest aircraft to that time, but the inevitable problems of a new design were met and solved, and in late December the Admiral was ready for testing. The aircraft measured almost 62 feet long, over 17 feet high, and had a wing span of 100 feet. Lake Erie and the Niagara River were

XPY-1 Admiral In February 1928 Consolidated won a $150,000 contract from the Navy in a flying boat design competition. The flattering Fleet decided to name the prototype the "Admiral," after Rear Admiral W.A. Moffett, who was instrumental in administering the competition and drawing up the contracts. (USN)

frozen over, and a new testing site was necessary. At a cost of over $10,000 and requiring 14 men, the XPY-1 was dismantled, and the pieces were loaded on three railway flatcars that needed to be routed to avoid impassable bridges and tunnels. On the day after Christmas it arrived at the Naval Air Station on the Anacostia River, near Washington, DC. On 10 January the Admiral made its first test flight with Navy test pilot Lt. A.W. Groton at the controls and Mac Laddon as an observer, as he was on all the first flights of his aircraft designs. After several shake down flights the Admiral was ready for a public demonstration, and on 22 January, with Lt. W.G. Tomlinson piloting, hull designer Capt. Holden Richardson as navigator, and Assistant Secretary of the Navy Edward Warner as a passenger the huge aircraft made a 655 foot takeoff run on the Anacostia River. The successful flight signaled the end for the Navy's large biplanes, and Fleet's successful entry into the flying boat field.

In June 1929, to Fleet's extreme chagrin, the Navy announced that, despite the fact that Consolidated had invested an additional $500,000 more for its development than the original $150,000 Navy contract awarded, it would accept bids from "qualified companies" to manufacture nine Admiral flying boats to Consolidated's design. To recoup its costs Consolidated was forced to bid for its own aircraft! The Glenn L. Martin Company, without any developmental costs, was able to under-bid Consolidated by $500,000, and was awarded the contract. Fleet refused to supply Martin with any of Consolidated's engineering drawings and data, and Martin was forced to extrapolate the engineering details from the prototype itself. Fleet's vindictive gambit delayed Martin's production of the nine aircraft (three P3M-1s and six P3M-2s) by 28 months, and the delay would tarnish Glenn Martin's standing as a major aircraft manufacturer.

During this time the Hall Aluminum Aircraft Company of Buffalo produced 29 all metal flying boats. The company was founded in 1927 by Charles Ward Hall, Jr., son of the aluminum production process developer Charles Ward Hall, and a vice president of the Aluminum Company of America. The younger Hall formed an engineering company that designed and fabricated duralumin wings for the Navy, and Hall would develop methods of aluminum fabrication that would transform the aircraft industry. When Fleet moved to San Diego Hall moved to Bristol, PA, but Hall and his company had always been an annoyance to covetous Fleet, as he made unsuccessful offers to buy it. In 1936 Hall was killed in a flying accident, and his son, Archibald, became president, but it was not until 1940 that Fleet bought the company. Hall would become an officer with Consolidated, and his company's engineers and technical staff would transfer.

Consolidated Enters the Latin American Market

Consolidated had spent $500,000 in the engineering expenses for the XPY-1, and with the expectation of receiving the Navy contract Fleet had bought the supplies and materials for its production. Again the astute Fleet had covered all possibilities with the XPY-1's convertibility to carry passengers as the "Commodore." Originally the aircraft was ordered by the Detroit & Cleveland Navigation Company to use on Lake Erie, but Latin America was seen as an opportunity for airline expansion. Capt. Ralph O'Neill, a World War I fighter ace with five shared victories with the 147th Aero Squadron, wanted to launch an airline with routes between North and South America, and had represented Boeing in the area by selling its aircraft there. Juan Trippe's Pan American Airways, with their Boeing-built flying boats, had already gained a strong entrée to the South American airmail, and soon passenger market. It was Trippe's government and Wall Street connections that would ultimately give Pan American a virtual monopoly in Latin America for decades to come. O'Neill concentrated on the continent's east coast, particularly Brazil, Uruguay, and Argentina, with its many harbors, estuaries, and rivers that were suited to operating flying boats. The Argentine government advised O'Neill that if he could secure strong financial backing it would be interested in establishing an airmail service on the Buenos Aires-New York route, and it seemed that Uruguay and Brazil would also then commit. Meanwhile Fleet had tried in vain to interest Trippe in purchasing the Commodores for Pan American, but Trippe had commitments to Boeing and its flying boats. In January 1929 O'Neill's idea came to fruition as James H. Rand, head of typewriter manufacturer Remington Rand Corporation of Buffalo, agreed to underwrite, through a consortium of investors, the design and manufacture of six Commodore flying boats for $150,000 each (plus spare parts), and also the formation of the New York, Rio, and Buenos Aires Line, Inc. (NYRBA). On 1 March Argentina officially signed the airmail contract, and Fleet had recouped his XPY-1 developmental expenses with an initial order for six Commodores, and went into profitability when an additional six Commodores were ordered, followed by two more in October. NYRBA was able to deliver a reliable air service, but there was a power struggle within the company, in which several of Rand's large investors had tried to gain control of the company from O'Neill. Rand, devastated by the stock market crash of

On 28 September 1928 Consolidated and NYRBA Airline representatives (L-R) George Newman (Factory Manager); Isaac Mac Laddon (Chief Engineer); Leigh Wade (Consolidated Chief Pilot); Col. Ralph O'Neill (NYRBA President); Larry Bell (General Manager); and William Gooch (NYRBA Chief Pilot) pose by the first Model 16 Commodore, the *Buenos Aires*, before its first flight. (Consolidated via Pima)

October 1929, did nothing to help O'Neill. Meanwhile, Trippe made inroads on the Argentine market and, with his influence on President Hoover's new Postmaster General, Walter Brown, was able to promote the idea that there should be only one American overseas flag airline. The Argentine government's exploitation of the rivalry between the two airlines and the stock market crash convinced the two airline companies that PAA should remain the operating company and buy out the stock of NYRBA. In October 1930 NYRBA was officially merged into Pan American. The Commodore proved to be a dependable aircraft, as nine years after they were built 13 of 14 were still flying (one burned in a hangar fire). Not only had Fleet had more than evened the score by making a $208,000 profit on the 14 Commodores Consolidated had built in 15 months, but the company gained valuable experience building large aircraft.

Even after recovering the costs of developing the XPY-1 by selling 14 Commodores, Fleet and Laddon were still piqued by its contract being awarded to the Glenn Martin Company, and decided to improve the de-

Model 16 Commodore After the Navy awarded the Admiral contract to the Glenn Martin Co. Fleet developed the XPY-1 as the Commodore for use on the Latin American market by NYRBA Airlines. Shown is the third production model, named *Havana*, being escorted by a Ford Trimotor. (Consolidated via Pima)

P2Y-1 Ranger Fleet decided to improve the Commodore design by enclosing the cockpit, adding larger engines with streamlined cowlings, removing many of its wires and struts, and suspending the floats from a short wing extending from the fuselage. The aircraft bore a striking resemblance to the famed Catalina. (Consolidated via Pima)

sign. They enclosed the cockpit, added larger engines with streamlined cowlings, removed many of its wires and struts, and the floats were suspended by a short wing extending from the fuselage. The result of the redesign was the XP2Y-1 Ranger, whose prototype was equipped with three engines (the third mounted on the top and center of the wing), and the first prototype flew on 28 March 1930. The third engine design was abandoned, and the 23 production P2Y-1s were manufactured with twin engines; the first was delivered on 1 February 1933. The longer range P2Y-2 succeeded the P2Y-1, and the Navy ordered 23—including 34 foreign orders over 57 Rangers were sold. The Ranger design bore a striking similarity to Consolidated's famed PB2Y Catalina, and became the Navy's stalwart scouting and patrol flying boat of the mid-1930s.

Consolidated and the Private Aircraft Market

After Lindbergh's New York to Paris flight in May 1927 there was a great demand for private aircraft. Consolidated had only its trainer designs to offer, and these were considered too large and too expensive for sale in the private market. Not one to pass up an opportunity, Fleet ordered head engineer Joseph Gwinn to develop the Model 10 business plane in 1928. The innovative five passenger aircraft was too cutting edge for the time, and the design was discontinued. Fleet then concentrated on adapting his PT-3/NY-2 trainers to a design that was commercially affordable. The result was the Kinner engine powered Model 14 "Husky Junior," which was manufactured by the newly created (on 1 February 1928) Fleet Aircraft Company—100% owned by Fleet. The company had purchased the Husky design and its manufacturing rights from Consolidated, and renamed it the "Fleet." Fleet's new company contracted 110 of the planes to be manufactured by his Consolidated Company on a cost-plus contract, and in the meantime had purchased a large amount of Kinner stock. As the company's sales manager, Fleet hired Lawrence Bell, who had been the general manager of Glenn L. Martin Company in Los Angeles, and then Cleveland. When Fleet hired Bell he had left Martin, and was a salesman in a Los Angeles second hand store. Fleet intended the Fleet airplane for the commercial market, but shrewdly built it to military standards, and the military air services purchased them as training aircraft, with the Army designating them as the PT-6, and the Navy as the NY2Y-1. With the success of the aircraft Fleet profited as Kinner's stock price climbed on the stock market due to his use of over 1,000 engines in the Husky design. His profit soon equaled the cost of the engines, and then each future engine installation would be at a no cost basis! Consolidated then issued 19,000 shares of company stock to purchase all Fleet's shares in his wholly owned Fleet

Aircraft Company, and Consolidated's shares were listed on the New York Stock Exchange.

Fleet decided to publicize his Fleet aircraft during a 15,000 mile cross-country promotional and sales tour in August 1929. He raised eyebrows when he announced that his secretary, Lauretta Golem, who was married to the Vice President of his Tonawanda Products Corporation, would accompany him. Fleet had a furtive romantic relationship with Golem, whom his close associates thought he would marry. During the final leg of the trip from Detroit to Buffalo the Fleet's engine malfunctioned with Lauretta at the controls in the rear cockpit. Fleet took over control of the aircraft, but it crashed in the emergency landing attempt. The next day Lauretta died of a broken neck and spinal injuries, and Fleet spent seven weeks in the hospital in London, Ontario. During his prolonged convalescence, Fleet named Larry Bell as company General Manager. Fleet then joined his parents on a New York to Panama to California cruise to recuperate. When he returned to work in November he hired Dorothy Mitchell, Lauretta Golem's niece, as his new secretary. It seems Fleet had an attraction to secretaries, as he married Dorothy in July 1930.

Fleet Enters the Mail and Passenger Plane Market with the Fleetster

In the late 1920s there was a need for a passenger and fast mail transport for the rapidly growing airline industry. Lockheed had introduced its streamlined wooden Vega in 1927, and it had influenced aircraft design at the time. Because Fleet was involved with the organization of the NYRBA Line to Latin America he authorized the design and production of the all metal fuselage Model 17 "Fleetster" passenger plane for use by NYRBA. The cantilever high wooden wing monoplane was clearly inspired by the Vega. The enclosed pilot's cockpit was located forward and above the six passenger cabin, and was streamlined into the wing's leading edge; it could accommodate a co-pilot or another passenger. The aircraft could cruise at 150mph (180mph top speed) powered by a 575 horsepower Hornet engine that was covered by an advanced NACA-developed cowling that increased airspeed by 15mph. About 25 Model 17 Fleetsters were built, with the major customer being the NYRBA Line.

A later version of the Fleetster was the Model 20, which was designed mainly for airmail use. It was distinguished by its parasol wing fastened to the fuselage by four struts about a foot above the fuselage. The pilot sat in an open (later closed) cockpit behind the passenger cabin. TWA leased, and then purchased seven Model 20s. Both the Model 17 and 20 were available as a landplane or twin-float seaplane. The Fleetster was somewhat of a failure, as the company could not duplicate Vega's successful

Fleetster Model 17 Because Fleet was involved with the organization of the NYRBA Line to Latin America he authorized the design and production of the all-metal fuselage Model 17 Fleetster cantilever high wooden wing monoplane, which was clearly inspired by the Vega. The pilot's cockpit was located forward and above the six passenger cabin. (Consolidated via Pima)

Model 14 "Husky Junior" was powered by a Kinner engine that was manufactured by the newly created Fleet Aircraft Company, which was 100% owned by Fleet, and had purchased the Husky design and its manufacturing rights and renamed it the "Fleet." (Consolidated via Pima)

Fleetster Model 20 A later version of the Fleetster was the Model 20, which was designed mainly for airmail use. It was distinguished by its parasol wing held to the fuselage by four struts located about a foot above the fuselage. The pilot sat in an open (later closed) cockpit behind the passenger cabin. (Consolidated via Pima)

PB-2A (P-30) Fifty of these two-seat, high altitude pursuit aircraft were the first aircraft to go into production at San Diego, because most of the parts had been previously manufactured in Buffalo, and the aircraft basically needed only to be assembled. (USAAF)

wooden design in metal. However, the Fleetster metal design and construction process was to be of value later to the company in fabricating their all metal designs.

The P-30 Fighter Establishes Consolidated as an Innovator

After the Detroit Lockheed Company went into bankruptcy many of its designers and engineers went to Consolidated Buffalo, and continued the development of the Lockheed YP-24, which Consolidated redesignated as the Y1P-25. The Y1P-25 was an all-metal two-place fighter whose development was impaired by crashes. However, the Army Air Corps (AAC) felt the accidents were no reflection on its design, and ordered four more sophisticated models designated the P-30 for service evaluation. The result was the first American production all-metal pursuit aircraft to feature a fully retractable landing gear, fully cantilevered wing, enclosed heated cockpit, controllable pitch propeller, and exhaust-driven turbo supercharger. The high altitude fighter had a rudimentary oxygen system, but the bulky flying suits made high altitude flights too awkward, and the rear gunner did not have a heated compartment. In 1936 Consolidated unsuccessfully entered a reconfigured P-30 in the AAC single seat competition. The two place pilot/rear gunner concept decreased performance, and ultimately the rear gunner proved to be impractical. However, the P-30 would later be the first aircraft to go into production at the new Consolidated San Diego plant, because most of the parts had been previously manufactured in Buffalo, and basically only needed assembly.

Consolidated Becomes a Major Industry Player with the PBY

During the first four years of the Depression (1929-1932), Consolidated's sales were $10.2 million, as compared to the $6.3 million in sales during its first five years in business. However, its earnings for the first five years were $2.1 million, and the company only broke even during the 1929-32 period, even though in 1930 it produced more aircraft (309) for more dollars ($4.3 million) than any other American aircraft company. In 1932 the company sold only 100 aircraft on sales of only $1.3 million, and it would not be until 1937 that sales would reach the 1930 level.

On 28 October 1933, both Consolidated and Douglas were awarded a contract by the Navy to build a 3,000 mile range successor to the P2Y-3 Ranger. The Consolidated entry was the XP3Y-1, which was an all metal high wing monoplane powered by two 825 horsepower Twin Wasp engines that were built into the leading edge of the wing center section, which was supported by a pedestal to the hull. Two struts on each side of the fuselage attached to the wing outboard of the engines and supported the wing to the hull. Two retractable floats were mounted on the ends of each wing, and were converted to wingtips upon retraction. The Consolidated XP3Y-1 was completed in the spring of 1935, but the Douglas XP3D-1 was ready a month and a half earlier. Both aircraft had almost identical performance data, and despite the Douglas time advantage Consolidated won the competition on a cost basis ($90,000 per aircraft versus $110,000), and was granted a $6 million, 60 plane production contract on 29 June 1935, the largest contract awarded by the government since World War I.

XP3Y-1 Catalina On 28 October 1933, Consolidated and Douglas were awarded a prototype contract by the Navy to build a 3,000 mile range successor to the P2Y-3 Ranger. The winning Consolidated entry was the XP3Y-1, which was an all metal high wing monoplane powered by two 825hp Twin Wasp engines. (Consolidated via Pima)

PBY Model 28 Catalina The PBY-1/5 was the most prolific and successful flying boat ever manufactured. During its production run from 1939 to 1945 it was produced in greater numbers than all other flying boats combined. Some 3,272 Catalina flying boats (1,854) and amphibians (1,418) were produced. (USN)

Consolidated representatives arrive in San Diego after Fleet agreed to move his plant from Buffalo. (L-R) Gordon Mounce, Consolidated's Western Sales Representative; C.A. Van Dusen, Production Manager; and Reuben Fleet and his son, David. (Consolidated via USAAF)

The production version was redesignated the Model 28 Patrol Bomber PBY-1, and was powered by two Pratt & Whitney R-1830-64 engines.

The PBY-1 through -5 was the most prolific and successful flying boat ever produced. In fact, during its production run from 1939 to 1945 it was produced in greater numbers than all flying boats combined. Some 3,272 Catalina flying boats (1,854) and amphibians (1,418) were produced by Consolidated plants at San Diego, New Orleans, and Buffalo, along with licensed versions to the U.S. Naval Aircraft Factory (Philadelphia), Boeing of Canada (Vancouver), and Canadian Vickers (Montreal). The name Catalina was coined by the British in November 1940, as they fulfilled a requisite that the names for all foreign aircraft were to be representative of the delivering nation, and the name of the resort island off the southern California coast was chosen. In 1941 the U.S. officially adopted names for their aircraft, and chose Catalina, along with Mustang, among others.

Consolidated Moves to San Diego

While patrolling the Tijuana border in 1911 during his Washington National Guard days, Fleet had become captivated with San Diego. During his ill-fated 1929 Fleet aircraft promotional junket Fleet had stopped at San Diego, and was so impressed with the city's new facility at Lindbergh Field that he offered to purchase it for a million dollars. While there he also acquired land in Mission Bay for a flying school. In April 1933 Fleet and Larry Bell visited the Los Angeles and Long Beach areas, which had previously made overtures to Fleet to move to their localities. Fleet, playing one city against another, contacted Thomas Bomar, head of San Diego's Chamber of Commerce Aviation Division, saying that Long Beach had made him an offer of free land on their municipal airport. Bomar had attempted to entice Fleet with San Diego's virtues since his 1929 visit, and told Fleet that the Long Beach land would be under water during the winter months, and was five miles from the ocean—a disadvantage in the flying boat business. Fleet and Bell then flew down to San Diego to meet with the Mayor, Bomar, the City Manager, and the Harbor Commissioner. After the meeting Fleet and Bell returned to Buffalo to consider moving to the West Coast, and to present the possible move to the Consolidated Board of Directors. Meanwhile, Los Angeles and Long Beach sent representatives to Buffalo to lure Fleet to their cities. When the city of Buffalo learned of

Fleet's possible defection, it also made offers to keep the company in place. Fortunately for San Diego, Emil Klicka, the city's Harbor Commissioner, who had heard Fleet during his California visit, stopped at Buffalo on 29 May 1934 during his spring vacation. The influential San Diego banker spent an hour with the Consolidated Board of Directors, and was so persuasive that on that same day the Board passed a resolution authorizing a conditional lease with the West Coast city. Fleet dispatched his son David and Vice President Charles Leigh to San Diego to contract to build a new factory at Lindbergh Field, and plan for the California end of the move from Buffalo. They retained architect L.B. Norman to design a modern aircraft factory using the basic element Fleet had observed during his visits to other new purpose-built aircraft and automobile factories: continuous, uninterrupted production from raw materials to a finished aircraft. The plant was to be 1,000 feet long and 275 feet wide, and total 275,000 square feet. In December Consolidated took construction bids and applied for a half million dollar loan from the Reconstruction Finance Corporation (RFC) to build the $300,000 plant, and spend the remainder of the loan on new equipment, and to move the company from Buffalo. The limit for a RFC loan

Thomas Bomar, head of San Diego's Chamber of Commerce Aviation Division, was instrumental in luring Reuben Fleet to his city. (San Diego)

The future site of the Consolidated San Diego factory in 1929, showing Lindbergh Field and the Ryan Aircraft factory, where the *Spirit of St. Louis* was built. (Consolidated via Pima)

The new San Diego Consolidated factory in November 1935. The plant was 1,000 feet long and 275 feet wide, and totaled 275,000 square feet. Consolidated took construction bids and applied for a half million dollar loan from the Reconstruction Finance Corporation (RFC) to build the $300,000 plant, then spent the remainder of the loan on new equipment, and to move the company from Buffalo. (Consolidated via Pima)

was $100,000, but Fleet and the San Diego faction influenced the area Congressman to persuade the RFC to grant the $500,000.

Fleet authorized $40,000 for the move, but it was imperative for Consolidated to make it as quickly as possible, as the company had been awarded two large contracts, one in December 1934 from the Army for 50 Model P-30 pursuit aircraft, and on 29 June 1935 for 60 PBY flying boats from the Navy. Initially, the move by a single shipment by sea via the St. Lawrence Seaway and the Panama Canal was considered, but was dismissed as too time consuming. However, Fleet used the sea route move as leverage in his negotiations with the railways to secure the best rates. The Buffalo factory continued production until mid-August, when its contents were sequentially loaded into 157 freight cars for shipment to San Diego, where they would be unloaded sequentially so that production could be resumed as soon as possible. Fleet selected about 300 key employees, paid their moving expenses, and promised jobs to another 100 if they paid their own expenses (another 400 would be hired in California). The employees drove from Buffalo to San Diego during the last two weeks of August, and the factory began limited operations by mid-September; the new factory was officially dedicated on 20 October 1935.

When the Buffalo city fathers learned that Fleet was actually going to leave the city it offered to finance a new aircraft company if Larry Bell would remain behind to head it. Bell resigned from Consolidated and remained in Buffalo, as did Robert Woods, to serve as Bell's new chief designer, and Ray Whitman, Fleet's long-time assistant. Bell planned to lease the Consolidated factory, which would become the Bell Aircraft Company, and would produce the P-39 Cobra fighter, designed by Woods. With the loss of Bell, Woods, and Whitman, Fleet named three new Vice Presidents, with Mac Laddon serving as Chief Engineer and Charles Leigh as Materials Supervisor, and then hired C.A. Van Dusen from the Glenn L. Martin Company, where he had served as their Works Manager.

The 50 PB-2A (P-30), two-seat, high altitude pursuit aircraft were the first aircraft to go into production at San Diego, because most of its parts had been previously manufactured in Buffalo, and the fighter basically only needed assembly. However, the contract for 60 PBY-1s, awarded only three months before the new factory was opened, was the most important contract at $6 million. The PB-2A contract was completed in July 1936, but the Navy placed a second order for 50 of the improved PBY-2 valued at $4.9 million to keep the Consolidated production lines busy. The Navy

A PBY flies over the new San Diego Consolidated factory (lower right) and adjacent Lindbergh Field. The Navy base at North Island is at the upper center of the photo. (Consolidated via Pima)

When the Buffalo city fathers found that Fleet was actually going to leave the city for San Diego it offered to finance a new company if Larry Bell would resign his Consolidated General Manager post and remain behind to head the new Buffalo aircraft company. (Consolidated via Pima)

Model 29 XPB2Y-1 The Coronado flying boat proto-type began as a single tail, but on 17 December 1937 test pilot William Wheatley flew the huge prototype for the first time, and was concerned about the aircraft's "directional instability." As a solution Consolidated engineers decided to add two small elliptical vertical fins placed adjacent to the single main fin on the front half of the horizontal stabilizer. Fleet personally flew the aircraft and found the new twin elliptical fin configuration helped, but did not solve the problem. (Consolidated via Pima)

initiated a new design competition for a long-range, four engine flying boat, and Consolidated was the winner, and was to produce a prototype (the XPB2Y-1) that would be called the "Coronado."

Prosperity brought problems, as space in the new factory was at a premium. For security reasons, and so as not to interfere with normal production, the experimental XPB2Y-1 Coronado prototype would have to be built in its own facility. Factory additions of 450,000 square feet of inside space and 170,000 square feet of paved area for outside assembly were financed by the issue of convertible stock, which raised $1.15 million. The PBY-2 proved to be such a success that on 3 October 1936 the Navy ordered another 66 of the improved PBY-3s with 1,000 horsepower Twin Wasp engines, only two days before the first of the 50 PBY-1s were delivered, and only two weeks less than a year after the dedication of the San Diego plant. Consolidated showed small profits in 1935 and 1936, but by the end of 1936 the Navy had ordered 176 PBYs, the company had an $18 million order backlog, and its work force had grown from 900 in 1936 to 3,200 the next year; finances were definitely on the upswing. In 1937 the Navy awarded a contract for 33 PBY-4s at $4.5 million. In 1937 and 1938 the company had sales of $12 million, but in 1939 the sales fell to $3.6 million, as after manufacturing 200 PBYs there were no new orders, and the work force decreased from 3,700 to 1,200 by the end of 1938 in anticipation of the decrease in orders. The Model 29 XPB2Y-1 Coronado prototype was having continual control problems with its tail configuration, and the first production order would not come until the end of March 1939, when the Navy ordered six of the deep-hulled PB2Y-2 patrol bombers; but the first would not be delivered until the end of December 1940.

Consolidated Enters the Four Engine Bomber Competition

By the mid-1930s the global situation had begun to change, with the rise of Hitler and Mussolini in Europe, and Japanese militarism in the Far East. In 1933 the disciples of Billy Mitchell's strategic air power theories had been promoted to levels of some importance in the Army Air Corps, particularly its research and development branch, the Air Materiel Command at Wright Field, Dayton, OH. Out of this branch came "Project A," a thorough feasibility study for a four-engined bomber that could fly 5,000 miles carrying a ton of bombs. However, also at the time the top echelon of the Army General Staff still was dominated by former cavalry officers, and on 14 April 1934 they grudgingly approved Project A, but not as an "offensive" weapon; instead one for "hemispheric defense." Project A in relation to the Long-Range Bomber program will be discussed in depth later.

Boeing Model 299

In a memorandum of 14 July 1934 the Air Materiel Command had changed its thinking, and decided that a second bomber that was not as grand as the Project A bomber could more easily be realized and put into production. The new AAC bomber was to have the same 2,000 pound bomb load, but its speed was to be 200mph, and its range was to be at least 1,020 miles, but 2,200 miles was much preferred. The AAC proposal was for "multiengines," which to the AAC meant two, but to Boeing it meant four. On 26 September 1934 the board of directors of the newly independent Boeing Airplane Company met for the first time after parent United Aircraft & Transport was finally dissolved. The new board bravely voted $275,000 to design and build a bomber to meet the new AAC specification. Boeing

Fleet and his engineers met and decided to delete the entire single tail section, and place a horizontal stabilizer on top of the rear fuselage, with dual round vertical fins and rudders placed at the ends. Each half of the horizontal stabilizer was canted at a 7.5 degree dihedral so that the lower one third of the rudder would not touch the water during takeoff. (Consolidated via Pima)

Model 299 Boeing built this low-wing four-engine monoplane to meet the new AAC bomber specifications: 2,000 pound bomb load, a speed of 200mph, and its range was to be at least 1,020 miles, but 2,200 miles was much preferred. (USAAF)

YB-17 The Model 299 was designated as the YB-17, and was to be a service test model. The production model was the Y1B-1, which rolled off the Seattle line on 2 December 1936. (USAAF)

President Claire Egtvedt assigned his project engineer, E.G. "Giff" Emery, with Ed Wells as his assistant, and Frederick Laudan as the construction supervisor to work on the Model 299. The bomber was to be a low-wing monoplane that would have four engines to power it, and was essentially an upscaled version of Boeing's streamlined Model 247 twin-engined airliner, which had been first flown in February 1934. Concurrently, Egtvedt ordered Emery to develop a four-engined airliner based on the Model 299 design, which was to become the Model 307 Stratoliner. With Emery running the Model 307 project, Egtvedt placed 24 year old Edward Wells as the project manager of the Model 299, which had been unofficially designated the "XB-17" by Boeing before it had been approved by the AAC. The Model 299 made its first flight on 28 July 1935, and the media was impressed by it size and dubbed it the "Flying Fortress." On 20 August project test pilot Leslie "Les" Tower flew it cross-country 2,100 miles to Wright Field for evaluation at an average speed of 232mph.

During testing at Wright Field the four-engined Boeing Model 299 was to challenge Douglas Aircraft's twin-engined DB-1 bomber, the XB-18 that had been developed from the company's successful DC-3 airliner design. From August and into October the AAC examined both bombers, and Boeing's better range and reliability earned it the lead in gaining a contract. On 30 October 1935 Boeing test pilot Les Tower and AAC pilot Maj. P.P. "Pete" Hill, and the test crew took off in the Model 299. But once it became airborne the bomber became uncontrollable, and as it passed over the end of the runway it crashed in a nearby pasture. Hill was killed on impact, but Tower survived with horrible burns and died 20 days later. Lt. Donald Putt was pulled from the burning wreckage and given little chance of survival, but Putt did survive, and four years later was to become the project manager of the B-29 program. Investigation showed that the ground crew had not unlocked the tail control surfaces, thus causing the crash that would put the Boeing program in jeopardy. The Douglas XB-18 had also done well in tests, and two of the twin-engined Douglas bombers could be manufactured for the cost of one Model 299. On 17 January 1936 the Army General Staff decided to order 133 production B-18s, and only 13 of the Model 299s now designated the YB-17 (the "Y" meant that the aircraft was not experimental, but a "service test" model that could, or not, precede production aircraft). Boeing put the now designated Y1B-17 (the 1 because they were purchased out of F-1 fiscal year supplementary funds) into production. The first Y1B-17 rolled off the Seattle line on 2 December 1936, and the last of the 13 was finished on 5 August 1937. One Y1B-17 was sent to Wright for testing, and the other 12 were assigned to the Sec-

ond Bombardment Group at Langley Field, VA, under Lt.Col. Robert Olds. The B-18 faded into oblivion, while the B-17 was slated to become America's four engine bomber.

The XB-24 is Contracted and Flies

By the autumn of 1938, Gen. H.H. Arnold, the recently appointed Chief of the Air Corps, while confident that the B-17 was a qualified success, was concerned that if war came Boeing would be unable to build sufficient numbers of the bomber. Arnold considered the possibility that Consolidated should manufacture the B-17 under license, and in December Mac Laddon and C.A. Van Dusen went to Seattle to discuss licensing with Boeing. They found that Boeing did not have enough work at that time to share orders, and moreover, the B-17 design was already four years old in an evolution of rapidly changing aircraft designs. The Air Corps had recently issued Type Specification C-212 for a bomber with a 3,000 mile range, 35,000 feet ceiling, a maximum speed of 300mph, and a bomb load of 8,000 pounds. Laddon and his engineering staff were confident that they could design a new bomber that would be able to carry the same bomb load as the B-17, but at higher speeds and longer range. Consolidated had experimented with the Davis Wing on its Model 31 deep-hulled twin engine flying boat, and found the wing improved performance by 20%. By the end of January 1939 Fleet sent Laddon and son David to Wright Field with specifications and primary data for the proposed Model 32 bomber (B-24). The Air Corps had made inquiries of Sikorsky and Martin, asking if they had any designs that could meet the C-212 Specifications, and neither had anything on the drawing board, as they had only three weeks to respond to C-212. However, Consolidated had a wooden mock-up ready

Model 32 XB-24 On 29 December 1939 the XB-24, piloted by William Wheatley and George Newman, first flew from Lindbergh Field. The prototype led to the Consolidated company flagship B-24 bomber that, by the end of the war, had 18,481 B-24s and variants built, the largest production run for any American bomber. (USAAF)

for AAF assessment on 1 February 1939. On 21 February the Air Corps declared that Consolidated was the only company that had a C-212 contender, and on 30 March awarded Consolidated a contract for a single XB-24 prototype (USAAC s/n 39-556), with a completion date of 30 December 1939. Since the world situation was deteriorating in early 1939, seven YB-24 service test aircraft with spare parts for $2.88 million were contracted in April, and 38 B-24As were added in August. On 29 December 1939 the XB-24 prototype, piloted by William Wheatley and George Newman, flew from Lindbergh Field on a 17 minute test flight.

Consolidated Wins New Contracts and Expands for B-24 Production
In September 1939 Adm. John Towers, Chief of the Bureau of Aeronautics, contacted Fleet, asking Consolidated to build 500 PBY-5s. Fleet advised Towers that Consolidated could fill the order in two years if the size of its factory was doubled. At the time the factory was only running at half capacity, and Fleet did not wish to invest any more company money, so he counter-offered to build 200 PBYs for $20 million if the Navy would build the new PBY factory. On 20 December the contract—the largest single military aircraft contract ever awarded to that time—was signed for the 200 PBYs, with the $20 million to be paid when the work was completed. The Navy let contracts to build a 441,000 square foot factory that would double Consolidated's plant capacity. With the machinery and associated equipment the cost was $2.2 million. In May 1940, with the war in Europe going badly for Britain and France, President Roosevelt authorized 50,000 new aircraft, and Consolidated spent $3 million to add 650,000 square feet to production, which then totaled 1.5 million square feet in factory capacity, and another 1.2 million square feet of paved outside area that could be used for assembly and final fitting in the good California weather. With the European and Pacific political situations threatening to escalate into a world war, and the B-24 coming online, there would have to be new factories built for its large-scale production. In November 1940 construction was begun on the government-financed 1.6 million square foot facility just north of Consolidated's San Diego main factory. Another massive $45 million, 3 million square foot government-financed facility to be operated by Consolidated to build four engine bombers and transports was to be built in Fort Worth, adjoining Lake Worth. In May 1941 the government decided to construct an 800,000 square foot B-24 factory near Tulsa, OK, that was to be operated by Douglas Aircraft. A third massive B-24 facility was to be constructed near Ypsilanti, MI. This $85 million Willow Run plant was to be operated by Ford Motor Co., and was originally to manufacture and supply parts for the Tulsa and Fort Worth B-24 factories, but later would fabricate complete B-24s. The Consolidated facility quickly expanded from 14,000 employees to 35,000 in 1941, and was adding 500 more per week. In April 1941 the government awarded Consolidated a contract for 700 B-24s worth $226 million. Sales had gone from the $3.6 million of 1939 to $95.5 million for 11 months of 1941, with a backlog of $755.5 million in unfilled orders. In 1942 a $28 million government-owned plant at Grand Prairie (Dallas), TX, was constructed to build B-24s under the supervision of North American Aviation. By the end of the war 18,481 B-24s and variants had been built, the largest production run for any American bomber. Consolidated-Vultee San Diego built 6,724, and Consolidated-Vultee Fort Worth built 3,034 to total 9,759 Consolidated-Vultee B-24s. Ford Willow Run built 6,792, Douglas Tulsa built 964, and North American Texas built 966. During 1944, its greatest year of production, Consolidated-Vultee produced more aircraft than any other manufacturer in the world! From Pearl

In December 1939 the largest single military aircraft contract ever granted to that time for the 200 PBYs was awarded to Consolidated. The Navy let contracts to build a $2.2 million, 441,000 square foot factory that would double the Consolidated's plant capacity. In May 1940 President Roosevelt authorized 50,000 new aircraft, and Consolidated spent $3 million to add 650,000 square feet to production that then totaled 1.5 million square feet in factory capacity, and another 1.2 million square feet of paved outside area.. In November 1940 construction was begun on the government-financed 1.6 million square foot facility just north of Consolidated's San Diego main factory, for large-scale B-24 production. (Consolidated via Pima)

Harbor to the victory in Europe the company manufactured 33,000 aircraft, which amounted to 13% of the U.S. output. In addition to the 18,482 B-24s, Consolidated-Vultee manufactured almost 900 PB4Y-1s, 739 PB4Y-2s (the single-tail Navy Privateers), 2,393 PBY Catalinas, and 216 PB2Y Coronado flying boats.

Fleet Sells Consolidated
By the early 1940s Fleet became increasingly frustrated with the government and military bureaucracy, and meddling that had occurred throughout his aviation career. This frustration began with his forced selling of 50 PT-1s for a $1 each for alleged "profiteering," followed by the government's award of his Admiral flying boat design to Glenn Martin, and culminated with the favoritism shown to Pan American and Juan Trippe in the South American route awards. Fleet became increasingly concerned by the specter of the automobile industry's incursion into the aircraft industry, especially with Ford building his B-24 design at the Willow Run plant. Also North American, allied with General Motors for B-25 production, and Martin with Chrysler for the B-26. The government's wartime excess prof-

Reuben Fleet and Navy Under Secretary Artemus Gates at the dedication of new factory facilities in October 1941. (Consolidated via Pima)

its tax made the building of a quality aircraft as economically as possible not a priority, and this factor would later become evident.

Throughout the years labor relations were a sticking point for Fleet and Consolidated. Beginning March 1934 Consolidated was subjected to a 57 day strike by the Aeronautical Workers Federal Union at its Buffalo factory, which was settled by arbitration under the same terms that were stated in the pre-strike labor contract. Less than a year after the move to San Diego the National Labor Relations Board (NLRB) was forced to order an election to determine if the AFL Machinists Union or Consolidators Association would represent the Consolidated worker. The AFL won by a large margin, and demanded wage increase concessions. Soon there was another bitter struggle between the AFL and the CIO over representation that affected Consolidated's bidding process with the Navy over PBY contracts. The NLRB ordered another election, which the AFL again won by a substantial margin, but not after much acrimony. In December 1940 Fleet antagonized pro-labor members of FDR's administration, and was forced into an unfavorable settlement with the International Association of Machinists (IAM). In June 1941 a new two year contract with the AFL Machinists Union was mandated on Consolidated by a mediation board, and by the government, which slowed payments to Consolidated, and then withheld them, coercing Fleet into signing. Even after this settlement Fleet was forced to take a stand on wages. After other San Diego aircraft companies (North American Aviation and Lockheed) were forced into a 10% pay raise by the AFL Machinist's Union, that union asserted that Consolidated should also do so, and authorized a strike, even though the newly signed contract did not provide for the raises, which Fleet thought would break his company. Fleet refused to negotiate with the union, and flew to Washington to take the issue to the National Defense Mediation Board (NDMB), whom he managed to infuriate during his first day there. After a bitter two day battle with the NDMB Fleet then took on the War Department, the Department of the Army, the Department of the Navy, and the Office of Production Management (OPM), led by Sidney Hillman, FDR's feisty new appointee. Fleet became so exasperated that he offered to let the government take over his company if they thought they could do a better job of running it. Finally the OPM relented, and a new one year union contract was signed with the government, assuming the wage increase in their aircraft contracts with Consolidated.

The Navy's order for 200 PBYs in 1939 increased Consolidated sales from $3.6 million to $95.5 million, and the company had a backlog of $775.5 million in orders. Consolidated Aircraft and Fleet were industrial icons, but the government and the War Department wanted the influential and autocratic Fleet removed from his position as Consolidated Chairman and President. They believed that the company had gotten so large that he was unable to make every decision for what they considered was his private fiefdom of 35,000 workers. But King Reuben did not feel that he was adequately compensated, and he was right. In 1941, Fleet's investment income amounted to $1.7 million, but Federal income taxes took 93%, and the state of California got another 6%, leaving Fleet with only $17,000. Fleet, the hands on entrepreneur, saw the proverbial handwriting on the wall, and sought to sell his controlling 34% interest in the company.

On 25 November 1941 Fleet reached a merger settlement with New York investment banker Victor Emmanuel, CEO of Aviation Corporation (AVCO). Emmanuel was a World War I Navy pilot, and was on the board of directors of Republic Steel and Vultee Aircraft, Inc. At the time there were rumors in aviation circles that would be substantiated later that Re-

In 1932 Gerard "Jerry" Vultee formed the Airplane Development Corporation (ADC), which occupied a plant at Glendale, CA, and built the single engine V-1 commercial airliner. In 1938 Vultee converted the V-1 into a dive-bomber, designated the V-11, and bought a new plant at Downey, CA. (Vultee via Pima)

public Steel Chairman of the Board, Tom Girdler, was also behind the merger. AVCO was a holding company, and one of the companies it controlled was Vultee Aircraft, Inc., a mid-sized Downey, CA, manufacturer of fighters and training aircraft, its most prolific and profitable aircraft being the BT-13/BT-15 trainer, of which 11,000 were produced.

In 1932 Gerard "Jerry" Vultee formed the Airplane Development Corporation (ADC) with the financial support of entrepreneur E.L. Cord of Cord automobile. ADC occupied a plant at Glendale, CA, that built the single engine V-1 commercial airliner, which was subsequently sold to American Airlines. However, the Federal Aviation Administration decided that all commercial aircraft were to be multi-engine, and Cord left the aircraft industry and Jerry Vultee to fend for himself. By 1938 world politics threatened peace, and Vultee converted the V-1 into a dive-bomber, designated the V-11. Orders soon were received from the Spanish Civil War combatants and the Chinese Nationalists, and Vultee bought a new plant at Downey, CA, that by 1938 had 500 employees. Vultee renamed his company the Vultee Aircraft Division of the American Manufacturing Corp. In January 1938 Vultee and his wife, Sylvia, were killed near Sedona, AZ, while flying home from Washington, DC. The company was reorganized a year after Vultee's death, and it began an expansion program. In 1940 AVCO was merged with Vultee Aircraft Division to form Vultee Aircraft, Inc., and that year the new entity merged with Stinson, which had plants in Tennessee and Michigan. By the time of the Consolidated merger Vultee Aircraft, Inc., had 10,000 employees at its Downey plant, and had contracts valued at $162,000,000, mostly for training aircraft from U.S., Peru and China. At the time of the merger Consolidated's contracts were valued at $750,000,000.

The merger agreement had Vultee purchase 348,882 shares of Fleet's personal Consolidated stock, and 440,000 shares from his family at 22-7/8's, plus a $2 cash dividend per share to bring the sale's total to the then enormous sum of $10,945,000. Ever the astute businessman, Fleet saved a 10% capital gains tax by completing the sale before 1 January 1942, when the capital gains tax rate was to be raised from 15% to 25%. Succeeding Fleet, who was both Consolidated's Chairman and President, was Tom Girdler, Republic Steel Board Chairman, as Chairman, and Harry Woodhead, Board Chairman of Vultee, as President. Mac Laddon remained as General Manager (he would become the Vice President by 1945), while Charles Leigh and Fleet's son, David, remained in San Diego. Girdler was the personification of the self made, ruthless entrepreneur, rising from a steel salesman to form Republic Steel in 1930. He built the company as a one man show by acquisition, modernizing existing plants, and exploiting labor, while deftly guiding it through the Depression. In 1937 Girdler's Republic Steel and three other of the so-called "Little Steel" companies (Bethlehem, Youngstown, and Inland) refused to sign a contract with the Steel Workers Organizing Committee (SWOC) of the CIO that had been signed by "Big Steel," the U.S. Steel Company, the leading American steel producer. The SWOC called a strike on the other Little Steel companies, but Girdler, who was vehemently anti-union, refused to close his Republic Steel plants, and trouble started at the Chicago plant. After initial union picketing that was dispersed by a police department that was clearly supportive of Republic Steel, about 1,500 SWOC sympathizers and their families gathered to show their support. About 1,000 members then marched toward the Republic plant, and were stopped by police, who fired into the fleeing crowd, killing 10 and wounding 30, with 38 more being hospitalized by injuries from beatings. The major newspapers portrayed the marchers as communist conspirators, and downplayed the evidence of police brutality uncovered during a Senate investigation. Just months before the Consolidated/Vultee merger, in August the Little Steel companies were legally forced to "cease committing acts of unfair labor practices," and a

year later signed their first labor contract with the U.S. Steel Workers of America. When Girdler took over as Consolidated-Vultee Chairman there was a possible threat of labor union problems, as Aircraft Local 1125 of the AFL Machinists Union held the bargaining rights for most of Consolidated's 30,000 workers, while the Vultee Downey plant had a contract with the CIO Auto Workers Union. However, President Roosevelt's unlimited national emergency declaration forestalled the threat, as the Consolidated contract ended on 27 May 1943, or the end of the emergency declaration, or whatever was shorter.

After the merger Reuben Fleet signed a five year agreement with Harry Woodhead to serve in an advisory and consulting capacity for $60,000 per year. The retaining of Fleet was taken by aircraft industry observers as an effort to rebut insinuations that the merger had been motivated by the War Department to force a change in management at Consolidated. An interesting provision in the sale was that Fleet's private secretary, Eva Wiseman, continue in her position, and soon thereafter Fleet and his wife, Dorothy, separated. In May 1944 Mrs. Fleet filed for divorce, citing "great mental suffering and bodily injury" (later dropped), and in 1945 received an unprecedented $1.555 million settlement and custody of their three young children. In March 1947 Fleet crashed his car into a tree, severely crushing his chest against the steering wheel. Two months later, the resilient Fleet, at 60 years old, and true to his "marries his secretary" proclivity, wed Eva, and after seven years of marriage the couple had three daughters. Fleet died on 29 October 1975 at 88 years old, married to Eva for a Reuben Fleet marriage record of 28 years.

The merger of Consolidated and Vultee was not formalized as ConVair or Convair until March 1943, but the two companies worked as an entity during the interim. The new company consisted of 13 manufacturing, modification, and operating divisions in 10 states, employing over 100,000 workers. The San Diego plant was the company's largest producer, manufacturing 8.2% of America's warplanes, and employing a peak labor force of 45,000 (40% women). The B-32 was known by the AAF as the Consolidated B-32 until the formation of the new company in March 1943, when it officially designated the bomber as the Consolidated-Vultee B-32. However, many AAF publications and documents referred to the bomber as the Consolidated B-32 until October 1945, but there were a few ConVair B-32 references in the popular media.

Consolidated head executives Chairman Tom Girdler and President Harry Woodhead observe Consolidated's high altitude chamber. The two men assumed their positions after Fleet sold Consolidated in late 1940. (Consolidated via Chana)

2

Early Development of the Long Range B-32 Bomber

Introduction

Lost in the chronicle of the successes of Reuben Fleet and the Consolidated Aircraft Company is the story of their very heavy bomber contender, the B-32. From its inception the B-32 design was only considered as a back up to the initially troubled, but favored and ultimately successful B-29 program. Consequently, with its huge, profitable PBY and B-24 contracts and promising post war B-36 program, perhaps the B-32 program was not given Consolidated's full attention during its development, and suffered the consequences of a slow and troubled development, supposed mediocre performance, lackluster combat record, and finally, its wholesale cancellation when the war ended. Just as the B-32 is a footnote in Consolidated's history, it has been a footnote in the chronicles of World War II aviation.

Pre-War Aircraft Procurement Policy

The Air Corps Act of 1926 was to establish a statutory means to procure new aircraft. It provided for a design competition that would lead to the purchase of one or more prototypes, the issue of contracts for "experimental" aircraft by the Secretary of War at "his discretion without competition," and competition where aircraft could be procured on grounds other than the first two provisions, with the Secretary able to "exercise discretion in determining the lowest responsible bidder." Another procurement possibility was for a negotiated purchase contract without competition of a design "of sufficient promise to justify immediate procurement." The Act required the use of a design competition, with the designs to be submitted to and evaluated at Wright Field, and a winner was to be selected and awarded a contract to build one prototype for service testing. If the service tests were successful a production order was then to be issued. However, design competition was effectively impractical, as when bids went out Wright Field received a large number of design proposals that the designers claimed met or exceeded the specifications. Until a prototype was built it could not be determined from the submitted design if specifications had been met and, if not, time passed and money was spent without result. Also, bidders were given inadequate time (several months) to design and submit their proposals, and once the winner was chosen its design had to be detailed; it was then often found that the original dollar bid was inadequate, and the manufacturer would lose money on the building of the prototype and production models. This ineffective design competition gave

way to the negotiated purchase contract, but the manufacturer with the winning bid also lost money, as they intentionally low-balled the bid, expecting to recoup this loss on the quantity production order. The Act made no provision for a quantity order, and a new bid for a quantity order needed to be issued; another manufacturer could then be contracted to build the winning design of another manufacturer. In June 1929 the Navy announced that, despite the fact that Reuben Fleet's Consolidated Aircraft had invested an additional $500,000 more for the development of the Admiral Flying Boat than the original $150,000 Navy contract awarded, it would accept bids from "qualified companies" to manufacture nine flying boats to Consolidated's design. The Glenn Martin Company was then selected to build Consolidated's flying boat. Manufacturers were reluctant to submit designs and bids, and Army Regulation 5-240 was resurrected from the mass of regulations to accommodate procurement. This Regulation stipulated that "competition might be avoided in certain special circumstances in which competition was impractical." By interpreting AR 5-240 to classify the manufacturer of an experimental aircraft purchased under the Air Corps Act of 1926 as the only source, that manufacturer could be awarded the production contract. Between 1926 and 1934 $16 million was awarded for contracts under the "experimental" provision of the Act, and $22 million under the "impractical competition" provision; both of which were entirely legal under the terms of AR 5-240. Each year (1926-1934), each procurement contract was on public record, and annual aircraft procurement reports were made to Congress—all were completely legal. Nonetheless, in January 1934 the *Washington Post* reported that the House of Representatives was about to investigate seven years of wrongful aircraft procurement by the War Department in violation of the Air Corps Act of 1926.

In late 1933 the ambitious Democratic Alabama Senator Hugo L. Black was aggressively investigating the federal subsidies to private airmail contractors that were U.S. airlines. Black, who would become a Supreme Court Justice in 1937, was so strident and vocal that the newspapers soon led the public to believe that most of the nation's airlines were guilty of flagrant wrongdoing and excessive profits. Since many of America's aircraft manufacturers were associated with airlines (e.g. Boeing/United Airlines) they were also incriminated by the newspapers. When the Navy and Army came to Congress to present their appropriations bill, in January and February 1934, respectively, both were attacked with accusations of allowing profiteering and excess profits by the aircraft manufacturers at the expense of the taxpayers. The Chairman of the House Naval Affairs Committee, Georgia Representative Carl Vinson, appointed a subcommittee headed by New York Representative J.J. Delaney to investigate the supposed widespread procurement corruption. After two months and hearing 800 pages of testimony the Delaney Committee's final report found that the charges against the Navy's procurement policies were unfounded, and were "prudent and practicable," and fostered competition. The Committee found that the major airframe manufacturers made only a very marginal 0.2% on cost profit on their sales to the military and commercial interests. The average profit earned by aircraft and engine manufacturers between 1926 and 1934 was also a not-too-excessive 9% on cost. Further figures showed that aircraft manufacturers lost an average of 50% on cost on "experimental" aircraft, and when combining these losses with production profits (if the aircraft went into production) the return was 11.5%, which was not considered excessive for the high risk involved. However, while the New York *Times* had headlined the Committee's appointment of Delaney and the upcoming investigation, and then printed titillating accusation feature articles during the Committee's investigation, it only spent one day reporting the story exonerating the Navy, and that was carried on page 15! To exacerbate the situation, one member of the Committee charged publicly that the majority had "whitewashed" the Navy, and then he wrote a minority report that reached the *Congressional Record*, while the majority report languished in obscurity. Of course, the newspapers cited this minority report, and referred to the "indication of new evidence of illegal procurement" alleged by the minority report author. Strangely, the majority members did not refute this minority report, and the misleading indication of the "new evidence" that would never surface.

In the turmoil the Air Corps also soon came under fire from South Carolina Representative John McSwain, Chairman of the Military Affairs Committee, who put New Hampshire Representative W.N. Rogers in charge of an eight man committee that took his name. In closed hearings the Rogers Committee found the Chief of the Air Corps guilty of "gross misconduct" and "deliberate and willful and intentional violation of the law," and the Air Corps both "inefficient" and "expensive," using "various subterfuges" for "pernicious" and "unlawful" procurement. It made the recommendation that there be a return to "aggressive design competition for experimental aircraft," and "competition on all contracts for procurement in quantity." Perhaps due to the closed nature of the hearings Congress did nothing about the Air Corps Act of 1926, as there was no public outcry. Congress did pass a law limiting aircraft manufacturers' profits, and provided for the recapture of all earnings in excess of 10% (but provided nothing to put a floor under losses). This excess profits law raised questions and a mandate for further revisions to it.

A new administrative procurement policy was devised by Assistant Secretary of War (1933-36) Henry Woodring, who would later serve as Secretary of War under Roosevelt (1936-40), resigning from office because he opposed Roosevelt's third term campaign. The policy essentially supported competitive bids, and thus circumvented the Congress from amending the Air Corps Act by statute. During fiscal 1933 the Congress appropriated $10 million for the Army Air Corps, but the new Roosevelt Administration, under the economic pressure of the Depression, impounded $7 million as an economic emergency measure. The AAC urgently needed more than 700 new aircraft to equip active units, and many more were needed to replace aircraft that were, or were going to be obsolete soon. At the end of the year the administration transferred $7.5 million to the AAC from the Public Works Administration (PWA). To expedite the purchase of the best aircraft available the AAC negotiated production contracts with the manufacturers of "top-quality aircraft" using Army Regulation 5-240, maintaining that the manufacturer was the "sole source" of the required aircraft. However, two companies complained about not getting the AR 5-240 negotiated contract awards. The Depression put the War Department under pressure to award contracts to a number of aircraft companies to keep them viable, and Assistant Secretary of War Woodring was forced to reconsider the contract awards. In order to award contracts equally throughout the aircraft industry, and also obtain aircraft of maximum performance at a minimum cost, Woodring was in a Catch-22 situation. Aircraft contracted on the basis of price competition would save the government money, but not insure purchasing aircraft with the best performance. On the other hand, aircraft contracted on the basis of having the best performance would cost more. Either way, the intention of spreading the wealth was not met, as whether contracts were awarded on cost or performance, most of the contracts tended to be awarded to a few efficient companies who had the best designs and production capacity. Woodring asked the Air Corps to devise a policy before Congress reconvened in January 1934. The AAC responded with the 1934 War Department Aircraft Procurement Policy, which had "competition" as its foundation. The AAC's solution was to allow each manufacturer to bid on its own design specifications, but the AAC required a minimum high speed, thus allowing competition as to performance, but disqualified all companies but those whose design proposals fell within a narrow margin of specified performance. The competition was also limited to companies that had previously submitted similar aircraft for approval to Wright Field for evaluation, so that there was some assurance that the submitted aircraft proposal had some design and safety substance behind it. The 1934 Procurement Policy went on to state that if the aircraft with the highest performance was not the lowest bidder the Secretary could award the contract "at his discretion to the best advantage of the Government." Each submitting company was required to supply a prototype for flight testing, eliminating "paper promises," and would provide a basis for an assessment of the aircraft for production contracts. The Secretary's timely submission of the 1934 Procurement Policy undercut a Congressional Committee that was infuriated over the alleged profiteering by the aircraft industry, and bent on amending the Air Corps Act.

Now the competition procedure was to mail a circular containing "type specifications in terms of the minimum acceptable performance." The aircraft's maximum performance was then left to the talents of the manufacturer's design team, whose design performance was to be verified by flight tests of the prototype aircraft. The AAC needed to require a necessary "degree of uniformity and standardization" on the aircraft industry to prevent the "collection of heterogeneous aircraft and equipment," and "insure a high degree of uniformity and interchangeability." The aircraft manufacturers were asked to submit designs based on the performance specifications issued by the AAC. With their invitations to the aircraft industry for designs and bids the AAC issued the *Handbook for Aircraft Designers*, and an "index of all pertinent Army, Navy, and Federal specifications for materials and subassemblies." In addition, the industry was required to use Government Furnished Equipment (GFE), which included instruments, armament, communications, oxygen equipment, etc., and use mandatory engine and propeller installations. The *Handbook* and use of GFE decreased the number of variables to be incorporated in the prototype design, and thus limited the range of the competing designs, thereby making the competition more evenhanded among the qualified competitors. In June 1936 the Secretary of War reported to Congress that the new policy was a success, as it had increased the number of bidders, and the designs submitted were far advanced compared to contemporary aircraft. But the question remained as to equating price to performance. To which bidder should a contract be awarded when one manufacturer submitted a superior design at a higher cost, while another submitted a much lower bid on an inferior design? If performance was the main prerequisite, then the manufacturer with the superior design could ask an unreasonable price for his design. During the design competition for an AAC transport the larger, twin engine Douglas DC-2, already in successful service as a commercial airliner, was clearly the far superior design over the single engine transport designs submitted by Curtiss Wright (Condor) and Fairchild (C-8). But the Douglas bid was $49,500 per aircraft, as compared to the $29,500 for Curtiss Wright and $29,150 for Fairchild. The transport design proposal stipulated that the primary consideration would be performance, not price, and the Douglas DC-2 was given the production contract. But Fairchild protested, and the Comptroller General deferred payment to Douglas, pointing out that the performance of the Fairchild transport "was far in excess of the minimum performance required." The Comptroller General did not realize that in combat, having the minimum acceptable performance would not be sufficient against the superior aircraft being designed in Europe. The CG believed that the AAC's competition was illegal, as it did not provide any method of establishing a precise relationship between cost and performance, and left the choice only on performance. The Secretary of War held that no formula could evaluate price vs. performance, and that the Air Corps Act of 1926 gave him legal discretion to make decisions regarding the weight of price versus performance when evaluating bids "in order to serve the best interests of the air arm." Meanwhile, Douglas delivered aircraft on the contract, but was not paid, as the disagreement between the CG and Secretary of War continued. The Attorney General was asked to intervene, and after four months ruled significantly in favor of the Secretary of War, and Douglas was finally paid. Even though the Attorney General had ruled in favor of the Secretary of War, AAC procurement officers realized that price would remain a problem with the Comptroller General and General Accounting Office. In order to expedite their procurement programs, and for their aircraft contractors to receive timely payments, the AAC agreed to include price as a factor for evaluation in all future competition. The AAC's evaluation proposal was to determine a "figure of merit" on the basis of performance that was to be divided by the dollar cost bid by the manufacturer. This "price facto" would favor the bidder with the lowest price and the highest performance. However, the War Department continued to be adamant that final selection would be the decision of the Secretary of War, and the figure of merit and price factor would serve as a guideline for the final selection.

With this procedure in place the manufacturers found that drawbacks lingered. The circulars (design proposals) had to be composed so that the manufacturers had enough design autonomy to incorporate innovations, but it also had to be specific as to the design requirements, so that the manufacturer knew what the circular required. To make the competition as fair as possible the manufacturers could not consult Wright Field engineers which, in turn, prevented Wright from offering suggestions that could enhance the design. The manufacturers were also not allowed to submit mock up aircraft to Wright for evaluation that could discover design de-

fects that could be more easily corrected in this mock up stage, rather than in the prototype phase. Changes in the prototype phase once it reached Wright Field could only be made by change orders to amend the contract, which was time and money intensive. The overriding factor in issuing a circular was getting a design into quantity production as soon as possible, and the AAC assumed that the manufacturers would submit a wholly developed prototype that would be ready to go into production. But to win the competition the manufacturers had to design aircraft with innovations that were not yet combat proven, and thus the prototypes tended to be more experimental in nature, and would later require numerous contract change orders (e.g. the B-29 and B-32). Prototypes were very expensive to build, especially four engine bombers, whose airframe costs could rise 300 to 400%, and the time for their fabrication increased from months to as much as two years during the 1930s. Also, the manufacturers always faced the possibility of not having their design and prototype accepted, and having to absorb the entire cost of the project, as there was a very slight chance that the rejected design could be sold to foreign air forces or used commercially. The manufacturers were caught in a Catch-22 situation, as they were forced into bidding simply because they needed the business in the poor economic environment of the Depression, and failure to enter the competition would result in leaving the manufacturer behind its contemporaries in developing combat technology. But then not entering competition would save them the costs of developing a design and building a prototype without out assurance of a contract. In the late 1930s the result was a declining number of bidders for government contracts, as the economic conditions improved and the large manufacturers were receiving contracts from commercial airlines and air transport. In 1938 manufacturers led by Consolidated Aircraft Corporation's Reuben Fleet suggested remedies to increase bidding. Fleet had once been a procurement officer for the Army in the early 1920s, and had been committed to solving the problems of aircraft procurement and legislation. Over the years Fleet had made several proposals that culminated in his suggesting that legislation be passed to authorize the War Department to procure aircraft in production quantities by negotiated contracts, rather than bids involving prototypes. Of course the War Department could not endorse this idea without rankling Congress and their desire for competition. And in a dilemma the government's usual solution was to convene another board to study yet again another revised procurement recommendation. The AAC and various aircraft manufacturers testified, and the new board recommended a solution that was a compromise between competition with prototypes and a simple design competition. Before issuing circular proposals for production aircraft the AAC would invite aircraft manufacturers to submit designs for evaluation. One or more designs would be selected and be granted experimental contracts for the construction of one or more prototypes. There was also the proviso that a quality data from losing designs could be purchased. Detailed type specifications would not be prepared until the winning design(s) passed the final mock up phase, allowing the AAC and manufacturers to discuss changes. Once the design was finalized the AAC was to issue its circular proposal for a prototype aircraft to be built by manufacturers interested in procuring a contract for the production aircraft. The War Department would subsidize the building of the prototype of the winning manufacturer(s). Usually the winner could expect to be awarded a production contract with his prototype, but other manufacturers who could afford to build a prototype to specifications could also enter the competition, and preclude any accusations that free competition was being thwarted. An impartial evaluation of the design was now based on the performance of the prototype, and was to reduce the number of design changes and get the aircraft into production sooner. Finally, a workable procurement proposal seemed to have been realized. The Chief of Staff approved the board's proposal in October 1938, but the threat of an impending European war soon made the proposal mute.

In February 1939 the chairman of the House Military Affairs Committee introduced a bill authorizing 6,000 aircraft for the fiscal year 1940 that was passed in April, authorizing $57 million for new equipment. The next day the AAC issued contracts worth $19 million to build 571 aircraft. In July, in response to an appeal by President Roosevelt, a request for a supplementary $89 million was authorized for immediate disbursement, and authorized an additional $44 million. On 10 August 1939 the AAC issued $86 million in aircraft contracts. By 1941 the same Congress that was so adamant about financial prudence and competitive bidding in 1934 was now voting billions of dollars for defense, and endorsing negotiated contracts to expedite the placement of contracts to meet the President's call for 50,000 aircraft. All the legislation from the Air Corps Act of 1926 onward, and all the boards and committees and their investigations and recommendations were to be invalidated by the Japanese attack on Pearl Harbor, and the procurement flood gates were to be opened.

The Air Materiel Command and the Long Range Bomber Requirements

In the early 1930s the Army Air Corps realized they needed a bomber with both speed and range. However, range was contingent on aircraft size; the more fuel carried for longer range meant a bigger aircraft and larger wing to carry the increased fuel supply. Large aircraft were dependent on the availability of sufficient power plant(s). In 1933 the requirements of a long-range bomber were discussed at Wright Field by chief engineer James Howard, his assistant Al Lyons, aircraft branch chief James Taylor, Hugh Kneer of the field service section, and Leonard "Jake" Harman, the Air Materiel Command representative. The group decided to categorize the future bomber types that would be required:

1) Wingspan, 75 feet; gross weight 15,000 pounds (that was already contemporary in the B-9 and B-10)
2) 100 feet span; 40,000 pounds gross weight
3) 150 feet span; 60,000 pounds gross weight
4) 200 feet span; 150,000 pounds gross weight
5) 250 feet span; 200,000 pounds gross weight
6) Etc.

In the fall of 1933 it was decided to disregard the No.2 category, and category No.3 was considered a feasible choice; it was to be identified as "Project A." Jake Harman drew up the requirement, and Gen. Conger Pratt of the Air Materiel Command authorized the money for engineering designs, then sent the request to Washington for approval. At the time strategic air power had few advocates, but long-range defensive patrol aircraft did have their proponents in Air Chief Benjamin Foulois and the Army General Staff. In 1933 Foulois directed his assistant, Brig.Gen. Oscar Westover, to fly missions testing the defense of the West Coast. Westover's report to the General Staff found the observation and patrol aircraft flying these missions to be "woefully obsolete." But he suggested that modern bombers flying in formation with increased speed and range could frus-

trate any "known agency." Pratt was able to sell the idea of the 5,000 mile bomber, as it could protect Alaska and Hawaii, and was a step in establishing a mobile GHQ Air Force.

In the early 1930s there was a dichotomy in the War Department. The conflict engaged the traditionalists, led by Army Chief of Staff Gen. John J. Pershing, who believed that the infantry ruled the battlefield, while the Army Air Arm, led by the defrocked Gen. Billy Mitchell, espoused the future role of air power in warfare. The government organized a number of boards and committees to study air doctrine and its role in future warfare. The most influential of these groups was the Baker Board Report of July 1934, which recommended America's national defense policy was not based on aggression, and its purpose was to defend the homeland and overseas possessions, with the Army fending off any invader until civilian forces could be mobilized. The Baker Report stated:

"The idea that aviation can replace any of the other elements of our armed forces is found, on analysis, to be erroneous. Since ground forces alone are capable of occupying territory, the Army with its own air forces remains the ultimate decisive factor in war."

Baker Board member Jimmy Doolittle voiced the minority dissent, supporting the separation of the Army and its air forces, and advocating the development of an air doctrine for its employment.

Although the Baker Board rejected an independent strategic air force, it did support the creation in March 1935 of a General Headquarters Air Force, which would be under the control of the Army commander in the field. However, there were conflicting opinions of the role of the GHQ Air Force. One was that it would be allocated and attached to field armies, and utilized under their direct control. Another view had the GHQ Air Force engaged as an integrated force, acting to further the mission of the Army. The view held by most airmen was to have it act as a unified force, not just to support the Army, but also to act beyond the realm of the Army with missions of its own. Maj.Gen. Frank Andrews was the CO of the GHQ Air Force, and forcefully advocated the airmen's point of view. As the possibility of a war in Europe approached the War Department was in a state of flux, and the GHQ Air Force and its concepts were replaced by ideas for-

Gen. Conger Pratt (R) of the Air Materiel Command authorized the money for "Project A" engineering designs, and sent the request to Washington for approval. Maj.Gen. Frank Andrews (L) was the CO of the GHQ AF, and held the point of view that the air force was to act as a unified force, not to support the Army, but to act beyond the realm of the Army with missions of its own. (USAAF)

mulated by the Joint Army-Navy Board that culminated in the First Strategic Air Plan (AWPD-1), which will be discussed later.

"Project A"

On 14 April 1934, Pratt released Harmon's Long-Range Bomber Requirement designated as top secret "Project A" for a bomber that could fly 5,000 miles (five times the range of the B-9 or B-10) at 200mph carrying a one-ton bomb load. No production was to be actualized, as Project A was more of a proof-of-concept than a production military bomber. On 12 May 1934 Pratt was authorized to begin negotiations for the initial designs. On the 14th he met with Boeing President Clair Egtvedt and Martin Works Manager C.A. Van Dusen (before Fleet hired him away from Martin the next year) at Wright Field. Pratt's aide, Jake Harman, explained the importance of Project A, and presented the ambitious proposal and outlined design and cost estimate procedures. He told the two company representatives that he would like to have their proposals by 15 June—only a month away! Sikorsky later entered the long-range bomber project with the XBLR-3, but it did not progress beyond the initial stages of development, and was not given the "B" (Bomber) designation. Back in Seattle Boeing began a flurry of activity by drawing up the preliminary design for its Model 294, which the AAC designated as XBLR-1 (eXperimental Bomber, Long-Range, Number-1). But a design obstacle was encountered in the proposed use of the four 850 horsepower Pratt & Whitney R-1830-11 Twin Wasp, 14-cylinder, 2-row radial engines, which would only provide the minimum power required for the projected weight of the aircraft. Another possible engine choice was four 1,600 horsepower 24-cylinder Allison XV-3420 liquid-cooled inline engines. The Allison V-3420 engine consisted of two of its V-1710 engines (e.g. 2x1710=3420) tied together by a single crankshaft to yield a V-24 (two V-12s). This engine had critical developmental problems, and was not available (until 1940). On 28 June Boeing was awarded a $600,000 contract to build its Project A design, which was then designated the XB-15, and Martin was given another $600,000 contract for its Model 145, to be called the XB-16.

Early VLR Bomber Concepts

Boeing XB-15

Engineering work began on this Boeing design in January 1934, and the result would be a single remarkable research model that was the largest aircraft ever built. On 29 June 1935 the Boeing proposal was officially designated the XB-15, with the AAC serial number 35-277, but it would not be ready until mid-1937. The XB-15 was an all-metal, 70,700 pound giant, with a 149 foot wingspan, an 87 foot, 7 inch length, and a 19 foot, 5 inch height. The aircraft was very similar in appearance to the B-17, except for the severe taper of its wing. It made its first flight on 15 August 1937, and the four 1,000 horsepower (rated) Pratt & Whitney R-1830-11 engines were found to be insufficient; thus, the XB-15 was underpowered, and its performance was mediocre. Its 197mph speed, rate of climb, and operational ceiling were each inferior to the Model 299, which had made its first flight on 28 July 1935, two years earlier than the XB-15. In the meantime, the Model 299 had been officially designated as the Y1B-17, and 13 had already been completed. Nonetheless, the design work on the XB-15 had provided Boeing engineers with beneficial experience toward the future development of the B-29, as the design was unique in many ways. It was the most heavily armed bomber ever built, as it was defended by three .30 caliber and three .50 caliber machine guns supplied with 7,200 rounds located in six turrets. It had the first 110-volt AC electrical system, with generators driven by two auxiliary power plants. It had a "comfort conditioned" living and sleeping quarters, including a kitchenette and lavatory for its crew of 10, including, for the first time, a flight engineer. There was a passageway leading through the thick wing for inflight servicing of the engines. The XB-15 project was continued as Model-294-2, the service test type that was designated the Y1B-20. In late 1937 the AAC ordered two more aircraft that were to be powered by the 1,400 horsepower Pratt & Whitney R-2180-5 engines. This proposed 80,000 pound model was similar in appearance to the XB-15, with a 152 foot wingspan and 90 foot length, but was canceled in the mockup stage. Later the original XB-15 had a large door cut into its fuselage, and continued its days as the XC-105 transport; it was based in Panama with the 6th Air Force. It would set several payload and load-to-altitude records, and flew relief supplies to earthquake victims in Chile before it was scrapped in 1945.

The Boeing XB-15 was an all-metal 70,700 pound giant with a 149 foot wingspan, an 87 foot, 7 inch length, and a 19 foot, 5 inch height. The aircraft was very similar in appearance to the B-17, except for the severe taper of its wing. (USAAF via Pima)

The Douglas XB-19 was a gigantic all-metal monoplane that measured 132 feet, 4 inches long, and its tail towered 42 feet above the tarmac. It weighed 84,431 pounds, and had the largest wing ever built at 212 feet. (USAAF via Pima)

Douglas XB-19

Meanwhile, the Very Long Range Bomber concept went off on a tangent with the Douglas XB-19. The design was initiated in 1935 as the XBLR-2, and one plane was ordered on 29 September 1936 to be powered by four new 2,000 Wright 3350-5 engines. It was designated the XB-19 by the AAC in mid-November 1937, and given the serial number 38-471. By mid-1938 work on the XB-19 had fallen behind schedule, and design changes had substantially increased its weight and decreased anticipated performance; realistically, the design was obsolete in view of contemporary advances in aircraft design. Douglas had spent a substantial amount of company funds on the project, and on 30 August 1938 requested to be released from the program, as it needed its design team to concentrate on more promising aircraft that could reach production. The Air Materiel Division persisted,. and ordered Douglas to complete the XB-19, which was to be used as a test aircraft. It required seven years of development before the bomber took flight for the first time over Clover Field, Santa Monica, CA, on 27 June 1941. Maj. Stanley Umstead and a crew of seven flew the bomber to March Field for testing and evaluation, first by Douglas, and then by the Army. Since the bomber was considered obsolete its "impressive" numbers—mostly its size and anticipated performance—were released to the press. Great public hoopla ensued:

"America's millions, given (its) breath-taking statistics, have probably been nursing a secret desire to hear that it bombed Tokyo" (Edward Churchill, *Flying Magazine*, August 1942).

Since it did not bomb Tokyo or anywhere else its "bigger job" as a flying laboratory was emphasized. President Roosevelt personally telegraphed congratulations to Donald Douglas on his company's accomplishment. The XB-19 that was tentatively accepted by the Air Corps in October 1941 was a gigantic all-metal stressed skin monoplane that measured 132 feet, 4 inches, its rudder towered 42 feet above the tarmac, and it weighed 84,431 pounds (162,000 pounds maximum gross weight). The bomber had the largest wing ever built at 212 feet and, like the XB-15, had 45 foot ailerons, and its eight-foot main tire retracted almost flush into the lower wing surface. A prototype tricycle landing gear was tested on a Douglas OA-4B Dolphin amphibian on loan from the Army, and then fitted to the XB-19. Initially it was to be powered by four 1,600 horsepower Allison XV-3420-1 24 cylinder in-line engines that were to power Boeing's model 247. The XV-3420-1 was two coupled V-1710 12-cylinder "V" engines driving a single propeller, but the engine ran into teething problems and, on 2 November 1936, Douglas decided on four 2,000 horsepower Wright R-3350-5 18-cylinder Cyclones. The XB-15 had a top speed of 224mph and a cruising speed of 135mph, and could carry 16,000 pounds of bombs internally; exterior bomb racks were able to carry 20,000 addition pounds. The aircraft had a crew of 16 that included an aircraft commander, pilot, co-pilot, flight engineer, navigator, radio operator, bombardier, and nine gunners. An additional crew of two flight mechanics and six relief crewmen could be accommodated in a special cabin with eight seats and six bunks built in the fuselage above the bomb bay. There were passageways built into the lower wing to give flight mechanics access to service the engines in flight. There was also a complete galley to prepare hot meals in flight. Defensive armament was an impressive total of 12 guns with 4,770 rounds of ammunition. The nose and top forward power turrets each contained one 37mm cannon and a .30 caliber machine gun. Single .50 caliber

machine guns were positioned in the powered rear dome, the two waist positions, a belly fairing, and in the tail. Two more .30s were at each side of the bombardier, and in the sides of the empennage. Self-sealing fuel tanks and protective armor for the crew were not included in the test model, but would have been placed in a production version, and would have further denigrated the bomber's performance. After Pearl Harbor, as a precaution against a possible Japanese attack, the bomber was flown to Wright Field, Dayton, OH, where it was painted in camouflage, and flew with loaded guns for its final test flights. In June 1942 the XB-19 was officially accepted, and the Air Force paid Douglas $1.4 million; however, Douglas had invested $4 million. Further testing was uneventful and mostly trouble free, except for the typical Wright 3350 engine cooling difficulties, which were solved by opening the engine cowl flaps during extended flights, and lowering the maximum speed under 16,000 feet. In 1943 the XB-19 was redesignated as the XB-19A when it was finally fitted with four Allison V-3420-11 engines that increased its top speed to 265mph. The XB-19A was tested at length, and was eventually converted to a transport; it remained the largest American aircraft ever built until the arrival of the Convair B-36 in August 1946. Its ultimate fate was to be scrapped at Davis-Monthan, Tucson, AZ, in June 1949.

The 1937-1938 "Superbomber" Requisites

In October 1937 the AAC Chief of Staff, Oscar Westover, decided to initiate informal design requisites for a "superbomber" that would succeed the B-17. The superbomber was to be much larger and heavier than the B-17, and also would be able to fly farther and faster with a heavier bomb load. Previously, scant attention had been paid to improving bomber operational efficiency by totally redesigning and cleaning up its airframe configuration, and making the fuselage larger to accommodate the interchangeability of fuel and bomb loads. The tricycle landing gear concept was in vogue with designers, and while it did ease ground handling, takeoffs, and landings, it added weight to the design (a ton in the case of the B-29). A superbomber that was to fly faster and farther would require the design of new and more powerful engines. Designers understood the means to increase range and speed was to fly at altitudes above 25,000 feet, but this presented problems of extreme cold and lack of oxygen, not only for the crew, but also for the engines. The engines would have to be "supercharged," which necessitated the compression and heating of the outside air used by the engines. The crew cabins would have to be "pressurized" to avoid the crew from having to wear warm heavy clothing, and to use oxygen equipment for long periods at high altitudes.

Aircraft companies were reluctant to take on new designs as, unlike today's cost-plus contracts, the AAC was by law only permitted to let fixed-price contracts, with no money paid in advance. Compensation was only made when the contracted aircraft was built and had flown. Aircraft companies had to use their own money to buy materials and tools, and also pay the salaries of their engineers and employees. The time from contract signing to prototype flight could range from months to years. Contracts had no "cost overruns clauses," and there was no guarantee that the prototype would be accepted for production.

Only four companies responded to Westover's request: Boeing in Seattle; Consolidated in San Diego; Douglas in Los Angeles; and the United Aircraft Sikorsky Division in Hartford. The design submissions were mediocre, and the Douglas design was considered the best of the lot. Even though Douglas was the only profitable company of the four at the time, its design was merely a lackluster upgrade of its new DC-2 airliner. Despite having four engine bomber expertise, Boeing's submission was nothing more than a reworked XB-15 design, whose mid-1930's technology was obsolete. Despite having been awarded the B-17 contract, Boeing had received no funds for that project, and was having problems on its early production phase, and the AAC refused to purchase more of the bombers. In fact, it would take a Federal loan in 1940 to keep Boeing from going bankrupt.

On 21 September 1938 Gen. Oscar Westover died in an aircraft accident. He was succeeded by Col. Henry Harley "Hap" Arnold, who had risen through the ranks, starting as a fledgling Lieutenant in the new Aeronautical Division of the Signal Corps in 1911. By the mid-1930s Arnold and other disciples of Billy Mitchell's theory of airpower had gradually gained prominent positions in the Army Air Corps, and were able to exert an "air" influence in the "horse soldier" dominated Army. When Arnold took over the AAC his bomber force consisted of 14 B-17s. In January 1939 President Roosevelt, after a review of American air power at Bolling Field, Washington, DC, requested the production of "500 bombers a month." On 30 March 1939 the AAC approved Consolidated's Model 32 design that would lead to the B-24. The Liberator would make its first flight on 29 December 1939, and join the B-17 as America's primary heavy bombers in the upcoming war.

The superbomber concept languished until late 1938, when Maj.Gen. Arnold called a secret meeting of AAC officers and aviation experts to discuss the future of the AAC, and the future of America's bomber strategy. Charles Lindbergh had visited Hitler's Germany, and was impressed and alarmed over the emphasis that the Luftwaffe had put on bombardment aircraft. Arnold asked Lindbergh to serve on a board headed by Brig.Gen. Walter Kilner, and was joined by Col. Carl Spaatz, Col. Earl Naiden, and Maj. Alfred Lyon. The Kilner Board issued its report in June 1939, and recommended that two engine light and medium bombers and a 2,000 mile four engine heavy bomber should be developed, along with another heavy bomber with a large fuselage that could carry bombs and/or enough fuel to give it a range of 5,000 miles. From the latter specification the B-29 and the B-32 would eventually be developed for hemispheric defense. The members of the Board thought that in a European war Germany would not only overrun the Continent, but also conquer Great Britain and then Africa, and perhaps establish bases in South America. If the Japanese began a war in the Pacific it would have to be fought over long expanses of ocean extending from Alaska to Hawaii to the Philippines, to as far away as Australia. In this scenario the B-17 would surely be inadequate, and the superbomber notion was revived. The role of the superbomber was not thought to be as a strategic bomber, but was to be a defensive bomber, able to fly long distances to strike an enemy advancing on the American Continents. The Board proposed a five-year research and development program for new aircraft and engines. Engine development was to focus on liquid-cooled engines with a range in horsepower from 1,500 to 2,400, and eventually increasing to 3,000hp. Although the Kilner Board recommendations were accepted by the AAC, at the time there was an isolationist sentiment in America, and the AAC could do nothing until Congress appropriated funds.

R-40B Contracts and the Role of the Air Materiel Command
For mostly good, and sometimes bad, the Air Materiel Command (AMC), headquartered at Wright Field, Dayton, OH, acted as a liaison between the taxpayer, the government, the Army Air Corps, and the aircraft industry in formulating military aircraft designs, developing these designs, purchasing the completed design, and placing them into production as soon as possible. The AMC did not design aircraft, but after receiving a list of requirements from the Air Staff it formulated performance, but not dimensional, specifications for the requisite aircraft. The Air Materiel Command's Procurement Division sent out requests to aircraft manufacturers to draft and tender designs for the specified aircraft. AMC engineers then considered the submitted designs, and consulted with the designers to determine if the proposal met specifications, was workable, and if the manufacturer was capable of producing the specified aircraft. If these criteria were met, then the manufacturer was contracted to build mockups and conduct wind tunnel tests, followed by contracts to build one or more experimental models. Finally, if the experimental model met specifications better than other contracted designs, the manufacturer was issued a contract to build the combat aircraft and then service test them.

The Air Materiel Command merged with the Air Service Command in 1944 to become the Air Technical Service Command (ATSC). The ATSC was made up of six divisions: Engineering; Procurement; Supply; Maintenance; Personnel; and Base Services. Of the six ATSC Divisions, the Engineering and Procurement Divisions had a direct affect on aircraft development and manufacture.

The function of the AMC Engineering Division's 10 extensively equipped laboratories was to research, develop, test, and evaluate every aspect of aircraft design, including those of the enemy. It had separate sections, such as Armament, Power Plant and Propeller, Aero-Medical, Radio and Electronics, etc. to study, test, develop, and approve equipment and systems in these sections. The Procurement Division evaluated design proposals, let contracts, and then followed up on the terms of the contract. At one time during the war this division had 40,000 contracts, with over 26,000 individual contractors comprising 400,000 plus items. The Production Section of the Procurement Division was responsible for the correct and timely supply of raw materials to over 15,000 manufacturers. It guaranteed the steady supply of combat-worthy aircraft into battle by providing for the expansion or construction of manufacturing facilities, dispersing government-furnished equipment (GFE) and parts, and obtaining and supervising subcontractors. Another responsibility of this division that would particularly affect the B-29 and B-32 programs, was its function to prescribe changes to aircraft and equipment as determined by flight testing and combat experience, and then incorporate them into the production line. Another Procurement section was the Quality Control Section, which employed thousands of officers and civilians to inspect and accept all aircraft, aircraft accessories, and equipment for the AAF. The inspection ran the gamut from raw materials to the finished article. Larger manufacturing plants often had a resident representative who supervised other inspection personnel who had been trained by the Division. There was a chronic shortage of ATSC Quality Control personnel to staff the thousands of factories doing defense work, and the factories also provided inhouse quality control that could range from meticulous to negligent.

R-40-B Contracts
Due to an energetic campaign by Maj.Gen. Henry Arnold in November 1939 Congress approved funding, and Arnold was authorized by Gen. George Marshall to let R-40-B study contracts (R-40-B translates as **R**equirement number **40**, **B**omber) for the Very long-range bomber. Capt.

Donald Putt of the Air Materiel Command at Wright Field established a statement of the military characteristics of the new bomber. The bomber was to have a range of 5,333 miles and be able to carry a bomb load of a ton over half that distance, and have a rather overly optimistic speed of 400mph. The high altitude strategic bomber was to be pressurized. In early 1940, after the experience of five months of war in Europe, the AAF saw that there were limitations in its earlier requirements, and issued another specification to succeed its R-40-B specs. The AAF restructured its heavy bomber requirements, requesting self-sealing fuel tanks, increased armor protection, and multiple turrets with heavier caliber machine guns and cannons. On 29 January 1940 the AAC sent the Request for Data R-40-B and Spec XC-218 to a number of aircraft companies that designed heavy bombers. The request was sent via mail marked as "Urgent" from Washington, DC. The companies were given 30 days to submit design proposals, and then were expected to finish a full-scale engineering mockup by 5 August 1940; the first completed aircraft was to be ready by 1 July 1941, and subsequent aircraft one month later. Four West Coast companies would submit designs: Lockheed and Consolidated of San Diego; Douglas of Los Angeles; and Boeing of Seattle. Again, none of the companies was motivated to submit far-reaching designs. Whatever resources they had available were being invested in expanding their factories and work force to build established, but mediocre, contemporary aircraft for the three American military services and foreign air forces that were at war, and in dire need of anything that could fly and fight.

On 8 April 1940 Boeing, Lockheed, and Douglas Consolidated (and later Martin) tendered their R-40-B proposals to the Air Materiel Command. The AAC Evaluation Board decided that all had met the requirements, and on 14 June all were awarded contracts to construct wooden scale models for wind tunnel testing and evaluation, and also were requested to furnish comprehensive engineering drawings and data, along with cost estimates. The Air Materiel Command initiated negotiations for price and delivery dates for a pair of prototypes with an option to purchase 200 production bombers. The Evaluation Board designated the proposals in order of preference: the Boeing proposal was designated the XB-29; the Lockheed XB-30; the Douglas XB-31; and the Consolidated XB-32. The contracts were valued at only $85,652, which was a pittance compared to the $3 billion dollar military aircraft allotment Congress had approved for 1940.

The Long Range Bomber Also-Rans
Lockheed XB-30

Lockheed based its proposal (Model 51-81-01 XB-30) on its triple-tailed Model 49 C-69 Constellation cargo/transport design that was, in turn, based on its Model 49 Airliner. The design was similar in dimension to the airliner, except for the lengthening of the nose, which was covered by Plexiglas for the bombardier, and the tail, which contained the two .50 caliber machine guns and a 20mm cannon. The design had a wingspan of 123 feet, a length of 104 feet, 8 inches, a height of 23 feet, 10 inches (at the vertical stabilizer), and an empty weight of 51,725 pounds (gross 86,000 pounds). It was powered by four 2,200 horsepower Wright R-3350-13 radial engines that were predicted to have a top speed of 450mph (cruise at 240mph), a service ceiling of 40,000 feet, and a range of 3,380 miles. It was to have an eight-man crew, with the pilot and co-pilot seated side-by-side under separate bubble canopies. However, on 6 September the Lockheed Board of Directors made a policy decision and withdrew its proposal from the superbomber competition.

Douglas XB-31

Douglas continued to rework its basic DC-4 transport design into the proposed XB-31, but their project never progressed beyond the drawing board. There was no XB-31 as such, but the designation denoted a series of engineering studies that created a range of shapes and sizes. The Model 423 was typical of the designs spawned from the bomber development of the commercial DC-4 airliner. The design was the largest and heaviest of all the proposals, and was submitted in the fall of 1941. It was to have a wingspan of 207 feet (five feet less than the XB-19), a length of 117 feet, 3 inches (only 3 inches less than the XB-19), and a height of 40 feet 5 inches (vertical stabilizer). It weighed 109,000 pounds empty, grossed at 176,000 pounds, and could drop 25,000 pounds of bombs through its double bomb bays. It was to be powered by four 28-cylinder 3,000 horsepower Pratt & Whitney R-4360 X-Wasps (later named the Wasp Major) radial engines to turn the huge 25 foot three-bladed propellers. The fuel load was 13,000 gallons, and its 450 gallon oil tank capacity exceeded the fuel load of many of the bombers of the 1930s! The eight-man crew was lodged in a beautifully streamlined, pressurized fuselage, with the pilot and co-pilot stations located in two small Plexiglas bubble canopies protruding from the top of the fuselage behind the nose. The potentially remarkable XB-31 never progressed beyond the design study phase, but some innovations shaped other later Douglas aircraft. The Douglas C-74 transport utilized the twin bubble canopies, and on a smaller scale the B-26 Invader tail assembly resembled the Model 423 tail.

Martin XB-33 and XB-33A

In late 1940, when the AAC was continuing to solicit high altitude twin-engined medium bomber designs, the Martin Company presented the Model 190, to be designated the XB-33, as a possible twin-engined replacement for its B-26 Marauder. The design featured a pressurized fuselage, and resembled Martin's recently developed PBM Mariner Navy Patrol bomber. It was slated to use two 1,800 horsepower Wright P-3350 engines, and was to measure 71 feet long, 22 feet, 6 inches high, and have a 100 foot wingspan. The continued evolution of the design caused a great increase in weight that precluded Martin from achieving the performance specifications required by the AAC. Martin set aside the XB-33 program, and expanded it to a four engine program, the XB-33A.

At the time Martin was in competition with Boeing and Consolidated for a long-range heavy bomber design, and felt its Model 190 showed promise. Martin was awarded a contract (AC-18645) to begin construction of two prototype XB-33A airframes. On paper the "Super Marauder" was to have a 79 foot, 10 inch fuselage, 24 foot height, and 134 foot wingspan (1,500 square feet). It was to be powered by four 1,800 horsepower Wright R-2600-15 Cyclones with two-stage GE CMC-3 turbo superchargers that were to give the bomber a top speed of 345mph at 39,000 feet (cruise at 242mph) over a range of 2,000 miles. The empty weight was 65,000 pounds (gross 98,000 pounds), with a bomb capacity of 10,130 pounds. The fuselage was to house a remote firing system that operated power turrets of twin .50 caliber machine guns in the nose, forward belly, and upper rear and tail. Three thousand rounds of ammunition fed the eight .50 caliber machine guns. The proposed performance specs were so promising, the AAC ordered 400 more XB-33As before the prototypes were built! But by this time the course of the war pointed toward a Japanese defeat, and the need for a third long-range heavy bomber was redundant, as the B-29 was proving itself over Japan, and the B-32 had been relegated to a non-player.

The XB-33A order was canceled, and the two unfinished prototypes were dismantled.

Boeing and Consolidated Awarded Long Range Bomber Contracts

Boeing and Consolidated were contracted to build the XB-29 and XB-32, not on a fixed cost basis, but on a cost plus a fixed 6% management fee basis. Once the contracted aircraft were finished the cost basis was the expense of salaries, materials, and depreciation, less any advances and progress payments. Boeing and Consolidated would receive a 6% fee of the total cost for managing the project. To give the companies an incentive to keep costs down it was to be awarded a percentage of the savings under the expected cost. The 6% essentially was the company's profit.

Boeing is Awarded the XB-29 Contract

From early 1938 Boeing engineers had been working on various superbomber designs (Models 316, 322, 333, 333A/B, 334, 334A, and 341), trying various engines (Allison V-1710, Wright X-1800, Pratt & Whitney R-2800, and finally the Wright R-3350), fuselage configurations, and wing designs. Boeing continued to evaluate its earlier Model 341 proposal, and made numerous improvements that led to the Model 345. Compared to the Model 341, the Model 345 was to reflect the exigencies of the European air war in its design. After working day and night for two months Boeing responded by sending the preliminary design for the Model 345 to Wright Field on 11 May 1940. The Model 345 was essentially a reworked Model 341, with a crew of 12 contained in a pressurized cabin. The Boeing design team worked in close association with the Flight Test and Aerodynamics Division to produce the most aerodynamic design possible. The fuselage skin joints were to be smooth, and all external rivets were to be flush. All "normal" protuberances, such as lights, thermometers, antennas, de-icers, drains, vents, and air scoops were to be streamlined, faired, or flush. The new design requirements increased the gross weight of the Model 345 to 112,300 pounds, which was 27,000 pounds more than the Model 341. The weight increase decreased its speed by 23mph (to 382mph), compared to the Model 341's 405mph (at 25,000 feet). The weight of the new remote armament system weighed 4,153 pounds, as compared to the Model 341's armament of 1,646 pounds. This ton and a quarter increase in weight required 1,680 pounds of additional fuel to carry the bomber over a constant range, while the newly added self-sealing fuel tanks weighed 3,000 pounds more, and required another 2,000 pounds of fuel. Generally, for each pound added to the Model 345 there was two-thirds pounds of fuel needed to carry it over the required range of 5,333 miles. To accommodate these increases the Model 345 had 17 feet more wingspan (141 feet, 3 inches), and was almost 16 feet longer than the Model 341. Edward Wells and Wellwood Beall of Boeing's Aerodynamics Department had continued their work on high lift wings from the Model 334A in August 1939, and developed the Boeing 115 Aerofoil. On the drawing board the Model 334A had a promising 124 feet, 7 inch very high aspect wing that was to be fitted with four 2,000 horsepower Pratt & Whitney R-2800 engines. The 115 Aerofoil had a wing area 70 square feet less than the 334A, and a wing loading of 64 pounds per square foot, as compared to the 334A's 47 pounds. The Boeing 115 Aerofoil had the potential of increased range due to its lower drag. The AAF was unconvinced about the wing, as it was concerned that, because of its high wing loading, its operational ceiling would be reduced, and would affect its takeoff and landing characteristics. After comprehensive wind tunnel tests a wing flap that would offset the high

wing loading was developed that precluded the Air Force's worries. The wing had an unusually high aspect ratio of 11.5, but was of a laminar flow type, which gave it a good lift/drag ratio. Compared to conventional wings the 115 Aerofoil was deep between the main spars, giving it greater strength, increasing the space for fuel tanks, and had more gradual stalling characteristics. The 115 Aerofoil was later developed into the 117 airfoil by George Schairer, and would help characterize the B-29. The bomber was supported by a tricycle landing gear with double wheels, with the main wheels retracting into the inboard engine nacelles instead of into the wing, as in previous models. It was powered by four new Wright air-cooled R-3350 twin-row radial engines, and more than met the one-ton bomb load over 5,333 mile requirement, as it was capable of an eight ton maximum bomb load over 6,950 miles. While the Model 341 mounted only six flexible manual .50 caliber machine guns, the Model 345 bristled with 10 .50 caliber machine guns and one 20mm cannon. The machine guns were mounted in pairs in four Sperry retractable turrets, and one pair plus a 20mm cannon were mounted in the power operated tail turret. The previous problem of pressurizing the gun positions was solved in a new innovative way. Instead of having the gunners positioned inside each turret they controlled the guns remotely via sighting periscopes from stations within pressurized cabins inside the fuselage.

At the time the Boeing engineering department was stretched thin, as the Boeing B-17 venture was ready for mass production, and the AAC was about to place an order for 250 B-17Es. Over the previous two years the preliminary design engineers and aerodynamic engineers had developed the Model 345 into the XB-29 design from performance specifications set by the Air Materiel Command, and issued by its Procurement Division into a detailed plan with dimensional specifications.

On 24 August 1940, before the mockup was even completed, the AAC was so impressed by wind tunnel data that it let a contract for two flyable Model 345 prototypes at a cost of $3,615,095. The first prototype was scheduled to be delivered in April 1942, and the second in June. The AAC redesignated the Model 345 as the XB-29 experimental bomber 29, as it was the twenty-ninth Army bomber since the Martin B-1 of 1918. Soon the mockup was approved, and wind tunnel tests of a detailed scale model were begun. The XB-29 was to be the largest and fastest bomber ever built at 116,000 pounds, and a cruising speed of 380mph (at 25,000 feet). The bomber would have a wingspan of 141 feet and a fuselage length of 99 feet. It would carry a crew of 10, with five in the nose cabin: pilot, copilot, engineer, navigator, and bombardier. Four would be in the rear pressurized

The AAC redesignated the Boeing Model 345 as the XB-29, which was to be the largest and fastest bomber ever built at 116,000 pounds and a cruising speed of 380mph (at 25,000 feet). The bomber would have a wingspan of 141 feet and a fuselage length of 99 feet, and would carry a crew of 10. (USAAF)

cabin: Central Fire Control gunner, two more gunners, a radio operator, and a lone gunner in the tail. The pressurized forward and rear cabins were to be connected by a crawl tunnel across the top of the bomb bay. The XB-29 was truly to be a superbomber, at twice the weight and horsepower of the B-17, and half again as large dimensionally.

The war in Europe was escalating, and Gen. Oliver Echols summoned Boeing President Philip Johnson and Earl Schaefer, the vice president of the existing Boeing-Wichita factory, to Dayton, but because of a threatened strike, Oliver West went in Johnson's place. At the meeting Echols told the two Boeing representatives that the AAC was going to contract for 512 B-17s and two XB-29s, and the Seattle plant would need to be doubled to accommodate the new B-17 production. When B-29 orders came in Plant #2 would have to be built in Wichita, as the B-29 would not be built on the West Coast. In order to get part of the Wichita plant built B-17 tails were to be fabricated there until B-29 production began. With the government contract in hand, Boeing was able to obtain loans and buy material from suppliers, and begin in earnest its long quest to develop the XB-29 into the finest bomber in World War II.

Consolidated is Awarded the XB-32 Contract

In response to the R-40-B request Consolidated had submitted drawings of its initial design to Wright Field, where wind tunnel tests were completed using a 1/35th scale birch wood model that had a 46 inch wingspan, and had a very different look from the final contracted model. To facilitate the wind tunnel tests the turrets and landing gear were removable to replicate their retraction, and the controls (elevators, rudders, and stabilizer) were movable. The tests uncovered that, while the twin-tailed configuration gave the bomber "satisfactory" longitudinal control, its directional stability was assessed as "insufficient." Although the tests led to many minor modifications that were incorporated in the contracted version, the twin tail configuration was not changed, and was to be the bane of the prototype.

On 6 September 1940 contract number AC 15549 ordered two XB-32 prototypes to be delivered. The first prototype (#41-141) was to be delivered in 18 months (March 1942), while the second (#41-142) was to be delivered three months later (June 1942). That same day contract AC15429 for two flyable XB-29s and a non-flying static test aircraft was let to Boeing.

In response to the R-40-B request Consolidated submitted drawings of its initial design to Wright Field, where wind tunnel tests were completed using a 1/35th scale birch wood mockup that had a 46 inch wingspan, and had a very different look from the final contracted model. To facilitate the wind tunnel tests the turrets and landing gear were removable to replicate their retraction, and the controls (the elevators, rudders, and stabilizer) were movable. (Consolidated via USAAF)

On 14 December 1941 the contract was revised to add a third flyable XB-29 and a third XB-32 prototype (#41-18336), which was to be delivered in March 1943. Consolidated designated the XB-32 as its Model 33, and named R.C. "Sparky" Seabold as Project Engineer. Seabold used the experience gained on this project later as the Project Engineer for Consolidated's giant post war B-36 bomber.

The contract stipulated that Consolidated submit a wooden model to the Air Materiel Command at Wright Field for wind tunnel tests. By December Consolidated had built revised mockups using new data from the previous Wright Field wind tunnel tests. The tests were conducted during the last 10 days of December. On 6 January 1941 the modified mock up, as suggested by the Wright wind tunnel tests, were approved by AAC inspectors, who had continued reservations about the twin tail configuration. On 17 April the engine mock ups were inspected and approved. In mid-June the AAC awarded a contract to build 13 YB-32 service test models for $221.7 million to be developed, and built along with the original three XB-32 prototypes.

3

The XB-32 Prototype

Description

The XB-32 had some family characteristics to its older B-24 Liberator sister, but in a beauty contest the XB-32 was the definite winner. It had the same fully cantilevered slim high aspect ratio Davis Wing mounted at the top of the fuselage, but the wingspan at 135 feet was 25 feet longer than the B-24. The wing center section was permanently attached to the fuselage, and the wing was constructed on two spars, with metal ribs and flush riveted stressed aluminum skin. Each wing had two Alclad-covered Fowler flaps that ran from the center section of the wing from fuselage to ailerons. The XB-32 had the same two vertical fins and rudders as the B-24, but with trim tabs mounted on the ends of the "horizontal" stabilizer, which was canted at a 7.5 dihedral like the tail assembly of the PB2Y Coronado. The B-32's four Wright R-3350 engines (R-3350-13 inboard and R-3350-21 outboard) produced 1,000 horsepower each more than the B-24's four 1,200 horsepower Pratt & Whitney R-1830s. The B-32 was designed to have a remote armament system controlled by crew enclosed in pressurized cabins, while the B-24 gunners, wearing oxygen masks, were located in manned turrets and gun positions. Despite having almost twice the gross weight of the B-24 at 101,662 pounds (65,000 pounds empty and 113,500 pounds maximum), the XB-32, in contrast to the B-24's 66 foot slab-sided

Each wing had two Alclad-covered Fowler flaps that ran from the center section of the wing from fuselage to ailerons. The XB-32 (41-141 shown) had the same two vertical fins and rudders as the B-24, but with trim tabs mounted on the ends of the horizontal stabilizer, which was canted at a 7.5 dihedral like the tail assembly of the PB2Y Coronado. (Chana)

The XB-32 (shown is the first prototype 41-141) had some family characteristics to its older B-24 Liberator sister, but in a beauty contest the XB-32 was the definite winner. The B-32's four Wright R-3350 engines (R-3350-13 inboard and R-3350-21 outboard) produced 1,000hp each more than the B-24's four 1,200hp Pratt & Whitney R-1830s. (Chana)

Despite having almost twice the gross weight of the B-24 at 101,662 pounds, the XB-32 (41-141 shown), in contrast to the B-24's 66 foot slab-sided profile, featured a sleek tapering 83 foot cylindrical fuselage with a maximum 9.5 feet diameter to accommodate the two pressurized cabins, which were separated by dual bomb bays equipped with hydraulic doors. The B-32's tricycle landing gear gave the bomber a more stately upright appearance, rather than the B-24's squat, low slung physique. (Chana)

The original XB-32 design had a rounded nose, but reverted to the stepped windscreen and a dome-shaped nose that gave the bomber a streamlined look, rather than the pug-nosed appearance of the stepped B-24 nose and cockpit sections. Shown is the second prototype, 41-142. (Chana)

The XB-32 (41-142 shown) had the same fully cantilevered slim high aspect ratio Davis Wing mounted at the top of the fuselage, but the wingspan, at 135 feet, was 25 feet longer than the B-24. (Chana)

profile, featured a sleek tapering 83 foot cylindrical fuselage with a maximum 9.5 foot diameter to accommodate the two pressurized cabins, which were separated by dual bomb bays equipped with hydraulic doors. Both the XB-29 and XB-32 had a pressurized tunnel that traversed over the top of its two bomb bays, and could be used at altitude. The two pressurized cabins were also connected by a catwalk that was supported by a heavy beam; it ran through the bomb bays, and was only used at low altitudes. The bomb bay doors were similar to the B-24 hydraulically powered roll up type. The original XB-32 design had a rounded nose, but reverted to the stepped windscreen and a dome-shaped nose that gave the bomber a streamlined look, rather than the pug-nosed appearance of the stepped B-24 nose and cockpit sections. The forward section had flush riveting, while riveting rear of the flight deck was the standard brazier head type. Each had a tricycle landing gear, but the B-32's gear gave the bomber a more stately upright appearance, rather than the B-24's squat, low slung physique.

The Davis Wing
The XB-32 inherited some resemblances to older Consolidated designs and borrowed from their innovations. Its designers gave it the same high aspect ratio, high-lift/low-drag slim Davis Wing that was pioneered on the Model 31 flying boat, and had established the B-24 as a rival to the B-17. In late 1937 Walter Brookins, the first civilian to be taught to fly by the Wright Brothers, intervened for David R. Davis, asking Reuben Fleet to talk with him about his radical new airfoil design, Fleet, who was always looking for new ideas, granted Davis an interview. Davis had been the partner of Donald Douglas in the Davis-Douglas Aircraft Company, but had formed a new association with Brookins. During the interview Davis, a brilliant engineer without a formal engineering degree, described his theories and the experimental work he had done. It was Davis' contention that there was a mathematically perfect airfoil section that could reduce drag to an absolute minimum. Previously airfoils were developed by placing them in a wind tunnel, and then calculating which one was the most efficient design. But Davis thought that instead of testing countless airfoil designs, why not begin with the perfect sphere and then test the successive tear drop shapes that were formed while it fell; similar to a falling drop of

water. Davis applied for a patent for his "fluid airfoil" principle, and continued to successfully improve and test it by using wing sections installed on automobiles driven at high speeds. Fleet told Davis he was very definitely interested in the design, but was not an aerodynamicist, and wished to have Davis' idea studied by his own staff. Davis hesitated, protecting his idea, but Fleet assured him that he and his company were honest and could be trusted. Applying pressure, Fleet told Davis the only way he would accept his idea was for him to come to an overnight decision. Of course, Davis really had no alternative but to accept, and allowed Mac Laddon, Consolidated's Chief Engineer, and George Schairer, the company's best aerodynamicist, to examine his airfoil.

Although initially unimpressed by Davis' non-engineering degree credentials, Schairer and Laddon both saw that Davis' ideas, though radical, were viable. On 10 February 1938 Fleet signed Davis as a consultant to Consolidated at $200 per month, working a minimum of eight days per month for six months. Consolidated agreed to pay the wind tunnel test expenses at the California Institute of Technology, and if the test results were satisfactory and the wing section was used on a Consolidated prototype aircraft, Davis would then be paid $2,500. If the wing were used on production aircraft then the Davis-Brookins Aircraft Co. would be paid one half of 1% of the airframe sales price, excluding the cost of the engines and Government Furnished Equipment (GFE), which calculated as equivalent to about $5 per aircraft. From October 1943 to February 1945 a royalty was paid on 8,801 Davis-Winged aircraft, including the Navy PB4Y-2 and the Air Force B-24 and B-32. Davis-Brookins received a grand total of $650 for the 130 B-32s that Consolidated built. To protect its competitive position Consolidated prohibited Davis from revealing data on his airfoil to any other aircraft companies or organizations of the Federal Government. Consolidated directed Davis to expedite receiving full patent protection on the pending patent application, but if the patent was judged invalid then the royalty payments were to stop. It has been reported that Davis inserted wrong coordinates on his patent application so that the true coordinates could not be duplicated (via Bill Chana).

At the time Consolidated wished to improve on its PBY design, and had the Model 31 twin-engined flying boat nearly ready to come off the

The Model 31 design was a deep-hulled flying boat that was so incongruous with its huge 22 foot deep hull it was nicknamed the "Pregnant Guppy." What made it even more incongruous were the two slender 55 foot Davis wings supporting the aircraft. (Consolidated via Pima)

drawing boards, and decided that the Model 31 aircraft offered an opportunity to test Davis' wing design. Davis fabricated a reduced scale eight foot wing section and tested it in the Cal Tech Guggenheim wind tunnel. Davis waited several weeks for the results before inquiring about the delay. He was told the wind tunnel did not seem to be performing correctly and the test had to be redone. Dr. Clark Millikan and other Cal Tech scientists were puzzled by the 102% efficiency of Davis' airfoil, as 90% had been considered the theoretical maximum. When the tests were repeated the results were the same, and were accepted, although no one, including the renowned Dr. Theodore von Karman, was able to explain the phenomenon. It would not be until April 1939 that Consolidated would allow Davis and Brookins to disclose that they had perfected a method to plot "near perfect curves for wing section." Consolidated had spent over $40,000 for the wind tunnel testing of the Davis Wing and never regretted the costs.

The Model 31 design was to be a deep-hulled flying boat powered by two 2,000 horsepower twin-row 18-cylinder Wright R-3350 radial engines that were to give the aircraft long-range at high cruising speeds, and would enable it to carry heavy loads. A commercial version was designed that was able to carry 52 passengers and a crew of five in a double deck cabin. The aircraft had extendable pontoons on its wings, and a fully retractable tricycle landing gear for beaching. In its design stage the surprising results from the Cal Tech wind tunnel test of the Davis Wing became available. After consulting with Laddon and Schairer Fleet made a momentous deci-

sion; instead of waiting for Navy design competition and bureaucracy he risked $1 million of company money by deciding to utilize the Davis Wing on the Model 31. Construction started in July 1938, and by May 1939 it was ready for testing. The aircraft was so incongruous with its huge 22 foot deep hull supported in the air by two slender 55 foot wings that it was nicknamed the "Pregnant Guppy." To reduce takeoff and landing speeds the Fowler type flap was utilized. On 5 May 1939 test pilot William Wheatley surprised onlookers when he lifted the large aircraft off the waters of San Diego Bay in a very short takeoff run, and reported that the flying boat handled like a pursuit aircraft in the air. Further testing demonstrated the Model 31 to have an increase in overall performance of over 20% compared to the PBY, with a top speed of 250mph, and an expected range to exceed 3,500 miles, as compared to the PBY's 170mph and 2,500 mile range.

In 1939 Schairer left Consolidated to become Boeing's Chief Aerodynamicist. In Seattle he and Eddie Allen, Head of Flight Testing and Aerodynamics, led Boeing engineers in the continued testing of the Davis Wing concept in their wind tunnels. Schairer was definitely influenced by the work at Consolidated, and suggested that the Davis concept that Boeing previously used on the Model 334A be retained, but decided that a different approach to the concept would be needed for the Model 345. They kept the long narrow taper of the Davis Wing, and developed the Boeing 115 wing for the Model 345, which evolved into the 117 wing on the XB-29, and eventually on the B-29.

XB-32 Receives Its First Tail

The XB-32 used the signature Consolidated twin tail configuration that had been used successfully on the B-24 Liberator design. However, closer inspection of the tail assembly of the XB-32 showed that each half of the horizontal stabilizer was tilted upwards in dihedral, which was the redesign of the PB2Y Coronado Flying Boat tail.

On 27 May 1937 the Bureau of Aeronautics awarded Consolidated a contract to build a long-range four engine flying boat, the Model 29 Coronado, XPB2Y-1 to -5 (Navy designation). On 17 December 1937 test pilot William Wheatley flew the huge prototype for the first time, and was concerned about the aircraft's "directional instability." The prototype was equipped with a single vertical fin and rudder that gave it dangerous lateral stability. As a solution Consolidated engineers decided to add two small elliptical vertical fins placed adjacent to the single main fin on the front half of the horizontal stabilizer. Fleet personally flew the aircraft, and found the new twin elliptical fin configuration helped, but did not solve the problem. Fleet and his engineers met, and decided to delete the entire single tail section, and place a horizontal stabilizer on top of the rear fuselage with dual round vertical fins and rudders (2/3s above and 1/3 below the stabilizer) placed at the ends. Each half of the horizontal stabilizer was canted at a 7.5 degree dihedral, so that the lower 1/3 of the rudder would not touch the water during takeoff. The design was successful, but later in the XB2Y-2, and then the PB2Y-3 to -5 production models, the dual round vertical fin was made more elliptical in shape. Because of the success of this tail configuration on the large Coronado the design was adapted for the large XB-32 design as a means to expedite designing the aircraft by the overburdened Consolidated engineering department.

Consolidated test pilot William Wheatley first flew the Model 29 Coronado in December 1937, the Model 31 Guppy in May 1939, and the XB-24 on its first flight in December 1939. (Consolidated via Pima)

The XB-32 used the signature Consolidated twin tail configuration that had been used successfully on the B-24 Liberator design. However, closer inspection of the tail assembly of the XB-32 shows that each half of the horizontal stabilizer was tilted upwards in dihedral, which was the redesign of the PB2Y Coronado Flying Boat. (Consolidated via LeVine)

Initial XB-32 Flight Testing

The first XB-32 prototype (41-141) was completed on 1 September 1942, and was ready for flight testing on 7 September, two weeks ahead of the XB-29, but still six months behind schedule. The delay was caused by pressurization, remote sighting, and turret retraction problems, but because both the B-32 and B-29 were the core of America's VHB bomber program the AAF stipulated that the tests begin immediately, even if the aircraft were tested "stripped." The first taxi tests were conducted on 3 September at Lindbergh Field, and four days later the aircraft was ready for its maiden flight. Test pilot Russell Rogers and co-pilot Richard McMakin, assisted by first and second flight engineers Harold Siegenfield and Henry Bomback, respectively, made up the minimal crew. Russ Rogers was the senior pilot in charge of all Consolidated pilots, and manager of experimental and production flight crews: flight engineers, radio operators, and navigators. Consolidated test pilots under Rogers were Douglas Kelly for production flight testing, and McMakin was the head of Overseas Delivery, which would become Consairway. Engineer William Chana had designed and supervised the installation of the flight test instruments, but test flight engineers were not allowed on the flight, and he was in radio contact with the aircraft in the air. The flight was a harrowing experience, as 10 minutes after take-off forces on the vertical tail surfaces fractured a rudder trim tab, setting up a tail flutter that caused the prototype to shudder severely. Rogers quickly turned across San Diego Bay and made an emergency landing at the Navy's North Island Field. Both pilots had to use both feet on the rudder pedals to curb the flutter. Bill Chana describes the problem:

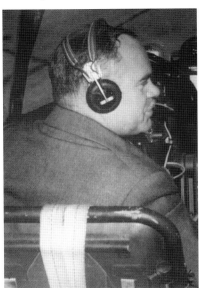

Russ Rogers was the senior pilot in charge of all Consolidated pilots, and manager of experimental and production flight crews: flight engineers, radio operators, and navigators. (Chana)

"The XB-32 had directional trim tabs conventionally located at the trailing edge of each rudder. But unconventionally, they were electrically operated, driven by a small electric motor and an actuating arm located within the rudder. Post flight inspection revealed that one actuator arm had failed, allowing a trim tab to float freely and flutter, thus driving the rudders into their violent gyrations."

The following day a ground test was conducted using the twin tail of the second XB-32 (41-142), which was nearing completion in the Experimental Shop. The twin tail was subjected to flight frequencies using external shakers. Outwardly the trim actuator and trim tab seemed to be dependable, but under the scrutiny of a strobe light Bill Chana reported: "You could see it bending like a rubber band." Modifications were made to the tail surfaces, and they were never to fail again, but this did not remedy the tail problems.

Testing was continued, and 41-141 continued to encounter a few major, and many minor, nagging problems. One modification after another was made to try to solve each problem as it occurred. During the testing Chana ordered a change to his flight test instrumentation control console. The next day he asked for the aircraft's electrical power to be turned on, and soon saw smoke flowing out of the flight deck hatch. He quickly had the power cut, and when he entered the flight deck he saw the wires at his station smoking. Until the mechanics arrived with fire extinguishers Chana huffed and puffed, trying to extinguish the now cooling wires. Chana's examination showed that, despite quality control inspections and sign offs, a wire had not been connected, and was grounded against the aircraft structure. A number of the XB-32's tests were speed power runs, and changes were continually being made to maximize the bomber's cruise and top speed. Each engine of the XB-32 had two exhaust-driven turbo superchargers located on the lower right and left sides of the nacelle. The hot exhaust gases were released directly aft to the nacelle surface, and into the line of flight, as designers believed that eight exhaust columns directed 90 degrees into the slipstream could cause drag and decrease airspeed. Porcelain coated steel deflector caps were fitted to the superchargers to deflect the exhaust gases rearward. A test using all eight deflectors was scheduled to test them at various power settings and at low altitudes. The test was to be conducted over the Imperial Valley, east of San Diego, near the Salton Sea. 41-141 flew 80 miles, crossed the 7,000 foot Laguna Mountains, and descended to about 1,000 feet over the desert, then began the first high power speed run. Chana checked the engine temperatures and found them to be normal. When he climbed up into the astrodome he saw that the porcelain covers were directing the hot gases aft as they were designed, but that the gases from the No.2 engine had burned away half of the landing gear doors' outer skin, heating them to a cherry red color. The fire was adjacent to the

Early mock up of pilot's side of cockpit XB-32 (30 September 1941). The forward upper controls are the throttles; below them are the round mixture controls, and aft (below the seat arm) are the inboard and outboard flap handles (flat ends) and the round landing gear control. (Consolidated via Chana)

Early mock up of co-pilot's side of cockpit. (Consolidated via Chana)

Pilot's and co-pilot's station with instrument panel and entrance to bombardier's compartment on the first XB-32. (Consolidated via Chana)

Co-pilot's station on the first XB-32 (Consolidated via Chana)

XB-32 Flight Engineer's Station. The four large dials above the panel are the Engine Torquemeter Indicators, and the triangular box above left is the Fuel Selector Panel. The round porthole is the Delreo 180 Degree Vision Lens. The levers on the back of the table are Turbo Supercharger Controls (left) and the Carburetor Mixture Controls (right). (Consolidated via Chana)

main landing gear tires, and only a few feet from the wing fuel tanks. To make maters worse, the No.3 nacelle appeared ready to catch fire. Chana informed pilot Russ Rogers of the situation, who cut the power to both engines, climbed back over the mountains, and made an emergency landing at Lindbergh Field. Once on the ground inspection showed that the fires would have been a serious threat if the power had not been reduced in time. The XB-32 had nacelle extension cones attached to the lower surface of the wing flaps. All four nacelle extensions were burned off, the rear section of all nacelles were charred, and the nacelle skin surfaces were buckled from the heat. Large sections of the outer aluminum skin and inner door frames were missing. The flaps were not damaged, as they were up during most of the flight.

During previous high speed test flights it was found that the landing gear doors, when closed, would crack open a few inches, causing drag. A temporary remedy while new doors were being designed and manufactured was to attach steel cables to the front and rear ends of the four landing gear doors, two on each nacelle. The eight cables were then run through the wing to the rear bomb bay, where each was attached to a strongly mounted eyebolt. Each cable had a turnbuckle to remove any slack, and to pull the landing gear doors tightly closed. After the landing gear was retracted the rear cabin observer was to enter the bomb bay and hook each cable to the appropriate eyebolt, then use a bar to tighten the turnbuckle to

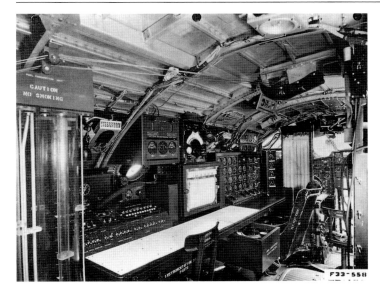

Bill Chana in the cone-shaped tail. (Consolidated via Chana)

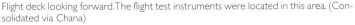

Flight deck looking forward. The flight test instruments were located in this area. (Consolidated via Chana)

tightly close the landing gear doors. The closing cable procedure took about 20 minutes, and about 15 minutes to remove the cables upon landing. In case of an emergency, the rear observer was to enter the bomb bay and cut the cables with a large cable cutter, and be prepared to duck the whipping cables once they were cut.

While these many problems were relatively minor, they and the XB-32 delays caused the AAF to cancel its order for the 13 YB-32 service test aircraft in early February. Even though the AAF maintained that it would add these 13 YBs to the first production contract, it was evident that there were major concerns about the entire XB-32 program. Fortunately for Consolidated, Boeing's XB-29 program was also suffering from serious teething problems, mostly involving the Wright R-3350 engine.

The XB-29 Prototype Meets Disaster: 18 February 1943

On 18 February 1943 the XB-29, piloted by renowned Boeing test pilot Eddie Allen, took off to the south from Boeing Field, Seattle, at 1209. Allen was to evaluate climb and level flight performance, and to measure engine-cooling figures with two and four engines operating. The test flight was to be restricted to 25,000 feet, as the Wright R-3350 Duplex Cyclone engines had previous problems with low nose oil pressures at high altitudes. Corrections made to previous problems were also to be assessed. Five minutes after takeoff, climbing at rated power through 5,000 feet, a fire was reported in the No.1 engine nacelle. Allen cut the mixture and fuel to the engine and feathered the prop, while Fritz Mohn, the flight engineer, closed the cowl flaps and discharged the Lux CO_2 fire extinguisher, and the fire appeared to have been extinguished. Allen turned the bomber back toward Boeing Field and descended for a routine landing from the north on Runway 13 to the SSE into a five-mph wind, rather than a downwind landing on the longer, 5,200 feet runway. After five minutes Allen radioed that he was descending at 2,400 feet, and asked for immediate clearance, as his No.1 engine had been on fire, and the prop had been feathered. He said that the trouble was not serious, but crash equipment should stand by. Two minutes later Allen radioed that he was over the Lake Washington Bridge, four miles NE of the field on the downwind leg. Turning left into the base

leg at 2,500 feet he corrected his altitude to 1,500 feet, passing over the heavily populated west shore of Lake Washington. The XB-29 continued a normal descent over Seattle at 1,200 feet, but heavy smoke and pieces began to come from the No.2 engine, and the stricken bomber was headed for Seattle's industrial and commercial area south of downtown. The bomber continued to head south, losing altitude as the fire spread across the wing into the bomb bay. Two minutes later an explosion occurred that could be heard on the ground. The radio operator peered into the forward bomb bay and saw that the center wing section forward wing spar was on fire. The control tower overheard the radio operator on his open microphone tell Allen:

"Allen, better get this thing down in a hurry. The wing spar is burning badly."

Prominent aviation engineer Eddie Allen (pointing center) meets with the Consolidated flight test instrumentation survey team visiting the Boeing factory in Seattle in late 1940. (L-R) H. Siebert, W. Chana, F. Zellmer, Eddie Allen, A. Bussey, G. Stetsuk, E. Stout, and H. Moe. (Consolidated via Chana)

On 18 February 1943 the XB-29 was being flown on a test flight over Seattle by Boeing test pilot Eddie Allen when it crashed into the Frye Meat Packing Plant, killing him and pilot Bob Dansfield, as well as nine valued scientific crewmen. The crash halted the B-29 program until an investigation was completed. (Boeing via Pima)

Allen's last message to Boeing Field was to order that the fire equipment be ready, as he was coming in with a wing on fire. Allen turned the XB-29 south on an oblique final approach at 250 feet, anxiously trying to reach the field, which was still three to four miles away. Witnesses later reported seeing the leading edge of the wing missing between the No.1 and No.2 engines (parts were later found on the ground). Two crewmen in the forward compartment tried to bail out, but their parachutes failed to open at the low altitude. The radioman, Harry Ralston, hit a high-tension wire, and his parachute snagged and he was strung over the wire. Flight Test Engineer Edward Wersebe jumped, but his chute never opened. At 1226, three miles from the runway, Allen tried to pull back on the controls into a left turn, but the XB-29 crashed into the Frye Meat Packing Plant, killing him, pilot Bob Dansfield, and the remaining seven crewmen on board. The crash and ensuing fire killed another 20 people, including workers in the factory and several firemen, and destroyed much of the plant.

The Allen crash devastated the Boeing XB-29 test program, as in eight years the company had lost three chief test pilots, three large experimental aircraft, and the 11 highly qualified men on Allen's XB-29. The crash was investigated from every angle, with witnesses questioned. Remnants of the aircraft were collected not only at the crash site, but also along the flight path, and were intensively examined. Thousands of hours of ground tests and engineering analyses were conducted. Changes obviously had to be made, but the post crash investigation and previous tests had shown that the B-29 airplane was aerodynamically and structurally reliable. There were 54 major and literally hundreds of other minor changes, usually found during flight-testing, that were recommended and assigned precedence to be evaluated. The major problems centered on the engines, nacelles, and surrounding structures that needed to be redesigned to isolate and minimize the fire potential. There were problems with the nacelle design, and incorporating the changes in the Fisher nacelle plants in Cleveland and Detroit were done without interrupting production. Reducing cowl flap length and the internal airflow decreased nacelle drag, and modifications were made to ventilation and nacelle drainage. The engine was to be fitted with a computer directed fire-control and extinguishing system that was nowhere near ready. The carburetor had to be replaced by fuel injection carburetors, and Minneapolis-Honeywell electric turbo regulators were added.

The propellers needed a better feathering system so they would not continue to turn out of control and cause fires. The changes necessary for the wing were the relocation of the filler heads and isolation of the fuel cells, additional bulkheads and ventilation of the wing leading edge, the seals in the firewalls and front spars were to be tightened, exhaust shroud cooling improved, and electrical equipment better fireproofed and ventilated. The changes recommended by the crash investigation report were incorporated into the R-3350 and nacelles, and would eventually benefit the B-32 program, which would not be plagued by the numerous engine-related problems of the B-29 program. It was the tail end of the bomber that would cause the B-32 its problems.

Crash of the First XB-32 Prototype: 10 May 1943

On 8 May the 30th test flight of the XB-32 prototype was scheduled with Richard McMakin at the controls to test the aircraft for the first time at the maximum allowable design gross weight of 100,000 pounds. For the test the takeoff point was planned to be at the 3,500 foot point on Lindbergh Field's 5,200 foot runway. The exact point was to be measured so that this distance could be compared to future takeoff points. The day was hotter than normal, and caused McMakin to modify his taxiing and takeoff procedure. The Wright R-3350 engine had a tendency to overheat after the pre-takeoff run up, so McMakin started the taxi run with a surge of power, brought the throttles back to idle, and coasted to the end of the runway. If the engines continued to overheat he was to request the tower permission to repeat this procedure in the opposite direction. When aerodynamics engineer William Chana found the CHT had cooled to safe limits McMakin asked the tower for immediate takeoff clearance, turned at the head of the runway, and took off into the wind. With optimal cowl flap setting the CHT remained in the green safe limits during climb and cruise, and this maximum gross weight test was successful.

On the 10th, after having Sunday off, Consolidated's flight test crew was scheduled for the 31st XB-32 test flight in the afternoon. The test was to be for maximum allowable design gross weight. Pilot Russ Rogers was to observe the test from the ground, with McMakin as the pilot, Donald Scott as the co-pilot, George Stetsuk as the power plant test engineer, William Easley as flight engineer, James Woodall as the aerodynamics engineer, William Chana as flight test instrument engineer, and James Scott as flight test engineer observer in the rear cabin. Flight engineer Easley, located at his station behind the co-pilot, had duplicate throttles and mixture controls, and had the only control of the turbo supercharger waste gates and propeller pitch. He monitored engine rpm, manifold pressure, oil pres-

Veteran Consolidated test pilot Richard McMakin was at the controls of the doomed XB-32, and was killed in the crash. McMakin had been Consolidated's chief flying boat test pilot, and had flown the aircraft on many of its previous 30 test flights. (Consolidated via Chana)

Six members of the plane's seven-man all-civilian crew escaped critical injury. The survivors were (L-R) Aerodynamics engineer James Woodall, Co-pilot Donald Scott, Flight test engineer observer James Scott, Power plant test engineer George Stetsuk, Instrument observer William Chana, and Flight engineer William Easley. (Consolidated via Chana)

sure and temperature, and torque pressure. Stetsuk sat just behind the pilot, facing outboard, and monitored critical engine instruments on his panel. Woodall monitored pilot's and co-pilot's instruments from his jump seat between the pilots. The air temperature had cooled from the previous Saturday, and the engine run up did not cause the CHT to rise into the red, despite having to wait in the run up area for about 10 minutes for a B-24 to land.

"It was 1:00PM according to the clock on my instrument control console. I was seated with my seat belt buckled, and keeping an eye on the airspeed indicator on my panel. 50mph...70mph...90mph.... I glanced up to look through the Del Rio lens, which provided a 360 degree fisheye view of the area outside the aircraft. You could see the rivet heads on the outside circumference that secured the window to the fuselage. It created a wide-angle image of the horizon. From this quick glance it appeared to me that the airplane was at a fairly high deck angle, which is the angle of the ship to the ground. 110mph...130mph.... We were now at takeoff speed.

Flight test engineer Bill Chana at his station. (Consolidated via Chana)

On all previous takeoffs, at 130mph I would unbuckle my safety belt and jump up into the astrodome chair. This gave me a good view to the rear, and I could tell if the engines were smoking due to a very rich fuel mixture. A proper fuel mixture was desirable to keep the engine cylinder head temperatures down. If necessary, I would report to the pilot and flight engineer which engine or engines were pouring out smoke. With the pilot's permission the flight engineer would reduce the mixture setting on the appropriate engine.

As I had done in the past, at 130mph I stood up, and was on my way to the astrodome. Just as I rose I was looking forward, and saw and felt a considerable amount of aircraft shaking. In my mind I immediately started spinning, and could feel excessive heat. The spinning became faster and faster, and the heat was getting hotter and hotter. I'm sure I gave a short prayer...could this be the end?....with all this heat, was this the entrance to the place down below? I learned later that this spinning sensation is the beginning of unconsciousness. When I couldn't imagine spinning any faster or the heat getting any hotter, I found myself standing on the ground. I saw a large plume of smoke off in the distance. It looked like the smoke was one or two blocks away. It probably was a lot closer.

Then I heard someone cry out 'There's a crew member!' I was walked to an ambulance, and they placed me behind the driver facing inward. I was puzzled. I couldn't identify the others that were being put into the ambulance. One person sat across from me, and two others were on stretchers. Everything was gray...were my eyes deceiving me?....were we cov-

(Chana)

Crash Survivors, Rescuers Honored by Convair Heads

Surviving crew members of Consolidated experimental bomber which crashed into the marine corps base recruit hut area May 10 are shown with some of the marines who rescued them, as Tom M. Girdler, board chairman, and Harry Woodhead, president of Convair, presented them with wrist watches in token of their bravery. Left to right, at marine base ceremonies, George Stetsuk, Don Scott, Staff Sgt. Robert Driscoll, Corp. Leo R. Gegg, Jack Scott, Pvt. D. M. Walker, James Woodall, Pvt. A. C. Spieth, William Easley, Pvt. George L. Armitage, William Chana and Woodhead. Two others who pulled the civilians from the burning plane, Pvt. William F. Bushnell and Pfc. William F. Landers jr., are now at distant posts.—(Official marine corps photo.)

(Consolidated via Chana)

ered with gray dust?...were the others in the ambulance members of our crew?....I couldn't tell. Nobody was talking as the ambulance pulled away. We were on the way to the Marine Base dispensary. My ambulance mates, it turns out, were U.S. Marines that had been hurt when the ship went through the fence into the Marine Corps Recruit Depot (MCRD)."

The 11 May *San Diego Union* headline read:

"S.D. Air Crash Kills 4, Hurts 63: Bomber Careens into Marine Base; Buildings Wrecked; Ship Catches Fire."

The leader of the article stated:

"Four persons were killed and 63 were injured yesterday when a Consolidated-Vultee Aircraft Corp. army-type experimental plane crashed through several temporary buildings at the Marine Base and burst into flame.
Killed instantly were the pilot, R.A. McMakin, about 33, manager of Consairway and Consolidated-Vultee manager of flight. Three Marines died later at the Naval hospital and at least 10 others were reported in serious condition. Six members of the plane's seven-man all-civilian crew escaped critical injury."

Flight Research Department Flight Engineer R. T. "Lindy" LeVine was an eyewitness, and described the fatal crash:

"I was scheduled to fly on this flight to be checked out on the flight engineer's panel by engineer Bill Easley, but Convair decided to put another flight test engineer aboard. There were too many in the crew, and I would have been in the way, so we decided that I would go on another flight where the flight deck would not have been so crowded. Mack (pilot McMakin) said, 'Sorry, Lindy, we will get you on the next flight.' So I went up on top of the wing of an XPB2Y-4 (Coronado) that was beached nearby for hull modifications, and sat on the wing with the rest of the guys to watch #1141 takeoff. Acceleration appeared to be normal for the gross weight (98,986 pounds). As it passed us, it appeared that the flaps were fully <u>retracted</u>—many people noticed it. #1141 rotated, but was unable to

clear the fence with its main wheels just barely off the ground and the tail skid dragging. It ploughed 800 feet into the Marine base barracks and then into the mess hall, raising a huge cloud of dust, splinters, debris, and feathers floating up from the bedding. All was quiet for a couple of seconds, and then whoof! The thing caught fire."

All four engines were torn from the wing, with the forward and rear fuselage and the wings and tail all separating, and strewn over a large area, including a Marine barracks. Thousands of gallons of aviation fuel from the ruptured wing tanks added to the conflagration. One of the buildings was a mess hall in which a training film was being shown to more than 50 recruits, who suffered the three fatalities and most of the injuries. McMakin's leg was amputated by the crash, and he quickly died of shock and massive blood loss, and could not be rescued because of the intense heat. The injured aircrew were Donald Scott, co-pilot, fractures and concussion; William Easley, flight engineer, burns and lacerations; George Stetsuk, power plant observer, burns and lacerations; James Woodall, aerodynamics observer, fractures and concussion; William Chana, instrument observer, burns and lacerations; and James Scott, engineer observer, fractures and concussion. It was later disclosed that the lives of two of the crew were saved by the heroic efforts of a Marine recruit who entered the flaming wreckage and dragged them to safety. Four other Marine recruits helped the other escaping crew from the aircraft, and extinguished their flaming clothing and parachutes. The recruits were personally thanked for their bravery in a ceremony, and presented watches by Consolidated-Vultee President Harry Woodhead and the survivors of the crash.

The Consolidated-Vultee press release from Woodhead described New Orleans native McMakin:

"As an airlines pilot, both here and abroad, he had a distinguished career. Not only was he unusually adept at the actual business of flying an airplane, but also he was an exceptionally gifted executive, a celestial navigator, and a practical engineer. As a test pilot on the experimental model which he was flying, he had proved himself and his ship. As a fearless man who called a trip across the Pacific a 'routine flight' he was without equal."

General view of the crash site showing the wrecked Marine barracks, where three Marines were killed and 63 injured. In the left center of the photo the striped tail can be seen, with the landing gear and wheels and nose section in the center near the smoke. (Consolidated via Chana)

The port landing gear and nose section. (Consolidated via Chana)

No.3 engine nacelle and fuselage nose section, including burned pilot's cockpit enclosure. (Consolidated via Chana)

Another press release stated that McMakin was a 1928 graduate of Parks Air College, and had been one of Consolidated's chief flying boat test pilots, making 515 landings in the XPB2Y-4 testing hull bottoms.

The accident report entitled: "XB-32 No.1 Airplane Accumulated Data and Summary of Accident, H.A. Sutton, R.R. Rogers, D.T. Kelly, W.S. Crockrell, T.P. Hall, Consolidated-Vultee Aircraft Corp., San Diego, CA, 14 May 1943, Declassified 16 September 1958" reported:

"This is a report of the accident to Consolidated-Vultee Model XB-32 No.1 Airplane, Serial No. R-1141, which took place on 10 May 1943, at approximately 1:32 pm, about 900 feet on the north side of the field approximately in line with runway #29, Consolidated-Vultee Aircraft Corp., San Diego California.

Preparation and Takeoff

Airplane prepared for flight 10 May 1943, at a gross weight of 98,986 pounds with a C.G. (Center of Gravity) of 28.7% MAC (Mean Aerodynamic Chord).

Airplane was taxied to the end of the field and there, in a customary manner, the engines were run up and the airplane proceeded to takeoff.

The airplane started conventional run, but at the end of the run the airplane did not takeoff but crashed into the Marine Base.

Possible Causes of Airplane Not Taking Off in Conventional Manner

Excessive airplane weight

Lack of power
Improper propeller setting
Lack of adequate control
Airplane stalled at end of ground run
Land gear failure
Failure of wing leading edge
Failure of flap operating mechanism
Improper flap setting.

Each of the possible causes was investigated forensically and through eyewitness accounts but a definite cause was never determined. The aircraft had been flown at the same gross weight in the previous test on 8 May. The flight engineer and other observers on board the aircraft ruled out lack of power and improper propeller setting. Although eyewitnesses observed that the aircraft raised its nose at the end of the runway to such an extent that the tail skid dragged it was determined that McMakin was making a last effort to clear the fence at the end of the runway. There was no evidence that the aircraft stalled or that the landing gear or leading edge of the wing failed. There was some evidence that there was either a failure of the flap operating mechanism or improper flap setting. Eyewitnesses reported that at the start of the takeoff the flaps were fully retracted and that the flap carriages in the wreckage were all in the fully retracted position. For a takeoff from the 3,200 foot runway with the existing weight and

Bottom view of tail assembly. (Consolidated via Chana)

Nose section with pilot's cockpit and No.3 engine nacelle. (Consolidated via Chana)

wind and temperatures the flaps needed to be in the 20-degree position. A 6,000 foot runway was required for a flaps retracted takeoff for the doomed aircraft. The flap position indicator recovered from the wreckage did not provide any definite information."

However, Bill Chana writes in his book *Over the Wing* (Pvt. Printing, San Diego, CA, 2003) that there were eight observers stationed along the field to measure the takeoff point, and half of the eight stated that the flaps were up when the aircraft passed their position, and the other half reported the flaps in the 20 degree takeoff position. Examination of the wreckage showed the flaps to be in the up position upon impact. Chana states that Frank Dolinski, a B-24 pilot standing with Russ Rogers on a ramp near the beginning of the takeoff, remarked, "There goes the -32 with its flaps up."

Ten years after the crash Chana came upon a declassified report to T.P. Hall, Convair's Chief Development Engineer, from investigator Petrus Carlson, entitled: "Investigation of possible operation of flap controls by possible fouling of the interphone cords or any object falling on the levers of the pilot's side and co-pilot's side." The document presented the possible cause of the accident. Chana reflected on the memo in his book:

"For ten years I had wondered why the wing flaps were up. The report contained a plausible answer. The report identifies the fact that the pilot and copilot each had an intercom jack box on the cabin wall outboard of their stations. Also the landing gear and wing flap operating handles were on both sides of the cabin in consoles just to the left and right of the pilots. This arrangement was necessary because the pilots were far apart, separated by a walkway leading to the forward bombardier's compartment in the nose. There were two flap handles in each console, one controlling the outboard wing flaps, and the other controlling the inboard flaps.

A sketch included in the report shows how it was possible for either the pilot's or copilot's headset and microphone cord to wrap around these handles. A slight pull upward could lift the flap handles, retracting the flaps. This condition was demonstrated and proven on the Number 2 XB-32 aircraft in the Experimental Shop. Although the landing gear and flaps were hydraulically actuated, their actuating handles merely engaged microswitches to start the action. The handles were centered by light springs. It took very little force to move the handles up or down.

Before XB-32 airplanes No.2 and No.3 were released for flight the flap operating controls were relocated. The switches were placed between the pilots on the structure above the aisle leading to the bombardier's area. In addition, the switches for the inboard and outboard flaps were joined so that all flaps acted together as one. It was only a few years ago that I learned of these changes while scanning XB-32 files in the archives of the San Diego Aerospace Museum.

In the ten minutes that Dick McMakin spent at the end of the runway assuring that all was ready for takeoff of flight 31, I'm sure that he or the copilot leaned inward towards each other several times to converse and to talk to Jim Woodall, who was seated between them. Such movement would have stretched the headset and mike cords which, if wrapped around the flap handles, would have retracted the flaps. That is all it would have taken to bring the flaps up after they had previously been set at 20 degrees for takeoff. The engine noise on the flight deck would have blanked out any sound associated with movement of flaps. There was no sound proofing on the cabin walls of this experimental bomber.

There was a flap indicator located in the lower left corner of the copilot's instrument panel that indicated the position of both the inboard and outboard flaps. This instrument was visible to Scott, Woodall, and McMakin. However, once the flaps had been set to 20 degrees for takeoff by using this instrument, there would be no reason to check it again prior to brake release. Takeoff check lists became more formal and more detailed following this accident.

Upon brake release, Dick McMakin advanced the throttles and made sure that the aircraft was directed straight down the runway. Jim Woodall was calling out airspeed, and Don Scott was guarding the throttles. When the airspeed reached 130mph McMakin pulled back on the control column to rotate the airplane to the takeoff attitude. The takeoff distance was expected to be about 3,500 feet. Before the pilot realized that the ship was not leaving the ground it would have traveled at least 4,000 feet down the runway. There was no possible way to stop this 100,000 pound aircraft in the remaining distance. McMakin pulled the throttles back the moment we went through the fence separating Lindbergh Field from the Marine Corps Recruit Depot (MCRD). Don Scott's first indication of trouble was when the throttles he was guarding came back and hit his knuckles."

The Second Prototype
At the time of the first prototype crash, the second prototype (41-142) was still two months from completion. The crash and this delay would trigger serious holdups in the XB-32 test program, and then production schedules, from which the entire B-32 program would never recover. Many valuable testing instruments were lost in the crash and had to be replaced, and there also was the loss of a large amount of testing data that would have to be laboriously repeated in the second prototype. R.T. LeVine, the flight engineer who was bumped from the fatal flight, was assigned to be the flight engineer on the second prototype. LeVine had extensive experience serving as the first flight engineer on Consolidated's large flying boat programs. While 41-142 was being readied, LeVine was asked to create a new flight engineering data "book" from scratch for the aircraft. He had copied some data from Easley's book, and was aided by Consolidated's experimental and engineering departments to complete the new book on time for the tests to continue.

This second aircraft, like the first prototype, was pressurized and equipped with Sperry remote controlled dorsal and ventral retractable turrets, and had a manned tail gun position. It was outwardly similar to the first aircraft, also being equipped with the problematical twin fin and rud-

2nd Prototype (41-141) (Chana)

der assembly. During its manufacture many internal modifications were made to improve the design. Previous to the start of Phase I testing a series of engine run ups was made. Under the command of pilots Russell Rogers and Beryl Erickson, with R.T. LeVine as the flight engineer, taxiing tests began on 1 July 1943, with the initial 30 minute shakedown flight made the next day. Most of the testing was done by pilot Beryl Erickson, and a number by Rogers and Philip Prophett, who was checked out later. Once the AAF accepted the aircraft 41-142 was flown by Air Force pilots Lt.Col. O.J. "Ozzie" Richland and Capt. Bretcher.

Beryl Erickson was to become one of America's outstanding post war test pilots, testing the B-36 Peacemaker and the B-58 Hustler. After joining Consolidated in 1940, he delivered PBYs from Consolidated's San Diego plant to the Dutch in the Netherlands East Indies, and then became a test pilot for the PB2Y Coronado and XP4Y Corregidor flying boat projects. In conjunction with his testing duties, he flew LB-30s (cargo versions of the B-24) for Consairway, a wartime air transport service organized by Consolidated and under contract to the Air Transport Command to fly cargo across the Pacific. However, on 10 May 1943, after the XB-32 prototype crashed, killing Consolidated test pilot Richard McMakin, he was transferred to the XB-32 program, and then was transferred to the Consolidated Fort Worth factory to flight test the B-32 production versions. Erickson reports:

"The second XB-32 was a good aircraft, with its pressurized cabins and high aspect Davis type wing. It was much like flying a four engine B-26 Marauder, which was a fast, maneuverable high wing, twin-engine attack bomber."

During the testing the rudder trim tabs continued to cause serious directional stability problems. Test flight engineer Lindy LeVine reported:

"They (the modified rudder tabs) also failed twice. It got pretty wild up there at 22,000 and 28,000 feet with a lot of tail flutter. The engineers finally got it fixed."

The second XB-32 continued to fly several more tests with its twin tail configuration, and then was sent to the experimental shop to have the B-29 tail installed. Tests with this new tail revealed that it did not provide adequate longitudinal and directional stability and control, which will be

3rd Prototype (41-8336) (Dembeck)

described in detail later. Lindy LeVine flew 61 flights in #2, including its last flight, piloted by Beryl Erickson, on 16 January 1946 to be scrapped.

The Third Prototype

The third B-32 prototype (41-8336) was finally ready for testing on 9 November 1943, nearly eight months late. By this time the Air Force had already taken delivery of its first production B-29, and the Superfortress had left little doubt that it could readily fulfill the AAF's high altitude, VHB specifications, and that the B-32 would not be needed as a back up. The B-32 was no longer to be part of Gen. Spaatz' high altitude strategic bombing campaign, which was to be the domain of the B-29s of the XXI Bomber Command, based in the Marianas. Thus, the B-32 program was further downgraded by the AAF, whose opinion now was that the XB-32 had too many unacceptable design problems that threatened the continuation of the program. However, too much was invested in the B-32 program to abandon it, and circumstances peculiar to the air war in the Pacific gave the program a second chance. In the Pacific heavy bombers took off from their bases to fly long distances to bomb their targets at low to medium altitudes. They did not have to rendezvous at 20,000 to 25,000 feet to avoid the accurate heavy flak that endangered bombers flying over Nazi-occupied Europe. Japanese radar, flak, and fighter opposition was far inferior to that of the Germans. So to get the B-32 into production and combat in its new heavy bomber role as soon as possible, the B-32 design was compromised. These changes were so comprehensive that they were essentially a total redesign of the B-32, and would essentially transform its character from an advanced high altitude strategic VHB bomber to an ordinary heavy bomber flying mundane tactical bombing missions like an improved B-17 or B-24.

In Phase II XB-32 testing, under the command of Lt.Col. O.J. Richland, prototype 41-8336 continued to experience rudder trim tab problems, and consequently Consolidated consented to an AAF engineering assessment of the two XB-32 prototypes in order to forestall the possible cancellation of the program. The first 13 flights were conducted to check the engines and surface controls. The XB-32 was then flown from Lindbergh Field to Muroc Air Base to test the bomber for overload takeoffs and landings and systems testing. Many of the flights in XB-32 No.3 were to operate and test the cabin pressurization system. The forward and rear cabins could be pressurized separately, and if both cabins were equally pressurized then the two bulkhead doors between the cabins could be opened, and crew members could traverse between the two cabins through the tunnel. Bill Chana relates an experience with the pressurization:

"On one flight we had an aircraft at 15,000 feet, and the cabin altitude at sea level. All of a sudden, with no warning, the cabin altitude jumped up to 15,000 feet, and again, without warning, it returned to sea level. This was not good for the ear drums or sinuses, or for that matter, the disposition of the crew. If the pressure in the forward and aft cabins were not exactly the same the bulkhead doors could not be opened, and sometimes, for the same reason, they could not be closed."

The AAF engineering report of 3 December 1943 found the B-32 to be "obsolete when compared with the 1943 combat airplane requirements." The B-32 requirement no longer included those of the sophisticated Very Long Range Bomber, as the B-29 had for all intents filled that role while the XB-32 languished. The report proposed many major changes:

Replacement of the twin tail with a single vertical tail.

Deletion of the pressurized cabins. The success of the B-29 caused a revision of the tactical role of the B-32 to one similar to that of the B-24 in the Pacific, and made the pressurization superfluous.

Replacement of the complicated and troublesome remotely controlled turrets by manned turrets, with the gunners wearing oxygen masks. Improved firepower (The Sperry remote system and the manned turrets are discussed later in the defensive armament section.)

Because of the Wright R-3350's problems there was to be a:

Total redesign of the nacelles.

Improvement in the fuel and oil systems.

Substitution of four-bladed propellers for the three-bladed propellers.

The extensive post crash investigation of the XB-29 prototype in February was of value in correcting the comparatively minimal XB-32 engine and nacelle problems.

The bombing system was to be improved by:

Installation of an M-series Norden bombsight and automatic flight control system.

Installation of the Emerson Model 128 nose assembly that was used by the B-24 to improve the bombardier's forward and side vision.

Installation of an all electric bomb release system.

Simplify maintenance by concentrating on accessibility, and standardize replacement parts and have them readily available.

The emergency exits were to be improved, which was simplified by the removal of pressurization.

Addition of heated wing de-icers.

Relocation of specified interior equipment.

Improved vision by adding scanning ports in the fuselage and improving the cockpit windows.

It Was the Tail!

The B-32 program was falling further and further behind schedule, while Boeing was quickly sorting out their B-29 problems. The B-29 program was favored by the AAF and the Air Materiel Command. The B-29 program was the better managed program, receiving the full attention from Boeing at the expense of their B-17 program. The Superfortress was continually being modified in the field while getting into simultaneous combat testing and training over Kansas during the so-called "Battle of Kansas." Meanwhile Consolidated, with an eye on the current bottom line,

concentrated its efforts on its B-24 Liberator production lines at San Diego and Fort Worth, and also monitored the Ford and Douglas B-24 production lines. Consolidated-Vultee saw that the B-32 program was no longer viable and had become a liability and, arguably, also made certain that the potential of its post war B-36 program would not be compromised.

Finally, after 25 flight tests with the Coronado-type twin tail, the third XB-32 (41-18336) was grounded in mid-1944 so that the Consolidated-Vultee design team could replace this tail with a single tail. Ironically, this was just the opposite circumstance that the prototype single-tailed Coronado encountered after it began its testing program and continued its career as a twin-tailed aircraft. The engineers had to forsake the better directional stability of the twin tail design to achieve the longitudinal stability and control of the single tail design, which the first two XB-32s lacked and had made them difficult aircraft to fly. The third prototype had its twin tail amputated, and a 16 foot 8 inch single tail was grafted onto the rear fuselage. The new tail was basically a modified B-29 tail that, unfortunately, also showed directional instability in several subsequent test flights when the remodeled third XB-32 flew again on 13 September. Further design re-evaluation determined that increasing the fin and rudder height to 19 feet 8 inches would finally provide the B-32 with much needed directional control, but at the expense of its flight attitude, which became mediocre but acceptable. The first two production B-32s (42-108471 and 472) were also fitted with the B-29 tail. They sat on the production line until this tail was removed, and they were fitted with the larger tail that gave the B-32 its "Big Tailed Bird" distinguishing characteristic. After the standard tail was installed 75 subsequent test flights were made to develop directional and horizontal stability and control. Altogether there were more than 120 test flights on the XB-32 No.3.

Ironically, in 1942 AAF studies found that the B-24 would also have greater stability with a single fin and rudder. Consolidated-Vultee tests in 1943 using a Ford-modified B-24D with a single fin and rudder proved the AAF conjecture, as the bomber had improved control, stability, and rate of climb. In April 1944 it was decided that all future B-24s were to be of the single fin and rudder variety, but this design change was added only to the B-24N, of which only seven were built before all Liberator production ceased. However, 740 independently developed single-finned, PB4Y-2 Privateer B-24 versions were built for the Navy. These Privateer tails looked very similar to the B-32 tail, and the two were often confused, especially after the war, when the Privateers were used for forest fire fighting, as there were a number of erroneous post war "B-32" spottings on remote Northwest airfields.

XB-32 Tail Gallery

During its lifetime the B-32 tail underwent a number of transformations, from its original XB-32 twin tail configuration to a single B-29 tail to its signature standard tall tail.

The third XB-32, 41-18336 was grounded in mid-1944 so that the Consolidated-Vultee design team could replace this tail with a B-29 single tail that, unfortunately, also showed directional instability in subsequent test flights after this remodeled third XB-32 flew again on 13 September 1944. (Smithsonian via Dembeck)

The XB-32 No. 1 and 2 prototypes used the signature Consolidated twin tail configuration that had been used successfully on the B-24 Liberator design. However, closer inspection of the tail assembly of the XB-32 shows that each half of the horizontal stabilizer was tilted upwards in 7.5 dihedral, which was the redesign of the PB2Y Coronado Flying Boat tail. (Consolidated via Chana)

The XB-32 twin tail configuration was developed from Fleet's earlier Model 29 PB2Y-1 Coronado patrol bombers (shown), whose prototypes ironically had continual control problems with their initial single tail configuration, and were fitted with a successful twin tail design. (Consolidated via Chana)

The B-29 tail being wind tunnel tested on a wooden mockup, as the Coronado twin tail configuration proved unsuccessful, and was replaced with a single modified 16 foot 8 inch B-29 tail that was grafted onto the rear fuselage. (Consolidated via Dembeck)

Right: Close up view of wind tunnel model with B-29 tail. This tail configuration was used on XB-32 No.3 and the first two production B-32-1-CFs (471 and 472). (Consolidated via Dembeck)

The third XB-32 (41-18336) flies over California with its new single standard B-32 tail after the smaller B-29 type tail failed (note that the last number of the 18336 has been deleted during the conversion). The other visible changes were the removal of the green house tail, which was faired over, and the addition of a mock dorsal turret. The aircraft had some interior equipment relocated, and its pressurization system removed. (Consolidated via Chana)

The first two production B-32s: 42-108471 (shown) and 472 were fitted with the 16.6 foot modified B-29 single tail with one rudder tab and a de-icer boot on the forward edge of the stabilizer. (Consolidated via Pima)

Later 471 was fitted with the larger 19.5 foot tail, which gave the B-32 its Big Tailed Bird distinguishing characteristic. This tail only had a single rudder tab, and all subsequent tails after 471 and 472 would have two rudder tabs. (Consolidated via Pima)

The twin rudder tab configuration was standard on the 10 B-32-CF-1s and 4 B-32-5-CFs, along with the 25 TB-32-5 and the 11 TB-32-10 models. Production was stopped on the eight B-32-5-CFs then on the production line until the extended tails arrived in early December 1943. This photo is of a T-32-10-CF trainer (499). (Consolidated via Stine)

Right: The standard tall, two rudder tab tail with the de-icer boot was standard on the final 4 TB-32-15s and all subsequent 74 B-32 models: B-32-CF-20, -21, -25, -30, and -35. Shown here is a TB-32-15-CF trainer (522). (USAAF via Stine)

472 refitted with its larger tail with one rudder tab. The aircraft was refitted with the standard two rudder tab tail, and can be seen elsewhere in a photograph of its belly landing during testing on 27 August 1944. (Consolidated via Stine)

In April 1944, it was decided that all future B-24s were to be of the single fin and rudder variety, but this design was added only to the B-24N, of which only seven were built before all Liberator production ceased. (USAAF)

After the B-24Ns were phased out, 740 independently developed single-finned, PB4Y-2 Privateer B-24 versions were built for the Navy. (USN)

4

The B-32 is Awarded a Production Contract

B-32 Contracts and Production History

A contract for 13 YB-32 service test models was approved in June 1941, but was later canceled, and the order was to be transferred to production aircraft. A limited initial production order for the B-32 had been made in March 1943, but after the single tail and armament modifications were made to the revamped third prototype, which was flown for the first time on 13 September 1944, the AAF revised its order to manufacture 300 B-32s and a small number of modified TB-32 transitional trainers. Since Consolidated-Vultee Fort Worth had no other contracts it began to slowly tool up to begin volume production of the B-32, but it was important that volume production not interfere with the remaining B-24 production and the important post war B-36 program. In August 1944, as B-24 production was winding down at Fort Worth, the first production B-32-1-CF to be flown was 42-108472 (on 5 August), while the first Fort Worth B-32-1-CF production aircraft (42-108471) was in the shop having extensive flight testing instrumentation installed. Production was delayed by so many changes in specifications, design, and equipment, and also by the "lack of cooperation" among Army Air Force organizations interested in the B-32, that as late as 29 November 1944, more than two years after the first flight test, only two B-32s had been built. Only 30 more were scheduled for production in December, but by the end of the year only five aircraft had

been delivered to the various service test centers. However, despite these production problems and the apparent success of the B-29, in early spring 1945 the company was forced to accelerate the B-32 program because of an unexpected order for 1,200+ B-32s at Fort Worth, and 500 planned for San Diego to be delivered that year.

Consolidated-Vultee's huge government-financed Fort Worth factory had the world's longest straight assembly lines, and would require 27,000 tools for the volume construction of the B-32. Each bomber required 59,290 purchased parts, 53,290 new material parts, 89,775 nuts and bolts, and 700,000 rivets. A total retooling was necessary for the stagnant B-32 program to become a volume program. This would be a sizeable undertaking on relatively short notice for an aircraft that had been radically changed physically and, in concept, had not been officially accepted until 27 January 1945, and also had not been combat tested.

Before the design and fabrication of the 27,000 manufacturing tools was begun the Consolidated-Vultee tooling and engineering departments broke down the bomber into basic components to facilitate the assembly line production techniques that Consolidated had pioneered in the aircraft industry. In order to coordinate all phases of the tooling program thousands of items of reference tooling, such as tooling masters, plaster mockups, and templates had to be planned, designed, and constructed. The assembly

Incomplete full-scale B-32 fuselage mock up. (Consolidated via USAAF)

B-32 full-scale flight deck mock up. (Consolidated via USAAF)

Full-scale mock up of the B-32 production model cockpit. Note that the pilot's pedestal is located on his right side, and that the control column is mounted on a pedestal, instead of being placed into the instrument panel. (Consolidated via USAAF)

Final cockpit of a production B-32. (Consolidated via Chana)

tools were designed so that they would be relatively independent from any movement in the supporting floor, and still provide the workers with the most accessibility. The Fort Worth factory was provided with an overhead monorail system that removed the completed assemblies directly upward from the jig for transport to the next assembly station. Importantly, the design of the manufacturing tooling was such that that it could be used by relatively unskilled labor. Also, since the B-32 was a new and untried bomber the Consolidated tooling department introduced a method of operation and type of tooling that provided for the integration of changes and modifications that had previously plagued production.

The success of the retooling is best illustrated by the paltry 74 B-32-CFs and 40 TB-32-CFs completed at contract cancellation on 18 September 1945, and the completion of the final dozen B-32s on production line on 12 October, when all B-32 production was terminated.

The Fort Worth Consolidated Plant

In 1939, in order to increase aircraft production, the National Defense Council (NDC) decided to adopt a plan that was first proposed during World War I to utilize the assembly line production techniques of automobile industry to manufacture aircraft parts and assemble aircraft. Consolidated and Douglas were slated to join Ford for the production of the B-24, North American with General Motors for the B-25, and Martin with Chrysler for the B-26. The advisory Commission to the NDC developed a plan to manufacture 12,000 additional aircraft by building a number of Government-Owned-Contractor-Operated (GOCO) defense plants manufacturing aircraft. The plan removed the investment risk for the contractor/manufacturer, and assured the rapid increase of aircraft production. A Plant Site Board (PSB) was established as part of the War Department to evaluate potential locations for new factories. Also, the Army Air Corps was to establish a flight training base adjoining each factory so that, ideally, the trained air crews could climb into completed aircraft at the end of the production line and fly off into combat.

The Defense Plant Corporation (DPC), under the Reconstruction Finance Corporation (RFC), was authorized to approve its first lease agreements for the construction of new aircraft assembly plants. The procedure

was to have the PSB contact aircraft manufacturers to carry out site surveys in pre-approved cities for suitable locations for the construction of government built factories that would be leased to them. President Herbert Hoover had formed the RFC when the banks failed in 1929. Hoover appointed Houston businessman Jesse H. Jones to head the RFC, which was expanded by President Roosevelt during the Great Depression. Jones became one of the most powerful men in the financial world, and is credited with restoring the American economy. In 1939 Roosevelt appointed Jones as Federal Loan Administrator (FLA), a position that also managed the RFC. In 1940, when Roosevelt decided to expand America's war economy, he named Jones as his Secretary of Commerce, but Jones also retained his position as head of the FLA. In the Act of June 25, 1940, Congress gave Jones and the RFC almost unlimited power in anything to do with the defense of America and its preparation for war. The power behind the RFC was its superlative legal staff, particularly Clifford Durr and Hans Klagsbrunn, who were responsible for the formation of the Defense Plant Corporation. The RFC was authorized to build factories and shipyards, to stockpile essential supplies and materials, and to pay subsidies to control prices. Jones mobilized industry to make America the "arsenal of democracy" by establishing such subsidiaries as the Defense Plant Corporation and Defense Supplies Corporation. Nearly one-third of the $25 billion invested in plant construction and equipment was supplied by the RFC directly, or by a greater degree by its defense related subsidiaries, especially the DPC, with its 2,300 investments totaling nearly $7 billion chiefly in the aviation industry and its auxiliaries. On 25 October 1940, the Defense Plant under the Reconstruction Finance Corporation approved its first lease agreement with Curtiss-Wright for the construction of new aircraft assembly plants at Buffalo, Columbus, OH, and St. Louis, each for between $12 and $15 million. A week later the DFC awarded Consolidated a $14.5 million lease agreement for a plant expansion in San Diego for the production of PBYs.

The decision to build the huge Consolidated factory at Fort Worth has been attributed to the influential publisher of the *Fort Worth Star-Telegram*, Amon Carter, Sr., who was a friend of President Roosevelt and Vice President Garner, and an acquaintance of Generals Arnold and MacArthur.

The massive government-financed Consolidated Fort Worth facility was built adjoining Lake Worth, and the plant and grounds covered more than 400 acres, with more than eight million square feet of paved working area, which made it the largest in the aircraft industry. The plant itself was the world's largest aircraft plant, measuring almost a mile long, and covering an area equal to eight city blocks; it had the world's longest straight line assembly lines (long building on right). The airfield in the photo is Fort Worth AAF (also known as Tarrant Air Field), and was originally built for B-24 training; when the B-32s arrived there was an immediate need for more spacious hangars, and wider and more heavy-duty runways, taxiways, and parking aprons. The airfield underwent a $65 million construction program. After the war the air field became Carswell AFB for SAC operations. (Consolidated via Chana)

In On 22 November 1940 Carter and the Fort Worth Chamber of Commerce began drafting a proposal to present Consolidated when, on the 26th Carter received an urgent letter from William Wheatley, Consolidated's chief test pilot. Wheatley wrote that Consolidated had been ordered to ferry 200 PBYs from San Diego to England ASAP, and required a layover stop at Fort Worth, and that Carter could expect a letter from Consolidated VP Edgar Gott outlining the requirements of the temporary base. By the next day Carter developed a plan to have everything ready for Wheatley's PBYs by 30 November. Carter's quick action would later play a positive role in Consolidated's decision to select Fort Worth as a factory site, as this temporary PBY stop over was located next to the proposed factory site.

Since the B-24 and PBY were critical to national defense Maj.Gen. George Brett, the AAC's chief mediator on site selection, ordered Rueben Fleet to choose one location and an alternate from the pre-approved list that favored Tulsa. Although Fort Worth was not on the pre-approved list, Amon Carter was resolute about bringing a B-24 plant to his home town. The Fort Worth Chamber of Commerce and Carter had fashioned an enticing proposal to present to Reuben Fleet. The proposal included an attractive site on the shore of Lake Worth on the western side of the city, along with substantial tax incentives, city financed access and utility improvements, and the pledge of a large pool of skilled laborers. The Consolidated President, accompanied by senior company official C.A. Van Dusen and Thomas Bomar of San Diego's Chamber of Commerce, visited Fort Worth as part of an inspection tour. Bomar, who had been instrumental in getting Fleet to commit to San Diego, accompanied Fleet to act as a liaison with the Chambers of Commerce of each possible site. Fleet saw the economic advantages of the Fort Worth proposal, and when he returned to San Diego he received a telegram from Gen. Brett saying that he needed to make an immediate decision for a plant location. Fleet wired back that Fort Worth was his choice, trying to influence Brett toward the Lake Worth site by pointing out the tax and utility incentives and labor pool. Brett responded that Fort Worth was not on the approved list, and asked "What's wrong with Tulsa?" Fleet replied that he had found that Tulsa was unsatisfactory, and Brett reminded him again that Fort Worth was not an option, and to select Tulsa. The two men argued back and forth by telegram, and finally a hearing was set for the PSB to settle the matter.

The Board selected, Tulsa and Carter was livid when he heard the decision. Carter had many friends and associates in Washington, and began a relentless lobbying campaign. He sent off a telegram to Roosevelt to disparage Brett's inclination toward Tulsa, but Roosevelt replied that the decision was up to the Army, and he could do nothing. Undaunted, Carter unleashed a crusade expounding the virtues of the Fort Worth site and pressuring congressmen, military leaders, and influential friends in the Roosevelt circle, including his good friend and Roosevelt Vice President John Nance Garner. Finally Roosevelt, prodded by Nance, gave in, and on 3 December the War Department announced that Omaha and Kansas City had been selected, and *both* Tulsa and Fort Worth would be receiving B-24 factories, with the Tulsa plant operated by Douglas. Ford was to supply these two factories with 100 airframe parts kits (in effect all the major B-24 components: fuselage, wings, tail, etc.) per month. Three days later, an Army contingent arrived in Fort Worth and officially sanctioned the Lake Worth site for Government Plant #4. But Carter still was not satisfied, as he learned that the Tulsa and Fort Worth factories would be identical in size. Carter counseled Roosevelt that Texas pride was at stake, as everything in Texas had to be the biggest. Roosevelt acquiesced and ordered that the Texas plant be extended by 29 feet to become the world's largest and longest manufacturing facility, being over a mile long.

On 28 March 1941 the Austin Company of Cleveland, OH, was contracted to build the $3 million plant. Groundbreaking ceremonies were held on a rainy 18 April, and were presided over by Carter, who had a sterling shovel made up for the event. Maj.Gen. Gerald Brant, CO of the Gulf Coast Training Center, proclaimed as he dug the silver spade into the ground, "We're digging Hitler's grave today." Construction began three days later.

In November 1941, when the construction of the new plant was well under way, Fleet stated:

"The story of B-24 production revolves around design, construction, and the placing into production of the huge new building recently begun at Fort Worth, which is constructed on the principle that the shortest distance between one finished bomber and the next is a straight line. Raw materials flow into one end of this mile-long defense plant, and completed subassemblies issue from the other. From there all sub-assemblies travel over a road to the final assembly line, which is mechanized to approach true mass production methods. At the end of the mechanized assembly line, the B-24s go into the yard area for final installation of internal fittings, engine and propeller adjustments, and testing, etc., prior to flight testing and final delivery to the Army Ferry Command."

The Fort Worth plant and grounds covered more than 400 acres, with more than eight million square feet of paved working area, which made it the largest in the aircraft industry. The plant itself was the world's largest aircraft plant, measuring almost a mile long, and covering an area equal to eight city blocks; it also had the world's longest straight line assembly lines. The painting of the outside walls of the plant involved approximately 1.25 million square feet of paint, equivalent to painting an area one mile long by one block wide. The entire plant complex exceeded its nearest competitor by more than one million square feet of floor space, and the plant's assembly lines were serviced by an overhead monorail system that was equivalent to 100 miles of track. The Fort Worth division operated its own railway line of several miles of spur track from the main line to the loading docks for freight cars inside the plant. The buildings were windowless, which required them to have the world's largest industrial air conditioning system that utilized 14,000 gallons of water a minute, which was equivalent to the average daily water consumption of Dallas and Fort Worth. There were 32,690 fluorescent lights, each five feet long, adding up to a total of 33 miles of lights. The plant was so large that supervisors toured the production lines on bicycles. The B-24s, and later the B-32s were able to roll off the production lines through the 200 foot doors, and were immediately ready for engine and flight tests without further delaying their start toward training or combat bases. The assembly lines were designed to incorporate modifications so that the B-32 did not have to be sent to outside modification centers, as did the B-29s, thus delaying their delivery for training and combat. Consolidated thus eliminated flying time,

delays due to bad weather, waiting time, and duplication of effort by setting up its modification department on the assembly line, and final modifications were made at the end of the line just before the bombers rolled out the door to the nearby Tarrant Training Center.

In the fall of 1940 the government had foreseen that the aircraft industry would conceivably not be able to supply the necessary aircraft if global war came, and considered the automotive industry as a possible source to supplement aircraft manufacture. Of course, the aircraft industry was concerned that this move could cause post war competition in their field. To allay these fears the government decided that the auto industry would not manufacture complete aircraft, but serve as a parts manufacturer and supplier. Initially Consolidated was to operate its Fort Worth plant and Douglas its Tulsa plant to assemble B-24 components called "knock down kits" (KD Kits), supplied from subcontractors. The knock down kit consisted of three large components: the aft fuselage; forward (nose) section; and center wing section, along with an assortment of smaller subassemblies. In May 1941 Ford was contracted to be the major subcontractor to build and supply KD Kits, which were to be built at its new Willow Run factory, near Detroit. Ford's components were to be shipped to and assembled initially at Consolidated's Fort Worth and the Douglas plant at Tulsa (North American was contracted in January 1942 to manufacture

Fort Worth plant a few days later, when several more B-32s were ready. However, by the end of 1944 only five aircraft had been delivered to the Air Technical Service Command (ATSC), and none to the AAF Proving Ground Command (AAFPGC) at Elgin Field, FL, which was to have a preliminary report on the bomber's operational limits ready by 15 February 1945. (Consolidated via Chana)

The Fort Worth plant tooling up for the first B-32 production in mid-December 1944 as the 3,034th and last Liberator, which had been signed by the production line workers, is at the end of the B-24 line. Production B-32-1-CF aircraft 42-108471 and 42-108472 were fitted with the modified B-29 tails, and 473 was being tested, so the B-32-5s in the photo are waiting until the extended standard tails arrived. (Consolidated via Chana)

After the first 14 B-32-1/-5-CFs were produced at Fort Worth, the next three production batches were the 40 TB-32-5/10/15-CF training aircraft. A TB is seen rolling out of the doors off the assembly line. (Consolidated via Stine)

and assemble its own B-24s at Dallas, instead of using Ford kits). Thus, the general B-24 production proposal stipulated that the bomber parts be fabricated at San Diego, Dallas, and Willow Run, and be assembled at San Diego, Dallas, Fort Worth, and Tulsa. The first Consolidated San Diego B-24Ds were rolling off the production line in April 1942.

Ford was initially contracted to supply 100 KD Kits consisting of all major B-24 components. Ford felt it could apply its automobile mass production techniques to manufacture these kits at a much lower cost per pound (e.g. aircraft were built for five to eight dollars per pound vs. 15 to 20 cents per pound for building automobiles). However, Ford did not anticipate the numerous changes to the design required by the AAF once on the production line, and became unwilling to produce more than a 60 day supply of kits, as they were concerned that the components would become obsolete by design changes. In late 1941 Ford experienced delays in tooling up and supplying kits, but the Consolidated Fort Worth and the Douglas Tulsa plants were soon to be completed and ready for the KD Kits. To fill the kit void both Fort Worth and Tulsa started operations using sub-assemblies supplied by San Diego, and their B-24Ds were essentially identical to the B-24D-COs manufactured by San Diego. Finally, by September 1942 Tulsa received its first Willow Run kits, followed by Fort Worth in January 1943 and Douglas in February 1943. By July 1943 Ford was supplying B-24E kits. During this period Consolidated San Diego and Fort Worth also continued to build their in house produced B-24s.

The huge Willow Run plant was ostensibly built as a kit and parts plant, but from the onset of the B-24 program Ford intended to build complete B-24s. But, to all intents and purposes, Willow Run was built as a complete production facility, and soon Ford was contracted to build complete static design B-24Es, but continued to supply KD Kits to Fort Worth and Tulsa. During its three years of operation the Willow Run plant produced 6,792 complete B-24s, supplied 1,893 others in KD Kit form to Fort Worth and Tulsa, and provided innumerable spare parts.

The Fort Worth plant would not be totally completed until the spring of 1944, but it continued to simultaneously assemble kit and indigenous B-24Es, and later the B-24 Hs and Js until May 1944, when it built its own B-24Js and the C-87 transport version of the B-24. During summer 1944 production was increased, and the Consolidated-Vultee Fort Worth plant contributed 3,034 of the 18,482 Liberators built.

Tarrant Field/Fort Worth Army Air (FWAAF)
With the initiation of construction of the vast Consolidated plant on 18 April 1941 Maj.Gen. Gerald Brant contacted the Fort Worth civic leaders

and Consolidated officials, expressing that he would like to see an air field built near the new factory site. Carter and the Fort Worth Chamber of Commerce soon chose a site adjacent to Knight Lake, acquired options on the land, and then moved the residents from their homes and cows from a pasture. The AAF site board arrived in September to assess the site, and preliminary negotiations were proceeding when the Japanese attacked Pearl Harbor. The attack hastened the transaction, and on 7 February 1942 land purchases began, and construction was authorized to contract the L.J. Miles Company of Fort Worth for the $6.5 million project, with Col. Bernard Thompson as the AAF CO of what was known as the Tarrant Field project. The first of 3,200 construction workers arrived on 15 March to begin the project, which was to become an ongoing undertaking throughout the war. Even though B-24s were being produced in the factory, the adjacent airfield and training facilities were slow in completion. The work was slowed by the need to place the 200 buildings on pilings to support them on the boggy land on the shores of the lake. Initial plans placed about 4,000 personnel on the base, but within months 1,200 additional personnel were stationed there.

The field was activated on 29 July 1942 under the command of Col. David Goodrich, but the field was not ready until 21 August. The initial cost was $9 million, providing three 150 foot wide concrete runways measuring 7,300, 7,000, and 5,643 feet that had 75 foot seashell and gravel

The Fort Worth Consolidated production line in full swing. The total of 118 B-32s were delivered, with July 1945 having the top monthly production at 21 aircraft delivered. The average cost per aircraft was approximately $790,000; $822,195 initially, and $731,040 later. (Consolidated via Dembeck)

shoulders. Seven hangars and large parking aprons were constructed, and all these facilities were thought to be capable of supporting the largest aircraft of the time, but would have to be reconstructed and augmented when the B-32s arrived. On 20 August the first cadre of 90 men arrived from Ellington Field, and was soon increased by 350 men from the AAF Recruit Center at Atlantic City, NJ. Living facilities and creature comforts had been sacrificed to complete the operational facilities. The men obtained their water supply from barrels, and food from local diners and hot dog stands.

Even the naming of the field was a labored process. Initially it was conveniently called the "runway next to the factory," and then Lake Worth Industrial Airport. But the military thought this name "too civilian," and designated it "The Army Air Force Combat Crew School." Soon this title was replaced by Tarrant Field, and then on 28 June 1942 when the base was assigned to the AAF Training Command it was designated as Tarrant Field Airdrome. Finally, in May 1943 it was renamed Fort Worth Army Air Field (FWAAF), AAF Pilot School (Specialized 4-Engine), which became the official designation. However, crews and the public continued to refer to it as Tarrant Field.

On 14 October 1942, eight-man B-24 crew transition training began. All crew members had graduated from their respective specialty schools and were allocated to combat crews. As the B-24s came off the production line they were towed immediately across the runway, where they were accepted by the AAF and assigned to training crews, saving days of ferrying to distant training fields. The same procedure was used for B-32 training, but B-32 training was shortened by using B-24 crews, which will be discussed later.

FWAAF was originally built for B-24 training, and when the B-32s arrived there was an immediate need for more spacious hangars, and wider and more heavy-duty runways, taxiways, and parking aprons. So at a time when AAF training fields were undergoing contraction and deactivation, FWAAF underwent a $65 million construction program under the direction of Maj. Chester Terry. In April 1945 two new hangars and two extra heavy wash racks were started, in June a heavy duty north-south concrete runway was begun, and in mid-July four taxiways were initiated, and the existing parking aprons were reconstructed. The hangars were 202 wide by 297 long and 117 feet high. The existing north-south runway was strengthened and widened from 250 feet to 300 feet.

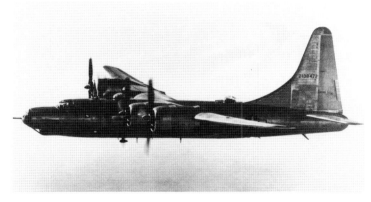

The first production B-32-1-CF to be flown was 42-108472 on 5 August 1944 by Consolidated Pilot Beryl Erickson, Co-pilot Gus Green, and Flight Engineer R.T. LeVine. (LeVine)

In 1946 the Strategic Air Command (SAC) took command of the base, and it became headquarters for the 8th Air Force. In 1948 it was renamed Carswell AFB after Fort Worth native Maj. Horace Carswell, who was awarded the Medal of Honor while flying a B-24 in World War II. The base was closed in 1993 for Air Force activities, and became Naval Air Station Joint Reserve Base Fort Worth.

The B-32 Doesn't Exactly Roll Off the Production Lines
The first Fort Worth B-32-1-CF production aircraft (42-108471) was not the first production B-32 to be flown, as it was in the shop having extensive flight testing instrumentation installed by a San Diego Consolidated factory crew. 471 was continually upgraded throughout its career, and was terminated essentially as a B-32-20-CF model. Among the modifications were flight instruments for the co-pilot, a second rudder tab, rear scanner windows, and the addition of various radar and navigation aids. It was experimentally fitted with extended horizontal stabilizer tips that proved to be ineffective, and were not put into use.

The first production B-32-1-CF to be flown was 42-108472 on 5 August 1944 by Consolidated-Vultee crew Pilot Beryl Erickson, Co-pilot Gus Green, and Flight Engineer R.T. LeVine. Erickson reports that Consolidated designers had been so weight reduction conscious that the strength of the fuselage was compromised, and during the first taxiing test some

The first Fort Worth B-32-1-CF production aircraft, 42-108471 was not the first production B-32 to be flown, as it was in the shop having extensive flight testing instruments installed by a San Diego Consolidated factory crew. (LeVine)

On 27 August 1944 472 was flown by the crew of Erickson, Green, and LeVine, and five other crewmen. The aircraft's main gear failed, and pilot Beryl Erickson brought the bomber into a smooth skidding landing that slowed to about 30mph when the fuselage parted at the junction of the canopy and top deck, and squashed down level with the top of the pilots seats. All eight crew members survived, but the aircraft was damaged beyond economical repair. (LeVine)

The news clip states: "Super Bomber in Belly Landing: It's a double salute of the wings of the two pilots who brought that new super bomber for a belly landing...." (Consolidated via LeVine)

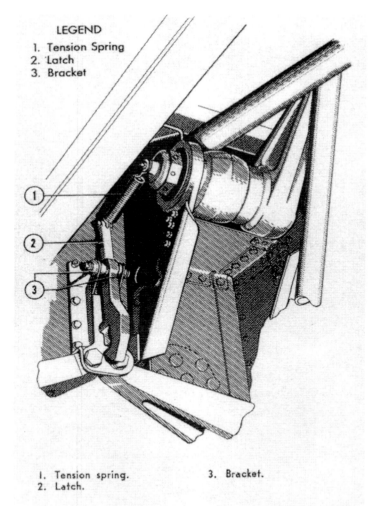

LEGEND
1. Tension Spring
2. Latch
3. Bracket

1. Tension spring.   3. Bracket.
2. Latch.

Figure 95—Main Alighting Gear Uplatch Assembly

The high "G" forces, and the aerodynamic forces of the dive pulled the main landing gear uplatches outward, and bent the nacelle doors just enough to move the latch rollers out of their tracks, shearing both struts. The wheels came down, whipped aft, and smashed into the rear of the nacelle. (E&R Manual)

cockpit windows cracked and crazed due to the flexing of the fuselage on the uneven runway. The aircraft had several other problems, and finally they were thought to be resolved, so test flight #6 was scheduled on the morning of 27 August 1944. The bomber was flown again by the crew of Erickson, Green, and LeVine. Also on board were Air Materiel Command observer Col. Thomas Gerrity and Robert Widmer, Consolidated Chief Aerodynamicist, along with a Consolidated assistant engineer who was to be checked out on the B-32 and two engineer observers. Gerrity had served as the CO of the 90th Bombardment Squadron on New Guinea in summer 1942, where he flew 49 combat missions. Upon his return to the U.S. in November he was assigned to the Air Materiel Command and became the project officer for the XB-32 program. The XB-32 had what Erickson describes as "maneuver control force problems" that Widmer solved by designing a new elevator tab, nicknamed the "banana tab." The new tab was to be tested during a 320mph dive at 3 to 3.5 Gs. Erickson was demonstrating pull-ups from maximum diving speeds to Col. Gerrity when the high "G" forces and the aerodynamic forces of the dive pulled the main landing gear uplatches outward and bent the nacelle doors just enough to move the latch rollers out of their tracks, shearing both struts. The wheels came down, whipped aft, and smashed into the rear of the nacelle. Flight engineer LeVine describes the incident:

"I felt a very sharp jolt. I looked out the window and saw that the right main gear was hanging loose, and when I looked out the left window I saw that the left gear had also failed. The bolt that held the universal joint to the drag strut had sheared, and the gear uplatches failed, causing both landing gears to unlock, allowing them to smash into the nacelles and then to hang down like two broken legs."

The crew prepared for a belly landing: draining the oxygen system; moving all loose equipment to the rear cabin; removing the rear emergency hatch; removing the ballast from the catwalk and throwing it out the opened bomb bays into Lake Worth; tying down the radio equipment with a rope; shutting off the fuel to the APU; and transferring the fuel from the inboard tanks to the outboard tanks to keep it as far away as possible from the fuselage. Erickson continued to fly to use as much fuel as possible, and to determine the safest and best possible landing procedure. He began the emergency landing at 1335 as the crew removed their parachute harnesses, neckties, and eyeglasses, loosened their shirt collars, and then took their assigned crash landing positions against the bulkhead, with parachutes placed to afford extra protection. The No.2 and No.3 inboard props were feathered so that a "live" propeller would not tear loose on contact with the ground and cut through the fuselage. On the final approach Erickson set the wing flaps to 30 degrees, extended the nose gear, switched OFF the fuel selector valves, battery, inverter, and the master ignition switch. It had been decided that the landing was to be on the grass, as Consolidated Engineering felt that landing on the concrete runway would create too much friction and cause a fire, but assured Erickson that the fuselage was strong enough to tolerate a belly landing. To test the smoothness of the grass an automobile tested it by driving at 70mph across it.

On the 95mph touchdown the crew felt the aircraft settle with the nose wheel and tail skid contacting the ground simultaneously. Erickson expertly brought the bomber into a smooth skidding landing, but as the aircraft came to a sudden halt there was a "very loud high pitched screech," and the collapse of the entire fuselage at about station 3.0. The number one

Beryl Erickson (L) and Gus Green on 26 March 1947 while testing the prototype of the B-36 Peacemaker at Fort Worth. (Consolidated)

On 21 November, the test flight crew took 473 up when turbo boost was lost in the No.2 engine, canceling the test. Once 473 landed the reason for the loss in boost was discovered; there had been a fire in the No.2 nacelle due to exhaust manifold failure. The fire had been on the outboard side of the nacelle, and thus could not be seen from the aircraft. The exhaust manifolds were too thin, and when operating under high power, the added back pressure of the turbo supercharger would crack the manifold, pieces would break off, and hot pieces would blow out through the cowling. (LeVine)

engine continued to windmill, and the number four engine stopped reluctantly after the propeller struck the ground violently about a dozen times. The fuselage had parted at the junction of the canopy and top deck, and squashed down level with the top of the pilots' seats. Many pieces of the overhead Plexiglas windshield broke and fell into the cabin. Gerrity, stationed at the fuselage fracture area, suffered a head injury, but Erickson and Green escaped injury. The other crew members survived with assorted minor bumps and bruises, but the aircraft was damaged beyond economical repair. There are reports (that Erickson says are untrue) that the aircraft was cannibalized, and all undamaged parts were returned to the Consolidated production line to fly again as part of other B-32s.

Erickson and Green encountered s similar situation on 26 March 1947 while testing the prototype of the B-36 Peacemaker at Fort Worth. Soon after takeoff the retracting hydraulic strut of the right main landing gear main brace failed and dropped the gear, smashing the rear of the #4 engine nacelle, and rupturing the fuel and hydraulic lines. It then swung back and forth in the slip stream, held only by the oleo strut and extender rods. There were 21,000 gallons of fuel on board that could not be dumped, and Erickson and Green flew the bomber over the area for six hours to consume fuel before landing. Meanwhile, the other 12 crewmen were ordered to bail out, but high winds caused injuries to nine of the 12 parachutists. Erickson and Green managed to safely land the huge bomber with no brakes or nose wheel steering due to the loss of hydraulic fluid. By landing the only prototype without damage the two pilots saved the B-36 program, which was behind schedule, over budget, and under political pressure.

The next production aircraft (42-108473, Number 3) was not ready until November due to production delays. On 21 November the test flight

crew of pilot Beryl Erickson, co-pilot Len Perry, engineer Lindy LeVine, and chief Consolidated aerodynamicist Bob Widmer took 473 up for a six hour test when turbo boost was lost in the No.2 engine at 14,000 feet. LeVine was unable to determine the cause, and Erickson canceled the test and returned to base. When 473 landed and taxied the men on the ground pointed at the No.2 engine, and the reason for the loss in boost was discovered. There had been a fire in the No.2 nacelle due to exhaust manifold failure that had not been detected by the fire detection system. The fire had been on the outboard side of the nacelle, and thus could not be seen from the aircraft. The exhaust manifolds manufactured by American Central Corp. were too thin, and when operating under high power with the added back pressure of the turbo supercharger would crack the manifold; pieces would break off, and hot pieces would blow out through the cowling. The B-32 test crews campaigned for an improved exhaust collector system, but their recommendations were not followed. This problem would continue to plague the B-32 program, and would cause the loss of 544 in combat while stationed at Yontan, Okinawa, in August 1945.

The AAF had planned to use the first 10 production bombers of the B-32-1-CF batch for testing. By early 1945 only five B-32s had been delivered to the various service test centers, and service testing was far behind schedule. The service tests were scheduled to be performed by the Army Air Forces Proving Ground Command (AAFPGC) at Eglin Field, FL, the Army Air Forces Tactical Center (AAFTAC) at Pinecastle Field, FL, and the Air Technical Service Command (ATSC) centers at Wright Field, Dayton, OH, Vandalia, OH, and at fields in San Diego and Fort Worth that were near the Consolidated factories. The particulars of the combat service tests will be discussed later.

5

While the B-32 Begins Production, the B-29 Begins Combat

While the B-32 program languished the B-29 program had problems of its own, mainly attributed to the Wright R-3350 engine delaying the availability of aircraft for training. In February 1944 the average airplane commander in the 58th Wing (XX Bomber Command) had less than 35 hours of flying time in the B-29 bomber, the program was behind schedule, and Gen. Arnold was most anxious to "commit the B-29 to combat as soon as possible." Aircraft were still being modified during March when the Command was ordered to move to the CBI. As a result of the constant modifications during the preceding six months the tactical squadrons sometimes had only one aircraft available to them for training.

Summary of Operations of the XX Bomber Command

The original Wright R-3350-5 engine was unreliable, and consequently was replaced by a later R-3355-23 type engine called the "war engine." Even this engine was unsatisfactory, and it was replaced just prior to going overseas with the R-3350-23A "combat engine." Estimates of B-29 losses anticipated in route to the CBI ran as high as 15%, primarily because of the unknown capabilities of the new engines. The movements overseas took place during the April, May, and June 1944, consisting of a move halfway around the world: Kansas, Maine, New Foundland, French Morocco, Egypt, and India. Fortunately, these new engines were far superior to the original model; consequently, the number of aircraft lost on the way was well within the calculated "risk."

The first "shake down" B-29 combat mission that was in range of B-29s taking off from bases in India was flown in early June against Japanese targets in Bangkok, Thailand. However, the XXBC had not reached its bases of operations against targets on Japan proper until the aircraft of the Wing took off in the middle of June on the flights over the Himalayan "Hump" to China. From there it could stage for the first attack by land-based aircraft into the heart of the Japanese Empire. Undoubtedly the sight of these huge aircraft was an invaluable morale factor for the Chinese armies fighting into their eighth year of war, and the reason for Arnold's acceleration of the B-29 program over the B-32 program. However, because of the logistical and combat mission distances involved the Japanese Homeland did not feel the true power of the B-29. The tenuous aerial pipeline of supply, called the "Hump," extending 1,500 miles from India over the "roof of the world" to Chengtu, China, could not logistically support the XXBC's operational capabilities. It is often forgotten that the beginning of this aerial pipeline in India was itself 15,000 miles from the United States, where the supply of materials originated to be transported by ship across the Pacific.

The first effort of the XX Bomber Command was primarily individual medium altitude attacks at night. Then in August, when the first production B-32 flew, daylight four-ship B-29 formations were attempted, because of the lack of accuracy achieved in the night mode of attack. The accuracy immediately improved, although the bomb load was decreased. In September the XXBC started flying 12-ship formations, again decreas-

The first movements overseas by the B-29s to the CBI began in April 1944, and combat commenced in May. The first B-29 of the XXI Bomber Command arrived at Isley Field, Saipan, on 12 October 1944. Shown are B-29s of the 39th Bomb Group taxiing on Tinian's North Field. (USAAF)

ing the bomb load, but showing an immediate return in more bombs actually placed on the target. This can be attributed to the use of selected lead crews for bomb aiming of their own bombs and the loads of 11 other bombers. In October there was an increase in the bomb loads, as better cruise control and piloting ability were realized from the augmented training program established by Gen. LeMay. It was during this month that, for the first time, Bomber Command achieved total destruction of a target (the aircraft depot in Formosa).

During the last two months of 1944, when there were only two production B-32s available, the Hump lift had been increased to an extraordinary extent, and the XX Bomber Command's allocation of fuel and ordnance from this lift had multiplied greatly. As a result the XXBC was able not only to multiply its efforts against the Japanese Homeland, staging from China, but by utilizing the time that the aircraft spent in the rear area (India) was able to multiply its effort substantially on the Southeast Asia Campaign (Singapore, Burma, and China) from Indian bases.

By January 1945, when the AAF was officially accepting the B-32, the XX Bomber Command had reached an experience level in which the various commanders of its units understood crew and aircraft capabilities, and were able to confidently dispatch missions with knowledge that the mission planning rationale they used was correct. Weather forecasts had become more reliable, bombardiers' accuracy was greatly increased, and the ability of the ground crews to maintain the aircraft and load them on short notice had become proficient.

In the latter part of January 1945, a decision was reached that VHB aircraft would relinquish their China bases and end operations against the Japanese home islands until they were able to move to Okinawa after its capture. During this month personnel and staging equipment belonging to the XX Bomber Command were evacuated from China back to India. Pending movement to its new Okinawan bases, the XX Bomber Command operated from India exclusively against targets requested by the Allied Supreme Commander Southeast Asia. These operations included mining of the water approaches to Singapore, and the mining of certain South China

ports. The precision bombing effort of the Command was utilized in most part in high explosive and incendiary attacks on targets in the Singapore area. However, a few limited effort missions were dispatched against targets in Burma. On 30 March the last mission of the XX Bomber Command was flown to Singapore, and the 58th Wing—the only VHB Wing of the XX Bomber Command—prepared to move its base to Tinian, under the command of the XXI Bomber Command.

Summary of Operations of the XXI Bomber Command

The 73rd Wing was the first of five wings of the XXI Bomber Command that were ultimately scheduled to go into combat. On 10 August 1944 the first service group arrived at Saipan to start preparation of the necessary facilities of the 73rd Wing base. The first B-29 of the Wing arrived at Isley Field, Saipan, on 12 October.

From the arrival of the first units, all efforts were intended toward getting the 73BW to bomb Japan as quickly as possible. However, problems of inadequate airfield and housing facilities, maintenance equipment, and limited supplies were to be overcome before the first mission could be conducted. The fact that the entire 73BW, including four Bomb Wings and four service groups, was stationed at one airfield created unique problems of organization and administration. Never before in AAF history had a total of over 12,000 personnel been located at one combat base.

According to the target directive from headquarters, 20th Air Force, Washington, the XXIBC was given the primary task of destroying Japan's aircraft industry, and the secondary task of supporting Pacific operations. In accordance with this directive, the first mission to the Empire occurred on 24 November, when 111 aircraft were airborne against Nakajima Aircraft Company plant at Musashino, near Tokyo. Attacking from 30,000ft, only 24 aircraft bombed the primary target, which was partially obscured by cloud cover, while an additional 59 dropped their high explosive bombs on the secondary target, the urban area of Tokyo. This attack marked the opening of an air operation that would be unparalleled in military history. At the time the future of the B-32 program not only looked very bleak, but was threatened with termination.

6

The B-36 is Conceived and Contracted

The influence of the XB-36/B-36 program needs to be broached, as it influenced the thinking and actions of Consolidated-Vultee officials in regard to the B-32. In 1940 the world situation was perilous, with Continental Europe under Nazi domination, Britain near defeat, and Japan making large gains in China, and threatening war in the Pacific. In response President Roosevelt and Army Chief of Staff, Gen. George C. Marshall, requested that Boeing and Consolidated submit proposals for a long-range intercontinental bomber capable of bombing European targets from North American bases. The requirements for the intercontinental bomber were that it had to carry 10,000 pounds of bombs 5,000 miles, and return at 300 to 400 mph. The B-17 had a combat radius of 1,000 miles, and the then secret B-29 and B-32 projects had ranges of 2,500 miles. Both Boeing and Consolidated engineers knew that they would have problems attaining the 10,000 mile range requirement with contemporary technology. When the secret competition began on 11 April 1941 Consolidated engineers had already developed their Model 35 four engine pusher-tractor design in August 1940, and thought the 10,000 mile range was feasible using the data obtained in their Model 35 studies. In November 1941 Consolidated submitted its design proposal to the Air Materiel Command at Wright Field to build two prototypes. The design had six pusher engines, and resembled the XB-32 with its circular fuselage, remote gun sighting stations, communications tunnel, Davis Wing, twin tail design, and a nose and cockpit design with stepped windows.

On 15 November 1941 the XB-36 contract (W535-AC-2232) for $800,000 (plus $135,455 for winning the design competition) was awarded for two XB-36 prototypes to be built in San Diego, with the first to be provided by May 1944, and the second six months later. The technical and monetary potential of the intercontinental bomber was significant, and Consolidated assigned some of its best engineering and managerial personnel on the project, perhaps at the expense of the B-32 program (the B-24 program was more or less at a fully developed, self-sufficient stage). I.M. Mac Laddon, developer of the PBY, was the executive vice president of Consolidated, but in fact was running the company, as Reuben Fleet was in the process of reaching an agreement to sell his shares in the company to Vultee. Work on the XB-36 commenced, and much of the technology that was used to develop the XB-32 was utilized in the XB-36: the Davis Wing; and the aerodynamics of aluminum skin joint bonding and weight control, along with the experience gained in the extensive wind

tunnel testing. By June 1942 the Consolidated San Diego plant was fully occupied with contracts for the B-24 and PBY programs, and the XB-36 program was moved to Fort Worth. But the work area there was not large enough, and it was not until early 1944 that a 90,000 square foot, 60 foot high facility ("the Experimental Building") was completed. San Diego was to be responsible for basic XB-36 design and wind tunnel testing, while Fort Worth was to engineer and manufacture the two prototypes, and then conduct their eventual flight testing. XB-32 chief project engineer R.C. "Sparky" Seabold was taken off that troubled program, and made chief engineer of the XB-36 program, which had more potential. By the end of 1942 the XB-36 program also encountered developmental problems, but in view of the current unfavorable war situation Gen. Arnold continued to give the XB-36 program "high priority"; this continued into 1943, when the fall of China seemed probable, and the projected use of VHB B-29s and B-32s from Chinese bases was placed at risk. With orders for only two XB-36s, new Consolidated-Vultee Chairman Tom Girdler informed the War Department that his company was having problems getting subcon-

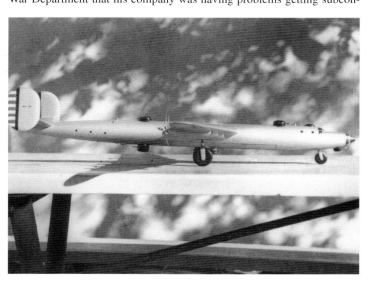

The lineage of the B-36 from the B-32 can be seen in this precursor of the XB-36, the Model 36. This wooden model shows the Davis Wing, the twin, dihedral tail arrangement, and the shape of the nose/cockpit area, with its birdcage windows. The original test model had six tractor engines instead of the six pusher engines of the production B-36. (Consolidated via Pima)

Consolidated-Vultee President Harry Woodward (R) presents test pilot Beryl Erickson an award for his work on the XB-36 during a postwar ceremony. (Consolidated via Pima)

tractors to accept orders for the limited XB-36 program. In July 1943 Gen. Oliver Echols, head of AAF procurement, issued a letter of intent to build 100 B-36s at Fort Worth, and in August 1944 100 production models were officially ordered (at $1.75 million each, including GFE at $500,000). To expedite the B-36 program—reducing developmental time by two years—it was decided to begin production before the two experimental models were ready for testing. However, in July 1944 Gen. B.E. Meyers of the Air Materiel Command informed Consolidated-Vultee President Harry Woodhead by letter that Consolidated-Vultee was to take:

"...positive and vigorous action to place the B-32 on Number One Priority from an engineering, tooling, and production standpoint, without reference to the effect this action may have on the XB-36 and B-36 programs."

As a result, by the end of 1944 the XB-36 was a year and a half behind schedule, but there were only a handful of completed B-32s available.

As the war intensified, Consolidated and the war industry in general faced a shortage of skilled and unskilled personnel, especially engineers, and this situation was aggravated when the Selective Service drafted unskilled and then qualified personnel. Consolidated at Fort Worth was overextended, especially in mid-1943, when it expanded its B-24 program, and was beginning to tool up for the B-32. All manufacturers were having problems obtaining raw materials and parts, and there was a domino effect in completing existing orders; at Consolidated-Vultee the XB-36, B-32, and B-24 programs all competed for parts and personnel. The company was in flux, as Reuben Fleet left the company except for a token advisory position, and Vultee executives, managers, and technical personnel had to be integrated into the melded company. With the capture and development of the Marianas air bases the B-29 program was increased to Number One Priority for engineering and production by Gen. B.F. Meyers at the Air Materiel Command, and the XB-36 and the B-32 programs languished. This was particularly critical for Consolidated-Vultee, as at the time B-24 orders and production were declining. As will be discussed later at length, Gen. Kenney's interest in the B-32 enabled Consolidated-Vultee to revive that program with Gen. Meyers' "positive and vigorous action" order to get the B-32 into production, while allowing the company to continue to develop the B-36 for the post war market. Consolidated-Vultee executives saw their B-32 production numbers stagnate, and also realized that the B-32 was not going to have a place as a postwar aircraft. Thus, the company indifferently produced 130 generally substandard B-32s while keeping the more promising, but troubled, postwar B-36 program viable.

As the B-32 contracts were terminated and, after six years of delay, on 8 September 1945 the first flawed XB-36 left the assembly line; it would not be until 11 months later on 8 August 1946 that it would make its first flight. Due to numerous continuing problems the aircraft was only sporadically tested into the spring of 1947. It would not be until 4 December 1947 that the upgraded YB-36 flew successfully. Ironically, the ill-conceived prop-powered B-36 also would not find a niche in America's postwar jet bomber strategy, despite being jury-rigged with additional jet pods.

7

B-32 Production and Production Revisions

B-32s built in Fort Worth were designated by the manufacturer's code suffix -CF, while -CO designated the aircraft built in San Diego.

B-32-1/5-CF

The first 14 Fort Worth production aircraft were run in two blocks:

B-32-1-CF (42-108471 to 480) 10 aircraft
B-32-5-CF (42-108481 to 484) 4 aircraft

All 14 of these aircraft were destined for the accelerated test flying programs, and no armament was installed. B-32-1-CF aircraft 42-108471 and 42-108472 were fitted with the 16.6 foot modified B-29 tails used on the second prototype, but were later given the extended 19.5 foot standard B-32 tail. Production was stopped on the eight B-32s then on the line until the extended tails arrived in early December 1943. The major revisions to this batch of aircraft (B-32-1-CF 42-108471 to 108480) were:

1) Standard tail with two rudder tabs.
2) The aileron control wheel travel was increased from 135 degrees to 150 degrees.
3) To increase their stability the elevator tabs were installed with cambered lower surfaces.

4) Replacement of the trailing edge over flap panels with those constructed of stronger 24ST aluminum.
5) The hydraulic uplatch mechanism on the main landing gear was modified after the 27 August accident.
6) The magneto cooling system was modified, and a magneto pressurization system was added.
7) The ammunition feed system for the nose and tail turrets was modified.
8) Installation of a AN/ARC-8 Liaison Radio Set.
9) Installation of a VHF SCR-522A Radio Set and a SCR-274 Range Receiver (instead of the SCR-274 Command Set).
10) Installation of the AN/ARN-7 Radio Compass (replaced the SCR-296-G Set.
11) Redesign of the radio operator's table.
12) Installation of the AN/AIC-2 Interphone System.
13) Installation of the AN/ARN-5 and RC-103 Instrument Approach System.
14) Installation of the AN/APN-4 LORAN Radio Navigation System.
15) Installation of the AN/APN-1 Radar Altimeter.
16) Installation of a combined radar/navigator's table.
17) Installation of the AN/APQ-5B Low Altitude Bombing Set and the AN/APQ-13 Radar Bombing Set.
18) Installation of additional generators and invertors for these new radar sets.
19) Installation of the SCR-729 IFF Set.

Changes in the four B-32-5-CF (Aircraft 11 through 14, 42-108481 through 484) were the same as for the above, plus the twin rudder tabs were standardized. Aircraft 42-108482 was also experimentally equipped with Sperry-built stabilized gun turrets and flown at Wright Field in demonstration flights.

Aircraft 42-108473 and 42-108479 were flown to Wright Field for flight and static load tests, respectively (479 had suffered an accident on 26 November 1944 before being flown to Wright Field). 42-108479 was load tested to failure in Wright's Static Test Building on 14 December 1944 and written off inventory. On 5 March 1945 a Lockheed C-60 stalled on takeoff and crashed into the experimental hangars at Wright Field, killing eight people and destroying nine aircraft, including 42-108473. Wright Field

Before and After. As was a common practice during WWII, the B-32 experienced the censor's air brush. On the right photo the Briggs A-17 nose and tail turrets, and the Martin A-3F-A top turret of 476 were air brushed out, as were the recess for the belly ball turret and the astrodome. The nose turret in particular has been very crudely erased. (USAAF via Dembeck)

evaluation considered the B-32 to be generally good with some construction shortcomings, and poor workmanship in several components. Aircraft 42-108478 was the first production B-32 assigned to the ATSC, and was based at Vandalia, OH, in December 1944 for evaluation. It was followed by two B-32-5-CFs (42-108481 and 482).

TB-32-5/10/15-CF
The next three production batches were built under the Army contract to supply 40 training aircraft designated with the TB prefix. They had no combat equipment, and were nearly 8,000 pounds lighter, giving the bomber much better performance. These 40 bombers were included in the following batches:

> TB-32-5-CF (42-108485 to 95) 11 aircraft
> TB-32-10-CF (42-108496 to 520) 25 aircraft
> TB-32-15-CF (42-108521 to 24) 4 aircraft

Major revisions in TB-32-5-CF (Aircraft 15 through 25, 42-108485 through 495) were:

1) Deletion of all defensive armament, with the openings in the fuselage for the turret installations faired over, and 750 pounds of ballast added to compensate for the weight loss.
2) Deletion of the AN/APN-4 LORAN set, AN/APN-1 Radio Altimeter, SCR-729 IFF, and AN/APQ-5 and APQ-13 radar sets.
3) A new fire seal adaptor flange for the R-3350-23 engine.

Major Revisions in TB-32-10-CF (26 through 50, 42-108946 to 520) were:

1) Redesign of the bombardier's entrance door to facilitate jettisoning (one-step).
2) Replacement of the SCR-269-G Radio Compass with the AN/ARN-7 Set.
3) Installation of engine fire extinguishers.

Major revisions in the third TB-32-15-CF (42-108521 to 24) batch were:

1) Standardize the empennage de-icer boots.
2) Redesign the glide-bombing system.

Aircraft 474, seen here at Tarrant Field, would be the first modified B-32-1-CF to roll off the Consolidated production line in early December 1944. It and subsequent B-32s had to wait for the standard tall B-32 tail with two rudder tabs. (USAAF via Dembeck)

B-32-20/21/25/30/35

The next and, what was to be the final, 74 bombers were the fully combat equipped, unpressurized models, B-32-CF-20, -21, -25, -30, and -35:

B-32-20-CF	2 aircraft	42-108525 through 108526
B-32-21-CF	1 aircraft	42-108527
B-32-20-CF	18 aircraft	42-108528 through 108545
B-32-25-CF	25 aircraft	42-108546 through 108570
B-32-30-CF	7 aircraft	42-108571 through 108577
B-32-35-CF	7 aircraft	42-108578 through 108584

After the completion of the TB-32 contract, the combat-equipped B-32-20-CF (Aircraft 55, 56, and 58 through 75/42-108525, 526, and 528 through 545) maintained the modifications made to the previous three blocks of TB aircraft, and the following modifications were added:

1) Reinstallation of all offensive and defensive armament.
2) Reinstallation of full radio and radar.
3) Installation of flak curtains.
4) Installation of improved and less complicated bomb hoisting equipment.
5) Installation of cargo-carrying platforms in the bomb bays.
6) Replacement of B-10 bomb shackles by B-7 shackles.
7) Addition of life raft stowage compartments on top of the fuselage.
8) Installation of jettisonable cockpit side windows.
9) Installation of scanning blisters on the rear fuselage for visual assessment of the main landing gear and engine nacelles.
10) Installation of cowl flap position indicators.
11) Replacement of the B-3 driftmeter by the AN-5763-40 type.

The B-32-21-CF (Airplane 57/42-108527) was the third B-32-20 built at Fort Worth, and was retained there for conversion as an experimental paratroop transport. All bombing equipment was removed, and benches were installed in the rear cabin and rear bomb bay. It was intended that the paratroopers would leave the aircraft through the forward bomb bay. The

There are some reports that the other two San Diego aircraft (44-904487 and 488) were built to shop assembled status, lacking combat equipment, and were declared FTI and flown directly from the factory to an aircraft disposal site. In close examination of the photo there appears to be two tails waiting behind the B-32, along with an additional cylindrical fuselage section against the left wall. (Consolidated via Chana)

paratroop carrier scheme was not pursued, and the aircraft remained at the factory until October 1945, when it was declared excess. Another scheme was to convert the B-32 into a target tow aircraft, but this ultimate affront to the B-32 project was not pursued.

The B-32-25-CF (Aircraft 76 through 100/42-108546 through 570) had two modifications to the fuel system, with the ability of two 750-gallon jettisonable, self-sealing auxiliary tanks to be added to the bomb bay (increasing fuel capacity to 6,960 gallons), and the addition of gas tight seals to the lower surface of the wing sections adjacent to the fuselage. The AN/APN-9 LORAN set was substituted for the AN/APN-4 set.

The B-32-30-CF (Aircraft 101 through 106/42-108571 through 577) was modified as follows:

1) Replacement of the Sperry A-17 nose and tail turrets with the stabilized A-17-A model.

Very rare photo of the obscure San Diego production B-32-1-CO (44-90486). For an unknown reason the San Diego plant was contracted to build three B-32 aircraft. Only one of these aircraft was fully completed (44-904486), which was built to late B-32-CF specifications, and was subsequently accepted by the Air Force on 27 July 1945. (Consolidated via Chana)

Very late Fort Worth production line B-32-40/45/50-CFs (42-108596 through 629). None of these aircraft were delivered to the AAF, and when the government terminated the Consolidated-Vultee contract all GFE (government furnished equipment) was removed, the engines were removed, and the aircraft broken up and sold to scrappers. (Consolidated via Chana)

2) The trailing edge of the wing was reinforced to correct its susceptibility for cracking.

3) Installation of AN/APQ-2, AN/APT-1, and AN/APT-2 countermeasures equipment.

4) Replacement of the AN/APQ-13 bombing radar with the improved APQ-13A set.

The B-32-35-CF (Aircraft 107 through 114/42-108578 through 584) was the identical to the B-32-30-CF batch, except for increased ammunition.

The final 10 B-32s—three from batch -30, and all seven from batch -35—were not fully completed when production was terminated, and were delivered as FTI (Flyable, Terminal Inventory). There is some evidence that these 10 aircraft could have been designated as B-32-40-CFs (42-108585 to 594).

Little is known about the B-32-20-CO built at Consolidated's San Diego plant, but it probably was a standard -20. For unknown reasons the San Diego plant was contracted to build three aircraft, batch number B-32-1-CO (44-90486 to 88). Only one of these aircraft was fully completed (Airplane 115/44-904486), which was built to late B-32-CF specifications, and was subsequently accepted by the Air Force on 27 July 1945. There are some reports that the other two aircraft (44-904487 and 488) were built to "shop assembled" status, lacking combat equipment, and were declared FTI and flown directly from the factory to an aircraft disposal site.

The total of 118 B-32s were delivered, with July 1945 having the top monthly production at 21 aircraft delivered. But this total could be raised to 130 *flyable* aircraft if the last 10 production B-32-40-CFs(?) and the two San Diego B-32-20-COs that were declared FTI are included.

If B-32 production had been continued there were several planned improvements. The exhaust was to be furthered modified to stop the continued engine fires, and fixed fire extinguishers were to be installed. Several of the last production models had oil shut off valves installed in the engine nacelle firewalls. The outboard engines were to have reversing propeller mechanisms added to aid in braking with the existing inboard re-

versing props. The next production models were to have stabilized nose and tail turrets. During the Philippines combat tests the B-32 bombardier's station had been graded (unfairly) as having poor visibility, and the new models were to have a newly designed compartment offering improved visibility.

The average cost per aircraft was approximately $790,000; $822,195 initially, and $731,040 later. The B-29-40-BA cost $971,373 initially, while the end-of-production B-29-90-BW was listed at $495,780. The original estimated cost of the World War II production run of 3,943 B-29s (5,092 on order were canceled) was $3.7 billion, resulting in an average estimated cost of $930,000 per bomber. This was 2.7 times more expensive than a 1945 B-17 when the Flying Fortress was nearing the end of its production run. As the size of the B-29 orders increased its manufacturers were able to lower costs per unit, because their mass production techniques and assembly line workers became more efficient, but this was not possible in the limited B-32 production run. When the pilot accepted his B-29 or B-32 he actually signed a form assuming financial responsibility for its cost if it were lost through his neglect!

In late 1943 Consolidated proposed that their B-32 bomber be called the "Terminator," and initially the Air Force accepted the name. However, in August 1944 the Official Technical Subcommittee on Naming Aircraft selected the name "Dominator," and the company agreed to the new name. In the summer of 1945 Assistant Secretary of State and Poet Laureate Archibald McLeish disagreed, as he felt Dominator was too totalitarian in connotation, rather than patriotic like Liberator, or robust like Superfortress. The State Department used its influence, and the name officially reverted to the original Terminator, but the B-32 will probably always be referred to as the Dominator.

The AAF Officially Accepts the B-32

Due to production and service testing delays the first B-32 was officially accepted by Fort Worth Army Air Field CO Col. H.W. Dorr on 27 January 1945. An official party of FWAAF officers and Consolidated-Vultee representatives taxied the B-32 from the factory production line across the run-

The B-32 was officially introduced to the general public on Air Force Day, 1 August 1945, when a formation of B-32s flew over Fort Worth during a morning and afternoon flyover, followed by an inspection at FWAAF of a parked B-32 (TB-32/514) that had a ramp built over and around it. (USAAF)

ways to the training facility. Included in the acceptance party was Col. Dorr, Lt.Cols. C.E. Jost, W.W. Holmes, and Fred Easley, Maj. Robert La Plante, and Lts. E.E. Reynolds and Matthew Lyle. In May 1945 delegates to the San Francisco Conference that had gathered there to form the future United Nations were shown the B-32, and at the same time newspaper, magazine, and technical writers were given a day long introductory program, including flights in the bomber. The aircraft was officially introduced to the general public on "Air Force Day," 1 August 1945, when a formation of B-32s flew over Fort Worth during a morning and afternoon flyover, followed by an inspection at FWAAF of a parked B-32 (TB-32/514) that had a ramp built over and around it. In his welcoming address

Col. Dorr emphasized "the cordial relationship that has existed between Fort Worth civilians and Army personnel since FWAAF was activated three years ago this month." He continued, saying:

"Today's open house is more than an Army Air Forces celebration. I look upon it as our joint tribute to the combat crews now bombing Japan, and to the men and women of our aircraft factories who helped build the largest and greatest air force in the world. But our job won't be completed until Japan has been decisively defeated. Until then, we here at FWAAF will continue training B-32 combat crews night and day. It will be up to you to give us the planes and equipment we need. Until Japan surrenders our combined efforts will make the Nips think every day is Air Force Day!"

Consolidated Company PR Photos

These four photos were released to the public of B-32-1-CF #476, the sixth production aircraft
off the line, which was used extensively for PR photos. (All USAAF)

Part Two

The Aircraft

B-32 Description

Performance (AAF Proving Ground Command Figures)

Weights

Empty	60,278 pounds
Design Gross	100,000 pounds
Maximum Allowable Gross	123,250 pounds
Recommended Maximum Takeoff Gross	100,800 pounds *

(*Restricted to 110,000 pounds during the ATSC Overseas Combat Test)

Ferry Range: 4,400 miles (w/o auxiliary bomb bay tanks)

Combat Range: 3,000 miles with 10,000 pound bomb load

Radius of Action:

Condition One:	1,300 air miles	**Condition Two:**	1,250 miles
Bomb Load:	10,000 pounds	**Bomb Load:**	20,000 pounds
Fuel Load:	5,460 gallons	**Fuel Load:**	5,460 gallons
Reserve Fuel:	655 gallons	**Reserve Fuel:**	490 gallons
Bombing Altitude:	29,600 feet	**Bombing Altitude:**	27,100 feet

Speed:

Maximum level at 30,000ft: 357mph

Maximum level at 5,000ft: 302mph

Normal Cruise: 290mph

Economical Cruise: 200mph

Landing: 118mph

Speed/Climb (at 100,000 pounds/military power/five minutes):

Altitude	(ft) Speed (mph)	Rate of climb (ft/min)
30,000	357	350
25,000	347	550
20,000	324	700
15,000	312	850
10,000	296	950
5,000	281	1,050

Speed/Climb (at 100,000 pounds/continuous power/unlimited)

Altitude (ft)	Speed (mph)	Rate of Climb (ft/min)
30,000	N/A	N/A
25,000	311	400
20,000	300	500
15,000	289	650
10,000	279	750
5,000	269	850

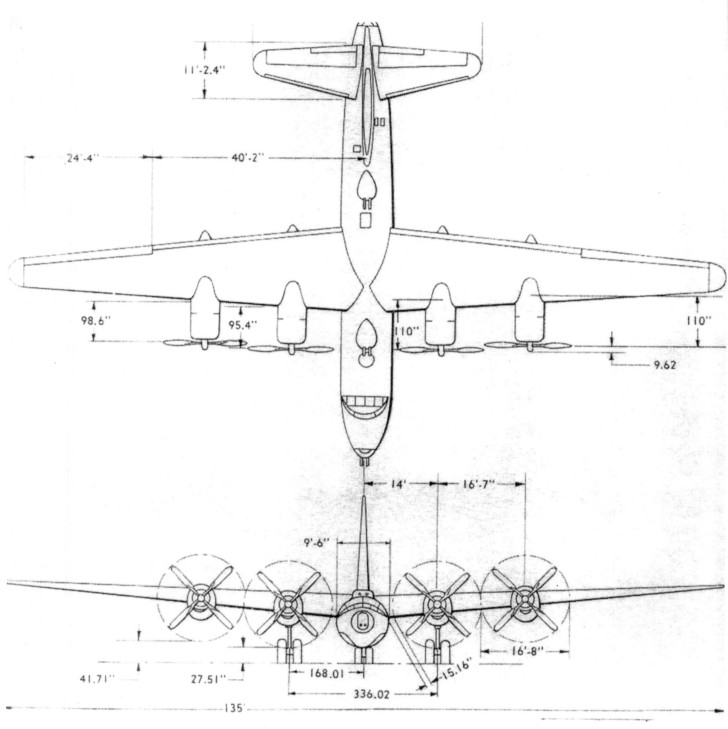

B-32 Specifications (E&R Manual)

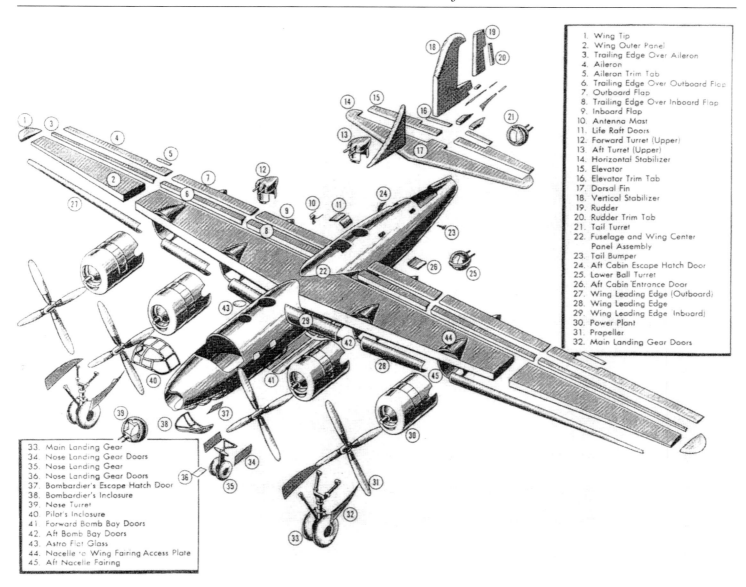

1. Wing Tip
2. Wing Outer Panel
3. Trailing Edge Over Aileron
4. Aileron
5. Aileron Trim Tab
6. Trailing Edge Over Outboard Flap
7. Outboard Flap
8. Trailing Edge Over Inboard Flap
9. Inboard Flap
10. Antenna Mast
11. Life Raft Doors
12. Forward Turret (Upper)
13. Aft Turret (Upper)
14. Horizontal Stabilizer
15. Elevator
16. Elevator Trim Tab
17. Dorsal Fin
18. Vertical Stabilizer
19. Rudder
20. Rudder Trim Tab
21. Tail Turret
22. Fuselage and Wing Center
   Panel Assembly
23. Tail Bumper
24. Aft Cabin Escape Hatch Door
25. Lower Ball Turret
26. Aft Cabin Entrance Door
27. Wing Leading Edge (Outboard)
28. Wing Leading Edge
29. Wing Leading Edge (Inboard)
30. Power Plant
31. Propeller
32. Main Landing Gear Doors

33. Main Landing Gear
34. Nose Landing Gear Doors
35. Nose Landing Gear
36. Nose Landing Gear Doors
37. Bombardier's Escape Hatch Door
38. Bombardier's Inclosure
39. Nose Turret
40. Pilot's Inclosure
41. Forward Bomb Bay Doors
42. Aft Bomb Bay Doors
43. Astro Flat Glass
44. Nacelle to Wing Fairing Access Plate
45. Aft Nacelle Fairing

Figure 4 — Major Component Assemblies

(E&R Manual)

1

Fuselage

General Description

The B-32 fuselage was 83.08 feet in overall length, with its circular cross section reaching a maximum diameter of 9.5 feet. It was of an all-metal semi-monocoque shell design, employing longitudinal stringers and longerons, circumferential stiffeners, and transversal bulkheads. The longitudinal stringers were usually spaced about six inches apart, with more employed in areas requiring extra strength. Longerons were used only to support loads around openings, such as bomb bays, access doors, and points where the skin/stringer arrangement was interrupted. Belt frames were 0.04 inch 24ST Alclad lipped channel that maintained the fuselage shape. They were spaced about 18 inches apart, and notched to cross over the stringers. The skin/stringer/bulkhead/belt frame structural design combination was utilized to disperse strength, rather than concentrate it in a few vital elements that would be subject to combat damage.

A smooth aluminum alloy stressed skin was of variable gauge (minimum was 0.025) that depended on local stress requirements. The skin was riveted directly to the bulkheads, ribs, and stringers, and the production models had the same riveting patterns as the XB-32s. Brazier rivet heads were used to attach the skin to the bulkheads, ribs, and stringers, with the exception being that flush head rivets were used forward of station 2.0 (where 3/16 inch and 1/4 inch rivets were used forward of the front spar, and 1/4 inch rivets aft of the front spar). The fuselage was composed of the following sections: nose cabin; nose wheel well cabin; flight deck; forward accessory cabin; bomb bay; rear cabin; rear accessory cabin; and tail cabin.

Fuselage Sections

Nose Cabin

This cabin extended from station 1.0 and 2.0. A molded transparent glass shell, extending from stations 1.0 to 2.0, formed the lower part of the nose, and provided the bombardier with downward vision. The turret formed the nose of the bomber, and occupied the forward part of the nose cabin, re-

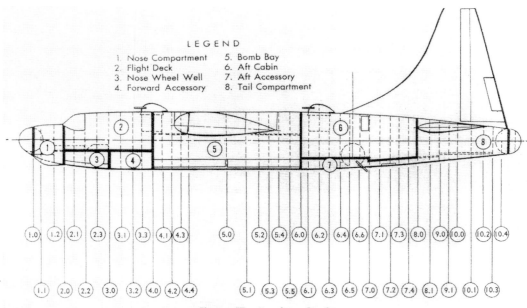

LEGEND
1. Nose Compartment   5. Bomb Bay
2. Flight Deck   6. Aft Cabin
3. Nose Wheel Well   7. Aft Accessory
4. Forward Accessory   8. Tail Compartment

Figure 57 — Fuselage Stations

(E&R Manual)

placing the greenhouse nose of the XB-32. It was the poor maximum vision (10 degrees below horizontal) for the bombardier in the XB-32 that caused production delays, as this field of vision could not be increased unless there was a "major change" in the design of the nose. Again, "there appeared to be a lack of cooperation and coordination of effort among the interested organizations" to change the nose situation. On 8 September 1944 a meeting was held in Fort Worth by the Air Technical Service Command (ATSC, the former Air Materiel Command) to revise and modify the nose position. The ATSC directed Consolidated-Vultee to increase forward and side vision for the bombardier by installing the Emerson Model 129 nose that was being used in the B-24. The ATSC set an 8 November date for the inspection of a mock up of the altered nose by Operations, Commitments, and Requirements (OC&R), with Materials and Services (M&S) and the Air Force Board (AFB) also to be represented at the mock up inspection. The general consensus was that that the mock up was a "satisfactory arrangement and should be incorporated." However, the Air Force Board did not concur, and it was not until 16 February 1945 that the B-32 Modification Board met at Wright Field, Dayton, and recommended that:

"...since it appeared impossible to devise a superior configuration which had superior fire power and visibility.... B-32 airplanes will be produced with a certain percentage of each of the two types of nose configuration...."

The bombardier and nose gunner were located in the two-tier nose compartment. Sliding panels at Station 1 separated the nose turret compartment from the nose section, and provided the entrance door to the turret. These panels, when closed, formed a wind bulkhead for the nose gunner, and provided him with a backrest. The bombsight glass in the bombardier's station was laminated, and equipped with a windshield wiper. While on the bombing run the bombardier was furnished with a kneeling pad, but otherwise he was stationed at the forward compartment settee. The bombardier's head clearance was about 4.5 feet, while the rear portion of this cabin had head clearance of about six feet. The bombardier's instruments and control panel were located to his left, and the oxygen panel to his right. The nose cabin also contained the turret's ammunition boxes, propeller voltage boosters, and parachute stowage rack.

Nose Wheel Well Cabin
The Nose Wheel Well Cabin extended from station 2.0 to 3.0, and included provisions for housing the nose wheel, the retracting mechanism, and nose wheel doors. An access door located between stations 2.0 and 2.2, on both

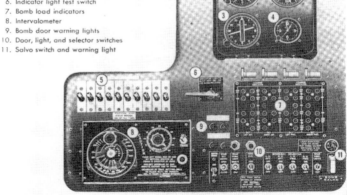

BOMBARDIER'S PANEL

1. Altimeter
2. Airspeed indicator
3. Flux gate compass repeater
4. Clock
5. Circuit breakers
6. Indicator light test switch
7. Bomb load indicators
8. Intervalometer
9. Bomb door warning lights
10. Door, light, and selector switches
11. Salvo switch and warning light

(E&R Manual)

1. Proportional Synchronizer   3. Turret Sliding Doors
2. Bombardier's Panel   4. Propeller Voltage Booster

Figure 59 — Right Side of Nose Compartment

(E&R Manual)

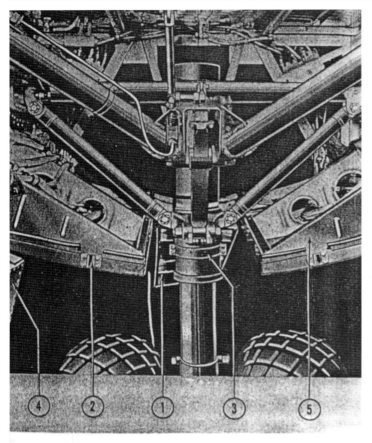

1. Strut Door Assembly
2. Nose Wheel Door Catch
3. Actuating Lug
4. Nose Wheel Well Door
5. Station 2.2

Figure 60 — Forward View of Nose Wheel Well Compartment

(E&R Manual)

Pilot's and co-pilot's station in early production model. (Consolidated via Chana)

sides of the fuselage was provided for servicing. Jack point plugs were attached to each side of the fuselage at station 2.0 and waterline 33 to 34. The cabin could be entered through the nose wheel opening, or by descending a removable ladder in the hatch leading through the flight deck floor. A flare chute was installed just of station 2.3 on the lower right side of the fuselage. The pitot mast and temperature bulb were located between station 2.0 and 2.1 on the lower left side of the fuselage.

Flight Deck

The flight deck cabin extended from stations 2.0 to 4.0, and included the pilot's and co-pilot's seats and flight controls, instruments, radio operator's station, navigator's station, and a settee bench, or a bunk in earlier models. The cabin was approximately 14.5 feet long, and had a maximum head clearance of 6.3 feet. A molded transparent glass shell formed the upper and lower part of this cabin, and extended from forward of station 2.0 to station 2.2.

Forward View of Flight Deck

L E G E N D

1. Navigator's Chair
2. Navigator's Table
3. Pilot's Chair
4. Sliding Enclosure Windows
5. Pilot's Enclosure
6. Main Instrument Panel
7. Copilot's Chair
8. Nose Compartment Passageway
9. Flight Deck Entrance

(E&R Manual)

Pilot's Station (USAAF)

The cockpit was so large and wide that it was termed the "pilot's compartment" in the *Pilot's Flight Operating Instructions*. In fact, it was so wide at 9.5 feet that the pilot and co-pilot were at arm's length, and sometimes had to communicate with each other over the interphone. Instrumentation was located in the traditional area in front of the pilot and co-pilot. Two control pedestals were located on the inboard sides of the two pilots, and a passageway leading to the nose cabin separated the pilots' seats. The flight engineer sat on the floor between the pilot and co-pilot, and was immediately available to monitor instruments. The flight controls were the conventional pedestal, cable-operated, dual controls for both the pilot and co-pilot. Throttle controls were dual, and located on both the pilot's and co-pilot's pedestal, and were conventional in operation. The Type-B electronic supercharger maintained proper carburetor inlet pres-

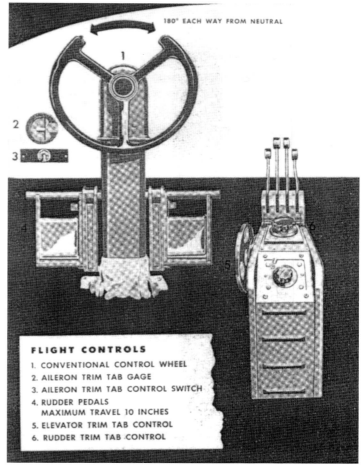

FLIGHT CONTROLS

1. CONVENTIONAL CONTROL WHEEL
2. AILERON TRIM TAB GAGE
3. AILERON TRIM TAB CONTROL SWITCH
4. RUDDER PEDALS
   MAXIMUM TRAVEL 10 INCHES
5. ELEVATOR TRIM TAB CONTROL
6. RUDDER TRIM TAB CONTROL

(E&R Manual)

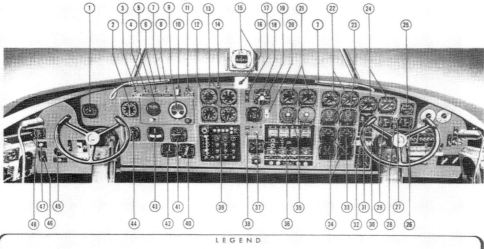

LEGEND

1. Pilot's Directional Indicator	13. Manifold Pressure Gages	25. Hydraulic Pressure Gage	37. Landing Gear Indicator Light
2. Airspeed Indicator	14. Both Inverter Failure Lights	26. Outboard Brake Hyd. Pressure Gage	38. Landing Gear Switch
3. Ball Turret Indicator Light	15. Magnetic Compass and Card	27. Brake Pressure Warning Light	39. Automatic Pilot Control Panel
4. Marker Beacon	16. Compass Light Rheostat Switch	28. Hydraulic Pump Override Switch	40. Fluxgate Repeater Ind. Compass
5. Turn Indicator	17. Alarm Bell Switch	29. Inboard Brake Hyd. Pressure Gage	41. Rate-of-Climb Indicator
6. Bomb Doors Indicator Light	18. Ignition Switch	30. Cowl Flap Switches	42. Radio Compass
7. AC Fluorescent Panel Lights	19. Flap Position Indicator	31. Oil Cooler Exit Flap Switches	43. Bank and Turn Indicator
8. Bomb Release Indicator Light	20. Flap Switch	32. Intercooler Exit Flap Switches	44. Altimeter
9. Gyro Horizon	21. Fuel Pressure Indicator	33. Cylinder Head Temp. Indicators	45. Aileron Tab Position Ind.
10. Bomb Salvo Switch	22. Main Oil Pressure Gages	34. Carburetor Air Temp. Indicators	46. Static Pressure Selector Valve
11. Salvo Indicating Lamp (Test)	23. Oil Temperature Indicators	35. Fuel Level Indicators	47. Turn and Bank Needle Valve
12. Engine Tachometers	24. Nose Oil Pressure Gages	36. Propeller Control Panel	48. Suction Gage

(E&R Manual)   **Figure 223 — Main Instrument Panel**

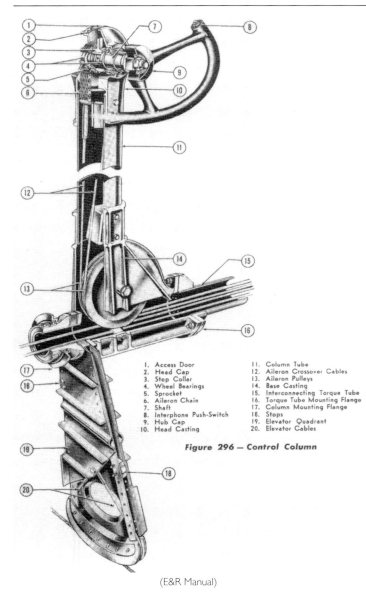

1. Access Door
2. Head Cap
3. Stop Collar
4. Wheel Bearings
5. Sprocket
6. Aileron Chain
7. Shaft
8. Interphone Push-Switch
9. Hub Cap
10. Head Casting
11. Column Tube
12. Aileron Crossover Cables
13. Aileron Pulleys
14. Base Casting
15. Interconnecting Torque Tube
16. Torque Tube Mounting Flange
17. Column Mounting Flange
18. Stops
19. Elevator Quadrant
20. Elevator Cables

Figure 296 — Control Column

(E&R Manual)

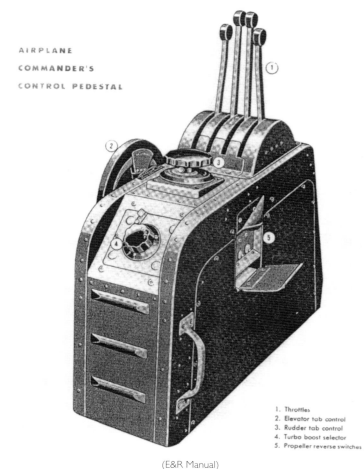

AIRPLANE
COMMANDER'S
CONTROL PEDESTAL

1. Throttles
2. Elevator tab control
3. Rudder tab control
4. Turbo boost selector
5. Propeller reverse switches

(E&R Manual)

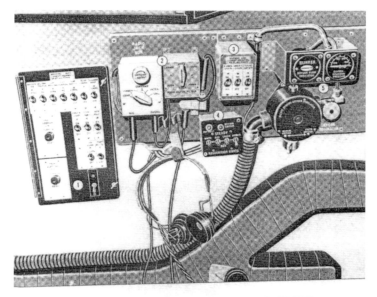

AIRPLANE COMMANDER'S CIRCUIT BREAKER PANEL

1. Circuit breakers
2. Radio jack box and filter
3. Circuit breakers
4. Recognition light control panel
5. Oxygen panel

(E&R Manual)

sure, and prevented the turbo superchargers from exceeding their safe limits. It also allowed the pilot to control engine power with only the throttles. The turbo supercharger boost selector (TBS) was mounted only on the pilot's pedestal. The elevator trim tabs were operated by two wheels, one on the outboard side of each control pedestal, while the rudder trim tab control wheels were located on top of both control pedestals. Both the elevator and rudder trim tabs were interconnected and conventional in operation. The aileron trim tab was actuated by a switch on the instrument panel to the left of the pilot, and was motivated by electric motors. The mixture controls were located only on the top of the co-pilot's pedestal. The wing flaps were controlled by a switch in the center of the instrument panel above the landing gear control, which had three positions: OFF, EXTEND, and RETRACT. The control lock lever was located forward and to the left of the pilot, and locked the rudder, elevator, and aileron in sequence. The aileron and rudder locked in the NEUTRAL position, while the elevator locked in the FULL DOWN position. In the LOCKED posi-

COPILOT'S

CONTROL PEDESTAL

1. Fuel quantity gages
2. Fuel pressure gages
3. Throttles
4. Rudder tab control
5. Elevator tab control
6. Mixture controls
7. Landing lights switches

(E&R Manual)

COPILOT'S CIRCUIT BREAKER PANEL

1. Circuit breakers
2. Oxygen panel
3. Radio jack box and filter
4. Circuit breakers
5. Circuit breakers

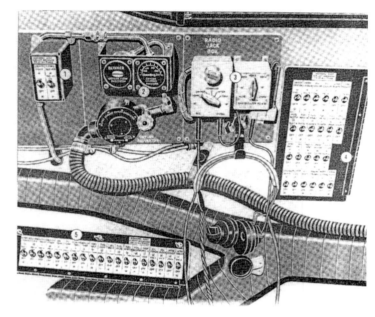

(E&R Manual)

AIRPLANE COMMANDER'S

AUXILIARY PANEL

1. Suction gage
2. Turn and bank needle valve
3. Static pressure selector valve
4. Aileron tab indicator
5. Aileron tab switch
6. Aileron tab indicator adjustment
7. Windshield wiper circuit breaker and switch
8. Formation, position, and tail lights switches

COPILOT'S AUXILIARY PANEL

1. Anti-icer flow controls
2. Battery switch
3. APP switches
4. Inverter switch
5. De-icer pressure gage
6. Engine priming and starting switches
7. Main inverter out warning light
8. Pitot heater switch
9. Tail de-icer switch
10. Carburetor air filter switches
11. Oil dilution switches
12. Wing anti-icer switch
13. Carburetor pre-heat switches
14. Forward cabin ventilating and heat controls

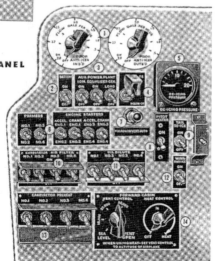

(E&R Manual)

(E&R Manual)

Aft View of Flight Deck

L E G E N D

1. Settee
2. Emergency Hydraulic Reservoir
3. Voltmeter Panel
4. Astroglass
5. Upper Forward Turret
6. Radio Operator's Table
7. Navigator's Panel
8. Bomb Bay Passageway
9. Navigator's Table

Flight Deck Aft View (USAAF)

1. Master Flux Gate Indicator
2. Radio Compass Indicator
3. Free Air Thermometer
4. Auto Pilot Turn Control
5. Flux Gate Gyro Caging Switch
6. Flux Gate Compass (A.C.) Circuit Breaker
7. Flying Suit Heater Circuit Breaker
8. Cockpit Light Circuit Breaker
9. Radio Compass Circuit Breaker
10. Flux Gate Compass (D.C.) Circuit Breaker
11. Table Light Circuit Breaker
12. Outside Air Temperature Thermometer Circuit Breaker
13. Altimeter
14. Airspeed Indicator

Figure 32 – Navigator's Station

(E&R Manual)

Navigator's Station (USAAF)

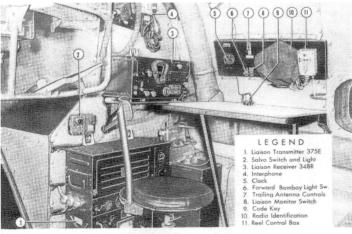

L E G E N D

1. Liaison Transmitter 375E
2. Salvo Switch and Light
3. Liaison Receiver 348R
4. Interphone
5. Clock
6. Forward Bombay Light Sw.
7. Trailing Antenna Controls
8. Liaison Monitor Switch
9. Code Key
10. Radio Identification
11. Reel Control Box

Figure 35 – Radio Operator's Station

(E&R Manual)

1. Radio Compass.   4. Altimeter.
2. Automatic Pilot Remote Turn Control.   5. Airspeed Indicator.
3. Free Air Temperature Indicator.   6. Master Fluxgate Compass.

Figure 224 — Navigator's Instrument Panel

(E&R Manual)

Radio Operator's Station (USAAF)

tion, the lever laid across the rudder pedals, making it known to the pilot that the lock was engaged.

The rear section of this cabin accommodated the navigator and radio operator (who also was the gunner for the forward upper turret). The navigator's station was located aft of the pilot's seat. The U-shaped radio operator's station was located aft of the navigator's station, and immediately forward of bulkhead 4.0. The emergency hydraulic reservoir and hand pump were located immediately forward of bulkhead 4.0 on the right side. The optically flat astro glass was located on the top centerline of the fuse-lage, directly behind and above the navigator's seat. It was used for astronomical navigation, and when opened inward could be used as an emergency exit. The forward top turret was located on the top centerline of the fuselage between stations 3.3 and 4.1. A trailing antenna was installed between stations 3.3 and 4.0 on the lower left side of the fuselage. An access door located between stations 3.1 and 3.2 on the floor of the flight deck provided accessibility to the forward accessory cabin.

Forward Accessory Cabin

The forward accessory cabin was located between stations 3.0 and 4.0, immediately aft of the nose wheel, and below the rear floor of the flight deck. The BTO (Bombing Through Overcast) radar turret, storage battery, turbo amplifiers, auxiliary power plant, and miscellaneous radio equipment were located in this cabin. The landing gear lights were contoured into each side of the fuselage between station 3.0 and 3.1.

1. Bulkhead 4.0   4. Hydraulic Brake Valves   7. Voltage Regulator Cage
2. Radio Compass Receiver   5. External Power Receptacle   8. Auxiliary Power Plant
3. Turbo Amplifiers   6. Inverter

Figure 63 — Forward View of Forward Accessory Compartment

(E&R Manual)

Bomb Bay

The tandem bomb bays were located in the lower central part of the bomber, extending from station 4.0 and 6.0, and were separated by bulkhead 5.0. A heavy truss crossed the entire 24.75 foot length of the bomb bay, and supported a 14.08 inch wide, roped-protected catwalk similar to that in the B-24; this extended through the center of each bomb bay, providing a supporting truss for the inboard bomb rails, and a passageway between the forward and rear cabins.

In the original pressurized XB-32 a small trolley mounted on tracks inside a 30 inch diameter tunnel provided a means of pressurized or unpressurized cabin-to-cabin transport. There were bulkhead pressure doors on each end of the tube. The occupant had to hoist himself head first on his back onto the cart, and pull himself via an overhead pulley rope system. If the aircraft were in a climb it was difficult, if not impossible, to move uphill from the rear to forward cabin, but movement in the opposite direction was easy, and the traveler had to be careful not to go too fast and end up on the floor of the rear cabin.

The outboard bomb bay rails were supported at their bottoms by compression trusses on each side of the fuselage. A horizontal X-type truss in the upper part of the bomb bays also increased the structural strength of each bomb bay. The forward X-type truss extended between station 4.0 and just aft of station 4.3, while the rear truss extended aft of stations 5.0 and 6.0. The lower part of the wing between stations 4.3 and 5.2 formed the upper part of the bomb bay. Some of the hydraulic equipment was installed in the upper part of the bomb bay section, and some of the oxygen bottles were located in the rear and extreme upper part of the bomb bay.

The bomb bay doors made up the entire lower surface of the bomb bay section, and were the same hydraulically operated roll-up doors used on Consolidated's B-24. The two doors for the forward bay extended from 4.0 to 5.0, and those of the rear bomb bay extended from 5.0 to 6.0. The doors were fitted with rollers at the fore and aft ends, and rolled in channel tracks located along the inner contour of bulkheads 4.0, 5.0, and 6.0. In opening, the flexible corrugated doors rolled in the tracks following the contour of the fuselage. A sprocket gear installed on a hydraulic motor shaft meshed with the corrugations in the bomb bay door to move each door. The bomb bay doors could be operated separately, and could be used as an emergency exit.

The removable bomb hoist assemblies could be attached to bulkheads 4.0 and 6.0, or the lower part of the bomb hoist rests on the catwalk. The

1. Brake Reservoir	4. Main Hydraulic Reservoir
2. Horizontal X Truss	5. Fuel Selector Valve
3. Main Selector Valve	6. Hydraulic Accumulator

Figure 64 – Overhead View of Forward Bomb Bay

(E&R Manual)

loop antenna was installed just aft of station 4.0 on the underside of the catwalk. The life raft doors were located on a shelf located in the top part of the fuselage between stations 5.4 and 6.0.

Rear Cabin

The rear cabin was a combination turret section and cabin section, and also contained facilities for relief crew members. It extended between stations 6.0 and 8.0, and had a length of 19.27 feet with a maximum head clearance of 7.58 feet. One entrance could be made from the bomb bay through a

LEGEND
1. Bomb Door Channel Track
2. Catwalk
3. Forward Accessory Compartment
4. Bulkhead 5.0
5. Bulkhead 4.0
6. Horizontal X Truss
7. Heating and Ventilating Duct
8. Cable Drum
9. Aileron Servo
10. Bomb Racks
11. Shackle

LEGEND
1. Horizontal Truss
2. Anti-Icing Fluid Reservoir
3. Heating and Ventilating Duct
4. Aileron Servo
5. Rear Spar
6. Oxygen Bottle
7. Main Shuttle Valve
8. Emergency Shuttle Valve

Figure 65 – Forward View of Bomb Bay

(E&R Manual)

Figure 67 – Overhead View of Rear Bomb Bay

(E&R Manual)

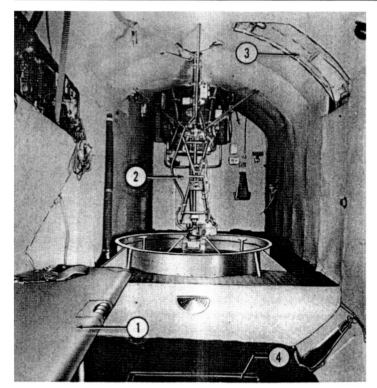

1. Horizontal X Truss
2. Anti-Icing Fluid Reservoir
3. Cable Drum
4. Rear Spar

Figure 66 — Fwd. View of Aft Cabin
(E&R Manual)

door that swung aft of bulkhead 6.0. Another entrance was provided through a drop-type door located between 7.1 and 7.3, and attached to beltframe 7.1. The door formed part of the fuselage contour, and could be jettisoned in case of emergency. A camera could be placed over this entrance for photography by removing the detachable circle portion of the door. A panel attached to the rear cabin floor folded over the upper part of this entrance and became part of the floor. An inward opening emergency exit with a window was located between stations 6.6 and 7.0 in the upper right side of the fuselage. Aft of station 7.0, the floor stepped down to a lower floor level. The upper turret was located between stations 6.1 and 6.3, while the lower turret was between stations 6.4 and 7.0. The static pressure discharge

LEGEND
1. Aft Cabin Entrance Door
2. Scanning Windows
3. Fire Extinguisher
4. Canteen Stowed
5. Door to Tail Compartment
6. Bulkhead 8.0
7. Portable Oxygen Bottle
8. Settee

Figure 68 — Aft View of Aft Cabin
(E&R Manual)

discs were installed on each side of the fuselage between stations 6.1 and 6.2. A bunk was located on the right hand wall. In early models this area contained the galley, which was a holdover from Consolidated's PB4Y Catalina design, and was only used on overnight flights.

Rear Accessory Cabin
The rear accessory cabin extended from station 6.0 to 7.0 below the flooring of the rear cabin. The retractable lower turret passed vertically through this cabin. Some oxygen bottles were stowed in this cabin.

Tail Cabin
The tail gunner was provided with a relatively large area, with very good visibility. The tail cabin extended from stations 8.0 to 10.4, with a length of 12.28 feet, and an average head clearance of about 3.75 feet. It was accessible from the rear cabin through a door in bulkhead 8.0, while a catwalk aft of station 9.0 provided an entrance to the tail turret. The tail skid was located on the underside of the fuselage between stations 9.0 and 10.0. The early XB-32 greenhouse tail gun was replaced by the Sperry tail

Greenhouse tail compartment of the XB-32. Note the numerous screws in the window frame. (Chana)

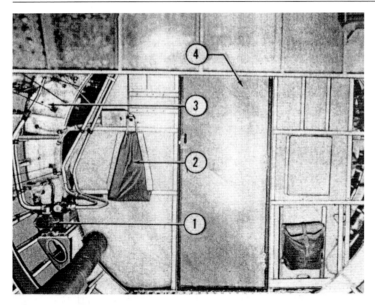

1. De-Icer Unit
2. Parachute Stowage Rack
3. Bulkhead 8.0
4. Door to Aft Cabin

Figure 70 — Forward View of Tail Compartment

(E&R Manual)

1. Catwalk
2. Ammunition Boxes
3. Tail Turret
4. Bulkhead 9.0

Figure 69 — Aft View of Tail Compartment

(E&R Manual)

turret; it was located on the extreme aft end of the tail cabin, and had an ammunition box located on each side of the catwalk. The tail compartment contained stowage for the tail gunner's parachute, on-ground engine, turret, and gun covers, along with pilot compartment and bombardier station window covers, jack pads, and various tool kits (propeller tool kit, two radio operator's kits, armorer's kit and tool roll, and the crew chief's kit).

Windows, Entrances, and Exits
Windows
Visibility from the pilot's and co-pilot's positions was described during testing as: "Poor over target; Fair during level flight and climb; Satisfactory while taking off and Excellent while taxiing and landing." Testing officers improved the overall visibility by increasing the vertical adjustments of the seats.

The pilot's and co-pilot's windshield was of a double pane plate glass designed so that heated air could flow between the panes for defrosting

A good photo of B-32 windows, doors, and covers on *The Lady is Fresh*. Seen are the pilot's side window, bombardier's glass, nose wheel entrance door, and two forward scanning windows. Dorsal and nose turret covers are in place. (USAAF via LeVine)

and de-icing. All of the forward cabin heated air supply could be passed through the double pane windshield by closing off all other forward cabin outlets, thereby forcing the complete airflow to the windshield ducts for ice removal. The pilot's and co-pilot's windscreens had a wiper controlled by a switch on the pilot's auxiliary panel. The remainder of the windshield was Plexiglas. An oval clear view panel was installed on the outboard sides of the pilot's and co-pilot's windows, and flipped down on hinges to open to give a clear view on landing and takeoff. The first 54 B-32s had an outboard window that slid aft, and could be jettisoned and used as an emergency exit. The final 74 had a window with an oval opening that could also be jettisoned. The B-32 windows allowed draughts in and leaked in the rain, especially the greenhouse windows of the early models.

Visibility from the bombardier's compartment was a continual problem, or perceived problem, throughout the B-32's career. The bombsight glass of the bombardier's enclosure was constructed of laminated plate glass, and was equipped with a windshield wiper controlled by a switch located on the bombardier's panel. The remainder of the bombardier's window was laminated Plexiglas. Heated air blast tubes were provided for the bombardier's panel, and also the navigator's astro panel.

The navigator's window was considered too small, and access to it was impaired by the location of the radar equipment and the width of the navigator's table. The astro/hatch arrangement for celestial navigation was considered unsatisfactory, because the navigator was unable to observe stars below 25 degrees altitude. Generally, access to all windows on the flight deck was obstructed by various radio and radar equipment.

There were three scanning windows in the flight deck fuselage and five in the rear cabin. Before the scanning windows were added to the sides of the rear cabin the rear turret was the only position from which the rear of the engine nacelles and undersides of the main wing could be monitored.

There was a defrosting system for the transparent areas: turrets, astro glass, and bombardier's station. The turrets were supplied with enough heat to warm them to the approximate temperature of the adjacent cabin. The pilot's and co-pilot's windshield was defrosted and de-iced by this system.

Curtains and Covers

Blackout curtains for all windows and a night flying curtain for the pilot's and co-pilot's stations were supplied for each aircraft. Blackout curtains for the three forward scanning windows were stowed, with the pilot's and co-pilot's night-flying curtain in the forward cabin on the left hand side of the nose wheel housing. Curtains for the five rear scanning windows were stowed in the rear cabin at the right of the rear door. The blackout curtain for the navigator's astro glass was strapped to the fuselage just to the left of the astro glass. Rollaway curtains and sun visors were installed at the pilot's and co-pilot's stations to eliminate glare. An anti-glare coaming was installed over the instrument panel to prevent glare on the instruments. Engine cover, turret and gun covers, and covers for the pilot's enclosure and the bombardier's station were stowed in the tail compartment.

Entrances and Exits

Entering a B-32 has been described as similar to "getting into a tall B-24." Entrance to the cabin was through a hinged drop-type door, opening downward, located between stations 1.2 and 2.0 on the left side of the fuselage, and when down served as a stair. It could be opened from the outside by depressing the flush-type door latch The door could be jettisoned by removing the two door supporting cables, and then pulling upward on the emergency lever, which pulled the pins out of the two hinges. When the door was closed it was flush with, and formed part of the fuselage. The nose cabin could also be entered from the flight deck by an opening under

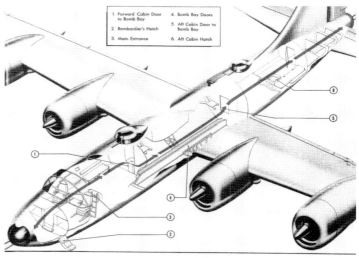

Figure 19 – Provisions for Movement of Personnel
(E&R Manual)

the center of the instrument panel, between the pilot's and co-pilot's control pedestals.

The forward crew (pilot, co-pilot, engineer, bombardier, radio operator, nose gunner, and later the radar operator) had several choices of entrance. Entrance to the flight deck could be through the nose wheel well by ascending a five rung ladder attached to bulkhead 3.0. This ladder was stowed on the flight deck behind the navigator's table, while a folding door covered the hatch. On B-32s Nos. 42-108481 onward a hatch in the flight deck floor opened to the forward accessory section.

The bombardier and nose gunner could enter the compartment via a drop-type hatch door that, when opened, formed a small stair. The flight deck could also be entered from the bomb bay by a removable stair step that was attached to bulkhead 4.0 and rested on the catwalk. The door between the forward cabin and the bomb bay was a drop-type that, when opened, formed a small stair from the flight deck to the catwalk.

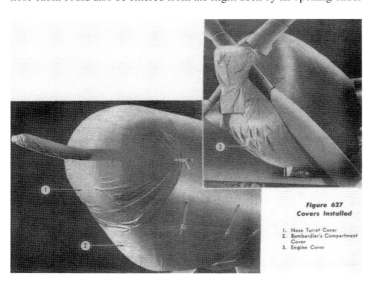

Figure 627
Covers Installed

1. Nose Turret Cover
2. Bombardier's Compartment Cover
3. Engine Cover

(E&R Manual)

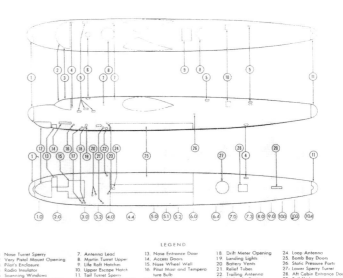

LEGEND

1 Nose Turret Sperry	7. Antenna Lead	13. Nose Entrance Door	18. Drift Meter Opening	24. Loop Antenna
2 Very Pistol Mount Opening	8. Martin Turret Upper	14. Access Doors	19. Landing Lights	25. Bomb Bay Doors
3. Pilot's Enclosure	9. Life Raft Hatches	15. Nose Wheel Well	20. Battery Vents	26. Static Pressure Ports
4. Radio Insulator	10. Upper Escape Hatch	16. Pitot Mast and Temperature Bulb	21. Relief Tubes	27. Lower Sperry Turret
5 Scanning Windows	11. Tail Turret Sperry	17. Flare Chute	22. Trailing Antenna	28. Aft Cabin Entrance Door
6. Astro Glass & Escape Hatch	12. Bombardier's Enclosure		23. Hydraulic Drain	29. Tail Skid

Figure 7 – Fuselage Access Doors and Inspection Plates
(E&R Manual)

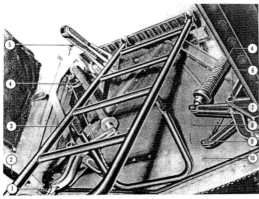

LEGEND
1. Actuating Push Rod
2. Hinge Assembly
3. Ladder to Flight Deck
4. Actuating Mechanism Spring
5. Closing Roller Lever
6. Actuating Mechanism Tube
7. Actuating Lever
8. Forward Accessory Compartment
9. Closing Mechanism Lever
10. Bulkhead 3.0

Figure 71 – Nose Wheel Door Mechanism

(E&R Manual)

Entrance to the nose turret was through a pair of sliding panels that formed a wind bulkhead located at station 1.0, then through the door of the turret that, when closed, acted as a backrest for the gunner.

The rear crew (three gunners: rear top, ball, and tail turret) entered the aircraft through a hatch located just center/aft of the retractable ball turret, the door swinging downward to form an entrance ladder. When entering through the forward bomb bay a catwalk was traversed to a drop-type door which, when opened, formed a small stair to the intermediate flight deck. From the intermediate flight deck another ladder led to the main forward crew stations. The nose gunner and bombardier climbed down through the pilot's station if they had not entered through their external hatch. On the XB-32 pressurized prototypes and some early production models a trolley was installed across the bomb bays, allowing a crew member to move to the rear cabin through a door located on the rear wall of the rear bomb bay.

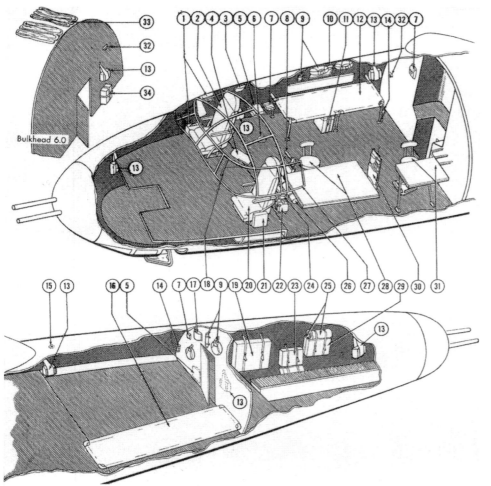

1. Very Pistol and Mount
2. Copilot's Seat
3. Copilot's Data Case
4. Sun Visor
5. Disposal Bags
6. Drift Signal Chute
7. First Aid Kit
8. Fire Axe
9. Water Canteens & Cups
10. Air Message Bags
11. Drift Signal Flare Stowage
12. Forward Settee
13. Parachute
14. Relief Tube
15. Alarm Bell
16. Aft Settee
17. Stowage Black-out Curtains --Aft Windows
18. Pilot's Windshield Wiper
19. Propeller Tool Kit
20. Pilot's Seat
21. Flight Report and Map Cases
22. Navigator's Signal Light
23. Radio Operator's Kits
24. Stowage Black-out Curtains, Aft Windows, and Pilot's and Co-pilot's Night-Flying Curtain
25. Armorer's Tool Roll and Kit
26. Navigator's Map Case
27. Sliding Clear-View Panel
28. Navigator's Chair & Table
29. Crew Chief's Tool Kit
30. Navigators Insert Case
31. Radio Operator's Chair and Table
32. Life Raft Release Handle
33. Life Rafts
34. Life Raft Radio

Figure 628 — Fuselage Equipment Locations

(E&R Manual)

Emergency Exits

Each crewman stowed his parachute near his workstation, and the principal emergency exit for all crew was through the bomb bay (if the bombs had been salvoed). On the B-32 the bomb bays could be opened, and nose landing gear could be extended simultaneously. The nose wheel well was the secondary exit for the flight deck, but only if the nose gear could be lowered and locked and, if not, the flight deck crew was to exit through either the bombardier's compartment or the camera hatch. Exit through the bombardier's hatch during flight after the nose wheel was extended created the possibility of a collision with the nose wheel door. Two static lines, one on the right side of the flight deck floor, and the other at the camera hatch, were supplied for assisted bailing out for wounded or unconscious crew. The rear crew was to exit through the primary exit rear bomb bay, and then the secondary center/aft hatch in the floor. The ball turret gunner could exit through his turret floor. The rear crewmen were alerted to bail out by an alarm bell located just forward of the stabilizer in the rear cabin.

Fuselage Equipment and Personal Accommodations

Seats

The pilot's and co-pilot's bucket seats had vertical, horizontal, fore and aft, and reclining adjustments, and had a full-width back, removable head rest, and armrests. From aircraft number 42-108475 onward magnesium seats were installed. The bombardier's compartment was furnished with a kneeing pad, but when not on the bomb run his seat was on the settee in the forward cabin. The navigator's and radio operator's chairs were swivel "posture-type" ("secretary") seats with no armrests, and a small pad for a backrest that had seat belts. Hand manipulated spring catches locked these chairs in four different positions. The navigator's chair was on slides, and movable parallel with the aircraft centerline, while the radio operator's seat was fixed to the floor.

The type S-2 seat parachute packs often replaced the cushions on these seats. All seats were equipped with Type B-14 lap seat belts and Type B-15 shoulder harnesses. When adjusting the seat belt care had to be taken to put the belt over, not through the parachute harness. An adjusting lever to the left of the seat locked the shoulder harness. The seat belt and the ends of the shoulder harness locked together at a quick release attachment in the center of the lap.

Settees

There were two settees on the B-32. The settee in the forward cabin had a backrest and seated two. The settee in the rear cabin was a bunk type that could be raised and fastened in the up position and seated four, or could be used as a bunk. The forward settee had two Type B-14 lap seat belts, and the rear had four.

Tables

The navigator's and radio operator's positions were equipped with half-inch plywood table tops, with the navigator's table equipped with a drafting machine. The combat test project navigator reported: "The B-32 is an airplane built around a navigator's table. It is the best arrangement that could be imagined. In my estimation all airplane designers should give the navigator's position in the B-32 special attention and learn a few things."

Data Cases

The navigator's map case was located on the forward edge of the navigator's table, and his insert case hung above the table to his left. The flight report and map cases were installed together near the floor to the pilot's left. The data case for the co-pilot was located at about head level to the right and behind the co-pilot's seat.

Toilet Facilities

There were two relief tubes, one in the forward cabin and one in the aft, both located on the port side and at the rear end of each cabin. Each cabin stowed disposable bags for bowel movements. In the forward cabin the bags were stowed on the cable guard forward of the settee, while in the rear cabin they were stowed on the right rear face of station 8.0.

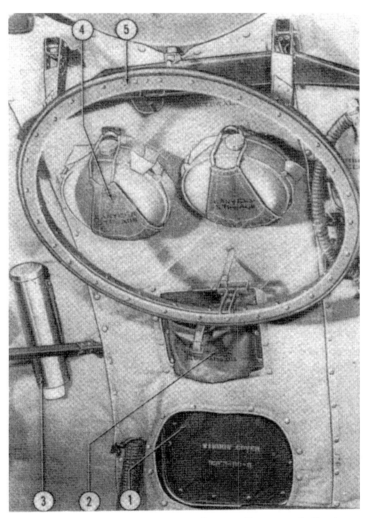

Figure 623 – Equipment Above Forward Settee

1. Black-Out Curtain Installed	4. Canteen	
2. Air Message Bags	5. Astro Glass, Open	
3. Cup Container		

(E&R Manual)

Drinking Water

The forward cabin had two one-gallon Stanley all metal heat-insulated thermos jugs and a paper cup dispenser on the left hand sidewall, and the rear cabin also had two similar jugs on bulkhead 8.0. The jugs had a spigot at the bottom and screw top with a metal cup/cap combination.

Soundproofing

The forward and rear cabins, bombardier's cabin, and the top forward gun turret were soundproofed. The soundproofing panels were made from Fiberglas, with the side facing the interior covered in wool that was an olive green color, described as a "soft, light-giving shade." The panels were fastened by "Mae West" spring snaps that snapped into holes drilled into the supporting structure.

Carpet

Carpet was provided on the flight deck and rear cabin. During initial tests the carpet was inadequately attached; several cutouts around some equipment proved to be too small, and interfered with some crew functions. The contractor easily remedied the defect by attaching the ends of the carpet more firmly and enlarging the cutouts.

Figure 561—Dinghy Transmitter and Case

An emergency radio Dinghy Transmitter SCR-578 was installed in the rear cabin. Nicknamed the "Gibson Girl," it was a self-contained radio set that was water resistant, and could float for a while without damage. It automatically sent out a SOS signal followed by long dashes, and could also be used as a transmitter. (E&R Manual)

Emergency Equipment

Alarm Bell

A switch on the pilot's instrument panel controlled an alarm bell located on the top of the face of bulkhead 7.1.

Parachutes

There were eight parachutes stowed on the bomber: one in the nose section; one behind both the pilot and co-pilot; one on the floor at the aft end of the navigator's table; one on the right hand side of the forward cabin near bulkhead 4.0; one on the floor of the rear cabin; one on the rear right hand face of bulkhead 6.0; and one on the rear left hand face of bulkhead 8.0.

Life Rafts

Two type A-3 life rafts with emergency accessories were installed in the top fuselage, forward of the rear turret in two large stowage compartments. Release handles were located on the right hand side of the aircraft in both the forward (at bulkhead 4.0) and rear (at bulkhead 6.0) cabins. When the handle was pulled out about three inches, ball fittings on the end of the release cable forced the locks of the life raft doors open, and at the end of their travel fell free from the lock mechanisms. When the cable had been pulled out another three inches ball fittings on the CO_2 cylinders were pulled free, and inflation of the life rafts began. The inflation forced the rafts into the water. They were installed to land right side up, and were fastened to the aircraft by a safety rope that would sever when the aircraft sank.

Life rafts could be released manually from the top of the fuselage. Small access doors with flush spring catches were located over each door handle. The handles had to be completely turned in order to release the ball fittings. A Plexiglas window was installed in each life raft door over the CO_2 cylinder for visual inspection of the linkage of the cylinder to the release cable, and installation of the ball fitting in the cylinder neck.

Life Raft Radio "Gibson Girl" Dinghy Transmitter SCR-578-A & B

An emergency radio transmitter, the "Gibson Girl" Dinghy Transmitter SCR-578-A & -B was installed in the rear cabin on the right hand side of bulkhead 6.0. The hourglass shaped SCR-578-A & B (later the AN-CRT-3) was known as the "Gibson Girl" after the 1890s glamour girl with an hourglass figure created by the artist Charles Gibson. The self-contained radio set was water resistant, and could float for a while without damage. It automatically sent out a SOS signal followed by long dashes, and could also be used as a transmitter. It was stowed with the right side life raft, and was accessible from the inside and outside of the aircraft; it was the responsibility of the radio operator after ditching. The 36 pound radio was contained either in one canvas case or two cases strapped together (the radio bag and accessory antenna bag). The carrying bag also contained a parachute in a compartment on top that would deploy when the ring was pulled as the bag was thrown out of the aircraft. The kit came with an instruction booklet for its operation and antenna deployment. Current for operating the radio was supplied by turning a hand crank that was dearly guarded, as there was only one. The antenna was raised either by a kite or hydrogen-filled balloon. The design was so successful that the Gibson Girl remained in service into the 1970s.

First Aid Kit
There were three first aid kits on each aircraft. Two were located in the forward cabin: one at the right hand cable guard, just forward of the forward settee; and the other on the same side, near the ceiling and aft of the forward settee. The third kit was located near the ceiling on the right hand side of the cabin.

Air Message Bags
Five air drop message bags were stowed in the forward cabin above the settee.

Pyrotechnic and Signal Equipment

Very Pistol
A type AN-M8 pyrotechnic pistol in a type A-2 holder was stowed on cable guard at the co-pilot's station, and a type A-8 signal flare container was stowed at the co-pilot's left. The pistol was operated by opening the breech and pulling out the unlocking lever. After inserting the signal flare the breech was relocked, and the loaded pistol was inserted into a mount installed at about the co-pilot's head level, and locked in a vertical position and fired to the outside. The pistol was not to be fired without the mounting, as its recoil was 216 pounds.

Drift Signal Equipment
The drift signal chute was located in the floor forward of the forward settee. The chute was covered by a spring-loaded cover, extended through the floor, and opened through the bottom of the fuselage. The day and night signal flares were stowed under the forward settee.

Navigator's Signal Light Type C-3A Aldis Lamp
To be discussed later in Interior Lighting

Fire Axe
The fire axe was stowed in the forward cabin to the rear of the nose wheel housing.

Tool Kits
The propeller tool kit, two radio operator's kits, armorer's kit and tool roll, and crew chief's kit were stowed in the tail section.

2

Wing and Tail

Wing General Description

The Donald Davis designed 135 foot span/1,422 square foot wing was shoulder-mounted, fully cantilevered, and internally braced. The stressed skin wing was manufactured of aluminum alloy and Alclad sheet, and was comprised of a front and rear main spar, bulkheads, stringers, ribs, and skin. Inspection doors and plates were located in the wing skin to give access to fuel and oil cells and other installations. The wing was made up of five basic structures: a permanently attached center section; two removable outer panels; and two wing tips. The leading and trailing edge sections, wing flaps, and ailerons were attached to these five basic parts.

Components
Wing Center Section

The center section was permanently attached to the fuselage by bolts and rivets, and supported the four engines and nacelles. The forward section of the front spar carried numerous systems lines extending from the fuselage to the nacelles. The interspar structure contained the fuel and oil cells, and the main landing gear. The rear spar carried wing flap and aileron control cables in its aft section.

The Wright R-3350 engine mounting was unusual, in that it was suspended from the rocker boxes. The loads were transmitted through the rocker shaft and rocker box, and then through the cylinder head. The nacelle lower rear cowling was riveted to fairing angles along the lower wing surface. The nacelle tail piece was separate from the rear cowling, and was attached with rivets to the lower surface of the wing flap. A sheet steel firewall extended across the entire nacelle cross section at the wing front spar.

The center wing section contained the four self-sealing fuel tanks. Each tank consisted of three self-sealing cells, connected consecutively rather than alternately, as on the B-24. The bomber carried 5,460 gallons, but about 90 gallons could not be used, as the four degree nose-up attitude of the bomber prevented it from being pumped to the engines. The wing interspar structure was designed to be fuel-tight.

Note: The engines, nacelles, and fuel system will be discussed in depth in later sections.

Wing Outer Panels

The outer wing panel was similar to the B-24, with only a minor difference in the shape of the wing tip and outboard end of the aileron. It was spliced

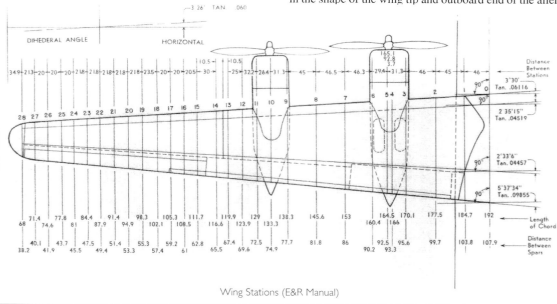

Wing Stations (E&R Manual)

to the center wing section with bolts, and was removable. Its leading edge section and outboard stub were attached with countersunk screws and were removable. The aileron was attached to the outer panel rear spar with five hinge brackets. The aileron trailing edge was attached to the rear spar angle with rivets, and was not easily removable.

Wing Tips
The wing tip was spliced to the outer panel at wing bulkhead 28 with bolts at the forward and rear attaching angles, and with countersunk screws along the upper and lower splice plates. The wing tip housed a running light at its extreme tip. Wing anti-ice hot air was exhausted through 21 holes in the wing tip lower surface.

Wing Leading Edge
The six main sections of the wing leading edge attached to the front spar of the center section. An overflap trailing edge section faired over each wing flap. Each section attached to the rear spar flange, and was supported by detachable struts anchored to the spar lower flange. The underflap trailing edge sections were riveted to the rear lower flange, and could not be easily removed.

Anti-icing of the leading edge of the wing was achieved by ducting hot air through the leading edge cavity and exhausting it through the front spar and wing tip. The air was heated in the nacelle heat exchangers by exhaust gases of the outboard engines. The de-icer/anti-icer system will be discussed in a separate section.

Fuel Tanks
Fuel was carried in four tanks, each of which was composed of three interconnected self-sealing cells. All of the tanks were installed in the wing center section interspar area, and had a total fuel capacity of approximately 5460 gallons. There were two main tanks per wing, each consisting of three cells: inboard, center, and outboard. The outboard main tank had a capacity of 1,005 gallons, divided into 316 gallons in the outboard cell, 380 gallons in the center cell, and 309 gallons in the inboard cell. The inboard main tank had a capacity of 1,725 gallons divided into 507 gallons in the outboard cell, 550 gallons in the center cell, and 668 gallons in the inboard cell. The cells were connected by a cell interconnector that passed

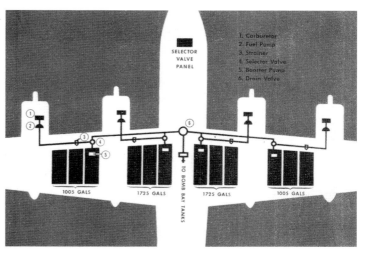

through both cell walls. The tanks were filled through a cast filler neck in the outboard cell. There was a vent on the top of each cell, and a cell access door on the bottom of each cell. Metal stiffeners formed a framework inside the cell to maintain its shape.

An electrically operated and controlled fuel booster pump (submerged type) was installed in the inboard cell of each tank. It provided fuel under pressure to the engine-driven fuel pump for takeoff, landing, and high altitude operation. From the booster, fuel was pumped through a strainer to the engine-driven fuel pump. This pump was installed on the engine, and maintained the proper fuel pressure in the fuel line to the carburetor. Under ordinary operating conditions each engine was fed from its respective tank. However, more than one engine could be fed from one tank through a cross-feed system, consisting of five solenoid operated selector valves and connecting cross-feed lines. The fuel was pumped out of the inboard cell to the engine with a strainer located in the fuel line.

Oil tanks
The self-sealing oil cells were installed in the wing center section within the front and rear spars between bulkhead numbers 6, 7, 9, and 10. The

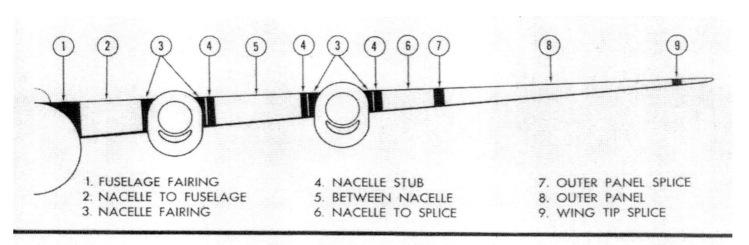

1. FUSELAGE FAIRING
2. NACELLE TO FUSELAGE
3. NACELLE FAIRING
4. NACELLE STUB
5. BETWEEN NACELLE
6. NACELLE TO SPLICE
7. OUTER PANEL SPLICE
8. OUTER PANEL
9. WING TIP SPLICE

Figure 17 — Wing Leading Edge Sections
(E&R Manual)

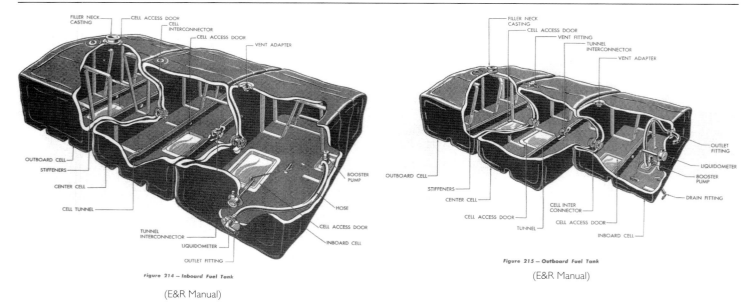

Figure 214 – Inboard Fuel Tank

(E&R Manual)

Figure 215 – Outboard Fuel Tank

(E&R Manual)

rectangular inboard cell had a capacity of 78 gallons, and the square outboard cell had a capacity of 73 gallons. The filler cap was surrounded by a scupper on top of the cell adjacent to a bayonet filling gauge. There was an access door located on the bottom of the outboard cell, and on the side of the inboard cell, while a vent was located on the top of each cell.

An oil hopper or accelerating well was installed in the cell between the inlet and outlet. It was 7.5 inches in diameter, and was constructed of synthetic rubber. As oil returned to the cell from the oil temperature regulator it was circulated through the hopper, and was thus prevented from mixing with the cold oil of the cell. As oil was consumed it was replaced from the cell, through holes in the bottom of the hopper. Any swirling action in the hopper was reduced by vertical fins located at its base.

Wing Flight Controls

Wing Flaps

Two Fowler-type wing flaps were installed in the wing center section trailing edge on each side of the fuselage. Together they spanned the entire center section from fuselage to aileron. The flaps were riveted assemblies of aluminum spars, ribs, and Alclad skin. Each flap traveled on steel tracks by means of three roller assemblies attached to the leading edge. The tracks were attached to, and supported by the wing rear spar. The flaps were operated by hydraulic motors and electrically controlled cables that passed through pulleys and anchored to the flaps. The two outboard and two inboard flaps were mechanically joined to form two sets of flaps, and the engine nacelles extended with the flaps. The maximum flap deflection was 40 degrees, and when extended increased the total wing area to 1,545 square feet.

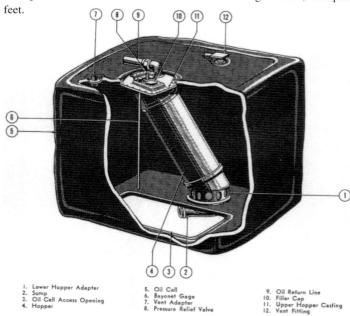

1. Upper Hopper Casting	5. Hose Connection	9. Vent Fitting	12. Pressure Relief Valve
2. Lower Sump Adapter	6. Sump Casting	10. Bayonet Gage	13. Oil Return Line
3. Oil Outlet Line	7. Hopper	11. Scupper	14. Vent Adapter
4. Outlet Fitting	8. Cell Access Door		

Figure 211 – Inboard Oil Cell

(E&R Manual)

1. Lower Hopper Adapter	5. Oil Cell	9. Oil Return Line
2. Sump	6. Bayonet Gage	10. Filler Cap
3. Oil Cell Access Opening	7. Vent Adapter	11. Upper Hopper Casting
4. Hopper	8. Pressure Relief Valve	12. Vent Fitting

Figure 212 – Outboard Oil Cell

(E&R Manual)

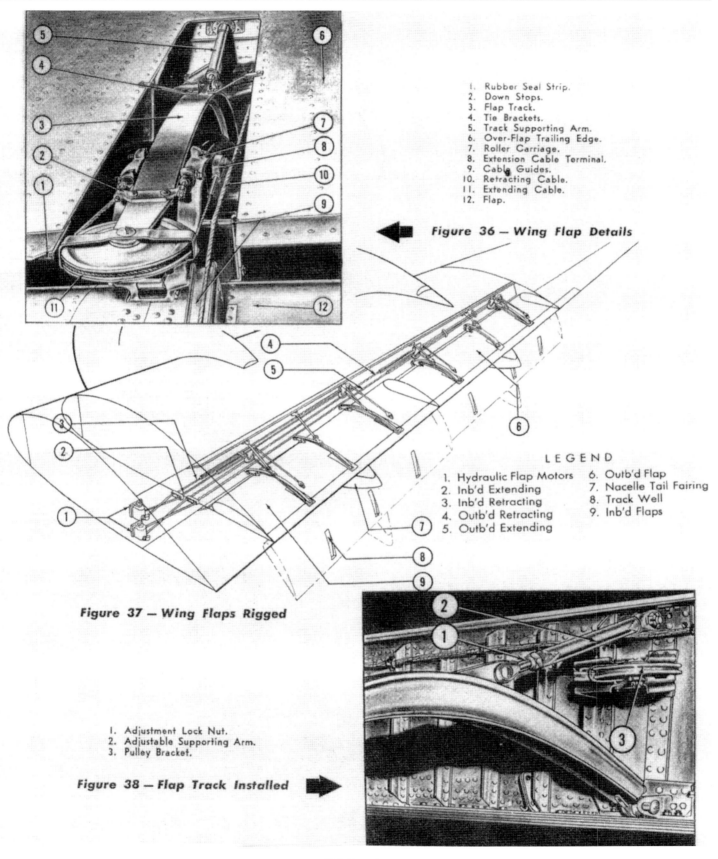

1. Rubber Seal Strip.
2. Down Stops.
3. Flap Track.
4. Tie Brackets.
5. Track Supporting Arm.
6. Over-Flap Trailing Edge.
7. Roller Carriage.
8. Extension Cable Terminal.
9. Cable Guides.
10. Retracting Cable.
11. Extending Cable.
12. Flap.

Figure 36 — Wing Flap Details

LEGEND

1. Hydraulic Flap Motors
2. Inb'd Extending
3. Inb'd Retracting
4. Outb'd Retracting
5. Outb'd Extending
6. Outb'd Flap
7. Nacelle Tail Fairing
8. Track Well
9. Inb'd Flaps

Figure 37 — Wing Flaps Rigged

1. Adjustment Lock Nut.
2. Adjustable Supporting Arm.
3. Pulley Bracket.

Figure 38 — Flap Track Installed

A toggle switch located near the center of the main instrument panel electrically controlled the flap unit of the hydraulic main selector valve. An indicator adjacent to the switch showed the flap positions, the left pointer indicating inboard flaps, and the right pointer indicating outboard flaps. Fluid from the main selector valve actuated two hydraulic motors that operated the flaps, one motor for the inboard engine, and the other for the outboard engine. In operation the hydraulic fluid flowed through flap lock valves before reaching the motors, unlocking the flaps for retraction or extension. The lock valves were needed to prevent creeping when the flaps were extended. A proportional flow divider acted in both up and down operations to synchronize travel between inboard and outboard flaps. Limit switches at the center of the track of the right outboard and left inboard flaps stopped the movement when both flaps were fully extended or retracted. Relief valves were integrated in the flaps up hydraulic system to prevent damage to the flap structure in the event that the hydraulic selector valve failed to return to neutral at the end of flap retraction. A warning horn sounded when there was insufficient flap extension at takeoff. The horn sounded if the engine throttles were advanced more than two-thirds of their full travel, and the flap extension was less than 18 degrees. Flaps were not to be lowered at airspeeds lower than 190mph IAS.

Aileron

The monospar ailerons were constructed of an aluminum alloy framework that was fabric covered, with the leading edge reinforced with Alclad sheet. The aileron attached to five hinge brackets on the outer panel rear spar, pivoted on prelubricated bearings, and had a maximum up or down deflection of 20 degrees. Static and dynamic balance was achieved by weights attached to the nose section. The aileron was actuated by a combination of push-pull tubes, bell cranks, and control cables. The aileron control cables were anchored to a quadrant mounted on the forward face of the rear wing spar at station 18. The aileron inboard push-pull rod operated directly from this quadrant. The outboard push-pull rod at station 24 was actuated through a small bell crank and main push-pull tube, located along the rear spar, and was attached to the control quadrant.

Aileron Tab

The aileron tab functioned to give servo-boost and/or trim to the aileron. The trim balance (servo) was mechanically produced by the control linkage, with the purpose of removing the load from the controls. It was constructed of aluminum alloy with an Alclad skin, and was hinged to the aileron at three points with prelubricated bearings. The aileron tab was actuated by an electric motor housed in the aileron, and a screw mechanism that operated a push-pull rod attached to the tab horn. The tab control switch and position indicator dial were located on the pilot's instrument panel.

Tail

General Description

During its development the B-32 had five different tail configurations. XB-32 #1 and #2 had a twin tail with a single rudder, and had a dihedral cant from the fuselage. The XB-32 #3 and the first two B-32-C-CFs (42-108471 and 472) were fitted with the 16.6 foot modified B-29 tails, with a single rudder and de-icer boots on the leading edge of the vertical and horizontal stabilizers. The remaining eight B-32-1-CFs were fitted with the extended

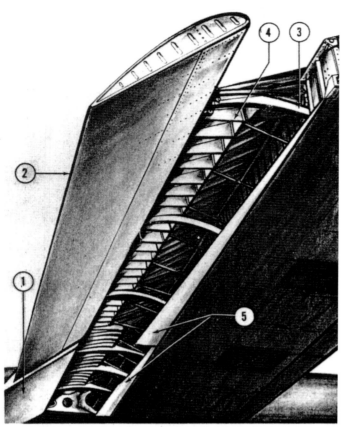

1. Inboard Flap.
2. Outboard Flap.
3. Flap Track.
4. Over-Flap Trailing Edge.
5. Under-Flap Trailing Edge.

Figure 35 — Wing Flaps Installed

(E&R Manual)

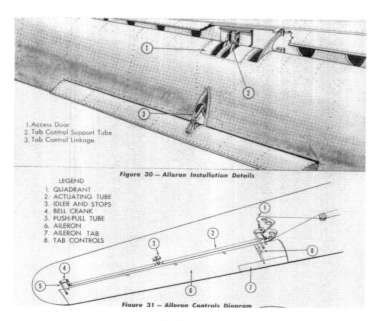

1. Access Door
2. Tab Control Support Tube
3. Tab Control Linkage

Figure 30 — Aileron Installation Details

LEGEND
1. QUADRANT
2. ACTUATING TUBE
3. IDLER AND STOPS
4. BELL CRANK
5. PUSH-PULL TUBE
6. AILERON
7. AILERON TAB
8. TAB CONTROLS

Figure 31 — Aileron Controls Diagram

(E&R Manual)

19.5 foot standard B-32 tail with a single rudder. The four B-32-5-CFs and the 36 TB-32-5s and -10s had the extended 19.5 foot standard B-32 tails with double rudders. The four TB-32-15-CFs, all the B-32-20-CFs, and all subsequent blocks had the standard tall tail with double rudders and de-icer boots on the leading edge of the vertical and horizontal stabilizers.

Components

The tail assembly consisted of a fully cantilevered stabilizer with dual elevators and tabs, and a single vertical dorsal fin with a rudder and tab attached. Each part was constructed of aluminum spars, ribs, and stringers covered with Alclad skin. The statically and dynamically balanced rudders and elevators were fabric-covered, with reinforced Alclad leading edges. The entire fin and stabilizer leading edge was de-iced by pulsating rubber de-icer boots. The main units of the tail were removable separately, or as an entire unit.

Stabilizer

The stabilizer was a single unit constructed of ribs, stringers, and skin riveted to two reinforced main spars. It was attached to the fuselage primarily by four fittings bolted to the stabilizer spars that attached to similar fittings on fuselage bulkheads 9.0 and 10.0. A horizontal and vertical shear plate that was riveted to the stabilizer leading edge at the airplane centerline was bolted to the fuselage bulkhead 8.0. Four elevator hinge brackets were bolted to the stabilizer rear spar.

Elevator

The aluminum alloy internal structure of the elevator consisted of a reinforced spar to which the nose and tail ribs were riveted. The elevator was covered with fabric, with its nose covered with Alclad skin. Each elevator nose section was slotted to accommodate the two stabilizer hinge brackets that inserted into female hinge fittings bolted to the aft side of the elevator spar. The two hinged elevators were joined together, and moved by an interconnecting torque tube that was supported by two hinge brackets that were bolted to the rear spar of the elevator. Each elevator had a combination trim and servo tab constructed of aluminum alloy ribs and skin, and was attached to the elevator auxiliary spar by a continuous hinge. The tab was moved by a push-pull rod operating from the tab cable drum and screw mechanism housed in the elevator.

Rudder

The aluminum alloy rudder consisted of a main vertical spar, to which nose and tail ribs were riveted. The nose and trailing edges were covered with Alclad skin, and the area in between was fabric covered. The rudder was inserted between the fin tip and the rear of the fin base. It pivoted vertically on two hinge brackets projecting from the fin aft spar that connected to the rudder torque tube. The rudder tab consisted of aluminum alloy ribs and skin, and provided trim for the aircraft and balance for the

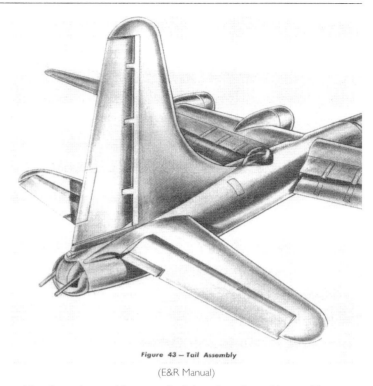

Figure 43 – Tail Assembly
(E&R Manual)

rudder. A continuous hinge attached the tab to the rudder auxiliary spar. Production models were fitted with one servo and one manual tab.

Fins

Main Fin

A single vertical and dorsal fin assembly was mounted on the aft end of the fuselage. The main fin was constructed of aluminum alloy, and consisted of two vertical spars, to which the horizontal ribs and stressed skin were riveted. The rear spar supported the rudder hinge brackets. An auxiliary front spar housed the four attaching angles for the dorsal fin attachment. The main fin attached to the stabilizer with four fittings anchored to the lower ends of the main spars. These fittings bolted to similar fittings on the stabilizer main spar. Pulsating rubber de-icing boots were fitted to the fin leading edge.

Dorsal Fin

The dorsal fin was faired to the main fin into the fuselage. It consisted of an aluminum alloy structure of vertical frames and ribs attached with stringers, and covered with riveted Alclad and magnesium alloy skin. A fairing angle around the bottom attached the dorsal fin to the fuselage with countersunk screws and nut plates. Four steel terminal fittings on the rear bulkhead were attached to fittings on the auxiliary front spar of the main fin. A gap cover faired the two fin assemblies.

3

Landing Gear

The landing gear of the B-32 consisted of two main gears and a nose gear, and was referred to as the "alighting gear" in the Erection & Maintenance Manual. A tail skid/bumper provided a cushion in the event of a tail down landing. Operation of all landing gear units was controlled from the pilot's and co-pilot's positions simultaneously by the means of a single toggle switch mounted on the center of the main instrument panel that electrically controlled a hydraulically sequenced actuating system. An electrical "tell-tale" lamp located near the switch indicated the position of the gear. Emergency operation of the landing gear was achieved by the use of the hydraulic switch-over and emergency selector valve.

Main Landing Gear General Description

The main landing gear was fully retractable, employing two cantilever shock struts located a short distance behind the center of gravity, and attached to two forged fittings mounted on the rear auxiliary spar of the main center section of each inboard engine nacelle. The dual wheels were mounted on the axle of an air-oil type shock strut that absorbed the initial shock of the landing. A hinge type drag strut connected the main shock strut and the forward auxiliary wing spar. When landing forces were exerted, either to the front or rear of the main landing gear, the tension and compression loads were transmitted to the forward auxiliary spar by the drag strut. The

landing gear "V" strut and the drag strut produced the smooth stable operation of the landing gear by correctly sequencing the travel and latching of the "V" and drag struts. Locking mechanisms locked the landing gear in place when it was extended or retracted. The dual wheels were equipped with dual duplex expander type brakes and heavy duty brake drums.

Operation of the Main Landing Gear
Normal Operation

The main gears were hydraulically operated, and when fully retracted were completely encased in the inboard engine nacelle. The landing gear control switch located in the center of the main instrument panel actuated a solenoid operated hydraulic selector valve that, in turn, actuated hydraulic jacks that extended or retracted the landing gear. The landing gear doors were mechanically connected to their respective landing mechanism to insure the correct sequence of operation. A green signal light adjacent to the gear control switch lit when all landing gear were down.

With the switch in the GEAR UP position, hydraulic fluid flowed from the main selector valve to the nose gear actuating cylinder through a restrictor that prevented too rapid a retraction of the gear. The actuating cylinder unlatched the down latch and retracted the nose gear. Fluid then flowed to the main gear down latch, unlocking jacks, disengaging the shock

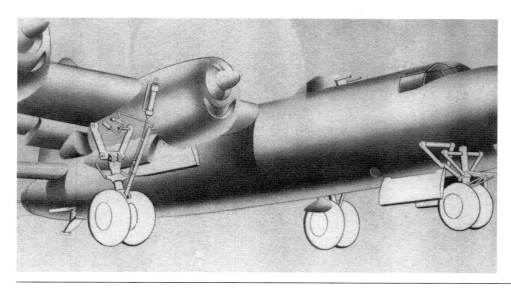

Landing Gear Arrangement (E&R Manual)

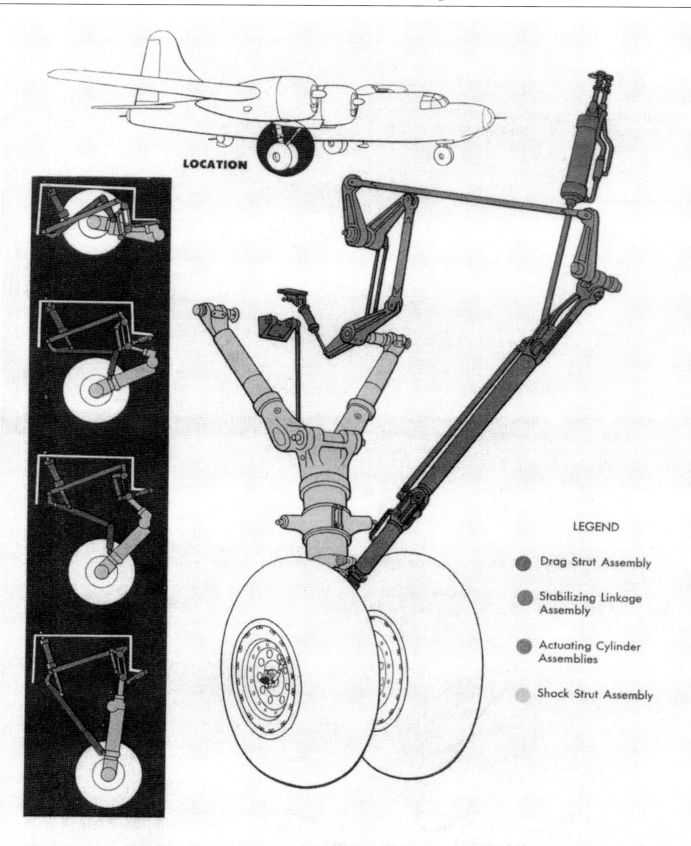

Figure 74 — Main Alighting Gear

LOCATION

LEGEND

Drag Strut Assembly

Stabilizing Linkage Assembly

Actuating Cylinder Assemblies

Shock Strut Assembly

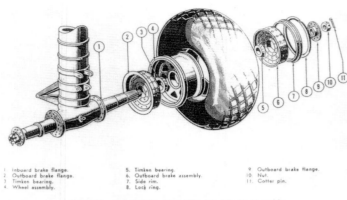

	Inboard brake flange.	5.	Timken bearing.	9.	Outboard brake flange.
	Outboard brake flange.	6.	Outboard brake assembly.	10.	Nut.
	Timken bearing.	7.	Side rim.	11.	Cotter pin.
	Wheel assembly.	8.	Lock ring.		

Figure 76 – Main Landing Gear Wheel and Brake Assembly

strut latch, and then to the main actuating cylinder. The initial travel of the main actuating cylinder disengaged the drag link latch, and the gear retracted. When the gear was up a spring-loaded hook latch engaged a roller on each gear to lock the gear up. Up-lock limit switches stopped the action when all gear were fully retracted and locked.

With the switch in GEAR DOWN position the action was repeated through the down lines, with the fluid first actuating the double unlatching jack and sequence valve to disengage the up-latch on the main and nose gear. The fluid then went to the actuating cylinders and the gear extended.

Emergency Main Landing Gear Operation

Electrical System Failure: The pressure control button was engaged, and then the landing gear selector valve button located above the catwalk, just behind the top rear turret between the first bomb racks, was pushed in and held until the landing gear was down and locked. The pressure control button was then released.

Hydraulic System Failure: The switchover valve control handle, located on the right side of bulkhead 4.0 (forward wall of the flight deck), was held in the EMERGENCY ON position. The emergency landing gear selector valve control, located inboard and under the switchover valve control, was moved to the ON position, and left in this position until the gear was down and locked.

Electrical and Hydraulic Failure: The switchover valve control was held to the EMERGENCY ON position, and the emergency gear selector valve control was moved to the ON position. The hand pump located slightly forward of the emergency selector valve control was operated until the landing gear was down and in the locked position.

Main Landing Gear Tires, Tubes, Wheels, and Brakes

Tires

Each main landing gear mounted two 56 inch, 16-ply, smooth contour tires (AAF Specification No. AN-C-55, type I) inflated to 77psi. The tires were replaced when the internal or side wall ruptured or broke, cuts or tread wear exposed the fabric casing, and damage to the beads extended through the outside rubberized fabric.

Tubes

The tubes were standard inner tubes (AAF Specification No, AN-I-14). Causes for replacement were cuts or rips of more than one inch, holes too large to patch safely, and large thin or chafed areas. The correct method for repairing an inner tube was to vulcanize the damage with a "hot patch," while a secondary method was with a "cold patch." The number of patches to a tube was to be limited, as the weight and distribution of too many patches could cause the wheel to become out of balance.

Wheels

The main landing gear wheels were Hayes (H-3-101M-1) 56 inch, smooth contour, type III, with no wheel fairings. A removable flange that formed part of the rim provided easy removal of the tire. Removable heavy duty brake drums were located in the inner and outer part of each wheel. Timkin roller bearings were installed in each wheel hub, and were packed with AN-G-3 grease for both summer and winter operations, but when continuous heat of over 100°F was prevalent AN-G-5 grease was used.

Brakes

Each main landing gear was equipped with a dual inboard Hayes (H-2-258-1) and outboard Hayes (H-2-259-1) brake assembly with a 20 x 2.75 Duplex Expander type tube. Each brake consisted of three major components: brake frame, expander tube, and brake blocks. The expander tube was equipped with a nozzle connected to the brake fluid source. The brake blocks were fabricated from a special material, and the number used corresponded to the number of inches brake diameter (20 blocks). The blocks had notches on their sides to engage with lugs on the brake frame, and had slots across their ends into which flat springs were inserted. The ends of these springs fit into slots in the side flanges of the brake frame, and these springs held the brake blocks against the expander tube to keep them from dragging when the brake was released. The brake was operated by brake fluid, as application of the brake would force brake fluid into the expander tube, which was restrained from inward and sideways movement. The fluid in the expander tube forced the individual brake blocks out radially against the brake drum. The brake blocks were held from rotating with the drum by lugs on the brake frame fitting into notches in the sides of the brake blocks. As soon as the pressure was released, the springs in the ends of the brake blocks forced the brake fluid out the expander tube.

The brake system consisted of two separate accumulator systems, so that the failure of one system did not result in a total brake failure. The accumulators provided fluid under pressure to two brake control valves. The left accumulator supplied fluid to the forward brake valve that controlled the inboard brakes of all main landing gear wheels. (Note: the inboard and outboard designation refers to the main landing gear strut.) The right accumulator provided pressure to the rear brake valve controlling the outboard brakes on all main landing gear wheels. Each wheel contained two expander tube brake assemblies, or a total of eight brake assemblies for the four main wheels. Each brake valve consisted of two independent control units, with each unit operating two brake expander tube assemblies. The brake valves were mechanically interconnected, so that pressure on the right hand brake pedal of either the pilot's or co-pilot's station would actuate all brake assemblies of the right landing gear. The accumulators were kept charged by an electrically driven hydraulic pump that was automatically turned on by a pressure control switch when the accumulator's pressure fell below 850psi. A warning light lit when pressures fell below 650psi. Two brake pressure gauges on the co-pilot's instrument panel indicated the available accumulator pressure for brake operation. The inboard brake pressure gauge indicated pressure in the left accumulator, and the outboard brake pressure gauge indicated pressure in the right accumulator.

If the pressure control switch or the switchover valve failed an override switch was provided. This switch was located under the accumulator warning light on the co-pilot's control panel, and when actuated it overrode all switches in the electrically driven pump circuit except the circuit breaker, allowing the electric driven pump to operate continuously to provide pressure in case of pressure control failure.

Parking Brakes

The brake pedals were located just above the rudder pedals, and pivoted from the same torque tube. The brake lock lever projected to the rear at the bottom of the pilot's instrument panel at his right and left pedal linkage. The parking brakes were set by depressing the pedals completely, pulling out on the lock levers, and releasing the brakes. The pedals were to remain in the depressed position when the parking brakes were ON (brake pressure gauges reading at least 850psi).

Main Landing Gear Doors

Two faired doors attached to the underside of each inboard engine nacelle by a pair of piano-type hinges, and completely enclosed the main gear inside the nacelle when the gear was fully retracted. The major components of the actuating assembly were a stabilizing linkage, an actuating linkage, and a latching mechanism. Each door had an individual operating link assembly, both of which were interconnected to the main shock strut via a common link. The doors moved down and away from the nacelle when extending, and were held in the down position by the link assembly when the gear was fully extended. When the gear was fully retracted the doors were automatically locked in the up position by a latch mechanism.

Drag Strut Assembly

The drag strut assembly connected to a collar on the lower end of the main landing gear shock strut through a universal joint. The opposite end was

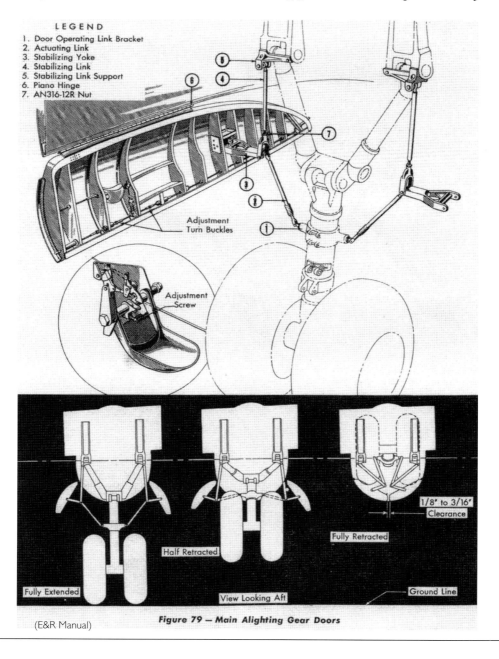

LEGEND
1. Door Operating Link Bracket
2. Actuating Link
3. Stabilizing Yoke
4. Stabilizing Link
5. Stabilizing Link Support
6. Piano Hinge
7. AN316-12R Nut

Adjustment Turn Buckles

Adjustment Screw

1/8" to 3/16" Clearance

Fully Retracted

Half Retracted

Fully Extended

View Looking Aft

Ground Line

(E&R Manual)

Figure 79 - Main Alighting Gear Doors

connected to a lever assembly that tied in with the horizontal retracting link and drag strut pivot shaft at the forward auxiliary wing spar. The function of the drag strut was to retract and extend the main gear by exerting force from the hydraulic jack to the main oleo shock strut. A secondary function was to lock the gear in the down position by an automatic locking mechanism (drag link latch) built in the drag strut at the trunnion point of the upper drag strut and the lower drag strut. During landing, the main strut was exposed to a force away from the line of flight, and this load was transmitted to the front auxiliary wing spar by the drag strut. After the initial force of landing, the main strut rebounded toward the line of flight, causing a compression load that was transmitted through the drag strut to the front auxiliary spar.

Nose Landing Gear

General Description

The hydraulically operated caster type nose landing gear was able to rotate through a full circle. Nose gear shimmy was eliminated by the use of two wheels mounted next to each other, and rotating on a shared axle. The axle turned on needle bearings installed in a knuckle, and was splined to the dual wheels. The action of the wheels rotating together in a straight line overcame the shock strut piston's inclination to shimmy.

The gear was equipped with an air-oil type shock strut that pivoted from two shafts installed in the right and left nose wheel beams, and were

connected to a trunnion attached to the top of the shock strut. The gear retracted hydraulically rearward and upward by a hydraulic jack connected to the shock strut trunnion and a cross tube assembly. A drag brace and a drag link assembly connected the lower part of the shock strut with the cross tube assembly to facilitate in extending and retracting the nose gear. A spring-loaded latch assembly attached at the knee joint of the drag brace and the drag link automatically locked the gear in the DOWN position. A spring-loaded latch assembly attached to the uplatch beam in the upper section of the nose wheel cabin locked the gear in the UP position. Fairing doors completely enclosed the nose gear into the forward section of the fuselage when the gear was retracted.

Normal Operation of the Nose Gear

The landing gear toggle switch, located on the center of the main gear instrument panel, was moved to the UP or DOWN position, directing electric current to a solenoid operated hydraulic selector valve. The solenoid plunger opened a port on the selector valve that led to the nose gear actuating jack line. The fluid pressure in the jack line increased, and was directed into the actuating cylinder, where the hydraulic pressure continued to build up to force the jack cylinder piston and rod to retract or extend.

Extension of the Nose Gear: During the extension of the nose gear, hydraulic fluid pressure was initially directed into a double unlatching jack located on the rear of the uplatch beam. The plunger of the double unlatch-

LEGEND

● Shock and Trunnion Assembly

● Down Lock and Drag Link Assembly

● Hydraulic Actuating Cylinder Assembly

● Drag Brace and Cross Tube Assembly

Figure 98 – Nose Landing Gear Assembly and Operation Diagram   (E&R Manual)

ing jack extended to contact the spring-loaded uplatch lever and forced it open, and the gear was ready to extend. The fluid pressure then flowed through the double unlatching jack to the in port of the main actuating cylinder where the pressure built up, forcing the extended piston and rod to retract into the cylinder. The nose gear mechanical actuating mechanism was connected to the cylinder rod, and when the rod was completely retracted the gear would completely extend. The gear was then locked in the DOWN position by a spring-loaded lock that was part of the knee joint of the drag link and the drag brace.

Retraction of the Nose Gear: A hydraulic cylinder connected the shock strut at the left side pivot shaft to an arm welded to the outer cross tube assembly. Force from the extension of the hydraulic cylinder piston rod caused the arm of the outer cross tube to rotate slightly and engage dogs on the outer cross tube, to mate with dogs on the inner cross tube. The first movement of the outer cross tube forced the latch actuating arm to disengage the down latch at the drag link and drag brace knee joint. After the down latch was disengaged, the hydraulic jack continued to extend, forcing the cross tube assembly to rotate, pulling the drag brace forward and up. Because the main oleo strut attached to the drag link, it followed the same direction until it was completely retracted and automatically locked in the up position.

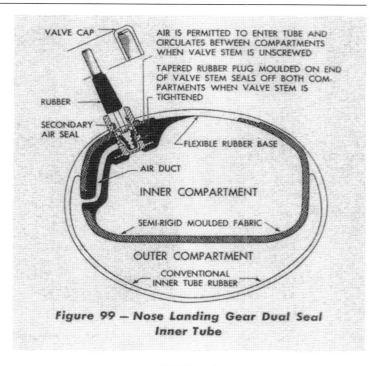

Figure 99 — Nose Landing Gear Dual Seal Inner Tube

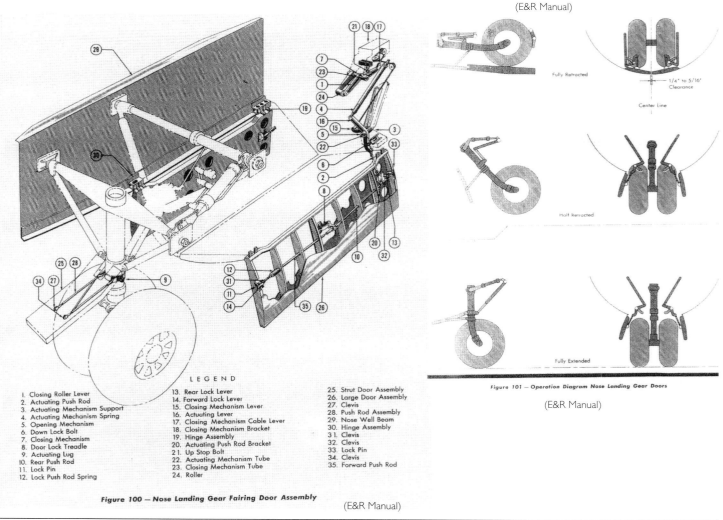

(E&R Manual)

Figure 101 – Operation Diagram Nose Landing Gear Doors

(E&R Manual)

LEGEND

1. Closing Roller Lever
2. Actuating Push Rod
3. Actuating Mechanism Support
4. Actuating Mechanism Spring
5. Opening Mechanism
6. Down Lock Bolt
7. Closing Mechanism
8. Door Lock Treadle
9. Actuating Lug
10. Rear Push Rod
11. Lock Pin
12. Lock Push Rod Spring
13. Rear Lock Lever
14. Forward Lock Lever
15. Closing Mechanism Lever
16. Actuating Lever
17. Closing Mechanism Cable Lever
18. Closing Mechanism Bracket
19. Hinge Assembly
20. Actuating Push Rod Bracket
21. Up Stop Bolt
22. Actuating Mechanism Tube
23. Closing Mechanism Tube
24. Roller
25. Strut Door Assembly
26. Large Door Assembly
27. Clevis
28. Push Rod Assembly
29. Nose Well Beam
30. Hinge Assembly
31. Clevis
32. Clevis
33. Lock Pin
34. Clevis
35. Forward Push Rod

Figure 100 — Nose Landing Gear Fairing Door Assembly

(E&R Manual)

Nose Landing Gear Tires, Tubes and Wheels

Tires

The nose gear mounted two 39 inch smooth contour 10-ply tires (AAF Specification No. AN-C-55, type I) inflated to 45-50psi and mounted on dual wheels. Unequal pressure in the dual tires did not have an adverse effect on the gear during takeoffs or landings. The maintenance and replacement of the nose gear tires was the same as the main gear tires.

Tubes

The nose gear tubes were Dual Seal inner tubes (AAF Specification No. AN-1-14, type I). The stiffer construction and greater weight of the Dual Seal inner tubes caused them to have a greater tendency to slip off the rim on landing impact than ordinary tubes.

the tire-assisted spring-loaded linkage located just forward of station 3.0 at the rear of each door. In the door opening sequence (strut extension), the tire descended and unlatched the door uplatch mechanism, and then the tire's continued downward movement forced the doors open. The door and tire remained in contact for about half of the door's rotation about its hinge line, at which time the "assist linkage" broke the tire to door contact, and the spring forced the door to its open position. The "assist mechanism" was a system of levers attached to a short torque shaft and a double coil compression spring that was constrained between a fixed pivot point, and a "floating" point located in a lever arm pivoting about and attached by a lever arm to the torque shaft. In the opening sequence, the door contacted by the tire began a clockwise torque on the torque shaft that compressed the spring until the "floating' spring end passed over the line of centers

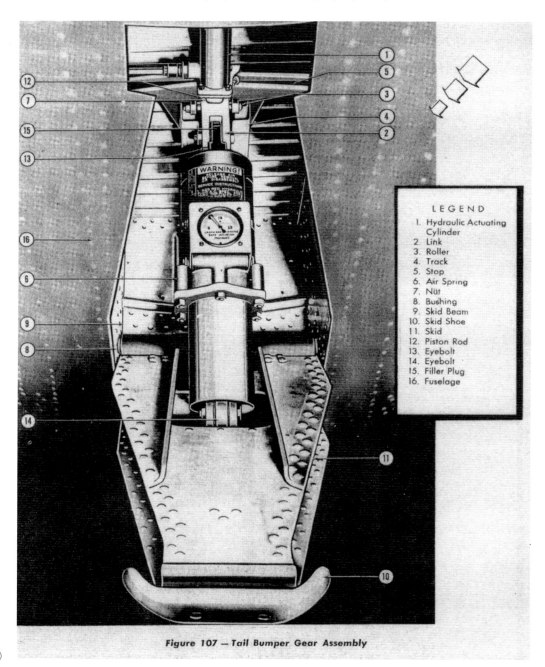

LEGEND

1. Hydraulic Actuating Cylinder
2. Link
3. Roller
4. Track
5. Stop
6. Air Spring
7. Nut
8. Bushing
9. Skid Beam
10. Skid Shoe
11. Skid
12. Piston Rod
13. Eyebolt
14. Eyebolt
15. Filler Plug
16. Fuselage

Figure 107 — Tail Bumper Gear Assembly

(E&R Manual)

The first production B-32-1-CF to be flown was 42-108472, which had many problems in its testing before crash landing on its sixth test flight on 27 August 1944. It appears in this photo that it was having hydraulic problems with its tail skid. (Consolidated via Stine)

between the torque shaft center line and the fixed end of the spring, which completed the door opening sequence. The door closing sequence was the reverse of opening, except that the tire contact was made by a roller-ended lever that, through a cable and pulley system, pulled the floating spring end across the line of centers. The spring then completed the closure sequence by causing a counterclockwise torque to the torque shaft that, through its attached lever and door push rod, pulled the door closed.

Tail Skid Gear and Air Spring

The tail bumper consisted of a forged skid mounted on the bottom side of an arm that pivoted from two machined castings installed in the after section of the fuselage. The unit was hydraulically operated with the landing gear, and fully retractable into the fuselage.

An air spring (Aircraft Accessories No. 24006) was built in the tail skid gear as a shock absorber. The spring attached to the skid at the lower pivot point, and to the hydraulic cylinder at the upper pivot point by a link fitting. The spring was approximately 16 inches extended and 10.6 inches compressed, giving a 5.4 inch stroke of the rod assembly. Dry air was compressed inside the cylinder assembly, and was measured by a pressure gauge on the top of the housing. About a pint of hydraulic fluid was used to lubricate the packing rings and piston rod guide.

Landing Lights

Two retractable landing lights were located, one on each side of the fuselage, at the bottom one-third of the fuselage, forward of the front bomb bay. Two three-position switches on the co-pilot's control pedestal controlled the landing lights.

4

The Wright Cyclone R-3350 Engine
Development and Factories

Introduction

The basic components of an aircraft are its airframe and engines. The success of the B-32 and B-29 programs hinged on the timely development, subsequent dependability, and mass production of the 2,200 horsepower R-3350 Cyclone engine designed and built by the Wright Aeronautical Division of the Curtiss-Wright Company of Paterson, NJ. The first XB-29 and XB-32 used the R-3350-5 that delivered 2,000 horsepower at 2,400rpm, but were subsequently fitted with the R-3350-13, rated at 2,200 horsepower at 2,800rpm. Later, a total of 162 R-3350-21s that also delivered 2,200 horsepower at 2,800rpm were ordered for the YB-29s, XB-32s, and XC-97s (a Boeing cargo spin-off of the B-29). The -21A (2,200hp/2,800rpm) was installed on the YB-29s, and the early B-29s and B-32s. The first R-3350 to be built in quantity was the R-3350-23, of which 1,366 were ordered. Early B-29 and B-32 production models used the R-3350-23 model built by Dodge-Chrysler/Chicago that delivered 2,200 horsepower at

2,600rpm. Once the problems of the -23 engine were remedied it was replaced by the -23A "War Engine." These -23A engines differed from the plain -23s, as they had aluminum cooling fins pressed into the cylinder barrels instead of the machined steel fins. A total of 22,385 R-3350-23As, also built by Dodge, were ultimately ordered. Late production B-29s and B-29As used the improved R-3350-57 engines that delivered 2,200 horsepower at 2,800rpm. The evolution of the R-3350 engine was slow and arduous, and was the major factor in influencing the development of the B-29 and the B-32. The problem with the Wright engine was not with the engine design, as much as the time constraints it was placed under as part of the accelerated B-29 project to solve the problems that were inherent in the development of any new engine.

Wright Cyclone R-1820 and R-2600 Engines

At a time when Pratt & Whitney dominated American aircraft engine manufacturing with its Wasp and Hornet engine series, Wright initiated its Cyclone engine series in 1923 with a Navy contract for two of the new radial engines. In 1929 Wright merged with Curtiss, and by 1932 the two engineering departments collaborated to produce the outstanding 9-cylinder 1,000 horsepower Cyclone F, designated the R-1820, that were to power the Douglas airliners and the B-17 bomber. Work on a 14-cylinder engine began in November 1935, and the Wright design department utilized the hard-learned lessons in the development of the R-1820. The 14-cylinder 1,600 horsepower Wright R-2600 Cyclone was the company's first successful two row air-cooled radial engine. It was used to power the Boeing 314 Clippers, and would become a major wartime aircraft engine used in the AAF B-25 and A-20 medium bombers, as well as the Navy's TBM/TBF and SB2C carrier bombers. A larger engine was needed to power the B-29 and B-32, and the Wright engineering department's developmental objective for the R-3350 was to produce one horsepower for every pound of weight. Wright engineers mounted two 9-cylinder R-1820 Cyclone engines together at a 90-degree angle from each other to form a "V," with its open ends facing toward the line of flight to yield a displacement of 3,640 cubic inches. Power from each engine was transferred through a common gearbox that combined the power of the two engines, and directed it into the propeller main shaft. While single Cyclone R-1820s had flown reliably over millions of airline and military miles, the new combined engine presented Wright engineers with a number of problems. The gearbox added

(Chrysler) Wright engine

weight, and there were two of every engine accessory: two carburetors, two superchargers, two air scoops, and dual fuel and oil lines. The dual engine had the standard 55 inch diameter, but its cowl needed to be much wider.

Wright R-3350 Development

Wright engineers soon realized the inherent problems of the R-1820 combination engine were significant, and went back to the drawing boards to design an entirely new 18-cylinder 3,350 horsepower flat engine that would become the company's financial backbone until well after the end of the war. Wright did not have enough engineers to devote to the R-3350 project, as they concentrated on the R-1820 and its employment in the pre-war DC-2 and DC-3 commercial market, which would reach 70%, and the later military market for the B-17. Also, at the time the potential and marketability of the R-2600 engine was thought to be greater than the R-3350. The company did not assign a large number of engineers to it until 1942, when it was compelled to do so by the awarding of the large B-29 contracts and its use by the B-32. As Wright and its parent company, Curtiss, rapidly expanded into huge manufacturing entities, Curtiss did not allow Wright management to make high-level decisions. The fact was that Wright executives were not qualified to assume undertaking a project of the magnitude of the R-3350, and consequently failed to support the project as forcefully as they should have. In the late 1930s, under the AAC's prototype/developmental contract system, there was no monetary motivation for airframe builders such as Consolidated, and engine builders such as Wright to hurry development of their products. Any improvement or innovation in the developmental process was expensive, and Wright had to assume these costs, knowing that there was no guarantee that the AAC would purchase the engine once it was ready. Wright could not expect financial help from its parent company, as Curtiss had not been profitable in the 1930s. It was not until 1940, when Congress allowed cost-plus contracts, that engines could be developed and produced without as much financial risk to the manufacturer.

Nonetheless work went ahead, and Wright engineers incorporated as many of the established Cyclone engine attributes as possible into the new engine. When it began its development in January 1936 the R-3350 followed the design and construction details of the R-2600. During 1937 and 1938, Wright engineers upgraded and hand-built the new engine in the experimental machine shop. The engine integrated traditional Cyclone steel-barrel cylinders with aluminum heads that increased the cooling area. They kept the Cyclone's strong steel crankcase and strong, light magnesium nose and supercharger sections. There were two banks of nine cylinders each with one master rod, and eight articulated rods directing piston power into a three-piece crankshaft. A 20-pinion reduction gear directed power into the propeller shaft at efficient speeds, and at a weight scarcely over one pound per horsepower. The R-2600 and R-3350 had the same bore and stroke, with the additional displacement gained by adding four additional cylinders (in two rows of nine). The R-3350 was an air-cooled, duplex engine that had 18 cylinders, with two radial rings of nine cylinders positioned around the crankshaft. The cylinder heads of the two cylinder rings radiated outward to be cooled by the air stream from the huge propellers. The R-3350 was rated at 2,000 horsepower for cruising and 2,200 horsepower for takeoff. The engine was twice as powerful as the R-1820 of the Flying Fortress, yet its 55 inch frontal engine exposure was the same size as the B-17, and provided equivalent cooling!

As mentioned, during the late 1930s the R-3350 was a low priority for Wright, as the company centered its attention on expanding its R-1820 and R-2600 Cyclone engine production. The R-3350 developed slowly from the Wright foundries to the machine shops, to assembly, and finally to the test cells. The testing and development of the R-3350 engine was very limited, and there was no significant production, as from 1936 to 1939 Wright delivered only seven to the Air Force. When Wright tested the first R-3350 in 1937 the initial problems arose. After running for 135 hours on a test stand the engine's reduction gears failed, and this problem was to continue until 1943. In 1939 two new problems with the exhaust valves and the cooling system occurred that also would never be fully remedied during the war. The R-3350 was scheduled to power the Martin Mars, Lockheed Constellation, and the Boeing Model 341, but it was not until May 1939 that it was first flown in the Douglas XB-19, and tests continued in that aircraft through the summer. In September 1939 the war in Europe began when Hitler invaded Poland, and the French and English demand for Wright Cyclone 9s and 14s increased dramatically. Wright was faced with a glut of orders for its proven R-1820 and R-2600 engines, and in less than two months it built new machine shops to accommodate these orders. These facilities almost equaled the size of the main Wright plant, and were in production by early 1940. The continued high demand prompted Wright to buy vacant silk mills in the Paterson, NJ, area, and these mills were quickly renovated and expanded into six plants and a new foundry to build more R-1820 engines. Wright expanded its main plant in Cincinnati, OH, that would build 50,000 wartime R-2600 engines, and also built its Lockland, OH, plant, which would be the largest single floor factory in America to exclusively manufacture the R-1820. Later Studebaker was licensed to build the R-1820, and it eventually built 60,000 to power the B-17.

In the R-40-B bomber design invitations of 29 January 1940, all five bidding aircraft companies offered their proposed aircraft to be powered by the Wright R-3350 engine: Boeing XB-29, Lockheed XB-30, Douglas XB-31, Consolidated XB-32, and Martin XB-33. The engine had been under contract by the AAC since 1936 (XB-19), and by the Navy from 1937 (for the Consolidated Model 31, Boeing XPBB-1, and Martin Mars APB2M-1). All five bidders had experimental aircraft in development using this Wright engine. The reason was that the displacement of the R-3350 was the largest of any contemporary engine, and had the potential for the greatest development. There were no other large contending engines under development at the time, except the Pratt & Whitney R-4360 and Allison's large liquid-cooled 1,600 horsepower Allison XV-3420-1 24-cylinder in-line engines. These engines were dropped from consideration, as they were in development, were too large and heavy, and did not provide any increase in power. So by default, on 15 April 1941 the Air Force issued contract No. AC-18971 to Wright for a future production of 30,000 engines, the largest and highest priority production program of the war.

Wright-Woodridge Plant

By the summer of 1943 the Wright-Woodridge Plant #7, near New York City (Dodge-Chicago was nowhere near geared up), was built in seven months to exclusively manufacture the R-3350 engine. Despite the supposedly "exposed" east coast location to possible enemy air attack, the large new 1.5 million square foot facility was chosen by Under Secretary of War Robert Patterson, Chief of Staff George C. Marshall, and Assistant Secretary of War Robert Lovett. They chose the site because of the availability of the nearby experienced labor pool and electric power in the area. Seventy million dollars had been invested in the Woodridge plant and machinery by the end of 1944. Plant #7 was scheduled to build 850 engines per month, with the first production engines slated for May 1943 (the first engines were actually shipped in July 1943). The plant was unusual, in that it was built entirely of poured concrete from the floor to the supporting pillars to the roof. The first Woodridge engines were hand-built on a single "pilot line," incorporating changes as they went. Wright engineers reasoned that once the design was frozen the final mass production assembly lines could be easily duplicated from the pilot lines. The first engine was built and tested in July 1943, and it was anticipated that by November all the changes could be incorporated into additional pilot lines/production lines, and relatively large numbers of combat engines could be turned out for the first B-29s coming off the Wichita production lines. But during the summer and into the fall R-3350 production met one delay after another, and there were not enough engines to go around for the B-29s, which were now going into an intensive training program over Kansas. The uproar reached Congress, which demanded to know why the R-3350 project fell so far behind schedule. Gen. Arnold was on the hot seat again with the B-29 project, and he made the R-3350 engine the top priority of the Air Force; he ordered a new board to investigate the engine program. Members of the board included future Supreme Court Justice Col. William Brennan, future mayor of New York William O'Dwyer, and founder of McDonnell Aircraft, James McDonnell. The board found widespread managerial ineptitude and indifference, and shortages in the labor force. Wright-Woodridge Plant #7 was scheduled to have 8,000 workers on the production line, but had only 3,300. Like other companies in the aircraft industry, Wright had problems attracting workers and then holding them after extensive training. Wright's reputation as an employer in the area did not help matters. It had broken a machinist's union strike in 1931, and throughout the 1930s fought the unions, and used every means to keep wages low. Wright had planned to attract workers from the New York Boroughs and Newark, but a starting wage of $0.60 per hour, the long commute, and better paying jobs in shipyards closer to New York and Newark left Wright with the dregs of the workforce to manufacture the most complex piece of mass produced machinery built at the time. To cope with this unskilled workforce Wright broke down as much production and assembly as possible into procedures that could be done by machines and watched by workers. Other jobs, such as testing and inspection, were simplified to the lowest common denominator. Wright did little to supervise or train their workers, but there was little work to do until the engine design was finalized. Low pay, an ineffective union, and little or no work led to low morale and excessive wasted time, loitering, absenteeism, and a high quitting rate. By September 1943 the situation at Woodridge became so bad that the War Department sent in advisors to turn things around. An improved training program was established, and workers were made to appreciate the importance of their jobs in the building of the engine of the superbomber that would win the war. Unskilled women and Negroes were also accepted into the workforce, and Wright transferred 300 skilled workers from other plants; the AAF also sent men to train new workers. Interchangeable engine parts were to be manufactured by new subcontractors at the Dodge-Chicago plant, and at government-financed Wright plant conversions at East Patterson and Fairlawn, NJ, and Lockland, OH. Gen. Arnold campaigned to have the government raise starting wages to $0.70 per hour, with raises for time on the job and bonuses for work produced. Perks such as child day care, bus

transportation to and from New York City, and cafeterias, banks, and stores also attracted new workers. In October the company hired 1,000 new workers to bring its total to 9,700 of the goal of 13,200. In November it seemed that 800 engines per month could be produced starting in January 1944, and the War Department withdrew its advisors and allowed Wright to manage the project at Woodridge. However, with their departure the problems did continue, and production lagged in the spring and early summer, after which the production lines finally churned ahead at the scheduled production rates.

Chrysler-Chicago Plant

The Navy had two important flying boat projects, consisting of 500 planes each, scheduled, requiring their variant of the R-3350 engine. The Consolidated XP4Y-1 was to be built at a new factory at New Orleans, and the Boeing XPBB-1 was scheduled for its new plant at Renton, WA. There were discussions about using the Navy version of the R-3350 engine, but Boeing and Consolidated were unable to make the necessary engine installation changes. It was determined that the new Chrysler Chicago engine plant could get tooled up to supply these Navy engines without jeopardizing its initial production schedules. However, the production totals of the flying boats were finally reduced, and Chicago's engine personnel were diverted to the B-29 and B-32 programs.

Chrysler was contracted to build a new factory complex on 450 acres on the west side of Chicago. The George A. Fuller construction company broke ground in June 1942 for 19 buildings covering 6.3 million square feet. Plant #4 housed the assembly areas and machine shops, and was the largest individual building in existence, as at four million square feet it was larger than the Pentagon. The building was remarkable, containing over 1,000 work bays measuring 30 x 38 feet. Located underground were 10 acres of lavatories, nine cafeterias, kitchens, and other services connected by two lengthwise and one cross tunnel. The complex also had the world's largest parking lot, which was a block wide and a mile long, and was capable of parking 8,000 automobiles. The other buildings contained administration, tool and die shops, magnesium and aluminum foundries, light and heavy forge buildings, a heat treating building, two powerhouses, and oil and chip recovery facilities. By 1944 $750 million had been spent on the Chicago-Dodge development, including $175 million on the land, construction, and equipment. Chrysler was to begin engine delivery in March 1943, but there were difficulties in starting up: buying the land, contracting architects, and then difficulties during construction. Chrysler

In June 1942 Chrysler broke ground for 19 buildings covering 6.3 million square feet on 450 acres on the west side of Chicago. Plant #4 was the largest individual building in existence, as at four million square feet it was larger than the Pentagon. (Chrysler promotional pamphlet)

then had problems obtaining engine blueprints and other data from Wright, which had few to provide, as the engine was under development and undergoing design changes. Crucial metals, such as aluminum, steel, and magnesium, were in high demand and short supply, and Chrysler President K.T. Keller was forced to ask for a July 1943 engine delivery date extension.

Dodge-Chicago continued to run into problems and delays in the fall of 1943. Dodge was tooling up before the engine had passed its type test, and as a consequence suffered an enormous 48,500 engineering changes that, of course, affected production schedules. The immense plant had been finished in April at a cost of $100 million, but shortages of machine tools, the relentless engineering changes, and problems in the exchange of technical data with Wright prevented Dodge-Chicago from setting up so much as a pilot line. After most of the design problems had been eliminated the first Dodge engine was finally produced in January 1944. The production line was fully equipped and manned, and from that point the engine manufacture moved efficiently, turning out 18,500 R-3350s by the end of the war. The Chicago operation was mammoth, with an average of 33,000 workers: 16,000 on the production line (8,800 on the day shift, 6,600 on the night shift, and 600 maintenance workers in the morning), and 17,000 on the managerial staff. Women comprised 36% of the labor force, and Negroes 20%, mostly in the hot, grueling foundry. The plant commonly surpassed production quotas, building not only engines, but also thousands of vital parts for the Wright Woodridge and Lockland plants. In November 1944 the plant turned out 1,079 engines, and by the end of the year the cost of an engine was down to $15,080. The number of new engines that did not survive hours of testing (called "penalty engines") dropped from 31% in early 1944 to 2% a year later. So good was the tooling set up at the Chicago plant that its parts were interchangeable with those from the Woodridge plant. When the Woodridge plant production faltered in the spring and early summer of 1944 the Chicago plant made up the deficit. Subcontractors supplied the electrical components, such as the generators, motors, magnetos, spark plugs, and wiring. Carburetors were also subcontracted.

In the Dodge-Chicago plant, engine production moved from the forge buildings, die shops, heat treating building, and the foundries to the machining and assembly buildings. The forge shop contained 41 hammers that weighed up to 35,000 pounds, and were able to strike with a force of 56,000 pounds to shape rough steel forgings, such as crankcases, master and articulating rods, and cylinder barrels. From the forge shops the slowly cooling forgings were moved to the heat treating building, where they were subjected to heating, cooling, and an oil bath. The Chicago magnesium and aluminum foundries poured more metal than any other plant in the world at capacity. The aluminum foundry produced intricate castings of finned cylinder heads in sand molds. Originally, Chicago was scheduled to tool up to produce forged cylinder heads that were preferred for better high altitude cooling, but was unable to do so because of the delays their set up for production would cause. Each die was half a cylinder head that was placed into molding sand, which was placed into the molding machine that compressed and vibrated the sand around the head die. The die was carefully removed, leaving its form in the sand. A binding liquid was sprayed on the delicate sand mold, and then the mold was placed on a slowly moving conveyor that moved it through a furnace for baking to harden it. The hardened mold was inspected, and then burned with a blowtorch to keep the poured metal from adhering to the sand. The other half of the cylinder head mold was fitted to its opposite, and the two were clamped together.

More than 9,000 machine tools were used in the Chicago-Dodge Plant. The photo shows cylinder head jackets being made. (Chrysler)

About 100 steel pins (1,400 in first production molds) were placed in the mold to keep it from breaking during metal pouring. The clamped mold then had aluminum poured into it, and after it cooled the clamps were removed, and the mold was pried open with a bar. The finned casting was removed from the mold and rough machined, inspected, and ready for fine machining and assembly in these automated plants.

The magnesium foundry produced the supercharger housing and the engine nose section. Caution had to be observed in the magnesium foundry due to the metal's inflammability, and the magnesium pouring pots were connected to temperature gauges that were constantly monitored. The molds

Engines were built on dollies, with parts and assemblies moving in from sub-assembly lines. (Chrysler)

had to be pumped full of sulfur gas and sprinkled with sulfur to keep oxygen away to prevent flare ups.

The main building contained the automated machining and assembly functions. The raw castings were machined, polished, and fabricated into subassemblies, and moved onward for final assembly. The completed engine was moved off the line on special mounts, and run on test cells for several hours. The Chicago engine testing facility had 50 test cells, where each engine underwent evaluation. The engines underwent preliminary "green" tests that gradually ran the engine up from 1,400rpm to full take-off throttle at 2,800rpm. Initial green tests lasted seven hours, but by 1945, after the engines became more reliable, this was reduced to 3.75 hours. Any failure of an engine or its auxiliaries during the green test caused the engine to be transferred for repair, and then it was put through the "penalty" tests. After the engine passed the green test it was returned to the factory for disassembly and detailed inspection of every part. It was then reassembled, and then retested for another 3.5 hours (later reduced to 2.75 hours) before it was shipped to one of the B-29 factories, or the Fort Worth B-32 plant for installation. Every month 2.25 million gallons of fuel were used for testing, but most of the power generated by the engines was recaptured by means of a unique power recovery system that resupplied one-quarter of the electric current used by the entire Chicago-Dodge facility.

By the fall of 1944 the Chrysler and Wright plants were exceeding the demand for the R-3350, not only for the B-29 and B-32, but also for the other aircraft mounting the engine—the Martin Mars flying boat, Douglas BTD Skyraider carrier borne attack plane, and Lockheed's Constellation airliner. There were so many engines produced that it was easier and less expensive to replace a worn engine with a new one than to overhaul it. By August 1944 R-3350 production had to be decreased, as engines had to be stored as the supply outstripped the demand.

Dodge Chicago supplied the majority of the R-3350s manufactured in WWII—18,413, as compared to Wright's 13,791—but the Wright engines averaged more time between overhauls (285 vs. 267 hours). In all, Wright and its licensees produced over 281,000 engines of all types by the end of the war.

Engine Model	Shipped 1937-40	Shipped 1940-45	Shipped Licensee	Total Shipped
975 Whirlwind	1,963	3,288	52,651	57,902
1820 Cyclone	7,770	34,192	63,789	105,751
2600 Cyclone	2,138	83,152	-0-	85,290
3350 Cyclone	17	13,791	18,413	32,221
Total	11,888	134,423	134,843	281,164

R-3350 Goes into Production
Wright received its first production order for the R-3350 in May 1941, when the AAC ordered 185 for its XB-29s and YB-29s. With all of the fundamental design changes, Wright did not have the engine available at that time, and would not have one until December 1941. The R-3350 design was nowhere near ready for the foundries, cutting equipment, and tooling that had been ordered, and thus, the government gave Wright a low priority to receive the machine tools and strategic metals that all defense contractors were clamoring after. Fortunately, the War Department continued to support the Wright engine program, and the exigencies caused by the Pearl Harbor attack benefited both the R-3350 and the B-29 programs. To meet the obligations of the R-3350 contract, Wright built a new plant at

Woodridge, NJ, exclusively to build the engine, and its entire Cincinnati factory production was also converted to the engine. In January 1942 the Chrysler Corporation and its Dodge Division were awarded a $314 million, 6% cost-plus-fixed-fee contract to build 10,000 R-3350 engines plus spare parts. When Dodge was awarded its contract there was the opportunity for the company to convert the cylinder head design from the forged to the better cast design, but due to delays in the delivery of tooling the existing cast design was continued. In March this contract was increased to 17,653 engines worth $594 million, and Chrysler was to construct a new factory on the west side of Chicago.

In the meantime, the B-29 program, and thus the B-32 program, were in jeopardy, and no one wanted to take responsibility. Army Air Corps and engine industry reputations and careers were at risk. Curtiss-Wright, the holding company for the engine, had swelled in size from 10,000 employees in 1939 to 140,000 in 1943, and was still expanding to become the second largest American military contractor after General Motors. But in the expansion Curtiss-Wright continued its archaic centralized management practices that controlled the 1939 company. The company's many divisions were not allowed any autonomy, and all decisions were to be made through corporate headquarters in New York. Curtiss-Wright Chairman Guy W. Vaughn, and top executives and investors were concerned over losing control of the company during its rapid wartime expansion, as they were looking to the post war, when its military contracts would be canceled, and peacetime endeavors would have to be pursued to stay in business. Consequently, military divisions like Wright Aeronautical found it difficult to draw top-flight executives and managers to fill what would be temporary war industry positions.

R-3350 Test Programs and Problems
In September 1942 three flight test programs commenced using the first 25 Wright R-3350-5 engines. The Consolidated XB-32 first flew on the 7th, and was followed two weeks later by the XB-29, while Lockheed flew its twin engine test aircraft, called the "Ventillation," at the end of the month. Very little is known about the Ventillation, except that it was a specially modified two engine Ventura bomber that was the seventh Ventura on the original British contract. It was kept at the Lockheed factory to test nacelle configurations for the Lockheed Constellation airliner, thus the combina-

Early B-29 and B-32 production models used the R-3350-23 model built by Dodge-Chrysler that delivered 2,200hp at 2,600rpm. Once the problems of the -23 engine were remedied it was replaced by the -23A "War Engine." (USAAF via Dembeck)

Lockheed Ventillation was a specially modified two engine Ventura bomber to test nacelle configurations for the Lockheed Constellation airliner, thus the combination of names. (USAAF)

tion of names. The Ventura's nose had to be shortened so it was cleared by the large diameter propellers. Over the next four months Wright furnished 65 engines for these programs. Due to the small number of test hours of the early lower powered engine's problems, some major, and many minor, problems soon appeared with the cooling system, reduction gear, and piston rings. The Wright service units spent many hours in the field making changes, mostly at Boeing, then at Consolidated, and a few at Lockheed. All engines shipped before 1 October 1942 had to have all cylinders removed and lapped. During takeoff the propellers developed runaway rpms measuring in the hundreds. Hamilton-Standard, the propeller manufacturer, and Wright discovered the problem was due to low oil pressure, and a stopgap remedy was to set the propeller stop at lower maximum rpms. The final fix was larger internal oil passages and increased oil pressures, which would only come with a newly designed, larger engine nose section. Moisture, particularly during rainy periods, was forced into the ignition by outside and inside pressure differentials, and interfered with normal function. To solve this problem Wright used filled harnesses and changed the materials in the ignition components. The original carburetor supplier could not maintain its contract numbers, and other manufacturers were contracted. When the engines were shut down large quantities of fuel were leaked and caused a fire danger (fixed by minor field changes). Also after engine shutdown, oil could leak past the pistons and cause a hydraulic lock at the bottom of the cylinders, which could cause damage on the next engine start (special instructions were issued for start up procedures). There was heat build up from the design of the nacelles, and from the two external superchargers that could cause exhaust fires. Most of these problems were no more than annoying, and were usually easily corrected. The most serious problem of the XB-32s was instances of extremely high oil consumption. However, a more serious problem soon emerged, as the test aircraft were unable to climb to altitude, and high altitude tests had to be suspended until an answer could be found. Investigation determined that, as the aircraft climbed the oil pressure decreased to unsafe levels. The solution was to increase the size of the external oil line from the rear of the engine to the nose, reducing oil pressure loss. But this fix would not come for four months, and finally, on 31 December 1942, the Boeing XB-29 finally reached 25,000 feet. The engines went through several configurations. Two reduction gear and two supercharger ratios were tested, as were

several different compression ratios and two different master rod locations. By the end of 1942 Wright engineers, designers, and their counterparts at component subcontractors had solved many problems, but in the meantime solving these problems had reduced the total flight testing times on the 26 engines involved in all three manufacturers test programs to 365 hours and 10 minutes:

Aircraft	Total Time
Boeing XB-29 #1 *	99:35
Boeing XB-29 #2 *	2:08
Consolidated XB-32*	131:12
Lockheed Ventillation+	132:00
Total	365:10

*=4 engine   +=2 engine

<cap>
2-04-07 XB-29 #1

The XB-29 #1 required 17 engine changes to reach the 99:35 total hours, and the highest flight time for any of these engines was only 19:35. During the test period the aircraft had encountered three total reduction gear failures and one partial failure, along with a fractured engine nose section on a ground test engine. The XB-32 results were better, because Consolidated utilized Boeing's experience gained earlier in the year, and the XB-32 was a lighter aircraft and caused less stress on the engines. The XB-32s used eight engines to accomplish the 131:12 testing hours, and suffered only one reduction gear failure, but the maximum XB-32 engine time was also low at 19:34. The Lockheed tests were much better, as the same two engines were used for the entire 132 hours of testing on both test aircraft, and no major problems were encountered during testing. This significant difference between the two-engine Lockheed and four-engine Boeing/Consolidated test models was due to having each XB-29/XB-32 engine fitted with two external superchargers for each engine nacelle, causing a concomitant increase in heat and mechanical complexity.

During the second week of January 1943 Wright did an extensive reexamination of its engine program. The reexamination findings permitted engine production to move forward, as most of the production and operational problems were found, and had been, or were in the process of, being remedied. However, time was of the essence. Wright's Woodridge, NJ, plant was still under construction, and then would need to have its machinery and tools installed and staffed by blue-collar laborers and technical personnel. The study determined that the new Woodridge plant, with

The XB-29 #1 had the worst engine testing results, requiring more than twice the number (17) of engine changes for 99 hours flight time vs. eight engine changes in 131 hours for the XB-32. (Boeing)

its new personnel and machinery, along with the complexity of R-3350 engine manufacture would require the strict maintenance of quality control.

Just as Wright had received its engine contract and was expanding its facilities, the company was beset by shortages in strategic materials that threatened to jeopardize the program. The East Coast foundries required core sand that was supplied from abroad, and at the time German U-boats threatened the shipment of the supply. A search for alternative local sources was conducted, but none could supply the volume or quality needed, and the foreign sand was scrupulously rationed. Other strategic materials used in engine manufacture were either threatened or in short supply, so Wright was forced to develop substitute materials, and once developed they required many hours of engine proof testing.

Both the B-29 and B-32 programs were hindered by the R-3350's problems, and consequently slowed their development during all of 1943 and into 1944. On 8 February 1943 the XB-29, flown by Eddie Allen, crashed due to engine fires that killed its crew and 20 people on the ground. A disgruntled Gen. "Hap" Arnold grounded all XB-29s and XB-32s, and formed the special Echols Board to investigate the engine's problems, conduct tests, and recommend changes. The Air Force Power Plant Laboratory at Wright Field was also assigned to investigate the causes of engine failure, and it compiled an extensive inventory of 82 instances of engine problems occurring between October 1941 and the end of February 1943. Individual engine problems were examined, Wright suggested a solution, and then considered the urgency of the change and its effect on production.

The Power Plant Laboratory findings were that the R-3350 engine design was viable, and that in time, with some basic suggested engineering changes, and given higher priorities, would be dependable, and could be put into mass production. Most failures occurred in the reduction gears or nose section of the engine, and these had to be corrected to attain high altitude operation and acceptable propeller rpm control at takeoff. The nose casting had thicker walls in some areas, requiring larger internal oil conduits, a larger oil pump and sump, and changes to the torque meter. The reduction gear required a new pinion carrier with closer tolerances, which was a very difficult manufacturing process. The machine tools and mass production assembly lines could not be set up until the suggested changes were completed and the engine design frozen. The parts for the first 13 engines shipped from the new Woodridge plant in July 1943 were machined by only one very skilled machinist working long shifts! There were over 2,000 changes made between January and November 1943, of which nearly a quarter caused expensive and time-consuming revisions in tooling that precluded any mass production.

After the installation of the dual turbo-superchargers on each engine the major potential problem of engine cylinder cooling, especially at high altitudes, emerged, and the lack of time prevented a resolution. The problem was exacerbated when the bombers were made combat ready, and their gross weights increased by five to eight tons. Also, each engine had a difference in drag that was caused by opening the cowl flaps to bring down its particular cylinder head temperatures to operating levels. These large differences in the drag of each engine, and concomitantly of each aircraft made formation flying very difficult. The Wright Engine Committee had anticipated this problem, as it had been remedied in the B-17 powered by R-1800 Cyclones during its high altitude missions over Europe by replacing cast cylinders with forged cylinders. The Committee recommended the same change from cast to forged cylinder manufacture in the Wright R-

3350, but there was insufficient forging capacity in the country to meet both B-17 and B-29 requirements, and the B-29 was sent into operational testing with this critical defect. The XB-32 was a much lighter aircraft, and at the time was not encumbered with combat equipment; therefore its R-3350 engines did not have any significant cooling problems. The production B-32s had an empty weight of 60,000 pounds, compared to the B-29's 78,000 pounds, and a gross weight of 100,000 pounds compared to the B-29's 135,750 pounds.

In the spring of 1943 there were only 32 R-3350s available to Boeing-Wichita, but they could not be used, as Gen. Arnold banned their use after the Allen crash. The first production B-29s rolled out of the plant without engines. The empty nacelles had cement blocks hung below them to balance the aircraft. The Wright Engine Committee decided that these engines could be modified to "flight status," so the Boeing-Wichita plant made a concerted, round-the-clock effort, and by 29 June 1943 the first production test flight was scheduled. The test flight work was temporarily halted at the Wichita factory, and the Wichita locals came to watch from a hill near the field. The impressive bomber was towed out, and the engines thunderously run up in preparation for takeoff. Just after the bomber lifted off smoke billowed out from one engine, and the flight had to be quickly aborted. Inspection on the ground showed the problem to be from a tiny oil leak around a small gasket in the engine nose section that flowed back over the hot exhaust and caused the heavy smoke. By 23 July 1943 143 engines had been shipped, but only 12 were -21 "combat" engines. Fifty of these engines were grounded because their Chandler Evans (Ceco) carburetors needed to be reworked, and another 29 were in the Wright service shops for modification. Once modified only 10 of these engines were declared "combat" ready, and were parceled out for flight (six to the Martin Navy program and four to Bell). Sixteen were only deemed suitable for "school" use and ground testing, and the other three were used for training or flight spares.

On 16 August 1943 a meeting was held at Boeing-Wichita to analyze and discuss the recent R-3350 tests, particularly the engine cooling tests. Comprehensive cooling tests had been conducted using the "combat" type R-3350-21s on the XB-29 #1. During ground testing problems that would later occur in combat were uncovered: burnt pistons and discolored, charred, burned, or seized parts. Flight tests established that the cowl flaps needed to be wide open for all ground running, and partially closed during take-offs. A revised takeoff procedure, considering the bomber's increased heavy gross weights, was tested and instituted, called the "War Emergency Rating." With the increased combat gross weights normal cruise power was not sufficient for climbing; a much higher power setting was necessary, and with it came the cylinder cooling problem, even with an auto rich mixture. A minimum climb rate of 180mph and a 1,400rpm limit was established and determined to maintain temperature limits.

By October 1943 the engine modifications and problems with the aircraft put everyone concerned with the program under great pressure to meet the original date to get the B-29 into combat. Aircraft for flight training were behind schedule, with only 21 B-29s delivered to combat units. The average flight time on these aircraft was about 70 hours (only one plane had 200 flight hours), and only seven had flown with "combat" engines (the highest time on any combat engine was 73 hours). Changes were continuing on a "routine" basis (e.g. the shortest time without interfering with the schedule), and production was rapidly increasing. Major engine and aircraft changes were accompanied by changes in the model "dash"

WRIGHT CYCLONE 18BA (R3350BA) SERIES AIRCRAFT ENGINE
Exploded View of a Typical Engine

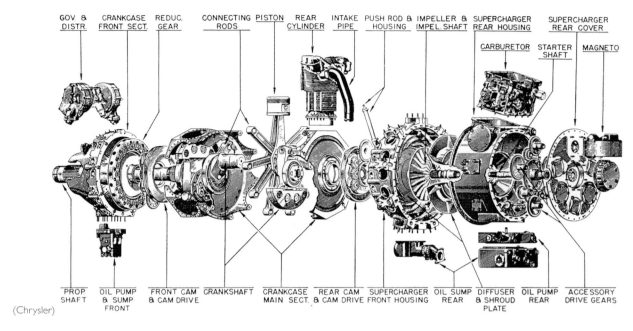

(Chrysler)

designation, so that it could be easily identified in the field. Since the B-29 program had a higher priority testing status, the delayed B-32 program benefited from the engine problem solving, and had fewer engine problems during testing. Because of the delays in getting the B-32 into production, the first aircraft off the line were equipped with the improved Model -21 and -23 R-3350s.

Wright Cyclone 18 R-3350 Described
The B-32 was powered by four, 18-cylinder Model R-3350-21 or -23 Wright Cyclone engines that were of the standard radial air-cooled conventional four-cycle design, with two staggered banks of nine cylinders each. The -21 and -23 were essentially the same, except for the installation of a torquemeter in the -21. Installation of the -21 was made in a number of the first production aircraft. The -23 was modified in accordance with Technical Order TO 02-35JA-8, with -10 and -12 to become the -23A, which was designated by a one inch yellow band around the nose of the engine. The modifications were numerous small changes that converted the engine from a training status engine (TSE) to a war status engine (WSE). The major change was the installation of ducted baffling and a rocker box cross over tubes for improved cooling.

R-3350 Wright Engine Gallery (Pima)

Legend:
1) Fuel Master Control (On fuel injected engines)
  Carburetor (On engines without fuel injection)
2) Fuel Injection Pumps
3) Magneto
4) Starter
5) Generators (2 on outboard engines)
6) Fuel Pump
7) Tachometer Generator
8) Rear Case Oil Pump
9) Oil Inlet Line
10) Oil Outlet Line

Specifications of the R-3350-23A engine were:

Type	18 cylinders, Wright Cyclone, staggered 2-row radial, air-cooled, geared drive, Supercharged, conventional 4-cycle
Length	76.26 inches
Diameter	55.12 inches
Frontal area	17.0 square feet
Weight	2,670 pounds
Weight/hp	1.21 pounds/horse power
Construction	3-piece steel crankcase, Cylinders with steel barrels with W-type aluminum alloy fins and cast aluminum alloy heads, one inlet valve and one exhaust valve (sodium cooled) per cylinder actuated by push rods, 2-throw 3-piece counterbalanced crankshaft supported in 3 roller bearings, Planetary reduction gear, ratio 0.44:1 or 0.56:1
Fuel Pump	AN4102 rotary, 4-vane, positive displacement
Vacuum Pump	Pesco rotary, 4-vane positive displacement (on engines 2 & 3)
Hydraulic Pump	Vickers 7 cylinder piston type (early aircraft) Pesco gear type (later aircraft) (on engines 2 & 3)
Supercharger	B-11 (B-31 later) G.E. Gear-driven, 2-speed supercharger, ratio 6.61:1 and 8.81:1 (two per engine)
Carburation	Chandler Evans (Ceco) Type 58CPB-4, fully automatic
Ignition	One Bendix-Scintilla DF18LN-1 dual magneto and one 18-point distributor. Two 28mm long reach spark plugs per cylinder. Shielded ignition system
Generators	Outboard Engines: P-2: 200 amp, 28-30 volt, engine-driven, DC with 2-speed overdrive

Inboard Engines:	R-1: 300 amp, 28-30 volt, engine-driven DC
Lubrication	Pressure feed, 60-70 lb/square inch Dry sump
Starter	Jack and Heintz JH-4E (later Eclipse E-95996)
Bore	6.125 inches
Stroke	6.3125 inches
Displacement	3.347 cubic inches
Compression Ratio	6.85:1
Fuel consumption (cr)	0.46lb/hp/hr
Oil consumption (cr)	0.020lb/hp/hr
Gasoline grade	100/130 octane (Specification No. AN-F-28)
Oil Grade (weight)	1120 (Specification No. AN-VV-O-446)
Oil grade (viscosity)	120 S.U. seconds
Output/displacement	0.66hp/cubic inches
Output/piston area	4.15 hp/square inches
Piston speed (max.)	2,946 feet/minute
Rating (takeoff)	2,200hp/2,800rpm/ at sea level
Rating (normal, low)	2,000hp/2,400 rpm/4,500 feet
Rating (normal, high)	1,800hp/2,400rpm/14,000 feet
Rating (cruising)	1,300hp/2,100rpm/no specific altitude
Military	2,200hp/2,600rpm /25,000 feet (for maximum of 5 minutes)

Temperature Limits

Conditions	Cylinder Head	Oil
Ground Operation	500°F	203°F
Takeoff Power	500°F	203°F
Military Power	500°F	203°F
Rated Power (1hr)	478°F	185°F
Rated Power (continuous)	450°F	185°F
70% Rated Power (cont.)	450°F	185°F

Engine Costs

Chicago-Dodge's initial estimate for the R-3350-23 was $25,314 per engine, plus a fee of $1,519. By the end of 1944 this figure was lowered to $14,500, plus a fee of $580, and further decreased for late model B-29s/B-32s to $11,537 for the -23 engine, and $12,954 for the -57 fuel injected model, despite its numerous engineering changes.

Consolidated's Engine Responsibility

Consolidated was responsible for the installation of the engine, its cooling, control, and supply of lubricating oil and fuel, but not for its structural safety or capability to function. During the XB-32 preliminary design phase the Consolidated Power Plant Design Unit initiated a thorough inclusive survey of engine problems relating to cooling, controls, superchargers, fuel, oil, exhaust, and fire. When the basic problems were identified they were delegated to specialist engineers that took their assigned problems back to their group to be analyzed and solved.

Engine Sections (Nose, Power, Supercharger, and Accessory)
Nose Section

The nose section housed a planetary-type reduction gear that reduced the propeller shaft rpm to 0.35 of the crankshaft speed. A propeller governor was mounted on top of the nose section. Wright engineers analyzed 82 engine failures occurring between October 1942 to February 1943, and the reduction gear was found to be a major cause, and several changes were made, especially to the pinion gears. A slowly responsive governor caused overspeeding that was corrected by increasing the size of the oil galleries in the nose, and increasing the size of the scavenge pump that increased oil flow.

The engines were provided with combination, inertia-direct cranking starters that could be of the Eclipse E-160 or 1416 direct cranking, or Series 48 type, which were powered by the P-2 generator. An ACCELER-ATE-START switch located on the flight engineer's switch panel controlled the starters. The starter switch had to be held in the ACCELERATE position until the flywheel had gained sufficient speed (in about 15 seconds), and then be moved to START to engage the flywheel and motor with the engine.

Power Section
Cylinders:

There were two staggered rows of nine cylinders each. The cylinders had a 6.125 inch bore, 6.312 stroke, and a displacement (capacity) of 3,347 cu-

Figure 128 – Front View of Front and Rear Row Cylinder Barrel Air Deflectors Installed

(E&R Manual)

bic inches. The cylinder head temperatures were measured by thermocouples at the No.1 cylinder in the rear bank, and the readings were sent to the pilot and flight engineer. The R-3350 cylinder design was similar to the R-2600 engine, being forged of a nitralloy barrel with Wright's aluminum "W" finned muff rolled into the outside diameter. The barrels were machined from nitralloy steel forgings, and had their inner surfaces nitraded, screwed, and shrunk into aluminum alloy heads. The cylinder head had a hemispherical combustion chamber with two inclined valves operating in bronze bushings shrunk into the head. The heads were cast, which would cause acute operational problems later.

The front and rear cylinders were staggered on the R-3350-5 engines used on the XB-32s. To save weight the cylinder heads were integral aluminum castings, with a lacework of W-type cooling fins cut into grooves on the exterior of the steel barrel as deep as four inches, and as little as 1/16 inch thick, spaced five per inch. The next nitralloy forged steel cylinder barrels had 40 cooling fins about 1/32 inch thick and 5/8 inch deep machined on the outside surface. Wright soon developed a better barrel design on its R-3350-13, -21, and -23A (war engines). Instead of cutting fins into the barrel, 54 thinner, deeper, aluminum fins were rolled into slots that increased the cooling area of the barrel by 45%. By rolling instead of machining the barrel fins the wall thickness of the barrel was reduced by half, saving Wright 24 million pounds of the scarce nitralloy. The total cooling surface on the 18 cylinders was 5,850 square feet, or 3,900 square inches per cylinder, which equates to the surface area almost equal to a 60 x 100 foot parcel of land! Although this number seems to be impressive, it was not enough to keep the R-3350 cool under high power climbs.

Valve rocker arm and springs were enclosed in housings cast integrally with the head. The combustion chambers were hemispherical, with two valves per cylinder. The exhaust was sodium cooled, with the exhaust ports on the front row of cylinders facing forward, rather than rearward, and this exhaust port positioning would later cause problems in the service life of the engine. The front cylinders exhausted forward into the front collector ring, while the rear cylinders exhausted into the rear collector ring. The front collector ring sections directed their exhaust through flexible couplings into the rear collector ring. The combined exhaust was then directed into the exhaust transition ducts on each side of the engine. The exhaust then passed through the left or right supercharger turbine wheels before exiting the flight hoods on each side of the nacelles. The pistons were the Wright "Uniflow" type, which had three compression rings and

three oil control rings (the bottom ring was inverted). The piston pins were case hardened with beveled ends, and were retained by coiled spring retainers held in small annular grooves at the ends of piston-pin holes. The Wright Engine Committee set up a program to test different types of piston rings. Because the early R-3350s had little flight time the choice of the best piston ring was delayed, and then it was further delayed by the demand for millions of piston rings for all the engines used in WWII. The single piece H-section master rods and eight articulated rods were machined from solid forgings. The main crank pin bearings were silver lead indium plated with steel backings, and fitted loosely in the large bore of the master rod. Master rod bearing and knuckle pin lubrication was improved via a bearing oil seal on each master rod. The chrome steel knuckle pin had nitrided bearing surfaces, and was center-drilled and tapered at one end to accommodate a locking screw. The chrome nickel steel articulated rods had split bronze bushings pressed into both ends. An Engine Test Stand Program was established to enable component transfer from one engine source to another either at production, modification, or overhaul.

The top three cylinders in the rear row (numbers 1, 3, and 5) were particularly exposed to exhaust valve seat erosion, with ensuing erosion of the valve guide boss at about 175 hours. A schedule was established to inspect the exhaust ports after 140 hours, and every 15 hours thereafter. If any evidence of erosion was found the engine was changed. The leaking of the exhaust ball joint for the front cylinders allowed the white-hot exhaust to be blown over the cylinder heads, causing overheating. Redesign of the ball joint mitigated the problem.

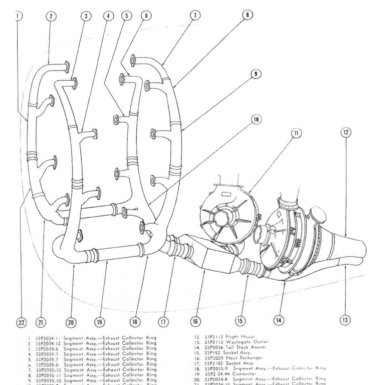

1. 33P2034-11 Segment Assy.—Exhaust Collector Ring
2. 33P2034-12 Segment Assy.—Exhaust Collector Ring
3. 33P2034-6 Segment Assy.—Exhaust Collector Ring
4. 33P2034-7 Segment Assy.—Exhaust Collector Ring
5. 33P2035-7 Segment Assy.—Exhaust Collector Ring
6. 33P2035-6 Segment Assy.—Exhaust Collector Ring
7. 33P2035-12 Segment Assy.—Exhaust Collector Ring
8. 33P2035-11 Segment Assy.—Exhaust Collector Ring
9. 33P2035-10 Segment Assy.—Exhaust Collector Ring
10. 33P2035-8 Segment Assy.—Exhaust Collector Ring
11. 33P2030 Turbosupercharger (Type B-31)
12. 33P2112 Flight Hood
13. 33P2113 Wastegate Outlet
14. 33P2036 Tail Stack Assem.
15. 33P152 Socket Assy.
16. 33P2029 Heat Exchanger
17. 33P2152 Socket Assy.
18. 33P2035-9 Segment Assy.—Exhaust Collector Ring
19. 33P2-34-44 Connector
20. 33P2034-8 Segment Assy.—Exhaust Collector Ring
21. 33P2034-10 Segment Assy.—Exhaust Collector Ring
22. 33P2034-47 Segment Assy.—Exhaust Collector Ring

Figure 160 – Exhaust System Complete

(E&R Manual)

Pistons

The pistons were full-trunk, heat-treated aluminum alloy die forgings. Half-dome heads were used to obtain the correct compression ratio. The pistons were cut for six piston rings (the sixth on the bottom); the top three were of the wedge type, and the next three were square cut.

Exhaust Collector Assembly

The exhaust collector assembly was fabricated from stainless steel sheet sections consisting of a forward collector ring and two connecting pipes. Exhaust from the front row of cylinders was collected by a ring located forward of the engine in the nose ring cowl. Exhaust from the rear cylinders was collected by a ring located aft of the rear cylinders. Front and rear rings were connected by two connecting pipes. Stub sections branched from the collector rings and attached to each of the 18 exhaust ports.

In all testing reports, the exhaust collector system was considered a major problem. Maj. Henry Britt of the Proving Ground Command reported:

"The B-32 aircraft as of 1 June (1945) had not been sufficiently mechanically proven to participate in flights over enemy territory. During a discussion with Lt.Col. Thomas Gerrity, ATSC, prior to overseas departure, a high altitude shakedown flight was suggested. Col. Gerrity stated that it was not necessary, as he knew what would happen; 'the exhaust collectors would fail.' They did, and they failed on the ferry flight (to the Philippines), and on a combat mission over Formosa. They were a repeated source of trouble, and a very definite flight hazard."

Crankcase

The three-piece (front, center, and rear) crankcase was originally an aluminum forging, but later was replaced by forged steel. The three pieces were machined and divided at the center line of the front and rear cylinders, and were bolted together internally. Steel retainers were installed on the inside diameter of the bearing support sections, except the rear, which contained the rear main bearing, oil seal, and oil distributor.

The forged chrome-nickel alloy steel crankshaft was of the two-throw split-clamping type, allowing the use of a single-piece master rod. The shaft was hollow throughout its length, and heat treated to withstand high loading and speed. Oil was transferred to the hollow crankshaft at the rear main bearing distributor for lubrication. The crank pins were nitrited to decrease wear. The three-piece clamping-type crankshaft was braced by three main roller bearings fastened on the shaft, and in the crankcase diaphragm. Two very large dynamic damper counterweights, one per row, were located adjacent to and directly opposite each crankpin. They were used to dampen vibrations, but in early models were insufficient, as crankshaft vibration was transmitted to the propeller shaft, causing the shaft to fatigue and fail. To remedy the problem eight (four front and four rear) counterweights, running at twice the crank speed, were placed radially around the crankshaft axis, and driven by the cam drive. The forward section was splined to accommodate the reduction driving gear and the front cam driving gear splines. A journal for the rear main roller bearing was formed by an extension on the rear section. It carried internal splines for the accessory and starter drive shaft coupling. The crankcase consisted of five main sections that were (from rear to front):

1) Front section: Constructed of magnesium alloy, and housed the propeller reduction gear assembly, the driving gears for the front lubricating oil pump, gearing for the distributors, propeller governor pump, and valve tappets and guides for the front row of cylinders.

2) Main section: Made up of three steel forgings that were bolted together internally.

3-4) Supercharger front and rear housings: Were fabricated from magnesium alloy, and provided room for the impeller, diffuser, induction passage to the impeller, supercharging drive gears, and all engine accessories.

5) Supercharger rear housing cover: The rear engine housing cover was machined from a magnesium alloy of the typical Cyclone pattern, and covered the engine accessories.

Valves

The small, one pound nickel steel valves were an engineering achievement. They opened ports through which millions of cubic feet of intensely hot gases were vented, and then closed these ports instantly to allow more gasoline and fresh air to be drawn into the cylinder. During the compression and explosion of this mixture the valves kept the ports tightly closed. At 2,800 engine revolutions per minute these valves opened and closed 1,400 times per minute. In the closed position the wide ends of the valves were part of the combustion chamber wall, and had to withstand the considerable force of the engine's power stroke.

There were two valves per cylinder. The intake valves had tulip shaped heads and solid stems, and the exhaust valves had mushroom shaped heads and hollow sodium cooled stems. The stem of the exhaust valve was hollow in order to contain liquid sodium to act as a cooling medium against the extremely intense heat of the exhaust. This hollow design had to be engineered to be strong enough to withstand the staggering forces hammering against it. The cam rings were driven off both ends of the crankshaft through intermediate gearing at one-eighth engine speed. The push rods were totally enclosed. One of the major R-3350 problems was valve failure due to high cylinder head temperatures and inadequate lubrication. Wright Field engineers corrected the problem with a revised system of oil crossover tubes that connected the cylinders in the same bank. Valve adjustment was critical, and compression checks were scheduled for every 50 hours, but some ground crews did them after every mission. Valve guides were to be inspected every 10 hours.

Ignition System

The dual Scintilla DF18LN-1 magneto was geared to turn 1.125:1 in a clockwise direction. It provided a double ignition from a single unit, employing the rotating magnet principle and stationary coils. Two radio shielded high-tension ignition cables conducted the current from the magneto to the two distributors mounted on top of the crankcase front section. Current from the distributor was conducted by radio-shielded ignition cable to the 36 spark plugs. The engine firing order was 1, 12, 5, 16, 9, 2, 13, 6, 17, 3, 14, 7, 18, 11, 4, 15, and 8.

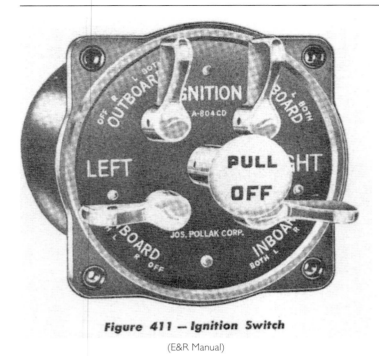

Figure 411 – Ignition Switch
(E&R Manual)

Carburetors

The front cylinders of the early Wright engines were inclined to run leaner than the rear cylinders due to poor carburetor mixture distribution, causing engine overheating and heavy valve wear. These carburetors were also prone to induction system fires. Bendix was the initial supplier for the downdraft carburetion units for the R-3350-21 "combat engine." But Bendix also was the major vender for many other types of engines, and the Chandler Evans Company (Ceco) was contracted to supply its Model 58-CPB-4 downdraft, fully automatic non-icing unit, which was mounted on top of the supercharger rear section. Initially the Chandler Evans carburetor had many production problems.

The flow of air delivered to the engine was controlled by the carburetor throttle, and was measured by an air meter. The air meter consisted of a rectangular parallel venturi with suction holes and impact tubes throughout their entire length to measure the flow of the entire airstream. The flow was indicated by the pressure differential between the impact tubes and venturi. The amount of fuel delivered to the engine was controlled by the fuel metering system, which operated as a function of the pressure differential obtained from the air meter. Since the air meter pressure differential was a relatively small force that had to be translated into fuel pressure variations in the fuel metering system, the venturi forces were amplified by a hydraulically actuated mechanism. The carburetor automatically compensated for the varying density of the air and special fuel requirements for acceleration. To the basic carburetor jet system an additional jet system was provided for idle, cruising, lean, and takeoff conditions, where special fuel mixtures were required.

The fuel was pumped to the carburetor inlet chamber at a pressure of 16 to 18psi. The inlet chamber was equipped with a vapor trap that automatically freed all vapor by allowing it to escape in small quantities through a weighted valve to the fuel tank. The fuel flowed through a strainer to a diaphragm operated fuel regulator valve. The fuel flowed from this regulator valve to the mixture control disc, which had holes that fed fuel to the jets. If the engine used a constant mixture for all operating conditions one jet would have been sufficient, but since it did not it was necessary to arrange the system using four jets. This system consisted of the "A" jet for minimum requirement (Automatic Lean); the "C" jet, which was manually opened in parallel with the "A" jet to supplement the fuel flow for Normal rich operation (Automatic Rich); and the "B" jet, also in parallel, which was spring-loaded to automatically enrich the mixture for full throttle or takeoff conditions. The "B" and "C" jets were in series with, and their combined output was controlled by the "D" jet, which limited the amount of fuel added for maximum power conditions.

The power output of an engine was determined by the air consumption, and therefore the fuel flow through the carburetor had to be proportional to the airflow. The increase in fuel flow with increase in airflow was accomplished by a variable hydraulic force located on top of the fuel regulator diaphragm. The pressure meter valve controlled this hydraulic force.

Fuel Injection

Throughout the war the AAF requested that fuel injection replace carburetors for better fuel distribution and extended valve life. Near the end of the war direct fuel injection solved the carburetor's problem of having some cylinders tending to run lean (low on gasoline content) due to poor mixture distribution. Fuel injection was made possible with the introduction of new steel alloys and machining techniques for producing plungers to tolerances of ten-millionths of an inch. The introduction of fuel injection involved a significant tooling problem, and the engineering and procurement sections at Wright Field did not want to interfere with factory engine production during the change over. The introduction of fuel injection was to start by November 1944, but there were the inevitable production setup difficulties that delayed its installation until late in the war. In all there were 6,427 engineering changes in adopting fuel injection. Once the fuel injection unit was ready, to facilitate its installation the engine and nacelle had to be removed, requiring up to 400 man hours, as the fuel lines were to be routed to accommodate the engine design. Engineers redesigned the routing of the fuel lines so that the fuel injection unit could be installed in two hours without removing the engine.

Fuel injection gave a more even fuel distribution at lower temperatures, better acceleration, there would be no carburetor icing at high altitudes (lessening the risk of fire). Fuel was injected into the late war R-3350-57 engine cylinders by two Bendix-Stromberg nine-plunger units directed by a master control unit that monitored the airflow entering the supercharger. The first unit supplied fuel to the front cylinders, and the second to the rear cylinders in accurately metered portions of fuel every twentieth of a second at 2,500psi through stainless steel tubing and atomizers into the combustion chambers. This arrangement enabled the fuel mixture to be adjusted if one row was running leaner than the other row. Again, Bendix was unable to meet the demand, and Bosch was contracted to manufacture fuel injection units for the R-3350-59 engines. There was an interchangeability problem between the two company's fuel pump control units and the air scoop, and Boeing, Bendix, and Bosch engineers had to collaborate to solve this problem.

Turbo Supercharger Section
Description

At sea level the weight of the earth's atmosphere is 14.7psi, but at 25,000 feet it decreases to 5.5psi. Greater air pressure creates greater air weight

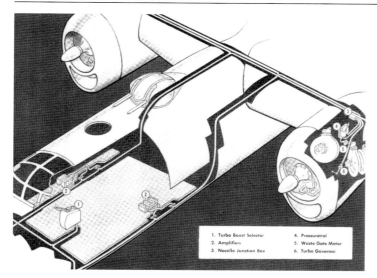

1. Turbo Boost Selector	4. Pressuretrol
2. Amplifiers	5. Waste Gate Motor
3. Nacelle Junction Box	6. Turbo Governor

(E&R Manual)

(density = pounds per cubic foot), and vice versa. As an aircraft flies higher the air pressure becomes less, and the air density becomes less. If an engine is to maintain its power at higher altitudes, it has to take in a higher volume of air from the outside to keep the weight of airflow from decreasing. By using a supercharger the weight of airflow can be maintained at the rated power output of the aircraft. This is done mechanically by pumping air into the engine carburetor at the required pressure, causing the carbure-

tor to add more fuel to keep the air/fuel mixture at the proper ratio. This increased amount of fuel and air, under greater than normal pressure, goes through the intake manifold, provides a greater charge to the cylinder, and increases the force of the piston's power stroke. The mean effective pressure in the cylinder determines horsepower.

Development
The need to increase power output at high altitudes, where atmospheric pressure is lower, led to the development of the supercharger. During WWII America was the only combatant to utilize the supercharger on a series production basis. Dr. Sanford Moss of General Electric was credited with designing the first practical aircraft turbo-supercharger, improving on a French idea. Early systems broke down after a few flights due to turbine or bearing failure from high mechanical and thermal loads. Research and development continued in the 1920s and '30s, and culminated in reliable designs that could be placed into production. General Electric produced the majority of American superchargers in WWII, with their Type B and Type C models. GE designed their superchargers to "maintain sea-level pressure at the carburetor from deck up to the rated altitude of installation."

Types of Superchargers and Intercoolers and Aftercoolers
Internal Supercharger
The internal supercharger was the one that was located between the carburetor and the intake manifold, and forced a charged mixture into the cylinder. The internal supercharger provided a uniform distribution of the fuel/air charge to the cylinder, and increased the density of the charge. It was built into the engine, and obtained its power by being geared to the crankshaft.

External Supercharger
The external supercharger was one that was located between the outside air and the carburetor, and forced an increased amount of air or compressed air into the carburetor. The external supercharger was a turbine (turbo supercharger) that was turned by the engine's exhaust gases.

Intercoolers and Aftercoolers
In using a supercharger with sufficient compression capacity to provide the full weight of air at high altitudes, it was necessary to cool off the air or mixture after it had been compressed. This was accomplished by using special radiators called intercoolers or aftercoolers, depending on their location in relation to the carburetor. Both methods, with their large radiator equipment, not only increased weight and drag, but also increased aircraft vulnerability, as it added another vital system that could be hit by enemy fire.

B-32 Turbo Superchargers
The B-32 mounted eight General Electric B-11 and B-31 exhaust-driven turbo superchargers—two for each engine—enabling each engine to maintain sea level horsepower up to 33,000 feet. Minneapolis-Honeywell electronic regulators controlled the carburetor air inlet pressure. The two superchargers on each engine operated in parallel, as a single supercharger was unable to handle the volume of air required for a single engine. There were provisions to shut down one supercharger when cruising at low power, where they were known to operate erratically. The turbo superchargers

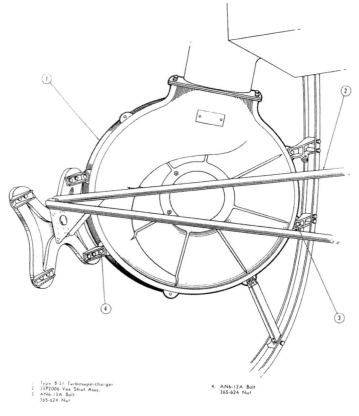

1. Type B-31 Turbosupercharger	4. AN6-12A Bolt
2. 33P2006 Vee Strut Assy.	365-624 Nut
3. AN6-13A Bolt	
365-624 Nut	

Figure 162 – Installation – Turbosupercharger

(E&R Manual)

were mounted vertically, one on each lower side of the nacelle, behind the firewall. The B-32 nacelles were recessed into the wing in an extremely clean installation. On normal turbo supercharger installations the turbine wheel was exposed, but the B-32 supercharger installation had only the exhaust stack protruding from the nacelle, and a panel called a shroud covered the remainder. The supercharger unit consisted of a single speed blower with a 6.06-to-1 impeller-to-crankshaft gear ratio. The front cylinders exhausted forward into a collector ring that was located inside the leading edge of the cowl, which then directed the exhausted air under the engine to the turbo superchargers. The turbo compressor released the air into an intercooler, and then it flowed into the down draft carburetor or master control unit (if the bomber was equipped with direct fuel injection). This supercharged air was then directed through a Chandler Evans (Ceco) Type 58 CPB-4 pressure carburetor mounted on top of the supercharger. The unit could maintain a pressurized fuel-to-air mixture of about 17 inches of mercury at 2,400rpm.

The supercharger system was extensively tested in B-17s, and was operational when it was installed in the B-29 and B-32. Later the R-3350 was the first Wright engine to be fitted with a Wright-designed gear-driven supercharger, replacing GE designs (GE continued to manufacture the impellers for the Wright supercharger), and the Wright design proved to be equal to the superlative Rolls Royce supercharger. During the war GE, aided by subcontractors Ford and Allis-Chalmers, manufactured 303,000 turbo-supercharger units.

Supercharger Construction

The supercharger consisted of three sections: the turbine, the compressor, and the oil pump bearing assembly. A single knob on the pilot's aisle stand controlled all the turbo superchargers. The Type B and C units used single-stage, centrifugal compressors driven by a single-stage axial-flow turbine. A common shaft supported on two bearings mounted the turbine wheel and impeller. Lubrication was provided by a two-section dry pump system that pumped oil through bearings. One dry pump section supplied pressurized oil to the bearings, and the other section returned the oil to the oil reservoir.

Turbine: Exhaust from the engine was directed to the nacelle or fuselage mounted turbine to aid in cooling it. A nozzle box (exhaust collector ducting) directed the exhaust gases through the nozzle blades, and then against the turbine blades, popularly called "buckets." The waste gate unit was located on the nozzle box that bled off excessive exhaust gases. The rpm of the turbine depended on the position of the waste gate, which controlled the amount of exhaust gases bypassed from the turbine nozzle box. If all the exhaust gases were permitted to flow through the turbine the result would be excessive boost pressures, especially at lower altitudes. The waste gate was a butterfly bypass valve that was initially controlled manually. Later, the turbo governor automatically regulated the waste gate to open when the turbine accelerated too rapidly, or when maximum safe speed (26,400rpm at 35,000 feet) was reached. Both exhaust waste gates on each engine were operated by a small reversible electric motor that automatically received power from the regulator system when a change in waste gate setting became necessary to maintain the desired manifold pressure. There were four amplifier units, one for each nacelle, and they were located two above and two below the navigator's table. This system encountered many problems, and required constant monitoring by the pilot or

flight engineer, especially during descent, when the danger of overboosting was greater. Installing automatic oil or electric servomotors solved the problem. The waste gate did cause some problems, as it stuck and resulted in a runaway turbine that could explode, sending pieces through the fuselage. The main reason for sticking was frozen moisture in the sensing lines leading to the regulator control. The problem was solved by the introduction of electronic regulators. Generally supercharger reliability was good, with most units running 400 hours between overhaul.

Compressor: A single-stage centrifugal compressor was mounted to the opposite end of the shaft. The compressor discharged air through a diffuser that converted kinetic energy from the impeller to potential (pressure) energy. Some type of intercooler cooled the high air temperatures from the compressors in order to delay the start of detonation resulting from the high charge temperature.

The high temperatures of the turbine system called for innovation in the use of high temperature alloys. Inconel alloy (nickel-chromium) was used extensively in the turbine to withstand the high temperatures, particularly in the vital nozzle box, which was fabricated from Inconel welded stampings. The turbine blades presented the greatest challenge because of the red-hot temperatures and centrifugal loads of 24,000rpm under which they operated. Because of the differential in thermal and mechanical demands placed on each blade and the retaining wheel, they were initially attached by a bulb-root attachment until methods of welding them to the wheel were perfected. The blade metal was vitallium-type alloy, Haynes Stellite 21, which was previously forged, and often failed until they were manufactured by the lost wax casting method.

Electronic Turbo supercharger Control: The electronic supercharger control system consisted of separate regulator systems, all simultaneously adjusted by a single turbo selector dial located on the pilot's aisle stand. Each system controlled the induction pressure of the particular engine through a Pressuretrol unit connected directly to the carburetor intake. The 115-volt, 400-cycle inverter supplied the electric power for the system. Each regulator included a turbo governor that prevented turbo overspeeding, both at high altitude and during rapid throttle changes.

The Mechanics of Supercharging: Supercharged engines were able to develop their takeoff power to an altitude determined by the maximum allowable speed of the turbine. At the critical altitude the waste gate would completely close, causing a maximum backpressure working against the engine. The result was the engine ran at sea level efficiency. Engine exhaust gases passed through the collector ring and tailstack to the nozzle box of each supercharger, expanded through the turbine nozzle, and drove the bucket wheel at high speed. A ramming air inlet duct supplied air to the impeller, which increased its pressure and temperature. However, in order to avoid detonation at the carburetor, the air supplied to the carburetor passed through the intercooler, where the temperature was reduced. The internal engine impeller, driven by the engine crankshaft, again increased air pressure as it entered the intake manifold. High intake manifold pressure resulted in greater power output. The amount of turbo boost was determined by the speed of the turbo bucket wheel, and the speed of the turbo bucket wheel was determined by the difference between the atmosphere and the exhaust in the tailstack, and by the amount of gas passing through the turbine nozzles. If the waste gate was opened more exhaust gas passed to the atmosphere via the waste gate pipe, and decreased the tailstack pressure.

Accessory Section: In the accessory section there was a succession of gear trains that operated the fuel, vacuum, oil, and hydraulic pumps, the generators, and the starter. The rear supercharger housing cover contained the components of the engine accessory section: tachometer; accessory gasoline pump; hydraulic and vacuum pump; dual magnetos; starter; two generators; and provision for spare accessory drive. Spur gearing drove all accessories, and were powered either directly from a gear on the rear of the accessory drive shaft, or indirectly through the pinion gears. All gears were machined from steel forgings, had hardened teeth, and functioned in bushings in the rear cover, allowing the entire unit to be removed with the cover. Bendix Scintilla dual-type magnetos were installed in each engine, and were individually controlled by switches by the flight engineer. They supplied ignition via a high-tension current to the distributors mounted in the nose.

Oil System and Engine Lubrication

Engine lubrication was of the dry sump full pressure type, in which all moving parts were lubricated by oil under pressure, except the piston pins, piston rings, propeller shaft thrust and radial bearings, crankshaft main bearing, and valve operating mechanism for the lower cylinders (all of which were lubricated by oil spray from oil jets, or by gravity feed). There was a pressure and scavenging pump contained in the same housing at the front and rear of the engine. The rear pump supplied the oil for the main bearings, the rear section, and part of the front section. The front pressure pump supplied oil to reduction gears, torque meter, and oil booster pump. Oil pressure pumps also provided oil to master rod bearings, knuckle pins, cam, supercharger drive mechanism, and accessory drives. All sections of the valve gear were lubricated automatically. Oil pressure operated the hydraulic, constant speed, full feathering propeller. Oil filters were included both in the front and rear oil sumps to remove dirt and foreign particles from the oil before it entered the lubrication system.

Independent oil systems provided constant lubrication and partial cooling for each engine and its accessories. Each system consisted basically of an oil cell, sump Y-drain valve, and oil temperature regulator. Each engine was supplied oil from an 85 gallon self-sealing tank located behind the firewall of each nacelle. The filler necks on the oil tanks were placed on the side of the nacelle, which made it impossible to overfill them, and also left space for expansion. On some models a 100 gallon reserve oil tank was located on the port side of the center wing section near the oil transfer pump and the oil selector valve. Oil was drawn from the oil tanks by two pumps, one located in the rear sump, and the other in the front sump. The sumps were machine-finished from magnesium alloy castings. The rear oil pump (rear sump), attached to the rear supercharger housing, was driven by a bevel gear that was integral with the spare accessory drive gear, and meshed with the oil pump drive shaft. Oil was supplied to the pump by an external line leading from the rear sump. After passing through the rear oil pump oil passed through an oil filter, pressure relief valve, and check valve. The front oil pump (front sump) was attached to the lower rear side of the crankcase front section, and passed through a similar filter to the check valve system. Excess oil from all sections of the engines drained into the front and rear sumps, where it was collected by two oil scavenge pumps in the rear sump, and a single scavenge pump in the front sump. Each sump had a drain plug, and a small magnet was incorporated in each plug to pick up metal chips from the oil. An oil temperature regulator (oil cooler) was located on the OUT line between each engine and its oil tank. The flight engineer operated it automatically or manually. It maintained uniform oil temperature to the engine throughout the various operating conditions. As oil returned to the cell from the oil temperature regulator it circulated through the hopper, and was thus prevented from mixing with the cold oil of the cell. The airflow through the oil cooler was controlled automatically by a temperature regulator, or could be manually regulated by the flight engineer by means of switches on his panel. In addition to engine lubrication, the oil system served to operate the propeller governor and propeller feathering. A bayonet gauge located on the filler casing measured the quantity of oil, while the temperature bulb located on the Y-drain valve transmitted the oil in temperature to the co-pilot's panel. Oil pressures were measured at the front and rear of the engine, and were transmitted to dual nose pressure and main pressure gauges on the instrument panel.

The standard 1120 (60wt) aircraft lubricating oil (Specification No. AN-VV-O-446) was a high viscosity fluid that was easily affected by cold. This property of the oil limited its use in high power engines in high altitude flight, and made engine design more difficult. At increasing altitude the high air content in the oil and the cavitation (i.e. choking) of the pumps limited the altitude the aircraft could attain. When the outside pressure became so low at high altitude the pumps ceased to operate. To remedy the situation engineers supercharged the oil tank and redesigned the line leading to the pump to reduce all possible pressure loss. In effect, this reduced the altitude inside the oil tanks, so they could operate. Also, if very low temperatures were encountered the flight engineer could dilute the oil with gasoline by switches that operated four solenoid valves to control the dilution of oil. These 37D6210-Rev E oil dilution solenoids were electrically-operated and remotely-controlled, and were installed on the right side of each nacelle, and located on a line leading from the fuel supply to the Y-drain valve.

Oil cells: (See Wing)

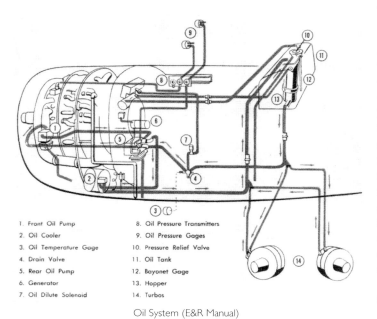

1. Front Oil Pump
2. Oil Cooler
3. Oil Temperature Gage
4. Drain Valve
5. Rear Oil Pump
6. Generator
7. Oil Dilute Solenoid
8. Oil Pressure Transmitters
9. Oil Pressure Gages
10. Pressure Relief Valve
11. Oil Tank
12. Bayonet Gage
13. Hopper
14. Turbos

Oil System (E&R Manual)

Fuel System

Selector Valves: The fuel valve control system was completely electrical, with the exception of the manual drain valve in the forward bomb bay. Four fuel selector valves directed fuel from the tanks to the engines, or into the cross feed lines. A fifth selector valve directed the fuel from the cross feed lines to the drain valves, and connected the left and right wing systems through the cross feed. The No.2 and No.3 selector valves and the drain valves were located on the front spar in the bomb bay area. The No.1 and No.4 selector valves were located on the front spar between the inboard and outboard engines. The control switch knob was rotated clockwise or counterclockwise for selection of any desired position of the valve ports. Any set of fuel tanks could either be drained, or used to supply all engines if necessary. Fuel could be transferred from any set of tanks by operating the booster pump of the tanks to be drained, and opening the ports of the fuel selector tanks to be filled.

Booster Pumps: Each fuel tank had a 24 volt DC electric motor operated booster pump submerged at the bottom of the inboard cell. The booster pump provided pressure to the priming solenoid for engine starting, supplied vapor-free fuel to the engine-driven pump at high altitudes, and acted as emergency fuel pumps in case the engine-driven pumps failed. The booster pump switches were located on the fuel pump panel, and had HIGH (21.5psi), LOW (8 to 10psi), and OFF positions.

Engine-Driven Fuel Pumps: Each engine was equipped with this pump. The pumps had a bypass valve that allowed the booster pump to pump fuel to the engine in case of its failure.

Fuel Pump: A type AN-4102 rotary, four-vane, positive displacement fuel pump was mounted on a pad on the left side of the accessory case of each engine. The pump consisted of a cast aluminum alloy housing containing a sleeve with an eccentric bore, in which a rotor with four vanes was driven by a drive shaft coupled to the engine drive gear. The pump was equipped with an integral, disc-type, spring-controlled, adjustable relief valve and bypass that maintained constant fuel pressure. When the fuel pressure was greater than the tension on the relief valve spring the valve was forced open, and the fuel was bypassed from the discharge side of the relief valve back to the intake side.

Gauges and Instruments: Each tank had a liquidometer fuel level gauge that had floats, whose position in the tank was transmitted electrically to dual indicators on the instrument panel. One indicator showed the fuel level in the right wing tanks, and the other the level in the left tanks. For checking fuel levels on the ground there were float-type gauges in the main gear nacelles for the outboard tanks, and in the bomb bays for the inboard tanks.

A fuel pressure transmitter was located in each nacelle, and was connected to the carburetor by a fuel pressure line. The pressure differential was transmitted to dual indicators on the instrument panel.

Vent System: The venting system maintained normal pressure in the tanks. The system either relieved excess pressure, or provided air to replace the fuel consumed. All of the vent lines ended at openings in the lower surface of the wing, slightly outboard of the No.1 and No.4 engines.

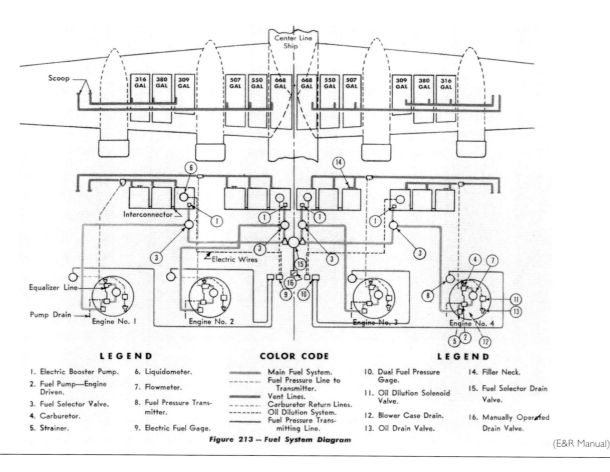

LEGEND

1. Electric Booster Pump.
2. Fuel Pump—Engine Driven.
3. Fuel Selector Valve.
4. Carburetor.
5. Strainer.
6. Liquidometer.
7. Flowmeter.
8. Fuel Pressure Transmitter.
9. Electric Fuel Gage.

COLOR CODE

Main Fuel System.
Fuel Pressure Line to Transmitter.
Vent Lines.
Carburetor Return Lines.
Oil Dilution System.
Fuel Pressure Transmitting Line.

10. Dual Fuel Pressure Gage.
11. Oil Dilution Solenoid Valve.
12. Blower Case Drain.
13. Oil Drain Valve.

LEGEND

14. Filler Neck.
15. Fuel Selector Drain Valve.
16. Manually Operated Drain Valve.

Figure 213 – Fuel System Diagram

(E&R Manual)

After a five-hour mission, one 3,000 gallon tanker and its four-man crew could service a bomber with fuel oil and oxygen in 25 minutes. (USAAF)

Fuel Transfer

Fuel transfer from one tank to another was done by opening the respective selector valves from the tanks to the cross feed lines, and turning the booster pumps to LOW for the tank from which the fuel was being transferred, and OFF for the tank being filled. The drain selector valve was to be on CROSSFEED.

Fuel Tanks (See Wing)

Refueling

After a five hour mission one 3,000 gallon tanker and its four-man crew could service a bomber with fuel, oil, and oxygen in 25 minutes (not all of the bomber's 5,460 gallons of fuel was used during a five hour mission). Three bombers serviced by four men per aircraft, with the fuel tanker refilling twice, could complete the servicing in 1:45.

Normal Fuel System Operation

The SOP for feeding each engine from its respective fuel tank was to set each selector valve to the TANK TO ENGINE position, and the drain selector valve to the CROSSFEED position, with the correct fuel pressure for flight being 16 to 18psi. This was also the correct procedure for takeoff and landing (if there was enough fuel for landing). On long missions it was necessary to transfer fuel from the inboard to the outboard tanks, as the latter did not have as much capacity as the inboard tanks. Normal procedure was to begin the transfer of fuel as soon as there was space in the tanks to do so. This procedure would constantly balance the fuel load. The Fuel Management Chart described the various methods of utilizing fuel in different tank to engine combinations, as well as methods of transferring fuel.

Engine Mounting

Vibration is a normal characteristic of every aircraft engine, and it is the principal source of vibration in an aircraft. In and of itself vibration is not damaging to an engine, but can adversely affect the propeller and nacelles. Aircraft instruments are very sensitive to vibration, and need shock absorbing mounts. Vibrations could eventually loosen bolts, rivets, and fittings on the hydraulic or fuel lines, causing leaks. Fuel pumps could fail, causing the engines to shut down, while hydraulic pump failures could affect gear, flaps, and brakes, causing takeoff and landing accidents. The great vibration of the Wright R-3350 engine caused the small resistors and resister clips of the propeller governor used in the engine feathering system to fracture and malfunction, and Wright engineers worked to redesign and improve them to solve the problem.

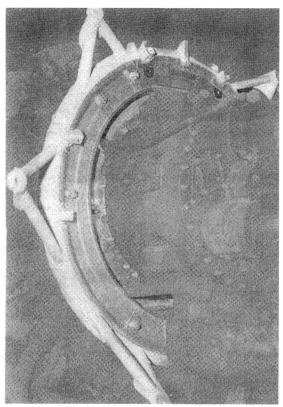

Engine mount L and R (E&R Manual)

It was the job of the Vibration Unit to locate and eliminate vibration, and Boeing estimated that its Vibration Unit eliminated about 70% of R-3350 engine vibration. In the preliminary design stage of development vibration engineers examined engine-propeller combinations, their installation in the nacelles, and the shock mounts cushioning the engine in the nacelles. Engine vibration was caused by the rpm of the turning engine, but not always in a direct proportion. Also, the engine was geared so that the propeller did not rotate at the same speed as the engine. The four propellers were each a source of vibration, and each engine had the internal vibration of its many moving parts. R-3350 mounting was unusual, in that it was suspended from the rocker boxes. The loads were transmitted through the rocker shaft and rocker box, and then through the cylinder head. This suspension system was effective, but made cylinder changes difficult.

Spark Plugs

The four engines of the B-32 contained 144 spark plugs, and to change the 36 on each early engine the propeller, cowl ring, and side panels had to be removed. Later cowls had removable side panels to make plug changes easier, and these panels were retrofitted on the earlier engines. Early spark plugs used mica as an insulating material, and its major source was in northeast India, which was being threatened by the Japanese. Champion Spark Plugs developed the ceramic insulating material that is standard in today's plugs. The spark plugs tended to foul at lower rpms, and condensation formed in the humid weather conditions; the engines had to be run up briefly after starting to clear it. Champion continually redesigned and improved its plugs, and found remedies to meet theater conditions.

Engine Cooling

The major problem with the R-3350 from early XB-29 testing and the loss of Eddie Allen and his crew was in flight fires and overheating, which would subsequently cause numerous B-29s to abort takeoffs, or to return to base prematurely. Engine cooling was such a problem in the early B-29s that airplane commanders quipped that they had as much tri-motor time on the bomber as four motor! However, engine cooling was not a major problem in the B-32 program, probably due to its lighter empty and gross weights.

The Wright R-3350 Cyclone 18 was the largest contemporary engine, weighing 2,595 pounds "dry weight" (e.g. without accessories), and measuring 55 inches in diameter and 75 inches long. The large bulk of the air-cooled radial engine needed to have outside airflow over it for cooling. (USAAF)

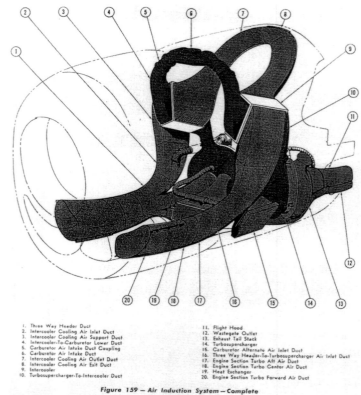

1. Three Way Header Duct
2. Intercooler Cooling Air Inlet Duct
3. Intercooler Cooling Air Support Duct
4. Intercooler-To-Carburetor Lower Duct
5. Carburetor Air Intake Duct Coupling
6. Carburetor Air Intake Duct
7. Intercooler Cooling Air Outlet Duct
8. Intercooler Cooling Air Exit Duct
9. Intercooler
10. Turbosupercharger-To-Intercooler Duct
11. Flight Hood
12. Wastegate Outlet
13. Exhaust Tail Stack
14. Turbosupercharger
15. Carburetor Alternate Air Inlet Duct
16. Three Way Header-To-Turbosupercharger Air Inlet Duct
17. Engine Section Turbo Aft Air Duct
18. Engine Section Turbo Center Air Duct
19. Heat Exchanger
20. Engine Section Turbo Forward Air Duct

Figure 159 – Air Induction System – Complete

(E&R Manual)

The Wright R-3350 Cyclone 18 was the largest contemporary engine, weighing 2,595 pounds "dry weight" (e.g. without accessories), and measuring 55 inches in diameter and 75 inches long. The large bulk of the air-cooled radial engine needed to have outside airflow over it for cooling. The induction system of an aircraft was the large system of ducts that was to supply and regulate air for the engine to "breathe." Air from the front of the cowl inlet was to be inducted to the carburetor, and while progressing through the induction system, air passed through filters, inter-coolers, and a number of openings to provide air to all portions of the engine requiring air-cooling. The primary design problem of the XB-29 and XB-32 was to provide the required airflow to cool the engines, and to eliminate unneeded airflow. Wright had several other engines—notably the R-1820s used in the B-17—in production, and several others were being built under subcontracts; thus, the Wright engineering department was unable to devote its full attention to the R-3350's early problems.

In the CBI and Pacific B-29s operated from bases where the ground temperatures radiating off the hot taxiways was often well over 120°F. This temperature exceeded the minimum carburetor air temperature for the engine, and caused the engines to strain and overheat. Normally 20 minutes of ground running time was the maximum, but when the weather became hot, to avert long taxi times B-29s occasionally had to be towed to the end of the runway before starting their engines. Overheated cylinders reduced the available power by 200 or more horsepower on takeoff. The lower rpm tended to foul spark plugs, which caused the bomber to taxi at a high rpm, causing the engines to heat to dangerous levels. Shorter taxiing times and takeoffs during cooler times of the day were the obvious remedies, but often were not viable. Champion worked on improved spark plug designs for theater conditions that were specially shipped by air and installed.

Early operational R-3350 engines were severely tested in the B-29 when they ferried very heavy loads of fuel across the Himalayan Hump from India to their new bases in China. Wright designers had anticipated that heavy loads were to be carried, but expected that the B-29 and B-32 would fly the first several hours at low altitude, gradually burning off fuel, becoming lighter, and gaining altitude (which the B-29 would do flying from the Marianas to Japan, and later the B-32s flying from the Philippines and Okinawa). But for the Hump flights the B-29s had to climb immediately to 20,000 feet, first because of the chronic Indian cloudy weather, and second to avoid the heavy Air Transport Command air traffic, primarily C-47s that had to fly at lower altitudes, and then to cross the world's highest mountains to China.

With the early R-3350 engines pilots had problems maintaining their engines on the right side of the power curve. Under ideal conditions a B-32 flew at 200 mph, with the cylinder heads at normal temperatures and the cowl flaps closed. If the flight engineer observed that the engine temperature had increased five degrees he opened the cowl flaps three degrees to bring the temperature down. However, the drag from the opened cowls caused the airspeed to drop, and the pilot then had to increase the power to regain speed, but this correction caused the engine temperature to rise again. Then, in a vicious cycle, the flight engineer would open the cowl flaps wider to lower the temperature, and the bomber would again slow down. To correctly adjust this situation, the pilot had to dive the bomber to get it back "on step." The "step" is that position of the airfoil at which the aircraft flies the fastest with the minimum power output. As the bomber in-

Air from the front of the cowl inlet was to be inducted to the carburetor, and while progressing through the induction system, air passed through filters, inter-coolers, and a number of openings to provide air to all portions of the engine requiring air-cooling. (LeVine via Dembeck)

creased its speed in the dive the pilot had to reduce power and close the cowl flaps. The increased airspeed and lower power setting cooled the engines, and put the bomber on the proper side of the power curve.

Engine cylinder head overheating remained a problem throughout the war, and the cowl flaps were a major cause and answer to the overheating problem. During taxiing, the cowl flaps were set to their widest opening of 26 degrees, while during landing they were set to 8 degrees. Cowl flaps were set for the highest permissible cylinder head temperature: 470°F for takeoff and 418°F for cruising. Cowl flap position was critical. If it were opened too wide drag was increased, and the bomber would drop behind the formation. If it was not opened wide enough the engine would overheat. Recommended cowl flap settings did not allow for discrepancies in instruments and in thermocouples, which were often out of calibration.

The cowling was composed of a fixed cowling ring, a set of side panels, 10 movable cowl flaps, and two immobile flaps on the top of the cowl. The cowl flaps were installed on each nacelle to electrically regulate the cooling of the engines via toggle switches on the flight engineer's panel. There was a thermocouple on each engine that was connected to the flight engineer's panel, and indicated the cylinder head temperature of each engine, allowing the flight engineer to regulate the cowl flaps for the desired temperature. Cowl flap position was indicated on a gauge on the flight engineer's panel. The cowl flaps and intercooler flaps were operated by

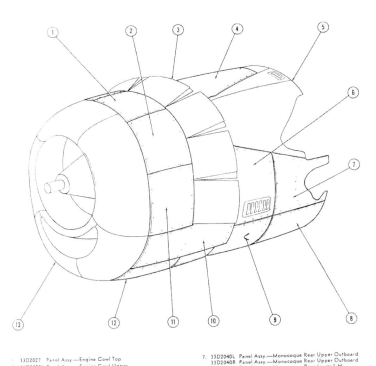

1. 33D2027 Panel Assy.—Engine Cowl Top
2. 33D2028L Panel Assy.—Engine Cowl Upper
3. 33D2003 Installation—Engine Cowl Flaps
4. 33D2034 Door Assy.—Monocoque Access
5. 33D2010 Structure Assy.—Monocoque
6. 33D2036L Panel Assy.—Monocoque Forward Upper Outboard
   33D2036R Panel Assy.—Monocoque Read Upper Outboard

7. 33D2040L Panel Assy.—Monocoque Rear Upper Outboard
   33D2040R Panel Assy.—Monocoque Rear Upper Outboard
8. 33D2039 Panel Assy.—Monocoque Rear Lower L.H.
9. 33D2038 Panel Assy.—Monocoque Forward Lower R.H.
10. 33D2030 Panel Assy.—Engine Cowl Lower Left Side
11. 33D2029L Panel Assy.—Engine Cowl Center
12. 33D2031 Panel Assy.—Engine Cowl Bottom
13. 33D2004 Cowl Assy.—Engine Nose

Figure 167 – Engine and Nacelle Cowling – Left Side

(E&R Manual)

means of flexible drive shafts interconnecting electrically driven jackscrews controlled by momentary contact (i.e. open-close) switches.

As a remedy it was recommended that the cowl flaps be shortened, and that the top two fixed flaps on each nacelle could be opened. More cooling air was circulated when the cowl flaps were shortened, which effectively rendered the cowl openings as larger, and exposed the engine to cooling air even when the flaps were closed.

Adjustable cowl flaps were installed on the flap support of each engine assembly to regulate the flow of the air through the engine power section for proper engine cooling. The flaps were adjustable from zero to 20 degrees. The cuffs on the propeller shafts increased the flow of air past the cylinders to aid in cooling the engine. The cuffs were particularly effective in ground operation. The cowl flaps were adjusted via a Lear-Avia electric motor located on the top right side of the engine mount, which drove interconnected flexible shafts through a gearbox. These shafts were connected to jack screws at each flap that opened and closed the cowl flaps when the motor was operating. The flaps were controlled from the co-pilot's main instrument panel by a spring-loaded toggle. Positive control

The cowling was composed of a fixed cowling ring, a set of side panels, 10 movable cowl flaps, and two immobile flaps on the top of the cowl. The cowl flaps were installed on each nacelle to electrically regulate the cooling of the engines via toggle switches on the flight engineer's panel. (LeVine via Dembeck)

of the flaps was provided by mechanical stops on the screw jacks and a limit switch assembly in the motorized unit.

There were other overheating fixes. After concentrating on the R-2800, the award of large engine contracts forced Wright to direct attention to the cooling problems encountered by the R-3350. It installed cuffs on the root of the propeller blades, improved cylinder baffle designs, added seals to increase airflow to the cylinders, modified collector ring installation, and improved valve cooling by designing inter rocker box lubrication lines to flood the valve stem, upper guide, and spring with oil to carry away the excess heat. Alterations were made to the engine and cowling ducting, and reduced the potential for backfiring and induction system fires. But it was mainly the changes to the cowling and cowl flaps, along with the induction system improvements and engine modifications, that enabled Wright to overcome the R-3350's overheating problems. Because the B-29 became operational first, and the success of its R-3350s was given high priority, the B-32 benefited from the engine fixes, and had a much lower combat testing incidence of engine cooling problems at high gross weights.

Engine Accessories

Starter
The first R-3350s had a shot gun starter that was installed on the B-19 and Consolidated Model 31 seaplane. The electric starter was installed on the three XB-29s and three XB-32s. In early model B-32s each engine was equipped with a combination inertia and direct cranking Jack and Heintz JH4E starter that was mounted on the engine accessory drive cover. The starter allowed either manual or electric cranking of the engine. The starter was operated electrically by a double-throw, momentary contact toggle switch. The starter switch, when held in the ACCELERATE position, operated the starter motor that accelerated the inertial flywheel to approximately 2,000rpm. When the starter switch was moved to START, the starter jaws and engine jaws engaged. A disc clutch in the starter functioned as a shock absorber and as a torque limiter, preventing excessive loads from damaging the starter or engine. The starter motor was in operation with the starter switch in either the ACCELERATE or START positions, and was able to maintain rotation of the engine after the energy of the flywheel had been expended. Engine cranking without the use of an electric starter motor was brought about by manually accelerating the flywheel with a hand crank. The hand crank operated in a gearbox on the crank support, where the rpm was stepped up and then transmitted to the flywheel gearbox by a flexible shaft. The starter needed to be cooled for one minute once it had been meshed before it was to energize again. A starter was not to be meshed for more than one minute.

The engines on later model aircraft were equipped with an Eclipse E-95996 starter and flexible shaft from the gearbox to a connector located on the lower side of the nacelle skin. An Eclipse No. E93231 portable external energizer driven by the auxiliary power plant applied power to a gearbox through the flexible shaft.

Generator
See Electrical System for detailed description.

Results of Combat Engine Testing
Despite multiple oil leaks throughout the engine that required substantial maintenance time, the engine operation was considered "satisfactory," especially considering the Wright's developmental problems. In the nearly

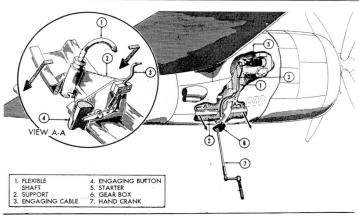

1. FLEXIBLE SHAFT	4. ENGAGING BUTTON
2. SUPPORT	5. STARTER
3. ENGAGING CABLE	6. GEAR BOX
	7. HAND CRANK

Figure 203 — Engine Starter Installation

(E&R Manual)

673 hours that the three B-32s had flown in 11 combat test missions and numerous training missions, only three engine changes were required. Two changes were due to lock washer valve failures in the reduction gear assembly, and the other was due to a swallowed valve. No cooling problems were noted, and cylinder head temperatures rarely exceeded 260°C, and could easily be held lower. Backfires—a previous problem—were infrequent, except due to faulty starting procedures. Blow by and compression problems were not encountered. Fortunately, the engine reliability negated the lack of spare engines available in the Philippines. Also nacelle assemblies, complete from the firewall forward, were in insufficient supply, and were required for the Service Squadron to be able to make overnight engine changes.

Equipment Lost Per Engine Loss

If the No.1 or No.4 engines failed then the following were lost:

> Fuel Pump
> Heat Exchanger
> Heat Exchanger for wing anti-icing

If No.2 or No.3 engines failed then the following were lost:

> Fuel Pump
> Hydraulic pump
> Generator
> Vacuum pump
> Heat exchanger for cabin heating

Fire Extinguisher System
Engine Fire Extinguisher System

The first 35 B-32s were built with a CO_2 fire extinguishing system of 24 CO_2 bottles; 12 cylinders were installed in the rear section of each of the outboard nacelles, with lines from six routed to each engine, and with outlets around the cylinders and in each engine accessory section. Each cylinder was charged to five pounds of gas. For operation four "T" handles, one for each engine, were located in the flight deck convenient to the co-pilot. The "T" handles had cables leading to the gas cylinders, and one pull on a handle discharged all six cylinders into the selected engine and accessory section of the nacelle.

Aircraft after No.35 had a one-shot fixed system installed, consisting of seven CO_2 bottles located in the rear bomb bay. In this system all the CO_2 was discharged into the selected engine nacelle by flipping one of the four guarded electrical toggle switches located to the right of the co-pilot. This system could not be operated manually. The CO_2 was directed by lines from each bottle: two lines into the turbo inlets of the induction system; two to the exhaust tail pipe shrouds; two to the nacelle accessory system; and one to the primary heat exchanger.

Fire Detector System

Each nacelle had a fire warning system consisting of tubing installed in the nacelles that, when subjected to a heat of 350°F, caused a tin alloy to melt and scatter beads, that then completed a circuit between the exterior copper conductor and the exterior copper plating that had not been affected. Then a warning light located in the flight deck indicated a fire in a specific engine. Four warning lights, and a set of test lights to indicate if the detector system was operable, were provided.

EQUIPMENT LOSS PER ENGINE LOSS

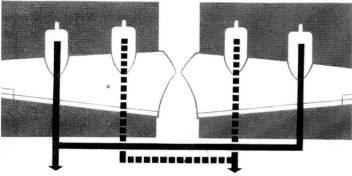

If No. 1 engine or No. 4 engine fails, you lose:

Fuel pump   Two-speed generator

Heat exchanger for wing anti-icing

If No. 2 or No. 3 engine fails, you lose:

Fuel pump   Hydraulic pump

Generator   Heat exchanger for cabin heating

Vacuum pump

(E&R Manual)

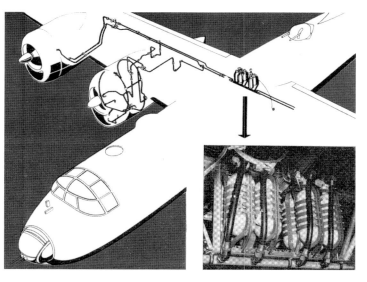

(E&R Manual)

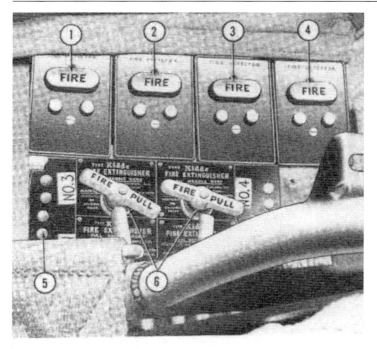

Figure 29 — Engine Fire Extinguisher Controls

(E&R Manual)

Portable CO₂ Fire Extinguishers

Two portable type 4TB CO_2 extinguishers were provided, one on the right flight deck floor between stations 2.0 and 3.0, and one in the rear cabin mounted on the right forward side of bulkhead 8.0. The fire extinguishers were held by mounting brackets and a snap clamp. The fire extinguishes were discharged by pressing the trigger in the handle after the horn was directed to the base of the flame.

Propellers

The four 16.67 foot Hamilton-Standard (a division of United Aircraft Corp.) hydromatic, constant speed, full-feathering electric, four-bladed hollow propellers (type C-644S-A22 and A24) were the largest fitted to an American production aircraft. The steel blades were painted flat black, with Hamilton Standard decals at mid-prop. There was a stencil near the hub end of the blade with the propeller specs, and there was a six inch yellow tip. The automatic control system was used to synchronize the four engines at the desired speed by means of a proportional synchronizer and alternator. The B-32's combination of the Curtiss automatic synchronizer and reverse thrust propeller was the first production installation of these features on a large land-based aircraft. The synchronizer had been previously fitted to Consolidated's PB2Y-3 Coronado flying boat, while the reversible propellers had also been used for several years to improve their water maneuverability. The synchronizer gave constant speed control for each of the four engines by altering the propeller blade angles, therefore maintaining accurate synchronization throughout various flight conditions. The two inboard propellers had a blade reversing mechanism to cause a reverse thrust to aid braking upon landing.

Publicity photo of 42-108471 at Fort Worth in November 1944 with (R-L) R.T. LeVine (1st Flight Engineer), P.F. Freckelton (Engineer), and L.C. Brandvig (2nd Engineer). The photo clearly shows the Martin Type A-3F-A top turret and 16.67ft Hamilton-Standard hydromatic, constant speed, full-feathering electric, four-bladed hollow propeller, which were the largest fitted to an American production aircraft. The bomb bay doors are open. (LeVine)

Propeller Components

1) Hub Assembly: The hub was spider-machined from a solid steel alloy forging. It served as a mount for six bronze slip rings, one of which was bonded to the hub and insulated from the remaining five rings. The other five rings—four blade assemblies and a slinger ring—were insulated from the hub and each other. The hub assembly was drilled and insulated to carry electric power conduits from the slip rings to the power unit. Five insulated brass connector rods carried electric current from the slip rings through passages in the hub to the contact rods at the front face of the hub. The contact rods were seated in a bushing assembly that transferred the current to the power unit to complete the electrical circuits to the electric motor. Seals were placed around the insulators to prevent grease from leaking through. A slinger ring and tubes for anti-icing were part of the hub assembly.

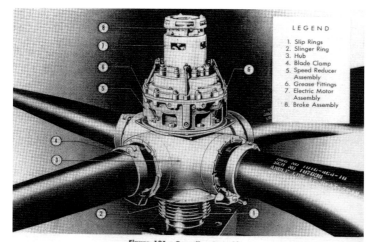

Figure 181 — Propeller Assembly

(E&R Manual)

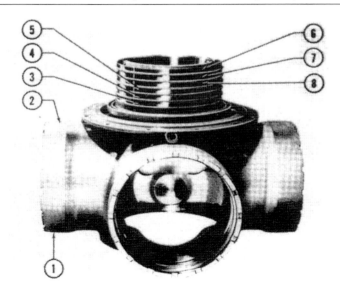

1. Hub.
2. Slinger Ring.
3. Increase RPM Slip Ring.
4. Feathering Slip Ring.
5. Reversing Slip Ring.
6. Bonding Slip Ring.
7. Common Slip Ring.
8. Decrease RPM Slip Ring.

Figure 182 — Hub Assembly and Slip Rings
(E&R Manual)

2) Blade Assemblies: The four hollow steel propeller blades contained shanks that were threaded inside to accommodate the bevel gears. Installed on the shank of each blade was a bearing assembly consisting of a stack of four individual angular contact type ball bearings, a seal, and a blade retaining nut that secured the blade in the hub socket. The bearing assembly allowed the blade to freely rotate in the hub under high centrifugal loads. A plug was installed in the blade gear to prevent hub lubrication from getting into the blade, causing an out-of-balance condition. A seal placed in the blade nut prevented the hub lubricant from escaping. The blade nut was slotted to take balance weight and the blade nut locking key. Aluminum alloy cuffs around each blade shank improved engine cooling. Collectors attached to the shank of each blade collected the anti-icing fluid, along the leading edge of the blade.

3) Brake Assembly: The brake assembly consisted of two solenoid-operated brakes that stopped the electric motor armature when the blades reached the selected angle. During increased rpm operation, one brake acted as a drag to prevent the rpms from increasing too fast. The brakes held the rpms constant when the propellers were operated at a fixed pitch. If the electric current failed, the brakes held the props at that angle.

4) Power Gear Assembly: The power gear, mounted in a steel adapter, was a spiral bevel gear that meshed with the blade gears. It was splined internally to engage with the splines of the low speed movable ring gear of the rear speed reducer. An angular thrust bearing absorbed the power gear thrust. The power gear assembly transmitted the torque force from the speed reducer through a system of bevel gears to the blade assembly to bring about a change of blade angle.

5) Power Unit Assembly: The power unit assembly consisted of a cut out switch, small reversible motor, a brake, and a speed reducer that were divided into two parts, the front and rear housings. The two stages of the planetary gearing were contained in these housings, while gaskets between the housings and seals at each end made the unit oil-tight. The unit was partially filled with oil having an extremely low pout point, which assured operation at high altitude and low temperatures.

Cut Out Switch Assemblies: The power unit cut out (or limit) switches were located in the rear housing. These closed circuit; spring-loaded switches were opened by cams that were tripped by cam segments. The cams controlled the low (17 degrees), high (57 degrees), feather (84.7 degrees), and reverse blade angle (-15.7 degrees) limits. The cams opened the cut out switches according to the degree of rotation of the movable ring gear at specified blade angle limits.

Electric Motor Assembly: The reversible electric motor bolted to the speed reducer front housing was of the series type, and had two field windings that provided for rotation in either direction. It received its power from the aircraft's power supply via the brush and slip ring assembly. The reverse feature allowed the increase or decrease of rpm, depending on the direction of the motor's rotation.

Magnetic Brake Assembly: The brake assembly was mounted on the front of the electric motor, and consisted of the inner and outer brake cage assembly.

Speed Reducer: The speed reducer converted the relatively high rpm and low torque of the electric motor into high torque and low rpm to produce the necessary force to change the blade angle.

6) Brush and Slip Ring Assemblies: The slip ring brush assembly was mounted in an aluminum housing bolted to the nose section of the engine.

Propeller Operation
Switches located on the main instrument panel controlled the propellers. For the propeller to operate automatically, the propeller master motor control switch was moved to the ON position, the control knob was turned

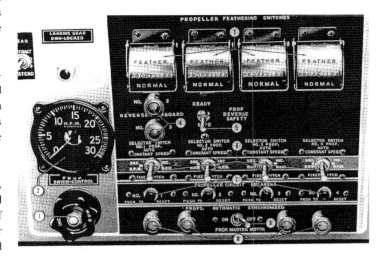

1. Synchroniser Control Knob.
2. Master Tachometer.
3. Feathering Switches.
4. Reverse Tel-Lights.
5. Reverse Safety Switch.
6. Selector Switches.
7. Circuit Breakers.
8. Automatic Tel-Lights.
9. Master Motor Switch.

Figure 200 — Propeller Panel

(E&R Manual)

until the desired rpm reading was indicated by the master control motor tachometer, and the selector switch for each propeller was placed in the AUTOMATIC position.

The propeller was operated electrically from the aircraft's power supply. The ideal engine speed could be selected manually by setting the master tachometer, after which the propeller control automatically maintained the selected speed by adjusting blade pitch, which then automatically synchronized all engines and propellers. During manual control the inboard propellers were furnished fixed pitch, and reverse pitch and feathering.

The electrical energy for changing propeller pitch passed through brushes mounted in a housing attached to the nose of the engine, to slip rings mounted on the rear boss of the propeller hub, and then to the pitch changing motor through connector leads to the hubs. A two-stage planetary gear speed reducer that drove a master bevel gear controlled the blade setting angle. A double field winding in the electric motor was designed to operate in either a clockwise or counterclockwise direction, reversing the pitch change.

In order to develop sufficient torque the electric motor drove a high ratio two-stage planetary type speed reducer. In the first stage, the action of the planetary gearing reduced the speed of the high-speed bell gear, but increased torque. A similar action was repeated in the second stage, with a further reduction of speed, but with enough torque to drive the single bevel power gear that meshed with the bevel gears attached to the shank of each blade.

The propeller blade angle was then able to be increased or decreased, as required, according to the direction in which the electric motor was made to rotate, and according to the duration of the motor rotation, as regulated by either the automatic constant speed control or the selective fixed pitch control.

A brake assembly consisting of an inner and outer brake held the blades at a selected angle. The outer brake was released by a solenoid connected in series with both the increase and decrease rpm windings of the motor, and was applied by spring forces acting against the rear outer brake when the motor was not running. The inner brake was released by a solenoid connected in series with the decrease rpm winding of the motor, and was applied by spring forces acting against the inner brake plate when the motor was not running, or when the blades were being rotated toward the low blade angle.

The cut out (limit) switches located in the rear housing of the speed reducer limited the high and low blade angles to within the flight range. The switches also stopped the blade angle change at the feather and reverse positions. The high and low cut out switches were effective in selective fixed pitch. The reverse and low angle cut out switches were effective in reverse pitch.

Reverse Pitch
The reverse pitch was used as a brake during landing by reversing the two inboard propellers. To reverse these propellers the throttles had to be placed at idling (800rpm), the mixture control to AUTOMATIC RICH, the reverse safety switch to READY, and the reverse normal switch (located under a spring-loaded door on the inboard side of the pilot's pedestal) was placed in the REVERSE position. During the reverse pitch procedure the throttle had to be maintained so that the engine tachometer would not drop below 800rpm at any time. When the reverse blade angle was attained, the reverse pitch amber tell tale light lit, the reverse safety switch was set to SAFE, and the engines were ready for braking. To return the engines from reverse they had to be idled at 800rpm, and the reverse-normal switch was returned to NORMAL. When the blades reached the low blade angle, as indicated by the green automatic tell tale light, normal propeller operation could be continued.

The advantages of the use of reversible pitch propellers were that it gave a high degree of directional control, and minimized landing roll and brake wear. However, the TB and B-32 aircraft had only the inboard propellers installed with reverse pitch, and it was recommended that it be installed on all four propellers, and that there should also be selective operation of the inboard and outboard propellers in case of engine failure.

The B-32 was the first land-based bomber to use the reversible propeller, and their success led to the decision to use them on the Martin-built B-29s of the 509th Composite Group of the 313th Bomb Wing Bombardment. It was considered important that the *Enola Gay* and *BOCK'S CAR*, carrying the atomic bombs, be able to stop quickly in case of malfunction during the takeoff run.

Feathering
A comprehensive description of propeller feathering and unfeathering is discussed elsewhere.

Systems

Hydraulic System

Unlike the B-29, which was an "all-electric bomber," the B-32 was a "hydraulic bomber." The B-32 was provided with:

1) Main (open center) system actuated by engine-driven pumps for normal operation,
2) Brake (accumulator type) system, containing a separate tank, pump, and lines.
3) Emergency system containing separate tank, selector valves, and lines. It was driven by electrically-driven pumps for use in the event of main system failure.
4) Turret system, with a completely independent unit for the extension and retraction of the belly turret.

The B-32's hydraulic system was powerful enough to raise the average automobile 17 stories in one minute. To reduce vulnerability the system was centrally located, and all the long vulnerable hydraulic tubes were protected by fuses that automatically stopped the flow of fluid to any line that was damaged in combat.

PRESSURE
LANDING GEAR
FLAPS
BOMB BAY DOORS

1. Open Center Pressure Gage
2. Shuttle Valve
3. Nose Gear Unlatching Jack
4. Nose Gear Cylinder
5. Restrictor
6. Engine-driven Pump
7. Disconnect Couplings
8. Check Valve
9. Filter
10. Main Reservoir
11. Return Line
12. Open Center Relief Valve
13. Check Restrictor
14. Main Selector Valve
15. Bomb Door Hydraulic Motor
16. Flap Lock Valve
17. Pressure Relief Valve
18. Flap Hydraulic Motor
19. Proportional Flow Divider
20. Main Gear Unlatching Jack
21. Main Gear Down lock Jack
22. Main Gear Auxiliary Cylinder
23. Main Gear By-pass Valve
24. Main Gear Cylinder

Main Hydraulic System

The main system provided fluid pressure for the landing gear, bomb bay doors, and the flap assembly. It was an open center system, meaning that the hydraulic fluid circulated freely in a completely closed circuit when no hydraulic mechanisms other than engine-driven pumps were operating. The system was centrally located to reduce vulnerability from battle damage, and the hydraulic lines were protected by fuses to stop the flow of fluid in case of perforation. Selector and brake valves were located as close as possible to the mechanisms they motivated to reduce line lengths. The valves were electrically or cable operated, with manual controls for emergencies.

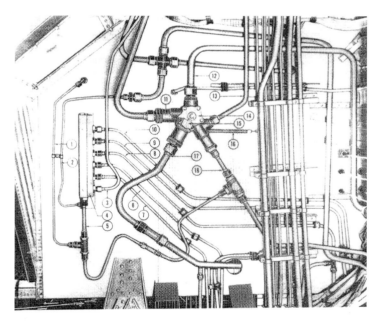

1. Emergency Pressure Gage Line
2. Emergency Selector Valve Return Line
3. Main Reservoir Refill Line
4. Emergency Selector Valve
5. Emergency Pressure Line
6. Bomb Doors "Closed" Line
7. Bomb Doors "Open" Line
8. Landing Gear "Extension" Line
9. Inboard Flap "Extension" Line
10. Outboard Flap "Extension" Line
11. Brake Reservoir Suction Line
12. Electric Pump Suction Line
13. Pressure Line to Accumulators
14. Switch-Over Valve
15. Limit Switch
16. Spring, Normal Valve Operation
17. Emergency Reservoir Suction Line
18. Electric Pump Pressure Line

Figure 369 – Hydraulic Installations – Aft Side of Bulkhead 4.0

The brake system consisted of two separate systems to compensate for the failure of one system.

Operation of any of these systems was controlled by a solenoid operated multiple selector valve that directed the flow of fluid from the main system to the actuating mechanism. Control switches were located on the pilot's and bombardier's instrument panels. Solenoids actuated both the selected operating valve and the pressure control valve, which operated simultaneously with all operating valve solenoids. The pressure control valve blocked the return flow, and directed pressure to the selected operating valve. When the hydraulic unit completed its travel (e.g. gear up), limit microswitches de-energized the solenoids, and all valves were returned to neutral. From the selector valve, return fluid from the units passed through a check valve back to the tank. The Main System consisted of:

Tank: The main system tank had a capacity of 3.1 gallons, and was located in the center of the forward bomb bay. The tank contained filters with relief valves (8psi) that bypassed fluid to the bottom of the tank in case of clogging. In an emergency the main tank could be filled from the emergency tank.

Pumps: From the main tank hydraulic fluid flowed through check valves and firewall disconnects to the two engine-driven pumps on No.2 and No.3 engines.

Main Selector Valves: Fluid flowed from the pumps through the disconnects, check valves, and filter, and past the main system pressure relief valves (set to 1,500psi) to the main selector valve. This valve was located under the upper bomb bay rack support beam in the forward bomb bay, and contained four separate solenoid-operated valves bolted together. Three of these were operation-controlled valves for bomb bays, flaps, and landing gear. The fourth was a pressure control valve that held pressure fluid for the selector valve when the operating valve was in use. The main system pressure gauge came from the unit (pressure) side of the valve. The main selector valve could be operated manually.

The hydraulics of the landing gear, bomb bay doors, brakes, and turrets are discussed in detail elsewhere.

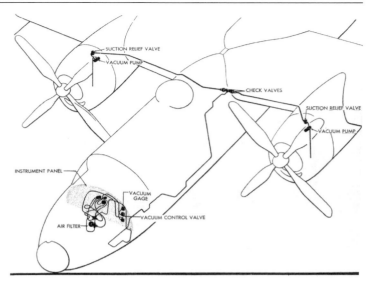

Figure 255 — Schematic of Vacuum System

(E&R Manual)

Vacuum System

The B-32 vacuum system operated the turn and bank indicator, directional gyro, and artificial horizon. The vacuum system consisted of:

Vacuum Pump: Each inboard engine (No.2 and No.3) was equipped with a Pesco No. 3P-207J rotary, four vane, positive displacement vacuum pump mounted on a pad on the left side of the accessory panel. The system automatically began to operate with the starting of either inboard engine, and normally both pumps supplied suction, but either engine alone could supply the system. The function of the pump was to operate air-driven gyroscopic instruments that required an air pressure lower than that of the at-

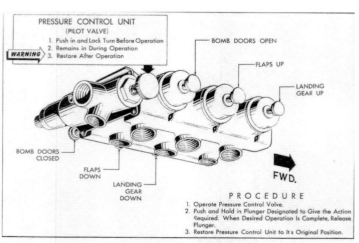

Figure 26 – Main Hydraulic Selector Valve

(E&R Manual)

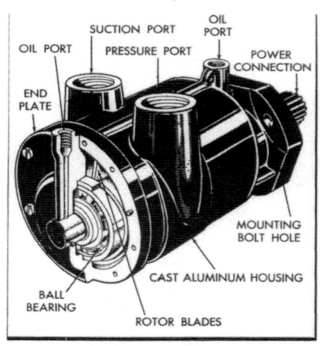

Figure 256 – Vacuum Pump

(E&R Manual)

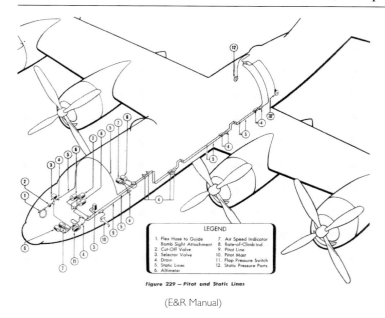

LEGEND
1. Flex Hose to Guide Bomb Sight Attachment
2. Cut-Off Valve
3. Selector Valve
4. Drain
5. Static Lines
6. Altimeter
7. Air Speed Indicator
8. Rate-of-Climb Ind.
9. Pitot Line
10. Pitot Mast
11. Flap Pressure Switch
12. Static Pressure Ports

Figure 229 – Pitot and Static Lines

(E&R Manual)

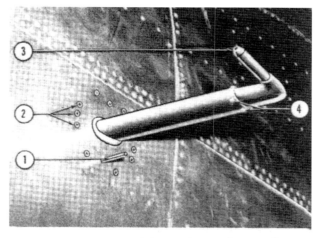

1. Free Air Temperature Bulb.
2. Mounting Screws.
3. Impact Pressure Opening.
4. Attaching Screws.

Figure 234 — Pitot Mast

(E&R Manual)

mosphere. The vacuum pump attained this pressure differential by creating a partial vacuum in the instrument. There was no selector valve to switch pumps in case of pump or engine failure, because check valves acted as automatic cross over valves to use the suction from the functioning pump.

Suction Relief Valve: The Pesco No. 3V-215-V suction relief valve protected the system from excessive pressure by maintaining the constant pressure of approximately 5 inches of Hg for the operation of air-driven gyroscopic flight instruments, as the change in the speed of an aircraft engine in flight resulted in a variation of the speed of the engine-driven vacuum pump, and thus there was a constant variation of the air pressure. When the vacuum on the suction side of the vacuum pump attained a preset force a diaphragm, held in place by a spring, opened and admitted air from the surrounding atmosphere.

Other Vacuum Valves, Gauges, and Filters: The vacuum control valve located on the pilot's auxiliary panel reduced the vacuum from 5 to 2 inches for operating the turn and bank indicator. The vacuum pressure gauge was mounted on the pilot's panel just above the control valve. Check valves near the junction of the two lines protected the instruments from a compressed air charge in case of a backfire. A screen type air filter in the nose, behind the bombardier's panel, protected the system from dirt and dust.

Pitot Static System

There were two pitot masts on the lower right and left side of the fuselage between stations 2.0 and 2.1 that supplied dynamic pressure for the co-pilot's, bombardier's, and navigator's airspeed indicators. Some of the early B-32s had only one set of flight instruments, and had only the left pitot mast installed. There was an electrical heating element controlled by a switch on the co-pilot's auxiliary panel that prevented ice formation inside the pitot tube, and holes drained away the water from the melted ice.

The normal source for the static pressure for the static side of the air speed indicators, and for the operation of the altimeters and rate of climb indicators was supplied from two openings, one on each side of the fuse-

lage forward of the wing. There were two selector valve switches, labeled STATIC TUBE: one on the pilot's auxiliary panel, and the other on the right side of the bombardier's station that, in the UP position, supplied the static pressure. In the DOWN position, labeled ALTERNATE SOURCE, the switch opened the line to a pressure source inside the cockpit in case of failure of the normal source.

Electrical System

The B-32 was equipped with a 24 volt direct power system, using the aircraft structure for the negative return and insulated cables for the positive conductors. There was a complete ring of three conductors in parallel around the fuselage that were interconnected adjacent to the front spar in the fuselage, with three parallel cables that formed a forward ring and rear ring inside of the fuselage power loop. Any one of the three cables was able to carry the power load in case of an emergency.

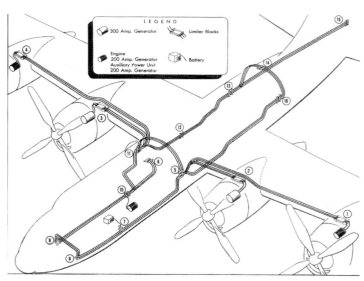

LEGEND
300 Amp. Generator
Engine 200 Amp. Generator
Auxiliary Power Unit 200 Amp. Generator
Limiter Blocks
Battery

Figure 399 – Electrical Power Sources and Distribution

(E&R Manual)

The switches and wiring for the control and indicating circuits of the B-32 were located in a different configuration than on other contemporary aircraft. They were located for isolation so that damage to the right side of the fuselage would only affect the outboard engine, while damage to the left side of the fuselage would only affect the inboard engines. Switches for engines No.1 and No.4 were on the right side of the pilot's compartment, while switches for engines No.2 and No.3 were on the left side. This arrangement was achieved by routing wiring for the outboard engines along the right side of the fuselage to the front wing spar, where wiring for engine No.1 crossed over to the left wing. Wiring for the inboard engine was routed along the left fuselage to the front wing spar, and wiring for engine No.3 crossed over the right wing.

Generators

The main power supply consisted of four generators of the self excited type: Engines No.2 and No.3 each operated one 300 amp, 24 volt DC type R-1 generator; and engines No.1 and No.4 operated two 200 amp, 24 volt DC type P-2 generators. All the generators were cooled by forced air through tubes connected to the intercooler inlet ducts. A two speed gear box was installed into the generator drive of the two outboard engines, allowing the generators to develop full load when the engines were operating at a low rate of speed. The two speed gear boxes began to operate when the engine speed dropped to 1,475rpm, and delivered their rated output down to as low as 800rpm, and disengaged when the engine speed reached 1,625rpm. The generators had an overload capacity of 50%, but it could not be overloaded for more than four minutes without causing serious damage. The DC power system was protected by current limiters instead of fuses. A solenoid operated clutch increased the generator drive ratio through a set of planetary gears. The solenoid circuit was completed by the fly wheel governor when the weights dropped due to the lack of centrifugal force. Each two speed gear box solenoid received power from the co-pilot's circuit breaker panel. These generators were cooled by an "air blast" tube connected to the carburetor air inlet duct, and were regulated for both voltage and equal load. A two-speed generator overdrive was built into the generators on the two outboard nacelles in order to maintain correct engine driven generator speed over a wide range of engine speeds. It was mounted between the pad and the generator. The overdrive had two gear ratios, and operated continuously to maintain the generator speed within its required limits, while the engine ignition switch was on. When the engine ignition switch was off the power to the overdrive unit was also cut off.

Battery

There was only one type F-1 (No.32198), 24 volt, 17 ampere hour battery that was connected to the aircraft's power network through a solenoid, and was controlled by a switch on the co-pilot's auxiliary panel. Twelve cells were connected in series to form a 24 volt battery. The battery was vented from the outside of the fuselage, and then back to the atmosphere. Its capacity was so small that it was easily discharged by even a short use by any electrical equipment. Its sole purpose was to start the APU. Electrical equipment was to be powered by the APU or an outside power source connected through the external power receptacle.

External Power Receptacle

The external power receptacle was located in the rear of the nose wheel well, and was connected to the fuselage power system through a solenoid switch.

Auxiliary Power Unit (APU), also called Auxiliary Power Plant (APP)

A type D-2, model 204 APU engine was a type V-32, four-cycle, two-cylinder, 10 horsepower gasoline engine that drove a P-2 generator. The APU delivered 10 horsepower at sea level, but the power output decreased with altitude. The unit was mounted under the flight deck just forward of the bomb bay, and was attached to its platform by four bolts on shock mounts. The main purpose of the APU was to supply electrical power during the ground check of the equipment, starting, takeoff, and during an in flight emergency. The APU was started from the battery or manually. The recommended procedure for the B-32 was to use an external power source for ground checks and starting, and to save the APU for taxing, takeoff, landing, and emergency power. The APU was to be running during all ground operations of the bomber and its equipment. It was started at least 10 minutes before takeoff and landing, so that it would have the necessary warm up cycle before assuming the power load required from it. The auxiliary power plant had to be running during taxiing, because the brake accumulators were charged only by an electrically-driven pump. The low capacity battery alone could not be depended upon to supply enough power to keep the accumulators charged for more than five minutes of braking, and more time was required for taxing. A manual altitude compensator located on the top of the power plant had a sea level, 5,000 feet, and 10,000 feet adjustment. The power plant's fuel supply was obtained from the No.3 tank's inboard fuel cell via a solenoid operated valve, but had its own oil supply, cooling system, and automatic controls. Exhaust gases were dumped overboard through a pipe that extended through the bottom of the fuselage.

A voltage regulator and a reverse current relay were installed to the right of the APU, forward of station 3.3. The APU had three switches (ignition, equalizer, and generator) that were mounted on the co-pilot's instrument panel to the right of the hydraulic pressure gauges, and had an additional ignition switch located immediately below its choke and throttle. The APU throttle could be controlled on the power plant itself, or remotely by a handle on the floor near the co-pilot's seat. The unit was started elec-

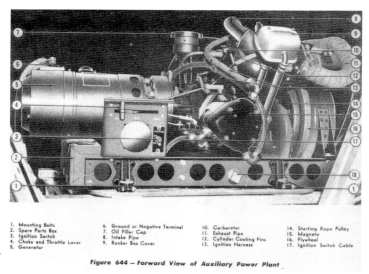

1. Mounting Bolts	6. Ground or Negative Terminal	10. Carburetor	14. Starting Rope Pulley
2. Spare Parts Box	7. Oil Filler Cap	11. Exhaust Pipe	15. Magneto
3. Ignition Switch	8. Intake Pipe	12. Cylinder Cooling Fins	16. Flywheel
4. Choke and Throttle Lever	9. Rocker Box Cover	13. Ignition Harness	17. Ignition Switch Cable
5. Generator			

Figure 644 - Forward View of Auxiliary Power Plant

(E&R Manual)

1. Exhaust Shroud	6. Oil Filler Cap	11. Ground Terminal "E"	15. Tachometer Drive
2. Exhaust Pipe	7. Cooling Holes	12. Voltage Regulator Control	16. Fuel Pump Outlet Line
3. Flywheel	8. Generator	Terminal "A"	17. Fuel Pump
4. Fuel Inlet Line	9. Equalizer Terminal "D"	13. Fuel Vent Line	18. Oil Drain Plug
5. Rocker Box Cover	10. Power Terminal "B"	14. Mounting Bolt	19. Sediment Bowl

Figure 645 – Aft View of Auxiliary Power Plant
(E&R Manual)

trically by the co-pilot, or manually by the crew. A 17-amp battery located next to the unit supplied power for starting, but this battery was too small to operate any other equipment without discharging. A solenoid valve located below the right inboard fuel cell supplied fuel to the power plant (when the generator switch was in the START or LOAD position).

Inverters

Two (MAIN and SPARE) 400 cycle, 750 volt ampere inverters with a 26 volt AC and 115 volt AC output and input of 25 to 28.5 volts DC were installed just aft of the main nose wheel well, and suspended below the floor of the flight deck. They had two voltages: 26 volts for the flux gate compass, and 115 volts for the TBS regulator, radio altimeter, radio compass, fluorescent lighting on the main instrument panel, and the drift meter. A toggle switch on the co-pilot's auxiliary panel controlled the inverters. The down position was for stopping and starting the main inverter, and the up position was for testing the spare inverter. Two red tell tale failure lights (one mounted on the co-pilot's auxiliary panel, and the other on the pilot's instrument panel) indicated that all AC power had failed.

Reverse Current Relays

There were five 24 volt reverse current relays (94-32278), one for each of the four engines located in each nacelle junction box, and the other reverse current relay was located next to the auxiliary power plant under the floor at station 4.0. The purpose of the relay was to connect the generator to the aircraft's electrical system when the generator voltage was sufficiently high. The relay opened automatically in case the generator voltage became lower than the system voltage, preventing a reverse current flow, which would happen if the engine speed was reduced to idling if the engine was not running.

Voltage Regulators

The regulators were manufactured by Delco-Remy, and consisted of two major parts: the carbon pile assembly, and an armature assembly. Voltage regulators, as their name implies, prevented the generators from fluctuating above or below the designated setting. Its purpose was to hold the

voltage of the generator within the limits of 24 to 28.5 volts for normal loads, and to equalize the voltage with that of the four generators. There were six voltage regulators (four on the TB trainers) for the engine generators, which were located on the rear wall of the flight deck under the generator panel. The APU voltage regulator was located to the right of the power plant aft of station 3.3, and was attached to the back of the relay box.

Lighting

Interior Lighting

Bomb Bay: The bomb bay was illuminated by 10 Type A-9 dome lights supplied with four spare bulbs. These lights were turned on or off at the radio operator's equipment panel in the forward compartment, or at the rear cabin's switch and circuit breaker panel.

Cockpit Lights (Spotlights): The cockpit was equipped with six Type C-4 cockpit lights that were small adjustable spotlights that supplemented the fluorescent lamps. These extension lights were located at the pilot, co-pilot, bombardier, navigator, and radio operator stations, and the forward cabin settee. Two spare bulbs were supplied in a box at the radio operator's station. They were contained in a cylindrical housing containing a 24-volt, T-3-1/4 bulb with a bayonet base. The light could be adjusted for either spotlight or floodlight effect by sliding the outer lens barrel.

Cabin Dome Lights: The forward cabin was equipped with one dome light, and was turned on or off from two switches: one located in the nose wheel well (so the cabin could be lit before entering), and the other located in the forward cabin next to the light. The auxiliary compartment under the flight deck between station 3.0 and 4.0 had a dome light that was turned on or off from two switches, one in the nose wheel well, and the other at the station 4.0 right hand switch panel, located just forward of the bomb bay. The rear compartment had a dome light that was controlled by two switches: one at the entrance to the rear cabin, and the other at the rear cabin camera panel.

Compass Light: The pilot's magnetic compass was controlled by a rheostat, and powered by the pilot's circuit breaker panel. The co-pilot's magnetic compass was located on his auxiliary panel, and was illuminated separately by a small self-contained lamp whose brightness was controlled by a lamp rheostat located on the co-pilot's instrument panel.

Table Lights: The Type A-6 flexible gooseneck, or Type A-11 three arm adjustable table lamp, lit the bombardier, navigator, and radio operator's station tables. The navigator's table was illuminated by a Type A-11 lamp with a variable rheostat for dimming, and was powered by current from the navigator's instrument panel.

Fluorescent Lamps: Two Type C-5 fluorescent lights fed from the pilot's 115-volt circuit breaker panel were fitted with fluorescent ultraviolet bulbs and adjustable filters, to vary or eliminate the amount of light that was projected on the pilot and co-pilot. Self-illuminating calibrations on the instruments fluoresced under ultraviolet light. These lights were controlled by a starter-rheostat that was provided with an OFF-DIM-ON and START position. To operate the lights, the knob had to be turned to the START position for about two seconds. When it was released the knob snapped to the ON position, after which it could be turned to the DIM position to reduce illumination. The bombardier's station was equipped with a fluorescent light supplied with a headband, and powered by the navigator's instrument panel.

Extension Lights: The Type B-7 extension light was provided with six feet of flexible cord on a self-winding reel, and an OFF-ON switch for a 3-candle power, 28-volt T-4-1/2 bulb. The housing was fixed at station 900 in the rear unpressurized compartment, and was used for lighting the APU and cameras.

Dome Lights: Type A-9 and the Type A-7
The A-9 was a reflector type lamp without a lens or cover glass. It used a 21-candle power, 28-volt, S-8 silver tip bulb with a single contact bayonet base. These lights were provided throughout the aircraft for general lighting: three in the forward pressurized compartment; two in the rear pressurized compartment; and three in the rear unpressurized compartment. The three dome lights in the forward and the one in the rear pressurized cabins were controlled by ON-OFF toggle switches that were integral with the lights. The dome light on the face of the aft wall of the rear pressurized compartment close to the bulkhead was turned ON or OFF from either side of the bulkhead. Dome lights in the unpressurized rear section were operated either by a switch accessible by the tail gunner, or a switch near the rear entrance door.

The A-7 was a reflector, vapor-proof light whose socket was hermetically sealed, and its cover glass lens was airtight. It used a 21-candle power, 28-volt, S-8 clear bulb with a single contact bayonet base. This sealed light was used in the bomb bay, where there could be gasoline vapor from the bomb bay fuel tanks that could be ignited. There were four lights in each bomb bay, with a type B-5A switch for the forward bomb bay located on the rear leg of the radio operator's table, and another B-5A switch located on the rear side of the rear pressure bulkhead near the door.

Aldis Lamps
The Type C-3A Aldis Lamp was a portable signal lamp equipped with interchangeable filters, and was stowed on the top shelf behind the pilot's seat. It was plugged into the 24-volt receptacle located on any electric flying suit outlet. An Aldis lamp with a clear or white lens (colored lenses were too translucent to permit enough light transmission) was used for fast and easy communications between aircraft during radio silence. There was a trigger ON-OFF switch on the lamp to aid in signaling a sequence of light flashes. The lamp had to be held close to the sighting blister, and be pointed directly at the receiving aircraft, with the position of the sun being considered. A special set of slow, deliberate flashes was devised that used letters and single letters called "prosigns" to transmit messages. The sender received the prosign "K" for "Go ahead" before sending, and after each word sent waited for the receiver to send the prosign "R" for "I understand."

Exterior Lighting
Landing Lights: The two Type B-3A electrically operated fully retractable white landing lights were flush mounted on the bottom of the fuselage below the level of the cockpit windows. The eight inch diameter all-glass 28-volt; 600-watt sealed beam was controlled by a reversible electric motor. Each was controlled by a three position switch (EXTEND-OFF-RE-

TRACT) located on the co-pilot's control pedestal. The lights went on automatically as they extended. They could be turned off in the extended position by using the OFF position.

Formation Lights: The B-32 carried nine Type C-1 blue formation lights with T-3-1/4 3-candle power bulbs. There were three formation lights on the top at the midline of *each* wing, extending equidistant outward from one located inboard of the outboard engine nacelle, and the other two outboard, and three on top midline of the fuselage, beginning at mid-wing, and ending just forward of the tail. These lights were controlled by a three position (BRIGHT-OFF-DIM) switch on the pilot's equipment panel (located next to his circuit breaker panel). This switch also controlled the position lights.

Position Lights: As was the AAF standard, the B-32 was equipped with the Type A-9 red (forward port wing tip), Type A-9 green (forward starboard wing tip), and Type D-1 white (below tail) position lights. The lights on the wing tips were contained in a transparent colored Plexiglas housing, and were controlled by a switch and fixed resistor on the pilot's aisle stand. The B-9A toggle switch gave the choice of BRIGHT-OFF-DIM. The white taillight had similar, but separate provisions.

Recognition Lights: Three Type E-2 (fore to aft in sequence about two feet apart: red, green, and amber) lights were located under the centerline of the lower fuselage forward of the bomb bay. The control box was located on the pilot's equipment panel (next to the circuit breaker panel). These lamps could be set for any of several combinations by means of individual KEY-OFF-STEADY switches on the aisle stand. Lights positioned to KEY could be keyed simultaneously by a push button key switch installed next to the recognition switches.

Bomb Release Light: During mass or pattern bombing a bomb release light, located on top of the fairing above the tail gunner's window, was used to signal bombers following in the formation that bombs were being dropped. It was controlled by a switch on the bombardier's panel. A white light went on when the bomb bay doors were fully open, and a red light

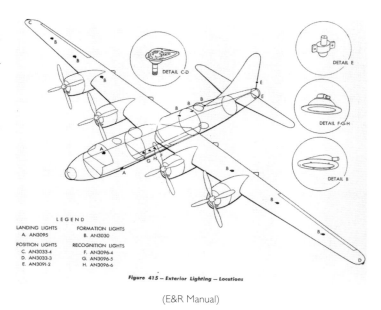

LEGEND
LANDING LIGHTS	FORMATION LIGHTS
A. AN3095	B. AN3030

POSITION LIGHTS	RECOGNITION LIGHTS
C. AN3033-4	F. AN3096-4
D. AN3033-3	G. AN3096-5
E. AN3091-2	H. AN3096-6

Figure 415 – Exterior Lighting – Locations

(E&R Manual)

came on during the bomb release period, and went out after the last bomb dropped.

Wheel Well Spotlights:
Three small Grimes-type A2301 spotlights lit the landing gear at night when it was in the extended position. A switch on the flight engineer's auxiliary panel controlled them.

Passing Light:
TB training aircraft possessed a red passing light located at the tip of the aircraft's nose.

Communications System
The combat test report on the B-32 stated:

"For the most part these installations were found to operate satisfactorily, but the positioning was generally poor, and numerous recommendations for re-positioning were made...."

It was also recommended that all controls be labeled to prevent mistakes. The general communications system in the B-32 consisted of the standard radio and interphone equipment to provide two-way communications with ground stations and other aircraft, interphone communications between crew members, and reception of radio range and marker beacon signals. Additionally, the B-32 also carried specialized equipment for automatic radio direction finding, and the recognition and identification of friendly aircraft. The communications equipment for the B-32 up to No. 42-108476 and 108478 included:

Interphone System	RC-36
Command Radio Set	SCR-274
Liaison Radio Set	SCR-287
Radio Compass Set	SCR-269G
Radio Identification Set	SCR-695
Radio Altimeter	SCR-718
Blind Approach Set	RC-103
Marker Beacon set	RC-193

The communication equipment for the B-32 No. 42-108477, 108479 to 108484 and 42-108525 onward included:

Interphone System	AN/AIC-2
VHF Command Set	SCR-522
Liaison Radio Set	AN/ARC-8
Radio Compass	AN/ARN-7
Range Receiver	BC-453
Radio Identification	SCR-595
Radio Altimeter	AN/APN-1
Blind Landing Equipment	SCR-570
Blind Landing Approach	RC-103
Blind Landing Approach	AN/ARN-5
Marker Beacon	RC-103
Long Range Navigation	AN/APN-4*
Radar Radio	AN/APQ-13
Radio Set	SCR-729
Indicator Equipment	AN/APQ-5B
Static Discharger Assembly	AN/ASA-3
Emergency Transmitter	SCR-578

*Replaced with AN/APN-9 after A/C No. 42-108545

Interphone System (RC-36 redesignated as the AN/AIC-2 in 1944)
The B-32 was so large and segmented that the interphone played an important role in the crew's combat efficiency. The interphone system provided intra-aircraft communications between the crew at the 14 stations, and allowed limited use of the aircraft's radio facilities. The 14 stations included:

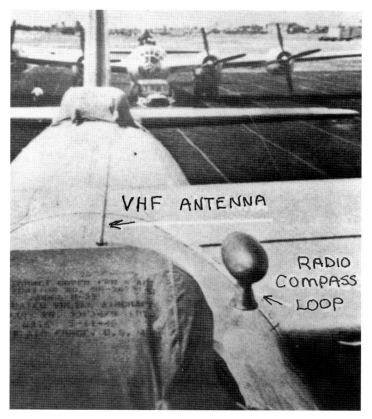

Service test experimental antenna installation on aircraft 535. (USAAF)

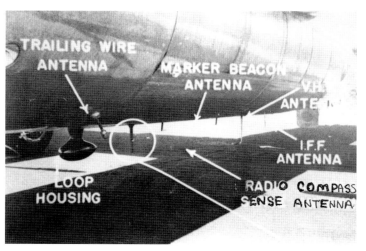

Standard antenna installation on aircraft 484. (USAAF)

1 Pilot	1 R.H. Bench Station	2 Aft Bunk Stations
1 Co-pilot	1 Forward Top Turret	1 Tail Gunner
1 Bombardier	1 Bomb Bay	1 Nose Gunner
1 Navigator	1 Aft Turret	
1 Radio Operator	1 Aft Lower Turret	

The interphone equipment included jack boxes, throat microphones, headsets and extension cords, a dynamotor, and an amplifier and filters.

Jack Boxes

Each of 14 stations was equipped with a Type BC-1366 Jack Box that contained a microphone and earphone jacks, a volume control knob, and a five-position selector knob that offered a choice of interphone channels, call position, radio compass, liaison radio, and command radio positions. Modulation of the command radio transmitter was possible at all positions, but the modulation of the liaison radio transmitter was possible only at the pilot's, co-pilot's, and radio operator's positions. The interphone system became operative when the battery switch was in the ON position, and remained in operation as long as there was power on the power system network. In the "CALL" position a switch connected the station to all other stations without regard to their respective selector switch positions. A spring was provided to return the selector to the "INTER" position to prevent the selector from accidentally being left in the "CALL" position. A limited control over the headset volume of the radio compass, liaison, and command radios could be acquired by manipulating the volume control of the jack box.

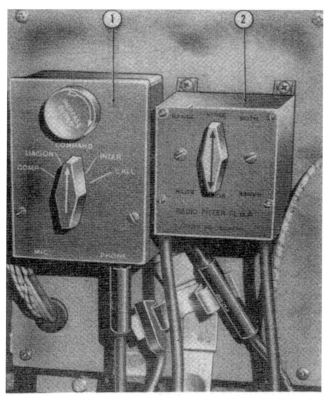

1. Interphone Jack Box BC-366   2. Interphone Filter—FL-8

Figure 526 – Interphone Jack Box and Filter
(E&R Manual)

Microphones and Extension Cords

The Type T-30 throat microphone found at all stations was a vibration receptive carbon-type microphone that was activated by mechanical vibrations from the throat area during speech. A brown elastic strap with a snap at the end held the vibration-receiving unit in place against the Adam's apple. A suffix at the end of the T-30 designation (i.e. T-30-Q) denoted the manufacturer: Q by Western Electric; R by Kellogg; S by Universal Microphone Company; and V by Shure Brothers.

"Push-to-talk" microphone switches were located on the aileron control wheels for the pilot and co-pilot, and in the ring sight of the top gunner. All other stations had the standard cord microphone push-to-talk switches that were located on the CD-508 extension cords to allow freedom of movement.

Headset

The HS-38 headset was the standard AAF set used in the war. It consisted of two adjustable brown leather-covered wire headbands, to which the Type ANB-H-1 receivers were attached. The earphones were padded with black or brown sponge rubber cushions to reduce outside noise interference. The twisted connecting cord ended in a red plastic PL-354 jack.

Amplifier

The Type BC-347 amplifier was mounted adjacent to the dynamotor at station 3.1, right hand, beneath the forward cabin bunk. It amplified the output of the type T-30 throat microphone. The single stage push-pull radio amplifier used one twin triode vacuum tube (tube VT-991). The output circuit supplied the 14 parallel headsets. The BC-347 was replaced by the AM-26/AIC.

Dynamotor

The type PE86E dynamotor was mounted adjacent to the amplifier, and supplied the amplifier plate voltage. The dynamotor system operated when the battery solenoid switch was closed. The DM-32-A replaced the PE86E.

Filter

The type FL8-A located at the pilot's and co-pilot's positions permitted selective reception of either voice or range signals, or both when they were being received simultaneously.

Interphone Procedure

There were procedures for the use of the types of interphone equipment used:

1) Hand-held microphone was to be held touching the lips.
2) Throat Microphone was to be worn snugly against the neck, slightly above the prominence of the Adam's apple, with the words spoken distinctly in a normal tone.
3) Headset was to be worn with the headband spread as far apart as possible, and pressed firmly over the ears to insure the best possible seal.

Interphone procedure and discipline varied from crew to crew, but was generally based on R/T procedure, and the pilot was responsible for proper interphone discipline. Interphone communication required that the speaker use a loud voice, but less than shouting, and was to speak more slowly and precisely than normal. Because the interphone and its continued sequences of messages did not involve mistaken identity the call up and sign off procedures were less rigid than with the R/T message. The use of procedure words and phrases that had clear and uniform meanings were to be used. For example, a few standard words in interphone communications were "acknowledge," "roger," "over," "out," "request," "standby," "wilco," etc. Routine interphone phrases were "Request ETA," "Fighters at ten o'clock," "Request ground speed (or airspeed)," etc.

Command Radio Sets: SCR-274 and SCR-522 (later)

SCR-274

The SCR-274 was a multi-channel aircraft receiving and transmitting set that provided plane-to-plane or short-range plane-to-ground communication (within a maximum range of 30 miles). If the interphone amplifier malfunctioned the command set could be used for intra-plane communication by switching the command transmitter control box switch to position "3" or "4," and switching the interphone jack boxes to "COMMAND." It also had Morse transmission capabilities. The command radio had three receivers, two transmitters, dynamotor and modulator, remote controls, an antenna relay switch, and an antenna.

The three receivers—BC-453 (190-550Kc), BC-454-A (3.0-6.0Mc), and BC-455-A (6.0-9.1Mc)—were located on a rack behind the co-pilot in the forward cabin, and were remotely controlled by the pilot. The type BC-450-A receiver controls were located on the pilot's radio control panel. The receiver control box had "CW"-"OFF-"MCW" switch, volume control, a tuning unit, and a three-position switch that isolated the receiver output, or connected it to either of the headset lines "A" and "B." The output of all receivers could be switched to "A" or "B," or may be on "A" while the others are on "B." Three type DM-32-A dynamotors located on the receiver rack unit furnished 250 volt current to the receivers, and were connected to the power system by a circuit breaker (AN3160-10) located at station 3.0 to the rear of the nose wheel below the flight deck.

SCR-522

The SCR-522 VHF Command Set provided two-way radio-telephone line of sight communication with other bombers in the formation, to rescue facilities, and to request and receive VHF D/F bearings within 100 miles of home base. Its range was limited to line of sight transmission (i.e. at 5,000 feet the line of sight is about 80 miles, and at 10,000 feet it increases to 120 miles, at 15,000 feet to 150 miles, and at 20,000 feet it is 180 miles). When long distances were involved relay aircraft could be provided to retransmit messages. Unlike other aircraft radios, VHF did not suffer from fading at altitude, but was susceptible to interference if ignition and other electrical systems were not efficiently suppressed. Amplitude modulated radio frequencies operated on one of four preset crystal-controlled channels in the 100-156Mc range. Both transmitter and receiver were simultaneously switched to any one of the four channels by pushing the appropriate channel selector. Only voice communications were available, but interphone communication was possible between two or more stations.

SCR-522-A

The SCR-522-A set was later installed. It was based on the Royal Air Force's TR1143 VHF (Very High Frequency) set, and consisted of the combination transmitter (BC-625-A) and receiver (BC-624-A) assembly housed together in a shock-mounted case under the floor of the rear pressurized cabin (at station 6.0), a dynamotor unit, and a push button control box. There was a BC-602-A radio control box at the pilot's aisle stand that provided complete remote control of the communications function. The PE-94-A dynamotor located next to the transmitter-receiver provided the DC voltage for the SCR-522 and control circuits. The VHF antenna made up the rear support mast for the radio compass antenna.

Liaison Radio Sets: SCR-287 AN/ARC-8

SCR-287

The liaison radio provided long-range code or voice communication with ground stations, or between aircraft. The radio operator controlled it, but all crew stations could receive the set's signal reception through their interphones, but only the pilot, co-pilot, and radio operator could modulate the transmitter. It consisted of a receiver, transmitter, and antenna equipment.

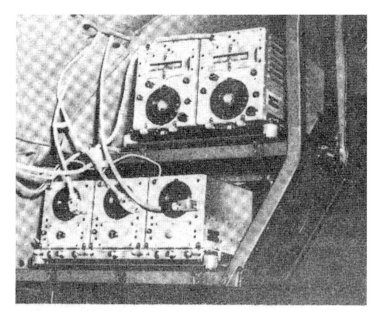

Command Receiver and Transmitter
(E&R Manual)

Figure 532 – Liaison Receiver BC 375A
(E&R Manual)

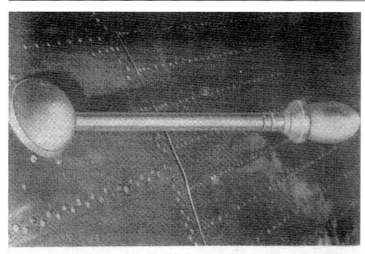

Figure 535 – Liaison Trailing Antenna
(E&R Manual)

Liaison Receiver BC-348-A: The eight tube, six band superheterodyne BC-348-A was mounted on the radio operator's table. The voltage was furnished by a self-controlled dynamotor positioned on the flight deck at station 3.3, and directly connected to the power network through a limiter at station 4.0.

Liaison Transmitter: A type BC-375E transmitter was located adjacent to the radio operator's table. Seven transmitter tuning units covering the range of 350 to 650 and 1,500 to 12,000Kcs were used as needed. The transmitter was supplied with 1,000 volts DC by a type PE-73-B dynamotor located at station 3.3.

Antennas: The liaison radio had fixed and trailing antennae, and either could be selected by using an antenna transfer switch (CVAC-SW-45-75) on the cabin 4.0 bulkhead above the radio operator. The fixed antenna utilized the aircraft's fuselage skin as a radiator. The trailing antenna W-106 wire was 250 feet long, and was wound by a RL-42B motor-driven reel mounted through an insulated retractable fair-lead located between stations 3.3 and 4.0. The reel motor had a BC-461 reel control box with an "IN" and "OUT" switch that was located at the radio operator's station. A cable operated counter denoted the length of cable unreeled. A red signal light at the radio operator's station indicated that the landing gear was being lowered before the antenna was reeled in.

AN/ARC-8

This later set provided long-range code or voice communication with ground stations, or between aircraft, and was controlled by the radio operator. The AN-ARR-11 receiver used a BC-348 receiver at the radio operator's station. It was capable of receiving CW, MCW, or voice signals with manual or automatic volume control. A built-in dynamotor furnished the high voltage necessary for operational. The transmitting equipment used the T-47/ART-13 transmitter, which was located at the radio operator's station, and operated on any one of 11 pretuned, automatically selected channels. The set used matched impedance fixed antenna, and a trailing antenna that was controlled by a switch below the transmitter. The fixed antenna extended from the right side of station 3.3 to the tip of the vertical fin. The trailing

antenna was wound on a motor driven RL-42 reel located on the left side under the flight deck and controlled by a BC-461 reel control box.

Radio Compass Set: SCR-269-G and AN/ARN-7

The radio compass was used for radio reception, homing, or for taking bearings on a radio transmitting station. The radio compass utilized signals transmitted from a range, commercial, or standard broadcast radio station to obtain directional or locational information. Under favorable conditions stations as far away as 250 miles could provide the necessary signal to operate this equipment, depending on the power of the transmitting station.

SCR-269-G

The SCR-269-G radio compass consisted of:

1) A 15-tube superheterodyne receiver located in the upper left section of the forward bomb bay.
2) Two control boxes located at the radio operator and co-pilot's stations.
3) CW-VOICE switch located next to the co-pilot's control box.
4) A relay to switch control from one box to another.
5) An automatic loop antenna located on the fuselage above the bomb bay.
6) A retractable whip antenna aft of the forward upper turret.
7) Direction indicators located in the pilot's instrument panel and navigator's position.

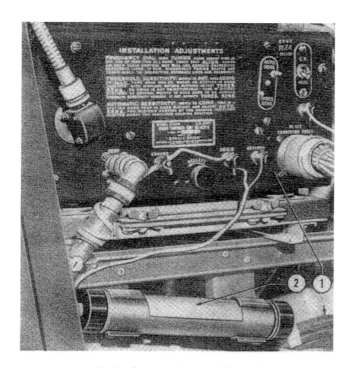

1. Radio Compass Receiver BC-433-G
2. Dehydrator Tube

Figure 531 – Radio Compass Receiver
(E&R Manual)

The type BC-433-G radio compass receiver was located below the flight deck at the left hand side of station 4.0. Either the pilot or navigator, by means of type BC-434-A control boxes, could operate it. It was only necessary to push the control button at the desired station to make that control the operating station for the equipment. It was powered by 400-cycle 115-volt AC current from the aircraft's inverters. The compass had a frequency range of 150 to 1,750Kc, and could be operated using either the loop or whip antenna, or both.

The type LP-21-A loop antenna was mounted in a streamlined housing on the bottom of the fuselage, just aft of station 4.1. The rotating coil or loop was maintained at a right angle to the signal by the driving motor in conjunction with the receiver. An autosyn transmitter sends the angular position of the loop to register at the pilot's and navigator's positions. The wire sense antenna was mounted on two masts on the bottom of the fuselage, approximately three feet aft of the loop.

AN/ARN-7

The AN/ARN-7 utilized a frequency range of 100 to 1,750Kc in four bands, with the frequency band in use visible on the two remote control boxes. The radio compass unit R-5/ARN-7 was located under the flight deck on the left hand side of station 4.0. Two remote boxes (C-4/ARN-7s) could be operated, one on the pilot's radio control panel, and the other at the navigator's position. The loop antenna (LP-21) was mounted on the bottom of the catwalk to the rear of station 4.1 in a streamlined housing that also contained a motor, compensator, and an autosyn transmitter in its base.

Radio Identification Set SCR-695

The SCR-695 IFF (Identification Friend or Foe), operating in conjunction with the fixed stub antenna installed on the lower surface of the fuselage,

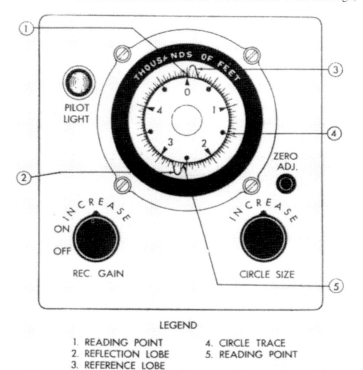

LEGEND

1. READING POINT   4. CIRCLE TRACE
2. REFLECTION LOBE   5. READING POINT
3. REFERENCE LOBE

Figure 536 — Radio Altimeter
(E&R Manual)

provided a means of identifying friendly aircraft. It consisted of a BC-958 power control box, BC-965 selector control box, BC-966A radio receiver, and a B0-767 indicator box. The battery side of the battery solenoid supplied power. The transponder was a beacon that beamed a coded response via the antenna when an aircraft came within range of the radar set. Aircraft emitting the proper IFF response were assumed to be friendly, but the reverse was not necessarily true, either because of equipment failure, or simply by not having its set turned on. The operation of the IFF was automatic once the ON-OFF switch located on top of the pilot's instrument panel, and in the IFF control box, was activated. The ON and OFF of the IFF varied with a particular mission, and was dependent on other operations in progress, and the dispersal of the U.S. Pacific Fleet. The SOI (Signal Operation Instruction) flimsies directed the operation of IFF equipment. The IFF used secret codes that were changed daily. To keep the secret apparatus from falling into enemy hands the set employed a destructor unit that consisted of a destructor "D" plug, two remote push button switches, and a crash switch and indicator. Both destruct switches had to be pushed together to send power to the "D" plug, which was denoted by two red indicator lights at the radio operator's station. There was an automatic crash switch at the radio operator's table that was tripped on impact.

The IFF had several other functions besides the IFF. It enabled home base radio to transmit bearings to the bomber up to 100 miles from that base. Generally, B-32 IFF operators would check the IFF from 500 miles out from any friendly base while returning home from a mission. It also enabled submarines to shoot a bearing on the bomber, determine its range, and inform naval radar equipment if the bomber were in an emergency situation.

Radio Altimeter SCR-718

The RCA SCR-718C provided the pilot with a visual indicator showing the position of his aircraft with respect to the height above the terrain below (from 0 to 40,000 feet). A vertical needle indicated the localizer course, while the horizontal needle indicated the glide path course. The indicator No. I-152A was located above the navigator's table, and the BC-778 radio receiver and transmitter were located at station 5.3, mounted on the fuselage framework above the catwalk. Two AT-4/ARN-1 antennas, one for transmitting and one for receiving, were located under the wing rear spar with the transmitter located on the starboard side of the fuselage, and the receiver on the port side.

The radio altimeter was used to determine the absolute altitude of the bomber for its bombing run and landing approaches, and was coordinated with the drift meter to determine ground speed and track. The 12- or 24-volt receiver was designed to operate at six fixed crystal-controlled frequencies, and when tuned to any one of them the receiver was capable of receiving continuous wave, radio frequency, and amplitude modulated at two frequencies. The type I-101 indicator provided a visual indication to the pilot of his lateral position in respect to the runway. When the receiver was tuned to the 90 to 150-cycle modulation of the field localizer transmitter it was audible in the headset, while the needle on the indicator produced a visual guide. If the aircraft were on course the needle was centered, but the needle deflected either to the blue (90-cycle modulation) or yellow (150-cycle) side of the dial. The modulations were received by a horseshoe shaped antenna located on top of the fuselage near the wing.

Marker Beacon Set: RC-193 and RC-43A (later)

The marker beacon receiver was ultra-high frequency radio equipment used as a navigating and landing aid, and gave the pilot visual indications that the aircraft was flying through the radiation field of a marker beacon transmitter. These transmitters gave the location of radio range stations, and indicated range course intersections, boundaries, and positions that were especially helpful in making an instrument landing approach. The length of the visual indication depended on the type of marker and the altitude of the aircraft. A station marker indication lasted about one minute at 10,000 feet with the aircraft flying at 150mph. The marker beacon transmitter locations and keying data were found on the Radio Facility Charts.

The aircraft marker beacon receiver (BC-357-B) was located in the bomb bay on bulkhead 5.0. The receiver was fine-tuned to ultra high frequency 75Mc signals. Its purpose was to automatically indicate signals received from instrument landing markers, fan-type and cone of silence markers, and other facilities using 75Mc horizontally polarized radiation. The antenna was mounted below the fuselage between the bomb bays, and was coupled to the receiver by a coaxial transmission line. As the aircraft flew over the conical field of the beacon transmitter an amber indicator light on the pilot's instrument panel flashed in synchronism with the transmitter keying.

Blind Landing Equipment SCR-570

The SCR-570 provided both lateral and vertical guidance to the pilot during landing operations. Lateral guidance was provided by the RC-103 receiver, which was made up of the BC-733 receiver, while vertical guidance was provided by the AR/ARN-5 receiver, which consisted of the R-89/ARN-5 receiver. Both of these receivers were located between the pilot's legs and the navigator's station, and were controlled from the BC-732 control box on the pilot's radio control panel. They operated on any of six preset frequencies. A DM-53 dynamotor supplied the high voltage.

Indicator Equipment AN/APQ-5B

The AN/APQ-5B was auxiliary equipment used in conjunction with the AN/APQ-13 radar set. This equipment was located between the co-pilot's legs, at the radio operator's station, and the bombardier's compartment.

Gyro Flux Gate Compass (GFGC)

The gyro flux gate compass was developed to satisfy a need for an accurate compass in long-range navigation. At the navigator's station there were many magnetic components, such as armor plate and electrical circuits, so that there were no desirable locations for a direct-reading magnetic compass. To remedy the problem a remote reading compass, with its magnetic

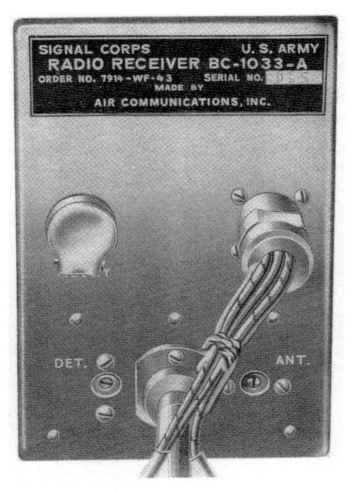

Figure 537 — Beacon Receiver

(E&R Manual)

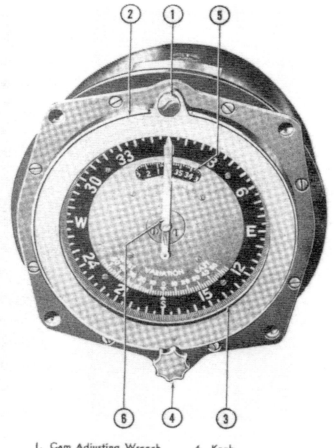

1. Cam Adjusting Wrench
2. Bezel Ring
3. Outer Dial
4. Knob
5. Uncorrected Dial
6. Pointer

Figure 418 — Flux Gate Master Indicator Compass

(E&R Manual)

component outside the navigator's area, was designed. This remote unit was a transmitter, while the unit used by the navigator was the master indicator. An auxiliary unit called the repeater indicator was placed at the airplane commander's station and other stations. The GFGC converted the earth's magnetic field into electrical impulses that provided precise directional readings that could be duplicated on instruments at all desired points in the aircraft. Unlike the magnetic needle, the GFGC would not go off its reading in a dive, overshoot in a turn, hang up in rough weather, or become frenzied in naturally magnetic regions.

The flux gate consisted of a flux gate transmitter, amplifier, and master indicator, and was powered by the aircraft's inverter, which supplied 26 volt AC. The system provided an accurate direction reading up to 65 degrees with horizontal, and within this angular limitation the readings were accurate, because of the electrically-driven gyro that maintained the operation of the flux gate in a horizontal plane. The master indicator and amplifier were unaffected by local magnetic disturbances, but the transmitter was located in the left wing to remove it from the magnetic materials in the fuselage.

In training manuals the three units of the GFGC were compared to the human brain, heart, and muscles. The transmitter was the brain, the amplifier was the heart, and the master indicator was analogous to the muscles.

The Brain: The main component of the transmitter was a magnetic-sensitive element called the flux gate, which received the direction signal by induction, and transmitted it to the master indicator. The flux gate consisted of three small coils arranged in a triangle, and each coil had a special soft iron core. The coil was made up of a primary (excitation) winding and a secondary winding, from which a signal was acquired. Each leg of the flux gate coil triangle was positioned at a different angle to the earth's magnetic field; the induced voltage was relative to the angle, and each leg produced a different voltage. When the angular relationship between the flux gate and the earth's magnetic field changed there was a relative change in the voltages in the three legs of the secondary winding. These voltages were the motivating forces for the GFGC master indicator, which supplied indications of the exact position of the flux gate in relation to the earth's magnetic field. Each coil had a direction sensitive component that could distinguish one direction from another (i.e. east from north, but not north from south). The combination of the three coils could combine their information to give a directional signal.

The Heart: The amplifier supplied different excitation voltages at a frequency to the transmitter and master indicator. It was mounted at the rear of the navigator's table, and a green light indicated that it was operating. There was a rheostat on the left side of the amplifier face for adjusting sensitivity. On long northerly flying missions the rheostat had to be adjusted more frequently to compensate for the increasing magnetic latitudes. The amplifier amplified the autosyn signal, which controlled the master indicator and served as a junction for the entire compass system. Power for the amplifier was furnished by the aircraft's inverter, and was converted to usable power for other units. The amplifier input was 400-cycle A.C., and various voltages could be used, depending upon the available power source.

The Muscle: The master indicator was considered the muscle of the flux gate system, as it provided the mechanical power to drive the pointer on the main instrument dial. It was located on the navigator's panel, and in-

corporated an adjustment dial to which the navigator could dial in magnetic variations. The pointer was driven by a cam mechanism that automatically corrected the reading for compass deviation, so that a corrected indication was realized on all headings. The pointer shaft was geared to another small transmitting unit in the master indicator that could operate as many as six repeaters in other locations. The amplifier, master indicator, and repeaters were not affected by local magnetic influences.

The installation of the GFGC was initially very unsuccessful, because excessive vibration in the wing caused chronic shorting of the transmitter. The problem was referred to the builder, Pioneer Instrument Company, who developed a new shock-absorbing mounting bracket that solved the problem.

Cabin Heating and Ventilating System
Outside Air
During low outside temperatures the vents were in a partially closed position to allow the maintenance of the correct amount of heated air for release from the cabin. When the outside temperature of the air was high the vent opened more fully, which allowed an increase in the rate of airflow through the cabin, therefore increasing the ventilating air supply. When the heating system was not in use ventilation was obtained by introducing fresh air from the outside through the same ducting that supplied heated air. This was achieved by dumping the heated air at the primary heat exchanger in the nacelle directly to the outside through the overboard dump duct. Fresh air passed through the system from the outside air supply through the intake scoops, and passed on in an unconditioned state through the distributing ducts in the cabins.

Air Intake Water Trap (No. 4C2096)
Rain water, or water formed from the condensation that collected in the air intake, was drawn off by a water trap installed as part of the air intake duct. The tap collected the water, and was drained through a tube welded to the outside of the trap.

Air Ducts
Intake scoops in the wing leading edge and fuselage (one to each secondary exchanger) supplied the rammed outside air for the forward and rear

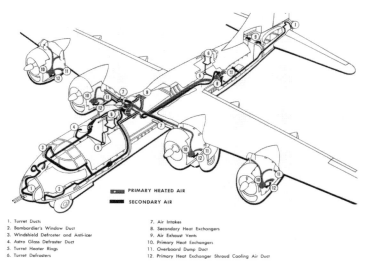

PRIMARY HEATED AIR
SECONDARY AIR

1. Turret Ducts
2. Bombardier's Window Duct
3. Windshield Defroster and Anti-icer
4. Astro Glass Defroster Duct
5. Turret Heater Rings
6. Turret Defrosters
7. Air Intakes
8. Secondary Heat Exchangers
9. Air Exhaust Vents
10. Primary Heat Exchangers
11. Overboard Dump Duct
12. Primary Heat Exchanger Shroud Cooling Air Duct

Cabin Heating and Ventilating System (E&R Manual)

Cabin Heat Duct
(E&R Manual)

secondary heat exchangers. Air ducts were used to route heated air from the primary exhaust gas heat exchangers in the inboard nacelles through the wing leading edges, between the inboard nacelles and fuselage, and furnished the heated air source to the secondary heat exchanges. In turn, cold fresh air was heated in the secondary heat exchangers, and was ducted to the forward and rear cabins through ducting systems.

Two main ducts running from the forward secondary heat exchanger along opposite sides of the forward cabin distributed heated air to the nose section. An auxiliary line from the right and left ducts forced heated air between the pilot's and co-pilot's double-paned windshield for defrosting and anti-icing. Another flexible auxiliary duct, also for defrosting, led to the astro glass in the upper fuselage.

In the nose section, an auxiliary duct entered on the right side running to the center line of the aircraft, where it was attached to flexible ducting in the nose turret. A flexible tube attached to the left side main duct exhausted heated air by direct application to the bombardier's window. The upper forward turret was defrosted from an auxiliary duct leading from the right hand main duct through a revolving heater ring attached to the floor at station 4.0. The upper rear turret was defrosted by an auxiliary duct that received heated air from the main duct through an arrangement similar to the forward upper turret.

A duct, running aft down the center of the bomb bay under the wing section, furnished the flow of air from the primary exchanger for heating the air in the rear cabin. A main duct leading from the underside of the rear cabin secondary heat exchanger to the floor on the left side of the fuselage ran rearward as far as the tail gun turret. An auxiliary line running from this main heating duct entered the lower ball gun turret.

Primary Heat Exchangers
The cabin heating system made use of rammed air heated by means of two primary gas heat exchangers in each inboard nacelle (No.2 and No.3), such as were used in the wing leading edge anti-icing system. The hot exhaust gases passed through closed passages in the exchangers, and the cold ram

air from the nacelle scoops circulated around these passages. The outlet flow of the exhaust gases from the heat exchangers went to the superchargers. Just to the rear of the primary heat exchanger was a Y duct with two outlets. One outlet led to the secondary heat exchangers in the fuselage that supplied both the forward and rear cabin, and the other led to an overboard dump door on the lower side of the nacelle. An outside air supply was introduced through air intakes in the wing leading edge, and was conducted through ducts to the two secondary heaters, where it was heated to 235°F maximum by heated air from the primary heat exchangers. The heated air was then led toward the cabin through ducts and distributed into the cabin via outlets located in the ducting, so as to evenly distribute it into the cabins.

Secondary Heat Exchanges (Airesearch No. 19117)
The two Airesearch secondary heat exchangers were of the vertical tube type, the tubes of which were joined to headers and support plates. Each secondary heater had an independent source of heated air, and each served different areas of the fuselage. The forward cabin secondary heater, located in the forward bomb bay, received a flow of heated air from the left inboard (No.2) nacelle primary heat exchanger. There it transferred heat to fresh air that entered through a scoop in the leading edge of the wing between the right inboard (No.3) nacelle and fuselage, and flowed through a duct around the closed passages in the secondary heat exchanger. This heated outside air then passed through ducts to the forward cabin, top turret, navigator's astro glass nose turret, bombardier's compartment, and the pilot's windscreens for de-icing. The rear cabin secondary heat exchanger received a flow of heated air from the No.3 nacelle primary heat exchanger, plus residue that was bypassed through the forward cabin heat exchanger. This primary air transferred heat to fresh air that entered the rear exchanger through a duct from a scoop in the leading edge of the wing between the No.2 nacelle and the fuselage. Then this primary heated air flowed out of the system through the overboard dump at station 6.3. The heated fresh air from the rear heat exchanger went to the rear cabin, upper and lower turrets, and the tail turret.

A valve controlled by an actuator at the Y ducts of the forward and rear secondary heat exchangers allowed primary heated air to flow through the heat exchangers, or to bypass the exchangers completely, routing the primary heated air out through the overboard dump outlet. Thermal switches on the actuator of this valve and the fuselage dump valve operated as a safety feature to bypass the secondary heat exchangers, and dump the primary heated air overboard if its temperature rose above a preset limit. When the air temperature dropped below the limit, the valves again would route the air through the heat exchangers. During combat, if both the primary

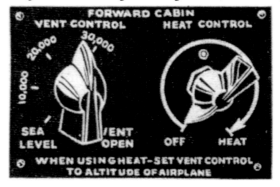

Cabin heating and ventilation control. (E&R Manual)

and secondary heat exchangers were damaged, the system was to be shut down to prevent the distribution of exhaust gas to the affected crew cabin.

Exhaust Vents

Exhaust vents on the rear bulkhead of the forward cabin allowed the used air in the cabin to flow overboard through outlets on top of the wing. Similar exhaust vents in the rear cabin routed rear cabin used air overboard through outlets in the fuselage just forward of the horizontal stabilizer leading edge.

Rheostats (GE No. CR2799-A113-N-6)

The forward and rear secondary heat exchanger systems were independent. The heat output was manually controlled and electrically operated by rheostats designated with OFF, HEAT, OFF, and VENT, located on the co-pilot's auxiliary instrument panel for controlling heating and ventilation for the forward cabin, and rheostats on the rear left hand side of the settee equipment panel for controlling the heating and ventilation of the rear cabin. Each panel had two rheostats, with those on the co-pilot's panel controlling the forward secondary heat exchanger and exhaust air outlet vent. The rear left hand settee panel rheostats controlled the rear secondary heat exchanger and rear cabin air exhaust outlet vent. One switch type rheostat was OFF-HEAT, and increased or decreased the heat output by varying the position of the valves in the secondary heat exchangers. The other rheostat was OFF-VENT, and electrically operated the actuator located at the cabin exhaust air outlet vent. Ventilation for these outlet vents was located at the top of the fuselage ceiling above the forward cabin heat exchanger, and in the rear cabin at station 8.0. For correct airflow the calibrations on the VENT rheostat dial read in altitudes, and were set approximately to the current altitude. The heat output could be manually regulated at the individual outlets installed in the ducts.

Actuators (Airesearch No. 25800)

Each secondary heat exchanger had one motor-driven actuator that operated the heated air intake valve by a jackscrew integral to the actuator. When the actuator was initiated by the bi-metal temperature control element, the jackscrew that was connected to the shaft of the heated air duct caused the valve to close over the opening to the heat exchanger, diverting the overheated air in the direction of the rear secondary heat exchanger. The rear secondary heat exchanger was also thermally controlled, and would be shut off by its actuator controlled valve, diverting the overheated air into the outside atmosphere through the overboard dump duct and overboard dump valve at station 6.3. A thermally controlled motor-driven actuator operated this dump valve, and excessive heat caused the actuator to open the dump valve, releasing the overheated air to the outside. As the temperature was lowered to its selected setting the valve was readjusted, allowing the heated air to follow its normal path and heat the cabin, if necessary.

Three air exhaust vent actuators—one in the forward cabin air outlet above the forward secondary heat exchanger, and two in the rear cabin air outlet on each side of the fuselage at station 8.0, below the horizontal stabilizer leading edge—operated the shutters in the vents to control cabin ventilation. Rheostats electrically controlled these vents through potentiometers located in the vents. The shutters were mechanically fastened to the screw jack of the actuator, and operated in a similar manner to those in the secondary heat exchangers.

Thermostat (Airesearch Type F-7)

Thermostats for limiting the maximum temperature were located on the secondary heat exchanger air outlets ducts. There was one thermostat to each secondary heat exchanger. A General Electric No. CR2799-B102 GI thermostat was also located at the heated air entrance to the dump duct at station 6.3. A temperature pick-up element attached to the thermostat tripped a switch in the thermostat, setting the actuator in motion, and placing valves in their proper position. The purpose of the thermostat at the secondary heat exchangers was to limit heated air to 235°F. The valves closed in the secondary heat exchanges, and simultaneously the dump valve at station 6.3 opened and would bring the temperature down to or below 235°F maximum.

Anemostat (Diffuser)

The anemostat was an air diffusion mechanism that assured draftless distribution of any volume of air at any velocity. It consisted of hollow flaring elements placed in a specific relationship with each other, with two of them acting as injectors only, and other elements having the dual function of ejectors and injectors. Adjustable anemostat jet outlets (types 7.5DJP and 10DJP) directed air over a wide angle, and the vane-equipped anemostat (type 10ADPS) were adaptable for a longer flow of air. Damper-equipped anemostats (types 7.5WS and 7.5ES-DL) were used for controlling the heat output. Anemostat defroster nozzles (types 7.5NV and 5NC) were used to direct and distribute air to the glass surfaces and turrets. Anemostats rotating heater rings with flexible ducts provided heated air for defrosting the upper forward and upper rear turrets. OFF-ON control knobs were located at the duct outlet to the turrets.

Ventilation

Ventilation was provided through the same system by controlling the valves in the Y ducts of the primary heat exchangers, so that the primary heated air was dumped overboard through the nacelle dump duct. Thus, the flow into the cabins was unheated fresh air taken in through the wing leading edge scoops.

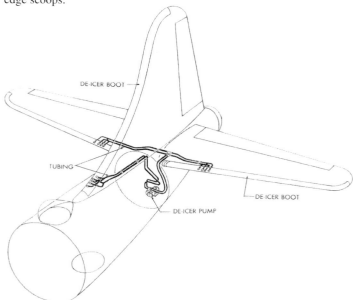

Figure 630 – Empennage De-Icer System

(E&R Manual)

De-icing and Anti-icing System

Empennage

The first 49 B-32s had the conventional *de*-icer boots on the leading edges of the horizontal stabilizer and fin. The following B-32s had thermal *anti*-icers in the tail, like those in the wing.

Empennage De-icer System

The B-32 *de*-icer system was the Consolidated-NACA design developed for the company's B-24 and PBY. The de-icer system consisted of de-icer boots, a pump in the rear accessory compartment, distributor valve, control and pressure gauge on the co-pilot's auxiliary panel, and another switch on the forward side of the pump. The portable de-icer unit (Eclipse type 1250X-1-A) was located in the rear accessory compartment, forward of the stabilizer, and provided for the distribution of air through tubing connected to the de-icer boots mounted on the leading edge of the empennage. De-icer boots installed on the leading edges of the stabilizer and fins consisted of a soft pliable rubber sheet, and a series of lengthwise parallel cells that were inflated with compressed air.

A toggle switch located on the co-pilot's instrument panel, or an auxiliary switch located at station 8.0 on the forward side of the unit, was flipped to the ON position to activate the de-icer, starting the air pump and distributor valve. The de-icers were inflated and deflated rapidly, with an inactive period between inflation of 37 to 40 seconds. As the center cell deflated the outer cells inflated, loosening the ice formed on the surface of the boots, and once loosened the ice was carried away by the slipstream. The pressure gauge on the pilot's auxiliary panel measured and indicated the air pressure when the de-icing system was activated. The de-icer conductive outer surface prevented static charges that could puncture the de-icer and interfere with radio reception. The conductive surface was restored by spraying the de-icer with Prenite-Graphite.

Empennage Anti-icer System

In later B-32s equipped with empennage thermal *anti*-icers, an alternate duct led off the primary heat overboard dump in the rear compartment to conduct primary heat to the tail. A three-way switch with OFF, ON, and MAX positions was located just above the wing anti-icing switch on the co-pilot's auxiliary panel, and actuated a valve that directed the heated air to the tail or overboard. In the OFF position the primary heated air was

The first 49 B-32s had the conventional *de*-icer boots on the leading edges of the horizontal stabilizer and fin. Beginning with TB-32 521, the following B-32s had standardized thermal *anti*-icers in the tail, like those in the wing. (USAAF)

directed out through the overboard dump outlet. In the ON position the primary heated air bypassed the rear secondary heat exchanger, and flowed through the ducts to the empennage, instead of out the dump. In the MAX position, the primary heated air bypassed both secondary heat exchangers and went to the tail. In the ON position the rear cabin received no heat, and in the MAX position neither the front nor rear cabin received heat. The crew was always to carry heated clothing when flying at high altitudes at low temperatures.

An overheat protective thermostat in the primary heat ducts to the empennage, located just to the rear of the dump valve, opened the dump valve and dumped the heated air overboard if it exceeded a preset temperature limit. When the primary heated air returned to a normal temperature the dump valve closed, and the heated air again flowed to the empennage anti-icing switch when it was in the ON position.

Wing Anti-icer System

The wing anti-icer system consisted of two heat exchangers, an air duct distribution system, and a thermostatic and actuator control valves. Two exhaust gas heat exchangers, one in each outboard nacelle (engines No.1 and No.4), furnished heated air to the wing tips, outer panels, and sections between the inboard and outboard nacelles. These heat exchangers functioned the same as the inboard heat exchangers, with the same thermal switch unit for dumping primary heated air if it exceeded the temperature limit. The exhaust gas heat exchanger produced heat by means of an interchange between hot exhaust gases that were passed through closed passages in the exchangers, and cold ram air that was circulated under pressure around these passages. The exhaust gases from the engine averaged 1,500°F for heating the ram air to an average temperature of 315°F. An outlet duct on top of the heat exchanger directed the heated air to the leading edge of the wing, or alternately, when anti-icing was not used, the heated air was led directly to the outside through overboard dump valves. Engine No.1 removed ice from the left wing, and Engine No.4 from the right. If either engine failed while icing conditions occurred, it would be necessary to shut off the de-icing system so that ice would not accumulate on one wing and not the other. Two similar heat exchangers, one in each inboard nacelle, furnished heated air for cabin heating. The heat equaled approximately 1.5 million BTUs per hour, which was equivalent to heating 25 five room houses for an hour, and required about 9,000 pounds of air per hour to the wing.

A toggle switch located on the co-pilot's auxiliary instrument panel activated the anti-icing system. With the switch in the ON position the valve at the nacelle Y ducts directed the primary heated air through an interspace formed by inner and outer leading edge skins. The air was then passed into the wing section proper through holes in the front web spar. It was then released overboard to the outside through holes in the rear spar web. In the wing sections between the inboard and outboard nacelles (where the fuel and oil cells were aft of the front spar), the "used" air was dumped into the nacelle area, instead of through the spar web, as was done in the outer panels. The wing tips required the heated air to be taken into the space between the metal skins at the bottom of the wing and exhausted to the outside through holes in the outer skin on top of the wing tip. The wing sections between the inboard and fuselage had no provisions for anti-icing. With the switch in the OFF position the Y duct valves routed the heated air out through the nacelle overboard dump flap.

LEGEND
1 Outer Leading Edge Skin   8. Exhaust Gas Heat Exchanger
2 Inner Leading Edge Skin   9. Ram Air Inlet Duct
3 Baffle Plates   10. Rear Ball Joint Cooling Air Duct
4 Thermal Control   11. Shroud
5. Dump Valve   12. Dump Flap Actuator
6. Carburetor Preheat   13. Exit Dump Duct
7 Heated Air Outlet   14. Dump Flap Actuator

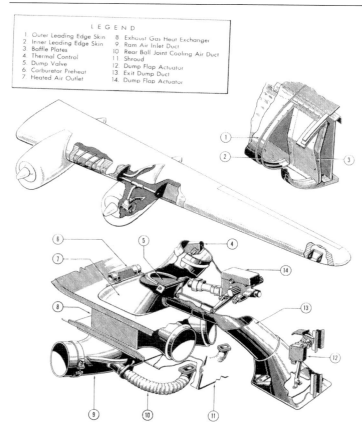

Figure 631 — Anti-Icer System

(E&R Manual)

Propeller

The propeller anti-icing system prevented ice accumulation on the propellers by spreading isopropyl alcohol (AN-F-13) along the surface of each blade. The fluid was carried in an eight gallon magnesium alloy tank mounted on the left hand top section forward of bulkhead 6.0 in the rear bomb bay. Two electrically driven fluid metering stainless steel (anti-corrosive) pumps (AN-6100-3) at the left of the tank distributed the fluid through lines to the slinger rings and their fluid collectors, which were integral parts of the propeller. The pumps were direct driven, positive displacement, rotor types operating at a normal pressure of 25psi. The right hand pump supplied the inboard propellers, while the left hand pump supplied the outboard propellers. Two rheostats on the co-pilot's instrument panel remotely controlled the output of the pumps to the correct pressure. The slinger rings were mounted on the rear side of the hub of each propeller. A feeder tube leading to the ring distributed the anti-icing fluid to the ring groove, and the centrifugal force of the revolving propeller moved the fluid through four tubes (one to each blade fluid along the leading edge of the blade, causing the fluid to spread over the blade area. Two rheostats mounted on the co-pilot's instrument panel controlled the output of the pumps to obtain the correct amount of alcohol flow. In combat tests the propeller anti-icing line chaffed and broke between the engine ignition harness and propeller slinger ring. The remedy was a steel welded nozzle assembly on the nose section of the engine, similar to that on the B-24.

Oxygen System

General

The B-32 oxygen system was a low-pressure demand type supplied by oxygen cylinders installed in the bomb bay and rear compartments. There were 14 oxygen stations, each equipped with regulators, a pressure gauge, a flow indicator and, in addition, there walk around bottles. The duration of the oxygen supply varied with the individual requirements of the crew, the altitude, and the equipment. Oxygen was to be used at 10,000 feet and above on all flights, from takeoff on all night time combat and tactical flights, and between 8,000 and 10,000 feet on all flights of four hours or longer.

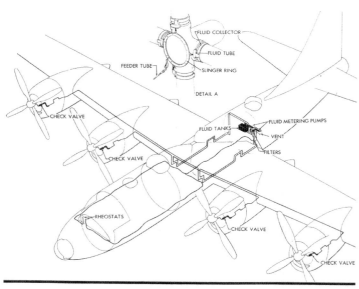

Figure 632 — Propeller Anti-Icer System

(E&R Manual)

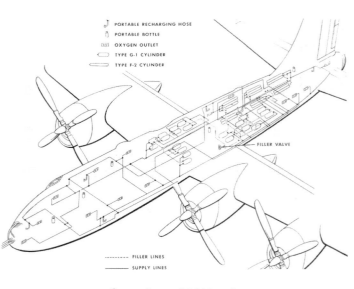

Oxygen System (E&R Manual)

Supply Line or Lines	Nose Turret	Bombardier	Pilot	Co-Pilot	Settee Forward Cabin	Navigator	Radio Operator	Upper Turret Fore	Upper Turret Aft	Sta. 6.1 - 6.2	Aft Settee Forward	Ball Turret Lower	Aft Settee Aft	Tail Turret
STATION														
A													●	
B				●										
C											●			
D										●				
A + B				●		●						●	●	
A + C		●									●	●		
A + D							●		●		●	●		
B + C	●				●				●		●			
B + D			●	●						●				
C + D		●				●				●	●			
Lines Normally Supplying Sta.	B, C	C, D	A, C	B, D	B	C, D	A, B	A, D	B, C	D	C	A, D	A	A, B

Figure 642 – Stations Supplied by Oxygen Lines

(E&R Manual)

Oxygen Cylinders (F-1) and Bottles (G-1)

Oxygen was necessary during unpressurized flight above 10,000 feet. At each crew station there was an A-12 demand regulator, K-1 pressure gauge, A-3 flow indicator, low-pressure supply warning light and filler, and distribution manifolding. There were 13 G-1 2,100 cubic inch shatterproof bottles that supplied 29 cubic feet of gas each to the low pressure A-12 oxygen demand Airco or Pioneer regulator unit. There were provisions for nine more cylinders, increasing the oxygen supply from 570 cubic feet to 830 cubic feet. The cylinders were filled from one filler valve located in the bomb bay, just forward of station 6.0 left. The entire system could be charged through a valve located on the forward wall of the rear cabin (a British adapter was included). In addition, there were 14 F-2 1000 cubic inch cylinders supplying 13.8 cubic feet each of auxiliary oxygen. The G-1 bottles were installed in the upper part of the rear bomb bay and under the floor of the rear crew cabin, just forward of the lower ball turret. The F-2 cylinders were installed against the right wall of the rear crew cabin behind the soundproofing panels. A two-way check valve was located at the outlet of each cylinder to prevent loss of the total oxygen supply due to damage of an individual cylinder. It was important that grease not come into contact with oxygen under pressure, as an explosion would occur.

The system was a low-pressure type, and when charged to 400psi, the duration of the oxygen supply depended on the requirements of the individual crewmen, their activity, the temperature, and the charge of the sys-

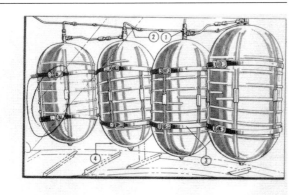

LEGEND
1. Check Valve
2. Oxygen Tubing
3. Cylinder Clamp
4. Oxygen Cylinder

Figure 635 – G-1 Oxygen Bottles and Tubing

(E&R Manual)

OXYGEN CYLINDERS IN THE B-32

Type	Installation	How Many	Approximate Size Diam.	Approximate Size Length	Vol., Cu. In.	Cap., Cu. Ft.*	Gen. Location	Specifications
G-1	Normal	13	12-9/16	24-1/2	2100	29.0	Sta. 5.4 to 6.4; 3 Ceiling, 10 under Fl. Deck	90-40321
G-1	Alternate	9	12-9/16	24-1/2	2100	29.0	Sta. 5.1 to 6.0 Bomb Bay Ceiling	94-40321
F-2	Normal	14	5-3/4	44-1/2	1000	13.8	Sta. 6.1 to 7.3 R. Above Floor	94-40356
A-4	Normal	5	5-1/4	7-5/8	104	1.44	3 For'd Cabin, 2 Aft Cabin	94-40376

*At standard temperature 21° C. (70° F.) and pressure (14.7 pounds per square inch).

(E&R Manual)

OXYGEN DURATION TO THE NEAREST WHOLE HOURS, ALL CYLINDERS CHARGED TO 400 PSI, AUTO-MIX ON (NORMAL OXYGEN):

Altitude in Feet	Normal installation: 13 G-1 and 14 F-2 cylinders. No. of men in crew 4	6	8	10	12	Alternate Installation: 22 G-1 and 14 F-2 cylinders. No. of men in crew 4	6	8	10	12
10,000	37	25	19	15	12	54	36	27	22	18
12,500	32	21	16	13	11	47	31	23	19	16
15,000	28	19	14	11	9	41	27	20	16	14
17,500	25	17	13	10	8	37	25	19	15	12
20,000	23	15	12	9	8	34	22	17	14	11
22,500	22	15	11	9	7	32	21	16	13	11
25,000	20	14	10	8	7	30	20	15	12	10
27,500	21	14	11	8	7	31	20	15	12	10
30,000	22	14	11	9	7	32	21	16	13	11
32,500	25	17	12	10	8	36	24	18	15	12
35,000	29	20	15	12	10	43	28	21	17	14
37,500	34	23	17	13	11	49	32	24	20	16
40,000	39	26	20	16	13	57	38	29	23	19

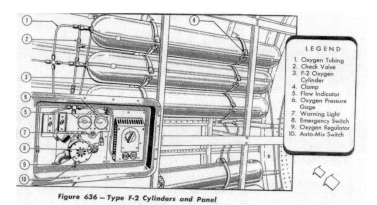

LEGEND
1. Oxygen Tubing
2. Check Valve
3. F-2 Oxygen Cylinder
4. Clamp
5. Flow Indicator
6. Oxygen Pressure Gage
7. Warning Light
8. Emergency Switch
9. Oxygen Regulator
10. Auto-Mix Switch

Figure 636 – Type F-2 Cylinders and Panel

(E&R Manual)

(E&R Manual)

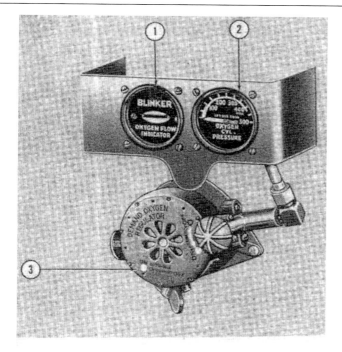

1. Flow Indicator   3. Regulator
2. Pressure Gage

Figure 34 — Oxygen Panel

(E&R Manual)

tem. The system could supply sufficient oxygen for eight men for 10 hours at 25,000 feet. When the nine additional cylinders were present the oxygen volume for eight men at 25,000 feet increased by five more hours. The zone between 20,000 and 30,000 feet was the least economical altitude for oxygen use.

Regulator Panels

The regulator panel was located close to each crewman's station: pilot's, co-pilot's, nose turret, bombardier's, forward settee, navigator's, radio operator's, forward upper turret, rear upper turret, three at the rear settee, and one each in the lower ball turret and the rear gun turret. The panels consisted of an A-14 demand type regulator, K-1 oxygen pressure gauge, warning light, and an A-3 flow indicator. There were pressure warning lights to warn of low pressure.

A-14 Oxygen Regulators

The Type A-14 pressure demand regulator—developed from the Aro Type A-12 demand regulator—was standardized in November 1944, and was manufactured by Aro or Pioneer. A demand regulator (sometimes referred to as the "diluter-demand regulator") was mounted at each station in the aircraft (two at the relief station). The demand regulator furnished oxygen on demand on inhalation, and no oxygen came out on exhalation. It had an auto-mix mechanism controlled by a lever on the side of the cover, and automatically mixed the correct quantities of air and oxygen, the ratio depending upon the altitude. When the lever was in the ON position, oxygen furnished below 30,000 feet was mixed with air. The quantity of the mixture depended solely on the breathing of the user. The dilution was con-

trolled automatically by an aneroid to furnish the correct amount of oxygen that the body requires for a given altitude. Above 30,000 feet the air inlet closed, and 100% oxygen flowed, even though the regulator lever was in the ON position. With the lever in the OFF position, 100% oxygen was furnished at all altitudes. This wasted oxygen, and the lever was never to be at the OFF position, except in certain emergencies. The flow indicator on the oxygen panel blinked open and shut as the oxygen flowed, and needed to be checked during the flight, as it was the only indication that oxygen was flowing regularly. A pressure gauge on the panel was to read 400 to 450psi.

A-3 Flow Indicator

The A-3 flow indicator was connected to the regulator, and when oxygen flowed the eye-shaped blinker on the oxygen panel gauge winked open and shut.

K-1 Pressure Gauge

The K-1 pressure gauge was of the standard Bourdon tube construction, and read from 0 to 500psi. It read between 400 and 425psi with full pressure ON at the before takeoff check. All gauges were to be checked against all other gauges on board, and any discrepancy over 50psi was to be reported. While in the ON position the oxygen gauge was to be checked often. When the pressure fell below 100psi (the 100 to 0 portion of the scale was marked in red lacquer) the supply was getting low, and the pilot was to be notified. The regulator did not function accurately under 50psi, and the portable walk around cylinder was to be used.

Check Valves

Check valves were used throughout the oxygen system to prevent back flow, and the resultant loss of the entire oxygen supply due to damage to any part of the system. There was a dual type check valve on each cylinder that allowed each cylinder to be filled through the filler line without back flow into the filler line. This dual valve also allowed the cylinder to empty into the system without back flow. There were check valves in the main supply line where it entered each crew station. If one or more cylinders was damaged or destroyed only the oxygen from those cylinders was lost, as the check valves prevented the movement of oxygen from the undamaged cylinders to the damaged cylinders.

Low Pressure Warning System

Low oxygen pressures under 100psi at the affected station were indicated on both the pressure gauge, and by lighting of the warning light. The warning signal was activated by the increase or decrease of oxygen pressure on a spring-loaded diaphragm that opened or closed an electrical switch.

Oxygen masks

The Type A-14 demand oxygen mask that entered service in mid-1943 was one of the best masks of the war. It was made up of a medium green rubber face piece, and a corrugated hose that attached to the regulator. An attaching strap ran along the bottom of the rubber face piece and held the mask to the face. There was a hook and tab on the right side of the mask for quick removal. Snaps and buckles on the right side of the helmet suspended the mask to the helmet. A microphone pocket was built into the mask just above the mouthpiece to accommodate the T-30 or ANB-M-C1 microphone. Excessive moisture accumulation from exhalation was a problem, and would

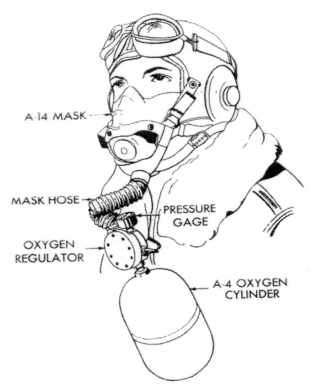

A-14 Oxygen Mask (E&R Manual)

condense and freeze inside the mask. A small electric heater was developed to be worn over the mask, and was used with the electric flying suit. The A-14 utilized the intermittent-flow principle, in which oxygen was supplied only when the wearer inhaled. With the inhalation there was a slight suction produced that caused the demand regulator to open and deliver oxygen to the mask. When the wearer exhaled the demand regulator automatically shut off, and the exhaled air passed out of the mask through a flutter valve. There was an A-14 mask and regulator stored in a cloth bag at crew stations, and was to be suspended on the flying helmet for use when the bomber was depressurized. The A-14 mask was continually improved, and in January 1945 the A-14A was standardized, and remained in use until well after the war.

The oxygen mask needed to fit perfectly, and each crewman had his personal mask fitted by the Personal Equipment Officer (PEO). It was stored in the supply room after each mission, where equipment personnel checked it for repair and cleaning. The mask check included inspecting the mask and straps carefully for worn spots, loose studs, or deterioration of the face piece and hose. The gasket was checked for proper seating on the male quick disconnecting fitting that was to fit snugly, requiring about a 10-pound pull to separate the two parts. The regulator hose was clipped to the flight jacket in such a way that the wearer was to be able to move his head fully without twisting, kinking, or pulling out the quick disconnects between the mask and regulator. Once this proper position was determined the PEO would sew a tab on the flight jacket on which to attach the hose. The mask was attached to the right side of the helmet. The knurled collar on the regulator was to be tight, and the diaphragm intact. The emergency valve was checked to see if oxygen flowed, and then the valve was closed firmly. To check the function of the flow indicator the tester breathed from the regulator normally in the Auto-mix OFF position. The Auto-mix was

then turned to the ON position, and the oxygen pressure was to be from 400 to 425psi. Checks were done on the walk-around bottles, mask function, and connections.

The mask had to fit tightly and have no leaks. The helmet and mask were put on carefully, and the edges of the face piece were slipped under the helmet. The crewman was told to shave every day, as short beard stubble could affect the fit of the mask. The mask could be checked for leaks by three methods:

- Mechanical leak detector: With the mask in place the crewman inhaled, held his breath, plugged the mask hose firmly into the leak detector, and released the bottom plate of the detector. If the plate descended in 10 seconds or less the mask had a leak.
- Suction test: With the mask in place the tester's thumb was placed over the end of the hose, and then the user gently inhaled. The mask was to collapse on the face, with no air entering.
- Sniff test: The inhaler was filled with oil of peppermint. The mask was to be plugged into the regulator hose, Auto-mix was to be turned OFF (100% oxygen), and several breaths of pure oxygen were taken. Then, with the eyes closed, the inhaler was held close to the edges of the mask. If peppermint could be smelled then there was leak.

The masks were to be cleaned frequently by washing them with soap and water.

D-2 and A-4 Walk Around Equipment
Each station was equipped with a portable, walk-around oxygen cylinder with a regulator and a recharging hose. There were two types of portable,

Portable Oxygen Bottle (E&R Manual)

walk-around oxygen equipment available on the B-32. The large yellow D-2 cylinders with carrying slings were provided for each of these crew positions: pilot; co-pilot; flight engineer; navigator; radar operator; and upper and right gunners. The remainder of the crew used the smaller green A-4 portable oxygen units that clipped to the flight jacket, and were able to supply 6 to 12 minutes of walk around operation. All crew members were to know the location of the units so they could be found easily in case of emergency, or in the dark.

Before each mission the bottle was to be checked. The outlet of the bottle was to be sucked on to check if it gave an easy flow, then it was to be blown into gently, then hard. Once the diaphragm was expanded there was to be positive and continued resistance. If there was only slight resistance the diaphragm was leaking, and the defective unit was to be replaced with a new bottle.

Each bottle had pressure gauges and regulators that furnished 100% oxygen on demand. The pressure gauges had to be closely watched for refilling (at 50psi), and they could be refilled onboard at one of the oxygen valves located at each crew station. To refill, the hose fitting had to be snapped on the nipple of the regulator until it clicked and locked. When the bottle was filled to the pressure of the aircraft system the hose was removed, and the mask could be plugged into the bottle.

The walk around bottle was always to be used when disconnecting from the aircraft oxygen system, and the crewman was instructed to hold his breath while switching bottles. The duration of oxygen supply varied, but did not last very long, and needed to be watched for recharging. It was always to be refilled after use. These bottles could be refilled at five locations: the bombardier's compartment; two places on the flight deck; and one location each in the rear crew cabin and tail section.

Bailout Bottle

The bailout bottle was a small, high-pressure (1,800psi) oxygen bottle with an attached gauge that furnished a continuous flow of oxygen. The cylinder was contained in a heavy canvas pocket, with tie straps to attach it to the parachute harness. It had a bayonet connector to be plugged into the adapter on the oxygen mask. If the crew was to bail out at altitude the mask was first to be connected to the walk around bottle while they headed for the emergency exit. Just before jumping the mask was disconnected from the walk around cylinder and attached to the bail out bottle, and the valve opened on the bailout bottle. In a free fall, to prevent the venturi effect from sucking oxygen from the mask the thumb was to be held over the end of the mask tubing.

Photographic Equipment

Provisions were made for the installation of a K-24 camera supported by an A-17 camera mount in the rear compartment of the fuselage. This consisted of a camera mount support assembly and an electrical junction box. The portable type support could be installed on the rear cabin floor between station 7.0 and 8.0, directly over the rear cabin entrance door. The camera support was elevated up from the floor, and held rigid by four brackets that were fastened to the floor by four quick-disconnect wing head studs. Shock mounts were installed on each of the four brackets at the attaching point to the camera mount support. Since the camera mount fit down over the main entrance door, it was necessary to disconnect two of the wing studs in order to enter through the door. A camera airseal made from nine ounce duck was designed to fit around the split ring of the camera mount and the opening of the entrance door to keep the windblast from entering. A drawstring was used for tying the airseal to the camera. An electric camera equipment panel was installed on the underside of station 7.2, and directly to the left side of the camera mounts support.

The camera was controlled from the bombardier's panel by a double-throw, single-pole switch with a fixed contact for automatic operation, and momentary contact for manual operation. The automatic operation of the camera was accomplished by placing the camera control switch in AUTOMATIC when the camera power was ON and the intervalometer was set. The manual operation of the camera was accomplished by holding the camera control switch in the MANUAL position. The camera operated as long as the switch was held in that position. There was an indicator light on the bombardier's panel of the PUSH-PULL type, and when the camera was operating the indicator light was green.

In combat tests the operation of the K-24 camera proved to be satisfactory, but provided strike photos of too small scale and inadequate coverage. The K-22 camera, with a B-3A intervalometer and A-11A mount, was recommended to replace the K-24.

6

Service Points and Fluid Levels

There were 12 major points for servicing fuel, oil, hydraulic, and anti-icing fluid levels.

Fuel

The fuel tank filler cap was attached by a chain to the top of the fuel tank, and had a flip up handle for unscrewing. It was spring locked, and was fully closed when the flip up handle was parallel to the leading edge of the wing. There was a filler point to fill the three outboard cells (located on the outboard cell), and one filler point to fill the three inboard cells (located on the outboard cell). The fuel was grade 100/130 (Specification No. AN-F-28). The capacity of each outboard tank (three cells) was 1,005 gallons, and each inboard tank (three cells) was 1,725 gallons. Personnel had to guard against explosions resulting from static electricity. When fueling from a fuel truck the hose and truck were to be grounded, and the hose nozzle held against the neck of the fuel tank. Personnel were to remove any metal objects from their pockets, and before climbing onto the wing they were to touch the wing surface away from the filler neck to discharge any accumulated static electricity.

Oil

There were four oil tanks located on the leading wing edge next to each engine. The capacity of each inboard tank (supplying the outboard engines) was 80 gallons, and the capacity of each outboard tank (supplying the inboard engines) was 73 gallons. Grade 1120 (Specification No. An-VV-446) was used, although grade 1100A could be used in cold weather.

Hydraulic Reservoirs

There were seven hydraulic reservoirs, with the first four reservoirs filled with hydraulic fluid Specification No. AN-VV-O-366, and the last three filled with hydraulic fluid Specification No. 3580M.

Main system: The main system was filled through the emergency hydraulic reservoir on the forward face of bulkhead 4. There was a switchover valve on this bulkhead that pumped fluid from the emergency reservoir into the main reservoir to a capacity of 3.07 gallons of hydraulic fluid Specification No. AN-VV-O-366. Personnel were to listen for fluid draining back into the emergency reservoir as an initial indication that the main reservoir was filled. A sight gauge was located nearby.

Emergency system reservoir: This reservoir, also located on the face of bulkhead 4, was filled to a capacity of 5.86 gallons of hydraulic fluid Specification No. AN-VV-O-366, to be determined by a black line on the sight gauge.

Brake reservoir: The landing gear needed to be extended, and the brake pedals depressed until all air was relived from the accumulators (the pressure gauge was to read zero). The reservoir was filled with 5.68 gallons of hydraulic fluid Specification No. AN-VV-O-366, as determined by a black line on a sight gauge.

Belly turret reservoir: The turret was to be retracted and filled with a capacity of 0.22 gallons of hydraulic fluid Specification No. AN-VV-O-366 as determined by a sight gauge.

Main landing gear shock struts: The pressure was to be relieved so that the pistons bottomed, and then were to be filled with hydraulic fluid Specification No. 3580M. Once filled the filler plug was replaced, and the cylinder recharged with compressed air.

Nose wheel shock struts: The pressure was to be relieved in the strut by backing out the filler plug on the top of the oleo cylinder, causing the strut to collapse. The strut was to be filled with hydraulic fluid Specification No. 3580M, the filler plug replaced, and the cylinder recharged with compressed air.

Tail bumper: The bumper was to be fully extended, and all air pressure released from the air spring. The air spring was to be detached, and the cylinder was to be filled until the hydraulic fluid Specification No. 3580M ran out of the filler hole. Once filled the spring was reattached and inflated to 600psi.

Anti-icing fluid

The filler tank was located on the aft side of bulkhead 6, with the tank located on the forward side. The tank was to be filled to the top of the filler neck (a gauge reading from 0 to 8 gallons was located on the right of the filler neck) with isopropyl alcohol (Specification No. 14082).

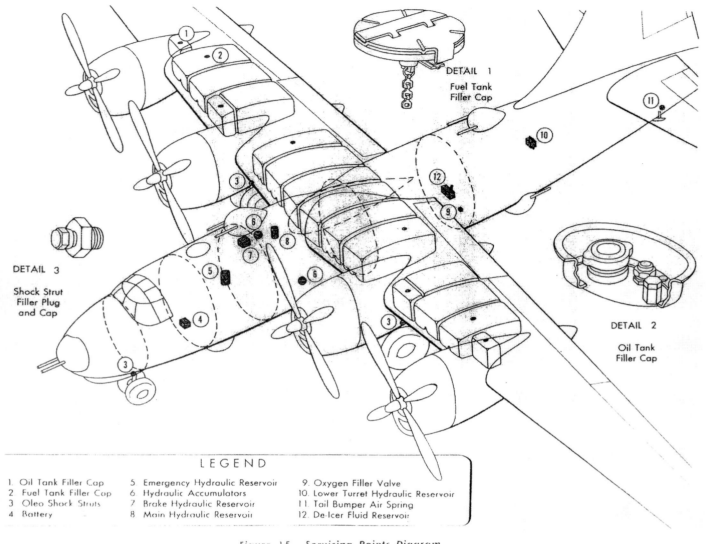

DETAIL 1

Fuel Tank
Filler Cap

DETAIL 3

Shock Strut
Filler Plug
and Cap

DETAIL 2

Oil Tank
Filler Cap

LEGEND

1. Oil Tank Filler Cap
2. Fuel Tank Filler Cap
3. Oleo Shock Struts
4. Battery
5. Emergency Hydraulic Reservoir
6. Hydraulic Accumulators
7. Brake Hydraulic Reservoir
8. Main Hydraulic Reservoir
9. Oxygen Filler Valve
10. Lower Turret Hydraulic Reservoir
11. Tail Bumper Air Spring
12. De-Icer Fluid Reservoir

Figure 15 – Servicing Points Diagram

(E&R Manual)

7

Bombing Equipment

AN/APQ-13 Radar Bombing Sets

Both the B-32 and B-29 were intended as high altitude VHB bombers, and the AAF anticipated the use of the AN/APQ-13 radar set (nicknamed "Mickey") for its navigation and bombing. In the ETO the AAF had used both the British H2S and American H2X (designated the APQ-15) beginning in the fall of 1943. In August of that year, the AAF decided to develop another new X-Band bombing radar set from "off the shelf" components, to be developed and built by Bell Laboratories and its Western Electric subsidiary, as well as MIT's Radiation Laboratory. The set was a 3cm unit, and operated in the 10,000MHz span to send out a narrow beam in the horizontal plane, and a wide beam in the vertical plane.

The B-32-1-CFs (42-108471 through 108480) were fitted with these sets, but during the production of the TB-32-5-CFs (42-108485 through 495) training version these sets were not installed. However, when the production of the B-32-20-CF and B-32-25-CF combat-equipped versions resumed they were equipped with the AN/APQ-13 radar sets. In July 1945 a B-32 AN/APQ-13 Suitability Test was conducted, and the B-32-30-CFs

(aircraft 42-108571 through 577) and subsequent CFs had these sets replaced with the AN/APQ-13A. Since the B-29 was combat-ready first it was fitted with the new AN/APQ-13 radar. The radar operator and the scope were located on the flight deck, but the physical unit was mounted elsewhere, and difficulties with air pressure, cold temperatures, and electrical problems occurred at high altitudes. The main unit was then mounted at the radar operator's station, except for the inverter, which was located beneath the floor near the radar operator, and the radio frequency unit, which was located in the barrel-shaped enclosure just behind the radar antenna dome. The 30 inch AS-53/APQ-13 radar antenna was mounted in a hemispherical radome that was installed on the bottom of the fuselage, behind the nose wheel doors. Wartime photos were usually censored, and the radome was painted out. The dishpan-shaped antenna (called a "spinner") was mounted on edge, and was rotated about its vertical axis, and it could be tilted through a small angle about a horizontal axis while rotating. The radome could be extended or retracted by the radar operator with a retracting motor located under the wing. The APQ-13 consisted of:

APQ-13 (1) Aircraft 471 shown with lowered early AN/APQ-13 Radar Bombing and Search radome. This set was superseded by the AN/APQ-13A on the B-32-30-CF models (42-108571 through 577). (USAAF via Dembeck)

APQ-13 (2) Close up of the AN/APQ-13 developed and built by Bell Laboratories, its Western Electric subsidiary, and MIT's Radiation Laboratory. The set was a 3cm unit, and operated in the 10,000MHz span to send out a narrow beam in the horizontal plane and a wide beam in the vertical plane. (USAAF)

Antenna Equipment	AS-53/APQ-13
Modulator	MD-12/APQ-13
Radio Frequency Unit	BC-1276-A
Synchronizer	SN-7/ APQ-13
Indicator	ID-41/ APQ-13
Control Box	C-71/ APQ-13
Inverter	PE-218-D
Rectifier	RA-90-A
Voltage Regulator	TF-12-A
Phasing Unit	CN-6/ APQ-13
Torque Amplifier	AM-19/ APQ-13
Azimuth Control Box	C-72/ APQ-13
Computer	CP-7/ APQ-13
Range Unit	CP-6/ APQ-13
Turn Control	GE 1027

Most of this equipment was located at the radar operator's station, except the radio frequency unit, the modulator, the JB-87 junction box, and the pressure unit, all of which were located under the flight deck, and the inverters and the J-66/A junction box, which were located in the bomb bay at station 5.0. The antenna equipment was in a retractable radome or radar antenna dome.

APQ-13 radar was less accurate than conventional optical bombing, with less than 1% of its bombs hitting within 1,000 feet of the aiming point. In early operations it was limited by the following:

The radar operators were hastily and insufficiently trained in the United States, which left them unable to evaluate the information depicted on their radarscopes in combat conditions. The radar operators also lacked sufficient navigation skills, and the aircraft navigator had to complete the computations required for bombing and navigation from his remote radarscope in the forward compartment.

The high bombing altitudes caused 25% of the airborne radar to malfunction, and the return signals at these altitudes were too weak to be of much use.

The strong jet stream winds at the high bombing altitudes limited the axes of attack to a downwind bombing run, which precluded the maximum use of the radar, as the target approaches with the more distinct radar markers were rarely used.

In the early combat missions from the Marianas the bomber's routes avoided the Japanese-held islands south of Japan to prevent early warning, and thus the radar operator and bombardier were unable to use these landmarks for navigational checkpoints. The B-29s were then left to fly over open water for seven hours with no checkpoints between takeoff and landing.

Dr. William Shockley, who was awarded the Nobel Prize for his invention of the transistor in 1956, developed a ground-based radar trainer. The complicated device was used at Smokey Hill AFB in early 1944 to train personnel for radar bombing in simulated bombing runs on Japanese targets. The radar operators were extensively trained in navigation and target identification utilizing clearly defined land-water contrast points. This improved intensive Stateside operational radar training, along with the initiation of low-level incendiary missions, led to conditions that were within the competence of the operators and capabilities of the equipment. Once

Japanese defenses diminished over the more important targets the smaller, virtually undefended cities were attacked, and radar was given primary consideration in mission planning. As time passed there was a continuous improvement in radar techniques when used in incendiary attacks. Improved target information and mission planning resulted in a satisfactory radar bombing accuracy. This satisfactory accuracy was not of the "pickle barrel" standard by any means. Post attack analysis documented that 18% of the bombs fell within 2,000 feet of the aiming point, 50% within 4,000 feet, and 75% within 6,000 feet, all of which were sufficient when using incendiaries to burn out large urban areas.

The B-32 AN/APQ-13 radar was tested in the combat suitability tests in the Far East with the assistance of Proving Ground Command personnel. Col. Frank Cook, CO of the combat test, submitted the following favorable report on the use of radar:

"The airplane appears to be well adapted to this type of employment. The highest latitude used for bombing during the combat test was 20,000 feet. Excellent results were obtained. Radar installation is favorable to radar bombing, as the flight deck arrangement allows close coordination among the radar-bombardier-navigator-pilot team. With properly maintained equipment radar operation has been excellent."

1Lt. Jack Whitener, the B-32 Radar Project Officer from the Proving Ground Command, reported:

"Radar equipment in the B-32 airplane was operationally suitable for navigation, search, and bombing."

However, Whitener also reported that during combat testing in the Far East the AN/APQ had many problems, and that the set was down or operating unsuccessfully 90 of 200 hours. This failure was attributed to faulty equipment, and to the lack of training of the combat test crew radar operators, which was to cause the most problems. In combat tests it was found that radar operators and LAB (Low Altitude Bombing) trained bombardiers were not sent overseas with the B-32s, and had to be trained by the 312th Bomb Group. The equipment problems were due to incomplete inspection before leaving the factory, modifications required but not done, and "inherent failure of parts of the equipment."

Bomb Bays

The B-32 had two tandem bomb bays (forward and rear) that were separated by the beltframe at station 5.0. The catwalk that extended lengthwise through the fuselage halved each bomb bay. The sections were designated, facing toward the nose, as the right half and the left half of the bomb bay, and each one-fourth of the bomb bay was a "half bay." The maximum number and weight of bombs was 20,000 pounds at 40x500 pounds. The heaviest single bomb was 4,000 pounds, and four could be carried at one time. Other possible bomb loads were: 12x1,000 pound bombs; 8x1,600 pound bombs; and 8x2,000 pound bombs. Bomb loads with less than 500 pound bombs were: 120x100 pound (AN-M30) by triple suspension from each 500 pound station; 80x260 pound fragmentation (AN-81) by double suspension from each 500 pound station; 40x250 pound demolition (AN-M57) by one bomb per 500 pound station; and 15x55 gallon Napalm filled gasoline drums (not used due to the danger from the all-way fuse igniter). The bomb bays could also carry four removable self-sealing bomb bay

The B-32 bomb bay doors opened by sliding upward along the curve of the fuselage, and were closed by sliding interlocking panels. (Consolidated via Chana)

tanks of 750 gallon capacity that were shackled to the bomb racks, one on each side of the catwalk, and were of the quick-disconnect type so they could be dropped in flight (to be discussed in detail). Each bomb bay half had provisions for two inboard and two outboard racks for bombs of 500 pounds or smaller. There were 48 shackling stations, with three stations per rack, but only two of the three stations on the outboard racks could be used at one time. Rack positions had to be changed for 1,000 pound bombs, and special racks had to be installed to carry 1,600, 2,000, and 4,000 pound bombs. The maximum bomb load was 20,000 pounds.

Bomb Bay Doors

During tests by the AAF Proving Ground Command "serious and repeated difficulties with the operation of the bomb bay doors was a common occurrence." The bomb bay doors on the test aircraft were found to be unsatisfactory, and the PGC requested the Air Materiel Command develop and install "a reliable and satisfactory" bomb bay door. However, the test aircraft supplied to the PGC were not later production models, and the Air Materiel Command informed the Army Air Forces Board that production models would have satisfactory bomb bay doors installed.

The bomb bay doors were opened by sliding upward along the curve of the fuselage, and were closed by sliding interlocking panels. The B-32 roll-up bomb bays did not snap open, and took 13 seconds for the four hydraulic motors to open or close the doors, causing a 9mph reduction in airspeed. A toggle switch on the bombardier's panel electrically controlled the hydraulic operation of the doors when the bombardier's master circuit switch was ON. When the switch was turned to OPEN it actuated the master selector valve solenoids, and the valve directed fluid into the doors' OPEN position. The fluid flowed through bomb door restrictors that metered into four hydraulic motors. The motors opened the doors, which were stopped by a microswitch when each bomb door was full open. The bomb bay doors also opened on operation of the salvo switches on the bombardier's panel, and on the rear bulkhead of the flight deck. If the

electric circuit failed the doors could be opened or closed by manual operation of the main selector valves. Limit switches on each door prevented bomb release until each door was completely opened.

Bomb Racks and Shackles

There were five types of bomb racks identified by a letter: "A," "B," "C," "D," and "E." On all five types there were racks for left hand and right hand half bays, made necessary by shackle hook arrangement and bomb shackle release A-4 controls. Left and right half bay racks could not be substituted for each other.

As an aid in memorizing designations of racks the catwalk was used as the origination point of sequence. For example, the type "A" was inboard (at the catwalk), and station 1 on the rack was the lowest station (closest to the catwalk). The nose arming control had to be forward, and the single hole in the bomb release receptacle had to be aft. There was a difference in the length of the spacers between the vertical beams and the shackle hooks. The shackles had to be placed so that the movement of the carrying hooks was from aft to forward. For this reason the forward spacer was shorter than the aft, making incorrect placement of the shackle impossible. The word FRONT was engraved on each shackle of all types. When the shackle was placed on the rack the end of the shackle on which the word FRONT appeared had to be toward the nose of the aircraft. When shackles were hung on the inboard racks in the right half bays, or hung outboard in the left half bays, with the word FRONT forward, the engraving was against the rack and not visible.

1. Type A Racks
2. Type B Racks
3. Type C Racks
4. Type D Racks
5. Hoisting Platform
6. Dollies

Figure 566 – Special Bombing Equipment

(E&R Manual)

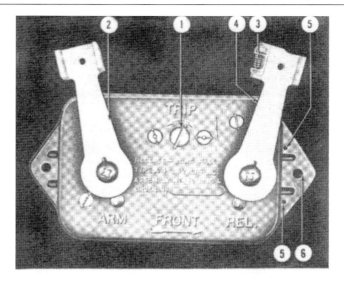

1. Trip Screw
2. Releasing Lever
3. Releasing Lever Ear
4. Arming Lever
5. Screw Hole Covers
6. Mounting Screw Hole

Figure 435 — Bomb Release, Type A-4 (Front)

(E&R Manual)

Vertical beams were the main supports for the structure, and were the parts that were attached to the bomber's structural members when the racks were installed. The holes for the mounting pins and bolts were at both the upper and lower ends of the rack. The racks were jig-drilled at the factory to insure ease of fitting and the security of mounting. When the racks were installed facing each other, the tops of the racks were the same distance above the ground. The difference in length corresponded to the difference in the distance they extended downward.

The type "A" rack was an inboard rack, and eight were provided for each bomber. Depending on the weight and type of bomb, either four or eight "A" racks were used. The rated capacity of "A" rack was 2,000 pounds.

Type "B" rack was similar to "A" rack, with the principal difference being their vertical length, and that the sections were much closer together on the "B" rack. They had the same identification nomenclature, with the arming controls forward and the release receptacles similarly placed. The

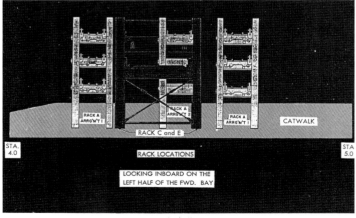

Figure 587 — Bomb Rack Locations

(E&R Manual)

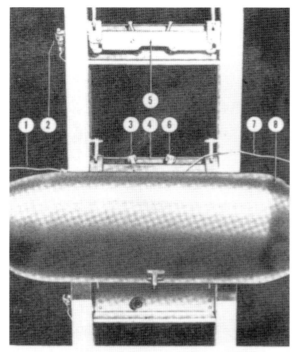

1. Nose Arming Wire
2. Bomb Control Release Type AN-A-2
3. Release Lever
4. Release Type A-4
5. Arming Lever
6. Shackle
7. Tail Arming Wire
8. 500 Pound Bomb

Figure 437 — Rack and 500-Pound Bomb Assembly

(E&R Manual)

"B" rack was the companion for "A," and they were always used together. They were placed exactly opposite and facing each other within the half bay. When carrying 500 pound bombs on all stations of rack type "A," stations #1 and #3 of rack "B" were in position to carry two 500 pound bombs. On "B," station #1 was between station #1 and #2 on "A," and #3 on "B" was between #2 and #3 on "A." Similarly, when 1,000 pound bombs were carried, station #2 on "B" was available at a correct distance between #1 and #3 on "A." Eight type "B" racks were used so that, when all were installed, there were 16 racks with a total of 48 stations. The type "B" racks were designed to carry two 500 pound bombs, or one each of 1,000 or 1,600 pound bombs. The maximum rated load capacity was 1,600 pounds.

Type "C" and "D" racks could be compared similarly to the "A" and "B" racks, and identifying nomenclature was the same. The "C" rack was the inboard rack, and had a greater length. It had only one station, at which a 1,000 pound or 1,600 pound bomb could be suspended by one D-6 shackle. Racks "C" and "D" were the only racks on which crossed brace wires were used. Type "D" rack was the outboard counterpart for "C," just as "B" was for "A." It faced "C' from exactly opposite in the half bay. The D-6 and D-7 shackles were similar. The D-6 was used on the "C" and "D" racks. The D-7 could only be used on the "E" rack, as the "C" and "D" racks were designed so D-7 shackles would not fit, and could not be suspended without alteration of the rack's suspension hooks or the shackles. The shackles were identified by their engraved identification, and also by their size and weight. The D-6 was 6.25 inches and weighed 9.4 pounds, while the D-7 was 7.125 inches and weighed 12.5 pounds.

The "E" rack was composed of three sections: inboard, outboard, and center sections. It was not only a bomb rack, but also a hoisting structure used in conjunction with the hoisting beam assemblies for loading 4,000 pound bombs.

When 1,000 pound bombs were carried stations #1 and #3 were the suspension points. All three stations could be used when carrying 500 pound bombs, while 1,600 pound bomb loading could only use station #1.

Rack Arrangements

Arrangement 1: The purpose of this set-up was to meet the need for a large number of bomb rack stations when the intended mission was to carry a large number of lightweight bombs. A total of 16 racks were used: eight of type "A" and eight of type "B." The inboard "A" racks carried three bombs each, and the outboard type "B" carried two bombs.

Arrangement 2: This arrangement, using type "A" and "B" racks, was intended to carry 500 pound bombs with hydrostatic fuses, 1,000 and 1,600 pound bombs. This method differed from Arrangement 1 in that only eight racks were used: one type "A" (inboard) and one type "B" (outboard) in each half bay. When 1,000 pound bombs were carried the type "B" (outboard) racks carried one each, and the type "A" (inboard) carried two for a total of 12. When 1,600 pound bombs were loaded each rack carried only one bomb (eight total for the aircraft).

Arrangement 3: "C" and "D" racks were used to carry 1,600 and 2,000 pound bombs in a plan similar to Arrangement 2.

Arrangement 4: This method was used to handle 4,000 pound bombs. It was similar to Arrangements 2 and 3, with the differences being the use of type E racks, and the use of bomb tail fin guides. The general loading procedure depended on:

> Type of racks required.
> Number of racks required.
> Type of shackles required.
> Number of shackles required
> Number of arming controls required.
> Number of shackle releases required.
> Stations to be used on each rack.

Bomb Rack Difficulties

The various types of bomb racks on the B-32 were not easy to interchange due to the improper alignment of aircraft fittings. In almost every case, when the racks were installed for the first time the holes needed to be redrilled and new fittings made. B-32 fuselage structural warping made it difficult to reinstall racks after removal. The space between outboard and inboard racks, and the spacing between outboard and inboard 500 pound bomb clusters and 500 pound incendiary clusters made it extremely difficult to reach the shackles in order to attach them to the rack when loading.

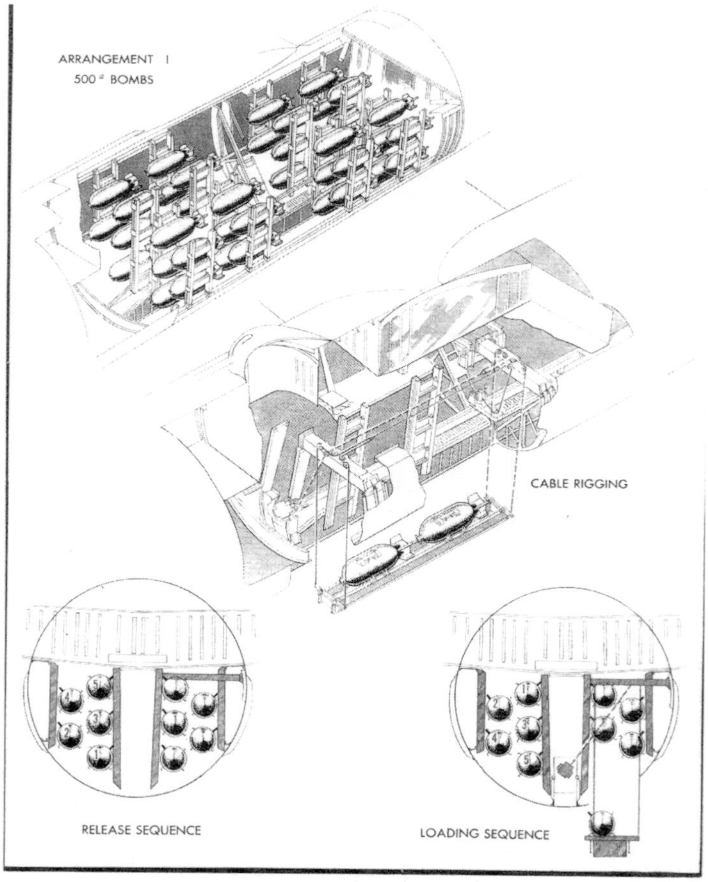

ARRANGEMENT 1
500# BOMBS

CABLE RIGGING

RELEASE SEQUENCE

LOADING SEQUENCE

Figure 591 – 500 Pound Diagram

(E&R Manual)

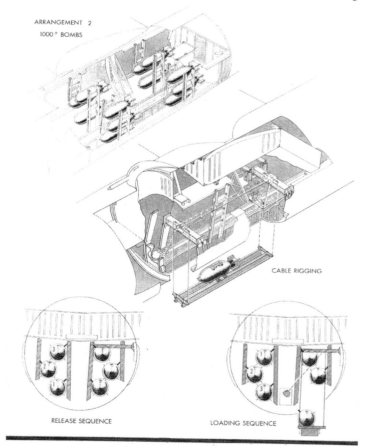

ARRANGEMENT 2
1000# BOMBS

CABLE RIGGING

RELEASE SEQUENCE

LOADING SEQUENCE

Figure 592 – 1000 Pound Diagram

(E&R Manual)

Bomb Hoisting Equipment

The bombs were loaded by means of a rectangular metal platform on roller chocks that carried two 500 pound bombs, or one larger size bomb. The platform was hoisted into the bomb bay, and the roller chocks were so positioned that the bombs were brought into proper position for hanging on the racks. The hoisting equipment consisted of structural units and equipment that were installed for the bomb hoisting (loading) operation, and removed when the loading was completed. They supplied the necessary strength inside the bomb bays to support the rigging and bombs. A hoisting beam assembly was used in each bomb bay: one at station 5.0 between the bomb bays, and the other at either end of the forward end of the forward bomb bay (station 4.0), or at the rear end of the rear bomb bay (station 6.0).

The hoisting beam was used laterally, extending outboard from a point above the bomb bay door, and was supported in position by outboard castings. The beam contained vertical, horizontal, and diagonal pulleys that were used as required by the bay being loaded and bomb size. The vertical pulleys were used in all procedures except 4,000 pound bomb loading. Horizontal pulleys were used in all procedures, and the loading of a 4,000 pound bomb required one per beam, while all the others required two. One or the other of the diagonal pulleys was used in each procedure.

For hoisting and placement of the bombs on their rack stations two C-3 hoist assemblies, a hoisting platform, two cradles, two A-1 slings, and a cable assembly were supplied to attach to the pulleys. The weight and type of bomb to be carried was the determining factor as to which equipment was to be used and where it was to be installed.

Bomb Loading Times

Bomb Type	Required Racks in Place	Required Racks to be Installed
40x500lb	3hr	4.5hr
12x1,000lb	1.5hr	3hr
8x2,000lb	1.5hr	3.5hr
40x500lb incendiary	2.5hr	4.5hr
80x260lb fragmentation	—	4hr
120x100lb	—	1hr

Bomb Loads

Single Suspension

40	100lb M30 General Purpose
40	500lb M64 General Purpose
12	1,000lb M65 General Purpose
8	1,600lb MK1 Armor Piercing
8	2,000lb M66 General Purpose
4	4,000lb M56 Light Case
40	500lb T4E4 Delayed Opening Fragmentation Clusters
36	500lb E46 or E48 Incendiary Clusters
40	E28 or E36 Incendiary Clusters

Multiple Suspension

112	100lb AN-M30 General Purpose (triple suspension)
112	100lb M12 Incendiary Clusters (triple suspension)
136	100lb M47A2 Incendiary Bombs (six per station on the center and top stations and five on the lower station of the inboard racks)
120	100lb M47A2 Incendiary Bombs (triple suspension)
80	260lb AN-M81 Fragmentation Bombs (double suspension)

A number of service tests were conducted investigating the multiple suspension of various bomb loadings. This photo shows 100 pound GP bombs in triple suspension on T-15 cluster adapters. (USAAF)

Cargo Carriers

Cargo was carried by the use of specially designed carriers that were installed in the bomb bays on each side of the catwalk. They were plywood bins reinforced with angles, steel plates, and wooden ribs. Each carrier was fastened to Type B-7 or B-10 shackles on two inboard and two outboard 500 pound racks. The bomb release or salvo switches could jettison the carriers.

Auxiliary Bomb Bay Fuel Tanks

The bomb bays could also carry four removable, interchangeable Good Year 2FI-6-4562 self-sealing 640 gallon (with a 20 gallon expansion capacity) auxiliary fuel tanks supported internally by fiber hoops. The tanks, with 2,560 gallons total capacity, were mounted two in each bomb bay, and were shackled to the bomb racks, one on each side of the catwalk. For loading into the bomb bays the auxiliary tanks were supported underneath by two special slings that were attached to the 500 pound bomb racks by B-7 bomb shackles, and A-2 bomb releases on each side of the bomb bay. The bomb hoist motor lifted the two tanks, one above the other, into each bomb bay.

Each tank had two outlet openings, but only one was used, depending on the location of the tank in the bomb bay, with the alternate opening closed by a cover. Each tank had a drain outlet on its bottom. All couplings were self-sealing and were of the quick-disconnect type so the tanks could be dropped in flight. Vent lines led from the top of each tank to openings in the fuselage skin over the bomb bay. There was a sight gauge located at the end of each tank near the center of the bomb bay.

Two three-way selector valves at fuselage station 5.0 directed the flow of fuel from the bomb bay tanks into the main fuel system at the manually operated drain valve. Each selector valve connected to two tanks, and to

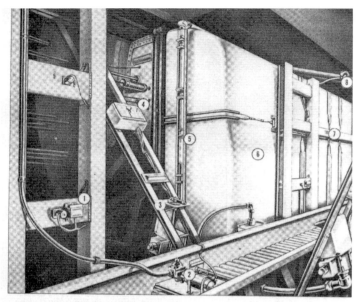

BOMB BAY FUEL SYSTEM

1. Toggle Switch	4. Pump Switch	7. Tank Supports
2. Booster Pump	5. Sight Gage	8. Vent System
3. Selector Valves	6. Fuel Tank	

(E&R Manual)

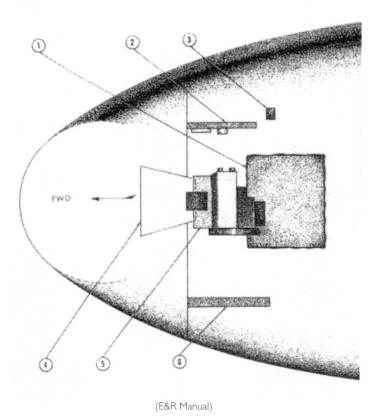

(E&R Manual)

Figure 434 - Intervalometer (E&R Manual)

the bomb bay system booster pump. The booster pump, mounted on the catwalk near the center of the bomb bay, was a standard engine-driven fuel pump mounted directly on an explosion-proof DC motor. Fuel from the bomb bay tank was transferred by setting the bomb bay manual selector valve to the desired tank. The bomb bay booster pump was turned ON, and the manual drain valve was OPENED. The drain selector valve on the fuel selector panel was turned to BOMB BAY or DRAIN. The selector valve was turned to CROSSFEED TO ENGINE for the engine or engines that the pilot wanted to operate on bomb bay fuel.

Bombing Controls

The bombardier's compartment was located in the lower part of the nose between the front turret and pilot's and co-pilot's control pedestals, and contained the bombing instruments and controls. The bombs were to be released as per the preset bomb release interval control, or the bombardier's SELECT switch. Auxiliary bomb controls outside the bombardier's compartment were two salvo switches: one was located at the pilot's left on his instrument panel, and the other was on the rear wall of the flight deck beside the radio operator's table. When a switch guard was removed and the switch was placed in the SALVO position the bomb bay doors opened, and the bombs were dropped according to the proper sequence, with a minimum interval (0.2 seconds) between releases. The SALVO overrode the bomb release interval control and the bombardier's SELECT switch.

Heavy Bomb Tests

On 21 April 1945 Order No. B4-5-1, coded the "Albert Project," for the use of 12,000 pound *Tallboy* and 22,000 pound *Grand Slam* bombs, recommended that the Armament Laboratory prepare experimental tests for these bombs using factory modified aircraft 42-108535 at the AAF Proving Ground at Eglin Field, FL. Provisions were to be made for the installation of one 22,000 pound and one 12,000 pound bomb, or two 12,000 pound bombs. Quick changeover suspension arrangements were to use two stainless steel straps, with each strap being fixed to one end of a removable beam, while the other end was attached to a bomb shackle hook. The bomb shackle was to be suspended vertically, and operated by a Type A-4 bomb release unit.

The 12,000 pound bomb was to drop vertically out of the airplane, while the 22,000 pound bomb was to drop at 17.5 degrees due to bomb bay space limitations. Hinged bomb bay doors would be needed in place of the sliding type. It appears from a memorandum of 16 June 1945, "Pull-Up Hoist for the B-32 Airplane," that the project was abandoned when Consolidated-Vultee was unsuccessful in developing an adequate hoist for raising the heavy bombs into the aircraft.

8

Combat Armament

Sperry Remote Gunnery System
Background and Development

The R-40-B study contracts of November 1939 called for a very long range bomber to operate at very high altitudes, and over long distances. The turret operators in the proposed bomber would have to suffer the cold at high altitudes, and use oxygen for long periods. All early turret designs, from the first enclosed turret mounted in the B-10 in 1934 to the huge contemporary XB-19 bomber, with its hydraulically assisted turrets, experienced the same problems. Besides operator discomfort, installation was complicated and difficult, the turrets were heavy and cumbersome, control was uneven, and visibility was limited. The Air Materiel Command promoted better turret and gunnery systems, particularly a system with remote turrets controlled by central fire control. The remotely controlled turret was particularly desirable, as its low profile reduced drag, and it could be used to advantage in pressurized aircraft. Also, using a remote gunnery system the crew would not have to use oxygen and be exposed to high altitude cold for long periods, as the engineers designed pressurized, air-conditioned crew cabins. This meant the gunners were comfortably stationed inside the cabins at sighting stations with the turrets and guns located outside.

Under the R-40-B specifications, both the B-29 and B-32 were scheduled to be equipped with pressurized crew cabins, and much time and expense was invested in its development jointly by Boeing (as the company had previous pressurization experience) and the Air Materiel Command engineers. On 20 March 1940 Sperry Gyroscope, Bendix, Westinghouse, and General Electric were requested to submit remote turret proposals. The first proposal concerning such a system was submitted by Sperry on 28 March 1940. The proposal covered one fire control system, consisting of two computers, three sets of gun controls, and a central switchboard. Gun turrets, auxiliary power plant, and permanent wiring were considered integral parts of airplane structure, and were not included in the proposal. Sperry quoted a price of $137,245 that was to be only the manufacturing cost, exclusive of development, and preliminary design costs. A contract to build a prototype system of this system was authorized by Purchase #160333, dated 1 April 1940. Six more systems were contracted for on 2 June 1941. Meanwhile, Bendix concentrated on developing both hydraulic and electric turrets for manned and unmanned use.

Development

Sperry Gyroscope was founded in 1910 by Elmer Sperry in Brooklyn, NY, and during the First World War he and his son Lawrence collaborated with the Navy to develop the first aircraft stabilizer, gyro-stabilized bomb sights, and automatic fire control systems. In 1918 Lawrence organized his own company, which often competed with his father's company until the younger Sperry died in an aircraft accident over the English Channel in 1924. Dur-

Only known Sperry P-4 Computer and Periscope in existence at the Cradle of Aviation Museum. (CAM via Hahn)

ing the 1920s Elmer Sperry relinquished the daily operation of Sperry Gyroscope to professional managers, and independently and unsuccessfully concentrated on the development of the diesel engine until the end of his life in 1930. However, during this decade Sperry Gyroscope became known as a "military think tank" renowned for its scientists and engineers, who developed numerous aircraft and marine instruments. In 1929 the Sperry Gyroscope was incorporated, and in 1933 the Sperry Corporation was incorporated as a holding company for many other smaller businesses, including Sperry Gyroscope, Ford Instrument Company, and Intercontinental Aviation, Inc. During the 1930s and 1940s Sperry collaborated with MIT and Stanford to develop the microwave technology that led to the development of radar. During WWII the company grew exponentially, and moved to larger facilities at Lake Success, Long Island, to develop computer controlled and stabilized bombsights, mobile airborne radar, automated takeoff and landing systems, automatic pilots and computing aircraft, and anti-aircraft fire control systems. The Varian brothers, Russell and Sigurd, who had invented the klystron tube that had led to the success of WWII radar, headed the brilliant Sperry scientific team. Soon Edward Ginzton, W.W. Hanson, and a contingent of Stanford University researchers would join Sperry to make the company's Research and Development facilities among the best in the world. Dr. Herbert Grosch was hired to join the Sperry Garden City Lab as a fire control scientist. Grosch would have a long and illustrious career, becoming one of the first computer scientists at the IBM Watson Laboratory, and was the author of Grosch's Law, which described the relationship between computer processing speed and cost. Grosch was assigned to design a double-ended aircraft periscope that was to be used on the top-secret pressurized B-29 and B-32, and the projected B-28 bombers. Grosch's job was to be the intermediary between Kodak/Hawkeye and its renowned optical expert, Rudolf Kingslake, and the Sperry/Garden City computer team, which knew nothing about optics.

In the original concept, Sperry was to build their Remote System for the B-28 bomber. In February 1940 the North American XB-28 (NA-63) design was contracted as a high altitude medium bomber to complement the company's B-25. When the prototype rolled out in March 1942 it bore little resemblance to the Mitchell, except for the twin engines and tricycle landing gear. It had a cylindrical fuselage ending in a large empennage topped by a single vertical tail. The cabin was pressurized by exhaust-driven engine blowers. The gunners sat directly behind the cockpit, aiming and controlling their dorsal, ventral turrets, and tail turret with the Sperry remote periscopic sights linked to mechanical computers. The sights protruded above and below the fuselage on either side of the fuselage centerline. The gunners could operate either dorsal or ventral turrets, depending on the master control panel settings. The tail turret was controlled from the right hand computer console. All turrets were equipped with twin .50 caliber machine guns. The design was not pursued beyond the prototype stage, as combat experience demonstrated that the B-25 had developed its low altitude bombing techniques to such a high degree that there was no need for a pressurized medium bomber to operate at high altitudes.

Sperry now had contracts for seven systems, and additionally was manufacturing turrets, gunsights, autopilots, and bombsights for several types of airplane. Soon Sperry found that it was going to be unable to meet all their delivery schedules on the various projects. The Air Materiel Division desired to maintain two sources of supply for fire control systems. It was decided, therefore, to have General Electric manufacture its own system that was to be used with the Sperry computer, and to have Briggs Body

Company, Detroit, Michigan, manufacture the Sperry-designed turrets. Briggs was given two contracts for turrets: 100 turret sets for B-29s, and 360 sets for B-32s.

Sperry was given five remote system contracts in all: contracts for 107 for B-29s; contracts for 360 for XB-32s; and a contract that provided for the conversion of the computers. It became evident that Sperry would not have the remote control systems ready in time to meet early deliveries of B-29s, and there was a faction that opted for building the first B-29s and B-32s without pressurized cabins, and adding manned gun positions similar to the B-17. General B.F. Meyers, Materiel Division, informed the Technical Executive, Wright Field, on 27 December 1941 that provision was to be made to supply at least the first 100 B-29s with locally controlled turrets. Fire control systems were to be installed as soon as they were accepted as satisfactory, and production was sufficient to meet deliveries.

Parts of the Sperry System were first installed on the B-17 for test purposes. Early reports revealed inadequate provision for keeping air on the computer and optical tubes dry, and the probable inefficiency of the drive control and gun charger at low temperatures. The major difficulty, however, was with the periscope sighting system, which had a limited field of view that made locating targets difficult. The apparatus was so unsatisfactory that plans for the use of the Sperry System were changed in March 1942.

The Air Staff sent Col. Kenneth Wolfe, head of the Wright Field Armament Section, along with Colonels Leonard Harman and Roger Williams of Wright Field to Seattle with orders to abandon the remote sighting system, install conventional turrets, and get the B-29 project quickly moving forward, as it was now favored over the B-32. The trio met with Boeing's Edward Wells and N.D. Showalter, who were adamant against installing conventional turrets in the B-29, as they knew that these turrets would reduce the bomber's aerodynamic integrity that they had worked so hard to achieve. The bomber was so aerodynamically clean that lowering the landing gear caused as much drag as the rest of the aircraft, and with conventional turrets the B-29 would not achieve the performance objectives the AAC had set. Over the weekend the Boeing engineers built wind tunnel models and demonstrated their remote turret/drag reduction point of view to Wolfe and Harman. After hearing Boeing's objections, as an alternative the Army Air Corps asked Boeing to use retractable turrets similar to the Sperry ball turrets used on the B-17 to reduce drag. The Boeing engineer's response was that besides the fact that there was not enough room in the B-29 design for ball turrets, their gunners could not be sustained in the freezing environment of these turrets. Williams had heard that

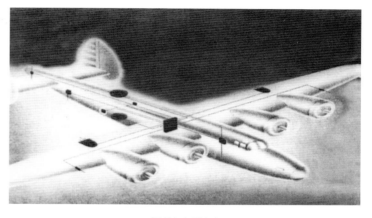

(CAM via Hahn)

General Electric was developing an electronic remote armament system, and recommended it be investigated as a solution to the remote turret dilemma.

Certain quantities of the B-29s were to be equipped with the General Electric system instead of the Sperry, and direct sighting used in place of the periscopic. It was believed by Experimental Engineering Section, Wright Field, that consideration should be given to making a like change in the B-32s. Considerable trouble was being experienced, too, in adapting the Sperry computer for use with the General Electric system in the B-28 type airplane. In view of these difficulties, Experimental Engineering Section, Wright Field, recommended that the Sperry facilities be converted to the manufacture of the General Electric system, that would then be standard equipment for all types of airplanes requiring remote fire control.

So both the retractable turret and the Sperry periscope concept were virtually set aside, and the decision was made to use the General Electric Central Station Fire Control System, which was now considered to be the only viable solution. Like the Sperry system, the early GE system also suffered from a limited scanning area through its periscope, and the gun controller had problems with orientation without a revolving seat or target locator that moved in conjunction with the turrets. The scanning limitation was solved by Bausch & Lomb, which developed a small double-ended reflector gunsight with a single eyepiece sighting station. In the General Electric sighting system the gun controller could rotate the sighting station in any direction during scanning. When the gun sighting station was engaged, its every motion was replicated by the turret(s). Central to the GE system were the selsyn generators on the sighting station that moved the selsyn control transformers on the turret. Each selsyn brought together the action of the turret and its guns. Each turret had two selsyn transformers controlling azimuth and two controlling elevation. The basis of the GE system was an optical reflector gunsight computer—located at four sighting stations in the fuselage—that would calculate lead azimuth and elevation angles, which were electrically transmitted to position non-retractable hydraulic turrets. The GE system eliminated the periscopes and the retractable turrets. (For a detailed description of the GE remote systems see my book: *The Boeing B-29 Superfortress: The Ultimate Look from Drawing Board to Combat*, Schiffer, PA, 2005.)

At a conference held at Wright Field in April 1942, it was definitely decided that the first three experimental B-29s were to be equipped with the Sperry system, but that the production models would carry General Electric equipment. The 100 Sperry systems already under contract were to be procured as "insurance"—as standby or alternate equipment. B-32s were to use the Sperry system, with the provision to change to direct (GE) sighting if that proved advantageous on B-29s. At the time no plans were made for the B-28s, pending a decision as to whether this type of aircraft was to be produced.

A report from Elgin Field, Florida, where the Sperry XB-20 type system was being tested on the B-17C, stated to the effect that the optical system and the spotting system needed changes, and that the whole system would not be effective at ranges over 500 yards if maneuvering was required of the plane while firing its guns. It was believed, however, that these difficulties would be remedied, and that the system was basically sound.

A later report that was submitted by the Proving Ground Command at Eglin Field on 30 December 1942 threw an unfavorable light on both remote systems. They found that neither was tactically suitable for defense of the B-29 and B-32 airplanes, and again recommended that provisions be made immediately to install locally controlled turrets in both airplanes. The disadvantages of the central station system were listed as follows:

1) Complexity of system and consequent maintenance problems;
2) Possibility of neutralizing entire system by a few hits;
3) Inability to defend against simultaneous attacks;
4) Inability to service guns quickly;
5) Inability to operate guns manually in case of electrical failure;
6) Limited scanning in Sperry system;
7) Unsatisfactory computer in General Electric system; and
8) Inherent inaccuracy in both systems due to parallax.

Only two advantages were found; namely:
1) Less weight, and
2) Greater ease of pressurization.

Shortly thereafter (January 1943) it was decided that locally controlled turrets would be used in B-32s, and that the plane would not be pressurized. Sperry and Briggs were notified on 13 February 1943 that their contracts for B-32 systems were canceled (360 fire control systems from Sperry, and 360 sets of turrets from Briggs). This left Sperry and Briggs tooled for full production, but only with contracts for B-29 systems (100 Sperry systems, and 100 sets of Briggs turrets). There were no requirements for the B-29 systems, except for "insurance" purposes. Production Engineering Section, Wright Field, asked that Materiel Command, Washington, make a decision in the matter, so that either installations could be planned or contracts canceled.

The B-29 Sperry contracts were not canceled; they were, in fact, augmented. Sperry held that the impending B-29 cancellations, along with the B-32 cancellations, would result in the loss of sources and of subcontractors, and it would be impossible to pick up production again in case there was a sudden demand for this system. Sperry suggested that their B-32 contract be changed to permit additional systems for the B-29 program. Major General O. P. Echols, who had "insisted upon the purchase of 100 sets of Sperry Central Station Fire Control Systems for B-29 airplanes as an insurance against a possible failure of the General electric Systems," and who thought that the Sperry system might prove to be superior to the General Electric, then recommended that Sperry's suggestion concerning the B-32 contract be adopted.

Accordingly, cancellations of Sperry and Briggs contracts for B-32 equipment were rescinded (22 February 1943), and the contracts were converted to provide for equivalent quantities for the B-29 series, making a total of 460 sets for B-29s. The converted systems were to be equipped with the auxiliary target locating sights recently developed by Sperry. These sights were provided for in a Change Order #7(?) to contract AC-25456, dated 31 August 1943, at a cost of $1,332,850. It was pointed out by Aeronautical Equipment Branch, Wright Field, that all Sperry systems were to be stored until such time as airplanes were allocated for installation of the equipment.

Production Division, Wright Field, asked Materiel Division, Washington, on 20 May 1943 if such an allocation was going to be made; if not, they recommended that the contract with Briggs for turrets be canceled. The value of the Sperry computers would not be jeopardized, since they could be used with General Electric turrets, and Briggs facilities would be released for the manufacture of local turrets, which were needed.

Materiel Command, Wright Field, informed Production Division, Wright Field, by authority of the Commanding General, Army Air Force, that no allocation of the Sperry system was to be made at that time, but that Sperry computers and sights would continue to be made for use with General Electric turrets. Briggs production of remotely controlled turrets, however, was to be slowed to conform to General Motors' production of B-29 planes.

In the meantime, tests of the Sperry system were proceeding at Eglin Field Proving Ground. Trial flights indicated that the system was entirely unsuitable for operational employment. The opinion of Wright Field, as expressed by Brigadier General C.E. Branshaw, was that the Sperry system was "coming in about third in this race, the winner being the General Electric system, and second place going to the locally operated turret installation." General Branshaw recommended, in the event it was decided to use some armament installation other than the General Electric, that locally controlled turrets be used, and that, in the interest of economy, and because the General Electric system was sufficiently developed so that Sperry equipment would no longer be required as "insurance," that the Sperry and Briggs contracts be canceled.

Materiel Division, Washington, did not agree that the contracts should be canceled. They considered it essential that the relative merits of the three systems be determined by actual air trials before a decision was made. General Electric was insistent that Wright Field not only follow through with tests of Sperry equipment at Marietta, Georgia, but that they participate in tests at Eglin Field to the extent that complete comparative reports could be made. Sperry protested, too, that adequate trials had not been made, and asked that a decision regarding cancellation be withheld for at least three months.

The test program was far behind schedule, due largely to difficulties with the YB-29 airplanes, which were frequently grounded because of various engine troubles, and conclusive comparative reports were never made. Production Engineering Section, Wright Field, reported 13 December 1943 that tests on General Electric equipment were just beginning, and that results would not be forthcoming until the middle of March 1944. It was expected that Sperry tests would be completed during February.

However, sufficient information on which to base a decision was available early in February, and a conference was called to analyze the B-29 armament program, and to determine a course of action concerning it. It was decided to initiate action immediately to cancel Sperry fire control equipment for B-29s, and to proceed with a plan for installing GE remotely controlled turrets. The two outstanding Sperry contracts—AC-25456 and AC-26160, for 460 sets of the Sperry system—were canceled as of 23 February 1944.

Description of the Sperry System

Despite the decision to use the untried GE system, Sperry and Grosch continued to develop the Central Station Computer System as a backup to the GE unit, as much time and expense had already been invested in its development. The Sperry system placed the gunner and the P-4 electromechanical analog computer, with its periscope sight, inside the pressurized fuselage, and the turrets outside, where they could be made smaller and retractable, resulting in a cleaner, more aerodynamic aircraft. The remote turret aiming system consisted of upper or lower sighting periscopes mounted on the P-4 analog computer base and turret selector panels. Sperry supplied

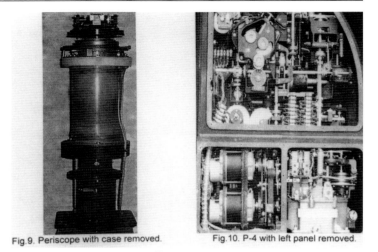

Fig.9. Periscope with case removed.   Fig.10. P-4 with left panel removed.

(CAM via Hahn)

the Central Control Computer Station and the entire gun turret works, with the turret hydraulics being built by its Vickers division. The computer was enclosed in a black 29.75 x 12 x 20 inch black cast aluminum case. The case contained an analog computer that was made up of three-dimensional cams, rate gyros, and ancillary equipment. There were two periscopes: one was approximately 29 inches long, and the other 38.75 inches—both were 5 inches in diameter. Each double-ended periscope with rotating heads permitted the sweep of a 30 degree cone of vision, covering both the upper and lower hemispheres with respect to the airplane. The periscopes were built by the Hawkeye Works of Eastman Kodak in Rochester, NY. The two different periscope lengths allowed the P-4 computer to be located in either single or dual configuration at different fuselage locations, with the shorter used in the upper position. The periscopes weighed between 100 and 125 pounds. The periscopes were located in small plastic domes at the top and bottom mid-fuselage of the bomber. The selector panels allowed the gun turrets to be switched among linked computers in case a turret or computer was inoperative.

Operation

The gunner sighted the target through the periscope, and tracked it with the power-operated computer that automatically, through the gun controls, rotated the turrets and elevated the guns. The periscope aiming system al-

Fig.4a. Forward turret control panel.   Fig.4b. Rear turret control panel.

(CAM via Hahn)

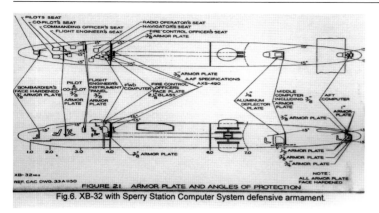

Fig.6. XB-32 with Sperry Station Computer System defensive armament.

(Sperry via CAM/Hahn)

lowed one central controller to direct as many as five turrets containing twin .50 caliber machine guns or 20mm cannons from a console in the forward compartment, near the navigator's station. Besides being able to transfer control to other gunners who were in better firing positions, on signals from spotters the controller was also able to switch from any turrets that were damaged or inoperable. Another scanner in the waist controlled the upper and lower turrets through a second periscope. With only two periscopes there was a lack of orientation on the target, and additional sighting stations had to be added. Two waist gunners scanned through ring and bead spotting sights in two fuselage blisters, and the bombardier had one in the nose compartment. Once these additional spotters had the target in their sights the controller was able to take over and track the target. If the target was seen broadside the determination of the wingspan was reasonably easy, but the target approaching from any other angle would cause the gunner to mentally calculate the trigonometry of the viewing angle in order to enter the wingspan into the computer. This auxiliary spotting sys-

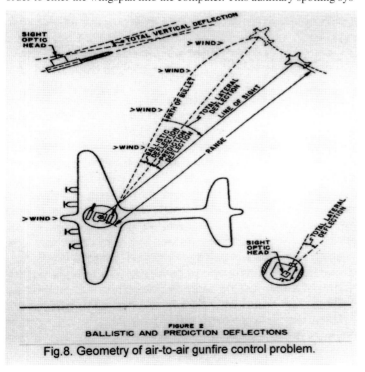

Fig.8. Geometry of air-to-air gunfire control problem.

(Sperry via CAM/Hahn)

tem involved a precise and well-practiced vocal communications system via the bomber's interphone. If the target was transferred the controller had to continue to align it in the lighted reticle of his sight, reconfirm the identity of the target, and use his memory of the specific data of the target aircraft to enter the wingspan into the computer (on the upper right hand side of the computer). The computer calculated corrections for altitude, speed, temperature, ballistics, deflection, and parallax to determine azimuth and elevation lead angles (range to the target was displayed on a dial on the left computer panel) to the selected gun turret needed to fire at an attacking aircraft. The analog computer could only direct one gun turret at a time to a selected target.

The controller continued to track the enemy by constantly keeping its wingtips centered in the sight by adjusting a dial, or by using a foot pedal. The foot pedal was connected to a rate gyro mounted on the base of the computer that measured the rate of change that, when multiplied by the range, determined the speed of the target along its flight path. The ballistics (drag coefficient) of the bullets of the guns was known, and their trajectories were computed. A dial (on the upper left of the computer) was set by the controller to the indicated airspeed, and the computer calculated true airspeed based on altitude. The computer could then calculate the gun turret lead angle at which the bullets and target would converge, and then set the gun turret in both azimuth and elevation to aim at that point. When the controller tracked a target across the zero-elevation midline (above or below horizontal) of the sight, a prism rotated the eyepiece field from the upper to lower periscope (or vice versa) and flip-flopped the target in the sight, which made smooth tracking difficult.

Testing

During testing a XB-29 equipped with the Sperry system was sent to Eglin, FL, for firing tests under Kenneth Eidnes, B-29 Director of Armament tests. The program was headed by Col. Paul Tibbetts, who would fly the *Enola Gay* on its atomic bomb mission over Hiroshima. There is a question concerning which XB-29 was used in the Sperry system testing. In the Eglin Armament tests it was probably the first XB-29 prototype that was used, as it was originally fitted with the Sperry system. However, in December 1942 XB-29 #1 developed so many engine problems in testing that it was detached from the testing program, and would not fly for another seven months. After XB-29 #2 was destroyed in the Eddie Allen crash in February 1943, XB-29 #3 was the only XB-29 available; this aircraft was used as Boeing's Flight Test Ship, and continued flying until 1947. The Sperry system was not used in the YB-29s, but the XB-32 #2 and #3 prototypes were equipped with them. In January 1943 the system was removed from the third XB-32 prototype, and experimental turrets were installed and tested. The second XB-32 continued as a test aircraft throughout the war, but it is not known if the Sperry periscopic sighting system was removed; however, both test flight engineers Bill Chana and R.T. LeVine cannot remember the defensive armament of the XB-32s, or find any mention of firing tests or armament equipment in that aircraft in their logbooks. The Pilot's Handbook for the XB-32 shows that the projected defensive armament consisted of three P-4 periscope gunsight computers, upper and lower turrets, rear mounted twin .50 caliber machine guns, a 20 mm cannon in each wing (mounted outboard of the outboard engines), and nose mounted .50 caliber machine guns. In early November 1943 future B-32s were to be equipped with manned dual .50 machine guns in the nose, upper and lower turrets, and in the tail position.

Problems

For the Remote Control Gunnery tests Sperry sent a technical representative to Eglin. In his book *Fire of a Thousand Suns* (Web Publishing, CO, 1995) gunner George "Bob" Caron describes his encounter with the Sperry system and the company representative:

"Tibbetts assigned Caron the task of evaluating the performance of the General Electric firing systems of the YB-29, which he knew as intimately as a surgeon knows gall bladders, against the Sperry remote-controlled hydraulic system of the XB-29, of which he knew nothing. In fact, few people did, other than the Sperry technical representative....

On their first meeting, the representative was waiting for Caron at the flight line, manual in hand."

The Sperry periscope was found to have several disadvantages. The principal drawback of the Sperry periscope was its small field of vision, as the eyepieces did not give a wide enough field without creating distortion. The plastic domes at the ends of the periscopes caused a systemic error in elevation calculation. The inner and outer surfaces of the dome were not concentric, and confused the computer. As discussed previously, to compensate for only two periscopes and the lack of orientation on the target other spotters were added on the bomber who could inform the controller of targets, but that entailed an involved vocal communications system via the bomber's interphone. The Sperry optical system had problems in the cold of high operating altitudes, and the optical prisms had to be heated.

The second problem was that Sperry had adapted the electromechanical analog computer they developed in conjunction with their Ford Instrument Division for use in their naval gun directors and AA fire control systems. The analog computer had no memory, and could track only one target at a time. If there were more than one target within the controller's field then he could only choose one. Also, having no memory the computer had problems tracking nearby targets, as it was unable to sustain calculations because of the rapidly changing relative ranges and angles to the target to compute the required lead azimuth and elevation angles. Only years later would high speed digital computers with memory be developed. The Sperry analog computer design was much larger and more cumbersome than the small optical gunsight computer (K-series), a small electromechanical bombsight computer the company was developing at the time. This computer had chronic malfunctions that were impossible to remedy in the air, and sometimes had to be sent from Florida back to the Sperry factory on Long Island for repair. The computer system also had problems functioning at low temperatures.

Testing determined the turret system to be unacceptable, as the nose and tail positions had inadequate firepower, and there was a blind spot forward of the wing tips. There also was a rear blind spot, as the tail turret was controlled by the waist spotter periscope, and an attack from directly behind the tail could not be seen from the waist periscope.

Failure

Despite the initial optimism surrounding the Sperry remote system, in March 1944, only days before the B-29 was to go into combat, the final Eglin report concluded that the system was unsatisfactory to defend either the B-29 or B-32 due to its vulnerability, complexity, and inherent inaccuracy, and was unsuited for unescorted missions where the bomber could be sub-

jected to focused fighter attacks. A month later, another Eglin report found the system "vulnerable" and "not functionally reliable," as it had many chronic maintenance problems that were impossible to correct during flight. The report concluded that the only benefit of the system was that it made pressurization easier and weighed much less than a conventional turret system, but the report held out hope that the system's problems would eventually be solved. Meanwhile, Sperry saw that its periscopic remote sighting system program was going nowhere, and pulled Grosch from the project; they transferred him to the vital computerized Mark-14 optical gunsight project. The Mark-14 allowed turret gunners in the B-24 and B-17 and, ironically, the newly reconfigured B-32 to automatically lead attacking enemy fighters. The Sperry system would continue to be tested and improved, and the problems would mostly be solved, but the GE remote system had been installed in the B-29s fighting over Japan, and the B-32 was relegated to heavy bomber status with conventional turrets installed. The Sperry Remote Gunnery Project was canceled, and it never saw combat. Today there is a P-4 computer and periscope on display at the Cradle of Aviation Museum Garden City, LI, NY.

Once it was decided to use the conventional turret system on the B-32 there were not any aircraft available to develop and test the new turret arrangement, and a Ford-built B-24J-20-FO (44-48802) was modified to carry the Sperry designed/Briggs built nose, tail, and ball turrets that were to be used on the B-32.

(Thanks to Mort Han and the Cradle of Aviation Museum (CAM) for the majority of the information on the Sperry System.)

Manned Turrets

General

The standard defensive armament of the combat-equipped B-32 was 10 .50 caliber M-2 Browning machine guns mounted in pairs in the five manned turrets. The nose, tail, and lower turrets were electric-hydraulic ball turrets designed by Sperry and built by Briggs, with the lower turret being fully retractable, as in the B-24. The two teardrop upper electric turrets were Martin-built. The TB-32 models were not equipped with defensive armament, but carried 700 pounds of ballast located in the fuselage just aft of the tail to compensate for the effect of this exclusion on the center of gravity.

On 29 November 1943 a four man AAF engineering assessment team was sent to the Fort Worth plant to inspect the armament of the XB-32.

Due to the early shortage of armed production B-32s, as the TB-32s were being built a small number of B-24Js were fitted with A-17 nose and tail turret for gunnery training. (USAAF)

B-32 TURRET DATA

Location	Type	SIGHT Tech. Order	Type	Tech. Order	AMMUNITION Rounds Per Gun	Boxes (Location)	BOOSTERS Type	Tech. Order
Nose	A-17	Manufacturer's Instructions	K-11	Manufacturer's Instructions	600	Bombardier's Compartment	H-1	AN-11-1-48
Tail	A-17	Manufacturer's Instructions	K-10	Manufacturer's Instructions	1,000	Fuselage	H-1	AN-11-1-48
Upper Aft	A-3-D		K-8	AN-11-35B-1	400	Within		Integral
Upper Forward	A-3-D		K-8	AN-11-35B-1	400	Within		Integral
Lower Ball	A-13-A	11-45G-1	K-4	11-35A-2	500	Hanger		None

FIELD OF FIRE

	Azimuth Deg.	Mils			Elevation Deg.	Mils	Interrupters
Nose and Tail	134	2385	at	(Max.)	60	1067	
	150	2662	at		0		Limit Stops Only
	122	2172	at	(Max.)	-60	1067	
Upper Forward and Upper Aft	Continuous		at	(Max.)	79	1405	
	Continuous		at		0		Yes
				(Max.)	-6.5	115	
Lower Ball	Continuous		at	(Max.)	10	178	
			at		0		Yes
	Continuous		at	(Max.)	-90	1600	

TURRET COMPONENTS — TYPE DESIGNATIONS

	A-17 Type	T.O. or Part Number	A-13-A Type	T.O. or Part Number	A-3-D Type	T.O. or Part Number
MOTORS						
Drive	FD-83			74831		5BA50LJ1
Gun Elevation	None					5BA50GJ1
DYNAMOTOR			R5702552	None		
AMPLIDYNE	None		None		AN-D191	
AMMUNITION BOOSTERS	H-1	AN 11-1-48	None			5-74877
FIRING SOLENOIDS	G-11	93-24706	G-11	93-24706	G-11	93-24706
GUN HEATERS	J-1	24864	J-3		J-3	

(E&R Manual)

Unfortunately, the XB-32 had left for San Diego, and only the mock up was available for inspection, so the team's report was very derogatory:

"Admittedly, it may not be feasible to arm operational aircraft to the point they can be expected to defeat every conceivable type of coordinated attack over indefinite periods of time. But it should be possible, for instance, to provide sufficient fire power to engage enemy aircraft making a simple two-plane simultaneous attack from below, and to provide for a nearly adequate supply of ammunition...." (Williams, Maj. J.C.E., Memo to Col. J.O. Guthrie, "B-32 Defensive Armament," 11 December 1943)

The assessment went on to state that the B-32 armament layout was unacceptable, as both the nose and tail positions lacked adequate firepower, and all the gun positions were not supplied with enough ammunition. It also found that there was a blind spot just forward of the wing tips that none of the turrets was able to cover. The assessment concluded:

"The defensive firepower is inadequate for a long-range bombardment aircraft operating beyond the range of fighter escort."

The visibility afforded to the nose, tail, upper forward, and upper rear turret gunners was considered excellent. However, the lower ball turret gunner's visibility was poor, which was characteristic of that turret.

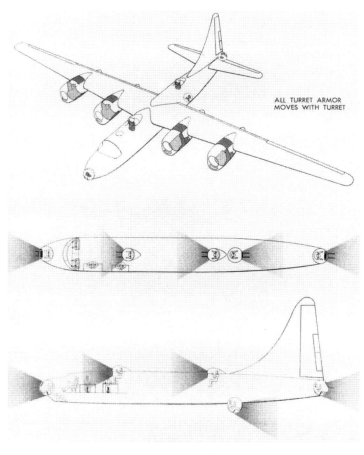

ALL TURRET ARMOR MOVES WITH TURRET

(E&R Manual)

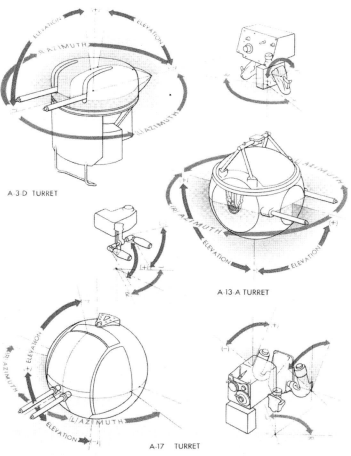

A-3-D TURRET

A-13-A TURRET

A-17 TURRET

Figure 603 — B-32 Turrets and Hand Control Units

(E&R Manual)

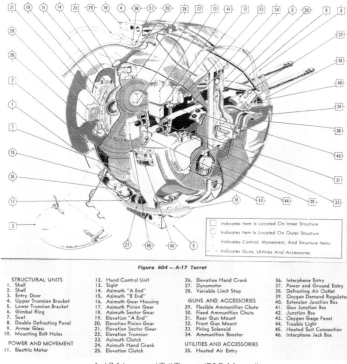

Figure 604 - A-17 Turret

STRUCTURAL UNITS
1. Shell
2. Shell
3. Entry Door
4. Upper Trunnion Bracket
5. Lower Trunnion Bracket
6. Gimbal Ring
7. Seat
8. Double Defrosting Panel
9. Armor Glass
10. Mounting Bolt Holes

POWER AND MOVEMENT
11. Electric Motor

12. Hand Control Unit
13. Sight
14. Azimuth "A End"
15. Azimuth "B End"
16. Azimuth Gear Housing
17. Azimuth Pinion Gear
18. Azimuth Sector Gear
19. Elevation "A End"
20. Elevation Pinion Gear
21. Elevation Sector Gear
22. Elevation Trunnion
23. Azimuth Clutch
24. Azimuth Hand Crank
25. Elevation Clutch

26. Elevation Hand Crank
27. Dynamotor
28. Variable Limit Stop

GUNS AND ACCESSORIES
29. Flexible Ammunition Chute
30. Fixed Ammunition Chute
31. Rear Gun Mount
32. Front Gun Mount
33. Firing Solenoid
34. Ammunition Booster

UTILITIES AND ACCESSORIES
35. Heated Air Entry

36. Interphone Entry
37. Power and Ground Entry
38. Defrosting Air Outlet
39. Oxygen Demand Regulator
40. Extension Junction Box
41. Gun Junction Box
42. Junction Box
43. Oxygen Gage Panel
44. Trouble Light
45. Heated Suit Connection
46. Interphone Jack Box

A-17 Nose and Tail Turret (E&R Manual)

The A-17 turret mounted the two .50 caliber M-2 Browning machine guns, the hand-controlled gun sight, and armor protection. The gunner, sitting on a small armored seat, faced armored glass and two thicknesses of plastic panels. (USAAF)

Once the B-32 was ready for combat training there were not enough armed B-32s available for gunnery training. This situation was due to initial design and production delays; the first 14 Fort Worth production aircraft (B-32-1 and -5-CF) were assigned to the accelerated test flying programs, while the next batch of 40 aircraft were the unarmed TB (TB-32-5/10/15-CF) training series. The final batch of 74 unpressurized bombers (B-32-CF-20, -21, -25, -30, and -35) were fully combat equipped models, but became widely available after the combat testing began. To remedy the situation several B-24Js were specially modified to act as surrogate B-32s mounting the B-32 turret arrangement.

The Sperry designed/Briggs built A-17 nose and tail turret were identical, except that the K-11 sight was used in the nose, and the Type-10 sight in the tail. (USAAF)

The A-17 turret consisted of two concentric structures. The 2.5 foot wide C-shaped center section that rotated around a lateral axis furnished vertical movement. It was entered through the rear, as seen in the turret in the second row. (USAAF)

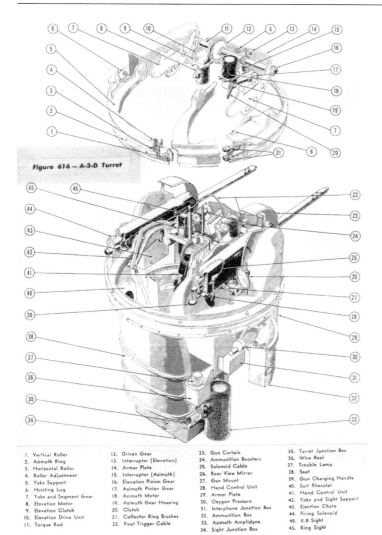

Figure 616 – A-3-D Turret

1. Vertical Roller	12. Driven Gear	23. Gun Curtain	35. Turret Junction Box
2. Azimuth Ring	13. Interrupter (Elevation)	24. Ammunition Boosters	36. Wire Reel
3. Horizontal Roller	14. Armor Plate	25. Solenoid Cable	37. Trouble Lamp
4. Roller Adjustment	15. Interrupter (Azimuth)	26. Rear View Mirror	38. Seat
5. Yoke Support	16. Elevation Pinion Gear	27. Gun Mount	39. Gun Charging Handle
6. Hoisting Lug	17. Azimuth Pinion Gear	28. Hand Control Unit	40. Suit Rheostat
7. Yoke and Segment Gear	18. Azimuth Motor	29. Armor Plate	41. Hand Control Unit
8. Elevation Clutch	19. Azimuth Gear Housing	30. Oxygen Pressure	42. Yoke and Sight Support
9. Elevation Clutch	20. Clutch	31. Interphone Junction Box	43. Ejection Chute
10. Elevation Drive Unit	21. Collector Ring Brushes	32. Ammunition Box	44. Firing Solenoid
11. Torque Rod	22. Foot Trigger Cable	33. Azimuth Amplidyne	45. K-8 Sight
		34. Sight Junction Box	46. Ring Sight

A-3-D Dorsal Turret (E&R Manual)

The A-3-D turrets provided for the mounting and servicing of two M-2 .50 caliber machine guns supplied with a K-15 sight and provisions for 400 rounds of ammunition each, and was actuated by 24-volt units that mechanically trained the turret and elevated the gun. (USAAF)

Type A-17 Nose and Tail Turrets

The Sperry designed/Briggs built A-17 nose and tail turret were identical, except that the K-11 sight was used in the nose, and the Type-10 sight in the tail. The turret was attached to the fuselage by a bracket at the top and a traversing gear housing at the bottom, with the entire ball moving left to right on pivot points incorporated by the attaching elements. The turret consisted of two concentric structures. The 2.5 foot wide C-shaped center section that rotated around a lateral axis furnished vertical movement. This section mounted the two .50 caliber M-2 Browning machine guns, the hand-controlled gun sight, and armor protection. In azimuth the entire assembly moved, while in elevation only the inner structure moved. The field of fire in azimuth was 150 degrees, and 120 degrees in elevation. Electrical power from the aircraft drove the constant speed electric motor, whose output was converted to hydraulic power that, through gearing, resulted in turret movement.

The gunner, sitting on a small armored seat, faced armored glass and two thicknesses of plastic panels that were not Plexiglas, but CR-39, manufactured by Pittsburgh Plate Glass Company. Between the panels there was a hollow space to allow the flow of heated air for defrosting.

Ammunition boxes for the 600 rounds supplying the nose turret were located beside and parallel to the windscreen in the bombardier's compartment. The 1,000 rounds for the tail turret were located inside the tail section just forward of the tail turret in boxes beside and parallel to the catwalk to the turret. The rounds were carried by flexible ammunition chutes. In the tail they ran through slings, and in the nose they ran across a shelf above the windscreen. The other turrets had integral boxes. The ammunition entered the turret through two openings located above and to each side of the rear entry door, and was fed through flexible chutes from two ammunition boxes that were mounted in the fuselage just to the rear of the turret. The nose and tail turrets were found to be the most important turrets in combat. In combat tests feeding difficulties and burned out turret clutches were major turret problems until remedied.

The B-32-30-CF (Aircraft 101 through 106/42-108571 through 577) turrets were modified by the replacement of the Sperry A-17 nose, and tail turrets with the stabilized A-17-A model.

Type A-3F-A Dorsal Turrets

Glenn L. Martin manufactured the dorsal turrets, designated as the upper forward and upper rear turrets, which were located on the centerline of the bomber in the top of the fuselage. Both teardrop shaped Plexiglas domed turret blisters were identical, and with the exception of the fire interrupter were interchangeable. The teardrop-shaped Plexiglas blisters faired the cupolas when the turrets were stowed in the fore and aft positions. These blisters and their thin, waterproof metal base plates were fastened to the turret chassis, and rotated with them. Aft of the turret and under the blister were non-moving, soleplate-shaped Alclad streamlined attachments connected to the fuselage.

Both turrets were mounted on cast aluminum alloy turntables that were driven by two 24 volt electrical motors that mechanically elevated, trained, and fired the twin M-2 .50 caliber machine guns. The turret drive was adjusted for average ranges of speed and load compounding before installation, but required adjustments in service. Tapped resistors used throughout the turret equipment permitted a wide variation of operating characteristics.

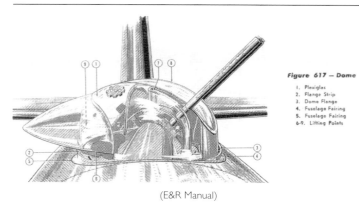

Figure 617 – Dome

1. Plexiglas
2. Flange Strip
3. Dome Flange
4. Fuselage Fairing
5. Fuselage Fairing
6-9. Lifting Points

(E&R Manual)

The turret provided for the mounting and servicing of two M-2 .50 caliber machine guns supplied with a K-15 sight, and provisions for 400 rounds of ammunition each, and was actuated by 24 volt units that mechanically trained the turret and elevated the guns. There were two hoppers, one for each gun, that collected the ejected cases and links, and expelled them downwards. The guns could be elevated 79-degrees above the horizontal, and depressed to a maximum of six degrees. The turrets had full 360-degree azimuths, but the interrupter gear limited the angles of fire. The interrupter consisted of a cam that meshed with the azimuth ring gear of the turret, and revolved at the same rate as the turret. The cam was engraved with an exact mini-duplication of the segments of the B-32 (e.g. the tail) that would come in line with the turret's guns. There were micro-switches connected to the cam that were closed as the turret revolved. When the turret reached a point where the guns would be crossing the bomber's tail, the engraved silhouette of the tail on the cam would cause the switch to open, and the guns could not be fired until the gun movement crossed the tail.

Type A-13-A Lower Ball Turret

The Briggs-built lower ball turret was a 44 inch spherical metal structure that could be suspended about 24 inches below the skin line of the aircraft, and could be retracted within the aircraft by means of a hand-operated hydraulic retraction assembly. Before the scanning windows were added to the sides of the rear fuselage this belly turret was the only means to view the rear of the engine nacelles and the underside of the wings. Generally, this turret consisted of two operating assemblies; the hanger and turret ball, which moved in azimuth with the trunnion ring, and in addition rotated in elevation by means of a self-aligning, top-mounting swivel assembly. It could be aimed in any direction in a hemisphere below the fuselage. Two M-2 .50 caliber machine guns were mounted in the turret, and were operated by a gunner who rode inside the turret, and was supplied by an external oxygen source. It had a K-4 gunsight, and was supplied by 600 rounds located on hangers fed by external ammunition feed boxes. If the

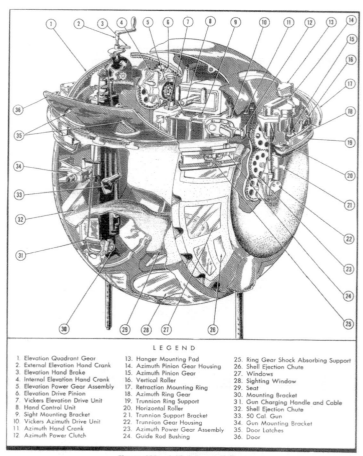

LEGEND

1. Elevation Quadrant Gear	13. Hanger Mounting Pad	25. Ring Gear Shock Absorbing Support
2. External Elevation Hand Crank	14. Azimuth Pinion Gear Housing	26. Shell Ejection Chute
3. Elevation Hand Brake	15. Azimuth Pinion Gear	27. Windows
4. Internal Elevation Hand Crank	16. Vertical Roller	28. Sighting Window
5. Elevation Power Gear Assembly	17. Retraction Mounting Ring	29. Seat
6. Elevation Drive Pinion	18. Azimuth Ring Gear	30. Mounting Bracket
7. Vickers Elevation Drive Unit	19. Trunnion Ring Support	31. Gun Charging Handle and Cable
8. Hand Control Unit	20. Horizontal Roller	32. Shell Ejection Chute
9. Sight Mounting Bracket	21. Trunnion Support Bracket	33. 50 Cal. Gun
10. Vickers Azimuth Drive Unit	22. Trunnion Gear Housing	34. Gun Mounting Bracket
11. Azimuth Hand Crank	23. Azimuth Power Gear Assembly	35. Door Latches
12. Azimuth Power Clutch	24. Guide Rod Bushing	36. Door

Figure 620 – A-13-A Turret Ball

(E&R Manual)

The rear fuselage compartment looking aft toward the internal ball turret apparatus. (USAAF)

Rare photo of a B-32 flying with its ball turret extended. (USAAF)

retraction mechanism was damaged or malfunctioned the gunner could yank on an overhead safety wire and pull out two pins, and the rear turret door would open; the occupant could fall out and, once clear of the fuselage, pull the parachute rip cord.

Arming the B-32
It took five men one hour to arm all the guns on a completely empty aircraft, while if the chutes were full it took 35 minutes. The combat test stated:

"Little difficulty has been experienced with the defensive armament on the airplane, with malfunctions at a minimum."

The only reported problems were feeding difficulties to the nose and tail turrets.

9

Controls

Power Plant Controls

Throttle Control

Conventional dual throttle controls were mounted on two pedestals, one for the pilot, and one for the co-pilot.

Turbo supercharger Control

The electronic Type B turbo supercharger control maintained the selected carburetor inlet pressure, and prevented the turbo superchargers from exceeding their safe speed limits. This control also allowed the pilot to control engine power using only the throttles. The turbo supercharger boost selector (T.B.S) was located on the pilot's control pedestal just behind the rudder trim tab knob, and was the control unit for the turbo superchargers. The T.B.S. dial was calibrated from 1 to 10, with the 8 to 10 area denoted in a red band. There was a latch stop on the dial at 8, but it could be released to allow the control to be turned to 10. Each number was a relative position, and did not indicate definite pressure values; they served as a reference, and were to be regulated as required to maintain the desired manifold pressure. The turbo supercharger control was calibrated for take-off power at position 8, but could be operated in the redlined area for normal rated power.

Mixture Control

The conventional mixture controls were located on top of the co-pilot's control pedestal (the pilot had none).

Propeller Control

The propeller controls were mounted on the center of the instrument panel. Blade settings were limited to: high pitch (57 degrees), low pitch (17 degrees), and reverse pitch (-15.7 degrees).

Intercooler Flap Controls

The intercooler flap control that provided carburetor air temperature control consisted of four switches on the instrument panel to the left of the co-pilot's control column. Each switch had three positions: AUTO, OPEN, and CLOSE. When the flaps were in the AUTO position the intercooler flaps were automatically adjusted to maintain carburetor air temperature at a predetermined value. The switches could be held in the OPEN or CLOSE position to override the AUTO control.

Cowl Flap Control

Four switches located on the instrument panel to the left of the co-pilot's control column controlled the cowl flap openings.

Fuel System Controls

The controls for the fuel system were located on top of the flight compartment directly over the co-pilot's station. The "Fuel System Management Chart" was consulted for operation of the fuel system.

Oil Cooler Controls

Four switches with three positions (AUTO, OPEN, and CLOSE) were mounted on the instrument panel to the left of the co-pilot's control column. When the switches were in the AUTO position the oil pressure was maintained at a predetermined value, but could be overridden in the OPEN or CLOSE positions.

Flight Controls

Conventional, cable-operated, dual controls were provided for both the pilot and co-pilot.

Wing Flap Control

The flap control switch was located on the instrument panel above the landing gear control switch, with a position indicated mounted to the left of this switch.

Aileron Tabs

These surfaces were operated and controlled electrically, with both trim and balance deflections incorporated. The trim tab mechanism consisted of an electric motor and position transmitter assembly housed in the aileron. The motor produced a trim deflection through a screw mechanism and push-pull tube attached to the tab. The operation of the motor was controlled by a toggle switch, and the position of the tab was shown by an indicator, both located on the left of the pilot's instrument panel. Balance tab deflection automatically accompanied aileron deflection by the tab linkage connection that was equal to and opposite to the deflection of the aileron.

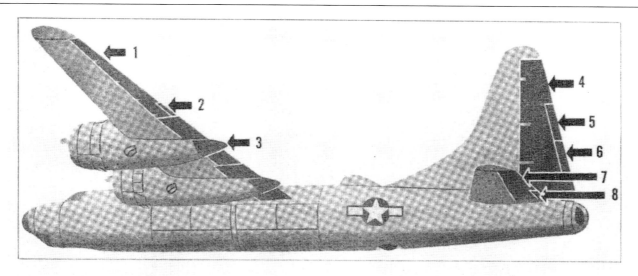

1. AILERONS • 20° UP AND DOWN
2. AILERON TRIM TABS • MANUAL TRIM DEFLECTION 10° UP AND DOWN
   SERVO DEFLECTION 20° UP AND DOWN
3. FLAPS • 40° (TOTAL)
4. RUDDER • 20° LEFT AND RIGHT
5. RUDDER TRIM TAB • SERVO DEFLECTION 8° LEFT AND RIGHT
6. RUDDER TRIM TAB • MANUAL TRIM DEFLECTION 10° LEFT AND RIGHT
7. ELEVATOR • 25° UP • 15° DOWN
8. ELEVATOR TRIM TAB • 10° UP • 14° DOWN

Note

Aileron trim tabs are operated and controlled electrically by a motor housed in each aileron. Tab balance (servo) deflection is mechanically produced by the control linkage, in order to take some load off the controls.

Flight Controls (E&R Manual)

Rudder Tab

The interconnected tab control wheels were mounted on top of both the pilot's and co-pilot's control pedestals. The tab linkage integrated automatic balance deflection of the rudder tab. Rudder trim was capable of reducing the control forces to zero with any one engine inoperative at any speed above 125% of stalling speed, with the remaining three engines delivering normal rated power. The rudder pedal stirrups were adjustable for pilot leg length.

Elevator Tab

The interconnected elevator control wheels were mounted on the outboard faces of the control pedestals. The elevator tab had no balance deflection.

Control Locks

A controls locks lever located forward and to the left of the pilot locked the rudder, elevator, and aileron in this sequence at about one-third intervals of the lever arc (the aileron and rudder lock in neutral position, and the elevator lock in the full down position. The surfaces were locked by pulling out the spring-loaded handle sleeve, and then swinging it upward. At one-third interval the rudder was placed in neutral until the lock pin engaged. The elevator was then put into the down position, and finally the aileron was put into the neutral position. The handle was released in the full up position after the lock clip was inserted below the handle sleeve. In the locked position the lever was positioned across the rudder pedal, restricting the use of the pedals, and making it obvious to the pilot that the controls lock was engaged.

Landing Gear Control

The landing gear control, located on the center of the instrument panel, had three positions: OFF, EXTEND, and RETRACT.

De-icing and Anti-icing Controls

Wing Anti-icing

The wing anti-icing control switch was located on the right side of the co-pilot's instrument panel.

Empennage De-icer

A toggle switch on the copilot's instrument panel, or an auxiliary switch on the forward side of the de-icer pump (located in the rear cabin, forward of the stabilizer) activated the de-icer.

Propeller De-icer

Two rheostats mounted on the co-pilot's instrument panel controlled the output of the pumps

Windshield De-icer and Defrost (See windshield de-icer)

10

Autopilot

C-1 Autopilot

The Minneapolis Honeywell C-1 Autopilot was an "electromechanical robot" that automatically flew the bomber in straight and level flight, or could maneuver it in response to fingertip controls by the airplane commander or navigator. The autopilot was powered by the rotary inverter, which was a motor generator unit that converted current from the aircraft's battery into 105-cycle A.C.

The autopilot control panel afforded the pilot with fingertip control, through which he could easily engage or disengage the system, adjust the sharpness or speed of its response to flight deviations, or trim the system for various weight and flight conditions. It consisted of various separate units interconnected electrically to operate as a system. The directional panel contained two electrical devices—the banking pot and rudder pick up pot—that signaled to the aileron and rudder section of the amplifier whenever the directional panel was activated by a change in course. The signals were amplified and converted by magnetic switches or relays into electrical impulses that caused the aileron and rudder servo units to operate the ailerons and rudder of the aircraft in the correct direction and amount to turn the aircraft back to its original heading. Likewise, if the aircraft's nose dropped the vertical flight gyro detected the vertical deviation and operated the elevator pick up pot, which sent an electrical signal to the elevator section of the amplifier. This signal was amplified and relayed by electrical impulses to the elevator servo unit that raised the elevators the correct amount to bring the aircraft back to level flight. If a wing dropped considerably, the vertical gyro operated the aileron pick up pot, the skid pot, and the up-elevator pot. The signals from the operation of these units were transmitted to their respective aileron, rudder, and elevator sections of the amplifier. The electrical impulses to the aileron, rudder, and elevator servo units caused each of these units to operate its respective control surfaces just enough to bank and turn the aircraft back to level flight. If a sudden cross wind turned the aircraft from its heading, the gyro-operated directional stabilizer detected the divergence and moved the directional panel to one side or the other, depending on the direction of the divergence. If the pilot wanted to make a turn, he set the turn control knob to the degree of bank and in the direction of the intended turn. His control command sent signals through the aileron and rudder sections of the amplifier to the aileron and rudder servo units, which operated the ailerons and rudder correctly to achieve a completely coordinated turn without slipping or skidding. As the aircraft banked the vertical flight gyro operated the aileron, skid, and up-elevator pots. The signals from the aileron and skid pots canceled the signals to the aileron and rudder servo units, and streamlined these controls during the turn. The up-elevator pot sent signals that caused the elevators to raise just enough to maintain altitude. When the intended turn was finished the pilot turned the turn control back to 0, and the aircraft leveled off on its new course. The directional arm lock on the stabilizer was energized by a switch in the turn control, and prevented the stabilizer from interfering with the turn by carrying out its normal direction correcting function.

Engaging the Autopilot

Before takeoff the turn control was centered, and all switches on the control panel were to be OFF. When the temperature was between 10°F and 32°F the autopilot needed to run up for 30 minutes before engaging. It could be warmed up on the ground prior to takeoff for immediate use after

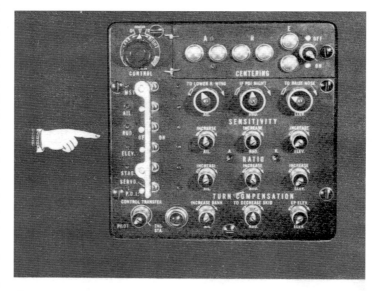

The C-1 Automatic Pilot

(E&R Manual)

takeoff by turning on the master switch during engine run up. The autopilot had to be OFF during takeoff.

Pilot Direction Indicator, PDI

After 10 minutes the Pilot Direction Indicator (PDI) switch was turned ON, and the aircraft was trimmed for level flight at cruising speed. The PDI was a remote indicating device operated by the PDI pot, and when the autopilot was used the PDI indicated to the pilot when the system and aircraft were correctly trimmed. When engaging the autopilot the aileron telltale lights were put out with the aileron centering knob, and then the aileron engaging switch was tripped. Once the ailerons were engaged on the autopilot, with the PDI centered, the autopilot could make aileron corrections automatically. The bombardier then disengaged the autopilot clutch, recentered the PDI, and locked it in place. The PDI remained locked and centered until the pilot had completed the rudder engaging procedure. The rudder telltale lights were put out with the rudder centering knob, and the rudder engaging switch was tripped. When the rudder was engaged the autopilot clutch was re-engaged, and the PDI lock released. The same procedure was then repeated for the elevator rudder. The final autopilot trim corrections were made, and if necessary the centering knobs were used to level the wings and center the PDI.

In-flight Adjustments and Operation

The master toggle switch of the autopilot turned ON all the autopilot electric motors, except the torque motor in the stabilizer. The servo-PDI switch controlled two circuits: it connected the PDI meter on the instrument panel to the PDI meter on the directional stabilizer; and it started the torque motor that opposed any force on the stabilizer gyro. The elevator, rudder, and aileron switches engaged their namesakes. C-1 was operating the pilot, and was to scrupulously analyze the action of the aircraft to be certain that all adjustments had been made correctly for smooth and precise flight control. When the two telltale lights in any axis were out it indicated that the autopilot was ready for engaging in that axis.

The centering knobs were electrical trim tabs that served two purposes. Before engaging, each centering knob was to adjust the autopilot control reference point to the straight and level flight position of the corresponding control surface. After engaging, the centering knobs were used to make small attitude adjustments.

The sensitivity control was comparable to the human pilot's reaction time. It was to regulate the amount of flight deviation the autopilot allowed before it would begin correction, e.g. speed of correction. When the sensitivity was set high the autopilot responded quickly to effect a correction for even the slightest deviation. If the sensitivity was set low, the flight deviations had to be relatively great before the autopilot made any corrections. There were three sensitivity increase knobs, one each for the aileron, rudder, and elevator, that were turned clockwise to increase and counterclockwise to decrease sensitivity.

1) The ratio control knobs regulated the amount of control movement applied by the autopilot to correct for a given deviation, e.g. amount of correction. The ratio control directed the speed of the aircraft's response to corrective autopilot actions. The correct ratio adjustment depended on airspeed. If the ratio was too high then the autopilot overcontrolled, and flight corrections were too great. If the ratio was too low then the autopilot undercontrolled, and the flight corrections were too small. The ratio panel resembled the sensitivity panel, with three increase knobs, one each for the aileron, rudder, and elevator.

2) Turn control knobs were used by the pilot to make coordinated turns when flying on autopilot. The navigator's and bombardier's stations also had turn control knobs.

3) The turn compensation knobs were electrical trim tabs for coordinating bombardier's turns, and were adjusted by having the bombardier disengage the autopilot clutch and move the engaging knob to the extreme right or extreme left. The aircraft then was to bank 18-degrees, as indicated by the artificial horizon. The recovery from this turn needed to be coordinated. If the PDI returned to center before the wings were level the rudder ratio needed to be decreased or the aileron ratio increased, depending on the speed of recovery. If the wings were level before the PDI was centered the rudder ratio was to be increased or the aileron ratio decreased, depending on the speed of recovery.

The control transfer knob transferred control of the aircraft from the pilot to the navigator. There was a light next to the control transfer knob that indicated who had control of the aircraft; when the light was ON the navigator had control, and when OFF the pilot had control.

Bombardier's Autopilot Controls

The autopilot clutch was located on the directional gyro at the bombardier's station, and was used to disengage the directional stabilizer. When the clutch was engaged the pilot, navigator, and bombardiers steered the aircraft, but when it was disengaged, only the bombardier could steer the airplane using his turn control. The bombsight clutch on the directional stabilizer engaged the bombsight and autopilot, allowing the bombardier to steer the airplane by turning the bombsight. When the bombsight clutch was engaged the autopilot clutch was to be disengaged. The bombardier used his turn control knob to turn the airplane when he had control.

The Effect of High Altitude on the Autopilot

At high altitudes of 30,000 feet and above there were several factors that affected the autopilot. High altitude affected the aircraft's normal flight characteristics, and the pilot had to compensate for these changes. The aircraft flew tail low, especially when fully combat loaded, and the controls became increasingly soft and the aircraft sluggish. Pilot control errors showed up more slowly and took longer to correct, and could take the aircraft far out of the formation before they were corrected. Low temperatures affected the autopilot, and it had to be properly warmed up and set up as soon after takeoff as practical. While in the climb the autopilot was to be adjusted with the necessary controls on the way up. At high altitudes the insulation of electrical wires lost efficiency and could affect the autopilot, and the generators needed to be checked periodically. The pilot had to know the characteristics of his aircraft under various conditions, be thoroughly familiar with the operation of the autopilot, and anticipate any correction the same as if he were flying the aircraft manually.

Formation Stick

The formation stick provided a means by which the pilot could maneuver the B-32 with the autopilot with easier, faster, and more efficient control, especially when flying in formation. The system consisted of two sticks and pedestal assemblies, two release switches, and one function selector

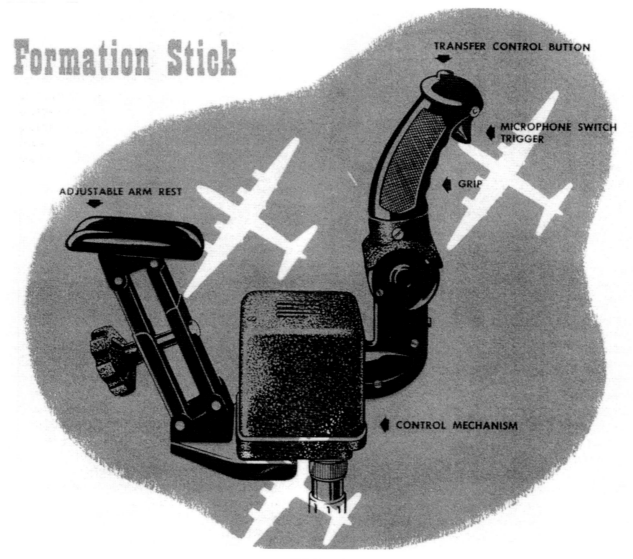

(E&R Manual)

switch located adjacent to the two pilot's seats. The formation stick assembly consisted of a fighter aircraft type stick grip, a control transfer switch button, and a trigger microphone switch. Two potentiometers picked up signals from the movement of the stick and transferred them to the autopilot amplifier. The control transfer button on top of the grip was used to transfer control of the aircraft from one stick to another. Only one stick had control at a time, and the pilot could override the co-pilot's transfer button and maintain control by constantly holding down his own control button. The release switches allowed immediate disengaging of stick and autopilot.

Part Three

The Crew and Flying the B-32

1

General

Most B-32 pilots and co-pilots were returned combat pilots, and only needed to review the basic principles of flying a large four engine aircraft, and familiarize themselves with the B-32, in particular. The USAAF encouraged teamwork and camaraderie in their bomber crews, that was to be instilled and then nurtured by the pilot. Officially the pilots of the B-29 and B-32 were generally referred to as Airplane Commanders, but unofficially and popularly they were called pilots. The B-32 Airplane Commander's Training Manual (Manual 51-126-7/15 July 1945) defines the pilot's role:

"Teamwork makes a good bomber crew. As the airplane commander you are responsible for achieving and maintaining teamwork. The proficiency of each crew member as part of the team is your responsibility, as much as is your ability to fly the B-32. To operate as a fighting unit at top efficiency you must know your own job and know your crew.

Knowing your own job means knowing all you can find out about your airplane, and developing the highest possible skill in operating it.

Knowing your crew means knowing the duties and responsibilities of each man, his qualifications for those duties, and the manner in which he performs them. Your co-pilot and aerial engineer, with whom you start your B-32 training, are the nucleus of your team. Begin your career as airplane commander by showing as much interest in their training as you can, and continue this policy with the rest of the crew when they join you later. Take a genuine interest in your men: learn something about their experiences, their families, their plans, and ideas. Help them with their personal problems, as well as their training progress.

As commanding officer of your small aerial army you must maintain crew discipline. Your personal interest in your men and your companionship with them can assure good discipline, rather than detracting from it if you handle it right. Be friendly and understanding, but be firm. Demonstrate that you know your job by the way you perform your duties. Be uncompromising in your insistence on the proper performance of crew duties before everything else. Make fair decisions after due consideration of all the facts, but make them in such a way as to impress upon your crew that your decisions are made to stick."

The pilots were to be completely familiar with the B-32 Flight Data Brief, which was a cheat sheet giving the pilot data on: Stalling Speeds; Limit Speeds; Takeoff and Best Climb Speeds; Engine Operating Data; Rated Power Service Ceiling; and Maximum Range Operating Speeds.

B-32 FLIGHT DATA BRIEF
(Estimated Performance, Not Checked in Flight)
(All Speeds Are Pilot's Indicated, MPH)

STALLING SPEEDS
(Power Off, Gear Down)

Gross Weight Lb.	Full Flaps 40°	3/4 Flaps 30°	1/2 Flaps 20°	Flaps Up 0°
80,000	106	113	117	131
90,000	111	118	122	137
100,000	116	123	128	144
110,000	120	128	133	151
120,000	125	133	139	156

TAKE-OFF AND BEST CLIMB SPEEDS

Gross Weight Lb.	Take-Off Speeds	Best Climb Speeds
90,000	118	172
100,000	123	178
110,000	129	183
120,000	133	188

TAKE-OFF: Wing Flaps 30°, Cowl Flaps 20°

CLIMB: Wing Flaps Up, Cowl Flaps 20° or as Req'd

RATED POWER SERVICE CEILING
(100 FPM Rate of Climb)

Gross Wt.—Lb.	Four Engine	Three Engine
80,000	39,000	34,000
90,000	37,500	30,000
100,000	35,000	25,000
110,000	32,000	18,000
120,000	28,000	9,000

LIMIT SPEEDS*—CLEAN AIRPLANE

Gross Wt. - Lb.	10,000 Ft. Alt.	20,000 Ft. Alt.	30,000 Ft. Alt.	35,000 Ft. Alt.
80,000	285	268	249	220
100,000	282	265	241	210
120,000	279	260	231	—

*For Design Load (2 - 1000# Bombs) Increase Speeds 10%.
*For Escape Condition (No Bombs, ½ Fuel) Increase Speeds 25%.

FLAPS DOWN ½ TO FULL 198
(Any Wt. or Altitude)

GEAR DOWN OR OPERATING 208
(Any Wt. or Altitude)

ENGINE OPERATING DATA

Condition	RPM	MAP	MIX	GPH
War Emergency Take-Off	2800	48	AR	1220
Military	2600	48	AR	1115
Normal Rated	2400	43.5	AR	945
Cruising	2100	33	AL	435
Cruising	2000	30.5	AL	370
Cruising	1900	30	AL	345
Cruising	1800	30	AL	325
Cruising	1700	30	AL	300

(See Reverse Side for Operating Limits)

MAXIMUM RANGE OPERATING SPEEDS
(For 3-Engine Operation, Reduce 5-9 MPH)

Gross Weight Lb.	Sea Level	10,000 Ft. Alt.	15,000 Ft. Alt. & Above
80- 90,000	181	178	176
90-100,000	190	186	182
100-110,000	199	193	188
110-120,000	206	198	194

C.G. Limits: 19% to 33% M.A.C.

Radar Extended Costs 5 MPH High Speed, 2% Range.

Stripped Airplane (No Radar, No Turrets) Adds 12 MPH. High Speed, 5% Range.

Minimum Speed With 2 Engines Out On One Side (Flaps Up): Power-Off Stalling Speed + 20 MPH.

(Airplane Commander's Training Manual)

2

Prefligt Walk Around Inspections and Preflight Checks

The preflight walk around inspection was divided, though not equally, by the pilot and the flight engineer. Generally, the pilot performed a 22 point counterclockwise inspection of the major exterior components starting at the left wing tip. However, the flight engineer was responsible for a much more comprehensive examination of the aircraft, having 106 inspections and responsibilities. He was to check instruments and components (in order) on the flight deck (40 inspections), then exit through the bomb bay to inspect the bottom exterior of the fuselage and wings (27 inspections), reentering the aircraft to inspect the bomb bays (10 inspections), move to the rear cabin (5 inspections) and then tail compartment (5 inspections), then exit the aircraft to inspect the top of the fuselage and wings (12 inspections). His final inspections were of the nose compartment (3 inspections), and then to recheck and complete several other exterior responsibilities (4 inspections).

<cap> 3-02-01 (See folder) Pilot's Walk Around Diagram

Pilot's Preflight Walk Around

1) Left wing tip: Check leading edge of wing tip for condition, and wing tip skin for cleanliness, freedom from wrinkles, missing rivets, and damage. Check running light to see that it is clean and undamaged. Walk around to the rear side of wing tip.

2) Left aileron: Check condition of aileron fabric and aileron hinges. Check condition of aileron tab.

3) No.1 nacelle and left outboard flap: Check nacelle for loose fasteners and evidence of oil leaks. Use a flashlight to look up into primary heat exchanger dump flap and make sure that Y valve is open, so that primary heated air dumps overboard. Check flaps for condition, flap hinges, and visible cables and pulleys for fraying. Check condition of wing between No. 1 and No.2 nacelles. Check stress plates for security. Check fuel cell area for leaks, particularly around selector valve area.

4) Left main gear. No.2 nacelle and left ill-board flap: Check oleo strut for proper inflation (2-11/16th inch clearance). Check gear accumulator pressure (normal 350 to 450 pounds). Check tire inflation, using gauge if practicable (normal pressure up to 100,000 pounds gross load, 77psi). Check tires for condition and slippage, and brakes for evidence of hydraulic leaks. Inspect all hydraulic lines in wheel well for security and evidence of leaks. Look for signs of fuel leaks in well, and check fuel drain cocks to be sure

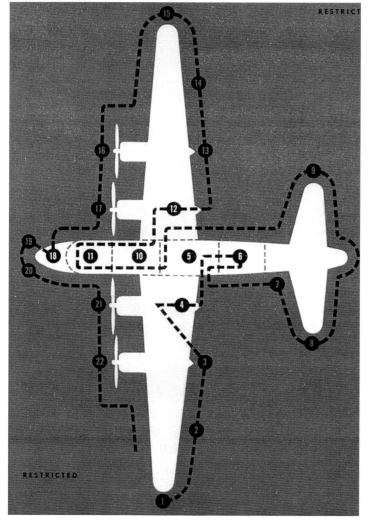

Pilot's Walk Around (Airplane Commander's Training Manual)

they are saftied. Check liquidometer gauge for fuel quantity. Check down locks for security, and see that ground locks are removed. Check shock strut down lock assembly, and latch release lever for clearances—approximately 1/8th inch each. Check No.2 nacelle and inboard flap as you did No.1 nacelle and outboard flap. Check fuel cell area for leaks. Enter rear bomb bay.

5) Rear bomb bay: Check flap cables and pulleys for fraying, and for proper tension. Check for hydraulic leaks around flap motors. Check condition of flaps, looking out along spar from top of bomb bay. Check all electrical and hydraulic lines for security. Check for evidence of hydraulic leaks throughout bomb bay, including area around bomb door motors. Check CO_2 and oxygen bottles, hand crank, gear box, prop anti-icer pumps, radio equipment, and any other necessary equipment present for security, proper stowage, and freedom from damage. Enter rear compartment.

6) Rear compartment: Check for proper stowage and security of equipment, including extra hydraulic and anti-icing fluid if present, as well as covers for nacelles, turrets, and windshields. Check lower turret for full retraction and security. Check presence and accessibility of parachutes, and inspect each pack for general condition of pack, elastics, ripcord pins, and seal. Look at inspection record card on each pack to be sure pack has been inspected and re-packed at proper time. Check scanning blisters for cleanliness. Check tail section for security of ballast in training ships, and for proper stowage and security of any other equipment carried there. Exit through bomb bay, left side.

7) Rear fuselage section: Check left side of rear fuselage for general condition. Check tailskid air-oil shock strut for proper pressure (550 to 650psi). Proceed aft to left side of tail.

8) Left side of empennage: Check left elevator and left side of rudder for condition of fabric and skin, hinges, and tabs. Check condition of tail de-icer boots, if present, looking for cracks and damage. Walk around to rear of airplane and check running lights and bomb release light for cleanliness and freedom from damage. Stand back from tail and note position of all elevator, rudder, and aileron tabs, and cross-check the positions of the tab indicators when you get up to the flight deck.

9) Right side of empennage: Repeat the foregoing checks on the right side of the rudder and the right elevator. Walk forward, checking condition of the right rear fuselage section. Note top turret for proper position. Then enter forward bomb bay.

10) Forward bomb bay: Inspect fuel selector valves and hose connections for security, and look carefully for signs of fuel leaks. Check liquidometer gauges for fuel quantity. Check main and brake hydraulic reservoirs for correct fluid levels. Check brake accumulators, main hydraulic selector valve, and all hydraulic lines and connections for security and for leaks. Check all electric and fuel lines for security. Look for leaks in fuel cell areas. Check fuel drain cocks for saftying. Inspect visible control cables for proper tension, and for signs of .fraying. Check recognition lights for cleanliness and freedom from damage, and lower antennas for security. Enter flight compartment.

11) Flight compartment: Check emergency hydraulic reservoir for correct fluid level. Check whole compartment for security and proper stowage of equipment. Check parachutes for presence and accessibility, and repeat the inspection of each pack, which you made on those in the rear compartment. Check positions of tab indicators to see that they agree with the positions of the tab surfaces. Check ignition and battery switches for OFF position so that you can safely check the props when you go out again.

Check Forms 1, 1A, and F (loading). Check for availability and proper stowage of maps and radio aid charts. Check spare light bulb and turbo fuse boxes to see that necessary bulbs and fuses are there. Check forward upper turret, if present, for security. Exit through forward bomb bay, right side.

12) Right main gear. No.3 nacelle and right inboard flap: Repeat the checks you made on the left gear, No.2 nacelle, and the left inboard flap.

13) No.4 nacelle and right outboard flap: Repeat the checks you made on No.1 nacelle and left outboard flap.

14) Right aileron: Repeat the checks you made on the left aileron.

15. Right wing tip: Repeat the checks you made on the left wing tip.

16) No.4 propeller and engine: Inspect nose section for oil leaks, or foreign matter wedged into scoops, or between cylinders. Check engine for general cleanliness. Check propeller for cleanliness, for nicks and abrasions, and for security of mounting. Look for anti-icer fluid leaks, and visually check the security of the anti-icing slinger ring.

17) No.3 propeller and engine: Repeat the checks you made on No.4 propeller and engine. Then enter nose wheel well.

18) Nose gear assembly: Check nose gear tires for condition, proper inflation (45 to 50psi), and slippage. See that wheels are in line with centerline of airplane. Check the oleo strut for proper inflation (3 1/8th inch clearance). Check down locks for security. Check hydraulic lines, pistons, and connections for leaks. Check for buckling of skin at suspension points, indicating beginning of structural failure from excessive torque loads. Exit nose-wheel well to right side.

19) Right nose section: Check general condition of right side of nose section. Check landing light for full retraction, and for cleanliness. Rub cover of static pressure source to drain condensation. See that pitot cover is removed. Walk around to front and check nose turret for proper position. If your airplane has no nose turret, check the passing light for cleanliness and freedom from damage.

20) Left nose section: Repeat the checks you made on the right nose section.

21) No.2 propeller and engine: Repeat the checks you made on No.4 propeller and engine.

22) No.1 propeller and engine: Repeat the checks you made on No.4 propeller and engine. Then assemble crew for inspection.

Even though the temperatures were often very hot on the ground, combat clothing was comprised of a heavy flight jacket, pants, fur-lined boots, leather helmet with built-in ear phones, an oxygen mask and throat microphone, three types of gloves (nylon, wool, and leather), a side arm and parachute harness, one-man life raft, and Mae West life vest. The ball turret gunner wore a back pack parachute inside his turret, while the other gunners stowed their parachutes and life raft pack nearby their stations

Flight Engineer's Walk Around Inspection
Remove pitot cover.
Enter Flight Deck and Check:
1) Check all switches on bombardier's panel for OFF position.
2) Check parachutes, if aboard.
3) Check Forms: 1 and 1A,
4) Set generator voltmeter to APU, all generator switches to OFF position.
5) Turn electric hydraulic pump control to OFF position. Check circuit breaker for ON position.

6) Check fire extinguisher.

7) Check oxygen pressure and masks, if aboard—six gauges: pilot's, co-pilot's, bombardier's, navigator's, radio operator's, and forward settee gauge.

8) Check ignition switches for OFF position.

9) Check all propeller switches for normal positions

10) Check all electrical units for OFF positions, landing gear and flap switches for neutral.

11) Check engine controls.

12) Check propellers clear, and turn battery on.

13) Start APU, idle with APU generator switch in LOAD position.

Note: If external power source is available, use it instead of APU for ground operation.

14) Check controls for freedom of movement and position, with assistance of another man checking outside.

15) Set tabs for right wing down, right rudder, and nose down.

16) Lock controls.

17) Set APU throttle to RUN position and check output.

18) Check cowl flaps and leave open.

19) Check propeller master motor and control knob, leaving control at 2800rpms.

20) Check propeller anti-icers.

21) Check instrument panel lights, landing lights, recognition lights, formation, passing, and running lights.

22) Open and close intercooler flaps manually. Then open or close flaps manually, depending on temperature, and set to AUTOMATIC position to check automatic operation.

23) Open and close oil cooler flaps manually. Then open or close manually, depending on temperature, and set to AUTOMATIC position to check automatic operation.

24) Turn fuel selector valves to TANK TO ENGINE position, and drain valve to CROSS-FEED.

25) Turn fuel selector valve circuit breakers to OFF position.

26) Turn No.1 booster pump to LOW position, and move mixture control out of IDLE CUT-OFF momentarily until you note a rise in pressure, then return mixture control to IDLE CUT-OFF. Turn OFF booster pump. Repeat this procedure on Nos. 2, 3, and 4 engines.

Note: This procedure checks the operation of the lock pins in the selector valves when the current is cut, thus insuring flow to the engine in event of solenoid failure. Avoid leaving mixture control out of IDLE CUT-OFF any longer than absolutely necessary because that procedure may produce liquid lock in the lower cylinders.

27) Turn fuel selector valve circuit breakers to ON position.

28) Check all other circuit breakers for ON position.

29) Set parking brakes and check accumulator pressure drop.

30) Check main and spare inverters, leaving switch in MAIN ON position.

31) Check AC voltage.

32) Check fluid level in emergency reservoir.

33) Turn hydraulic pump control switch to ON position, and check brake pressure.

34) Lower inboard and outboard flaps with emergency hydraulic system.

35) Open bomb bay doors with emergency hydraulic system.

36) Return all selector switches to OFF and switchover valve to BRAKE SYSTEM ON.

37) Check brake over-ride switch;
check all
electrical switches for OFF position.

38) Turn pitot heat to ON position for 10 seconds; then to OFF.

39) Turn APU and battery switches to OFF position.

40) Turn electric hydraulic pump control switch to OFF position.

Exit Through Bomb Bays and Check:

1) Lower exterior of airplane.

2) Pitot mast for heat.

3) Control access plates.

4) Nose wheels, tires, strut, for inflation and condition.

5) Nose wheel well and mechanism.

6) Circuit breakers under flight deck, station 3.0.

7) Turbo amplifiers, spare, and battery.

8) Main wheel well and mechanism, including accumulator in wheel well.

9) Main wheels, tires, struts, and gear mechanism for condition and inflation.

10) Outboard fuel tank level indicator.

11) Brake bleeder valve.

12) Chocks in place for quick removal.

13) Cables, pulleys, and turnbuckle safetying under the flaps.

14) Exhaust bolts, through flap opening.

15) Condition of aileron fabric.

16) Tabs, for right wing down.

17). Fuel cell vents and access plates.

18) Flaps, upper surface, for rubbing.

19) Oil cooler air exit and flap for position.

20) Engine and cabin air intakes.

21) Fuselage and empennage, including rupture discs for CO_2 bottles.

22) Tailskid and shock strut inflation,

23) De-icer boots, if installed.

24) Control surface fabric on empennage.

25) Tabs, for right rudder and nose down.

26) Other side of airplane: repeat inspection.

Enter Bomb Bays and Check:

1) Forward compartment: APU controls and unit, brake valves, hydraulic units and lines.

2) Fluid leveling main and brake reservoir.

3) Accumulators.

4) Control cables, pulleys, turnbuckles, tension regulators, and attachments.

5) Hydraulic units; selector valve, hydraulic pump, pressure .switch, etc., and selector valve relay circuit, breaker for ON position.

6) Inboard fuel tanks fluid level indicators, fuel lines, and fuel valves in bomb bays.

7) Access plates under center section.

8) Flap cables, drums, and .motors.

9) Aileron control locks, autopilot servo unit, and CO2, bottles.

10) Propeller anti-icer tank for leaks.

Enter Aft Cabin and Check:

1) Anti-icer fluid level and reservoir filler cap.

2) Oxygen pressure and masks, if aboard.

3) Fire extinguisher.

4) Turrets locked.

5) Hatches closed.

Enter Tail Compartment and Check:

1) Empennage attachment bolts.

2) Control cables, pulleys, control locks, and attachments,

3) All loose equipment for proper stowage.

4) Tail turret locked.

5) Return to cockpit and set tab controls to neutral. Turn battery on to set aileron tab; off after operation.

Climb on Top of Airplane and Check:

1) Aileron fabric.

2) Aileron tabs for neutral.

3) Fuel and oil quantity and proper installation of caps.

4) Engine cowling and fasteners.

5) Engine exhaust bolts through cowl flap opening.

6) Carburetor, for leaks, with mixture control on and booster pump on HIGH.

7) Antennas for security.

8) Intercooler flaps for proper position.

9) De-icer boots, if installed, and tabs on empennage for neutral.

10) Turrets.

11) Life rafts,

12) Clean windshields.

Enter Nose Compartment and Check:

1) Propeller control units and cables.

2) Security of all lines and instruments behind instrument panel.

3) Nose turret locked.

Exit Airplane and Check:

1) Pull props through six blades.

2) Re-check position of control tabs.

3) Make certain that access ladder is removed from nose-wheel well before taxiing, and that bombardier's hatch is securely locked.

4) Remove gear locks prior to engine starting.

Pilot's/Co-pilot's/Engineer's Duties After Entering the Flight Deck

The pilot needed to fulfill the instructions included in the "Weight and Loading Data" (T.O. AN 01-1B-40) and check Form F (also known as Weight and Balance). For best aircraft operation the center of gravity (CG) had to be as near 25% MAC (Mean Aerodynamic Chord) as possible, with the forward CG limit 19% and the aft limit 33% MAC. If the aircraft did not fall between these limits the pilot would have difficulty getting into step, and would require excessive trim, which would slow the airspeed and increase fuel consumption. Form F (Weight loading) and Crew Inspection (In transition training a crew inspection was done by the pilot in "accordance to CFTC Memorandum 50-2-4"):

Pilot to check Forms 1 and 1A.

Pilot checks Instrument Approach Procedures, "Radio Facility Charts," and other pertinent data current and in good condition.

Pilot to sign Exceptional Release (if necessary).

Pilot and co-pilot check through their windows to check if the wheel chocks are in place, and covers are off the pitot masts.

Pilot and co-pilot check for correct fluid levels in main, brake, and emergency hydraulic supply reservoirs. Check anti-icing fluid levels and reserve supplies of both anti-icing and hydraulic fluids.

Pilot and co-pilot check that control cables and pulleys are free from interference from cargo or stored equipment, and cargo properly secured.

Pilot and co-pilot check oxygen system fully serviced.

Pilot and co-pilot check fuel and oil quantity.

Engineer switches landing gear NEUTRAL

Co-pilot calls out electrical units, and each responsible crew member switches electrical unit (except generators) OFF to prevent placing a detrimental load on the battery when the switch was turned ON.

Co-pilot turns battery switch ON. Note: The battery switch was to remain OFF as long as an external power supply was connected to prevent damage to the battery relays and wiring, which could happen if the battery had a higher voltage than the outside power source.

Co-pilot starts Auxiliary Power Unit, and it is to continue to run until after takeoff.

Co-pilot places APU generator switch in the LOAD position after the engine was running

Keep the equalizer switch OFF until the engine generators were charging.

Turn inverter switch to MAIN, and never turn them OFF while the engines were running.

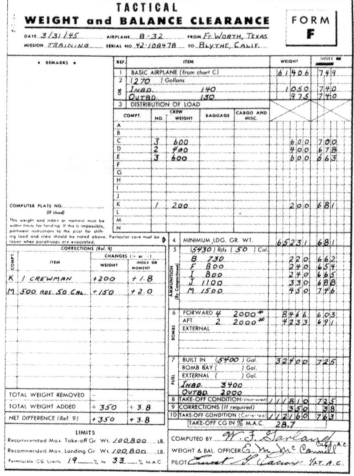

(FOR TRANSPORT AND CARGO MISSIONS, USE OTHER SIDE)

(Airplane Commander's Training Manual)

AC voltage 100 to 125 volts.

Leave generators ON at all times, except when they are not functioning, or when required to be OFF for electrical system repair.

All circuit breaker switches ON (each crew member checks circuit breakers at his station).

Engineer turns propeller master motor ON.

Engineer turns propeller selector switches AUTOMATIC (a green tell tale light indicated correct switch setting).

Engineer turns propeller reverse safety switch for SAFE.

Engineer turns propeller reverse control switch for NORMAL.

Engineer turns the hydraulic pump motor switch ON.

Co-pilot checks brake pressure gauges for minimum pressure (850psi), and pilot sets parking brakes. Accumulator pressure at a minimum 850psi. Brakes were to be operated until the accumulator pressure dropped below 850psi, and the cut-in (to be 850 plus 50 minus 0) and cut-out (1030 plus 50 minus 0) pressures were to be noted. The co-pilot's electric hydraulic override switch OFF.

Pilot and co-pilot UNLOCK controls.

Pilot and co-pilot move the control wheel in all extremities, and have crew members visually check all control surface movement.

Pilot and co-pilot move rudder full right and left.

Pilot or co-pilot sets altimeter. Check barometric setting and altitude indication.

Pilot or co-pilot sets and wind airplane clock.

Pilot turns automatic pilot OFF.

Pilot and co-pilot move engine controls through their operating range to check free action.

Engineer sets the Intercooler AUTOMATIC, but continues to watch carburetor, cylinder head, and oil temperatures.

Co-pilot visually checks cowl flaps OPEN LEFT and OPEN RIGHT.

Engineer sets oil cooler flaps to AUTOMATIC in warm weather, and MANUAL CLOSED in cold weather until the oil temperature reaches normal, and then place in AUTOMATIC.

Use carburetor air filters when engines operated in dusty areas.

Wing anti-icers OFF.

Tail de-icer switch OFF.

Propeller anti-icer system OFF.

Carburetor preheat controls COLD position.

Heat exchanger exit flap OPEN.

MASTER and INDIVIDUAL ignition switches OFF.

Engineer turns turbo booster selector at 0.

The service crews—two men per blade—were to pull the propeller through six blades to determine that liquid locks did not occur in the cylinder bottoms. If locks occurred a plug was removed from each cylinder bottom to drain the liquid. Once the liquid was drained, and before the plug was replaced, e crew was to pull the propeller through four blades to open the intake valves and release any fluid that could be trapped in the intake manifolds.

Special Checks for Night Flights

Check operation of all interior and exterior lights.

Check glare curtains.

If a rapid climb to above 10,000 feet was planned the crew was to use oxygen from takeoff.

Scanner (Gunner) Duties on the Ground

1) Participate in the crew inspection, and take position at a wing tip for engine start up.

2) Check flight controls on signal from pilots.

3) Post fire guards for starting engines.

4) Pull wheel chocks after engines are started.

5) Re-enter aircraft, take positions in rear compartment, and stand by on interphone.

6) Check interphone with pilot before taxiing.

7) Check flaps for 20 degree positions before takeoff.

8) Call pilot after take-off when gear is up, flaps are up, and if engines show smoking or torching.

9) Call airplane every 15 minutes to report condition of engines.

10) Call pilot on landings, reporting main gear and tailskid down, and flap positions.

11) Check flaps on running takeoffs for 20 degree positions.

3

Starting and Engine Warm Up

General

Before starting the engine the pilot and co-pilot each checked their side of the aircraft for an "all clear," and a thumb up from the crew chief. After the pilot set the throttle the co-pilot and engineer started the No.3 starboard engine first, as it drove the hydraulic system. The No.2 engine also drove the hydraulics, but the co-pilot could observe and control engine No.3 more readily. Once No.3 was functioning satisfactorily engines Nos.4, 2, and 1 were started in sequence. Once all the engines were turning, checks were made on the engine-related instruments (e.g. oil pressure, head temperatures, etc.). The pilot then made an interphone check of all crew position readiness.

Engine Starting Procedure

A ground crew fire guard was to be posted clear of the propeller of the No.3 engine that was to be started first, and a scanner was to be at the starboard wing tip. The co-pilot was to look out his window to check that this was done. The wheel chocks were to be removed upon signal from the pilot and co-pilot.

The co-pilot set all four fuel selector valves in the TANK TO ENGINE position, the fuel booster pump control switches LOW, master ignition switch ON, and all individual ignition switches OFF before starting engines.

The pilot retarded the throttle to the 1,000 to 1,200rpm position, as the throttle controlled the amount of air delivered to the engine during starting. If the throttle was opened too far the fuel mixture would be too

lean for starting, and if it weren't opened far enough the fuel mixture would be too rich. In cold weather, or at bases located at higher altitudes, the throttle was to be set at the lower end of the 1,000-1,200 limits.

The co-pilot would hold the No.3 accelerating switch to the desired position for 10 to 12 seconds, announcing, "ACELERATING No.3." Over acceleration turned the starter too fast and could burn it out, while under acceleration would not turn the engine fast enough to start it. Allowed the starter to cool for one minute once it had been meshed before it was energized again. A starter should not be meshed for more than one minute.

While continuing to hold the accelerating switch, the co-pilot would then hold the No.3 engine crank switch, announcing, "CRANKING No.3."

After the prop turned through two revolutions the co-pilot held the No.3 engine primer switch, while the engineer turned the ignition switch to BOTH position. The B-32 priming switch activated a solenoid-operated primer valve connected to the fuel line that shot raw fuel, unmetered by the carburetor, into the blower section. The engine impeller had to be turning over for proper distribution of the priming spray. The engines were not to be primed before the starter motor was engaged to prevent an accumulation of fuel, causing a liquid lock.

After the engine fired it was to be run on primer alone until about 800rpms, and it was certain that the engine would continue to run. Mixture controls IDLE CUT-OFF until the engines were turning over to prevent fuel from draining into the cylinder bottoms and causing a liquid lock.

After the engine was running on primer the mixture control was to be moved from IDLE CUT OFF to AUTO RICH, releasing booster and primer.

A ground crew fire guard was to be posted clear of the propeller of the No.3 engine, which was to be started first, and a scanner was to be at the starboard wing tip. The co-pilot was to look out his window to check that this was done. (USAAF)

If the engine stopped the mixture control was to be immediately moved back to IDLE CUT OFF.

After the engine was running the co-pilot and engineer checked the oil pressure; if the main oil pressure did not reach 40psi within 10 seconds, or nose oil pressure did not register 45psi within 30 seconds, the mixture control was to be immediately moved back to IDLE CUT OFF.

After a momentary advancing of the throttles to 1,500rpm to clear out the engine, the throttle was to be readjusted to obtain 1,000 to 1,200rpm until the oil temperature reached 55°C or, in an emergency, until at least a 10 degree rise was indicated. Quick movements were to be avoided to prevent backfires and induction system fires.

Once the engine was running smoothly with the mixture control in AUTO RICH the booster pump was turned OFF, and the co-pilot checked the oil pressure and reported, "No.3 IN; OIL PRESSURE CHECKED," which indicated that he was ready to start No.2 engine.

Hand Cranking Starting
There was a hand crank and portable gear box for starting the engine without the electric starter. They were stowed in the rear bomb bay, with the gear box under the catwalk, and the crank on the rear bulkhead. The props had to be pulled through at least one half turn in the normal direction to insure that the starter and engine jaws were not engaged. The gear box was inserted into the socket on the under side of the nacelle, and the hand crank was inserted into the gear box. The manual meshing button on the nacelle was pushed to lift the starter brushes off the commutator. After about 95 turns of the crank the flywheel reached an operating speed of 2,200rpms. After the crank and gear box were removed the meshing button was pushed again and held there until the engine started.

Engine Warm Up
If practical, the aircraft was to be headed into the wind during engine warm up to provide uniform cooling of all the cylinders.

The co-pilot turned the APU equalizer switch ON, which connected the APU generator in parallel with the engine-driven generators and equalized the electrical load.

The flight engineer sat in the entrance to the bombardier's compartment between the pilot and co-pilot. (USAAF via Dembeck)

The engineer turned ON engine No.1 and No.4 generators. These outboard generators were initially used, as they had a two-speed drive that gave full output at rpms as low as 800. At 2,000rpms the voltmeter was to read 28 to 28.5 volts for each generator (the generators were normally to remain ON at all times).

The engines were to run at 2,000rpms, 28 to 30 inches Hg with the propeller selector in AUTO CONSTANT SPEED, and the master motor at 2,800rpm. This speed and power range was sufficient to check the magnetos, spark plugs, and propeller controls.

Engineer checked oil pressures: rear section 60 to 70psi; nose section 45 to 50psi; and fuel pressures 6 to 18psi.

Engineer checked the magnetos. With propeller selector switch in AUTO, he turned the individual magneto switch to LEFT MAGNETO and looked for a drop in rpm. He returned the switch to both, and waited for the engine to increase rpm. He then moved the switch quickly to RIGHT MAGNETO, and again looked for a drop in rpm. The acceptable rpm drop between BOTH and RIGHT and LEFT was 100rpm.

Zero turbo boost run up. With the turbo boost selector at 0 the throttles were moved to full open with one at a more than 2 inches Hg between engines.

Check vacuum pumps on No.2 and 3.

Idle engine at 800 to 1,000rpm.

After the engines were run up they could be idled between 800 and 1,000rpm.

Engineer: Changed the inverter switch from MAIN to SPARE to check voltage (100 to 125), then moved back to MAIN.

Set oil cooler controls to AUTOMATIC when the oil temperatures reach normal (140°F plus or minus 30°F).

Operated wing flaps to the full down and full up positions.

Turned on command radio to contact control tower. Set transmitter and receiver to correct frequency. Turned volume control on jack boxes to correct output. Set selector switch on filter box to VOICE or BOTH, and the selector switch on the jack box to COMMAND.

The scanners were to reenter the aircraft, and the crew was to be at their takeoff stations.

Contact control tower for taxi and takeoff instructions.

Accessory, Temperature, and Pressure Checks
Oil pressure: rear 60 to 70psi, and nose 45 to 50psi.
Oil temperature: 130 to 185°F.
Cylinder head temperatures (CHT): Maximum 500°F.
Fuel Pressures: 16 to 18psi
Check tachometers.
Hydraulic pressures (brakes): minimum 850psi.
APU operating
Check clock.
Check compass.
Check free air temperature indicators.
Check landing gear DOWN LOCK light (green for down).
Recheck vacuum: 3.75 to 4.25 inches Hg at 1,000rpm.
Check ball turret indicator lights for turret retraction.
Check wheel chock removal.

4

Taxiing

Taxiing Instructions

After signaling the ground crew to remove the chocks the pilot released the brakes, and allowed the aircraft to start moving. Because of the nose wheel configuration it was necessary that the aircraft be moving before any turn was made. The use of brakes was to be minimal, as overuse could cause excessive overheating, possible brake expander failure, and the loss of the brakes. The B-32 was taxied like any other large tricycle gear aircraft. Turns were to be made in the largest possible radius to minimize nose wheel tire wear, and to make the turn easier. The two nose wheels were fixed to the axle so that they rotated together, eliminating nose wheel shimmy without the addition of a shimmy damper unit. However, without the shimmy damper there could be nose wheel tire loss when sharp turns were made. The bomber was to be stopped with the nose wheels in line with the aircraft centerline to minimize side loads on the nose gear during engine run up, and at the start of taxiing. The flight engineer set the engines to turn over at 800 to 1,000rpms, which would move the aircraft using minimal throttle and braking. The inboard engines were to be CUT when taxiing long distances or down wind, where engine rpms may be insufficient to prevent fouling of the spark plugs, and yet maintain taxiing speed. Because of the huge 32 foot high tail assembly taxiing in a crosswind could cause problems, and leg muscle was needed by the pilot to keep control.

Checks After Taxiing to Runway and Ready for Takeoff

Note: This check needed to be made as quickly as possible to prevent excessive CHT.

The B-32 was taxied like any other large tricycle gear aircraft. Turns were to be made in the largest possible radius to minimize nose wheel tire wear, and to make the turn easier. (USAAF)

Stop aircraft and set parking brakes.

CLOSE bomb bay doors.

Close and secure all hatches.

Uncage directional gyro and artificial horizon.

Set directional gyro to correspond with magnetic compass.

Check that all generator switches were ON.

Check main inverter switch No.1 ON.

Set booster pump control switches to HIGH.

Set fuel tank selectors to TANK TO ENGINE.

Check master tachometer for 2,000rpm, and the prop selector switches for AUTOMATIC.

Check mixture controls for AUTO RICH.

Check cowl flaps FULL OPEN.

Set oil cooler shutters AUTOMATIC.

Engineer sets intercooler shutters AUTOMATIC, but continues to watch carburetor, cylinder head, and oil temperatures.

Set carburetor preheat to COLD.

Extend wing flaps to 30 degrees.

Return flap switch to NEUTRAL.

Set trim tabs: aileron, elevator, and rudder 3 degrees right.

Operate rudder control full right and full left.

Operate elevator control full forward and full rear.

Rotate aileron control wheel full right and full left.

Run up each engine, and check the turbo boost selector setting before turning onto the runway.

Set turbo boost selector to 0.

Advance one throttle to the full open position, then turn the turbo selector control to 8, or until a manifold pressure of 49 inches was reached.

Retard the throttle, leaving the turbo boost selector at 8, or at the required position to obtain 48 inches Hg.

Advance throttle of each remaining engine individually until 49 inches Hg developed. Close each throttle, leaving the turbo selector at 8, or at 49 inches Hg.

Check that all crew members were in position and braced for takeoff, and that all guns were trimmed fore and aft.

5

Takeoff

Normal Takeoffs

Once tower clearance was obtained the brakes were released, allowing the aircraft to roll onto the runway using a wide sweeping turn, and using as little runway distance as possible. The pilot would use the outboard engine to turn and align the aircraft with the runway. Throttles were opened slowly and smoothly until rudder directional control was effective, after which the throttles were moved to full OPEN at 2,800rpm and 49 inches Hg. The co-pilot was to follow through on the throttles to be certain they were in FULL FORWARD. A fair amount of rudder was often needed at first, and about halfway down the takeoff run the controls would begin to be effective, and nose wheel steering was no longer needed. The use of brakes during takeoff run slowed the airplane, overheated the brakes, and lengthened the takeoff run. During the takeoff the engineer was to maintain the check of the M.A.P. and engine rpm to make sure that maximum rpm was not exceeded. If the manifold pressure needed to be reduced during takeoff, the reduction was accomplished by pulling back the desired throttle. The maximum allowable CHT during take of was 260°C for only five minutes. If the CHT ran high either during ground operation, or during the takeoff run, the pilot needed to use a longer ground run and attain airspeed of 200mph or more as soon as possible after takeoff. The B-32 had rapid acceleration, and thus a comparatively short takeoff run. During testing it was determined that at 111,300 pounds gross weight the ground roll was 3,675 feet, and at 121,300 pounds it was 4,550 feet. As the speed increased to about 70 to 80mph the pilot was to ease back on the control column to attain takeoff attitude, which was determined by field conditions, loading, and pilot experience. The pilot needed to keep in mind the approximate takeoff and power on stalling speeds at various weights with 20 degree flaps:

Crosswind Takeoff

Despite its large tail, crosswind takeoffs were considered not particularly difficult in the B-32. Aided by the inherent stability of the tricycle landing gear to keep the aircraft moving straight ahead, the pilot had to lead with the upwind throttle and use rudder pressure to hold the bomber straight on the runway. It was standard practice to move the aircraft off the runway at speeds of 5 to 10mph higher than normal, preventing the possibility of bouncing off the ground and dropping back, hitting the landing gear with a sideways stress.

Scramble Takeoff

If an immediate takeoff were required, as soon as the oil pressure steadied and the oil temperature rose 50°F it was safe to scramble. Oil dilution could be used to speed oil pressure steadying.

Emergency Takeoffs

The directional control of the large rudder and good flight characteristics of the B-32 made it easier to manage during engine failure during takeoff than other four engine bombers. In case of engine failure the pilot needed to get directional control with the rudder and aileron first, then correct the trim tabs without letting the wing with the dead engine drop. The engineer was to retract the landing gear immediately, and then raise the flaps 5 to 8 degrees, where they were left until the aircraft was ready for landing. Airspeed needed to be maintained, if necessary and possibly by nosing down to pick up speed. Once the pilot gained control and achieved safe airspeed he could reduce power and prepare to make a turn. If possible, the turn was to be made away from the dead engine, but if he had to turn into the dead engine, he was to be sure to maintain airspeed and trim into the turn.

APPROXIMATE TAKEOFF AND POWER-ON STALLING SPEEDS AT VARIOUS WEIGHTS WITH 20° OF FLAPS

GROSS WEIGHT	TAKEOFF IAS	STALLING SPEED IAS
90,000 LBS	118	95
100,000 LBS	123	100
110,000 LBS	129	105
120,000 LBS	133	110

(Airplane Commander's Training Manual)

After Takeoff

At 130mph Indicated Airspeed (IAS) the bomber would begin to fly, and the stick could be eased back to begin climbing. As airspeed was gained the B-32 was responsive, unlike the B-24, which was mushy. The pilot was instructed not to be overly anxious to gain altitude immediately after take-off, but he needed to be sure to get enough height to clear any obstacles at the end of the runway. As soon as the aircraft was definitely airborne he was to apply the brakes smoothly to stop their rotation BEFORE signaling gear UP to the co-pilot, and return the landing gear switch to OFF when the gear was UP. The scanners in the rear compartment reported that the gear was up on both sides, while the engineer checked the nose wheel up-lock from the bombardier's compartment and reported to the pilot. In preparation for the climb the pilot decreased the engine rpm to 2,400 and set turbo boost selector to 43 inches Hg. Once the wheels were up and at 160 IAS the wing flaps were retracted, which caused the aircraft to nose down, and the pilot had to be prepared to correct the trim. An extended climb was not to be initiated until IAS of 180mph or better was maintained for correct engine cooling using the climb power settings:

    2,400rpm: 43 inches (max.)
    2,300rpm: 39 inches
    2,200rpm: 35 inches

"They WARNED me these B-32's were quick on the take-off!"

(Airplane Commander's Training Manual)

6

Climb and Cruising

Climb

For operational flights the power was set at predetermined settings as worked out on climb control charts. After power was set engineer rechecked CHT and adjusted the cowl flaps correspondingly. The maximum CHT in climb was 480°F. If possible the cowl flaps were to be kept closed to attain engine cooling with a higher airspeed. Once the climb had been established the APU was shut off, and the equalizer switch turned to OFF. However, during night operations using turrets, radar, lights, radios, etc., the APU was to be left ON. On reaching 1,000 feet the engineer set the fuel booster pumps, one at a time, to LOW. However, once above 10,000 feet they were to be turned ON again. It was recommended that the scanners report the condition of the engines every 15 minutes.

Because the B-32 was designed as a long range, high altitude bomber, reaching high altitude was a crucial part of its mission. In its climb the bomber flew through changing outside conditions, such as decreasing pressure and temperature, using continuous high power settings and consuming extra fuel. The Pilot's Manual stressed that "smooth flying technique becomes increasingly important if you want to stay in formation, or get maximum performance from your airplane." The pilot needed to keep the aircraft trimmed, and to use "some degree" of flaps to increase the effi-

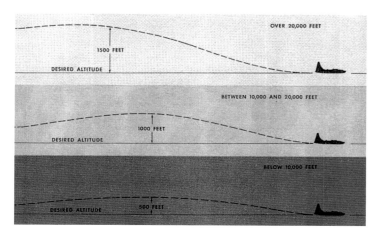

Cruising altitude was to be approached from above (never below), in both speed and altitude, by climbing above the desired altitude, then leveling off, and maintaining climbing power until the aircraft was at or above the desired cruising speed before reducing the power. (Airplane Commander's Training Manual)

ciency of the climb. With the Davis Wing 5 degrees of flaps produced the most efficient lift-to-drag ratio. With experience the pilot would learn how much flap to use, and at what point in the climb to use it to gain increased rate of climb at the same airspeed. Above 20,000 feet 5 degrees of flap was always recommended. When using the autopilot to climb the pilot needed to make adjustments to it to insure a smooth and efficient climb. Although the temperature was much lower at higher altitudes, the aircraft's cooling system became less efficient because of the decrease in air density. It was important that the co-pilot and engineer keep track of the cylinder head temperatures and engine instruments. If all CHTs were running high during a sustained climb the pilot was to hold the climbing power setting and level off until the CHTs returned to normal, and then restart the climb at higher airspeed. This technique gave a better rate of climb than if the cowl flaps were opened at the previous airspeed. If the CHT continued to run high then the cowl flaps were to be adjusted to remedy the situation.

The initial rate of climb was 1,200 feet per minute, and the bomber could reach 15,000 feet in 15.4 minutes, and 30,000 feet in 38.3 minutes. For long range cruise missions climb was to be at rated power, 42 inches of Hg, and 2,400rpm, regardless of the gross weight. Rated power climbs would give a more economical operation than climbs at lower power settings. This was because rated power settings would get the aircraft to cruising altitude, where AUTO LEAN mixtures could be used more quickly. Fuel pressure readings had to be monitored carefully and kept in operating limits, as the increase in altitude and the concomitant decrease in atmospheric pressure caused an increase in the volatility of the fuel, and thus increased the possibility of vapor lock at higher altitudes. To prevent this situation the pilot needed to set the fuel booster pumps to LOW above 10,000 feet, and if extra pressure was needed they were to be turned to HIGH. It was the pilot's responsibility to be sure that his crew donned their oxygen masks, and that the aircraft was warm enough for them to function efficiently.

Cruising

For any operational mission, fuel and power management were to be planned in advance using climb and cruise control charts. The factors affecting cruise control to be considered were weather, wind, turbulence, altitude, and changes in altitude, weight, drag, power settings, trim, and engine management. While one or two of these factors probably would not affect the aircraft's range and endurance, the combination of all could mean the failure of the mission, and the pilot and engineer were responsible for reducing each adverse dynamic to a minimum.

Cruising altitude was to be approached from above (never below), in both speed and altitude, by climbing above the desired altitude, then leveling off, maintaining climbing power until the aircraft was at or above the desired cruising speed before reducing the power. For cruising altitudes below 10,000 feet the pilot was to climb 500 feet higher, and then drop down to the desired altitude. For cruising altitudes between 10,000 and 20,000 feet the climb was to be made to 1,000 feet above the desired altitude, and for altitudes above 20,000 feet the climb was to be 1,500 feet, keeping in mind that 5 degree flaps were to be used for flights above 20,000 feet.

When the pilot reached the top of his climb, he was to maintain the climbing power and a zero rate of climb until the necessary airspeed (about 210mph with high gross loads) was reached. He was then to set the predetermined cruising power and nose the aircraft slightly downward into a shallow dive to the cruising altitude. The aircraft was then to be carefully trimmed, the elevators used to maintain cruising airspeed, and the power adjusted slightly to maintain altitude. If the pilot decreased the power before he reached sufficient airspeed there could be an increase in CHT, and the cowl flaps would need to be opened for cooling, which caused excessive drag, additional decrease in airspeed, and increased fuel consumption, and the controls would become sluggish due to the high angle of attack.

The automatic pilot was used most of the time while cruising, and often was used during climb to altitude. Normal cruising required 34 to 35 inches of boost and an IAS of 180mph. Stall signs in the B-32 were not as apparent as with the B-24, but once in a stall the nose dropped easily and rapidly downward. The control column was automatically snapped forward, and held the aircraft straight until speed was regained to 180 to 220mph, depending on the aircraft's weight. From this point recovery was accomplished by gently pulling the column back and easing the power. Cruising speed was normally 180mph, with redline at 240mph at 118,000 pounds weight, and 330mph at 100,000 pounds at 20,000 feet. Combat test crews found no difficulty in handling the aircraft. Due to its good flight characteristics, it was possible to check out crews on the B-32 very quickly, especially those who had previous B-24 experience. The official test report stated: "Handling characteristics of the airplane flying in formation have proven excellent." Propellers, because of their rapid, synchronized response, were used for power control in formation flying. Pilots expressed surprise at the desirable low control forces for this size aircraft.

Maximum Endurance Cruise

Plainly, the procedure for flying the many hours of a long mission was to fly at the airspeed at which the engines used fuel at the lowest possible rate. The conservation of fuel was accomplished when the least amount of engine power was used to keep the aircraft flying. The specific airspeed depended on the gross weight of the bomber, and was somewhat less than the IAS for the maximum range; it was determined by the cruise control charts. The pilot flew a constant IAS, and maintained the optimal altitude by the use of power. The rpm was set at 1,400, and the necessary manifold pressure was pulled to maintain airspeed and altitude. The pilot reduced airspeed as the aircraft's gross weight was decreased by fuel usage. The less the aircraft weighed, and the lower the altitude at which it flew, the longer it would fly.

Maximum Range Cruise

The B-32 was designed as a VHB bomber, and maximum range was the bomber's most important cruise type. Maximum range cruise was flown at the speed and altitude that yielded the most mileage per gallon of fuel used. In calm weather the airspeed in maximum endurance cruise was higher than that used in maximum endurance cruise. When a little additional power was added to the settings for maximum endurance there was a relatively large increase in airspeed compared to the increase in fuel consumption. As power was further increased both airspeed and fuel consumption increased, and as power settings were advanced to the higher ranges, the increase in airspeed over fuel consumption fell off rapidly. The pilot and engineer used the maximum range cruise control charts to determine the band of airspeeds in which the maximum miles per gallon could be achieved.

The optimum airspeed for maximum miles per gallon was not sufficient, as it had to be converted into maximum ground miles, which meant considering the effect of the wind. In a headwind the aircraft was to be flown at the upper limits of the band of airspeeds determined by the cruise control charts, and with a tailwind the aircraft was to be flown at the lower limits. However, the lower airspeed limits were difficult to use in formation flying. The formation leader needed to fly at an airspeed at the lower end of the band, enabling other aircraft in the formation to stay within the economical range of airspeeds, despite the constant airspeed changes they had to make to stay in formation.

Just as it did in maximum range cruising, the weight of the aircraft significantly affected the airspeed for maximum endurance cruising. Once the pilot and engineer determined the correct airspeed for the gross weight it was maintained at all altitudes, varying power as necessary. In descending in maximum cruise, the recommended cruising airspeed was to be maintained, and the power reduced to the lowest allowable power settings in order to extend the range.

Because the B-32 was designed as a long range, high altitude bomber, reaching high altitude was a crucial part of its mission. The Pilot's Manual stressed that "smooth flying technique becomes increasingly important if you want to stay in formation or get maximum performance from your airplane." (USAAF)

7

Formation Flying

Formation flying was based on two principles: to provide the greatest striking power in both time and degree, and to provide the greatest protection. The formation could bomb the target with the greatest concentration of bombs in the shortest possible time while offering the greatest number of mutually defending guns concentrating their fire on the attacking enemy. The disadvantages of formation flying were that it required its pilots to fly more precisely and skillfully than in individual flight. Good formation flying depended as much on good leadership as it did on the ability of the wing men to hold position. A thorough briefing on formation positions, power settings, assembly procedure, and timing was required. The formation leader had to forewarn the members of anticipated maneuvers, but the individual pilots also had to anticipate changes, and use smooth coordinated power to hold their positions. The leader had to fly as smoothly as possible using the power settings at the lowest range of the best cruise band on the cruise control chart. The aircraft response to changes in power

and airspeed varied noticeably with changes in altitude and load. For example, under similar conditions it took twice as long to make a given correction at 25,000 feet as it did at 5,000 feet. The formation leader used five basic formation signals:

- Assume Normal Formation: The signal was a slow, repeated rocking of the wings.
- Open Up Formation: The signal was a fishtail, or yaw to the right and left.
- Attention: The signal was a repeated and rapid aileron flutter used on the ground and in the air to attract the attention of all aircraft, and to stand by for radio messages. When on the ground at takeoff it meant, "Ready for takeoff."
- Change Formation: The signal was a dip of the right or left wing.
- Prepare to Land: The signal was a series of small dives or zooms.

Formation flying was based on two principles: to provide the greatest striking power in both time and degree, and to provide the greatest protection. (USAAF)

8

Night Flying

The flight manual stated:

"Your airplane and everything in and about it operates exactly the same at night as it does in the daytime. Everything, that is, except you. Your own vision is the only thing affected by the darkness. But this fact merely means that night flying requires more exacting technique on your part. Darkness, in affecting your vision, puts limitations on your judgment of distance, altitude, and speed."

Night Ground Operations
When taxiing at night the landing lights were to be used alternately to reduce the load on the electrical system, and to prolong their life. The flight deck lights were to be dimmed as low as possible to reduce glare and aid forward visibility. Turns were to be made with the inside landing lights on. In crowded taxiing areas a ground crewman walked ahead of each wing tip to direct taxiing by signaling with a flashlight. An observer was posted in the astrodome to help watch ground traffic. At any indication of brake trouble the pilot was to stop immediately and call to be towed off the runway, as defective brakes had a high probability of causing an accident at night. The pilot was to get tower clearance before crossing any runway, and if he were in doubt where to turn check with the tower. During run-up the aircraft was to turn off the landing lights to conserve the electrical system and avoid overheating the lights. After the preflight check unnecessary flight deck lights were turned off, and the pilot checked that all the crew were at their takeoff stations.

Night Takeoffs
After getting tower clearance for takeoff before taxiing onto the runway the pilot used his landing lights briefly to line up straight on the runway, being sure the nose gear was straight. Once lined up the landing lights were flashed down the runway long enough to check that it was clear. If the pilot had good visibility with clear ground references takeoff was visual, but with poor visibility and no visible horizon the takeoff was to be

by instruments. Once on instruments the pilot was to stay on them, and not try to fly half instruments and half visual. During takeoff the pilot was to maintain proper airspeed, and a constant heading that was to be held until sufficient altitude was reached to make a turn. Before making the turn the pilot was to be "particularly careful" to maintain his heading when braking the wheels and bringing up the gear.

Night Flight Precautions
Of course, the principal problem of night flying was visibility, and the pilot was to rely on his instruments as his primary reference, and not depend on scattered lights to orient him with the terrain below. The instruments were to be checked more frequently than in daytime.

Night Landings
On the different legs of the traffic pattern compass headings were to be flown. The pilot judged the start of the turn onto the final approach by the appearance of the runway lights. Along the base leg, the runway lights looked like a single row of lights. The start of the turn onto the approach was initiated the moment the two rows of lights seemed to separate. A medium turn was then made, and then a complete roll out from the turn was made just as the two rows of runway lights were squared away at full width. Low approaches were to be avoided at night, and constant airspeed, rate of descent, and glide maintained by making slight changes in power and altitude. The landing lights were most efficient from about 500 feet, and were helpful in locating the ground. The pilot was not to sight down the beam, but use the whole lighted area ahead and below for reference. The runway lights were to be used as a secondary reference, as the landing lights used alone could cause the pilot to level off for landing too late. But using the runway lights alone could cause the pilot to level off too high, especially if there was haze or dust over the field. If the pilot was uncertain of the final approach he was to use a little more power to prevent stalling out high. This increased power was to be maintained until making ground contact. The pilot was to avoid cutting power too high or too soon.

9

Flight Characteristics

General

The flight characteristics of the B-32 were considered "thoroughly satisfactory," with "all control pressures and responses excellent for an airplane of this size." The bomber "accelerated rapidly, both on takeoff and when power was applied in flight."

Control Surface Characteristics

Rudder: Even though the rudder was the heaviest of the controls there was no delay in its reaction, even at low speed. Rudder trim was considered adequate, and a few degrees of rudder trim eliminated the yaw caused by the loss of an outboard engine; 7 degrees would correct for the loss of two engines on the same side at cruising speeds and power settings.

Ailerons: The aileron control was considered sensitive and light, and undesirable yaw produced by aileron drag upon entering and leaving turns was slight. The aileron was effective at the low speeds of takeoff and landing, but caution had to be used not to use excessive aileron control at low airspeeds. Aileron tab control was activated via an electric switch and was very sensitive.

Elevators: The elevators were described as "smooth and light as an AT-6....almost." The elevators became effective early in the takeoff run, and gave a positive response in a stall. The elevators were the only controls without servo tabs, but they did not need them. There was some mushiness of the elevator trim tabs, and it was necessary for the pilot to be careful when trimming the bomber at altitude, but they were satisfactory at low altitudes. During banking up to 40 degrees elevator pressure was normal, but in banks above 40 degrees the elevator pressure increased rapidly, and it was difficult to hold banks of 60 degrees or more. Therefore pilots were warned not to make steep banks in the traffic pattern, or anywhere close to the ground.

Flaps: When the flaps were lowered there was a noticeable tendency for the aircraft to nose up, and a similar tendency to nose down when the flaps

were raised. To compensate for this condition the pilot had to make "fairly large" changes in elevator trim tab settings. When the flaps were retracted after takeoff or lowered for landing the pilot preferred to first use the elevator trim tabs to give him more time to adjust the flaps. With any given load, full flaps would lower the power off stalling speed 25%. The pilot was instructed to use 5 degrees of flap for flights above 20,000 feet, as this setting improved flight characteristics at altitude. For maximum performance at takeoff 40 degrees flaps gave the aircraft the shortest ground run, and the shortest distance for clearing obstacles at the end of the runway.

Restricted Maneuvers and Airspeed Limitations

Restricted maneuvers, referred to as "Prohibited" maneuvers in earlier manuals, were: loops, rolls, spins, Immelmans and vertical banks, and inverted flight. Banks were restricted to 60 degrees while flying the lighter TB-32 training aircraft, and to 30 degrees in operational aircraft carrying a gross weight of 120,000 pounds. An airspeed of 330mph was not to be exceeded at 100,000 pounds gross weight, and 240mph at 118,000 pounds (full fuel and bomb load). These banking and airspeed numbers were based on Technical Order restrictions based on structural limitations, and did not consider practical operational factors. Spins were a prohibited maneuver, but if the aircraft went into a spin, the conventional multi-engine aircraft remedies were used for recovery.

Stalls

The stalling characteristics were considered "as good and, in some cases better than, those in many smaller airplanes." The stalling characteristics of the B-32 were clean, and indicated by a severe tail shake three to five miles above the stalling speed. A slight rolling movement before the actual stall could develop as a result of an intermediate stall in or around the aileron. During the final phase of the stall a tendency for aileron snatch could be noticed. It was recommended that if the stall was allowed to progress after first noticing the tail shake, the wheel should be held firmly in order to prevent any whip that might be transmitted to it from the aileron. The complete stall was followed by the aircraft falling straight forward, without any tendency to spin.

10

Landing

Approach

The pilot notified the flight deck crew of the approach, and checked to see if they were on station. The co-pilot then advised the crew in the rear compartment by interphone of the approach, and were told to prepare for the landing. The crew acknowledged and reported they were on station. The Before Landing Checklist was to be completed before the aircraft was opposite the tower into its downwind leg, so that the pilot could be planning the placing of the base leg. The timing of the turn onto the base leg was to be about 30 seconds past the end of the runway. The tower was to be contacted as the aircraft turned onto the base leg so that the tower could give the pilot additional instructions if necessary. The Before Landing Checklist included:

The pilot called the tower for landing instructions and an altimeter setting. Turrets retracted.

Trailing antenna reeled IN.

The pilot turned the autopilot OFF.

The engineer set the intercoolers to AUTOMATIC.

The co-pilot started the APU 10 minutes before landing, giving it time to warm up. He then turned the equalizer switch ON, and placed the APU generator switch in the LOAD position after it began running.

Generators ON.

The engineer checked that the brake system hydraulic pump switch was ON and checked the circuit breaker.

The co-pilot metered the brakes until the pressure dropped to 850psi, and then checked that the electric hydraulic pump cut in at returned pressure at 1,030psi.

The engineer checked that all fuel tank selector valves were in the TANK TO ENGINE position, with the drain valve in the CROSSFEED position.

The engineer turned all four booster pumps to HIGH.

The engineer set the mixture controls to AUTO RICH.

The co-pilot pulled up the APU throttle to the RUN position, and reminded the co-pilot to check it regularly. The engineer was to continue a check on the APU voltage.

At the direction of the pilot the engineer lowered the wing flaps to 10 degrees (at speeds below 190mph IAS). The scanners checked the flaps from their blisters, and reported their operation to the co-pilot.

At the direction of the pilot the engineer lowered the main gear at IAS

below 190mph; otherwise, the nose gear might not extend enough to lock. A green tell tale light indicated when the gear was down. The landing gear switch was to be returned to NEUTRAL after the gear was down and locked. As soon as the engineer tripped the landing gear switch, and before the gear was down, he increased the propeller synch-control to 2,400 AUTOMATIC CONSTANT SPEED on master tachometer. The increase was necessary because the wheels caused considerable drag, and additional power was required.

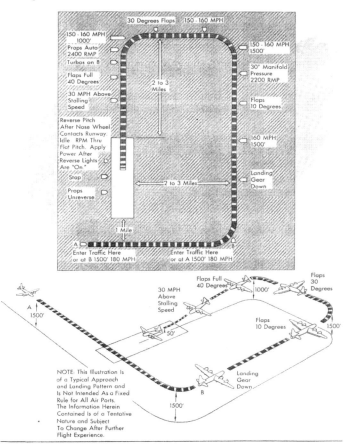

Figure 24 – Traffic Pattern

(Airplane Commander's Training Manual)

*STALLING SPEEDS

Power-off—Gear Down

Gross Wt.	40° Flaps	30° Flaps	20° Flaps	0° Flaps
80,000 lbs	106	113	117	131
90,000 lbs	111	118	122	137
100,000 lbs	116	123	128	144
110,000 lbs	120	128	133	151
120,000 lbs	125	133	139	156

*Estimated figures, not flight checked.

(Airplane Commander's Training Manual)

Gear check-down and locked. The bombardier was to visually check that the nose gear was down and locked, while the scanners called over the interphone to report the main gear and tailskid were extended. The tailskid was checked through the tailskid access door.

The engineer and co-pilot kept a running check on the engine instruments and CHT, and cracked the cowl flaps as needed.

The engineer checked brake accumulator pressure (minimum 850psi.). The amber brake pressure warning light indicated when the brake pressure fell below 650psi.

Final Approach

The turn into the final approach was to be started early to avoid making a steep turn, or going past the runway and having to S back. To reach a point just short of the runway the approach glide angle was controlled by adjusting the power. The pilot set the turbo on 8, while the engineer set the propeller synch-control for 2,400 rpm on the master tachometer. At the direction of the pilot the engineer extended the flaps to full landing position at 40 degrees, and returned the flap switch to NEUTRAL when the flaps were down. The scanners reported the flap position to the co-pilot over the interphone. The pilot would have no difficulty if he had to go around with full flaps down. The engineer moved the propeller reverse safety switch from SAFE to READY.

Normal Landings

The combat test report stated: "The airplane has proven to be easy for average crews to land." The Pilot's Manual stated:

"Consistently good landings in the B-32 require a combination of good judgment, technique, and timing. Still, this airplane is easier to land than other large airplanes. Its landing characteristics are consistently good in normal, crosswind, and emergency landings."

The pilot was to bring the aircraft down on the first one third of the runway by using the power carefully to adjust the approach glide, and then had to correctly time the flare out. A crosswind turn was made, the power was slightly decreased to set up the final approach at 150-160mph, and full flaps (40 degrees),†then 30 inch boost and 130mph IAS, keeping the aircraft's IAS about 30mph above power off stalling speeds. The flare out was started about 150 feet above the ground, but the altitude varied with wind velocity and the individual pilot's technique. If the pilot broke his approach too soon, or used too little airspeed, the aircraft tended to sink and slam into the runway, but if he broke the approach too low or used too much airspeed the aircraft tended to fly onto the runway. As the bomber came over the runway the throttles were eased back slowly and smoothly, so that the aircraft decelerated without sinking. The nose was slowly brought up as the aircraft settled, and a two-point landing was made, usually very gently, at about 95 to 105mph. The nose gear was eased down onto the runway before elevator control was lost. There was a "little shrug" caused by nose drift as the nose gear touched the ground. The propeller reversing mechanism was engaged from NORMAL to REVERSE, and the throttles pushed forward to LOW. The propellers were never to be reversed until ground contact was made. As the propeller blades twisted from a positive angle through zero, and then to a negative angle the throttle was to be accelerated quickly, causing the inboard propellers to push air with a 4,000+ horsepower negative thrust to bring the large bomber "quickly and remarkably steadily" to an easy stop within 1,200 feet. The inboard throttles were somewhat longer than the outboard throttles, which made handling easier in reverse pitch. However, if the runway was long, and other aircraft were

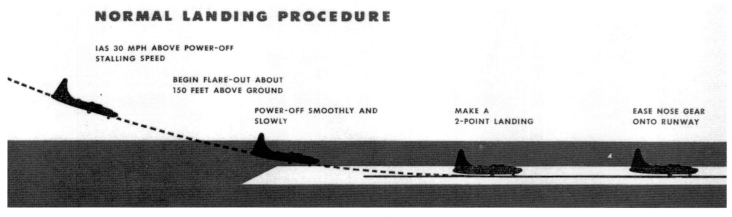

NORMAL LANDING PROCEDURE

IAS 30 MPH ABOVE POWER-OFF
STALLING SPEED

BEGIN FLARE-OUT ABOUT
150 FEET ABOVE GROUND

POWER-OFF SMOOTHLY AND
SLOWLY

MAKE A
2-POINT LANDING

EASE NOSE GEAR
ONTO RUNWAY

(Airplane Commander's Training Manual)

landing closely behind, the landing roll was allowed to be long. With the prop-reversing mechanism emergency landings were possible on short runways, such as fighter strips. This prop-reversal also prevented ground looping on wet or icy landing fields. The prop reversing mechanism could be used to correct direction with the opposite throttle from the conventional non-reversing props. If the aircraft started to move to the left the No.3 throttle (right throttle) was advanced, and if it moved to the right the No.2 throttle (left throttle) was advanced. The brakes could be used if necessary, but the reverse thrust was so effective that the ground roll was appreciably slowed by it without braking. The reverse props were most effective when used early to reduce the initial landing speed, and lost its effectiveness as the speed decreased. The reverse props were not to be used for parking the aircraft or other ground operations, except landing, as without the ram cooling of landing speeds the reverse operation quickly overheated the engines.

During the landing roll the engineer set the cowl flaps to FULL OPEN, and their position was checked by the pilot and co-pilot. The engineer RETRACTED the wing flaps, and then returned them to NEUTRAL. As the aircraft speed dropped to 50-60mph the pilot directed the engineer to switch the propeller reverse from REVERSE to NORMAL, and the propeller reverse pitch safety switch was moved from READY to SAFE. The engineer set the propeller controls to 2,800rpm AUTOMATIC, and he returned the turbo selector to 0. The booster pumps were turned to OFF, and the elevator trim tabs were returned to NEUTRAL. The engineer turned OFF the No.2 and No.3 generators, as they did not generate power at low rpms of taxiing. The landing roll distances were measured for brakes only, propeller reversal and a combination of both simultaneously. During testing (at 90,000 pounds gross weight), using the brakes only, the average ground roll was 5,600 feet; using propeller reversal only it was 4,300 feet, and using a combination it was 3,250 feet. The propeller reversal option on the B-32 was found to be very beneficial, as it gave a high degree of directional control, and produced a minimum landing roll with minimum brake wear. Initially reversible props were used on the two inboard engines, but testing results caused the recommendation that they be used on all engines.

Go Arounds

The go around was to be avoided if possible, but go arounds in the B-32 were relatively safe and easy, as the aircraft responded quickly to the pilot's sudden demand for increased power. During a go around the pilot had to consider several critical factors: engine failure; full flaps and gear down being in effect; low initial speed; winds; and low altitudes. The pilot needed to keep the tower notified of his position, and if his aircraft was in trouble the pilot was to inform the tower well in advance so that the field could be cleared. He was to maintain correct spacing of his aircraft in the traffic pattern, and proceed in the pattern so that other following aircraft would not be forced to go around. The pilot always had to be ready for a go around due to circumstances out of his control, such as accidents on the runway, misunderstandings from the tower, or the need for an immediate emergency landing by another aircraft. If the aircraft had touched down when a go around became necessary the pilot was to proceed as for a touch-and-go landing.

During a go around the engineer set the synch control to 2,400rpms, and the pilot advanced the throttles to FULL OPEN. He then gave the engineer orders to put the gear UP, and as it was moving up the engineer

was to raise the flaps to 20 degrees, with the scanners checking and reporting both the gear and flap positions. The airspeed was to be increased to at least 160mph as soon as possible, if necessary nosing down to get 160mph if altitude was sufficient. The engineer and co-pilot kept a running check on the CHTs, and adjusted the cowl flaps as needed. After safe airspeed was attained with the gear and flaps up the pilot readjusted the power for a normal climb and traffic pattern.

Crosswind Landings

The recommended technique for a crosswind landing in the B-32 was a combination of crab and upwind wing slightly low. Even though the B-32 had good aileron, rudder, and elevator control during the landing approach, the bomber took longer to respond to control pressures due to its weight. The pilot needed to anticipate control, and employ the normal amount sooner, rather than employing more control pressure later, when it was more urgently needed. The crucial phase of the crosswind landing was at the instant the aircraft contacted the ground, as ideally the aircraft was to make ground contact with zero drift and head straight ahead down the runway.

During a crosswind landing the pilot was to fly the normal traffic pattern, with the base leg moved out past the end of the runway approximately a half mile farther than for the normal landing, thus allowing more time to establish a heading to give the correct ground track. The approach was to be slightly longer, and the last one third of the approach was to be lower than normal. This extra time and lower approach was used by the pilot to line up the runway, and to accurately estimate drift. The flaps were at FULL as usual. On the approach the pilot crabbed slightly into the wind, and lowered the upwind wing to help decrease drift. Just as the bomber touched the runway, the pilot applied rudder and aileron pressure to level the wings and align the aircraft with the center of the runway. This maneuver had to be timed correctly, with the pilot anticipating control, and using some throttle on the outboard engine of the low wing to help raise that wing. Once on the runway the nose wheel was to be lowered as soon as possible to gain the stability advantage of the tricycle landing gear.

Low Visibility Landings

The low visibility, or close-in landing, was not only necessary when visibility was too low to make a normal visual pattern landing, but also when there were no radio facilities for an instrument approach, and when no alternate field was available.

The procedure for a low visibility landing was for the pilot to contact the tower and obtain a careful briefing on field conditions. The pilot preferred a left hand landing pattern, as that would place him always looking down on the field side. The approach was to be in the direction in which the aircraft was to be landed, and at an altitude as high as the ceiling and visibility would allow. The aircraft was to be trimmed, and the power set at 160IAS. The pilot flew the aircraft down the runway, noting the elapsed time if necessary, and then made a 180 degree turn at the end and flew a reciprocal heading. After flying 15 to 20 seconds beyond the head of the runway the pilot made another 180 degree turn, lowering the flaps, and slowing the aircraft to 30mph above stalling speed to make a normal approach and landing. The service manual admonished: "DANGER: Never walk in the path of the wheels. This airplane will run over you just once."

11

After Landing

Securing the Aircraft

After the brakes were cooled the pilot set the parking brake by depressing both brake pedals fully, then pulling rearward the parking brake handle located to the right of the his right rudder pedal. After the brakes were set the chocks were placed fore and aft of the landing gear tires. The engines were idled at 1,000rpm until the CHT was reduced to 400°F. The engine rpms were increased to 1,200 for 30 seconds to properly scavenge oil, and then the pilot stopped the engines by moving the mixture controls to IDLE CUT OFF. The cowl flaps were left FULL OPEN until the engines were cold (212°F). AFTER the engines were stopped the master and individual ignition switches were turned OFF, and ALL electrical units were turned OFF, except circuit breakers and generators. The pilot aligned the flight controls, and then locked them in the following order: rudder, elevators, and aileron, so that all controls were not movable in any direction. The control column and pedals were to be securely locked. The engineer turned the APU switch to NEUTRAL, and then turned the equalizer and battery switches to OFF. Then the co-pilot pushed the APU throttle down to IDLE, and after a short time turned the APU ignition switch to OFF. Many pilots elected to open the bomb bays with the bomb salvo switch as an emergency exit in case of fire, and also to ventilate any accumulated fuel fumes.

Towing

Towing lugs were provided on the forward part of the nose gear strut, and on the aft sides of both main landing gear struts. The nose gear lug could be used for towing on level ground, but for longer distances on inclines the main landing gear lugs were used with a tow bar attached to the nose gear, so that tow men could steer the aircraft from that point. For towing the following personnel arrangement was observed: one in the pilot's seat; one near the aircraft's nose; one at each wing tip; and one at the tail. Signals were relayed from the various crew members to the man at the nose, who was to be visible at all times to the tow tug operator and the crew member in the pilot's seat.

Mooring

In case of high winds, it would be necessary to use type D-1 "dead man" moorings Two tie down points were provided on the under surface of the wing outer panels, with four lines extending from each point. Enough slack was to be left to prevent damage to the wing in case a tire(s) went flat. The nose wheel towing lug (one line), main gear towing lugs (one line forward and one line aft), and the tail skid (two lateral lines) could also be used for mooring points.

Protective Covers

When the oil dilution was completed and the props cleaned the gun, engine, wing, and propeller covers were to be installed. Gun and engine covers were stowed in the tail compartment, while wing and prop covers were ground equipment.

TOWING AT NOSE GEAR

Tow Bar or
Steer Bar

Attaching
Point

Figure 14 – Towing Diagram

(E&R Manual)

Mooring diagram (E&R Manual)

12

Emergencies

General

It was the pilot's responsibility to check that all crew members had life vests and the correct parachute type, that they were properly fitted, and that everyone knew how to locate them and knew how to use them. The crew was to know where the nearest exits for bailout and ditching were located, and ditching and bailout drills were to be conducted periodically.

Engine Failure

On Takeoff

When engine failure occurred on takeoff the pilot was to immediately apply rudder and aileron to counteract the yaw caused by the unbalanced power conditions, and not allow the wing with the dead engine to drop. Power was to be used to improve directional stability (49 inches manifold pressure maximum). Airspeed was to be maintained, putting the nose down if necessary and possible until sufficient airspeed was gained. The gear was to be retracted, and the propeller on the bad engine feathered. As airspeed increased the wing flaps were to be raised gradually in stages. After these initial problems were overcome the trim tabs were to be used to reduce the forces on the controls, and the excessive engine power reduced.

In Flight

If an engine failed in flight the pilot had to use the control surfaces to counteract the yaw, keep the wing with the defective engine high, feather that propeller, and close the cowl flaps. When correcting yaw sufficient rudder was used first, and then the aileron, but too much aileron would cause the aircraft to be flown in a forward slip, making it impossible to maintain safe airspeed. After yaw was corrected the tabs were used to relieve the strain on the aircraft. Power was used to improve directional control if the use of tabs was ineffective. The flaps had to be used without sudden operation in either direction. At low speeds all turns were to be made with the two operating engines down and pointing toward the center of the turn. If the engine failure occurred at high altitude excessive power was not to be used to maintain the original altitude, and the aircraft was to be allowed to descend into denser air, where it could hold altitude with less power. When a long flight was to be made with any of the engines out, fuel was to be transferred or used from the tanks of the inoperable engine(s).

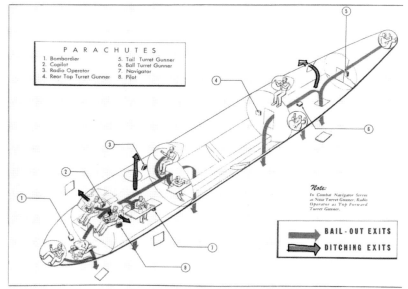

(Airplane Commander's Training Manual)

Figure 25 – Emergency Exits and Parachute Stowages

Feathering and Unfeathering Propellers

Feathering

Four feathering switches protected under a Plexiglas panel were located near the upper part of the propeller panel. When feathering a propeller the throttle was to be closed, and the feathering switch moved to FEATHER. The mixture control was to be in IDLE CUT OFF, and the booster pump and fuel selector valve OFF. Once the propeller stopped wind milling the ignition switch was to be turned OFF, and then the generator was shut OFF to complete the feathering.

Unfeathering

The throttle was closed, and the mixture control on IDLE CUT OFF. The fuel selector was placed in the desired position, and the booster pump turned ON. The feather switch was returned to NORMAL. The propeller selector switch was held in INCREASE RPM until the engine tachometer indicated about 800rpm, and then was released to the FIXED PITCH position. The ignition was turned ON, the mixture control moved to AUTOMATC RICH, and the throttles OPENED until the engines idled from 1,000 to 1,200rpm. The throttles were maintained in this position until the oil temperature and pressure were normal. Once the engine was warm the propeller selector switch was moved to AUTOMATIC, and the throttle and mixture controls readjusted to the normal flight settings. The generator was then turned ON.

Landing With One or Two Engines Out

With an engine(s) out the pilot was to approach from an altitude of at least 1,000 feet, keeping the approach leg close to the field and maintaining sufficient airspeed, and was to notify the tower of his difficulty as soon as possible. The emergency landing procedure was to fly the traffic pattern at a higher altitude, and continue at safe airspeeds: at least 160mph for one engine out; at least 170mph for two engines out; and all the speed available for three engines gone. The pilot was to avoid overshooting the runway, especially if two engines were out. In the traffic pattern the pilot used 8 to 10 degrees flaps, and the landing gear was to be kept up until the final approach. The aircraft was trimmed for lower power condition (if two engines on one side were inoperable the main power was to be placed on the good inboard engine). Once a successful landing was assured the flaps were to be lowered to FULL DOWN, and with the power set a normal landing procedure carried out.

Emergency Landings with Hydraulic System Failure

With hydraulic system failure the emergency hydraulic system was to be used to lower the landing gear, and with full flaps. However, the pilot had to remember that neither could be raised in case of a go around, and this would cause excessive drag and excessive CHT, with possible engine fires and failure, and a crash. It was imperative that the pilot land on the first try.

Emergency Landing with Gear Up

During gear up landings the general crash landing procedures were to be followed (see below). If both the nose and main gear remained up the pilot was to use the normal landing attitude, and slide the airplane in on its belly. If the main gear was down and the nose gear up, or flapping, the pilot was to land in the normal attitude, but was to hold the nose up as long as possible, and then lower it as gently as possible. With one main wheel down, the nose wheel down or up, the pilot was to land in the normal attitude, but

with the wing slightly down on the down wheel side. The other wing was to be held up as long as possible, realizing that there would be an abrupt ground loop when the wing hit the ground. The opposite brake was to be used to minimize this ground loop. With the nose gear down and the main gear up the normal belly landing procedure was to be used, realizing that the nose gear would rip a hole into the fuselage.

Crash Landings

After trying all the possible emergency procedures to correct the emergency, the pilot needed to decide whether the situation required a crash landing or bailout. The rule of thumb was to bail out unless there was a reasonable assurance that a crash landing would be successful. Once the decision to crash land was made the crew was notified, and emergency radio procedures immediately began. All unnecessary removable equipment was to be jettisoned to lighten the aircraft and prevent injury on impact. Among the objects to be jettisoned were: bombs (jettisoned in SAFE, over uninhabited or enemy territory), bomb sight, sun visors, radio receiver, navigator's table, seat back and drafting machine, cup container, map case (save maps, if necessary), transmitters, liaison set, head sets, portable oxygen units and oxygen hoses, and ammunition and ammunition boxes. Things that were to be saved were fire extinguishers, axes, flashlights, first aid kits, and any radio equipment that could aid in rescue. If it was possible the pilot was to fly until the fuel supply was less than 200 gallons per tank. The top hatches and windows were to be removed and stowed, or jettisoned, and the bomb bay and bottom hatches closed, and the bottom turret retracted. At this point the pilot had the option of offering those crew members not involved in the landing the choice of bailing out. The seated crew in the flight deck was to fasten their seat belts, while the remainder of the crew was to assume their crash landing positions. The bombardier was to vacate his position. Once in their crash landing positions the crew was to look directly to the rear of their station for poorly stowed or loosely installed equipment that could batter them during a sudden stop. The pilot was to make a long approach so that all the emergency procedures could be completed. The pilot lowered FULL flaps, LOWERED the gear, turned OFF the APU, and CUT the battery, ignition, and generator switches, feathered the inboard engines to prevent a blade from cutting through the fuselage, and shut OFF the fuel boost. Just before the landing the fuel selector valves were CLOSED, leaving about 10 to 15 seconds of fuel remaining in the lines. Just before hitting the ground the pilot warned the crew, pulled the throttle all the way back, placed the mixture controls in IDLE CUT OFF, and then gradually opened the throttles to clear the fuel from the carburetor. The possibility of a stall had to be kept in mind while the aircraft was high off the ground. Too much airspeed was better than not enough. The landing attitude had to be approximately level, with the tail slightly low. After coming to a stop every crew member was to leave as quickly as possible, taking fire extinguishers and axes with them. If hatches jammed the axes were to be used to chop holes in areas marked on the fuselage as "Cut Here for Emergency Rescue."

Ditching

The decision to ditch was entirely that of the pilot. The actual ditching procedure depended on the physical condition of the aircraft and crew, the loading of the aircraft, the area of ditching (e.g. radio silence in enemy waters), and the weather, none of which could be anticipated in advance. The success of the ditching therefore depended on the skill and judgment of the pilot and crew. However, ditching drills were repeated until every man automatically knew his duty and the duties of his crewmates, and nothing was overlooked.

The pilot announced the "Prepare for ditching in XX minutes" order to the crew over the interphone. The navigator plotted the aircraft's position, and the radio operator sent out distress signals and his position, and notified Air-Sea Rescue. The chance of being rescued after ditching was directly proportional to the efficiency of the emergency radio procedure. The radar operator moved into the bomb bay, set all racks on the ready position, and then returned to the forward cabin and salvoed bombs, cargo carriers, and/or auxiliary fuel tanks. The radar operator turned off the salvo switch, and called the pilot to close the bomb bay doors, or closed them manually. The flight engineer, radar operator and gunners collected all disposable equipment (including the detachable radio and radar sets located behind the pilot and co-pilot) and equipment that could break loose and launch dangerously through the cabin, and jettisoned it through the bomb bay. The radar operator, flight engineer, and gunners installed the ditching beams in the bomb bays. There were 16 ditching beams: four stowed on the forward side of bulkhead 6 in the bomb bay, and 12 in the rear cabin. These beams, when installed, contoured with the inner surface of the bomb bay doors, and greatly increased the structural strength to withstand impact when the aircraft hit the water. The lower hatch was closed and secured before ditching, as were the fuselage doors to the bomb bays. The nose turret door, and the fuselage door behind it, were closed in case the nose turret Plexiglas window collapsed. The landing gear and the belly turret were to be retracted. The bombardier's station was vacated.

The top escape hatches were opened to prevent jamming on impact. The navigator's optical flat was removed by chopping off the hinges using the fire axe. In the rear compartment, the emergency hatch on the right side of the fuselage was opened. If the sea was calm the side windows of the pilot's stations could be jettisoned before impact. The radar operator, flight engineer, navigator, and bombardier distributed ditching jackets in the forward compartment, and the gunners did so in the rear cabin. There were 11 ditching jackets: four stowed in a bag in the rear cabin, just behind the

escape hatch on the right hand side; and seven under the navigator's table in the forward cabin. The crew held the jackets to their bodies, reducing the possibility of injury while being tossed about the cabin upon impact with the water.

The crash stations were selected with consideration to the number of crew and the equipment in the cabin. The crew was instructed to brace themselves with the crash, not against it. A crewman braced his back against a solid structure, and never tried to absorb the shock by extending his arms or legs forward against the structure. The pilot announced "Brace for impact" as he ditched with full flaps at 10 to 15 miles per hour above stalling speed and level flight.

Every crew member knew the location of his ditching exit. The pilot pulled a leather thong to jettison the window at his left and exited through it, while the co-pilot did the same on his right hand side. Crew in the forward cabin escaped through the astro hatch, and those in the rear cabin left through the upper escape hatch.

After the initial impact, and when forward motion stopped, the life rafts needed to be released. Release handles were located in the flight deck on the rear bulkhead, and in the rear compartment on the front bulkhead, both on the right hand side of the fuselage. Life rafts were in a compartment forward of the rear turret, and could be released from the outside of the aircraft by operating the handles on the hatch covers and opening the CO_2 release valve. A mooring line that would break if the aircraft sank secured each raft. A crewman in the rear compartment was responsible for recovering the rafts.

During the escape procedure from the aircraft the waterproof and buoyant emergency radio transmitter was thrown out of the top hatch. The crew left the aircraft through the top emergency hatches, carrying as many emergency articles as time permitted. After leaving the aircraft the crew inflated their life jackets. The rafts were brought alongside the aircraft by the mooring lines, and boarded by stepping, not jumping, into them. Once all the crew was inside the life rafts the rafts were tied together, and if the aircraft continued to float the life rafts were to remain in the vicinity. The emergency radio was to be used as soon as possible, being careful to keep

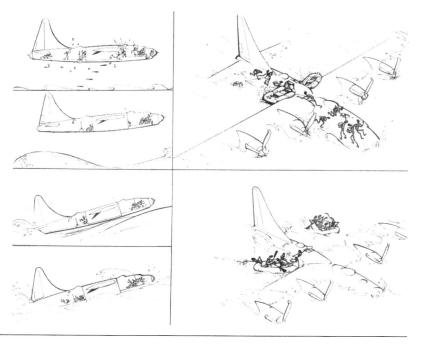

Ditching (Airplane Commander's Training Manual)

the antenna out of the water. The distress signals were to be transmitted in three minute international periods, 15 and 45 minutes after the hour.

Bail Out

It was solely the pilot's decision whether or not to abandon the aircraft, and once the decision had been made, the pilot tripped an alarm bell by a switch on his instrument panel. The alarm bell was located on the face of bulkhead 7.1, just forward of the stabilizer in the rear cabin. The alarm bell and interphone messages signaled for a prearranged and practiced emergency exit routine to be carried out. The prepare to bail out alarm signal was three short rings, indicating that the crew were to retrieve their parachutes from their stowage locations and help one another, inspecting parachutes and harnesses. The radio operator was instructed to send out distress messages.

The alarm signal to abandon the aircraft was one long ring. For bail out the pilot set up the autopilot; reduced power for a descent rate of about 1,000 to 1,500 feet per minute; set airspeed 30mph above stalling; and locked the throttles. If the crippled bomber were still under control the pilot was to reduce airspeed as much as possible to ease the exit through the aircraft's slipstream.

The bomb bays were the primary exit for all the crew, as they were the easiest to use. The bomb bay doors and the nose wheel well doors could be opened simultaneously. Bomb bay doors were to be opened so that any bombs could be salvoed conventionally by the bombardier, or by operating either of the bomb salvo switches accessible on the flight deck. One salvo switch was located on the pilot's panel, and the other on the forward face, left hand side of the rear wall of the flight deck. The bomb bay doors could also be opened by manual operation of the main hydraulic selector valve, or by the use of the emergency hydraulic system. The camera hatch was the secondary rear compartment exit, and the nose wheel well was the flight deck secondary exit. Before using the nose wheel well as an emergency exit during flight the nose wheel had to be extended and locked.

If the hydraulic system was damaged and there was no power to operate the bomb bay doors, or lower the nose wheel, then the camera hatch in the rear and the bombardier's hatch in the nose were to be used. If the bombardier's hatch was to be used as an exit during flight it was necessary to do so before the nose gear was extended to prevent the possible collision with the nose wheel well door. Exit through the nose wheel well was nervewracking, because of the proximity of the props.

System Failures

The B-32 was equipped with a dual independent hydraulic system that lowered the landing gear, opened and closed the bomb bay doors, and lowered the wing flaps. Single independent hydraulic systems were installed to raise the landing gear and to retract the flaps. The brake system was the pressure type, equipped with dual accumulators. Landing gear, bomb bay doors, and flaps could be moved in either direction by manually operating the main selector valve, in the event of electrical failure. However, the aircraft had no emergency means to raise the landing gear or flaps if hydraulic failure should occur.

Landing Gear, Flaps, and Bomb Bay Doors

The main hydraulic selector valve, located above the catwalk just behind the front top turret in the forward bomb bay, had to be operated manually in case of failure of the landing gear, flaps, or bomb bay doors. The appropriate pressure control button of the selector valve was identified by its position at the front or rear of the row of plungers on the hydraulic selector valve. The front of the main selector valve (looking toward the rear of the aircraft, left to right) contained the front of the main pilot valve, plungers for the bomb bay doors OPEN, for flaps UP, and for landing gear UP. The rear of the main selector valve contained (left to right) the back of main pilot valve, and the plungers for the bomb bay doors CLOSED, for flaps DOWN, and for landing gear DOWN. A coil spring was installed around the stem of the plunger. The plunger for the designated action was pushed in, and held in until the required action was completed and then released.

The open center and emergency systems were independent systems when the switch-over valve was in the normal position. The engine-driven pumps supplied power to the open center system, which operated all hydraulically activated equipment, except the brakes. The brake system obtained its power from the electrically driven pump. The switch-over valve in the emergency position diverted fluid from the emergency reservoir into the emergency system lines. A micro switch on the back of the switch-over valve turned on the electric-hydraulic pump that supplied power for the emergency system. The electric-hydraulic pump was in continuous operation during the period the switch over valve was in the EMERGENCY ON position. The appropriate emergency hydraulic valve on the emergency hydraulic selector valve was operated. If the hydraulic selector valve operation of the electric hydraulic pump failed to function the hand pump was to be used as the back up.

Brakes

The normal brake pressure range was from 850 to 1,080psi. With the initial brake pressure of 1,080psi, four full brake applications could be achieved by the use of the accumulators alone. A pressure of 850psi gave two brake applications. At no time was a brake application to be attempted with less than 850psi. A brake pressure warning light and an override switch were located at the co-pilot's panel. This switch operated the electric hydraulic motor, overriding all units except the circuit breaker. If the electric hydraulic pump failed to operate the hand pump was to be used until enough pressure was obtained.

Emergency Bomb Release

The bomb bay doors could be opened and the bombs released by the bombardier in the normal manner, or the bombs could be salvoed using either the salvo switch on the pilot's panel, or the salvo switch in the box on the rear flight deck wall. If the bomb bay doors opened and the bombs failed to salvo, the bombs could be released manually by tripping the release lever, or by using a tool to force the release lever of each bomb shackle past the hinge ear of the bomb rack release unit.

Fires

The B-32 and B-29, with their Wright R-3350 engines, were tagged with the bad reputation for fires. The B-32 Pilot's Manual stated, "Don't approach your B-32 so fire conscious that you fly with one hand on the wheel and the other on the fire extinguisher."

Engine Induction System Fires

Generally, induction system fires were confined to the induction system when they started, and if dealt with soon enough by the correct procedure they could be extinguished without engine loss. Induction system fires were usually caused by a series of backfires. These backfires were produced during ground operations, during initial takeoff by rapid changes in throttle openings, and during cruising when manual leaning was attempted. Induction system fires were indicated by sudden changes in manifold pressure and rpm, and then the recovery or partial recovery of the loss of manifold pressure and rpm due to windmilling. This was followed by heavy black smoke from the engine exhaust and, in the final stage, heavy white smoke from the engine exhaust. During ground operations a series of backfires were considered the cause of induction system fires and indicated too lean a mixture. Flames and black smoke from the exhaust tail stack indicated too rich a mixture.

When any crew member spotted an engine fire he would immediately broadcast "FIRE in (applicable engine)" using the CALL position on the interphone, and then repeated the engine number. The pilot would immediately CLOSE the throttle on the engine on fire, and the co-pilot moved the mixture control to IDLE CUT OFF, turned the booster pump to OFF, and the fuel selector valve to OFF. If the smoke stopped immediately the engine power was applied smoothly and normally, with the exhaust being carefully watched for smoke. If the smoke did not stop in about 10 seconds the pilot feathered the propeller of the affected engine, and the co-pilot closed the cowl flaps to decrease the drag on the airplane.

Nacelle Fires

Nacelle fires were identified by smoke or flame around the nacelle, particularly around the cowlings, or coming from the cowl flaps, and not from the exhaust alone. However, an induction system fire could become a nacelle fire and proliferate to the wing and fuselage. Fuel, oil, and foreign material in the nacelle were fire hazards, and careful inspections and cleaning were carried out before each flight. The carburetors were inspected for leaks, and excess oil was cleaned from the nacelle. Inspections were made of all oil and fuel line connections, of the oil induction system for leaks, and of the oil dilution solenoid for correct seating.

When a fire was observed in a nacelle the pilot CLOSED the throttle and feathered the propeller, and the co-pilot moved the mixture control to IDLE CUT OFF, shut OFF the fuel supply at the fuel selector panel, and OPENED the cowl flaps. When the engine stopped turning the pilot immediately turned OFF the ignition switch and generator. The co-pilot pulled up the T handle on the fire extinguisher for the affected nacelle. On B-32s prior to No. 42-103506 the CO_2 supply was sufficient to quench a fire in all four engines. On B-32s No. 103506 and above, a "one shot" fixed type system was used that discharged the entire CO_2 supply to extinguish a fire in any one engine.

Cabin Fires

Cabin or bomb bay fires could be caused by electrical problems, advanced engine fires, or crew carelessness. Smoking was not allowed on the ground or during takeoffs or landings, fuel transfer, or at any time when fumes were detected. Hydraulic and oil spills were to be cleaned up, and rags, paper, and other waste was to be removed.

Fire extinguishers were located in the forward cabin on the cable guard behind the co-pilot's seat, and in the rear cabin on the rear bulkhead wall to the left of the door. A fire axe was strapped on the rear side of the nose wheel in the forward cabin. When a cabin fire occurred, all the windows and vents were to be closed, including the cabin doors to the bomb bays, and all electric units were shut off.

13

Pilot Comments on Flying the B-32
1Lt. Robert Kirk

After taking advanced ROTC I graduated from Indiana University in December 1942, and was commissioned as a 2nd Lieutenant, Infantry at Fort Benning, Georgia, April 1943. I transferred to Army Air Corps for pilot training in November 1943 in Class 44G, Southeast Training Command, and received my wings at Turner Field, Georgia, August 1944. During Advanced Training I flew the B-25 instead of the AT-10, and flew the B-24 in Transition Training at Maxwell Field, Alabama, and then combat crew training at Mountain Home Army Air Base, Idaho. Upon completion of crew training my crew was one of 16 transferred to Langley Field, Virginia, for H2X/LAB training, which was low altitude bombing by radar. We staged at Hunter Field, Georgia, for duty in China, but orders were canceled on the day before departure, and we returned to Langley; we were then transferred to Tarrant Army Air Field, Texas, which later became Carswell AFB. We needed only two months to transition to the B-32. The Flight Engineers came in before us, as they were not part of the B-24 crew. The pilots and co-pilots arrived for an eight week course, with the first week in ground school, and then about three weeks in transitional flight training.

The first thing that got my attention when I first saw the -32 was the single tall stabilizer, and then the large size of its long cylindrical fuselage when compared to the boxy B-24. The stabilizer was even taller than the later Navy Privateer version of the B-24, but I never did understand the reason for the even larger tail on the B-32. Once inside the plane we could actually stand up inside the spacious flight deck, which was like a small room compared to the flight deck of the B-24. It contained the pilot's and co-pilot's flight controls, instruments, radio operator's station, navigator's station, and a bench. The co-pilot sat adjacent to me, and we were separated by a passageway that led to the nose; the flight engineer sat on the floor between us to monitor instruments. In the -24 we were almost shoulder to shoulder. The distance between us was not so wide that we had to communicate with each other over the interphone, as the -32 was a relatively quiet aircraft compared to the -24, and certainly to the noisy -25, with its short exhaust stacks. The pilot's and co-pilot's control pedestals were located on our inboard sides. The instrumentation was located in the usual position in front of the pilot and co-pilot. The flight controls were the conventional pedestal, cable-operated, dual controls for both the pilot and co-pilot. The standard throttle controls were dual, and located on both the pilot's and co-pilot's pedestals. The flight deck had room for everybody.

The navigator's station—located behind the pilot's seat—had a drop-down table of a size that he could spread his charts. As with the -24, the Flight Engineer was required on the -32 to be responsible for the maintenance and proper functioning of the aircraft before flights, and then the monitoring of the instruments and engines, as well as the balance and distribution of the gasoline supply while in the air. He didn't have to constantly moni-

tor the cylinder head temperatures of the -32's engines, as we didn't have any of the overheating problems that beset the B-29s because of all their additional weight of the pressurized cabins and turrets, in addition to the fuel and bomb loads. When the B-29 had overheating problems, the cowl flaps had to be cracked open to get air on the engines, and that cut down their speed, which increased their fuel consumption. It was a Catch-22 situation. I also thought the electrical outlets for plug-in of the hot meal canisters wasn't a bad an idea.

Transition to the B-32 was very smooth, and I personally found flying the -32 easier than flying the B-24. Since we flew later in the B-32 program we flew production version B-32s, and not the TB training models. On north takeoffs from Tarrant this takeoff procedure was not appreciated by the residents on top of the hill on the other side of Lake Worth, as we were climbing at almost roof top level. The landing gears were raised, and the brakes applied to stop the spinning tires. The flaps were retracted in small increments until the aircraft was flying cleanly. The -32's controls were smoother and more responsive, and to me it was more like flying a B-25. When you flew the -24 in formation for several hours you were one tired soldier when you got back on the ground. I always felt the -32 was a more forgiving aircraft than the -24, but this is not to say that you could fly along making a series of errors in the -32; the -24 was quick to try to get the upper hand in any situation. I had only one what I would consider a real emergency in a -32, but I believe I was able to get out of it with less difficulty than if I had the same problem in a -24. To get the B-32 on step wasn't a problem, as the plane could be flown to the selected altitude and leveled off smoothly right there. With the B-24 I had to climb 500 feet above the selected altitude, and then had to decrease altitude easily to the on step altitude. I found the airspeed of a -32 somewhat surprising. There was a Naval Air Station located in the nearby Dallas area, and on several occasions a couple of Navy pilots flying F6F Hellcat fighters would join us for a period of formation flying. They could do this without having to drop flap to compensate for differences in airspeed. We did a little preliminary formation flying before the program was ended, and found the -32 to be easy to maneuver. I never went into a stall, intentionally or unintentionally. I never went looking for trouble. I made the landing check during the downwind leg, and once over the end of the runway I eased the throttles back and brought the nose up slowly until the aircraft settled. The aircraft had a high landing speed, and you had to keep the nose up, being careful not to break off the nose gear. The touchdowns were usually very gentle, and once the nose wheel was down and rolling the propellers were reversed, but only if you had the aircraft going straight down the runway. The engineer threw the prop reversing switch on the pilot's command. The throttles were moved forward, and the aircraft slowed down quickly and evenly. The reversing propellers were a great innovation on the -32, and worked so well that the navigator had better have tied his maps down!

The only problem I ever had with the -32 was when the line chief "red X'd" the aircraft, meaning that it could not be flown. I went back to operations, who called in the line chief, who said everything had been corrected. I took the plane up, and one by one the engines began to fail; by the time I landed I had four dead engines. But that was not the fault of the manufacturer, but of a miscommunication between the line chief and his ground crew. When I flew B-24s I noticed a difference between the -24s manufactured by Consolidated and North American and those by Ford Willow Run. Those built by Consolidated and North American flew like airplanes, and those built by Willow flew like automobiles.

I never regretted going into the B-32 program. I went where they sent me. In my opinion the B-32 was an excellent aircraft that came on the scene too late to be effective operationally. It had the same Davis wing design and the Wright engines as the B-29, and could have flown combat missions with a heavier bomb load over longer ranges than the B-29. But it was too little, too late. At the end of the war I flew B-32s up to Walnut Ridge to be scrapped. It was very disheartening to see these fine aircraft cut up for scrap.

Part Four

The B-32 in Combat

1

B-32 Training

Aircrew Training

In October 1944 the AAF Training Command was requested to prepare a training program for future B-32 air and ground crews. Since the Headquarters of the Army Air Force's Training Command, under Lt.Gen. Barton Yount, was located at FWAAF, the B-32 was assigned directly to the AAF Training Command. Previously, new combat aircraft were handed over to one of the "Training" Air Forces for transitional crew training. FWAAF was one of the few AAF pilot schools to undertake a complete aircrew training program (from pilot transition to phase training for entire B-32 crews) within one training facility. The entire B-32 training program was coordinated by Col. H.W. Dorr and Col. H.M. Wittkop, CO of the 31st Flying Training Wing. Lt.Col. Fred Easley was the director of training and operations, and was assisted by Maj. Robert LaPlante as director of flying. Lt. E.S. Paxton was assigned to prepare the engineering procedure manual. The B-32 Flight Crew Transition Training School was activated by the 2519th Army Air Force Base Unit (AAFBU) at FWAAF in October 1944. At this point only three B-32s were available to be sent to FWAAF, and engineers from Wright Field established an Accelerated Service Test Branch there to find any bugs in the bombers through extensive testing. Pilots for the Accelerating Testing Branch were Capt. James Banks and Lts. Jack Frost, John Nett, Russell Newell, Francis O'Shaughnessy, Francis Session, and Julius Walker, who were all experienced B-24 pilots, and had little trouble adapting to the larger and faster B-32.

The 2519th did not receive its first B-32 (TB-32-5-CF/42-108485) until 27 January 1945, but soon more were on the way, as Consolidated-Vultee production increased. From that date until 6 July 1945 the Unit received nine TB-32-5-CFs (42-108485, 487, 488, and 490 through 495), 25 TB-32-10-CFs (42-108496 through 520), four TB-32-15-CFs (42-108521 through 524), 18 B-32-25-CFs (42-108551, 553, 555 through 670), and one B-32-20-CO (44-90486). Just as with the Accelerated Service Test units, the AAFPGC and AAFTAC did not receive B-32s for testing.

Fourteen pilots were selected to form the nucleus of FWAAF's new B-32 training instructor's school, and would later help organize the first flying training squadron. These pilots were Maj. William Smith, Capt. H.J. Saabye, and Lts. Maynard Alterfer, W.S. Berry, R.J Juttner, J.N. Hoffner, B.J. Kamross, R.E. Morris, F.N. Mortenson, C.W Pace, R.A Pietrowski, R.B Smith, F.J. Wicnieski, and F.L. Wallen. In 1945, as the war in Europe became more one-sided, the Air Force was able to expedite B-32 training by transferring many B-24 crews that had completed transitional training with the Fourth (Training) Air Force, and assigning them to B-32 transitional training in the January and February training programs. Fourteen trained demonstration crews were sent from the Fourth Air Force to train at Fort Worth. Also, many experienced B-24 combat pilots were shanghaied (the feelings of most of these pilots) into the B-32 program. Therefore, the prospective B-32 pilots and co-pilots had previously flown anywhere from 100 to 1,000 hours in B-24s. Because of their B-24 experience the crews only required two months to transition to the B-32.

The 2519th did not receive its first B-32, TB-32-5-CF (42-108485), until 27 January 1945, but soon more were on the way from the Consolidated production line, including 555 pictured here. The 2519th received 39 TBs and 19 production B-32-CFs. (USAAF via Pima)

Pilots and Aircraft Commanders in the U.S. B-32 Training Program

Pilots	Airplane Commanders	Airplane Commanders
Capt. Ralph Bilby	Capt. L.M. Schoennauer	Capt. Robert Smith
1Lt. Henry Wildgen	Capt. R.B. Hill	Capt. Eustice McKee
Capt. Frederick Clarke	1Lt. L.E. Williams	Capt. Richard Myers
Capt. Earl Foster	1Lt. D.G. Dennison	Capt. Joseph Sharp
1Lt. Claude Garner	1Lt. H.H. Hammersly	Capt/ Arthur Stenzel
Capt. Irving Christiansen	1Lt. V.W. Plageman	Capt. Jack Watson
Capt. Vola Dunham	Capt. L. Hagen	2Lt. Jack Gurak
Capt. Donald Davies	2Lt. M.N. Ritter	1Lt. Calvin Fuller
2Lt. John Keller	1Lt. A.E. Sprague	1Lt. Glenn Dolie
Maj. Stanley Rearson	1Lt. D.B. Chads	1Lt. Louis Hedstrom
Capt. Glen Penrod	Capt. George Kent	Maj. Powell Taylor
1Lt. Christopher Cammack	2Lt. James Crump	Capt. Maynard Ingalls
1Lt. Kenneth Althen	2Lt. Lester McGraw	1Lt. Elmer Csernits
Capt. Kieffer Parker	1Lt. Burrell Fletcher	1Lt. Otto Matzke
	2Lt. James Frank	1Lt. Ray Piret
	2Lt. Robert Green	1Lt. David Meyerholtz
	1Lt. Oscar Gustus	1Lt. James Graham
	2Lt. Robert Hacker	1Lt. Theodore Unland
	2Lt. George Amthor	1Lt. Lee Milton
	2lt. Donald McKenna	Capt. Howard Mauger
	1Lt. Chandler Robinson	Capt Edwin Wood
	Maj. Harry Brown	1Lt. Andrew Balogh
	Capt. Sidney Conley	2Lt. Joe Howell
	Capt. I.H. Young	2Lt. Duane Dotzler
	1Lt. Charles Jackson	1Lt. Norman Flooring
	1Lt. William Kingerly	2Lt. Edwin Allen
	1Lt. Bernard Lee	2Lt. Stanley Bailey
	Capt. Alfred Hyde	Capt. Raymond Stotler
	1Lt. Robert Zenishek	Capt. Walter Vollberg
	1Lt. Jack Ellison	Capt. Richard Saurbier
	1Lt. Lorenza Murray	Capt. John Priday
	Capt. Harry Zink	1Lt. William Koch
	1Lt. Loren Cornish	1Lt. William Murphy
	1lt. Dominic Brindisi	1Lt. Edward Craig
	1Lt. Leo Bradford	1Lt. Albert Morris
	1Lt. James Carson	1Lt. Wesley Swope
	2Lt. Edward Tostanoski	1Lt. James Sawyer
	2Lt. Frank Abbott	1Lt. Elmer Dyer
	Maj. Floyd Whitlow	1Lt. Alton Owens
	1Lt. Douglas Frederickson	1Lt. Cecil Poss
	Capt. Donald Proctor	1Lt. Alton Schmidt
	1Lt. John Quebe	2Lt. George Robinson
	1Lt. Richard Smith	F/O Ronald Jordon
	1Lt. Richard Nilsson	1Lt. Robert Kirk

Maj. William Bailey was the first ground school director, and developed the ground school program using notes from his inspection of the B-32, as well as visits to B-29 training bases. Capt. E.O. Wiitala and his staff developed the cruise control program, which had been found to be a necessity for flying long distances in the Pacific Theater. Lt. Eli Canady was appointed to head the ground school engineering department, teaching the pilots the operation and mechanics of the Wright R-3350 engine.

The transition training began with the flight engineer, who was not part of a B-24 crew. Unlike the B-29 flight engineer, who was an officer, the B-32 flight engineer was an enlisted man. The first three enlisted men sent to San Diego to study the B-32 and commence the special aerial engineer's training course established by Consolidated-Vultee were M/Sgts. Emil Gabrys, William Gauthier, and Clyde Sharrer, who were all former experienced line chiefs, and had years of experience as flight engineers maintaining four engine aircraft. These three sergeants would form the nucleus of the flight engineer program. The flight engineer arrived two weeks earlier than the rest of the crew for a 10 week training course concentrating on maintenance and aircraft systems.

Two weeks later the pilot—at that time called the airplane commander by the AAF (as was the B-29 pilot)—and co-pilot arrived to take an eight-week course, spending the first week in ground school. In the next three weeks the pilot spent 50 hours of transition flying time in the TB-32, and the co-pilot flew 25 hours, and spent another 25 as an observer. Emphasis during this phase was on what the training crews called "circuits and bumps," as it consisted of takeoffs, following the traffic pattern and landings in a continuous cycle. Meanwhile, during the first month the various specialists, navigator, bombardier, radio/radar operators, and gunners were dispersed to study the application of their individual skills on the B-32. During the last four weeks of training the entire crew was gathered together at FWAAF, where they flew 80 hours of crew time: 40 hours in a TB-32, and 40 hours in a combat-equipped B-32. After the crews had completed their transition training and were ready to complete their training, the original Training Command plan was to transfer them to the Fourth Air Force and the 426th AAFBU at Mountain Home, ID. The 426th received its first two B-32-25-CFs: (42-108550 and 549) on 26 May 1943, followed by two more B-32-25-CFs: (42-108550 and 552) on 30 May, and a single -25-CF: (42-108554) on 6 June. The AAF changed its plans, and all five B-32s and their crews were sent back to the 2519th AAFBU at Fort Worth on 27 June to complete their training under the AAF Training Command. B-32 transition training, like the rest of the program, was beset with many difficulties, beginning with the shortage of aircraft, and continuing with the aircraft's chronic mechanical problems.

The most serious B-32 problem was engine fires, which had also plagued the B-29 program; however, the B-32 program was to suffer far fewer engine fires. On 8 March 1945 TB-32-5-CF (42-108495) was making a series of training takeoffs and landings from FWAAF. The aircraft's eight man crew consisted of observers Cpl. L.J. Powell and S/Sgt. S.D. Krodell; crew chief S/Sgt. M.J. Hartings; instructor engineer S/Sgt. W.G. McDiffett and student engineer S/Sgt. H.A. Keller; student airplane commander Lt. F.O. Bock; student pilot Lt. C.N. Purlee; and instructor/pilot Lt. M.G. Alderfer. During the seventh landing a crewmember reported the smell of smoke, and although no fire could be found, Lt. Alderfer left the traffic pattern to try to gain altitude to further check for a possible fire. At 5,000 feet a fire was reported in the No.3 engine. The fire could not be extinguished or the propeller feathered, and the crew was ordered to bail out. Alderfer continued to try to extinguish the fire, but several minutes later he also bailed out. Post crash investigation recommended that Alderfer should have landed and then checked for the fire. Sgt. Krodell described his bailout:

Three TB-32s (no turrets) flying formation for a publicity photo, probably during training along the Texas coast. (USAAF via Stine)

"Well, if my ripcord had been welded in, that jerk I gave it would have got it out. I told my girlfriend not to ever complain again about nylon stockings. That nylon chute over me looked better right there than on any women's legs."

No one was injured in the bailout, and most of the men flew their regularly scheduled flights the next day.

Two days later, as previously described, B-32-1-CF (42-108475) crashed due to an uncontrollable engine fire. A series of minor engine fires followed, and finally the problem was traced to defective engine fire seal adaptor flanges. The engine mount ring was replaced on all aircraft, and engine fire extinguishers were installed on all subsequent production models. In April three TB-32s suffered serious damage when the main landing gear collapsed on landing. The flight engineer caused one of the losses (42-108488 on 25 April) when he raised the gear instead of the flaps, but the other two—42-108487 (on 22 April) and 108510 (on 29 April)—were blamed on defective main gear shock strut locking mechanisms. At AAFPGC Eglin, FL, 42-108484 suffered yet another gear failure on 26 April. Then, on 5 May, two more aircraft (42-108499 and 108531) were damaged due to main gear collapses. The training command grounded all TB-32s and B-32s, and over the next three weeks these aircraft had modified Bendix lock down latches installed. In 8,500 hours and nearly two million miles of flying training these mishaps were considered better than normal for a new aircraft by Consolidated-Vultee. Aircraft 487 would again be off flying status for repairs due to an accident on 14 August 1945.

The B-32 underwent continuous design changes and modifications throughout its existence, sometimes numbering in the hundreds per week.

On 8 March 1945 TB-32-5-CF (42-108495) was making a series of training takeoffs and landings when at 5,000 feet a fire was reported in the No.3 engine that could not be extinguished, and the crew and then the pilot bailed out. (USAAF via Pima)

The 2519th Supply and Maintenance Branch met problems obtaining replacement parts for its TB-32s when it found that the ordered part had been discontinued or modified, so as to be useless for that particular batch of aircraft. The bombardier's cabin bulkhead that had been damaged on the TB-32-5-CF (42-108488) that crashed due to a gear collapse on 25 April could not be replaced, as the similar part was being manufactured to different specifications. Meanwhile, aircraft 488 languished as Consolidated-Vultee had to fabricate a special new jig to build the part. Once repaired 488 was involved in another accident on 12 July that caused it again to be off flying status. The combat test report stated:

"The maintenance requirements on the airplane were much less than expected. This has contributed much to the success of the project to date."

From 26 May to 30 June 1945, 74.3% of the aircraft were in commission, while the remaining 25.7% represented maintenance time. The maintenance facilities and handling equipment were very limited, causing an increase in maintenance time. Items that were considered scarce were: exhaust stacks, chevron clamps, stack nuts, and overflaps, which all needed constant attention. The maintenance report concluded: "However, in general the maintenance items are not considered excessive."

The B-32 training centers were able to deal with the persistent problems, and provide a continual supply of competent aircrew and maintenance personnel. By October 1945, when the B-32 program was terminated, the AAF Training Command had graduated 240 pilots and co-pilots, and more than 140 flight engineers.

TB-32-CFs Assigned as Training Aircraft with the 2519th AAFBU, Fort Worth Army Air Field, TX (Station ID Code: OM)

AAF Serial #	Field #	AAF Serial#	Field #	AAF Serial #	Field#
42-108 511	11	42-108512	23	42-108493	35
42-108 488	12	42-108510	24	42-108515	36
42-108 490	13	42-108507	25	42-108498	37
42-108 491	14	42-108513	26	42-108504	38
42-108 492	15	42-108506	27	42-108508	39
42-108 497	16	42-108499	28	42-108514	40
42-108 485	17	42-108494	29	42-108520	41
42-108 496	18	42-108518	30	42-108523	42
42-108 501	19	42-108517	31	42-108524	43
42-108 500	20	42-108509	32	42-108516	44
42-108 503	21	42-108519	33	42-108522	45
42-108 505	22	42-108502	34		

TB-32-5-CF (42-108485 to 495) 7 of 11 aircraft
  (not assigned: 486, 487, 489, and 495)
TB-32-10-CF (42-108496 to 520) 25 of 25 aircraft (all assigned)
TB-32-15-CF (42-108521 to 24) 3 of 4 aircraft (not assigned: 521)

Note:
1) B-32-5-CF 42-108483 with a Field Number of 03 was assigned.
2) There is a discrepancy in the number of TB-32-5s assigned, as records show that 9 were sent (including 486 and 489).
3) There is a discrepancy in the number of TB-32-15s assigned, as records show that all four were sent.
4) The 2519th AAFBU also received 18 B-32-25-CFs (42-108551, 553, 555 through 670) and one B-32-20-CO (44-90486). 551 was off flying status for repairs after an accident on 12 July 1945.
5) In early training the OM field numbers were not painted under the cockpit, and the field number alone was not painted on the tail.

Ground Crew Training

The problem of securing personnel for maintenance and servicing of the B-32 was not as difficult as for the B-29. The B-32 was simpler to maintain than the B-29, because it no longer had pressurization or central fire control. B-29 mechanics could easily be transferred to the B-32, as both aircraft were powered by the Wright R-3350 engine. Additional maintenance training was unnecessary, as the B-32 turrets were basically similar to those used on the B-17 and B-24, and could be serviced by and maintained by men transferred from these aircraft. Hydraulics and electrical installations were also similar to comparable equipment on the B-24.

The maintenance program was initiated by Lt.Col. C.E. Jost, Lt.Col. William Holmes, and Maj. Clyde Stephens. Work on ground training and maintenance schedules began in the fall of 1944 when FWAAF CO Col. H.W. Dorr assigned 1Lts. Everett Reynolds and Matthew Lyle to examine the B-32 from an engineering perspective. The two lieutenants were very qualified for the project, as Reynolds was a returned B-24 combat pilot with many hundreds of hours of combat flying time, and Lyle was a graduate of the AAF Engineering School at Yale. Their first duty was to inspect the first B-32s off the Fort Worth Consolidated-Vultee production lines and consult with the Company engineers there. They then transferred to Consolidated-Vultee's San Diego plant for additional study, and on their return to FWAAF instructed their knowledge of the bomber to maintenance officers.

In late October 1944 the B-32 technical school was established at Keesler Army Air Field near Biloxi, MS, which had been functioning as the AAF's training base for B-24 mechanics. Since the B-24 was a Consolidated Aircraft Company bomber it was the reasonable choice to send prospective Consolidated-Vultee B-32 mechanics there. The B-32 Airplane and Engine Mechanic School was activated by the 3704th AAFBU at Keesler Field in October 1944. Soon the Engine Training School was activated by the 3502nd AAFBU at Chanute Field, IL, and a Consolidated-Vultee operated Maintenance Training School activated by the 3712th AAFBU at Lindbergh Field in San Diego. Since the San Diego training school was adjacent to the B-32 factory, in addition to their 19 courses 1,800 ground crewmen were placed on the production line for "on the job training."

At the technical schools the instructors and students were beset with shortages of training aids, such as parts to be studied (i.e. engines) and technical manuals, but the most important shortages were complete B-32 aircraft! Gen. Wilson's mid-December 1944 report on his investigation of the B-32 program touched on the problems of the technical schools and improved their situation. Finally they received odd parts (e.g. landing gear, early model R-3350 engines from a B-19, pilot and co-pilot pedestals) and some technical orders and factory parts catalogs. In February 1945 Keesler received a TB-32-5-CF (42-108489) that was assigned to the mechanics school to become a maintenance trainer. But it was not until March 1945, when the B-32 program was prioritized, that the situation improved con-

TB-32 Gallery

TB-32-CFs assigned as training aircraft with the 2519th AAFBU, Fort Worth Army Air Field, TX, were coded with the station identification code, OM. However, in early training the OM field numbers were not painted under the cockpit, and the field number alone was not painted on the tail. (All USAAF via Stine)

siderably. In July and August 1945 Keesler graduated 138 mechanics and 60 engineers. A total of 146 engineers were graduated from all the AAF schools when training was terminated in September 1945.

Two B-32 mobile training units (46th and 47th) were formed, and the training of unit instructors was completed by July 1945 under the direction of liaison officer L.W. Brown as part of the AAF Western Training Command, headquartered at Denver. Each unit was comprised of 11 enlisted men and one officer, and had an experienced crew chief and specialist for every phase of maintenance on the B-32. The units were to train ground personnel in the field on the latest operational and maintenance procedures, factory modifications, and approved shortcut combat maintenance procedures. Each unit had operating mockups, cutaways, schematic drawings, factory diagrams, latest technical orders, training films, and special instructional devices. The mockups were not models, but actual aircraft parts built to demonstrate the operational and maintenance features particular to the B-32. These mockups were engineered by Consolidated-Vultee, and built by the Curtiss Wright Technical Institute at Glendale, CA, and when they were completed they were flown to FWAAF by C-47s. These mockups were quite sophisticated, and included an electrical system that showed all essential components; a full-sized prop designed to demonstrate synchronization and the blade angles; operating cutaways; actual full-sized engines driven by an electric motor; a turbo supercharger that showed the influence of altitude and manifold pressures under different operating conditions; the C-1 autopilot; a fuel system that showed the complete transfer of fuel; a Fluxgate Gyro Compass; a hydraulic system; armament system; and instrument panel.

2

Testing Production B-32s

Combat Test Directive

The official general AAF directive for the functional and tactical testing of production B-32s was not issued by the Air Material Command until 15 August 1944, via a letter from Brig.Gen. Orval Cook, Chief, Production Division of the Air Materiel Command, Dayton, OH, to Brig.Gen. E.L. Eubank, the President of the Army Air Forces Board, Orlando, FL. The letter directed that aircraft #42-108476 and 477 be assigned to the PGC, and aircraft 478 and 483 be sent to the AAFSAT for testing. A pilot and ground crew transition course was to be conducted at the Fort Worth Consolidated-Vultee factory. The company was to draw up an outline for testing the B-32, and submit it to the ATSC that, in turn, sent it to the Army Air Forces Board. With the 48 Group Plan no longer viable and the B-29 embarked to India and China, the AAF was determined to scrupulously test the plagued Dominator, even though it meant further delaying its deployment into combat. The test directive required an agenda of at least 200 flying hours to assess the B-32's flight and landing characteristics, combat performance, operational and bombing capabilities, armament, internal equipment, maintenance and servicing requirements, and its possible use for long-range weather reconnaissance. The tests were scheduled to be under the direction of the Air Forces Board, and performed by the Army Air Forces Proving Ground Command (AAFPGC) at Eglin Field, FL, the Army Air Forces Tactical Center (AAFTAC) at Pinecastle Field, FL, and the initial tests by the Air Technical Service Command (ATSC) centers at Wright Field, Dayton, OH, Vandalia, OH, and at San Diego and Fort Worth, which were near the Consolidated-Vultee factories. The test directive ordered the close liaison between the ATSC and the AAFPGC. It required that a representative of the ATSC be present during the conduct of the armament tests by the Proving Ground Command at Eglin. The Project Office, Bombardment Branch, Production Engineering Section was to inform the AAFPGC of any unsatisfactory results. The Tactical Center and the School of Applied Tactics also took part in the tests. Generally, throughout testing, with some early lapses and then more in the latter phases, these organizations cooperated and coordinated successfully.

On 5 June 1944, to prepare for the testing of the B-32 at the Proving Ground Command at Eglin, FL, the PGC sent one officer and six enlisted men to the Consolidated-Vultee Factory at Fort Worth for a "familiarization visit" to obtain information on the aircraft. An AAF officer and Consolidated-Vultee technical representative were to pass on information and answer questions.

All test directives to the PGC were submitted by the Air Forces Board after originating from Operations, Commitments, and Requirements (OC&R), Materiel and Services (M&S), Headquarters of the AAF, and from the Air Technical Services Command (ATSC). When the test directive arrived at the PGC its Commanding General ordered test programs by various testing organizations within the PGC. The various test reports were prepared, and from these the B-32 Final Service Test Reports were formulated. During the testing the PGC provided specific information and preliminary reports to requesting organizations. Abbreviated weekly progress reports were submitted to Headquarters, AAF, to the AAF Board, and to the ATSC. Weekly status reports were made on each B-32 test aircraft. These status reports were to include: 1) all tests currently being conducted on each test aircraft; 2) percentage of completion, and estimated date of completion of each test; 3) weekly flying time completed; 4) weekly status of the test aircraft; 5) maintenance and operational difficulties; and 6) other priority tests being delayed. A Preliminary Report on the operational limits of the B-32 was requested by the OC&R Division on 15 February 1945, but because there were no B-32s available for testing this request was amended to 8 March 1945 (later advanced to 15 March).

By late 1944, the PGC was the official operational suitability testing agency responsible for the testing program and findings for the B-32, and ultimately did not recommend combat use of the B-32. It was the Air Staff that had recommended the establishment of the B-32 training program, and committed the bomber to combat in order to salvage a program that had cost millions of dollars in production, training, and testing, all approved and urged by the Commanding General of the Air Force, Hap Arnold.

Wilson Report

The delays in the B-32 program caused a lack of production aircraft for the testing program, and the Air Force was not about to place the bomber into combat before the testing program was completed. AAF headquarters delegated Brig.Gen. Donald Wilson, Assistant Chief of Staff OC&R, to conduct a thorough investigation of the B-32 situation. In his 14 December 1944 memo Wilson stated:

"A definite decision on the cancellation or adoption of the B-32 into the Army Air Forces is dependent upon results of performance, operational suitability, and tactical tests to be run by ATSC and AAF Board. Test programs have been prepared by the AAF Proving Ground Command. Provided expected availabilities are realized (e.g. aircraft-author), the progress of the tests will be sufficiently advanced by April 1945 to indicate the suitability of the B-32 for the AAF Program."

Wilson recognized the many problems with the B-32 program, but prudently acknowledged that the AAF had too much invested in the program, both monetarily and militarily, to cancel it until its service tests were complete. He recommended that the B-32 not be included in the 48 Group Plan, but that it be continued on an experimental basis, and that accelerated service tests be completed by 15 February 1945. Wilson allotted 13 of the 40 B-32s scheduled to be completed by the end of March 1945 to testing, and the remainder to training. He recognized that the "operational and tactical suitability of the B-32 was problematical, and will remain so until completion of tests." He recommended that B-32 crew training continue until the final fate of the B-32 was determined in the service tests.

Wilson concluded that the tactical and suitability tests be expedited (the end of February 1945) so that the final determination of the disposition of the B-32 could be determined: either the B-32 would be abandoned, with the aircraft on the production lines (100 to 150 aircraft) being completed and some use found for them; or to use the B-32 to replace the B-17 and B-24, and increase production to meet this demand.

By late December 1944, nearly two months before the beginning of combat suitability testing by the Proving Ground Command, and after Wilson's report, the AAF Headquarters was making definite plans to commit the B-32 to combat in Europe. On 16 December 1944 Brig.Gen. F.H. Smith, Deputy Chief of Air Staff, informed his Assistant Chief of Air Staff, Training that he was to "....take immediate action to put into effect the training plan required for the conversion of five B-24 groups now in the MTO to B-32 groups." Ten days later Smith informed his Assistant Chief of Air Staff, Operations, that he was to prepare plans for the employment of B-32s in the ETO to replace B-24 and B-17 groups as soon as the B-32 became operationally available. Operations, Commitments, and Requirements was informed by Smith that the B-32 was not to be deployed to the Pacific prior to the victory in Europe.

The Very Heavy Bomber Program was under scrutiny in early 1945, as Brig.Gen. Lauris Norstad, Chief of Staff of the 20th Air Force, was visiting the Pacific to examine the "needs and activities" of the VHB Program. The Office of Operations, Commitments, and Requirements used Norstad's findings to make recommendations on modifying the B-32 program, if it were not canceled entirely. On 11 February 1945, Col. Jack Roberts of the OC&R issued the following summary of the B-32 program:

"....there is considerable controversy at the present time as to the ultimate disposition of the B-32 airplane. As with all new airplanes there is great opposition to the B-32. In the past, opposition to such airplanes as the P-38, P-47, and P-51 has proven quite unjustified.... This may or may not be true with the B-32. It is unfortunate in this respect...that the B-32 is already rolling off the lines in increasing quantities while we have yet to test it. It is most important, therefore, that we expedite current testing of this airplane in order that we may properly plan for its use, or if found advisable halt its production."

On 1 March 1945, the same day that the APG issued its preliminary findings to Headquarters, AAF, Gen. Hap Arnold was reported to have asked several questions concerning the B-32 program: "Why are we building the B-32?"; "Why must we have another nose on the B-32?"; and "When are we going to get this settled?" In response the OC&R issued a memorandum that recommended that the production of the B-32 be terminated, and that B-32s currently in production be used for administrative, experimental, and cargo service. Five days after this recommendation was made the OC&R was asked to provide a more detailed answer to Arnold's questions. There were over 50 major modifications suggested by various organizations to make the existing B-32s operationally suitable. The most undesirable element of the B-32 was its "nose problem." The OC&R submitted the list of unsatisfactory characteristics to the Chief of Air Staff for transmission to Arnold.

There was a struggle between the various testing organizations for aircraft allotment The AAF planned to use the first 10 production bombers of batch B-32-1-CF for testing, and the first B-32 delivered was 42-108472. Aircraft 42-108478 was the first production B-32 assigned to the ATSC, and was based at Avenger Field, TX, in December 1944 for evaluation, and was followed by two B-32-5-CFs (42-108481 and 482). As late as mid-February 1945 the Proving Ground Command had not received its second aircraft for testing.

As described earlier, on 27 August 1944 the first production B-32 (42-108472) was test flown by Capt. Beryl Erickson and co-pilot Gus Green. They encountered problems with the main landing gear uplatches, and belly landed the aircraft successfully without fatalities; however, the crash was fatal to 472, as it was written off. Due to production delays it was not until 22 November that the next B-32 (42-108475) was delivered, and by the end of the year only five more aircraft were delivered to the various testing centers. Again the B-32 program was threatened with cancellation. The B-29s of the XX Bomber Command had flown their first combat mission over Bangkok, Thailand, in early June 1944, and were staging missions against the Japanese Homeland from advanced bases in China. The pro-B-29 factions in the AAF felt that the B-32 transition training of experienced pilots and other crewmembers would impede the B-29 program, which was now established and expanding at a great rate, as more and more Superfortresses were rolling off the production lines and from the modification centers into combat. The few B-32s that had been delivered had suffered an abnormal number of mechanical failures, and there were accusations of substandard manufacture and poor quality control by Consolidated-Vultee at the Fort Worth plant; the company was also beset with delays caused by belated deliveries by its subcontractors. R.T. LeVine, who had been Consolidated-Vultee's first Flight Engineer beginning with their four engine flying boat program, has stated:

"The B-32 was basically a very good offensive weapon, but during wartime in Fort Worth the quality of workmanship in some areas needed to be *vastly improved*. Also, the quality of some subcontractor products was not good enough to meet company standards. The mass hiring of labor, which was in short supply, led to the employment of some very unskilled, untrained, and careless workers, which showed up in the quality of the aircraft produced. So, we test flight crews had to be *very careful* in preflight inspections of the aircraft. I could cite many examples! We had many in flight 'adventures' due to the poor workmanship that were corrected after landing by more skilled mechanics. That is what flight test crews are for!"

Test pilot Beryl Erickson adds:

"The B-32 design was basically flawed, in that in order to make the aircraft as light as possible the skin was too thin, and there were not enough rivets. The fuselage of the XB-32 flexed so much that on the first taxi tests the cockpit windows would crack as the fuselage flexed over even a moderately rough surface. The aluminum skin should have been thicker, and more fuselage stiffeners added."

However, the best Brig.Gen. M.E. Gross, Chief of the Requirements Division, could say about the B-32 in a memo of 29 August 1944 was:

"....it is believed...there is nothing basically wrong with the airplane...that cannot be fixed."

He went on to state:

"...(the B-32) should be completely fixed, as far as its inherent flying qualities are concerned, before it is turned over to the services, even at the expense of production."

The AAF acknowledged Wilson's program-saving proposals, and on 31 December 1944 it directed the AAF Proving Ground Command at Elgin Field, FL, to have a preliminary report on the bomber's operational limits ready by 15 February 1945. The AAFPGC was unable to issue its report on time, as all B-32s had been delivered to the Air Technical Service Command (ATSC), and it had none to test. It was not until 30 January 1945 that the AAFPGC Squadron E of the 611th AAFBU received its first B-32-1-CF (42-108477/Field Number 581), and not until 22 February that the second

B-32-5-CF (42-108484/FN 580) was delivered. The AAFPGC had to make do testing these two aircraft until a third B-32-25-CF (42-108547/FN 591) was delivered in May. Later the AAFPGC received two more B-32s, 42-108535/FN 589 and 42-108574/FN 596.

By October 1945 the ATSC had received a total of 18 aircraft: two B-32-1-CFs (42-108477 and 478); two B-32-5-CFs (42-108481 and 482); seven B-32-20-CFs (42-108525, 526, 533, 535, 540, 541, and 542); one B-32-25-CF (42-108546); and six B-32-30-CFs (42-108571 through 576). The AAF Tactical Centers received one B-32-1-CF and four B-32-20-CFs (42-108534 through 538).

The AAFPGC, ATSC, and AAFTAC continued service tests on the B-32 until it was canceled in October 1945. Most of the scheduled tests were completed, although several were canceled because there were not enough aircraft available. The tests that were completed:

5 June 1945: Photographic Suitability of B-32 Aircraft.
6 July 1945: Operational Suitability of B-32 Bombing Equipment (1st series).
26 July 1945: Test of the Multiple Suspensions of Bombs.
30 July 1945: B-32 AN/APQ-13 Installation Suitability.
28 August 1945: Operational Suitability of B-32 Aircraft (All testing done by B-32 #108477)
28 September 1945: Operational Suitability of B-32 Communication Equipment
4 October 1945: Tactical Suitability of B-32 Aircraft.

The tests that were canceled:

22 September 1945 "Albert Project," for the use of 12,000 pound and 22,000 pound bombs.
28 November 1945: Bomb Handling and Loading.
Determination of Bomb Release.
Operational Suitability of Armament Installation.

Flight Test Crew of first and second production B-32s at Consolidated, Fort Worth (L-R Standing): L.C. Brandvig (2nd Flight Engineer), unknown AAF (observer), Beryl Erickson (Flight Captain), L.B. Perry (Co-pilot), Victor Allwardt (Flight teat engineer), Lindy Levine (1st Flight Engineer), (L-R kneeling): R. Horn, Robert Bryden and Leonard Sutton (Test Instrumentation Installers). All were from Consolidated, except Perry and the AAF Observer. (LeVine)

Flight Test Crew of B-32 No.3: 42-108473 November 1944 (L-R) L.C. Brandvig (2nd Flight Engineer), Robert Bryden, R. Horn and Leonard Sutton (Test Instrumentation Installers), Lindy Levine (1st Flight Engineer), L.B. Perry (Co-pilot), Victor Allwardt (Flight teat engineer), Beryl Erickson (Flight Captain), and unknown AAF observer. (LeVine)

Faulty Materiel and Flawed Manufacture Plague the B-32

Before the flight testing of the first B-32 (108471) in September 1944, a preflight inspection revealed that screws were hanging loose from the underside of its wing stress plates, and consequently all the screws in the six plates under each wing had to be removed and reinserted before the flight testing could begin. The factory then had to check thousands of screws on all production B-32s that had their fuel cells installed. When 471 was taxied out for its second test flight there was a grinding sound, and test pilot Beryl Erickson slowed down to see the nose wheel continue to roll down the runway. After being towed back to the hangar an inspection showed the inner bearing of the right nose wheel had become so extremely hot that the axle twisted off. The cause was determined to be that a worker at subcontractor Menasco had not removed the machining chips from the axle hub, and they had worked their way into the inner bearing, causing it to become red hot. All nose wheels on all production line aircraft then had to be removed and inspected. Electrical problems arose, caused by poor quality soldering and poor connections, and were to become the aircraft's major difficulty during the overseas combat tests and missions. It is interesting to note that in July 1945 the XB-36 program came under the scrutiny of Brig.Gen. L.C. Craigie, head of the Air Materiel Command, who expressed concerns that Consolidated-Vultee "quality control had gotten of hand during the war years."

During a static test of the B-32 at Wright Field in February 1945 there was a failure in the subject aircraft below the 100% limit of the ultimate load. The Air Technical Service attributed the failure to "faulty workmanship during the manufacture of the airplane" (Capt. Mattison, Test Officer, and Maj. Little AAF Board, entry 19 March 1945). The report stated that the longeron joints near the lift raft well were "very poorly made."

On 23 March 1945, ATSC test aircraft B-32-1-CF (42-108475), piloted by Capt. Robert Quinn, was flying a high altitude firing test with Gus Green as co-pilot. At 17,000 feet the instruments for the No.1 engine failed, followed by those of the No.2 engine. Soon the two engines became erratic and began to surge. The flight engineer reported a fire in the wing between the fuselage and No.2 engine. Quinn tried unsuccessfully to extinguish the fire, and found that when the fuselage skin was touched it gave off electric shocks. He emptied another fire extinguisher into the mounting fire without result. Quinn gave the order to bail out, but the bomb bay doors would not open. Flames burst into the forward cabin, and the six crewmen located there were forced to bail out of the bombardier's hatch. The three crewmen in the rear bailed out through the rear hatch, which was covered by a sheet of flame, causing severe burns. Quinn was the last to leave, and just in time, as his parachute was scorched on the way out. All crew members survived the bailout.

The repeated failures and poor workmanship encountered by various testing organizations led to a major investigation of the "adequacy and efficiency of B-32 inspection." The investigation was requested by Headquarters, AAF, after it "became apparent that B-32s accepted by the Consolidated-Vultee factory in Fort Worth were showing consistent evidence of improper acceptance inspection." On 7 May 1945 Brig.Gen. John Phillips, Chief of the Materiel Division, Materiel and Services, reported to Wright Field that B-32s were rolling off the Fort Worth assembly lines with:

"...many rivets missing, and with such tools as crowbars and wrenches found in wing sections. It is reported that recently a flashlight was found in the supercharger ducting after the airplane was accepted. It is further reported that Fort Worth Army Air Field has been forced to change engines with less than 10 hours of operating time." (B-32 Inspection at Fort Worth, Texas)

As a result of these problems an air inspection survey was initiated at Consolidated-Vultee, Fort Worth, for the week 1-8 May 1945 to determine the quality of the factory inspections, and to assure the AAF that only aircraft conforming to contract specifications would be accepted. The report issued on 12 June 1945 was titled "Inspection of the Consolidated-Vultee Aircraft Corporation, Fort Worth, TX." It noted that the company was manufacturing both the B-32 and B-36 "at the same time in the same place." The report stated that there were almost 9,500 employees on the Fort Worth production line, 876 factory inspectors, and 113 AAF inspectors. The report found that the major problem with B-32 production was:

"...the numerous and constant design changes in the aircraft, sometimes running as high as 300 to 400 per week. Such changes included major and minor design changes, and important alterations in production drawings. This condition obviously imposed a heavy burden on production and inspection."

The report found a "definite lack of coordination" between Consolidated-Vultee and the Board of Inspectors. It stated that "numerous defective parts were continually being produced. Often, the removal of tools from production had been delayed or refused on the grounds that the parts were critical production items. Identical parts, however, were lying in salvage cribs, rejected."

The B-32 program was not the only Consolidated-Vultee program having quality control problems. The company's PB4Y-2 Privateer was a modification of the successful B-24 Liberator, and was built at the San Diego Lindbergh Field plant. On 22 November 1944 PB2Y-2 (BuNo 59544) rolled off the assembly line, and was to be flown by a company crew prior to its acceptance flight by the Navy's Bureau of Aeronautics Representative (BAR). The six man crew lifted the Privateer off the runway and, while climbing to altitude, the outer left wing panel tore away. The loss of the wing panel caused a precipitous loss of the little altitude the aircraft had gained, and it crashed into a ravine on Portal Loma, killing all six men on board. The wreckage was removed and inspected. The investigation had shown that factory workers had failed to install 98 bolts that were to secure the outer wing panel. On 24 November Consolidated-Vultee announced that it had terminated four employees; the men who were responsible for installing the bolts, and those who had inspected and signed off on the completed work. On 4 December 1944 the Bureau of Aeronautics reduced the number of PB4Y-2s deliverable on the contract by one, and reduced the amount paid to the company by $155,000. Most damning to Consolidated-Vultee was on 5 January 1945 a San Diego coroner's jury voted 11-1, finding Consolidated-Vultee was guilty of "gross negligence" in the six deaths.

During the B-32 investigation of rivet installation, "numerous instances of defective riveting patterns were observed throughout the entire construction of the B-32s." It was found that the cause was the use of insufficient dull jigs for rivet patterns. Consolidated tried to overcome this problem by having their riveters place the missing rivets by drilling holes free-hand and placing the rivets. This resulted in "sloppy, incorrect spacing, and in a lack of edge distance."

Even though the service test aircraft had been inspected before being officially accepted, the B-32 service test program uncovered multiple mechanical problems, design deficiencies, and difficulties with the internal equipment. To remedy these deficiencies each aircraft received a daily seven hour inspection while on the production line. After being accepted the aircraft underwent 12 hours of inspections after 25 hours of flying time, while 50 and 100 hours of flying required 24 hours of inspections. Despite the thoroughness of these inspections many bugs continued to occur in the B-32, which Consolidated-Vultee maintained was "normal" for any new production aircraft. As the bomber's problems continued the allegations of poor workmanship and quality control persisted. The two AAFPGC test aircraft had so many problems that they were "out of commission" 82% and 59% of the time, respectively! R.T. Lindy LeVine states:

"During the company's vast expansion of its war time manufacturing facilities, thousands of unskilled aero workers were employed with insufficient training, which meant lousy workmanship—and it showed! It was not only Consolidated-Vultee, but also faulty workmanship from the sub-contractors. The main examples of this were very poor quality exhaust collector rings, and poorly manufactured nose wheel strut and wheel assemblies."

The most serious problem was the heat exchanger, which was located under the nacelle, where any leaking engine oil would drip onto it and cause fires. Engine nacelle fires were started by exhaust stack failure, as the stacks were too thin, and would blow out due to high back pressures when the supercharger blower was at full power at high altitudes. This malfunction was the cause of the loss of two bombers in training in March. The problem was never corrected, as by the time the B-32 reached combat it was flying at relatively lower altitudes where the supercharger would not develop high back pressures.

The following improvements were suggested for new production models as a result of the initial service tests. The exhaust system was modified to prevent engine fires. Fixed fire extinguishers were to be installed as early as models TB-32-15-CF. Oil shutoff valves were placed at the engine nacelle, while firewalls were to be placed in the last few production models. The entire engine system was modified to stop chronic oil leaks. It was suggested that all four engines be fitted with the prop-reversing mechanism. The bombardier's compartment was redesigned to increase visibility. Other problems were inadequate mechanical sub-systems, inconveniently located instruments and controls, and high interior noise levels. The flight deck was drafty, and the cockpit could leak in rainy weather. Most of the problems found in the service tests were resolved in later production blocks through design revision or improved quality control.

The 12 June report concluded that "even within the limits of articles that were regarded as 'acceptable,' the quality level of the B-32 airplane was only fair." It stated higher quality was "not possible because of the numerous design changes, inadequate tooling, and ineffective cleanup." The report characterized Consolidated-Vultee quality inspections as "consistently inadequate, as was evidenced by the number of discrepancies uncovered by Army inspection...."

The poor quality of the B-32s "was clearly reflected" in the aircraft delivered PGC for testing. Col. L.O. Peterson, Acting Chief of the Requirements Division, OC&R, stated:

"...the installation and inspection deficiencies...of the B-32 can only be attributed to inferior workmanship and inspection.... In instance after instance the Command was required to delay testing until inadequacies of various kinds were corrected at the Command."

The slowness of Consolidated-Vultee in delivering acceptable B-32s delayed the original PGC testing schedules. The first official directive for the testing program was sent to the PGC on 20 September 1944, and the PGC activated its B-32 testing program six days later. However, the first aircraft available for testing (108477) did not arrive until 29 January 1945! Even after it had been delivered, testing in it was delayed until 12 February by instrumentation, adjustments, and modifications. On 10 February 1945 Brig.Gen. Grandison Gardner, PGC CO, told Col. N.F. McKee of the OC&R: "I wish I could give you a lot of encouragement, but I am afraid we are going to be slow, mainly because the airplane is not quite finished." When the second B-32 (108484) arrived on 22 February, testing in it could not be started until instrumentation and equipping were completed, and until a number of "deficiencies" were corrected. By the time testing began Headquarters, AAF would not tolerate any further delays, and urged that PGC begin preliminary testing immediately.

Test aircraft 477 was down 70 days during the first 123 days it was tested. From 29 January to 3 August 1945 the two test aircraft, except for the time they were down for the installation of test equipment, were down 82% of the time for 477 and 56% for 484. The delays were attributed to a list of 22 reasons that ended with the statement:

"Such delays were common in the testing of all types of aircraft, though the number and character of the B-32 delays were reflective of the airplane itself, to an unusual degree."

Previously, the PGC had been notably successful and commended by Gen. Arnold on its accomplishments in the testing of the B-29 and other heavy bombers. Peterson remained convinced that with the B-32 program the PGC was working against "unavoidable handicaps, and was not unnecessarily or excessively delayed," and responded again to Wilson on 8 May 1945. He was able to present an analysis showing that the PGC was not unduly slow in its testing of the B-32, which Gen. Wilson accepted as a satisfactory explanation of the PGC testing program, and no further questions were then raised concerning the PGC's conduct of tests.

Many major design and maintenance problems were found during the PGC test missions. "Serious and repeated difficulty with the operation of the bomb bay doors was a common occurrence." The bomb bay doors on the test aircraft were found to be unsatisfactory, and the PGC requested that the Air Materiel Command develop and install "a reliable and satisfactory" bomb bay door. The engine exhaust system also encountered numerous problems. The metal used to construct the exhaust was too thin to withstand the combined effects of excessive vibration and high temperatures. Failures also occurred in the mounting flanges, and near the individual welds joining the segments, which were also prone to cracking. The

No.4 engine of aircraft 484 suffered extensive damage when heat burned through an exhaust segment during takeoff. There were five fires in the accessory section of the engine nacelle aft of the fire wall. The fires were started when oil leaked and collected in the shrouding around the heat exchanger. Several induction system failures occurred. There were hydraulic system failures during takeoff, making it impossible to retract the landing gear and flaps. At high gross weights this was "critical," as it made emergency go-arounds dangerous, as the pilot would have difficulty gaining safe altitude and airspeed. Over 20 oil cooler collector exit flap actuators were replaced during testing.

A majority of the PGC's testing to determine the suitability of the B-32 as a very heavy bomber concerned the bomb installations in the aircraft. Six comprehensive tests of the B-32's bomb installations were planned and activated. Because of the sudden end of the war, and the lack of production aircraft, only three of the tests were completed. The conclusion of the PGC concerning the bombing suitability of the B-32 was:

"...The suitability of the airplane as a bombing platform was entirely satisfactory, and its ability to maintain straight and level flight was good. The C-1 (autopilot) performed satisfactorily on bombing runs, and provided good response to corrections. Bomb bay turbulence was not sufficient to affect bombing accuracy, and the B-32 could carry the same single suspension bomb loads as the B-29 airplane. The airplane's good features, however, were limited by the defects in the bombing equipment. Preparation of the airplane for a bombing mission (rack installation and bomb loading) was a generally slow and difficult procedure. In the air, target identification was impeded by insufficient visibility, and the operating conditions on the bombing run were not conducive to accuracy. Faulty bomb bay door operation introduced the possibility of release failure. Finally, when the bombardier was not sighting independently, lack of visibility made it extremely difficult to see the lead airplane's release."

As discussed previously, the PGC considered the bombardier's position had:

"...insufficient visibility and poor positioning of the instruments and controls, and the bombardier was subjected to extreme (physical) discomfort."

After testing the PGC concluded that:

"...the B-32 airplanes tested were not operationally suitable...because of continual bomb bay door failures, insufficient bombardier's vision, continual engine accessory malfunctions, engine exhaust system failures, and the presence of numerous structural weaknesses and instances of faulty design."

The conclusion reached about the problems in the PGC testing program was that they were:

"...essentially problems inherent in the aircraft itself, or in the lack of coordination evidenced in the preparations for the use of the airplane...and in delays of production and deliveries of the aircraft. As has been indicated, the principal and unique factors in the testing of the B-32 aircraft were factors originating outside the Proving Grounds Command."

Despite deficiencies in quality control service, test reports praised the aircraft's good takeoff and landing characteristics, its excellent low speed directional control, its quick control response, its excellent ground handling characteristics (due to its reversible inboard propellers), its stability as a bombing platform, and the ease of maintenance of its sub-systems. Transition training pilot Robert Kirk found the B-32 to be much better than the B-24s he had flown previously, and easy and enjoyable to fly. The line crews found the bomber to be easy to maintain, and commended the accessibility to the engines and systems.

Continued Domestic Testing of B-32 Operational Suitability
The report on the Operational Suitability of Bombing Equipment in the B-32 was issued by the PGC on 6 July 1945. The conclusions reiterated previous findings:

"From the standpoint of bombing suitability, the airplanes tested fall short of desired standards at several major points in the operational sequence. Preparation of the airplanes for a bombing mission, i.e., rack installation and bomb loading, is generally a slow and difficult procedure. In the air, target identification is impeded by inadequate visibility, and the operating conditions on the bombing run are not conducive to accuracy. Faulty bomb bay operation then introduces the possibility of release failure. Furthermore, when the bombardier is not sighting independently, lack of visibility makes it extremely difficult to see the lead plane's release. The airplane's good features are its bomb capacity, stability, and response to control on the bombing run, and the absence of severe bomb bay turbulence. However, the defects in the bombing equipment sharply limit the advantage which can be taken of these desirable features."

Closely tied to the combat test of the B-32 were other tests being performed by the PGC and other organizations to:

"...provide full information on the aircraft that was now effectively out of the experimental stage and regarded as a combat weapon."

By the beginning of April 1945 the PGC had completed more than half of its operational suitability tests. At this point Headquarters, AAF requested an advanced "unbiased" report on the minimum number of changes and modifications that the PGC considered "essential for immediate use of the B-32 in combat." The PGC response was a list of 33 necessary modifications. Late in May 1945 Col. D.C. Smith, Headquarters, AAF requested that PGC CG Brig.Gen. Grandison Gardner submit a statement to Gen. Arnold "as to the comparative combat worth of the B-32 to the B-29." The request was considered "very hot," and needed ASAP (e.g. tomorrow). Particularly valued were statements from pilots who had flown both aircraft, and other officers who were "competent to make such opinions." Gardner quickly furnished a report from PGC pilots who had combat experience with the B-29 and had flown the B-32 in tests. The opinion of these pilots was "further and inescapable, evidence that the B-32 was not an efficient combat weapon, particularly by comparison with the B-29." Gardner's report was carefully prepared and assigned an index number of 100 as the standard performance represented by the superior B-29.

Gardner Report Comparing the B-29 to the B-32

B-29	Comparative B-32	
100	Overall Bombing Suitability	50
100	Bombardier's Compartment	25
100	Bombsight Operation	20
100	Bomb Release System	90
100	Bomb Racks	60
100	General Bomb Bay Door Operation	00
100	Bomb Hoisting and Loading System	50
100	Bomb Flight	15
100	Suitability as a Bombing Platform	100
100	Radar	90
100	Defensive Armament Suitability	150
100	Ease of Over-all Aircraft Maintenance	90
100	General Aircraft Suitability	75

B-32 vs. B-29 General Aircraft Suitability 75%

Range: 80%

Bomb Load: Same

Flight Characteristics:

Handling during taxiing: Inferior

Takeoff: Same

Climb: Same

Level flight: Slightly superior

Evasive action: Superior

Landing: Superior

Speed and adequacy of operation of trim controls:

Rudder: Same

Elevator: Slightly inferior

Aileron: Superior

Suitability of Instrument Flying: Same

Cockpit visibility: Slightly inferior

Cockpit Arrangement: Inferior

Oxygen supply: Same

Flight and engine instrument arrangement: Same

Pilot and crew comfort: Vastly inferior

Ease of formation flying: Superior

Heating system efficiency: Definitely inferior

Night flying: Inferior

Two and three engine handling: Superior

Takeoff distance: Superior

Landing roll: Superior

Flak protection: Inferior

Time of service and number of men to service: Inferior

Emergency provision for gear and flap retraction: None in B-32

By chance, a bombardment conference attended by 80 officers returning from combat was being held at the same time at the Tactical Center at Orlando, FL; they were given a chance to fly the B-32 and B-29, and were asked to submit an evaluation of the Dominator compared to the B-29. Their consensus was "nearly unanimous that the B-29 was 'far superior' to the B-32."

With most of the test results overwhelmingly unfavorable to the B-32, on 26 May 1945 Brig.Gen. A.C. Strickland, President of the AAF Board, recommended that:

"Inasmuch as the B-32 apparently has no outstanding advantages...and the B-29 can perform any mission of which the B-32 is capable....and missions of which the B-32 is incapable, the Army Air Forces Board sees no justification for the purchase of the B-32, and therefore recommends that its manufacture be discontinued."

On 28 May 1945 Maj.Gen. Kenneth Wolfe, Chief of Engineering and Procurement, ATSC, added that the B-32 "...is obviously not in the class with the B-29," and that of all the pilots in that command who had flown both aircraft "none considered the B-32 comparable to the B-29."

All the negative B-32 test results and multitude of problems recorded by the PGC and ASTC, as well as those from other organizations, were compiled into a single significant memorandum submitted by Brig.Gen. William McKee of the OC&R to the Chief of Air Staff on 30 May 1945. McKee had been consistently a B-32 program adversary, and had previously tried to have the program canceled. The memorandum was the final confirmation that the "B-32 was not suitable for combat, that the aircraft was not needed, and that immediate cancellation of the B-32 program desirable." McKee concluded that "considerable monetary savings will result...by discontinuance of the B-32 program." Brig.Gen. Patrick Timberlake, Deputy Chief of Staff, backed up McKee's savings contention by stating that if the B-32 program were terminated with the 162nd aircraft, instead of the planned 313th (recently reduced from 713 aircraft), a savings of $43.3 million would be realized. Timberlake, however, did not suggest the immediate cancellation of the B-32 program, as did McKee. Despite the best efforts of the OC&R and McKee B-32 production continued, as did the conversion of B-24 groups. Most importantly, by this time the B-32 combat test mission had reached the Philippines

3

War Plans for the B-32

AWPD-1 and the *Casablanca Conference*

Both original contracts for the B-29 and B-32 were too optimistic, and both aircraft fell far behind scheduled delivery. The first XB-32 model was not ready for flight until September 1942—six months late, but still two weeks before the XB-29. Because of the delay the AAC requested that the XB-32 testing be started "as soon as possible, even if the aircraft must be flown in a 'stripped condition.'"

Despite lagging behind schedule, the B-29 and B-32 continued to play an important role in the AAC's prewar long range bombing plans for the predicted air war over Europe. The urgency of rearmament increased on 22 June 1941 when the German armies invaded Russia. On 9 July 1941 President Roosevelt sent a letter to the Secretaries of War and Navy, asking them to prepare "an estimate of overall production requirements required to defeat our potential enemies." To forestall the War Plans Division from preparing a plan that would relegate the Army Air Force into a supporting role to the Army, Arnold's Air Chief of Staff, Brig.Gen. Carl "Toohey" Spaatz, and member of the 1939 Kilner Board, formed the Air War Plans Division (AWPD). The AWPD was to be headed by Lt.Col. Harold George, who was CO of the Second Bombardment Group, and the newly appointed Chief of the War Plans Division. Also appointed was Lt.Col. Kenneth Walker, Chief of the War Plans Group; Maj. Haywood Hansell, Chief of the European section of the War Plans Group; Lt.Colonels Lawrence Kuter, G-3 from the General Staff, and Orvil Anderson and Howard Craig. The responsibility of the AWPD was to formulate a general plan for the employment of air power to defeat the Axis that would utilize air power to its fullest capability. The AWPD was to determine the size of the air forces required to defeat Germany first, and then defeat Japan. Their plan, called AWPD-1, was submitted to the Army General Staff War Plans Division on 12 August 1941. Generally, it called for 24,500 combat aircraft, of which approximately 10,000 were to be four and six engine bombers. On 11 September 1941 Gen. Marshall accepted AWPD-1, and the B-29 and B-32 were an important element in the plan. In 1939 the Kilner Board had recommended that the future B-29s and B-32s were to be hemispheric bombers, intended to operate from American bases. But by early 1941 Britain appeared to be safe from German invasion, and if the United States entered the war, English and American planners envisioned the Very Long-Range (VLR) Bomber to operate from bases in England and the Mediterranean to bomb Germany. In those dark days AWPD-1 projected that by summer

1944, 24 B-29 and 24 B-32 groups would be sent to bomb Germany from England and Egypt as part of the "48 Very Long-Range Group Program." Also as part of this plan, several B-24 groups in the MTO would initially transition to B-32s and B-29s as soon as the bomber's service tests were completed. Then the remaining Eighth and Fifteenth Air Force B-17 and B-24 groups in the MTO and ETO would transition to the two new very long range bombers. Gen. Spaatz also saw the bomber as a weapon against Japan in a future war in the Pacific that seemed to be inevitable, so also embodied in AWPD-1 was the provision for two B-29 and B-32 groups to be available to bomb Japan from Luzon if the Japanese entered the war. This was the beginning of the "Europe first" strategy, in which the Anglo-American alliance concentrated their efforts against Germany. Until Germany was defeated Japan would be contained in a defensive battle, in which naval forces would predominate. Even after the great post-Pearl Harbor Japanese successes American long-term air strategy focused on Europe. AWPD-41 (15 December 1941) and AWPD-42 (9 September 1942) both deployed the B-29 and B-32 to Europe, after which they would be transferred to Pacific bases that were captured in the island battles to bomb

The *Casablanca Conference* in January 1943 continued the Europe first strategy, approved a Combined Bomber Offensive against Germany, and projected that the B-29 and B-32 would take part in the offensive. Shown are FDR and Churchill (sitting) and (standing L-R) Lt.Gen. Henry Arnold, Adm. Ernest King, and Gen. George Marshall representing the U.S., as well as Lt.Gen. Hastings Ismay, Adm. Sir Dudley Pound, and Air Chief Marshall Sir Charles Portal. (National Archives)

Japan. The *Casablanca Conference* in January 1943 continued the Europe first strategy, approved a Combined Bomber Offensive against Germany, and projected that the B-29 and B-32 would take part in that air offensive. The plan was to deploy Very Long-Range bombers in shuttles between North Africa and England. Maj.Gen. Ira Eaker of the 8th Air Force was to develop a Combined Bomber Offensive, and in March 1943 requested a tentative deployment schedule for the B-29 and B-32 groups. By early 1944 both the B-29 and B-32 were experiencing developmental problems, and it was apparent that the 48 Group Plan could not be implemented on schedule; Arnold advised Eaker that the VLB groups, now called VHB (Very Heavy Bomber) groups, would be sent to the Pacific. By early summer most of the B-29's problems had been worked out, and the potential of that bomber becoming a true "Superfortress" was realized. The AAF issued an unusual directive, allowing the B-29 to be tested in combat, rather than tested domestically first, and the bomber was on its way to China for combat testing. Meanwhile, the B-32 program was in a shambles. It lacked aircraft for testing and training, and those that were available had numerous and reoccurring problems.

In August 1944 the AAF issued a test directive that stated that the B-32's combat suitability had to be tested before it was assigned to operational units. However, by April 1945 the problems and controversy encountered by the B-32 program made the prospect of combat suitability testing improbable. The AAF Proving Ground Command was the only testing organization authorized to conduct this test, but the Proving Ground Command's previous experience with the B-32 led it not only to object to the test, but to oppose the bomber's introduction into combat altogether.

Gen. Kenney Rescues the B-32 Program
In February 1945 the Acting Chief of Air Staff, Brig.Gen. Patrick Timberlake, stated "The B-32 in its present form is not an acceptable bomber...due to the bombardier visibility problems, and the aircraft's weight." But despite Timberlake's poor assessment, too much time and money had been invested in the B-32 program, and in the spring of 1945 the B-32 was considered combat ready, but no high level decision had been reached on the combat mission of the B-32, or orders issued for B-32 groups to be formed or converted.

In light of the decision not to deploy the B-29 to Europe in January 1944, Lt.Gen. George Kenney, the influential commander of the Far East

Lt.Gen. George Kenney (USAAF)

Air Forces (FEAF), personally traveled to Washington, DC, to present his case for the 5th Air Force to be assigned B-29s to bomb the important oil refineries in the Netherlands East Indies, which produced a large percentage of Japan's aviation gasoline. In August 1943 his B-24s of the 380th Bomb Group had successfully bombed Balikpapan, and Kenney used the potential of these raids to validate his request for the B-29. Throughout the war Kenney had hounded Arnold for more aircraft. Realizing he would not be able to obtain the P-47 and P-51 from Europe, he lobbied for the P-38 fighter, which was unwanted and only moderately successful there. In the Pacific the P-38 was to become the most successful Army Air Force fighter of the war, boasting the top two American fighter aces of the war in Dick Bong (40 victories) and Tommy McGuire (38). In his book *General Kenney Reports*, Kenney describes the meeting:

"I wanted some B-29s, which would be coming available in a few months, and explained that, with their heavy bomb load of 20,000 pounds, as compared with the 8,000 pound capacity of the B-24, and with double the range, I could destroy the oil refineries in the Netherlands East Indies, and the Japs would be unable to keep the war going. Arnold would not make any promises, but said that if I had a runway big enough to take them by July he might let me have 50 B-29s at that time."

Kenney began his campaign to get the B-29s by lengthening the field at Darwin, Australia, to 10,000 feet, and constructing facilities there to accommodate an optimistic 100 Superfortresses. At the end of March, Maj.Gen. Lawrence Kuter arrived at Kenney's headquarters and told him that it was the popular opinion among the top echelons of the Air Force in Washington that B-29s operating out of the Marianas could bomb the Japanese Homeland and knock Japan out of the war before the Philippines were captured. Furthermore, Kuter said that Arnold and the Joint Chiefs of Staff were espousing the bypass of the Philippines in February 1945 for a direct attack on Formosa. Kenney continues in *General Kenney Reports*:

"In spite of the fact that Washington knew that I was ready to operate B-29s out of my new airdrome at Darwin against the oil refineries at Balikapan, which my information showed was producing most of the aviation fuel for the Japanese, the first 100 B-29s were going to the China theater, where half of them would haul gasoline from India across the Himalayas to the fields in China, from which the other half would operate. The next groups would go to the Marianas when the Navy captured them and had airdromes built to receive them. Kuter said Washington's information was that Palembang, which could be reached from India, was a bigger producer of aviation fuel than Balikpapan, which was considered of much less importance.

I remarked that I hoped no one expected me to cheer either the decisions or the beliefs that he had voiced."

July came and went, and no B-29s were delivered to Kenney. During a visit on 6 August by Maj.Gen. Barney Giles, Arnold's Chief of Staff, Kenney influenced Giles to send a telegram to Arnold asking for the B-29s. In Arnold's quick reply Kenney was told he would receive no B-29s, as they had been placed under the direct control of the Joint Chiefs of Staff and the newly formed 20th Air Force. Kenney reconciled himself to continuing raids on the NEI oil fields with his B-24 heavy bomber units, and concentrating on supporting the invasion of the Philippines.

However, on 14 March 1945 Kenney again returned to Washington, ostensibly to confer about the FEAF's administration of the air war in the Far East, but in reality to reargue his belief that very heavy bombers flying from bases that were within the control of his command could bomb Japan to help end the war. Kenney had written to Arnold asking to transition his B-24 units to B-29s, arguing that each Superfortress could deliver two and half times more bombs (10 tons instead of four) at twice the range (3,000 miles vs. 1,500) than the Liberator. Arnold had suffered a heart attack and was recuperating in Florida, and Kenney again met with Barney Giles, who told him again that the B-29s were going to the 20th Air Force in the Marianas. The single-minded Kenney reconciled himself that he would not receive the B-29, and would have to settle for the B-32. Giles said that Consolidated-Vultee was manufacturing about 200 B-32s, but they had not been assigned, and that Kenney could have them.

Kenney and his staff flew to Miami to meet with Arnold on 17 March, and asked for enough B-32s to equip one heavy bomber group. Kenney backed his request for the B-32 with the contention that, although the bomber was having developmental problems, it was in production and combat crews were being trained, and it would be a shame to squander the time and money already invested in the Dominator. Kenney continued by stating that the bomber was immediately available, and could be combat tested by deploying them to the FEAF. He went on to maintain that if the B-32 proved successful production could be increased, but if it failed the program could finally be terminated, and its resources diverted to the B-29 program. Arnold, who believed that the B-32 was an improvement over the B-17 and B-24, was pleased that the troubled and now superfluous bomber could perhaps find a niche. He ordered two combat-equipped B-32s flown in to nearby

Bolling Field to acquaint himself and his staff, and Kenney and his staff with the bomber through demonstration flights. On 18 March aircraft 42-108477, piloted by Maj. Henry Britt, flew in from Eglin Field, and was met by Lt.Col. Stephen McElroy of the OC&R, who informed Britt that the aircraft would be inspected the next day at 1000. Later that day aircraft 42-108478 arrived from Wright Field with Col. Frank Cook and Lt.Col. Thomas Gerrity at the controls.

On the 19th both aircraft were taxied to maintenance hangars for cleaning prior to the 1000 inspection time. There was not enough time to clean 477, which was to be the focus of the inspection. The two aircraft were then taxied for inspection, but the day was spent with only interested staff officers from the OC&R, M&S, and ATSC examining the two aircraft.

On 19 March 1945, at an Air Staff meeting, Maj.Gen. Donald Wilson, Assistant Chief of Staff, OC&R, reported that a commitment to provide Kenney with B-32s probably could not be met by May 1945 due to continued delays in B-32 production, and the unfavorable test findings of the PGC. Lt.Gen. Barney Giles was firm in his promise to Kenney that B-32 delivery could be met, and that he would personally get together with Arnold to discuss the situation.

On the 20th, at 0900, the Arnold and Kenney entourages, Maj.Gen. Oliver Echols (M&S); Maj.Gen. Bennett Myers (ATSC); Brig.Gen. Donald Wilson (OC&R); Brig.Gen. John Phillips (M&S); Maj. P.B. Baird (M&S) and Lt.Col. D.E. Bailey (OC&R) gathered at Bolling. Also present were three members who would play an important part in the combat test mission: Col. Frank Cook (ATSC); Lt.Col. Stephen McElroy (OC&R); and Maj. Henry Britt (PGC). The group held a meeting that Maj. Henry Britt described:

"The officers present for the demonstration mission held informal conferences on the flight deck of the Eglin Field B-32. The purpose of the mission was revealed. Gen. Kenney wants to take the B-32 and operate it off the B-24 fields in the South East Pacific.... Gen. Kenney stated that he had been to see Gen. Arnold, and that he could save him from a Congressional investigation if he could give him 200 B-32s instead of canceling the contract. Operations, Commitments, and Requirements wanted to stop the program entirely. Gen. Kenney said he could give them the answer on the B-32, and if the airplane proved to be no good production would be ceased. Operations, Commitments, and Requirements could at least answer an investigation saying it (the B-32) was given a try. Kenney requested that two B-32s be sent to the Philippines as soon as possible so he could get his personnel acquainted with the airplane, as well as test the airplane as to the suitability for runways and operation conditions of the South West Pacific. They agreed to do that. After this conference Kenney and Arnold questioned each crew member of the Eglin Field B-32."

Britt's comments are enlightening, as he mentions the possibility of a Congressional investigation of the B-32 program as a likely reason for Arnold's continuance of the B-32 program and its commitment to combat testing. Kenney describes his first encounter with the B-32:

"I returned to Washington, and the next day inspected and flew in the B-32. It was a nice job, about 20 miles per hour slower than the B-29, but could carry 10 tons of bombs from Clark Field (Philippines) to Kyushu (Japan)."

Unable to secure B-29s for his V Bomber Command, Lt.Gen. George Kenney (R), the influential commander of the Far East Air Forces (FEAF), personally traveled to Washington, DC, to present his case to AAF Chief Gen. H.H. Arnold (L) that the V Bomber Command be assigned B-32s, and thus rescued the B-32 program. (USAAF)

Arnold commented on his discussions with the B-32 crews and his conclusions:

"In general they were fairly well impressed, that it was a decided improvement over the B-17 and B-24, and that there might be a use for it. Whether or not there will be a use for it depends on whether it could operate in the theater that it was intended for off the fields that they have, without any extensive new construction or additional construction, and also whether it was able to deliver the same number of tons of bombs per month that the airplanes that they now have over there are delivering. If it couldn't do that it wasn't a satisfactory airplane. If it could, or deliver more, it was a better airplane than the ones that they are using."

The PGC noted that Gen. Arnold was:

"...more interested in what the pilots and enlisted men of the (demonstration) crews had to say about the airplane...than he was in...any of us (PGC personnel) up here were able to tell him." (Note that the PGC was never in favor of the B-32.)

On the 21st the Eglin crew was scheduled for an inspection by Lt.Gen. Barney Giles and Brig.Gen. Lauris Norstadt. Col. McElroy conducted the inspection, and then flew the two generals on a 30 minute flight, during which Giles and Norstadt took control of the aircraft. Giles reported that he did not like the bombardier's visibility, and asked Britt if he was on the mock up board for the nose design of the B-32. Britt "proudly stated that Eglin Field was not responsible (for the nose)."

After several days of demonstrations, conferences, and deliberations Arnold told Kenney that if he wanted the Dominator he would continue its production until two B-32 groups could be equipped. Kenney reports: "I told Giles to line them up for me, and Arnold's proposition was set up as an approved project." On 27 March Maj.Gen. N.F. McKee, Acting Chief of Staff OC&R, reported that:

"Gen. Arnold has made the decision that he will continue...production of the B-32, and that initially we shall begin the conversion of B-24 groups in the Pacific to B-32s."

On 27 March Arnold ordered extensive combat tests, designated Special Project 98269-S, for the B-32, with the rationalization that the B-24 needed to be replaced in the Pacific, and that the B-32 could deliver the heaviest possible bomb load on Japan in the shortest time, helping to shorten the war. A press release in *Skyways* magazine stated:

"...The Dominator should be regarded not so much as a 'sister ship' to the Superfortress, but as a specially adapted, highly superior replacement for the same company's B-24 Liberator."

Arnold's decision is described in "Testing the B-32: September 1944 -October 1945:"

"It was an unalterable, if embarrassing, fact in the spring of 1945 that the B-32 program was continuing, in spite of its involved and anomalous record of delay, disagreement, and dissatisfaction; it was an inescapable, if

incomprehensible, reality that B-32s were still rolling, however slowly, off the assembly lines, untried and, conceivably, in the eyes of a potential Congressional investigating committee, unjustified. It is evident that the combat test mission was seized upon as the best means at hand to justify the continuation of the B-32 program. At this time the B-32 (although originally intended as a substitute aircraft to the B-29, but in actuality incomparable to the Superfortress other than for publicity purposes) was redesignated as a 'heavy bomber.'"

On 29 March, in the only meeting of the Air Staff he attended between 1 January and late June 1945, Gen. Arnold spoke at length on the B-32 to the Air Staff in order to justify his decision to continue the program:

"Paralleling the importance of the B-29, another type of aircraft is developing to the point where it must be employed to the maximum extent possible. With these two types the Army Air Forces have a weapon which is not comparable to any other type.... We are trying to win the war in the shortest possible time. To aid this, the B-32 must replace the B-24 in the Pacific in order to bring the maximum striking force against Japan.... We will need every B-29 and B-32 possible to stop the war soon."

The Decision to Continue the B-32 Program and Conduct a Combat Test

Although PGC testing had shown the B-32 program to be in trouble, an unusual decision was made to continue the program—immediately—by testing an aircraft that had been found "operationally unsuitable" for combat, in combat! To conduct a combat test of an aircraft in actual combat was an unusual undertaking in Air Force chronicles, as only the B-29 had ever been so committed. The decision was a repudiation of B-32 test conclusions (e.g. program cancellation) of the PGC, Air Force Board, OC&R, and other testing organizations. On 5 April the PGC submitted a list of minimum change requirements to the OC&R to be carried out before the aircraft was committed to combat. Maj. Henry Britt states "Only the least important of these requirements were accomplished" before the B-32 was sent to the Philippines.

ATSC is Assigned the Combat Test Mission
During the March B-32 conferences Gen. Kenney suggested to Gen. Arnold that one or two B-32s be immediately sent to the Philippines to determine the possibility of operating the aircraft off B-24 fields, to introduce the bomber to the Fifth Bomber Command, and to examine the problems of converting B-24 groups to B-32 groups. It should be noted that in its new role the B-32 was intended to operate from B-24 fields, and it was never considered that it would operate from the B-29 fields. Kenney also proposed that Col. Frank Cook of the ATSC act as the project commander. In his report Maj. Henry Britt commented that there were factions (e.g. PGC) that felt that the combat test gave the ATSC an immediate opportunity to seize control and revive the lagging B-32 program, and justify its efforts to keep the program alive when other organizations had been earnestly recommending its cancellation. OC&R informed the PGC that the primary purpose of the B-32 Operational Suitability Test was to demonstrate the aircraft's operational unsuitability, and that it wanted PGC personnel to conduct the tests. As the combat testing program was prepared a number of other organizations besides the PGC and ATSC became involved, includ-

ing the Army Air Forces Board, Tactical Center, Air Transport Command, Training Command, OC&R, and the Consolidated-Vultee Corporation. Normally, the Army Air Forces Board would be the most suitable agency to supervise this type of project. Brig.Gen. A.F. Strickland, President of the Board, made the Board's position clear that the ATSC would be in command:

"It is the opinion of the AAF Board that, since the ATSC will be conducting testing of the B-32 aircraft in the cited theater of operations, with Col. Cook as Project Officer, that the name of the mission should be changed from Operational Suitability Test to some other more suitable title. Further recommend that AAF Board, PGC, and ATSC personnel attend as observers, with only the ATSC submitting the final report, and with the AAF Board, PGC, and ATSC personnel to write memorandum reports for the information of their respective commands only."

The Board's recommendations were accepted, and the combat test was redesignated from the Operational Suitability Test to Project 98269-S (Special Project of 3 B-32s for the FEAF). The ATSC was responsible for the "organization and general direction" of the test, and that their final report be submitted to Headquarters, AAF, through the PGC and AAF Board. Maj.Gen. Donald Wilson of the OC&R insisted that the final report go through these two organizations so that the ATSC "would not have a completely free reign" over the project.

On 7 April 1945 Headquarters, AAF ordered the PGC to supply a complete crew and B-32 aircraft to the FEAF, and "be prepared to demonstrate to the personnel of the FEAF the combat suitability of the B-32." The ATSC's final report submitted to the OC&R was to include:

"...type of tests and demonstration conducted, runway requirements...gross weights at which the aircraft was operated, and maintenance and operational difficulties encountered."

By late April 1943 personnel had been assigned to the project, and Col. L.O. Peterson of the OC&R requested three aircraft to be supplied by Consolidated-Vultee. A schedule was set up, with 5 May as the date to move the aircraft from the Consolidated-Vultee Fort Worth factory to the staging area in California; 12 May as the date for flying from the staging area to the jump off point (California); and 15 May as the jump off date.

On 11 May, during a meeting in Manila, Philippines, including: Kenney; Barney Giles, now Deputy Commander of the 20th Air Force, taking over for Maj.Gen. Millard Harmon; Maj.Gen. Robert Douglass, CO of the 7th Air Force; and Maj.Gen. Curtis LeMay, CO of the XXI Bomber Command, the disposition of the Army Air Forces in the Pacific was discussed. Giles asked Kenney how he would coordinate bombing attacks on Japan with the B-29s once his B-32s were operating from Okinawa. Kenney suggested that B-29 targets should be east of Kobe, and B-32s west of that line. If either of the two Air Forces wished to operate in the other's territory, notification was to be made at least 24 hours in advance. Both men thought that a unified command would be optimal, both operationally and logistically, but that order would have to be issued through Washington, where there was no unified command, either.

Part Five

Combat

1

B-32s are Deployed to the Philippines

Once the decision was made to conduct combat tests there was a discussion about which aircraft should be assigned to the project. Initially, it was contemplated that one or both 477 and/or 484, which were assigned to the PGC, would be sent to the Far East. On 28 April 1945 Gen. Donald Wilson was of the opinion that neither of these two aircraft was suitable for combat testing, and was concerned with the slow progress of the entire B-32 program, which was impeding the efficiency of the PGC's testing program. He wanted to know "Why was the program taking so long?" On 30 April 1945 Col. L.O. Peterson of the OC&R, who was monitoring the B-32 program, relayed a memo describing the down times and problems of test aircraft 477 and 484 to Wilson, who was not at all happy over the memo. Col. Jack Roberts of the OC&R answered Peterson's memo by stating that Peterson did not answer Wilson's "Why?," and that he only raised a "host of other questions." Roberts concluded:

"If you are satisfied that these tests are being conducted expeditiously...explain. If you are not satisfied...initiate corrective action...Gen. Wilson feels that the time consumed is excessive, and he wants you to either do something about it, or else convince him that it is necessary."

Once Arnold authorized the deployment of the B-32 to the Pacific the pace of the program increased. Arnold had selected Col. Frank Cook of the ATSC as the commander of the test detachment, which was comprised of 33 personnel: 13 from the AAFPGC (Eglin Field); four each from the ATSC, AAFTAC, and from the Consolidated-Vultee factory; three from the ATC; two each from the AAF Board and AAF Training Command; and one from the AAF Office of the Assistant Chief of Air Staff for Operations, Commitments, and Requirements. Cook asked Consolidated-Vultee flight engineer R.T. LeVine to go to the Philippines to be the flight engineer on his aircraft, and also to conduct ground school, and to be the squadron technical advisor representing Consolidated-Vultee.

List of Crews: B-32 Combat Evaluation Teams

Airplane #1 (532)
1) Pilot	Col. Frank Cook	(ATSC) Project Commander
2) Co-pilot	Capt. Byron Boettcher	(ATSC) Officer in Charge of Crew
3) Flight Engineer	Mr. R.T. LeVine	(CVAC) Field Service Representative
4) Navigator	??	(ATC)
5) Radio Operator	??	(ATC)
6) Radar Operator	1Lt. Erland Maurer	(ATSC-Warner Robins)
7) Gunner	Cpl. Harold Van Der Dussen	(AAFPGC/Eglin)
8) Crew Chief	T/Sgt. G.W. Davis	(ATC/Fort Worth AFB)
9) Crew Chief	M/Sgt. G.B. Thacker	(ATC/ Fort Worth AFB)
10) Passenger (pilot)	Mr. E.C. Graham	(CVAC)

Airplane #2 (531/528)
1) Pilot	Maj. Henry Britt	(AAFPGC/Eglin) Officer in Charge of Crew
2) Co-pilot	1Lt. Jack Whitener	(AAFPGC/Eglin)
3) Flight Engineer	T/Sgt. Charles Sims	(AAFPGC/Eglin)
4) Flight Engineer (alt)	Mr. Jack Leet	(CVAC)
5) Navigator	? Malcolm Boynton	(ATC)
6) Radio Operator	Sgt. Kenneth Spargo	(AAFPGC/Eglin)

7) Bombardier	1Lt. Jack Cropper	(AAFPGC/Eglin)
8) Mechanic	S/Sgt. Thomas Sims	(AAFPGC/Eglin)
9) Gunner	S/Sgt. James Crews	(AAFPGC/Eglin)
10) Gunner	S/Sgt. Wayne Dowding	(AAFPGC/Eglin)
11) Relief Pilot	Lt.Col. Stephen McElroy	(OC & R)

Airplane #3 (529)

1) Pilot	Col. Frank Paul	(ATSC)
2) Co-pilot	Capt John Houston	(AAFSAT) Officer in Charge of Crew
3) Flight Engineer	T/Sgt. William Franklin	(AAFSAT)
4) Navigator	1Lt. William Lambert	(AAFSAT)
5) Radio Operator	Sgt/ Russell Schmidt	(AAFSAT)
6) Mechanic	Sgt. Thomas Laven	(AAFPGC/Eglin)
7) Mechanic	Sgt. Ralph Burgess	(AAFPGC/Eglin)
8) Gunner	S/Sgt. Raymond Wozniewski	(AAFPGC/Eglin)
9) Observer	Maj. J.C. Bishop	(AAF Board)
10) Observer	Capt. W.H. Corrie	(AAF Board)
11) Passenger	Mr. John Stuck	(CVAC) Aeronautical Engineer
12) Passenger	??	(AAFPGC/Eglin)

A three man radar maintenance team from ATSC/Warner Robins was assigned to accompany spares flown in by the ATSC.

Col. Frank Cook of the ATSC would seem to be a good selection for B-32 Project Commander, as he had experience in the B-29 program beginning in mid-1939, when as a Lt. Colonel he was a representative of the AAC and Air Materiel Command in meetings with Boeing representatives in the initial stages of B-29 design adapted from the company's Model 341. Cook would later head B-29 production engineering. In April 1944, after it had been decided that the B-29 was to be flown against the Japanese, the ninth YB-29 (136963), named *Hobo Queen*, was piloted by Cook. It was flown from Wichita to Miami under secret orders, and then headed south over the Atlantic, then north to Gander, Newfoundland, for refueling, and then flew non-stop to Horsham, St. Faith, England. Within an hour after its arrival the bomber was discovered and photographed by a Luftwaffe photo-recon aircraft, which was part of the point of the mission—to make the Germans believe that the B-29 would be deployed to the ETO. This YB-29 also was to test a new radar bombing system over France as a prelude to "*Project Ruby*." The project was to conduct a limited number of B-29 missions to bomb the *Kriegsmarine* U-boat pens at Farge, Germany, with the RAF 12 ton "Tall Boy" bomb in the summer of 1945. After spending several weeks in England the *Hobo Queen* flew directly to the CBI, arriving at Kharagpur on 6 April 1944, and the second B-29 to reach the theater. The bomber was assigned to the 462BG, and *Hobo Queen* was the only YB-29 to see combat, acting as a tanker to transport gasoline across the Himalayan "Hump." Cook left the B-29 project, and was assigned to head the B-32 combat test program, to be called the "Cook Project."

The Fort Worth to Philippines ferry crew of 529 *The Lady is Fresh* before leaving Fort Worth on 12 May 1945 (L-R): Col. Franklin Paul (Aircraft Commander), John Stuck (Tech Rep), Capt. John Houston (Co-pilot), William Lambert (Navigator), unknown AAF representative), Maj. J.C. Bishop (AAF observer), Capt. William Corrie (AAF Observer), and maintenance men: Laven, Burgess, Franklin Schmidt, and Wozniewski. (LeVine)

The Fort Worth to Philippines ferry crew of 532 *Hobo Queen II* pose before leaving Fort Worth On 12 May 1945 (L-R): Gunner/Mechanics G.B. Thacker and Harold Van Der Dussen, Flight Engineer Lindy LeVine, Instructor Pilot E.C. Graham, unknown ATC navigator, Airplane Commander, Col. Frank Cook, Co-pilot Capt B.K. Boettcher, and Radio/Radar Operator, Capt. Erland Maurer. (LeVine)

Hobo Queen II (532) piloted by Col. Frank Cook, B-32 Overseas Project Commander, takes off from Fort Worth on 15 May 1945 on the way to Mather Field, CA, and then on to cross the Pacific for the Philippines. (LeVine via Dembeck)

In view of the previous dissention among the various testing organizations, and the opinion of OC&R that the main purpose of the combat test mission was the continuation of operational suitability testing of the B-32 (that was a PGC role), it was not unexpected that there would be problems through the life of the project. The failure of the Army Air Forces Board to monitor the project and the participating testing organizations led to the consensus that the ATSC and Cook would use the test as an opportunity to prove that it had been justified in its efforts to keep the B-32 program viable when others, especially the PGC, categorically recommended its cancellation.

The test detachment was ordered to assemble at the Consolidated-Vultee Fort Worth factory by 1 May for processing and familiarization with the three B-32-20-CF test aircraft: 42-108531 (unnamed); 42-108529, *The Lady is Fresh*; and 42-10532, *Hobo Queen II*. The 13 PGC members left Eglin on 24 April, and reported to the temporary overseas project headquarters at Fort Worth. At the time Col. Cook, the Project Commander, had not arrived, and the project was under the direction of Lt.Col. Thomas Gerrity of the ATSC, who had assigned the personnel and aircraft, dispersed information and guidance instructions, and scheduled the preliminary procedures. PGC personnel had been assigned to all three aircraft instead of a single aircraft, which they had anticipated. A successful protest was made by Maj. Henry Britt, the senior PGC officer, and most of the PGC personnel were assigned to 531. Prior to the final AAF acceptance of the three aircraft intensive classes were held for all personnel. Once the aircraft were accepted each crew flew three shake down flights, one of which was an 18 hour fuel consumption flight. However, on 3 May Britt, with co-pilots Stephen McElroy and Jack Whitener, flew a 12 hour fuel consumption test. On landing 531's right landing gear did not lock, and the aircraft ground looped, causing extensive damage. Britt and his crew were then assigned aircraft 42-108528, which had been a company armament test aircraft at Fort Worth, and was not in top condition, as noted by Maj. Britt on his initial inspection. Fuel cell leaks, tachometer failures, loading difficulties, and other troubles delayed final acceptance of 528 until 11 May, as the aircraft was rushed through inspections and repairs.

The original staging area was to be Savannah, GA, which was then changed to Topeka, KS, at the request of the ATSC, because of its proximity to Fort Worth. Then the staging area was again changed to Fourth Air Force station, Mountain Home, ID, because of Topeka being a Second Air Force station, and the Fourth Air Force being responsible for the final B-32 training responsibility. The last change was made about 1 May, when a

decision was made to stage the aircraft from Fort Worth to Mather Field, CA, outside Sacramento, to begin the trans-Pacific ferry flight on 16 May.

Aircraft 532 and 529 left for Mather on 11 and 12 May, respectively, and 528 left on 13 May, performing a 12 hour range flight, flying a circuitous route via Little Rock and Corpus Christi. 528 had malfunctions in all four tachometers, the No.1 oil temperature gauge, the No.2 main oil pressure gauge, and the No.3 nose pressure gauge. Its radar equipment became unserviceable, and was not repaired until the aircraft arrived in the Philippines. The final problem on the flight occurred on the landing approach at Mather, when Britt was unable to extend the landing gear electrically, and it had to be cranked down manually. At Mather each crew member was processed and issued personal equipment. Any aircraft "discrepancies" (problems) were corrected by Air Transport Command mechanics. Accompanying the bomber crews were specialists and factory representatives to help indoctrinate the 312th on the B-32. The maintenance parts and supplies were to be shipped by air, and would arrive about the same time as the B-32s. However, all the spares for the B-32 were mistakenly shipped to Biak, New Guinea, so Flight Engineers R.T. LeVine and Jack Leet gathered parts from the Consolidated-Vultee factory and loaded them into specially built cargo bins that were hung from the bomb bay racks. This spares kit weighed 793 pounds, and contained six pairs of chevron exhaust clamps, an oil cooler flap actuator, one fuel pump, and one generator relay.

The 386BS (312BG) supplied mechanics to service the new B-32s at Floridablanca. The mechanics had previously worked on the squadron's Douglas A-20 medium bombers. Since the B-32 servicing equipment was misdirected to Biak, New Guinea, B-24 equipment had to be adapted, such as the jacks placed under the nose. (LeVine)

The three bombers were to be flown overseas by flight commander Col. Cook (532), Maj. Henry Britt (528), and Col. Frank Paul (529). The B-32s were to hop across the Pacific via the B-29 ferry route: Hawaii (Honolulu John Rogers Airport); Kwajalein via Johnson Island, then to Guam (Harmon Field); and finally to their destination on Luzon (Clark Field and Floridablanca). The original route was to be through New Guinea to the Philippines instead of Kwajalein through Guam, as thus the spares were left at Biak. While the *Hobo Queen II* and *The Lady is Fresh* left Mather on 15 May, Britt's 528 was delayed with mechanical problems for two days while crew chiefs and technical representatives tried to resolve them. Cook and Paul piloted their Dominators to Hawaii, with Cook's 532 having a problem with falling oil pressure in the No.3 and No.4 engines on the way. Consolidated-Vultee flight engineers recognized the problem as an indicator gauge—not actual pressure—malfunction, and told 532 pilots Cook and Boettcher to watch the oil temperatures, and if they remained stable not to worry, even when the pressures continued to fall. Once in Hawaii LeVine corrected the problem by punching a hole in the oil pressure transmitter to allow the oil to get into the capillaries and keep them full, and then attached a fitting to the line, where the pressure would then match the cockpit gauge reading. At Honolulu inspection of Col. Paul's 529 discovered a safety washer collected in the No.3 engine oil strainer and the engine was changed, and 529 was not to encounter any other major problems during the trip to the Philippines. The two aircraft flew to Guam, with the only problem being with the packed lunches provided at Kwajalein, which were so bad that they had to be "salvoed to the fish."

Britt's 528 departed from Mather on 17 May at 0100, and arrived in Hawaii at 1300. During the flight the Loran and radar equipment failed, the APQ-13 and radio compass operated only intermittently, and the turbo flux gate compass and the pilot's magnetic and repeater compass all showed deviations from the flux gate compass. Thus, on its flight to Hawaii, 528 flew 150 miles off course due to the compass deviations. An overcast prevented navigational sun shots, but Britt's navigator was finally able to pick up a homing beacon from Hawaii with its radio compass. Once in Hawaii the plane was given a thorough inspection that was completed on the 19th. Takeoff for Kwajalein via Johnson Island was scheduled for 0700 on the 20th, but a bad oil leak developed in a cylinder of the No.1 engine, and takeoff was delayed for several hours. The No.2 generator also continued to cause electrical problems, but the bomber was pronounced ready for the trip to Kwajalein, where it flew without trouble.

The following day, 22 May (as the International Date Line had been crossed), five minutes after takeoff from Kwajalein, 528's oil temperature on No.3 engine passed into red, and the pressure began to fall, as the oil cooler flap on the No.3 engine had stuck in the closed position—Britt returned to base. Upon landing the heavily loaded (111,000 pounds gross weight) aircraft the plane stalled at 120mph about two feet off the ground, and hit and damaged the tail skid. The oil flap was jury-rigged three quarters open, and Britt left for Guam via Eniwetok later that day, where he joined the other two B-32s at Harmon Field.

At Guam the crews spent their time performing minor repairs and adjustments, and picking up information on VHB operations in the Pacific from the B-29 staff. On their takeoff from Harmon Field on 24 May the runway was blocked by a crashed B-29, leaving just under 5,000 feet for takeoff. Showing off to the B-29 personnel stationed there, both *Hobo Queen II* and *The Lady is Fresh* easily took off over the crashed B-29 and headed toward Clark Field.

Col. Frank Cook's 532 *Hobo Queen II* arrives at Clark Field, Philippines, after a hop across the Pacific via the B-29 ferry route: Hawaii (Honolulu John Rogers Airport); Kwajalein and Guam (Harmon Field); and then on to Luzon. Originally, the route was to be through New Guinea to the Philippines, instead of Kwajalein through Guam. (LeVine)

At Harmon 528 remained in depot for repairs, and left Guam on the 25th. On takeoff Britt found one or more engines had dead cylinders that were not revealed on power run up. The underpowered 528 just barely cleared a 300 foot hill at the end of the runway, but power seemed to return to normal, and 528 did not return to base. Several hours out the seal on the No.1 engine driven fuel pump developed a leak, resulting in a steady fuel leak that caused a serious fire hazard. The leak was closely monitored during the flight, but the engine was not feathered.

When the three aircraft landed at Clark Field they had a total flying time of 175 hours. During the ferry flight to the Philippines Britt found 32 mechanical failings in 528, mostly due to incorrect wiring, instrumentation malfunction (all radar was inoperative), and poor workmanship. He also noted broken structural parts, disintegration of interior surfaces, cracks in the skin and rib formers, and fuel leaks during the entire flight. Britt stated that:

"...this airplane was the poorest combat airplane...(he) had ever flown, and that from his experience with the B-32 (e.g. 531 and 528), and that this was the rule rather than the exception with the B-32."

The newly arrived *Hobo Queen II* receives a going over upon its arrival at Clark Field on 24 May 1945 from curious 312BG personnel. (USAF via Pima)

The Lady is Fresh arrives at Clark Field (L-R): Co-pilot Capt John Houston (officer in charge of crew); mechanic Sgt. Thomas Laven; Sgt. Russell Schmidt; and navigator 1Lt. William Lamberton. The three B-32s left Mather Field on 12 May, and *The Lady is Fresh* and *Hobo Queen* arrived at Clark Field on the 24th, with Maj. Britt's troubled 528 arriving the next day. (LeVine)

312th Bomb Group Insignia (USAAF)

The other two aircraft suffered 31 failures or inoperative conditions (18 in 532 and 13 in 529) on their way to the Philippines.

B-32s Arrive in the Philippines
The B-32 crews were met at Clark Field by Gen. Ennis Whitehead, CG of the 5th Air Force, and Col. Merritt Burnside from the V Bomber Command, who had been assigned by that Headquarters as the B-32 project officer. The B-32s were assigned to the 386th Bomb Squadron of the 312th Bomb Group (Light) of the 5th Air Force's Bomber Command. The History of the 386BS for May 1945 prepared by 1Lt. Rudolph Pugliese stated in the "Local Interest" section:

Changeover to the Dominators
The hottest rumor that this outfit had ever been exposed to began to materialize in May, and convinced us that there may have been something to

what was being discussed in all latrines. We were going to change over to B-32s, the new super bomber! Running true to form, the Group was about to prove its versatility again, and was selected by General Arnold to become the world's first B-32 combat group. This squadron was to be the first of its type in the Air Force. Operating as a P-40 unit at Gusap (New Guinea) in December 1943, we changed over to A-20s in January, and now we were at it again; this time our planes were the new Dominators, counterpart to the Superfortresses."

The 312th called themselves the "RoArin' 20s," with the "A" of RoArin' over the 20s on the insignia to indicate their use of the A-20. This insignia was modernized and replaced in November 1956. The Group was made up of four Squadrons, each assigned a code based on playing card suits: 386th (Clubs); 387th (Diamonds); 388th (Hearts); and 389th (Spades). On the A-20s the white card suit was placed on the rear olive painted fuselage behind the National Insignia. On the B-32s the black-colored card suite was

386th Bomb Squadron Insignia (USAAF)

The 386th Bomb Group was made up of four Squadrons, each assigned a tail code based on playing card suits. The 386th BS was assigned the club suit, as seen on this unidentified B-32 taking off from Yontan. (LeVine via Dembeck)

Lt. Col. Selmon Wells (L), Col. Robert Strauss (center), and Brig.Gen. Jarred Crabb (R) as Wells takes over as 312BG CO on 10 March 1944. (USAAF)

Capt. William Barnes (shown) and 1Lt. Rudolph Pugliese were sent on detached service to the B-24 equipped 43rd Bomb Group at Clark Field to familiarize themselves with the maintenance and operation of a heavy bomber, and were on hand at Clark to indoctrinate the three B-32 crews. Barnes would die in the crash of 544 on 28 August 1945. (USAAF)

placed on the forward part of the vertical stabilizer, just above the fuselage. The 386th Bomb Squadron insignia was a waving skeleton riding a bomb. This insignia was modernized and replaced in June 1955. The Group remained in New Guinea until November, when it was transferred to the Philippines, from where it began operations in late January 1945. After flying out of airdromes on Mindoro, Leyte, and Luzon, the Group moved to Floridablanca, Luzon, in mid-April to assume a ground support bombing role. The 312th Bomb Group was commanded by Lt.Col. Selmon Wells,

who had succeeded the original CO, Col. Robert Strauss, on 10 March 1945. Wells had flown 141 low-level A-20 missions as the CO of the 389th Bomb Squadron. With the transfer of many 386BS personnel in spring

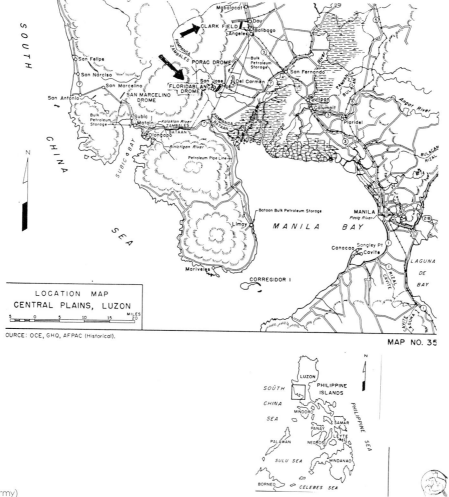

Floridablanca, Luzon, P.I. (U.S. Army)

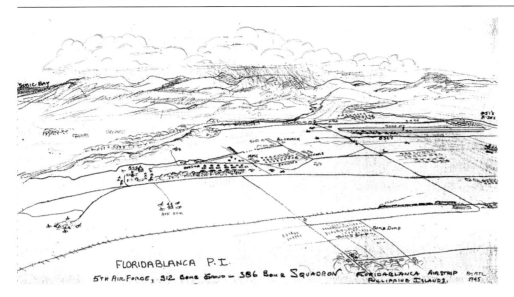

FLORIDABLANCA P.I.
5TH AIRFORCE, 312 BOMB GROUP - 386 BOMB SQUADRON FLORIDABLANCA AIRSTRIP BY RTL PHILIPPINE ISLANDS. 1945

(Drawing by R.T. LeVine)

1945, Capt. Ferdinand Svore had succeeded 312th BG veteran Richard Wilson as 386th CO, and would primarily be in command of the ground echelon of the squadron.

Floridablanca was a former Japanese air field built on a sugar cane plantation north of Manila, and 25 miles to the southeast of Clark Field, which was located on the Central Plains of Luzon. To the west of the field was a valley with the foothills of the Zambales Mountains bordering on it. The 312th moved to Floridablanca on 16 April 1945, and flew its first A-20 mission on the 20th. The Japanese field was a grass field, but by mid-March 1945 U.S. Army Engineer Aviation Battalions began construction of the first of two 7,000 foot runways that were originally scheduled for Porac Drome. By early May one runway was prepared for temporary use, and by mid-May it was paved with asphalt and ready as an all-weather runway, with clear approaches at each end to accommodate the B-32s. The B-32s were to be stationed on the east side of the N-S runway, and the A-20s and P-51s were posted on the NW side; the control tower was located midway. The B-32 crews were to be assigned to the new screened buildings built for, but never occupied by, the 90th Bomb Group, which flew B-24s.

To service the B-32s 312th ground maintenance, armament and ordnance, radio and instrument personnel, and two intelligence officers (Capt. William Barnes and 1Lt. Rudolph Pugliese) were sent on detached service to the B-24 equipped 43rd Bomb Group at Clark Field. They were assigned to acquaint themselves with the maintenance and operation of the B-32 bomber in the field. Until the B-32s arrived the 386th continued to fly their A-20s against Japanese targets, but once the B-32s were in the Philippines the 386th's A-20s, and their pilots and gunners, would be transferred to augment the other three 312th squadrons. Since the 387th Squadron was scheduled to be the next B-32 Squadron, the 386th's A-20s were transferred to the 388th and 389th Squadrons.

Capt. Barnes and the 386th personnel were to be stationed at Clark Field to indoctrinate the three arriving B-32 crews while their B-32s underwent four days of maintenance and preparation for their test combat after their long overseas flight. The 386th personnel familiarized themselves with the bomber, and observed bomb loading and general aircraft demonstrations. While 312th Group Commander Lt.Col. Selmon Wells was technically in charge of the combat test, he was ordered to work closely with Cook in implementing the combat test program. Wells was to furnish support personnel and services for both the aircraft and their crews, while his intelligence staff was to choose targets and provide data on them. Cook was to make the ultimate target choice, and control the deployment of the individual bombers. During the test program both Wells and Cook were to draft independent weekly reports on the program, and at the end of the test submit a critique and conclusion.

Unidentified B-32 taking off from Floridablanca, which was a former Japanese air field built on a sugar cane plantation north of Manila, and 25 miles to the southeast of Clark Field on the Central Plains of Luzon. To the west was a valley with the foothills of the Zambales Mountains bordering on it. (USAAF via Dembeck)

2

B-32s Enter Combat from the Philippines

On 26 May Col. Burnside met with the three B-32 crews for orientation. Since Britt's 528 Eglin crew was the only complete crew, two B-24 crews less pilots and co-pilots were assigned to the other two aircraft for combat tests. After the baggage racks were unloaded inspection and maintenance were started, and all armament equipment checked. The armament inspection revealed several serious problems. The bomb rack salvo had been incorrectly wired so the bombs could not be salvoed, and the salvo system circuit switch was wired in reverse. The bomb racks in the right hand forward bomb bay would not fire, because the electrical leads were too short and never had been connected, and the ends were merely taped over. Inspection of the nose and tail turrets found that the azimuth and elevation inputs had been reversed. The inspection report stated:

"These deficiencies indicate poor workmanship on the part of Consolidated-Vultee, and either very poor company and Army inspection or, which is worse, none at all."

While at Clark Field, the 386th was scheduled to fly its first B-32 mission on the 29th against Japanese positions in the town of Antatet, in the Cagayan Valley, in northern Luzon, 190 miles away. Capt. Barnes briefed the crews with an assemblage of high-ranking officers, press correspondents, and photographers present. The press was under strict censorship regulations, and was not allowed to release any information on the top secret new bomber. That morning the three B-32 guns were armed with .50 caliber ammunition, their bomb bays loaded with nine 1,000 pound demolition bombs each, and their tanks fueled with 3,000 gallons of gasoline, to give each aircraft a gross takeoff weight of 97,900 pounds. The bombers were crewed by the normal complement of 10 plus three observers. Running true to form, 528 developed trouble, this time with its superchargers, and Britt was forced to taxi the bomber off the runway. Inspection revealed that the No.1 and No.4 turbo controls were reversed. The other two bombers took off successfully, and arrived over the target at 10,000 feet without any anti-aircraft or fighter opposition. The first bomber dropped its load

1Lt. Rudolph Pugliese conducts the first combat briefing for the 386BS before the first B-32 mission from Clark Field on 29 May 1945. (USAAF)

Hobo Queen II (right) taxies out first as *Lady is Fresh* (foreground) starts her starboard inboard engine, as the first B-32 mission begins on 29 May 1945. (USAAF)

Lady is Fresh taxies to the runway on the first mission. (USAAF)

Hobo Queen II takes off, and was followed by *Lady is Fresh*, but 528 aborted on take off due to a runaway supercharger, and did not take part in the mission. (USAAF)

on the center of the town, followed by the second bomber, which hit the northern end of the town, after which the two bombers loitered over the target only long enough to take strike photos. The aircraft returned to Clark Field 2:35 hours later. Post strike ground liaison reports and strike photos deemed the mission to be successful. The official press report written by 1Lt Rudolph Publeise stated:

"World's First B-32 Raid
The outstanding raid of the month, and probably the most notable in this theater, was the B-32 strike on May 29th. Two of the three B-32s assigned to the 386th were sent on a mission to Antatet, in the Cagayan Valley. If the Japs below took time to peek out of their foxholes, they must have been amazed to see 18 1,000 pounders dropped from only two planes. Bombing

B-32 BOMBERS HIT FROM LUZON BASES

New U. S. Superplane Striking Japanese on Formosa and Along the China Coast

NEW YORK TIMES

UNDER KENNEY'S COMMAND

7-29-1945

First Attack by Craft, Much Like B-29 in Power, Range, Was Made on May 29

By JAMES E. HUTCHESON
Associated Press Correspondent

ABOARD A B-32 BOMBER, over Luzon, Philippines, Sunday, July 29—The giant new B-32 bomber has participated in strikes against widely spread Formosa targets by day and in night-time sweeps along the China coasts seeking Japanese shipping. The Army permitted these disclosures today. The new Super-Bombers made their first combat runs exactly two months ago today against Japanese positions on Luzon.

NEW B-32 BOMBER IN RAIDS ON JAPAN

Developed From Battle Lessons, Plane Is Hailed as Adding Punch to Attack

LOAD VARIETY IS STRESSED

Reversible Propellers Make for Agility on Ground or in Air—Suicide Squads Scorned

By JOHN STUART

from 10,000 feet was excellent. All bombs 100% on target, scoring direct hits on a house, and damaging a large tin-roofed warehouse.

More to Come
This, the first B-32 raid in the world, was the forerunner of future operations in the Pacific. The 386th Bomb Squadron, a P-40 dive bomber outfit 16 months ago, was selected to become the first combat B-32 Squadron in the Air Force. Our A-20s, along with their pilots, were transferred, and gunners were transferred out and assigned to the other three Squadrons in the Group. New crews, civilian factory representatives, and specialists joined the squadron, and preparations were under way to convert the 386th Bomb Squadron (Light) to a Very Heavy Bomb Squadron.

Rudolph Pugleise, 1Lt.AC"

After the mission Col. Merritt Burnside, commander of the operation, called the B-32 a "top notch weapon," and stated that "they performed perfectly, and justified all predictions." (The first mission is described in more detail later as part of the 12 Combat Test missions reports.)

On the 30th the 386th Squadron was redesignated "VH," or a Very Heavy Bomb Squadron, and it was to be transferred to Floridablanca Field to establish its Headquarters there. The 386th was to take over the administration, bivouac, and training area formerly occupied by the 90th Bomb Group. The next day the three B-32s arrived at Floridablanca, along with the civilian B-32 technical, radar, and instrument specialists. Also arriving from Clark were pilot navigators culled from B-24 units at Clark to begin transition training on the B-32s. Col. Cook inaugurated a comprehensive technical ground school for mechanics, radar, and radio operators. Gunners were given familiarization training on the B-32's defensive armament system. By the time of their next mission the 386th Squadron would have six pilot and navigator combat crews for the three aircraft. That same day Brig.Gen. Jarred Crabb, commander of the Fifth Bomber Command, delineated the combat tests in a letter to 312th commander Wells. The tests, popularly known as the "Cook Project" after Col. Frank Cook, were to cover three phases: engineering, maintenance, and "suitability as a combat weapon."

The Cook Project
The engineering phase was to "compile data indication modifications which would materially improve the airplane's reliability or combat suitability." Recommendations would be made to the headquarters of both the AAF and ATSC. The maintenance phase would also "compile data from which a summary of maintenance experience encountered during the test" would be used for "a guide for future maintenance personnel and supplying data to the Air Service Command." The combat suitability phase was to include handling qualities under as many varied conditions as possible, any special requirements for safe operations, and an "appraisal of the offensive and defensive capabilities of the airplane." The ground and flying instructions were to run concomitantly, with the tests having precedence over instruction.

The personnel conducting the tests were to be "employed exclusively in B-32 matters." They were to "assist the group commander in instructing flying and ground personnel on the operation and maintenance of the B-32 airplane." The safety of the bombers was to be the primary consideration throughout the tests. Col. Cook was to have the final decision on any

aircraft's airworthiness, and none were to be flown without his approval. Crabb set a 1 July completion date for the tests. In the June *Combat Narrative* Pugliese writes:

"Every precaution was taken to preserve these three planes; they were given the same careful attention a mother shows to her newborn child."

In his letter Crabb included a significant appendix entitled "Exhibit A: The Program for Combat Test of the B-32 Airplane," composed by Crabb's A-5, Col. Merritt Burnside. Exhibit A was divided into five sections: General, Object, Scope, Schedule, and Record and Reports.

The General section reiterated the body of Crabb's letter, adding that the test would consist of about 30 sorties on enemy targets using the three B-32s on hand. Photographs were to be taken and used in the test report "to illustrate the conclusions reached as to engineering, maintenance, and operational matters." The Object of the test was stated as:

"Determination of the suitability of the B-32 airplane as a combat weapon for use of the V Bomber Command under the conditions encountered in its present and contemplated operational area. Conclusions will be based upon the use of combat crews of average ability."

The Scope of the tests was to include:

Servicing requirements: Suitability of bomb loading equipment, together with number of men and time required for servicing gasoline, oil, bombs, ammunition, oxygen, and miscellaneous.
Suitability of ground maintenance equipment.
Requirements for the airdrome and its taxiways and hardstands.
Aircraft handling qualities using pilots of average ability during takeoff and climb, in formation, in various weather conditions, and at various gross weights.
Effectiveness of defensive armament.
Capabilities of the airplane in emergency operations. Conclusions should be reached as to proper emergency procedure in case of mechanical failure, including bailing out and ditching.
Suitability of offensive armament:
Visual bombing.
LAB bombing.
H and X bombing.
Suitability of navigator's equipment and navigator's position for day and night flying using DR (Dead Reckoning) and celestial navigation with radar aids.
Suitability of radio equipment and radio operator's position.
Suitability of the arrangement of instruments, controls, and equipment.
Combat radius of actions for various loadings, altitudes, and missions.

A Schedule of missions was outlined as an intended guide, and could be changed by the group commander "in the interest of efficiency to dovetail the test program with the training school, which runs concurrently, to take advantage of weather conditions, or other similar reasons." Eleven missions were listed and described:

Mission 1:   3 airplanes-8x2,000 pound bombs-altitude 15,000 feet-release by single ship-reduced fuel loads.

Mission 2: 3 airplanes-40x500 pound bombs-altitude 10,000 feet-formation release-reduced fuel loads.

Mission 3: 3 airplanes-12x1,000 pound bombs-altitude 20,000 to 25,000 feet-release optional-reduced fuel load.

Mission 4: 3 airplanes-40x500 pound incendiary clusters-altitude 15,000 feet-opening altitude 5,000 feet formation release-reduced fuel loads.

Mission 5: 3 airplanes-LAB night formation-dispatched singly-20x500 pound bombs-fuel load to reach Formosa Straits-or China coast.

Mission 6: 3 airplanes-F2X daylight mission-6x1,000 pound bombs-altitude over weather-individual release-fuel for maximum combat radius within gross weight limitations of the airplane and airdrome.

Mission 7: LAB night mission-same as Mission 5.

Mission 8: 2 airplanes-4x2,000 pound bombs-altitude optional-method of release optional-fuel for maximum combat radius within gross weight limitation of the airplane and airdrome.

Mission 9: LAB night mission-same as Mission 5.

Mission 10: 2 airplanes-10x1,000 pound bombs-altitude optional-method of release optional-fuel for maximum combat radius within gross weight limitation of the airplane and airdrome.

Mission 11: 2 airplanes-4x2,000 pound bombs-altitude optional-method of release optional-fuel for maximum combat radius within gross weight limitation of the airplane and airdrome.

The Records and Reports included a daily journal that included engineering, maintenance, and operations. Burnside instructed that any matters requiring immediate attention be dealt with by personal contact, telephone, or via a provisional report. The OC&R, ATSC, ASA (Air Services Activities), AAFPGC, and AAF Board were to submit their reports through the HQ of the FEAF, and that the final report be submitted to the FEAF HQ (in six copies).

It was evident from this letter and its appendix that the fate of the B-32 rested in the hands of the 386th Bomb Squadron and their ability to conduct the combat tests within the constraints of the test limitations and their personal capabilities.

Crabb's letter had authorized the formation of B-32 ground schools to operate with the flying program. The Consolidated-Vultee factory representatives were to establish a ground school and on-line indoctrination. This request came as a surprise to the Consolidated people, as Col. Cook originally told J.R. Lund, Consolidated-Vultee's Military Training Chief, that there would be no need for these schools. Despite the short notice, a successful ground school was set up by 2 June by Consolidated-Vultee personnel R.T. LeVine, John Stuck, and Jack Leet. The civilian factory representatives established technical classes with specialized courses in navigation, radar, radio, turrets, and bombsights, training B-24 and A-20 crews. Despite the lack of instructional material, the Consolidated-Vultee reps conducted a successful training regimen. The factory reps continued the training until a group of 10 USAAF men from the Military Mobile Training Unit arrived and set up their ground school on 21 July.

Veteran combat crews from the 22nd Bomb Group (B-25, B-26, and B-24), 43rd Bomb Group (B-26 and B-24), 90th Bomb Group (B-26 and B-24), 380th Bomb Group (B-25 and B-24) arrived at the now Very Heavy 312th Bomb Group for transition training. Mechanics, radio, ordnance and armorers arrived from Service Groups and V Bomber Command. Additional highly trained personnel arrived from Replacement Centers, and from the States. On 1 June the 386th had 20 officers, 249 enlisted men, and six civilians, and by the end of the month the roster increased to 55 officers, 370 enlisted men, and nine civilians. The roster was filled by the personnel that left San Francisco, and those of the 386th who had been stranded in Leyte aboard their LCI for four months, and finally landed in Manila on 6 June.

In the 11 days before the combat tests were initiated, Col. Cook's *The Lady is Fresh* flew training flights during six days, and Col. Paul's *Hobo Queen II* flew on seven days. However, Squadron records show no flying time for Maj. Britt's beleaguered 528, which probably was being serviced. Once in the Philippines 386th Squadron records show that 528 was also flown by Lt.Col. Stephen McElroy, the AAF HQ representative, who flew with Maj. Britt on the trans-Pacific flight. McElroy had been assigned to the B-29 program at Clovis, NM, before being assigned to a staff position in the bombardment branch of the OC&R Division of the Headquarters AAF in March 1944, where he was promoted to Lt. Colonel, and was assigned to the B-32 suitability test program. McElroy retired from the AAF as a Brigadier General in July 1967.

Combat Test Missions

There were 11 combat test missions, flown with 22 sorties totaling 142:10 flying time. Even though the 29 May mission was flown three days before Crabb's combat test directive, it was included in the final "Combat Suitability Mission Records." The following are the official narrative reports of the Combat Suitability Mission Records as prepared by 386th Squadron Intelligence officers Capt. William Barnes and 1Lt. Rudolph Pugliese, and taken directly from microfilmed copies of these reports:

Mission 1, No. 149-A-11 29 May, 1945
Airplanes: 529, 532 (note: airplane 528 aborted on takeoff due to a runaway supercharger)
Bomb Load: 9x1,000 pound demolition bombs per aircraft
Fuel Load: 3,000 gallons
Crew: 10 plus 3 observers per aircraft
Gross weight: 97,900 pounds
Distance to target: 190 miles
Duration of Mission: 2:35 hours
Narrative Report of Mission
The morning of the 29th of May marked the third epoch-making day in the life of the 386th Bombardment Squadron in less than 18 months of combat operations. The first occurred on Christmas Day 1943, when the 386th Bomb Squadron (L) flew its first mission with P-40Ns. On February 25, 1944, 12 A-20s of the 386th Bomb Squadron (L) flew a ground support mission in the Cape Rigny region of New Guinea to begin the softening up process prior to the Yawla Plantation landing. Today, two B-32s of the Air Forces' most versatile Squadron took to the air to aid our forces in the drive toward the Cagayan Valley. Mission No. 149-A-11 is the aerial dreadnoughts to attack Antatet, (1659'45"N-12144'10"E) in the Cagayan Valley. The target was a worthy one, since it contained one general officer, over 50 men, and several 75mm howitzers, in addition to being the Nip Supply Division Number Two for their troops resisting our advance in the Belete Pass area. Careful planning was required, because the target was within 2,000 yards

of Philippine guerilla troops, who have occupied the territory as far East as the Magat River.

At 1030/I the "Dominators" took off from Clark Field, and after making a circle to join formation, flew to the E. coast of Luzon and over Baler Bay, where all turrets were tested, firing out to sea. The B-32s then flew directly to the target. One circle was made to positively identify the target. At this time a large warehouse with a new metal roof was observed in the SW corner of town, and another large warehouse that had been revetted was seen just E. of the first one.

At 1200/I, on a 45 degree run from 10,000 feet, the first combat attack by a B-32 was begun. The strike was perfectly executed as planned, with the planes at no time passing over our own troops. It was also necessary that the bombs fall nowhere except in the assigned target area, because guerilla patrols had crossed east of the Magat River in the vicinity of the target. The nine 1,000 pound inst. GP bombs exactly covered the north portion of town for its entire length of 1,800 feet. The second plane, also on a single ship run, unloaded its nine 1,000 pound bombs on a 50 degree run as planned, to get complete coverage of the town with blast and bomb fragments from the two strings of bombs. On this run the central blocks of the town were covered just as perfectly as was the north section. A direct hit was scored on a house in the center of the string, and the large tin-roofed warehouse was badly damaged. There was no A/A or interception encountered. CAVU weather prevailed over the target, and photos were taken before and after bombing.

After the attack the planes reformed and returned directly to Clark Field. With the exception of .three scattered clouds at 10,000 feet over Belete Pass the weather was CAVU on the return. The big bombers landed safely at 1305/I.

Strike photo taken from the *Hobo Queen II* of the first bombs dropped by a B-32 in WWII during the raid on Antatet in the Cagayan Valley, Luzon. (USAAF)

Author's Note: Britt's 528, on its attempted takeoff, had the manifold pressure on the No.1 engine rise to 65 inches, causing the aircraft to swerve to the left. The left brake dragged badly, which further caused the aircraft to swerve off course. Britt cut the No.1 and No.2 throttles and applied full throttle to No.3 and 4, but the No.3 manifold also went to 65 inches, and the aircraft swerved across the runway in the opposite direction. Britt averted a crash and brought 528 under control at the end of the runway. Lt.Col. Selmon Wells, CO of the 312BG, flew as an observer on this mission with Col. Cook's 532.

Mission No. 2, No. 163-A-6, 12 June 1945
Airplanes: 529, 532 (Note: airplane 528 did not participate due to being grounded for an engine change)
Bomb Load: 40x500 pound demolition bombs per airplane
Fuel Load: 3,350 gallons.
Crew: 15 per airplane
Gross Weight: 110,000 pounds
Distance to Target: 380 miles
Duration of Mission: 4:00 hours
Narrative Report of Mission
On the morning of 12 June Basco Runway on Batan Island was the target for two B-32s of the 386th Bomb Squadron; FFO 163-A-8 directed the mission.

At 0930/I the Dominators took off from Floridablanca and flew to Lingayen Gulf. From there they followed the west coast of Luzon to Cape Bojeador, and thence to Batan Island. No A/A was expected, so the planes made two passes per plane on a single ship run. Prior to the attack Basco Runway appeared rough but serviceable. The first B-32 over the target unloaded half of its 10-ton load of 500 pounders at 1117/I on a 65 degree heading from 16,000 feet. The bomb started in the center of the runway, three-fourths of the distance from the north end, and trained to the extreme north end of the runway. The second string started on the west side of the runway at the same position as the first string and fell across the runway, with the last five bombs hitting just east of the northern one-third of the runway. The second B-32 made its first run on a 160 degree heading from 15,500 feet. Dropping the bombs in minimum train, the plane put 50 percent of its first string of bombs on the east center of the runway. The second run was made on an 80 degree heading at 1138/I Again using minimum train, 65 percent of the second string hit the northeastern portion of the runway. A total of 80x500 pound inst. GP bombs were expended, rendering the runway definitely unserviceable. No A/A or interception was encountered. Photos were taken over the target.

As the planes were leaving the target, a boat similar to a DE was observed traveling at about 20 knots on a 300 degree heading. The boat changed its heading to 90 degrees shortly after it was sighted.

The weather throughout the mission was good. En route there was three tenths alto cumulus from 6,500 feet to 10,000 feet, with a second layer from 12,000 feet to 16,000 feet. Four-tenths alto cumulus from 6,500 feet to 11,000 feet with 15 miles visibility prevailed over the target. On the return, three tenths cumulus had dropped to 3,000 feet base and 6,500 feet tops, the second layer dropping to 11,000 feet.

The planes returned over the same route and landed safely at 1330/I. After the planes were parked, the report was received that one plane had been holed in the left stabilizer by a bullet similar to a .50 cal. After the repair work had begun, it was found that the damage was caused by a bomb fragment from the previous day's practice mission. Author's Note: The 5th Air Force Bomber Command narrative stated, "The Batan Islanders are probably trying to figure how so many bombs came from two planes." Also, it was evident from the strike photos that the K-24 camera provided photos too small in scale and of inadequate coverage. It was recommended that the K-22 camera should be standard on all new B-32s arriving in the theatre.

Mission No. 3, No. 164-A-13, 13 June 1945
Airplanes: 528, 532 (Note: 529 did not participate due to having stabilizer damaged by a bomb fragment on a previous practice bombing mission.)
Bomb Load: 12x1,000 pound demolition bombs per airplane
Fuel Load: 4,000 gallons.
Crew: 10 plus 4 trainees and 1 observer per airplane
Gross Weight: 106,800 pounds
Distance to Target: 480 miles
Duration of Mission: 6:25 hours
Narrative Report of Mission
On the morning of 13 June, two B-32s took off to bomb the runway at Koshun airdrome as directed by Mission No. 164-A-13. This was to be the first B-32 strike over Formosa. Taking off at 0800/I with 12 half ton bombs

Strike photo of the second B-32 mission on 12 June; the Basco Runway on Batan Island was the target for two B-32s (529 and 532), as 528 did not participate due to being grounded for an engine change. (USAAF)

in their bomb bays, the planes got directly on course and headed North over five-tenths cloud coverage.

Although the target was partially obscured by eight-tenths cloud coverage, bombing was done visually from 12,000 feet from 1100/I to 1115/I. In single ship passes, on a 162 degree bomb run the first plane dropped all 12 bombs, nine of then hitting the leading edge of the strip, the last hitting the west side of the runway. The second plane dropped nine bombs down the center of the south half of the strip. Three bombs hung up on 528, and were salvoed off the south coast of Formosa (1214E, 2115N.) at 1148/I.

No opposition was encountered over the target, and after an uneventful trop back, the planes landed at the base at 1425/I.

Author's Note: The Fifth Air Force Bomber Command Combat narrative for June 1945 (page 91) stated that after the first three combat missions:

"From the operation of three planes it is hard to draw any conclusions as to functional difficulties which might be encountered in large scale operations. But from the tests it seemed that the B-32 was even more suited to the Pacific war than the B-29. This is mainly due to the increased range and payload over the B-29." The narrative went on to state: "Aside from this minor happening (e.g. the hang up of three bombs) the 32s had not as yet developed any serious bugs in their trial runs. The Command was, in fact, anxious to get more planes."

On 14 June 528 flew a practice mission at 13:30 piloted by Boettcher, with Sill as the co-pilot, and the aircraft returned with the No.4 engine feathered. Post-flight inspection showed a spark plug hanging out of the engine due poor maintenance on the part of the 386BS, who were A-20 mechanics.

Mission No. 4, No. 166-A-6, 15 June 1945
Airplanes: 529, 532 (Note: airplane 528 did not participate due to dinghy life rafts not being installed in the airplane.)
Bomb Load: 8x2,000 pound demolition bombs per airplane
Fuel Load: 3,600 gallons.
Crew: 10 plus 4 trainees and 1 observer
Gross Weight: 106,400 pounds
Distance to Target: 520 miles
Duration of Mission: 6:00 hours
Narrative Report of Mission
Taito Sugar Mill was the target for the night of 15 June for two B-32s as directed by FFO 166-A-6.

At 0800/I the big airplanes took off, and proceeded along the west coast of Luzon, and then north to Formosa. The flight to the target was made over .2 to .4 strato cumulus clouds ranging from 5,000 feet to 6,500 feet. The attack was made from sea to land to avoid any weather that might have built up over the mountains west of the target. At 1138/I from 1,500 feet the first plane unloaded its eight 2,000 pound GP 1/10 nose and .025 tail fusing bombs on a run of 310 degrees. These bombs fell in a riverbed 2,000 feet northeast of the target, causing no damage. The second plane, which made a 360 degree turn over the water, made its run at 1148/I from 15,000 feet on a 315 degree heading. The eight bombs from this plane blanketed 800 feet of the southwest center of the sugar refinery. The bombs fell among the larger warehouse buildings and the alcohol plant in this portion of the target. Prior to the bombing, these buildings were reported

Hobo Queen II takes off from Floridablanca. (USAAF)

to be in good condition. Photos were taken over the target. The weather was favorable over the target, with .4 strato cumulus from 5,500 feet to 7,000 feet and 15 miles visibility.

The first plane over the target received no A/A fire, but the second received about 20 bursts of heavy and inaccurate fire that were on level, but behind the plane. No damage was caused.

Both planes broke to the right, reformed over the water, and over .4 strato cumulus at 6,000 feet returned directly to base, where they landed safely at 1400/I.

Author's Note: After this mission Brig.Gen. Jarred Crabb sent the following congratulatory message:

"Congratulations upon your successful completion of the first four Baker dash Three Two strikes in history. It is most commendable that these missions have been run without mishap or delay concurrently with a big training program. The Three One Two Group continues to uphold its reputation for versatility.

(Signed) Crabb"

The 312th had called itself "The Air Force's Most Versatile Group," as it had first flown P-40s in 1943, A-20s in 1944, and now B-32s in 1945.

Mission No. 5, No. 167-A-7, 16 June 1945
Airplanes: 528, 529, 532
Bomb Load: 40x500 pound incendiary cluster type bombs per airplane
Fuel Load: 3,600gallons.
Crew: 10 plus 2 trainees and 1 airplane commander
Gross Weight: 112,000 pounds
Distance to Target: 520 miles
Duration of Mission: 5:30 hours
Narrative Report of Mission
Taito, on the southwest coast of Formosa, was selected by Bomber Command as the fourth target in the further experimentation of B-32s, and the training of the crews. FFO 167-A-7 ordered that the planes carry a maximum bomb load of 500 pound incendiary clusters.

At 0800/I, on the morning of 16 June 1945, the planes took off, lifting their 20,000 pound bomb load easily into the air. Flying a close formation, they headed directly for the target through clear weather, with visibility up to 20 miles. Forty-five miles from the target rope was thrown out, and five minutes later each plane threw out strings of rope every two minutes until they reached the target.

At 1030/I. still in formation but about 500 feet apart, the Dominators made their attack. Bombing was done visually over a one-tenth to two-tenths cloud coverage of strato cumulus topped at 4,000 feet. The run was made on a course of 310 degrees from an altitude of 19,000 feet. Bomb coverage was perfect. Dropping a total of 120 clusters at 100 foot intervals, the bombardiers attained excellent coverage, dispersing their bombs throughout the heart of the town.

Crews were enthusiastic over the results of this Taito "Tokyo Treatment." Taito was an inferno of smoke and flames that completely enveloped the center of town. An accommodating breeze spread the fires northward to cover the sections of town that the bombs missed. Smoke was rising up to 4,000 feet by the time the planes left the target. Two hours later the 43rd Bomb group passed by Taito, and reported that the fires were still burning intensely, and smoke was trailing 25 miles away.

A burst of heavy ack-ack was observed over the target to the right of, and on the same level as the formation. No damage was done, and no further opposition was encountered.

The planes returned safely, and landed at the home base five and one-half hours after takeoff. The bomb bay doors on one of the B-32s could only be opened on EMERGENCY. The catwalks inside the bomb bays showed permanent shear wrinkles due to the heavy bomb load.

Note: During Missions 5, 6, 9, 10, and 11 "rope" was dropped in units at various intervals. Small bundles of metallic foil strips were used over Europe to counter German radar: first "Window" by the British over Hamburg in July 1943, and then "Chaff" by the Americans that fall. This particular metallic foil was found to be ineffective against the Japanese radar frequencies, and on 9 January 1945 the XXIBC countered Japanese searchlight radar by using a type of aluminum jamming Chaff called "Rope." Packages of 6 inch wide by 400 foot long strips of foil were dropped by hand in bundles when the searchlights or radar controlled anti-aircraft guns were to be encountered. The bundles would separate in the slip stream, and long strips floated down behind the bomber; the searchlight radar homed on them instead of the bombers. Rope proved to be very effective, but its only problem was that there was not enough of it in the Pacific.

It was not until the fifth mission on 16 June 1945 that all three B-32s (528, 529, and 532) were able to bomb a target, which was Taito, on the southwest coast of Formosa. (USAAF)

The fifth mission was the only one to utilize incendiary bombs (500 pound clusters). The photo shows 484 dropping M47A2 incendiary clusters at 0.1 second intervals during bombing suitability service tests. (USAAF)

Mission No. 6, No. 168-A-4, 17/18 June 1945
Airplanes: 532 (Note: Due to the fact that the mission was a night LAB shipping search, only one airplane participated.) Practice missions were flown by 528/1:30 hours and 529 /2:30 hours.
Bomb Load: 9x500 pound demolition bombs
Fuel Load: 6,060 gallons
Crew: 10 plus 3 trainees and 1 airplane commander
Gross Weight: 111,900 pounds
Duration of Mission: 12:00 hours
Narrative Report of Mission
In order to disrupt the Jap shipment of troops and supplies between Hainan Island, Liuchen Peninsula, and Indo China, one B-32 was assigned by FFO 169-A-4 to conduct an armed recco in the Tonkin Gulf area, west of 111 degrees Longitude. In the event that Nip shipping failed to venture out, Haikow Town on the north tip of Hainan Island was assigned as a secondary target.

The Dominator took off at 1900/I and flew over the South China Sea, arriving at the assigned search area at 2300/I. A thorough search was conducted from about 8,500 feet. Most of the land areas around the Gulf were blacked out, but on the coast of the Liuchen Peninsula, a string of about six lights was observed along what appeared to be a pier in Nau-Sa-Bay. No suitable shipping targets were picked up, and at 0248/I in the morning of 18 June on a heading of 10 degrees from 8,500 feet, 9x500 pound GP bombs were dropped at Haikow Town on a visual run. The bombs were observed to hit the town just west of its center, but no results other than the bursts from the bombs were seen. During the run one unit of rope was dropped every 15 seconds for a distance of 15 miles on each side of the target. No searchlights, A/A, or interceptions were encountered.

Throughout the trip the weather was favorable. En route to Hainan Island there was a .3 strato cumulus layer at from 2,000 feet to 6,000 feet, with 10 miles visibility. In the Tonkin Gulf area the layer had thinned to .1 at from 3,000 feet to 4,000 feet, giving almost perfect weather for the search. On the return there was .4 strato cumulus at 8,000 feet, which was building in towering cumulus.

No sightings were made on the return, and the B-32 landed safely at 0745/I.

Author's Note: It was during this long range mission that the first true test of the B-32 radio communication was conducted. The B-32 radio operator was to call hourly, giving weather reports, and all were received, and no contact was lost. Maj. George Balassee, 312th Communications Officer, wrote:

"Needless to say the operation was convincing that the radio used in this maneuver was capable of sending and receiving a readable signal from a radius as far as the Dominator will fly."

On 18 June Col. Stephen McElroy wrote a letter to Col. Dale Smith at the Headquarters of the OC&R discussing the "considerable improvement in the situation." McElroy stated that the V Bomber Command now only expected one B-32 Group of three squadrons, and that the "final determination of the utilization of the airplane has not been made, doubtless pending the results of the combat test." He thought the bomber would be used as a LAB airplane, with "occasional" use as a high altitude bomber. He stated that the bombing results had been excellent, "Being much better than expected." Bombardier visibility was "definitely marginal, but the airplane has proven itself to be a stable bombing platform on missions of 10,000, 15,000, and 20,000 feet."

Mission No. 7, No. 170-A-3, 19 June 1945
Airplane: 528, 529, 532, (Note: 528 was delayed for one hour due to electrical trouble)
Bomb Load: 529: 12x1,000 pound demolition bombs
 528 & 532: 9x1,000 pound demolition bombs
 (Note: 532 had a bomb bay fuel tank installed from its previous mission)
Fuel Load: 3,600 gallons
Crew: 11 per plane
Gross Weight: 529: 103,600 pounds, 528 & 532: 101,100 pounds
Distance to Target: 540 miles
Duration of mission: 6:50 hours

The Lady is Fresh parked at Floridablanca. The photo shows the AT-17 nose turret, the bombardier's station and open entrance door, the cockpit windshield with oval opening and wiper, the open, two scanning windows, rolled up bomb bay doors, and the R-3350 engine with the reversible 16.67 foot Hamilton-Standard four-bladed hollow propeller, which was the largest fitted to an American production aircraft. (Claringbould)

Narrative Report of Mission

In an attempt to disrupt rail traffic along the east coast of Formosa three B-32s were designated by FFO 170-A-3 to bomb railway bridges at Paiyapai, Rokuryo, and Ikegami. The bomb load was 1,000lb GP, .01 second delay bombs, 12 in one plane, and nine in the other two.

Flying in close formation, the superbombers had excellent weather enroute to Formosa. Ceiling and visibility were unlimited, with a .3 undercast of strato cumulus at 3,000 to 6,000 feet. After passing Taito the planes turned inland, and each made for one of the bridges.

The crews were briefed to destroy the two southernmost bridges (Paiyapai and Rokuryo) first, and if they had any bombs left to bomb the bridge at Ikegami. However, the crew decided to split up, each taking one of the bridges.

Three bombing runs were made by 532 on Paiyapai. Three bombs were dropped in the first run from 10,000 feet on a 205 degree heading. One near hit was scored. The second pass was made at Rokuryo on a 210 degree heading from an altitude of 9,800 feet. The three bombs fell 80 feet east of the bridge. The last three bombs, dropped on a 220 degree heading, missed the bridge by 200 feet.

Ikegami Bridge was bombed by 528 on three runs from altitudes of 9,500, 9740, and 9,640 feet, respectively. The first two runs failed to bring any results, with three bombs dropped on headings of 257 degrees and 274 degrees. The third run at 282 degrees produced two near hits with three 1,000 pounders. The crew was unable to determine whether or not direct hits were made because of the smoke and bursting bombs that obscured any results.

Aircraft 529 made two runs over Paiyapai by dropping three bombs on the first and two on the second. Bombing from 10,500 feet on a 195 degree course, the three fell 500 feet northeast of the bridge, and the next two hit the riverbed 50 feet east of the target. The remaining seven bombs of this plane's 12 were dropped on Rokuryo. Two bombs missed the bridge by 100 feet, but near misses were scored with three bombs on the following run. The last two bombs fell 200 feet east of the bridge. Photos were taken of the bombings.

Two puffs of medium ack-ack were fired at B-32 528, bursting at about 5,000 feet. The first were reported to have come from a town, either Shinko or Senkeo, which had an L-shaped sea wall around it. No damage was done.

It was noted that the strip at Tuapo appeared to be serviceable. The city of Taito was burned out as a result of the Dominator fire bomb attack of 16 June.

The flight back was completed without any mishap or unusual occurrence. The planes landed at the base at 1430/I.

Chronically troubled 528 rests at Floridablanca (LeVine via Dembeck)

528 had problems during the flight. The bomber took off 35 minutes late due a load relay problem that failed to operate while using the APU. Mechanics were able to repair the problem, and the bomber bombed the Ikegami Bridge. After the bombing run the No.3 engine ran rough and had to be feathered for most of the return trip.

Mission No. 8, No.171-A-3, 20 June 1945
Airplanes: 528, 529
Bomb Load: 4x2,000 pound demolition bombs per airplane
Fuel load: 5,000 gallons
Crew: 11 per airplane
Gross Weight: 108,000 pounds
Distance to Target: 700 miles
Duration of Mission: 7:55 hours
Narrative Report of Mission

As directed by FFO-171-A-3, two B-32s of the 386th Bomb Squadron took off at 0700/I on the morning of 20 June to attack the railroad yards at Suo. The big planes each carried 4x2,000 pound bombs.

Along the coast of Luzon, and north along the east coast of Formosa the weather was good, with unlimited visibility and .5 cloud cover at 4,000 feet. However, at Karenko the weather began closing in, and by the time Suo was reached the undercast was solid from 5,000 to 7,000 feet. Unable to hit this target without getting too low for safety, the Dominators headed for the secondary targets: RR bridges north of Taito. The first plane reached Paiyapai Bridge (the first bridge north of Taito) at 1115/I, and from 10,000 feet on a 205 degree heading dropped its load. Over the bridges the weather was closing in fast, and just as the bomb release point was reached a cloud obscured the target. The bomb hit 3,000 feet southwest of the bridge. By the time the second plane reached the bridge it was closed in, so the B-32 headed for Tamari Town (2237N-12110E), and two large warehouse buildings there. On a 355 degree run from 4,300 feet at 1204/I the 4x2,000 pound instantaneous GP bombs were dropped. Direct hits were scored on the warehouses, which were located in the west center of town. The warehouses were demolished, and a large column of black smoke came up to 1,000 feet, and was still rising as the plane left the target. Photos were taken of both attacks. No A/A or interceptions was encountered.

When the planes turned south from Suo, they noted that the town of Kosoku (2427N-12149E) showed signs of extensive activity. There was a group of five warehouse type buildings near the coast with a railroad spur running into the group. From the coast a good jetty projected out into the bay.

The trip back to base was made under clear weather conditions from Taito. The planes landed safely at 1455/I.

Author's Note: 532 was held on the ground due to turbo problems on all engines caused by a flash voltage surge after the battery was damaged by the pilots starting the engine without the APU.

On 21 June 529 flew on a transition training flight, but 532 and 528 did not fly due to the turbo and then APU problems on the latter, and turret malfunction on the former. The times on the three aircraft were: 528: 122:35; 529: 146:30; and 0532: 136:45. Totaling 405:50 hours, or 230:50 overseas time.

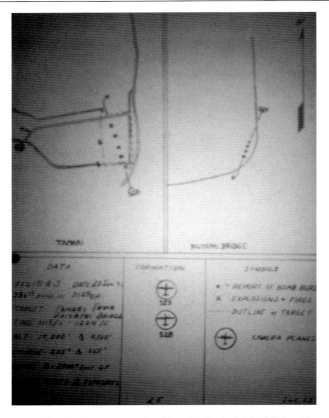

After each mission drawings were made of the raid. On the left is 529's bombing run on Tamari Town, and on the right is 528's run over the Paiyapai Bridge. The dots are reported bomb bursts. (USAAF)

Mission No. 9, No. 173-A-3, 22 June 1945

Airplanes: 528, 529 (Note: Airplane 532 was held on the ground due to supercharger wiring difficulty)

Bomb Load: 528: 40x500 pound demolition bombs & 529: 78x 260 pound fragmentation bombs

Fuel Load: 4,000 gallons

Crew: 11 per airplane

Gross Weight: 528: 114,000 pounds and 529: 114, 540 pounds

Distance to Target: 555 miles

Duration of Mission: 6:40 hours

Narrative Report of Mission

The central refining and distillery buildings of the Heito Butanol plant and nearby heavy gun position were the targets assigned to two B-32s by FFO No. 173-A-3. One plane carried 40x500 pound inst. GP bombs, and the other was loaded down with 78x260 pound frags. Each plane was assigned to one of the targets.

Lady is Fresh 529, piloted by Col. Frank Paul, lands after one of the combat test missions. (LeVine via Dembeck)

The flight en route was made over .3 to .4 coverage of strato cumulus based at 3,000 feet, and built up to 12,000 feet. The first landfall at Formosa was made for Heito. Bombing weather was excellent, with ceiling and visibility unlimited.

Carrying the frags, 529 went in first to bomb the gun position; the run was made from 15,000 feet on a course of 240 degrees. The bombs missed the target by about 200 feet, and trained diagonally across the military barracks in the area. The frags were observed bursting among the barracks, probably causing a considerable amount of damage.

Aircraft 528 hit the butanol plant with its load of quarter tonners on a 220 degree bomb run from 15,000 feet. Thirty bombs were dispersed over the length of the target, and 10 bombs that failed to drop over the target were salvoed immediately after the pilot made his breakaway. There were three large explosions among the buildings of the plant, followed by fires emitting black smoke up to 5,000 feet.

Both crews reported intense, heavy A/A fire that came close enough to rock the big planes. 529 dropped rope before and during its run and reported inaccurate fire. 528 did not use any radar counter measures and encountered A/A correct as to altitude and course, with accurate tracking through the run. No damage was sustained by either plane.

Fires were observed in two towns between Heito and the coast that were the results of heavy bomb group attacks. Heito strip appeared serviceable, although there was a bomb crater in the east end. Heito north and Koshun strips were also serviceable.

The planes returned on schedule, and landed at the base without experiencing difficulty of any sort.

Author's Note: Upon landing A/A hits were found on 528's heat exchange pipe of the No.2 engine, burning a hole in the No.2 nacelle and cracking the trailing edge of the wing. The inboard flap and the right hand side of the outboard flap were damaged, and had to be repaired with .020 24ST. Further inspection showed that the bomb bay door rollers had to be replaced by using B-24 rollers. All work was done by the 49th Service Squadron.

Mission No. 10, No. 175-A-6, 23/24 June 1945

Airplanes: 532 (Note: Due to the fact that the mission was a night LAB shipping search, only one airplane participated)

Bomb Load: 9x5,000 pound demolition

Fuel Load: 6,000 gallons

Crew: 11

Gross Weight: 111,000 pounds

Duration of Mission: 11:00 hours

Narrative Report of Mission

One B-32 was assigned to attack enemy shipping in the Macao-Canton River Mouth area on the night of 23/24 June, as designated by FFO 175-A-6.

Although an unidentified ship was sighted on the scope, it was outside of the blind bombing zone, and no attack was made. A further search was fruitless; no other shipping could be picked up, so the secondary target, Sanchau airdrome, was hit.

There was a .6 cloud cover at 7,000 feet over the airdrome, but the target was easily picked up and bombed by H2X at 0157/I. Six quarter ton bombs were dropped from 10,000 feet on a heading of 210 degrees. Due to the overcast, only one bomb burst was observed west of the center of the strip. No results could be determined. Three bombs hung up, and were salvoed in the water one mile southeast of Sanchau Island. Twenty units of rope were dropped, one every 10 seconds, for seven miles on each side of Sanchau Drome.

From a position at 2100N-11140E, on a northeast heading, a green light was observed about two miles off the right wing. The light stayed in this position for about one-half hour and then disappeared.

No opposition was encountered, and after an uneventful trip back the plane landed at home base on schedule.

Author's Note: On the *Queen's* return it was found that a bomb had damaged the right rear bomb bay door when it was dropped, breaking the three roller castings. During the 24th 529 flew a 1:50 hour transition flight, buzzing the field and making four landings.

Mission No.11, No. 176-A-1, 25 June 1945
Airplanes: 529 & 532 (Note: Airplane 528 did not participate due to a hole burned through the nose ring cowl of the No. 2 engine on a previous mission)
Bomb Load: 529: 12x1,000 pound demolition bombs
532: 9x1,000 pound demolition bombs (Note: This airplane carried only nine bombs because a bomb bat tank was installed on a previous mission)
Fuel Load: 4,500 gallons
Crew: 11 per airplane
Gross weight: 529: 109,000 pounds & 532: 106,500 pounds
Distance to Target: 744 miles
Duration of Mission: 7:30 hours
Narrative Report of Mission
The railway bridges north of Hatto Railway Station at Kiirun, Formosa, a vital link in the transportation route to Matsuyama and Tainoku, were assigned to the 386th Bomb Squadron as the target on 25 June. The planes were loaded, as per FFO 176-A-1, with half ton instantaneous GP bombs.

The crews were carefully briefed on the possibility of intense anti-aircraft fire, and warned that the run would be critical. They were also warned that interception was probable from local airdromes, and the absence of fighter escort added to the hazards of the mission.

The planes took off on schedule, flying over a .4 cumulus overcast built up to 10,000 feet. At the southern tip of Formosa they headed northwest up the East Coast, and arrived at the target three minutes late. The 750-mile flight was made in three and a half hours.

Kiirun was closed in with .8 alto stratus undercast, but 532 bombed visually through a hole that suddenly appeared below. Nine bombs were dropped from 20,000 feet on a 09 degree run, and hit about 1,000 feet northeast of the bridge.

Hobo Queen II and *The Lady is Fresh* parked at Floridablanca. (Claringbould)

Aircraft 529 did not bomb the primary because of cloud coverage, so it bombed the town Giren as a target of opportunity. Its 12 bombs, dropped on a 185 degree run at 20,000 feet, landed in the center of the town, damaging several buildings.

Neither A/A nor interception was encountered over the targets, much to the relief of the crews. Both planes dropped rope on their bomb runs, six units at eight second intervals. 529 took photos of the bombing.

No sightings were made, and after an uneventful trip back the planes landed at the base, completing the 1,500 miles round trip in seven and one-half hours.

Test Mission Summary
After two weeks in June, the 386th Bomb Squadron, unofficially known as the "B-32 School," had completed the B-32 combat test as prescribed by the FEAF. The missions had included 20 sorties, 140:36 combat hours, the dropping of 433 bombs weighing 133.27 tons, and the firing of 1,500 rounds of .50 cal ammunition. The first two missions were over the Philippines, while seven missions were over Formosa, and missions No.6 and No. 10 were long range single plane sorties to the South China coast. The June 1945 *312th Bomb Group Combat Narrative* stated:

"The change over (from A-20s to B-32s), however radical, is not the difficult task it appeared at first blush.... The B-32 is no longer an unknown. It has been tried and tested."

Combat Test Reports
There were three major reports submitted on the combat suitability test of the B-32, and there was a wide range of different opinions, conclusions, and recommendations reported to the various AAF organizations concerned with the testing.

Cook's Report to the V Bomber Command
Col. Frank Cook, the Project Commander, was generally favorably impressed with the B-32's combat suitability. He indicated from his point of view that the number and magnitude of "critical" items was "surprisingly" small. He observed that:

"...a long list, including many difficult critical items, is not required, as has been the case with other VHB programs...."

On 17 July Cook forwarded his report on the combat test of the B-32 and the training effectiveness of the 312th Bomb Group to Brig.Gen. Jarred Crabb, the Commanding General of the V Bomber Command. The report contained five Annexes (A through E) totaling 32 pages that encompassed all the specifics of:

"(A) Engineering, maintenance, and supply, (B) Suitability as a combat weapon, (C) Combat test and directive and program, (D) Combat suitability mission record, and (E) Loss of flying time." Included in the Annexes was "information covering the summary of maintenance experience, which will provide a guide for future maintenance personnel and supplies data of value to ATSC activities."

Servicing times and airdrome requirements were included. Handling qualities, and appraisal of offensive and defensive capabilities of the airplane were covered, and were described as "proven, or appear excellent." The annexes listed numerous, but generally minor, problems with various components and systems, followed by a list of "Clean Up Items" that were recommended remedies for the listed problems.

Although the Wright R-3350 continued to be a problem in the B-29 program, the B-32 Combat Test Report stated:

"Outside of oil leaks throughout the engine, which have required considerable maintenance, engine operation has been quite satisfactory. A total of three engines have been changed to date: two because of lock washer failures in the reduction gear assembly, and one because of a swallowed valve. No cooling problems seem to exist. Head temperatures seldom exceed 240°C indicated, and could be held lower. Backfires, except due to faulty starting technique, have been no problem. Blow by and compression problems have not been encountered."

The "Suitability as a Combat Weapon" annex was the most important, as it evaluated the characteristics of the bomber as follows:

"1) Handling Qualities: Combat test crews, and the 11 crews now being checked off are having no difficulty with the handling of the airplane. Due to the ease of the transition to the airplane it has been possible to check these crews out rapidly.

Takeoffs: Takeoff distances at 110,000 pounds have been running from 3,000 to 5,000 feet. As the airplane must be definitely lifted off, some crews are taking more run than necessary. Excessively long takeoff rolls are a characteristic technique used by B-24 and B-25 organizations in the theater. Takeoffs are always made to the north on the present operating strip, as the airplanes are parked at the south end. This gives downwind takeoffs at times. No difficulties have been experienced getting off the 7,000 foot strip (just extended to 8,000 feet).

Landings: The airplane has proven to be easy for average crews to land. Two tail skids have been broken, which can probably be expected during transition. Otherwise there have been no difficulties.

Formation Flying: Handling characteristics of the airplane flying in formation have proven to be excellent. Vision seems to be entirely adequate, although formations larger than three ships have not been flown. The best power control for formation flying is with the propellers, as their response is rapid and synchronized. It would be a distinct improvement for formation flying if a propeller control lever were installed at the throttle quadrant at both the pilot's and co-pilot's positions. Control forces during formation flying are very satisfactory. Pilots have expressed surprise at the desirable low control forces for the size of the airplane.

Stability: Under all conditions of loading used to date no deficiencies in longitudinal or directional stability have been noted.

2) Airdrome requirements for safe operation: The strip should be 8,000 feet long, and at least 150 feet wide, with good shoulders; 200 to 300 feet is desired. The taxiways should be at least 50 feet wide. The hardstands should be at least 120 feet wide and 195 feet deep. The reverse pitch propeller installation is used every time the airplanes are parked in their hardstands, and turn around facing directly toward the taxi strip. They are then backed into the hardstands 20 or 30 feet. This allows the narrow taxiway width noted above.

3) Offensive Capabilities:

A) Medium and High Altitudes, Visual and Radar Bombing: The airplane appears well adapted to this type of employment. The highest altitude used for bombing during the combat test was 20,000 feet. Excellent results were obtained. The radar installation is favorable to radar bombing, as the flight deck arrangement allows close coordination between the radar-bombardier-pilot team. With properly maintained equipment radar operation has been excellent. The question of bombardier's visibility is covered in Annex A. As noted, the limited vision afforded the bombardier has not detracted from the number of bombs put on assigned targets. Radar assisted approaches are used consistently. This is necessary in any case due to the common scattered broken cloud cover.

B) Bomb Load: The bomb load that can be carried by the airplane is roughly two and a half times that of the B-24. The number of ground and air personnel required per airplane is the same for B-32 groups as for B-24 groups. This means that, based on effort and hazard to personnel and equipment, the airplane has a 250% efficiency advantage over the B-24. All personnel in the theater concerned with the B-32 have quickly recognized this fact. In addition, the airplane is about 50 miles per hour faster, and has range capabilities greatly exceeding those of the B-24. All fuel consumption checks have indicated that the latest cruise control data gives accurate fuel consumption predictions.

A summary of operations in the Fifth Bomber Command during 1944 shows the following bomb loads carried by the airplanes used in this theater:

Airplane	Avg. Tonnage/Airplane/Sortie
B-24	2.094
B-25	0.636
A-20	0.658

Lighter loads for the B-24 LAB missions and long missions for the capabilities of these three types have decreased the average tonnage figures. In the comparison with the above, one B-32 airplane carried 10 tons for the same or greater radius than that of the above missions.

If it can be assumed that the above tonnage figures are representative of what can be expected in the future missions, one squadron of B-32s carrying 10 tons of bombs per airplane will, on average, carry the same loads as 57 B-24s, 189 B-25s, and 182 A-20s. If the B-32 tonnage is dropped to six tons (maximum load of 1,000 pound bombs) these figures become 34, 112, and 109, respectively.

4) Defensive Capabilities: No fighter opposition was encountered during the combat test, so factual conclusions as to the adequacy of the defensive armament are not warranted. Outside of the feeding and clutch problems with the nose and tail turrets, it appears that the defensive armament installation is adequate. The disposition of the turrets is optimum for angles of defensive fire, and for minimum interference with the internal arrangement of the airplane. Ammunition capacity meets accepted requirements."

It is interesting to note that, although the B-32 was a very heavy bomber and a challenger to the B-29, the combat tests results compared the B-32 to the B-24, B-25, and A-20, which it was now intended to replace.

McElroy's Report to the OC&R

Lt.Col. Stephen McElroy of the AAF Office of the Assistant Chief of Air Staff for OC&R, who accompanied Maj. Britton to the Philippines in the troubled 528, also reported on the tests: "Report on Special Project 98269S, 2 July 1945." His report can be considered essentially neutral He stated that the B-32:

"...in its present condition was suitable for operations in this theater at altitudes up to 20,000 feet if there is no fighter opposition, and icing conditions are not encountered."

However, before the B-32 could be considered combat ready in the Pacific to act as a heavy bomber with the FEAF, he recommended that the bomber's engine exhaust stacks needed modification to solve the chronic overheating and fire problems, that the heating systems needed improvement for high altitude, unpressurized bombing, and that the nose and tail turret ammunition feeding systems often malfunction and needed to be improved.

In his summary McElroy reported that there were eight points in favor of the B-32: 1) Load carrying ability; 2) Bomb loading provisions; 3) Bombing platform; 4) Takeoff ability; 5) Flight handling characteristics and formation flying ability; 6) Curtiss electric propellers; 7) Flight deck arrangement; and 8) Power package unit.

McElroy also listed eight disadvantages of the B-32. Among those were the limited bombardier visibility, bomb bay doors that had given "considerable trouble," and the location, arrangement, and installation of flak curtains. The aircraft's structural flexibility was a "particularly unfavorable condition." The structural flexibility of the B-32 was due to the original weight-saving design by Consolidated-Vultee engineers. The flex was such that it resulted in the improper fit of escape hatches and entrance doors after a few hours of operation. It caused serious leaks throughout the aircraft during the rains of the monsoon season. Water leakage caused increased malfunctions and maintenance of electrical and radar equipment. The lack of pressurization was a "definite handicap in operating conditions over 20,000 feet." McElroy described the malfunctions of the nose and tail turrets at length, especially the improper feeding of ammunition to these turrets. He mentioned the lack of storage space for cameras, radios, parachutes, and mechanic's kits. The major portion of his complaints about the bomber included the 40 plus "clean up items" that were "obviously necessary."

Probably the most significant of McElroy's remarks was:

"The introduction of a bombardment aircraft to the theater before operational suitability tests were completed, plus the additional load on the theater in meeting new maintenance and supply demands... were a major limitation and disadvantage.

This remark echoes the beliefs of OC&R, which had long wanted the cancellation of the B-32 program. It must be noted that Project Commander

Col. Frank Cook of the ATSC did not mention the introduction of the B-32 to combat before operational suitability tests had been done as a disadvantage.

Britt's Report to the PGC

The report of Maj. Henry Britt of the PGC on the combat suitability of the B-32 was basically negative, and much more conservative in its estimation of the B-32 in its current condition as suitable for combat. Britt was probably the officer on the project who was most familiar with the qualities and faults of the B-32. Unlike the Cook and McElroy Reports, Britt did not qualify his finding that "the B-32 in its present condition is not a suitable combat weapon to pursue the war against Japan." However, Britt listed six modifications that could be done to reach that objective:

Complete change in the design and type of exhaust collector rings.
Installation of a satisfactory heating, ventilation, and de-icer systems.
Clean up the electrical system problems.
Solve the bomb bay problems.
Solve the nose and tail turret ammunition feeding problem.
Install flak curtains.

The test mission failed in its purpose, in that each of the three submitted reports that came from Cook (ATSC), McElroy (OC&R), and Britt (PGC) were subjective, and reflected the pre-existing opinions of the submitters and their affiliations. Both the OC&R and PGC were firmly of the opinion that the Far East tests could have been better conducted in the United States.

The Truman Committee and Gen. Arnold on the B-32 Program

As discussed, in the spring of 1945 the various AAF organizations presented data that, at the time, the B-32 was unsuitable for combat, and unnecessary in the scheme of the future of the air war in the Pacific, as the B-29 had fulfilled the VHB role there. But Gen. Hap Arnold, Commanding General of the Army Air Force, was reluctant to write off the Dominator program, which had consumed vast amounts of time and money. Throughout the war Gen. Arnold was never specifically asked to justify his decision to continue the B-32 program, to test the aircraft in combat, and then to operate it in combat, despite the advice of a number of his staff officers and organizations. He then continued the program when all the results of the B-32 Combat Suitability Test demonstrated that the B-32 was unfit for combat.

The Senate Special Committee Investigating the National Defense Program—the so-called "Truman Committee"—was formed in March 1941, and during its first three years was chaired by Missouri Senator Harry S. Truman, who conceived the idea. Although senior military officials were opposed to the Committee, Congressional leaders advised President Roosevelt that it would be better to have a sympathetic Democrat like Truman make official inquiries, rather than those who might attack his administration. To limit the investigation it was funded by a paltry $15,000 per year budget. The Committee was formed to investigate the terms of defense related contracts and the methods of awarding them for the manufacture of articles and facilities, and then to monitor and improve production programs. Much of the Committee's wartime effort involved uncovering and exposing corruption and mismanagement, and during Truman's energetic tenure hundreds of hearings were held and millions of dollars were saved. As a result, his enhanced image brought him to public and political attention, and the Democratic Party nominated Truman to replace the controversial Vice President Henry Wallace on the 1944 ticket, and then to the Presidency after Roosevelt's death.

The bungled B-32 program was a prime target for Truman's aggressive Congressional Committee, and Arnold found a way to vindicate the B-32 program when Kenney offered to take the B-32s and have his V Bomber Command use them as mid to low altitude heavy bombers. As Maj. Henry Britt stated during the March 1945 Washington demonstration of the B-32 to Arnold and Kenney:

"Gen. Kenney stated that he had been to see Gen. Arnold, and that he could save him from a Congressional investigation if he could give him 300 B-32s instead of canceling the contract.... Gen. Kenney said he could give them (Congress) the answer on the B-32, and if the airplane proved to be no good production would be ceased. Operations, Commitments, and Requirements could at least answer an investigation saying it (the B-32) was given a try."

The continuation of the B-32 program was so important to Arnold that on 29 March he spoke at length on the B-32 to the Air Staff in order to justify his decision to continue the program in the only Air Staff meeting he attended between 1 January and late June 1945.

The influential and powerful Arnold had been instrumental in restoring American airpower to make it the most powerful in the world. The success of the B-17 and B-24 bomber programs and the P-38, P-47, and P-51 fighter programs far outshadowed the handful of questionable AAF aircraft programs. At the time the once troubled B-29 program had become an unqualified success, and Arnold was virtually untouchable. He had previously testified before the Truman Committee to defend his approval of the procurement of the controversial large cargo seaplane, the Kaiser-Hughes HK-1 "Spruce Goose," which was the topic of both public and Congressional debate in 1943-44. The Truman Committee heard Arnold justify that project and many others that were in development at the time:

"I let contracts for anything which offered a probability of speeding victory. I would be the last to claim that this process was economical in dollars. In fact, I have never claimed war was economical."

The Truman Committee supported Arnold's claim in an official statement:

"It is only natural that in so vast a program there have been many mistakes. Perfection must not be expected in war, where it is better to use wasteful methods than to risk having too little." But added: "All that can be fairly asked is that reasonable care should be taken to keep waste and mistakes at a minimum."

The Truman Committee reviewed the AAF development, procurement, and testing programs, and issued a slap-on-the-wrist statement obviously directed at the PGC, which had been organized to test the combat suitability of aircraft:

"The Committee in a previous aircraft report called attention to the large number of different...planes that are being produced. The efficiency of many of these has never been proved on fighting fronts.... The Committee believes that...where ever possible, changes should...be made to reduce the number of models, and to concentrate production on proven models."

This statement was made at a time when the B-29 and B-32 programs were the only examples of aircraft approved for production before comprehensive testing. The B-29 program had proven a success, but the parallel B-32 program still languished five years after its start. The Truman Committee stated that the global military situation at the spring of 1945 was such that:

"Experimentation should continue for the purpose of developing and proving new models, but we should not attempt mass production of an entirely new model...until after it has been tested and proved."

Why didn't the Truman Committee apply this statement to the B-32 program, which had been awarded a large production contract and was yet to be tested? It appears that the intervention of Generals Kenney and Arnold did save the B-32 program, not only from cancellation, but also from more intense Congressional investigation, which could have been embarrassing to Consolidated-Vultee, and possibly affect the post war B-36 program, which was being developed on adjacent production lines.

The *Lady* and *Queen* Art Gallery

On 24 June 532 had its new *Hobo Queen II* painting finished on its port side. The dark-haired *Queen* was framed by a cloud, and was sitting barefooted in a green pasture with a fence, house, and outhouse in the background. The *Queen* was wearing a very revealing sheer halter top and a very short skirt. The lettering was yellow, and each letter appeared to be stitched onto the fuselage. The Fifth Air Force artists were paid $25 for their work. Soon *Lady is Fresh* had her shabby portrait redone. The original *The Lady is Fresh* was painted on the nose of 529, and was replaced by another painting placed further aft in the same location as that of the *Hobo Queen II*. The lettering was red, and the blond *Lady's* two piece swim suit was red and white stripes, and she wore sandals.

After the Combat Tests: More Training

Intensive air training missions were flown following the conclusion of the combat test missions. During this transition training period six combat crews had been selected for the Special Project personnel from B-24 pilots and navigators from the theater and 312th Bomb Group. Also, several pilots and navigators were transferred from the 20th Combat Mapping Squadron for B-32 training. During June 12 combat crews had transitioned to become B-32 qualified. The later B-24 pilots and navigators in this transition program were considered not as well trained in the B-32, possibly because they were veterans and had accumulated enough points to go back to the States, and were perhaps understandably apathetic about checking out in a new aircraft. These indifferent and inadequate new B-32 pilots were then used as instructors to train new pilots. Twelve crews and aircraft from the United States were scheduled to arrive, but were never transferred to fly combat in the Pacific. Maj. Britt flew 528 on 27 June for 1:20 hours; Col. Paul took 529 up on four training flights on consecutive days beginning 27 June for flights of 3:30, 1:10, 1:45, and 2:00 hours, while Col. Cook took

The original *Hobo Queen I* was a YB-29 flown by Col. Frank Cook during his stint in the B-29 program. The first B-32 *Hobo Queen II*, wearing only a bowler hat, was painted under the cockpit, had her name in red lettering, and sat with a red kit with white polka dots tied to a stick. (Claringbould)

A late war photo of *Hobo Queen II* with a new 5th Air Force emblem painted on the tail. (Claringbould)

532 up for two flights on 28 June for 1:00, and 30 June for 1:45. The aircraft continued to have problems. In just two days the maintenance logs reported problems with landing gear retraction (528 on 28 June), induction fires (528 on 29 and 30 June), oil leaks (529 on 29 June and 528 on 30 June), generator and turbo problems (532 on 29 June), nose ring (532 on 30 June), and so forth. However, L.T. LeVine writes in his diary that these were "all the troubles of normal maintenance."

Meanwhile, transition training was continuing on the ground for engineers, radio and radar operators, and gunners. After the 387th Squadron had completed 30 A-20 missions in 24 days in June it received orders to transfer its Douglas bombers and crews to the 388th and 389th Squadrons on 4 July, and begin B-32 training. For the next two weeks the remaining 387th personnel attended the B-32 schools, followed by two weeks working on B-32s on the flight line. Meanwhile, the A-20 contingent of the 312th Bomb Group was to continue a heavy schedule of ground support operations for MacArthur's troops battling Japanese General Yamashita's tenacious army fighting in northern Luzon.

The larger revised and more flamboyant *Hobo Queen II* was surrounded by an array of antennas and scanning windows. The new hatless brunet *Queen* was just as nude, and was framed by a background of white clouds. She was sitting with her kit bag next to her on a carpet of green grass with a picket fence in the background. The yellow block lettering was made to appear to be stitched onto the fuselage. The new nose paintings were done by talented 5th Air Force artists at Floridablanca for $25 in mid-June 1945. (LeVine)

The first *Lady is Fresh* painting became scruffy, and was replaced by another painting placed further aft in the same location as that of the new *Hobo Queen II*. The new painting was larger and much more artistic. The blond *Lady* was posed similarly, and still was wearing the same two piece red and white striped swim suit, but different sandals. The lettering was red script. (LeVine)

Consolidated-Vultee sent factory technical representatives to deal with the problems the B-32 encountered in combat. From the photo the nacelle cowling appears to be removed, probably due to the chronic exhaust collector troubles. (Note: the negative of this photo was damaged by mildew) (LeVine)

Scaffolding for B-24 maintenance were commandeered. In the foreground is a crated Wright R-3350 engine waiting to be installed. (LeVine via Dembeck)

The first *The Lady is Fresh*, in red script, was originally painted on the nose of 529 above the bombardier's window She was a blond wearing a red and white striped two piece swim suit and sandals. (LeVine)

During the month 12 transferred crews took part in transition flights and practice bombing. The total time of each bomber since arriving on 26 May was: 529 flying 218:10 hours; 532 flying 190:10 hours; and 528 again lagging behind with 164:25 hours. With only two combat missions in July the majority of the 357 hours flight time that month was flown in training. By the end of the month there were enough crews trained to man a complete B-32 squadron. LAB Ground and Air Training had top priority. Link flight simulator training, supplemented by a B-25 trainer installation, was followed by flight training. M/Sgt. A.L. Butler was assigned as the Line Chief of the Engineering Section, while three B-32 Flights ("A," "B," and "C") were set up with the following Flight Chiefs: Flight A, M/Sgt. J. Knox; Flight B, M/Sgt. Fleming; and Flight C, M/Sgt. Kozora. During this time the lack of spare parts became serious, and there was an increase in engine fires, exhaust stack cracking, and landing gear failures. The Maintenance Section and Crew Chiefs did yeoman's duty in keeping the bombers repaired and flying. Since the spares for the B-32 were sent to Biak, New

Hobo Queen II (532) undergoing maintenance at Floridablanca. Note that the rear bomb bay doors have been opened, cowling panels are stored on a cart in the foreground, and a spare R-3350 waits on dolly on right of photo. (LeVine via Dembeck)

Guinea, the crews soon ran out of parts from the parts kits flown in by the original three B-32s. R.T. LeVine:

"We had to beg, borrow, or steal parts from other B-24 or C-47 combat outfits that we could modify for use on our B-32s. So all the mechanical problems were not the fault of the airplane. Eventually, the parts in Biak arrived on an LST about a week after the war!"

Missions Nos. 12 and 13: 6 and 13 July 1945: The Last Missions from the Philippines

During July the B-32s flew only two missions. A mission to the Haito alcohol plant was scheduled for 4 July, but was canceled when 528 and 532 experienced mechanical problems on the ground. 528 had an inoperable pressuretrol, and on 532 someone had hung a head set across the volt-meter taps and shorted out the voltage regulators. Mission No. 12 was flown on the 6th with the three B-32s: 528 and 529 carrying 12x1,000 pound bombs, and 532 carrying 9x1,000 pound bombs. The trio took off at 0815 on a 520 mile flight to bomb a sugar refinery at Tako Town, on Formosa. The bombing results were poor, as only six of the 33 bombs hit the target, with the Squadron history noting that a "guest bombardier" from HQ signaled the drop using H2X radar. One of the aircraft was hit in the radome by heavy AA fire. Lindy LeVine reports that the guest bombardier was the Chief Bombardier of the V Bomber Command, who:

"...ordered all bombs to be dropped on his release. Most of the bombs fell into the ocean, missing the target. The other two B-32 bombardiers said that they could see that he was going to miss. When he got back he officially complained about the 'poor vision' of the B-32 bombardier's station. This 'big excuse' gave the B-32 the reputation of having inadequate vision from the bombardier's position."

On the 13th 529 took off on Mission No. 13, which was a night LAB mission, but soon returned due to bad weather.

On 29 July the AAF officially unveiled the "giant new Super-Bombers" to news correspondents gathered at Floridablanca with a two hour demonstration flight, piloted by Col. Cook and co-pilot 2Lt. H.W. Rehm. Among Cook's statements quoted in an article by James Hutchison in the July 29, 1945, *NY Times* were:

"The big plane has virtually fingertip control." To prove his point Cook permitted correspondents to fly the bomber "as it responded surprisingly easily to an amateur's touch."

"The B-32 takes off almost like a fighter, lifting off gracefully from its tricycle wheels after a run of 3,500 feet."

"The new plane can carry a larger bomb load faster and farther than its little brother, the B-24 Liberator."

The article described the B-32 raids as:

"...exceedingly accurate against bridges, airfields, and industrial plants. The Formosan town of Taito was so completely fired by B-32 incendiaries that waves of following Liberators withheld their bombs." Cook went on to say, "As additional B-32s arrive, they will be added to the Far Eastern Air Forces assaults against Japan...carrying sizable bomb loads for long distances at speeds of 300 miles an hour."

3

Move to Yontan, Okinawa
August 1945

On 23 July Lt.Col. Selmon Wells received Movement Order No. 369 from 5AF Headquarters, ordering the transfer of the 386th and 387th Squadrons and Group Headquarters to Okinawa. By 30 July Capt. Woodrow Hauser, 386th Communications Officer, was ordered to be ready to lead the advanced echelon to Okinawa. Meanwhile, the B-32s continued their training flights during the month. On 1 August the FEAF Table of Organization officially designated the 312th as a Heavy Bomb Group, effective on the 15th.

By early August the 386th and 387th had their equipment packed and ready for land transport to Subic Bay, Luzon. On their arrival at Subic the LSTs had not appeared, and the men had to set up overnight camp on the beach until the LSTs arrived. The next morning the 387th loaded onto LST 745, and the 386th onto LST 801. Early in the morning of 6 August the LSTs left on their weeklong trip to Okinawa. During the voyage the men heard news reports of the dropping of the atomic bomb on Hiroshima, and the prospect of a Japanese surrender in the near future. The news of the atomic bombing of Nagasaki on the 9th reinforced the hope for a Japanese surrender. The LSTs reached the coast of Okinawa on the 11th, but were not ordered to land until the next day. The advanced echelon moved to the north end of the new base at Yontan.

Yontan Airfield was located just over a mile from the west coast of Okinawa, at the top of the relatively flat southern one third of the island. It had been an operational Japanese airfield that was captured in the late morning of the first day of the invasion, 1 April 1945. There were three existing runways, and the first priority was to get one runway operational for fighters, so that fighter-bombers could support the bloody ground battles that did not officially end until 15 August. Engineers filled in bomb craters, and graded and added a coral-based extension to increase the runway length to 5,000 x 200 feet. At the end of April construction was started on the heavy bomber runway, and this first bomber runway that was completed on Okinawa was 7,000 x 100 feet, and surfaced with coral; it was ready on 17 June. A second 7,000 x 150 foot runway surfaced with bitumen ran parallel to the first, and was operational at the end of August. A total of 189 standard hardstands were dispersed over the base.

Meanwhile, Group HQ and the flight echelons of the 386th and 387th were getting ready to move to Okinawa. At this point the records are incomplete, as several typhoons hit Okinawa in September and October 1945, destroying 312th Group records pertaining to the B-32s on Okinawa. However, R.T. LeVine's aero diary clarifies the confusion. On 30 July 530,

Hobo Queen II (shown) and 528 made the 1,000 mile trip to Yontan, Okinawa, arriving in the late PM on 11 August. Both bombers had minor mechanical problems to be corrected after arrival. (USAAF)

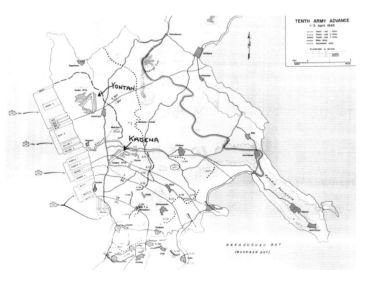

Yontan Air Field (U.S. Army)

Yontan Airfield was located just over a mile from the west coast of Okinawa, and had been an operational Japanese airfield with three existing runways, which were lengthened and improved so that there could be fighter-bomber support during the ground battles. At the end of April construction was started on the heavy bomber runway. This first bomber runway completed on Okinawa was 7,000 × 100 feet and surfaced with coral, and was ready on 17 June. A second 7,000 × 150 foot runway surfaced with bitumen ran parallel to the first, and was operational at the end of August in time for the 386th's B-32s. (USAAF)

The smoke in the background is from a P-61 that was attempting to land at Yontan with a raging fire on board. The pilot headed the Black Widow off shore, and the three crewmen bailed out and were picked up by a rescue boat. Yontan lies on a flat coastal plain, as can be seen in this photo. (LeVine)

piloted by Capt. Byron Boettcher, arrived at Floridablanca from the States at 1845, and the pilot announced 14 more B-32s would be arriving in the future. Between 4 and 10 August preparations were made at Floridablanca to transfer the bombers to Okinawa. Mechanical checks were made, and all aircraft were fitted with bomb bay fuel cells that were not connected. The preparations were interrupted by the news of the atomic bomb attacks on Hiroshima and Nagasaki. It appears that 532, *Hobo Queen II*, and 528 made the 1,000 mile trip to Yontan, arriving in the late PM on the 11th. Both bombers had minor mechanical problems that had to be corrected after their arrival. *The Lady is Fresh* (529) was grounded at Floridablanca by a fire that destroyed the three way header of an engine; a spare was not readily available, and would delay the bomber's arrival. 530 was also delayed at Floridablanca due to rudder problems, but arrived with 543 at 12:15 on 12 August, followed by 539 and 544 at 16:30. 578 arrived the next day to put seven B-32s on the island. The troubled *The Lady is Fresh* (529) got its new engine installed and arrived on 20 or 21 August. On 4 September 531

finally arrived from Floridablanca to put the final total of nine B-32s on the island after training was canceled on 1 September, and the B-32 Project was called back to the States on 10 September. 531 had been scheduled to be one of the original three B-32s to fly to the Philippines, but had suffered a main gear failure on the conclusion of a 12 hour fuel consumption test flight, and was replaced by Britt's ill-fated 528. Since 531 arrived late it did not participate in combat, but probably did fly some training missions. All the B-32s at Okinawa were B-32-20-CFs, except 42-108578, which was a B-32-35-CF. 42-108543 was named *Harriett's Chariot* by pilot Lt. Lyman Combs, and also displayed a large map of the state of Indiana, as well as the names of 15 crewmembers on the side of the fuselage.

The War Draws to a Close
After the *Enola Gay* dropped the atomic bomb on Hiroshima on 6 August the Japanese were given a surrender ultimatum in accordance with the unconditional surrender terms of the Potsdam Declaration. Despite the hor-

Lady Is Fresh (529), with pilot Collins Orton (left), co-pilot Lt. William Tursellino (second right), and Pvt. Jack Scott (far left). The prop and the cowling are removed on the inboard port engine, indicating engine maintenance. (LeVine).

Jack Leet, John Stuck, Lindy LeVine (Consolidated factory flight engineers) and pilots Capt. John Clark, Maj. Henry Britt, and Maj. J.C. Bishop. (LeVine)

rific destruction and the threat of another atomic attack the Japanese balked, and a meeting of Prime Minister Suzuki and the Supreme Council for the Direction of the War, to be followed by a meeting of the full Cabinet, was not held until the morning of 9 August. The debate in the Supreme Council was divided by the "peace" faction, led by Foreign Minister Togo and Prime Minister Suzuki, and a "war" faction, led by War Minister Anami, and as the deadlocked meeting was to be adjourned it was announced that B-29 *Bock's Car* had dropped its atomic bomb on Nagasaki. Togo and Anami spoke before the full cabinet, but the deadlock continued and Suzuki, Togo, and members of the Supreme Council had an unprecedented meeting late that evening. After hearing both factions, early the next morning Emperor Hirohito told the Council, "This is unbearable for me. But the time has come to bear the unbearable." The full cabinet still had to ratify the Emperor's decision, and several hours later it unanimously voted their affirmation. The Japanese Foreign Ministry informed the Allies that the Japanese government, at the command of the Emperor, was ready to accept the terms of the Potsdam Declaration, provided that the sovereignty of the Emperor was not compromised.

This Japanese condition to their resolute unconditional surrender ultimatum caught the Allies by surprise, and while the Allies considered the proposal President Truman ordered that the naval and air offensive continue in the Pacific. Meanwhile, Anami and the war faction were not ready to bear the unbearable, and there were plots, counterplots, and threatened *coup d'etats* within the Japanese military and political structure that continued into the morning of 14 August. Truman and Gen. George Marshall lost patience with the Japanese impasse, and Marshall sent a secret directive to MacArthur in the Philippines and Gen. Carl Spaatz, Commander of the Strategic Air Forces on Guam, calling for the resumption of maximum B-29 operations against Japan. Spaatz authorized four B-29 wings to attack Japan. Meanwhile, Kenney received the Marshall message, and he ordered Lt.Gen. Ennis Whitehead to resume V Bomber Command operations immediately.

Last Missions
Missions No.14 & 15, 13/14 (night) August 1945
As soon as the B-32s arrived at Yontan they were sent out on two missions on the night of 13/14 August. The first mission sent 528 out on a low level shipping search over the China Sea, where a small vessel was sunk. When

528 landed at Yontan its No.1 engine caught fire, but the pilot was inexplicably directed by the ground controller not to extinguish it. The nacelle and associated wiring and ducting were totally destroyed, and were later replaced by one from 539.

The second mission sent two B-32s on an armed reconnaissance of the Tsu-Shima Straits. One bomber, carrying 9x500 pound GP bombs, searched along southern Korea and northwest Korea without making any sightings. The second bomber dropped 9x500 pound GPs on a 75 foot sloop, attacking from 2,000 feet at 0530/I and scoring two near misses that resulted in a list, causing the crew to abandon ship in a small boat. Continuing its search in the area, the B-32 attacked a 150 foot boat with four masts and three hatches at 0600/I. The bomber fired 4,000 50 caliber rounds and caused damage of an unknown extent. The bomber reported no AA fire or enemy fighter interception. The recce report stated there were many small ships lying close to the shore of the islands off the southern Korean coast.

Mission No.16, 15 August 1945
On 15 August two B-32s were dispatched on reconnaissance over Korea and Honshu to monitor Japanese aerial activity. The bombers were recalled when the Japanese agreed to American surrender terms and a cease fire was declared. A cease fire had been ordered, as the Emperor had made an unprecedented radio broadcast commanding his subjects to "endure the unendurable and suffer the insufferable."

Mission No.17, 16 August 1945
The Far Eastern Air Force (FEAF) ordered the 386th to fly a series of photo recons to observe and report on the Japanese compliance with the cease fire conditions. On the 16th *Hobo Queen II* and *Harriett's Chariot* were sent on a photo recon over Tokyo to survey airfields on which paratroops could land preceding occupation troops. Despite the cease fire, the formation was fired on by inaccurate AA fire, and then was attacked by 10 enemy interceptors. The B-32 gunners claimed two Japanese fighters probably destroyed. 543 had a No.2 engine leak on the flight back to base, but the pilot did not feather the engine.

On the 16th eight B-32s on Okinawa had the following total flying hours: 532 (276:10); 529 on Luzon (260:00); 528 (238:00); 530 (117:55); 539 (94:00); 543 (81:40); 578 (61:45); and 544 (60:05).

An unidentified B-32 lands after a mission from Yontan. Note the wing from a burned out B-24 in the photo foreground. (LeVine)

Impressive forward view of an unidentified B-32 at Yontan. (Claringbould)

Hobo Queen II (532) taxiing past a Curtiss C-46 Commando transport with a 386BS Douglas A-20 following (far left). (LeVine via Dembeck)

Mission No. 18, 17 August 1945

On the 17th four B-32s (*Hobo Queen II*, 539, 543, and 578) took off at 0545/I on a photo recon mission (Mission No. 229 A-10) over northeast Tokyo. Each of the four bombers was to complete photo runs along three of the 12 assigned flight lines, which were to be two miles apart and end at Chiba. The other three bombers were to be on standby in case one of the bombers was unable to complete its photo runs. As the bombers approached Kyushu the Radar Counter Measures operators intercepted signals of Japanese radar-controlled AA activity. The formation arrived over southern Tokyo Bay at 1015/I, and each plane left the formation and flew two miles from each other to photograph its assigned area. The assigned area was blanketed by six- to nine-tenths strato cumulus cloud at 3,000 feet, making the photo runs difficult.

At 1030/I the B-32 piloted by Lt.Col. Wells was about to enter its assigned area when it was intercepted by a brown-green Japanese Army Air Force Tojo that slow-rolled next to the B-32, and then split-S'ed, making a firing pass from two o'clock. Wells turned his bomber into the attack, and his nose gunner sprayed the Tojo with twin .50cal machine gun fire to

chase the Japanese fighter away. At the end of the run heavy but inaccurate AA fire was received over Chiba.

The cloud cover prevented the B-32s from photographing their assigned zones, and they diverted to photograph secondary airdromes at Imba, Katori, Miyakawa, Matsudo, Kisarazu, Hanedam, Tomika, and Yokosuka. During the runs over Kisarazu and Imba radar controlled AA gun-laying signals were jammed by rope, and heavy but inaccurate AA fire was thrown up. As 543 was starting its photo run into Yokosuka it encountered heavy but inaccurate fire at 12 o'clock low, but as the plane continued its run it was bracketed by 50 to 60 bursts of radar tracked AA fire that hit the No.4 engine nacelle and the port wing flap. At 1135/I, as 543 continued its mission, 10 Japanese fighters were spotted at 20,000 feet just south of Yokosuka. The Japanese peeled off and made single plane passes. As a Tojo made a pass from 12 o'clock the B-32 nose gunner reported that his tracers had scored hits, damaging the enemy fighter, which rolled away from the battle. Another Tojo attacked from two o'clock level, and as it turned in and crossed over the bomber's forward top turret its gunner scored hits on the attacker's engine, causing it to roll away, losing altitude emitting puffs of black smoke from its engine, giving the B-32 gunner a probable victory. As the attacks on 543 continued the Dominator's tail turret guns jammed, and its pilot put the bomber into a shallow dive at full power on a southerly heading toward the sea. One Japanese pilot zoomed in at 4 o'clock low, past the tail, and was fired upon by the upper rear turret without effect. The other Japanese fighters remained safely at long range of the ineffective rear of the bomber, and sporadically pulled their noses up and fired long range shots at the bomber. They managed to put 20mm holes in the right flap and left wing tip, and 12.7mm holes in the rudder tab. Finally the Japanese broke off their attack, returning to base and allowing the B-32 to escape.

As the attacks on 543 continued, 539 was also under attack, and slowed by an exhaust collector failure. 539 sustained a hit on the No.4 engine that was feathered, and then suffered damage to the port outer wing panel about three feet from the tip, a hole in the aileron tab, followed by hits on the starboard outboard flap, and the No.3 engine exhaust pipe broke, damaging the inboard nacelle.

The Japanese fighters appeared to respect the 10 machine guns in the B-32's five turrets, and were content to fire at long range, causing a num-

On 17 August, 543 was starting its photo run into Yokosuka when it encountered heavy but inaccurate fire at 12 o'clock low, but as the plane continued its run it was bracketed by 50 to 60 bursts of radar tracked AA fire that hit the No.4 engine nacelle and the port wing flap. (LeVine via Dembeck)

Damage from Japanese fighter cannon fire to the port wing of 539 during the combat of 17 August. (LeVine via Dembeck)

ber of hits, but 532 was able to return to Yontan despite some minor mechanical problems.

Meanwhile 578, following 543, was attacked by five "Tojos and a Tony" at 1135/I, just northeast of Yokosuka, in a running quarter hour aerial battle. The Tony made the first pass from 5,000 feet above, diving below and then pulling up, making an ineffective firing pass from 6 o'clock. The upper rear turret gunner fired and hit the Tony in the engine and cockpit. The stricken enemy fighter began to trail smoke while rolling over into a steep dive before disappearing into the clouds below in a sheet of flame. The Dominator had scored its first aerial victory. The bomber's nose guns jammed, and one Tojo made a high firing pass from 2 o'clock, but broke quickly away. Another Tojo made a pass from below, pulling up in a firing pass with the ball turret firing at the Tojo as it broke away. The tail turret malfunctioned, but three trailing Tojos did not take advantage of the situation and made ineffective long range attacks. Again the Japanese were reluctant (perhaps because the war was over) to close on the bristling guns of the B-32, with only one attack pressed as close as 500 yards, and 578 suffered no damage. During the attack the B-32 made a left circling turn and headed north toward the *Hobo Queen II*, which seemed to be in danger. Once it was determined that the *Queen* was all right 578 took evasive action and headed east. The Japanese broke off their half hearted attack, and at 1215/I the four bombers regrouped and turned toward Okinawa. The B-32 gunners had expended 4,000 rounds of ammunition and claimed a victory, a probable, and a damaged. All four B-32s returned safely to base, but 543 and 539 had sustained damage. Although 543 had incurred the heaviest damage it was superficial and simple to repair, and would soon fly again. Because of the lack of spare parts it was decided that 539 would be cannibalized and would never fly again, and sat beside the Yontan tarmac until the end of the war.

A footnote to this mission was reported by Henry Sakaida in his book *Winged Samurai* (Champlin, AZ, 1985). A postwar interview with Japanese ace Saburo Sakai reveals that his last mission of the war was against the B-32s on 17 August 1945. Sakai stated:

"Our commander told us that the war was over, and that we were not to go out looking for trouble. But he also added that should the Americans dare fly over us and we wanted to get them, he wouldn't stop us. Then

around noon, we received word that some American bombers were flying over Tokyo. That really provoked us, and we said, 'Let's go get them!' and piled into our planes."

Sakai could not remember if he flew a Zero or George that day, but it appears that the American gunners misidentified the George for a Tojo. According to Japanese records all of their fighters returned to base from combat that day.

Mission No. 19, 18 August 1945

In the pre-mission briefing on the 18th, the Dominator crews were alerted in view of the experience of the previous day's mission and, despite the cease fire, they could expect enemy fighter attacks, and were to stay away from Hiroshima in particular. *Hobo Queen II* headed the day's photo reconnaissance mission, flying again over the Tokyo area, and was followed once more by 578 and the quickly repaired 543, while 544 replaced the damaged 539. A B-24 recon conversion F-7B of the 20th Long Range Photo Reconnaissance Squadron was to join the Dominators over the target, but since the F-7B cruised more slowly than the B-32s it left Okinawa earlier. Five hours after takeoff 543 and 544 developed engine oil leaks and returned to base. *Hobo Queen II*, piloted by Captain James Klein, and 578, piloted by 1Lt. John Anderson, flew at 20,000 feet, two miles apart over Choshi, which is located on southeast Honshu. Without the tardy F-7A they photographed Shimoshizu, Kicroshi, Miyakawa, and Imba Airdromes on their first run, and turned to make two more photographic passes. However, Anderson reported that his camera shutters were frozen, and that he was descending to a warmer altitude, and was seen descending toward Hiroshima. Onboard RCM detected Japanese radar tracking during the entire run, and fire control radar signals in the Tokyo area. An intense AA barrage was thrown up near the Miyakawa Airdrome on the first run, but it fell about 1,000 yards behind the two ship formation.

Klein made his second pass, and reported that Japanese fighters were taking off from a field just north of Tokyo. As the *Hobo Queen* returned several miles south of Choshi for the final photo run fighters were seen to be approaching, and Klein ordered Anderson to rejoin the *Hobo Queen*. There was no response from Anderson, but soon a waist gunner on the *Queen* reported seeing 578 at about 10 to 12,000 feet below. From 22,000 feet Klein put the B-32 into a shallow dive to 430mph, exceeding the "never exceed" speed of 357mph. As the two bombers joined up they were intercepted from behind (south) by a mixed bag of 14 Tojos and Zekes. The Tojos went after the *Hobo Queen* first, with three fighters diving successively from 11 o'clock. The upper rear turret gunner bore the brunt of the attacks, and his return fire discouraged the Japanese, who each broke off their attacks. A Tojo made a close-in climbing attack from 3 o'clock, but the ball turret gunner drove off this attack. Another Tojo attacked from the rear at 4 o'clock low, but was forced to break off to the left by the tail gunner's fire. Three head on closing attacks were made against the nose position. The nose turret gunner's .50 caliber bullets hit the first fighter as it attacked from 1 o'clock, causing it to half roll on its right wing, and begin to smoke on its slow descent. The gunner would claim a probable. The second fighter attacked from 11 o'clock, but broke away prematurely, and passed over both bombers. The third fighter made another indecisive attack, and also broke off early and passed over the formation.

Meanwhile, Anderson's 578 was enduring an even more concerted, but seemingly unorganized, attack by circling Tojos and Zekes that made

On the mission of 17 August 539 was under attack and slowed by an exhaust collector failure. 539 sustained a hit on the No.4 engine that was feathered, and then suffered damage to the port outer wing panel about three feet from the tip, a hole in the aileron tab, followed by a hit on the starboard outboard flap, and the No.3 engine exhaust pipe broke, damaging the inboard nacelle. Because of the lack of spare parts it was decided that 539 would be cannibalized, and would never fly again; it sat beside the Yontan tarmac until the end of the war. (LeVine via Dembeck)

On 18 August 1945 1Lt. John Anderson's 578 underwent a concerted Japanese fighter attack, with its gunners shooting down two enemy aircraft to mark the last aerial combat for the B-32, and 578 shot down the last Japanese aircraft of WWII. However, 578's crew suffered the last AAF KIA druing the war. (USAAF via Dembeck)

Sergeants Davis and Fry (R) are joined by Lindy Levine to repair 578's one dead No.3 engine, and others that suffered damage of some sort. There were numerous holes in the wings and fuselage, and damage to the left and right hand scanning blisters, and the upper Martin turret was shot out. (LeVine)

Sergeants L.H. Fry (L) and G.I. Davis point to three fresh victory flags on 578 after the 18 August mission, as the turret gunners claimed three Japanese fighters shot down, but one was a probable. The cost was high, with one crewman dead, one seriously injured, and one suffering a minor injury. (LeVine)

one individual attack after another, keeping 578's gunners busy calling out attacks. Tail gunner Sgt. John Houston sprayed several attackers with his turret guns, driving them off. A Jap was able to slip in to fire a number of rounds that hit the No.3 engine, encouraging the other fighters to converge on the crippled bomber. The engine suffered a sudden drop in oil pressure, and Anderson was forced to feathered it. The nose turret gunner had trouble getting his guns to elevate, but after several passes over the nose one enemy fighter made the mistake of crossing level and took several hits, and it began a smoking descent for a probable kill. A Zeke was able to close slowly to 1,000 yards on 578's tail before Sgt. Houston spotted it and began to fire. His third burst hit the fighter, which exploded into small pieces for a certain victory, his second in two days. Two photographers, Sgt. Marchione and S/Sgt. Lacharite, on temporary assignment from the 20th Long Range Photo Reconnaissance Squadron, were in the rear compartment removing film from their cameras when a fighter dashed in from 3 o'clock low and put several 20mm shells into the rear scanner's hatch. Both S/Sgt. Marchione and Sgt. Lacharite were critically wounded in both legs. Marchione collapsed, but Sgt. Lacharite, despite his wounds, was able to move Marchione to another area to administer first aid. Another Japanese fighter bore in from 9 o'clock and hit the bomber, wounding Marchione again. 2Lts. Donald Smith and Thomas Robinson worked frantically to save Marchione, who died 30 minutes later to become the last AAF airman KIA of WWII. The Japanese continued to attempt single attacks, but without much resolve when they met any return fire. Sgt. James Smart, the upper rear turret gunner, had been successful in beating off several attacks, and was finally able to hit an attacker coming in too close at 3 o'clock. The Japanese fighter rolled over in a slow dive and exploded under the bomber for 578's second victory of the day. Smart's satisfaction was short lived, as a Japanese fighter was able to attack from 9 o'clock and hit his turret. Smart was wounded in the left temple and forehead, and was unconscious as he was removed from his inoperable turret. Fortunately the Japanese, with four losses, decided not to press any further attacks and withdrew. When the F-7B arrived it continued inland into Japanese territory without fighter opposition, but was unable to complete its mission, as it was hit by flak.

The end of a successful mission, as an unidentified B-32 lands at Yonton. (LeVine via Dembeck)

On 28 August, at 0545 five B-32s were assigned to a special 18-hour communications mission that was to be the last B-32 mission of the war. The first four bombers lumbered off, but as 544 (shown), piloted by 1Lt. Leonard Sill, moved slowly down the Yontan runway the No.3 engine lost power. The bomber was almost airborne when Sills decided to abort the take off. The decision was too late, as the bomber plunged into a coral pit at the end of the runway in a fiery crash. Besides the pilot and co-pilot, 11 other crewmen were lost. (LeVine)

Hobo Queen II arrived at Yontan first after 11.5 hours, undamaged and without casualties, but 578 limped in at the same time as the F-7B, and was allowed to land first, as it suffered more battle damage to crew and aircraft: one crewman dead; one seriously injured; one suffering a minor injury; and the bomber had one dead No.3 engine, and others suffering damage of some sort. There were numerous holes in its wings and fuselage, and damage to the left and right hand scanning blisters, and the upper Martin turret was shot out. Anderson landed 578 successfully, and the mission was to mark the last aerial combat for the B-32—578 shot down the last Japanese aircraft of WWII.

Author's Notes:
Note 1: There have been many discrepancies in this mission and the number of Japanese aircraft shot down due to an International News Service reporter who dispatched his flawed story to the U.S. news organizations and *Time* Magazine. The above account has been gleaned from the official mission transcript.

Note 2: The last fighter vs. fighter combats took place on 15 August after Fleet HQ announced the cease fire. However, Adm. Halsey ordered Navy fighters on CAP that day to "investigate and shoot down all snoopers in a friendly sort of way." The Japanese lost 30 aircraft after the cease fire, 25 to the Navy and five to the Air Force. The last fighter victory of the war was apparently scored by Ens. Clarence Moore of the *BELLEAUWOOD*. At 1400 Moore shot down a Judy that was closing on the Task Force. That day four 5th Air Force P-38 pilots of the 35th Fighter Squadron of the 8th Fighter Group were escorting two PBYs over the Inland Sea on an ASR mission and shot down five Franks in the air battle, which occurred at 1215. In that battle Lt. Duane Keiffer was the Air Force's last fighter combat casualty of WWII when he was hit and unable to bail out of his Lightning.

Mission No. 20, 25 August 1945
On the 25th 528, 532, 543, and 544 were sent on an 18 hour cover mission to the Tokyo area. 543 turned around soon after takeoff, as its landing gear could not be retracted, while 532 turned back due to an oil leak and malfunctioning turbo. As the other two bombers approached Japan they found the area was socked in by a typhoon, and the mission was turned back. On landing 532 hit and broke its tail skid.

Mission No. 21, 27 August 1945
Two days later 578 and 543 prepared to fly a recon mission, but both bombers soon returned with mechanical problems. The nose wheel on 578 would not retract, and inspection showed that faulty maintenance was the cause. The main landing gear on 543 also would not retract, as the old drag strut unlatch link problem again occurred, and was found to be broken on both gears.

Missions No. 22, 28 August 1945
On 28 August, at 0545 the repaired 578 and 532 were joined by 528, 529, and 544, and were assigned to a special 18-hour communications mission over Atsugi and Tokyo that was to be the last B-32 mission of the war. The bombers were fully loaded with fuel for the long mission, and weighed 115,000 pounds for their takeoff in the predawn darkness. Beginning at 0430/I the first four bombers lumbered off at one minute intervals, but as 544, piloted by 1Lt. Leonard Sill, with 1Lt. Glen Bowie in the co-pilot's seat, moved slowly down the Yontan runway its No.3 engine lost power. The bomber was almost airborne when Sills decided to abort the takeoff. The decision was made too late, as the bomber, loaded with almost 8,000 gallons of fuel in full wing tanks and bomb bay tanks, plunged into an 80 foot deep coral pit at the end of the runway in a fiery crash. Besides the pilot and co-pilot, 11 other crewmen were lost, including Capt. William

The burned wreckage of 544 lying at the bottom of an 80 foot deep coral pit. (LeVine)

I Lt. Leonard Sills. (LeVine)

Barnes, 312th Intelligence Officer, and Capt. Woodrow Hauser, 312th Communications Officer, who had been with the Group since it entered combat. Post crash investigation found the old exhaust collector problem had resurfaced, as the No.2 engine lost its takeoff boost power. Sills thought he was losing the entire engine and its power, and chose to abort, when he probably could have taken off and climbed out on three and a half engines. Erland Maurer describes the day:

"When MacArthur landed in Japan to sign the surrender papers, three B-32s were assigned to go to Japan for communications and photo reconnaissance. I lived in a tent with the flight crew of one of the planes. I asked Lt. Sill if I could go along. He said, 'No problem.' The night before the mission he told me I could not go. I was outranked by two captains and a major from the group. The navigator was bumped by a navigator that needed one more mission to complete his tour. That left just two of us in the tent the morning of the mission. We slept until about 6 o'clock, when someone stopped by to tell us that Lt. Sill's plane had crashed on takeoff. We could see the smoke from our tent. There were 14 (13, author) men on that plane. The war was over. They were just going for a joy ride. We were in a stupor. Finally we got to the crash scene, but we didn't stay long. It burned for 24 hours. If this had been during the war, everyone would have taken it differently, shrugged their shoulders, and carried on.

The funeral was the saddest thing I had ever experienced. It wasn't unusual to see someone walk away and toss their cookies. The next thing the navigator and I had to sort out their belongings and sell what we could. We went through their personal papers to be sure there wasn't something that would cause any problems, like letters from a girlfriend, when it was sent home. All of them were married, so we had to write a letter to their wives. That was the worst part. There was no form letter that would cover the situation. Lt. Sill was married and had one child. He was a mortician, just beginning practice when the war started. What I said in the letter I don't remember. We sent home one complete uniform, personal effects, and money ($250) from the sale of their personal property. Lt. Sill had a radio that sold for big bucks. We had to take care of them. What a way to end the war." (Memoirs of Erland Maurer)

529 returned soon after takeoff, as the nose wheel would not retract, and landed over the burning wreckage of 544. The other three B-32s con-

tinued the mission, and after 11 hours during the return leg 528, following its previous bad habits, developed No.2 engine problems south of Kyushu. The pilot, 2Lt. Collins Orton, and co-pilot, F/O John Clark, tried unsuccessfully to correct the problem, but about half an hour later engine No.4 also developed similar problems. Both engines quit, and the underpowered aircraft lost altitude. The crew jettisoned everything it could but to no avail, and Orton gave bailout orders at 1930 when the other two engines failed. The 13 crew members bailed out about 200 miles south of Japan and east of Amaro Shima, in the Ryukus, just before it exploded. The crew was briefed that the Navy had stationed destroyer pickets at 50 mile intervals north of Okinawa, almost to the coast of Japan. Two U.S. Navy destroyers, DD 569 *Aulick* and DD 553 *John D. Henley*, both on picket duty, heard the Mayday, and the *Aulick* picked up nine and the *Henley* rescued three. Corp. Morris Morgan was never found, and Staff/Sgt. George Murphy died of internal injuries from a parachute malfunction on board the *Aulick* before it returned the survivors to Okinawa five days later. Post-mission investigation placed the blame for the failure of all four engines on water contamination in the fuel (via LeVine).

Jack Munsell, an engineer/gunner on 528, described his rescue (*Friend's Journal*, Summer 2000):

"We all bailed out of the rear camera hatch door opening after the door was jettisoned.

My parachute opened OK, Praise the Lord. I saw the B-32 fly into the North China Sea and blow up.

You cannot judge your distance over water, since there is nothing relative, so one second I was floating down, and the next second I was under water. My Mae West inflated, because I punctured the two small CO_2 (carbon dioxide) cylinders, and this brought me up to the surface. It was slightly after sunset when I managed to inflate my one man life raft by puncturing another larger CO_2 cylinder. I got on top of the raft only to discover that it was upside down. I had to get into the water again to turn it right side up.

It was beginning to get dark. I could not see any destroyers, but there was a PBY sea plane flying over. This was great, but it could not land and pick me up, as the sea was too rough. I was happy to see the PBY, because this meant they had our location, and perhaps would pick us up tomorrow. The life raft was equipped with some canned fresh water, a signal mirror, and ocean dye markers, which I intended to save until tomorrow when it was daylight, and they could be seen by search aircraft. I pulled in my parachute, which was still under water, and which I was still connected to. I intended to use it tomorrow as a sunshade, cover, or whatever came up that would be useful.

When it became real dark, a search light was turned on by one of the destroyers, and began to sweep the ocean in a circular manner. It went over me a couple of times. Apparently they didn't see me due to the rough seas, and because I was four or five miles away. I got out the signal mirror, which was supposed to be used in daylight by reflecting the sun's rays...I thought about using the sun signal mirror to reflect the ship's searchlight glare. It didn't work on the first attempt, but looking through the aiming cross on the mirror I pointed it toward the searchlight, and I was able to catch their attention. They zeroed in on the source of the mirror's light and sent a small boat out to pick me up. It seemed like it took forever to get to my life raft. They tied a rope to a designated swimmer, and he dove into the ocean water, got to my raft, and the sailors in the small boat pulled on

Direct from Tokyo left Yontan on 31 August, piloted by Col. Frank Cook. (USAAF via Dembeck)

At the end of August aircraft 530 was ordered to fly to New York City carrying early surrender photos on a good will flight. The B-32 was rechristened *Direct from Tokyo* by painting that name under the pilot's window. The bomber was painted silver, and its turrets were removed and faired over. The 312th Group *Roarin' 20's* insignia was painted on the nose behind the turret, and a large 5th Air Force Patch was painted under the *Direct from Tokyo* name. (Cherry via Dembeck)

the rope and drew me plus the swimmer over to them for the trip back to the destroyer (USS *Aulick*)."

Direct from Tokyo Good Will Mission, 31 August 1945

At the end of August aircraft 530 was ordered to fly to New York City carrying early surrender photos on a good will flight, and return two weeks later. The bomber's turrets were removed and faired over, and it was painted silver; behind and under the pilot's window the words *Direct from Tokyo*

were painted. The 312th Group *"Roarin' 20's"* insignia was painted on the nose behind the turret, and a large 5th Air Force Patch was painted under the *Direct from Tokyo*. The men of the 312th were told they could write one letter that was to be delivered by the bomber. At 0030 on 31 August *Direct From Tokyo*, piloted by Col. Frank Cook, left on its first leg to Kwajalein Atoll, then to Honolulu, and on to Mather AFB, CA. In a Letter to the Editor to *Air Force Magazine*, November 1980, Brig.Gen. C.R. Bullock claims that *Direct From Tokyo* was carrying the Japanese Peace Treaty documents signed at Manila to Washington, DC.

Epilogue

Conclusion of the B-32 Program

The sudden end of the war in the Pacific made further plans for the use of the B-32 unnecessary. The interim B-32 combat reports had reached AAF Headquarters by mid-June 1945, and the final reports were submitted in mid-July, and were received by August, coinciding with the end of the war. Thus, the only action required on the B-32 program was its cancellation, which was initiated on 18 September, and it was officially declared terminated on 12 October 1945.

On 10 August 1945, in a final review of the B-32 program, OC&R issued a memo entitled "Production and Use of the B-32 Airplane." The review made three major statements:

The development and procurement of the B-32 parallel to the B-29 was justified in view of the pressing need for larger bombers to successfully prosecute the air offensive against Germany and Japan.

The B-32 was superior to the B-17 and B-24 in bomb carrying ability and combat range, but was definitely inferior to the B-29.

In view of the design and performance deficiencies of the B-32 and the availability of the superior B-29 in large numbers for the post war Air Force, the termination of the B-32 program was justified.

The OC&R disregarded the testing and improvement of the B-32 in the continental U.S. by various AAF agencies and Consolidated-Vultee, and its more or less successful use in the Far East as a heavy (not VHB) bomber, replacing the B-17 and B-24. Nonetheless, the OC&R assessment can be considered definitive of the B-32 program.

The frustration and eventual dissatisfaction with the B-32 stemmed from the interminable delays in its development and production. The testing organizations had their patience worn thin during the pressure of war, resulting in a unanimous bias against the bomber from its earliest stages. Also, it is the B-32's eternal misfortune that it was developed as a Very Heavy Bomber alongside the B-29, and in the comparisons that inevitably followed the B-32 never met the VHB requirements that the B-29 finally met and exceeded to become the bomber that arguably won the war in the Pacific.

Fate of the Okinawa B-32s

On 1 September all B-32 training was discontinued on Okinawa. On 6 September the B-32s had the following flying hours: 532 (316:05); 529 (285:45); 528 (262:00); 531 (133:15); 530 (120:10); 578 (117:00); 539 (104:00); 543 (102:25); and 544 (71:45). 544 was destroyed in Sill's crash, 528 had been ditched on 28 August, and 530 left on the 31st. On 9 September 532 *Hobo Queen II* suffered an unflattering accident. During line maintenance an electrician mistakenly cross-connected the power to the wing flaps solenoid and the landing gear actuating solenoid. During a ground taxiing run, when the flaps were selected the nose gear unlocked and slowly retracted as the flight engineer desperately tried to stop the accident. Over the next days, to add insult to injury, the *Queen* was then dropped, not once, but twice, first when a hoisting clutch failed, and then after a hoisting chain linkage broke. The forward fuselage suffered extensive damage, and she was left on Okinawa after being declared beyond economical repair. On about 10 September the bombers were to be readied to return to the States. Air Transport Command requirements for the flight mandated that the ball turret be removed, and as much equipment as necessary be stripped from the aircraft. On 17 September Yontan was hit by a minimal typhoon, but the remaining six B-32s survived the winds, and were ready to leave during the second week in October. However, on 9/10 October the airfield was ravaged by the eye of another larger and stronger typhoon, whose 120-150mph winds did considerable damage to facilities, and destroyed many of the Group's records. Col. Paul's 529 was damaged, but the other bombers survived the winds. Capt. John Houston led the five remaining B-32s back to the States at 2300 on 14 October. The repaired

Hobo Queen II returning from a mission at Yontan. This bomber flew more missions and more hours (316:05) than any other B-32. (Claringbould)

On 9 September 532 *Hobo Queen II* was taxiing to the line when its nose gear retracted, because an electrician mistakenly cross connected the flap solenoid power and the nose gear actuating solenoid. During the ground run, when the flaps were selected the nose gear unlocked and slowly retracted. Over the next days, to add insult to injury, she was then dropped, not once, but twice, when the hoisting clutch failed and the hoisting chain linkage broke. The forward fuselage suffered extensive damage, and she was left on Okinawa after being declared beyond economical repair. (LeVine)

Hobo Queen crew chief George Davis (R) poses with his wrecked bomber. At the time the crew roster above his head lists Maj. J.E. Miller as the Flight Commander, taking over from Col. Cook, Capt. B.K. Boettcher, and Lt. R.L. Heise as the pilots. (LeVine)

529 was the last B-32 to leave Okinawa on the 16th. The B-32 would never see combat again, and as soon as the Okinawa B-32s reached America they were flown to the Kingman, AZ, aircraft disposal site for scrapping. Upon reaching the States most of the B-32 crews left the service, while Col. Frank Cook returned from his flight on *Direct from Tokyo* to Okinawa and took over as CO of the 312th from Lt.Col. Selmon Wells, who was rotated home. The 386th was officially deactivated on 18 December 1945 at Ft. Lewis, WA, but was redesignated as the 386th Bombardment Squadron (Very Heavy) on 14 July 1947, and assigned to the 10th Air Force in Reserve.

Fate of the Postwar B-32s
In June 1945 the Air Force had canceled the remaining 1,213 B-32 contracts, along with the planned 500 from the Consolidated-Vultee San Diego plant. I.M. Laddon, Consolidated-Vultee Executive Vice President, informed the B-32 Flight Research Department that all flight testing and other expenses being incurred on the XB-32 and B-32 Research Program were to be stopped at once. After V-J Day the AAF had no further plans for the B-32, and on 18 September 1945 production was canceled. On 12 October all Consolidated-Vultee production was discontinued after Fort Worth had built 74 B-32-CFs and 40 TB-32-CFs, while San Diego built the three prototypes and one (possibly three) B-32-COs. The B-32 was never sold to a foreign air force; because of its poor reputation for mechanical problems, and because even before the end of the war it was considered obsolete, the Dominator was not a candidate to continue in military service, or for the postwar commercial market. All flying B-32s were ordered to fly to the nearest disposal location, and all non-flyable aircraft were to be scrapped in place and delivered to the scrapper. San Diego B-32s 44-90487 and 488 and Fort Worth 42-108585 through 594 were to be flown directly to the disposal sites.

Aluminum was very expensive to process from natural ore, as it required a large amount of energy. However secondary aluminum, on a weight for weight basis, derived from scrap required only about 5% of that energy. Different types of aircraft had different construction and percentages of aluminum and non-aluminum metals. The normal WWII bomber contained about 75 to 80% aluminum, and was thus valuable as an inexpensive source of aluminum. Usually the first step in the aircraft scrapping process was to remove the engines and other valuable reusable and resalable equipment that had not been removed by the Air Force. These items included instruments, life rafts, fire extinguishers, oxygen equipment, etc., which was sorted and stored. The propellers were removed so that the landing gear could be retracted in order that the aircraft could sit flat on the ground to be more assessable to the workers. The propellers were pure aluminum alloy, and were not sent to the smelting ovens. The aircraft was methodically dismantled, with the easily detached items, such as the control surfaces, bomb bay doors, turrets, etc., being removed first. The aircraft was then cut into manageable pieces, mostly by oxy-acetylene cutting torches. However, the fuel tanks were removed by axes, as they could contain explosive gasoline vapors. The pieces were sorted for processing, with the steel and aluminum pieces separated. Since it was virtually impossible to completely separate both metals the Sloping Hearth Furnace was developed. These furnaces were relatively easy to construct, and were built at the aircraft disposal area. The furnace was a 15 to 20 feet tall, 6 to 8 feet wide square brick chimney with sloping internal walls and a melting chamber at the bottom. There was a platform at the top of the chimney leading to a door in the chimney wall. Here aircraft parts were inserted and slid down the sloping walls toward the melting chamber, which was heated to 1,300°F, and which would melt the aluminum, but not the steel, as that had a much higher melting point. The molten aluminum was drawn off through holes in the bottom of the furnace and kept in the molten state in a holding container so that any remaining iron residue could be removed. The aluminum was poured into ingots that were not pure aluminum, but contained about 3-4% copper, which was the alloying component in Dural aluminum.

In the fall of 1945 the powerful Reconstruction Finance Corporation (RFC) was the government department charged with the disposal of surplus military aircraft and aircraft equipment. In late 1945 the RFC had six storage fields: Augusta, GA; Altus and Clinton, OK; Kingman, AZ; Ontario,

CA; and Walnut Ridge AK. Most of the aircraft would be scrapped, as there was little civilian demand for obsolete military bombers or fighters. However, some foreign governments, such as some Central American countries unable to manufacture aircraft, purchased some of the more up-to-date types. Some were sold to start-up airlines, such as Slick Airways of Texas, which bought eight C-46 transports. Once the aircraft were parked, row upon row, they were stripped of parts and equipment (such as radar equipment, bombsights, guns and ammunition, etc.) classified as "combat," "restricted," or confidential." Parts, equipment, and engines were sold to foreign governments. By the spring of 1946 the disposal of aircraft was transferred to the newly formed Surplus Property Administration (SPA) of the War Assets Administration (WAA). The WAA was first headed by Lt. Gen. Edmund Gregory, but was soon succeeded by Maj.Gen. Robert Littlejohn, who had been Eisenhower's Quartermaster General in Europe. The WAA and 26 Congressional committees were charged with selling over 100,000 aircraft, 1,164 warships, and 21,000 tanks and guns, along with such ephemera as millions of shoes and socks, 24 million folding chairs, and seven million tubes of toothpaste, for a total value of $34 billion. Although a dedicated and efficient administrator, Littlejohn was a stormy figure in charge of a project that inevitably led to corruption and scandal. He encountered difficulties with Congress in the fall of 1947 and tendered his resignation, to be succeeded by Col. Jess Larson. In 1945 the RCF's first chief of the Surplus War Aircraft Division was George Adams, who was in charge of transferring aircraft to the six storage fields.

After being unable to sell surplus aircraft in large numbers, on 10 June 1946 the WAA advertised for bids for scrap and salvage on the remaining 20,000 plus aircraft stored around the country. The advertisement stated that the aircraft were "ineligible for certification by the CAA, and could not be used for flight purposes. They are offered for sale as is for the value of component parts and basic metal contents." The bidding was to close on 1 July 1946 at WAA offices in Washington, DC, with each of the six depots to be sold to different bidding companies. The winning bidder was to pay 10% initially, and then make monthly payments; they were given a specified time to complete the scrapping and clear the fields. All the successful bidders formed the Aircraft Conversion Company (ACC), and these companies ultimately recovered 200 million pounds of aluminum, which was retailing at five cents a pound in June 1946, but the high civilian demand for the metal soon raised the price per pound to 22 cents. Also recovered were 1,000 ounces of platinum (mostly from engine magneto points) and 80,000 ounces of silver. The scrapping venture was very profitable, as the six partners had invested $6.58 million for a return of $40 million.

Kingman Disposal

Kingman Army Air Field, located in west central Arizona, was then under the Air Service Technical Command. It was in the process of closing down when provisions were made to convert the base to a temporary storage and scrapping base called Sales Storage Depot No. 41, to be administered by the War Assets Administration. In early 1945 700 officers and men were transferred from Stinson Field, TX, to receive surplus military aircraft, and either sell them to the private sector or scrap them for parts and melt the rest into aluminum ingots. Later, an additional 600 men were stationed at the field to dismantle or scrap an anticipated 15,000 aircraft. The first aircraft were flown in on 10 October 1945, and by the first of the year there were almost 4,700 (including 2,205 B-24s and 1,640 B-17s) aircraft stored

at Kingman awaiting their fate, and more were scheduled to arrive. The military personnel were reduced to 281 by the end of December, and the field was deactivated in early 1946. The WAA attempted to sell aircraft and sold only 16, mostly AT-6s, before mid-1946, when the WAA Deputy Regional Director, John Taggart, announced that a bid process would be initiated to scrap 8,000 aircraft at Kingman and Ontario, CA, with the bids to be submitted by 1 July. The Martin Wunderlich Contracting Company of Jefferson, Missouri, was awarded the WAA contract to continue the scrapping privately. It purchased 5,483 aircraft for $2.78 million, and was given 14 months to complete the scrapping. In August 1946, after Wunderlich received its contract the Los Angeles WAA office informed the company it was taking bids on the gasoline and oil remaining in the aircraft, which totaled over three million gallons! Wunderlich argued that it had purchased the whole aircraft, including the oil and fuel, and that the original WAA ads included nothing about the fuel and oil being sold separately. Wunderlich was awarded the fuel and oil, but the media heard of the dispute and investigated both the scrappers and government, resulting in accusations of ineptitude, corruption, and bribery. At its peak Wunderlich was scrapping 35

Kingman Army Air Field, located in west central Arizona. The Martin Wunderlich Contracting Company was awarded the WAA contract, purchasing 5,483 aircraft for $2.78 million. Wunderlich was given 14 months to complete the scrapping. Shown are hundreds of B-17s and B-24s. (Kingman Air Museum)

Aviation historian William Larkins took this photo of 38 B-32s stored at Kingman in February 1947. (Larkins via Kingman Air Museum)

Aircraft #480, the tenth production model, awaits scrapping at Kingman. (Larkins via Kingman Air Museum)

aircraft per day, and by the time the scrapping was completed about 70 million pounds of aluminum ingots from over 7,000 aircraft had been shipped from Kingman. On 3 December 1948 the WAA finished at Kingman AAF by conveying nine buildings and the airfield to surrounding Mohave

County. During its stay the WAA had sold 400 buildings, disposed of $850,000 of personal property, and "processed" 5,634 aircraft.

Walnut Ridge Disposal
Walnut Ridge Army Air Field was located in the rural northeast corner of Arkansas, and construction started in June 1942; it served as a Flight Training School throughout the war, after which it was shut down. In late 1945 the base was reopened under the WAA and used as a storage/disposal site. The base was said to contain as many as 4,300 aircraft at one time, and they covered all 1,800 acres of the base. The scrapping operation was contracted to the Texas Railway Equipment Company, a subsidiary of the global Brown & Root Company of Houston, TX. The company removed the equipment and smelted over 5,000 aircraft during a two year period. The TB-32s and B-32s used for training at Fort Worth were sent to Walnut Ridge in batches of three to six at a time. Robert Kirk recalls landing on the short runway and being thankful for the reversible props. The ferry pilots and crews would be flown back to Fort Worth to repeat the process.

Davis-Monthan Storage and Disposal
When the AAF canceled the B-32 contracts there were about 66 B-32s (B-32-40, -45, -50, and -55-CF models) on the Consolidated-Vultee Fort Worth production line The last six fully equipped B-32s (42-108579 through 584) were declared excess upon delivery in September and October, and were flown directly from the Fort Worth production line to the Walnut Ridge

Since it was virtually impossible to completely separate steel and aluminum the Sloping Hearth Furnace was developed. The furnace was a 15 to 20 feet tall, 6 to 8 feet wide square brick chimney with sloping internal walls, and a melting chamber at the bottom. There was a platform at the top of the chimney leading to a door in the chimney wall, where the aircraft parts were inserted and slid down the sloping walls toward the melting chamber, which was heated to 1,300°F, which would melt the aluminum, but not the steel, which had a much higher melting point. The molten aluminum was drawn off through holes in the bottom of the furnace and kept in the molten state in a holding container, so that any remaining iron residue could be removed. (Kingman Air Museum)

This photo was found in the Kingman Air Museum collection with no caption. Since there are no accident reports involving B-32 ground fires the supposition is that this unfortunate B-32 was used for fire fighting practice. Note the numerous hammer dents on the nose. (Kingman Air Museum)

Hundreds of B-17s await their fate on the 1,800 acres of the Walnut Ridge Disposal Site, located in the rural northeast corner of Arkansas, where as many as 4,300 aircraft were stored at one time. (WRAAF Museum via Harold Johnson)

Aerial view of P-40s and P-47s with their engines removed stacked like cords of wood awaiting the scrapper to take them to the smelters. On the horizon are bombers, some with tall tails that may be B-32s. (WRAAF Museum via Harold Johnson)

TB-32s OM95, 4K78, 4K79, and OM40 (42-108514) with a P-40 nose and P-39 nose gear in right foreground, and two B-24s in right background. 80 to 82 B-32s and TB-32s were scrapped at Walnut Ridge after the war. (USAAF via Dembeck)

4M88, 4M90, and 4M98 at Walnut Ridge. The .50 caliber machine guns have been removed from the A-17 nose turret, and the opening taped over on the aircraft in the right foreground, which makes the aircraft a CF production model. (USAAF via Dembeck)

4M95, unidentified, and 4M79 with two P-40s and four more TB-32/B-32s in the background. (USAAF via Dembeck)

A P-47 and P-38 are framed under the wing of a condemned Dominator. (USAAF via Dembeck)

Three (OM20, OM12, and OM10) of the 40 TB-32s built awaiting an unknown fate at Davis-Monthan circa 1947. Originally four aircraft were sent to Davis-Monthan to be preserved. (USAAF via Dembeck)

Only B-32-1-CF (42-108474) *Flaming Mamie* was reserved for future display at the Air Force Museum, but in August 1949 it was inexplicably declared as excess and scrapped while in storage at Davis-Monthan. (Smithsonian via Dembeck)

Tail end view of front to rear: 42-108500 (OM20), 42-108488 (OM12), and 42-108497 (OM10). (USAAF via Dembeck)

disposal site. Four TBs (488, 497, 500, and an unidentified aircraft) were sent into storage by the 4105th AAF Base Unit (Aircraft Storage) at Davis-Monthan, Tucson. B-32-1-CF (42-108474), used in the accelerated flying test program, was reserved for future display at the Air Force Museum, but in August 1949 it was inexplicably declared as "excess" and scrapped while in storage at Davis-Monthan. Ten or 12 "shop assembled" B-32s—10 from Fort Worth (42-108585 through 594), and possibly two at San Diego—were declared as "terminal inventory," and were flown to disposal sites. Fort Worth Consolidated-Vultee contracted the Metals Reserve Company (MRC), a government operated subsidiary of the RFC, to remove the engines and all GFE (Government Furnished Equipment) from the 50 unfinished B-32s (42-108595 through 644). Consolidated-Vultee test pilot Beryl Erickson remembers that the engines of Dominators on the Fort Worth line were literally pulled from their mountings to crash useless to the factory floor. The aircraft fuselage, wings, and tails were then dismantled and loaded on railway flat cars, and shipped to the large MRC smelter at Texas City, TX, for scrapping.

TB-32 (489) was sent to Kessler AFB for use at the mechanic's school and became non-flyable, and remained there—most likely in the crash res-

Only OM20 remains, but the scrappers have started its destruction. These aircraft were scrapped, and only (42-108474) remained to be preserved. (USAAF)

Another photo of 474 at Davis-Monthan. Note the B-29 in the left background. (USAAF via Pima)

Only known photo of TB-32 (489) in July 1946, when it was sent to Kessler AFB for use at the mechanic's school; it became non-flyable and remained there, most likely in the crash rescue training course, and was sold for scrap sometime in 1947. (Bell via Dembeck)

cue training course—and was sold for scrap sometime in 1947. On 5 March 1945 42-108473 was destroyed in the experimental hangars at Wright Field. At least three B-32s (472, 475, and 495) were lost in testing or training, and three B-32s (528, 532, and 544) were lost in combat. An educated guess from the sparse records available indicates that of the 128 (or 130) flyable B-32s and TB-32s built the final disposition has at least seven lost in training or combat: one at Kessler; six going for storage at Davis-Monthan, Tucson; the Kingman depot received at least 38 flyable B-32s for scrapping; and the remaining 75-78 were sent to the depot at Walnut Ridge, AR, for disposal. By the end of 1947 there were only five B-32s at Davis-Monthan that had not been scrapped.

Today there is no complete B-32 in existence. In June 1947 pen manufacturer Milton J. Reynolds announced that he wished to purchase a surplus B-32 from the War Assets Administration for a planned round-the-world flight over both the North and South Poles, but Reynolds never purchased the aircraft. However, Reynolds did purchase a B-26, and with pilot Bill Odom did complete a record setting round-the-world flight. All that remains of the B-32 program today are two Sperry A-17A nose turrets, one in storage at the Smithsonian's Paul Garber Restoration Facility at Suitland, MD, and the other was on display at the Minnesota Air and Space Museum in St. Paul until it was sold to a private party in California in 2001. The other B-32 relic is a memorial to aviation pioneer John J. Montgomery. It is the slender end of a Davis static test wing panel from a B-32 erected on pylons pointing majestically to the sky. It is located on Otay Mesa, near San Diego, where Montgomery allegedly made the first flight in a heavier-than-air aircraft in 1883.

Legacy of the B-32

In the development of the B-32 project Consolidated-Vultee designers and engineers had been working in new areas of aerial technology that could be applied to their post war projects. Postwar American airpower strategy gave precedence to the development of the strategic bomber. It has been alleged that after the AAF chose the B-29 as its VHB bomber and deployed it to the CBI in March 1944 that Consolidated-Vultee downgraded the B-32 program, and caused it to fall behind schedule to concentrate on surreptitious preparatory groundwork on the giant post-war B-36 "Intercontinental Bomber." The XB-36 project had been contracted on 15 November 1941, and design work began in San Diego, but was transferred to Consolidated's Fort Worth Division in August 1942 for detailed design and the construction of two prototypes. The Peacemaker was to have a gross weight of 265,000 pounds, pressurized cabins, six 3,000 horsepower engines, and a range of 10,000 miles carrying 10,000 pounds of bombs (or 4,600 miles with 72,000 pounds of bombs). R.C. "Sparky" Seabold was the Project Engineer for both the B-32 and XB-36 bombers, and maintained that Consolidated-Vultee management gave the B-36 project low priority during the war, as current production of the B-24 and B-32 was ordered not to be affected. However, by mid-1944 it was evident to Consolidated-Vultee that the PBY was obsolete, the B-24 was at the end of its usefulness, and the B-32 had met its maker in the B-29. The success of the

Two turret remnants of the B-32 program. The right turret was on display at the Minnesota Air and Space Museum in St. Paul until it was sold to a private party in California in 2001. The other turret is in storage at the Smithsonian's Paul Garber Restoration Facility at Suitland, MD. (Minnesota Air & Space Museum and Smithsonian via Dembeck)

The last B-32 relic is a memorial to aviation pioneer John J. Montgomery. It is the slender end of a Davis static test wing panel from a B-32 erected on pylons pointing majestically to the sky. (Pima)

B-29 made it evident that the Superfortress would continue as part of America's post war strategic Air Force. Under pressure Consolidated-Vultee was obligated to continue its post-war future with the ill-conceived prop-powered XB-36 that, ironically, was scheduled to replace the B-32's nemesis, the B-29 Superfortress, as America's global bomber. Meanwhile, in 1943 Boeing had begun preliminary studies on the turbojet-powered bomber, and completed a Model 450 mock-up in 1946. By December 1947 Boeing had two swept wing XB-47 bomber prototypes powered by six jet engines ready, and the Convair B-36 was soon obsolete, even though Consolidated-Vultee engineers unsuccessfully attempted to upgrade by attaching supplemental jet engines.

The Convair B-36 was soon obsolete, as by December 1947 Boeing had two six jet engine, swept wing XB-47 bomber prototypes ready. (USAAF)

Bibliography

Books

Alexander, Thomas, *Wings of Change*, McWhiney, TX, 2003.

Andrade, John, *US Military Aircraft Designations and Serials Since 1909*, Midland Counties Pub., UK, 1979.

Birdsall, Steve, *Flying Buccaneers*, Doubleday, NY, 1979.

Bridgeman, Leonard, (ed.), *Jane's All the World's Aircraft 1945/46*, Arco, NY, 1970.

Caron, George, *Fire of a Thousand Skies*, Web Publishing, CO, 1995.

Clarington, Michael, *Forty of the Fifth, Aerothentic*, Australia, 1999.

Chana, Bill, *Over the Wing: The Bill Chana Story*, Pvt. Printing, CA, 2003.

Clarington, Michael, *Forgotten Fifth*, Private Printing, Australia, 1999.

Craven, W.F., and Cate, J.L., *Army Air Forces in World War 2, Vol. IV: Men and Planes*, University of Chicago Press, Chicago, 1948.

Craven, W.F., and Cate, J.L., *Army Air Forces in World War 2, Vol. Pacific: Matterhorn to Nagasaki*, University of Chicago Press, Chicago, 1948.

Freeman, Roger, *American Bombers of World War 2 Vol.1*, Hylton Lacy, UK, 1973.

Green, William, *Famous Bombers of World War 2*, Doubleday, NJ, 1959.

Grosch, Herbert, *Computer Bit Slices from a Life*, Third Millennium Books, CA, 1991 (www.columbia.edu/acis/history/computer)

Hans, Mort, *The Sperry P-4 Periscope and the Central Station Computer System*, Cradle of Aviation Museum, 2005.

Harding, Stephen & Long, James, *Dominator: The Story of the Consolidated B-32 Bomber*, Pictorial Histories, MT, 1984.

Haugland, Vern, *AAF Against Japan*, Harper, NY, 1948.

Holley, Irving, *Buying Aircraft: Materiel Procurement for the Army Air Forces*, US Army Special Studies, Wash. DC, 1970.

Kenney, Gen. George, *General Kenney Reports*, Duell, Sloan, Pearce, NY, 1949.

Jones, Lloyd, *US Bombers*, Aero, CA, 1974.

Maurer, Maurer (ed.), *Air Force Combat Units of WW-2*, Watts, NY, 1969.

Maurer, Maurer (ed.), *Combat Squadrons of WW-2*, Dept. of the Air Force, AL, 1969.

Munson, Kenneth, *Aircraft of WW-2*, Doubleday, NY, 1972.

O'Leary, Michael, *Consolidated B-24 Liberator: From Production Line to Frontline*, Osprey, UK, 2002.

Sakaida, Henry and Sakai, Saburo, *Winged Samurai*, Champlin, AZ, 1985.

Smith, Jim and Malcomb, McConnell, *The Last Mission*, Broadway Books, NY, 2002.

Stout, Wesley, *Great Engines, Great Planes*, Chrysler Corp. MI, 1947.

Sturzebecker, Russell, *The Roarin' 20': The History of the 312th Bomb Group*, Pvt. Printing, PA, 1976.

Thole, Lou, *Forgotten Fields of America: Volume II*, Pictorial Histories, MT, 1999.

Thole, Lou, *Forgotten Fields of America: Volume III*, Pictorial Histories, MT, 2003.

Wagner, William, *Reuben Fleet and the Story of the Consolidated Aircraft Company*, Aero, CA, 1976.

Weal, E.C., *Aircraft Engines of the World, 1945*, Pvt. Printing, NY, 1945.

White, Gerald, *Billions for Defense*, U. of Alabama Press, AL, 1980.

Wolf, William, *USAAF Jabos in the MTO and ETO: American Fighter-Bombers of World War Two*, Schiffer, PA, 2003.

Wolf, William, *Victory Roll: The American Fighter Pilot and Aircraft in World War Two*, Schiffer, PA, 2001.

Wolf, William, America's *Very Long Range Bombers, Volume 1: The Boeing B-29 Superfortress*, Schiffer, PA, 2005.

Magazines and Newspapers

Adams, John, "Time Traveler: Gerard "Jerry" Vultee", *Downey Eagle*, 4 February 2000.

Aeroplane, 1 August 1947.

Air Enthusiast Quarterly, "Rival to the B-29," #48, December 1992.

Air Force Magazine, "B-32, the Liberator's Big Brother," September 1945.

Air International, "Plane Facts: Superfortress Backup," February 1979

Air News, October 1945.

Ashley, Tom, "Super Liberator," *Southern Flight*, August 1945.

Birdsall, Steve, "Arizona Sundown," *Wings*, December 1969.

Bullock, Brig.Gen. C.R., *Force Magazine*, November 1980.

Chicago Daily Tribune, "4 killed, 63 Hurt by Plane," 11 May 1945.

Chicago Sun, "Bomber Hits Camp; 69 Hurt," 11 May 1945.

Childs, James, "How the Great War on War Surplus Got Won-or Lost," Smithsonian Magazine, December 1995.

Eagle, "AAF Releases Details of Deadliest Aerial Weapon," Volume 4, Special Edition, 1945.

Eagle, "B-32 Crews Trained in Sight of Plant," Volume 4, Special Edition, 1945.

Eagle, "B-32 Dominator Built Without Delaying B-24 Liberator Job," Volume 4, Special Edition, 1945.

Eagle, "B-32 Spare Parts Shipped Before Planes," Volume 4, Special Edition, 1945.

Eagle, "First Flight in 1942 was Secret," Volume 4, Special Edition, 1945.

Eagle, "Fort Worth 'Home' to B-32!" Volume 4, Special Edition, 1945.

Eagle, "Work Begins in 1940 Toward Newest of Superbombers," Volume 4, Special Edition, 1945.

Flight, "B-32 Shot Down Last Enemy Plane during WWII," August 1989.

Flying Review International, May 1965.

General Dynamics Magazine, "B-32 Dominator," December 1980.

General Dynamics Magazine, "B-32 Dominator was the Last Bomber Built for WWII," ND.

Harding, Stephen, "Reluctant Dominator," *Airplane Monthly,* Part 1, April 1989.

Harding, Stephen, "Reluctant Dominator," *Airplane Monthly,* Part 2, May 1989.

Harding, Stephen, "Flying Terminal Inventory," *Wings,* April 1993.

Hehs, Eric, "Beryl Arthur Erickson, Test Pilot," *Code One,* October 1992.

Impact, USAF, September 1944, "B-32 Dominator."

Hutchinson, James, "B-32 Bombers Hit from Luzon," *N.Y. Times,* July 29, 1945.

Johnson, Frederick, "Dominator: Last and Unluckiest of the Hemisphere Bombers," *Wings,* February 1974.

Larson, George, "B-32 Dominator: Alternative to the B-29 Superfortress," *Friend's Journal,* Summer 1999.

Littrell, Gaither, "Consolidated-Vultee B-32," *Industrial Aviation,* September, 1945.

Pacific Observer, "In the Home Stretch of the Pacific War," *Skyways,* July 1945.

Munsell, Jack, "Dominator Mission," *Friend's Journal,* Summer 2000.

O'Leary, Michael, "Hobo Queen II," *Air Classics,* May 1995.

Perkins, Frank, *"The Crash That Saved the B-36,"* Fort Worth Star Telegram, 13 March 1997.

Sack, Maj. Thomas, "About That B-32 on Our Front Cover," *Air Force Magazine,* September 1980.

San Diego Tribune Sun, "Plane Falls on Marine Base," 11 May 1945.

San Diego Union, "San Diego Air Crash Kills 4, Hurts 62," 11 May 1943.

San Diego Union, "Consair-Vultee Deal Confirm: Fleet to Stay," 26 November 1941.

Stuart, John, "B-32 Applies War Lessons," *N.Y. Times,* July, 29, 1945.

Stuart, John, "New Bomber in Raids on Japan," *N.Y. Times,* July 28 1945.

Skyways, October 1945.

Tarranteer, "B-32 Is Unveiled Today as Visitors See Newest AAF 4-Engine Bomber," 1 August 1945.

Tarranteer, "32's Demolish Japanese Base on First Run," 1 August 1945.

Tarranteer, "B-32 Climaxes Consolidated's Air Pioneering," 1 August 1945.

Tarranteer, "B-32 Spare Parts Shipped Overseas Ahead of Planes," 1 August 1945.

Tarranteer, "First FWAAF Personnel Had 'Rugged' Existence," 1 August 1945.

Tarranteer, "Four GIs Use Production Line System to Make Exact Scale Models of B-32s," 1 August 1945.

Tarranteer, "Huge Building Program Readies Field for B-32s," 1 August 1945.

Tarranteer, "Nothing tiny About B-32; Here is Impressive Data," 1 August 1945.

Tarranteer, "Only One Major Accident in 8,500 Hours for 'Sweet' B-32," 1 August 1945.

Tarranteer, "Personnel Worked Hard Pioneering B-32 Training" 1 August 1945.

Tarranteer, "Short Cut B-32 Combat Crew Training Hailed as Another 'First for the FWAAF," Sgt. Earl Rives, 1 August 1945.

Tarranteer, Unique Mobile Training Units Formed Here Feature Mockups to Speed B-32 Training," 1 August 1945.

Trimble, Robert, "America's Mystery Bomber," *Air Classics,* September 1981.

Veronico, Nicholas, "Failure at the Factory," *Warbirds,* March 2005.

Y'Blood, William, "The Second String," *AAHS Journal,* Summer 1968.

Y'Blood, William, "Unwanted and Unloved," *Air Power Historian,* Fall 1995.

Microfilm

USAF Archives: Microfilm B0231, USAF, "312th Bomb Group History," AFSHRC, Maxwell AFB, AL.

USAF Archives: Microfilm A0597, USAF, "386th, 387th and 388th Bomb Squadron History," AFSHRC, Maxwell AFB. AL.

AFSHRC Archives: Microfilm A2607, "Testing the B-32: September 1944 -October 1945," Maxwell AFB, AL.

USAF Archives: Microfilm A7508 USAF, 5th Air Force Bomber Command History, April-June1945, AFSHRC, Maxwell AFB. AL.

USAF Archives: Microfilm A7509 USAF, 5th Air Force Bomber Command History, July-August 1945, AFSHRC, Maxwell AFB. AL.

Manuals

Consolidated-Vultee Aircraft Company, *Model B-32: Erection & Maintenance Manual: Alighting Gear,* Ft. Worth, TX, 1945.

Consolidated-Vultee Aircraft Company, Model B-32: Erection & Maintenance Manual: Auxiliary Power Plant, Ft. Worth, TX, 1945.

Consolidated-Vultee Aircraft Company, *Model B-32: Erection & Maintenance Manual: Bombing Equipment,* Ft. Worth, TX, 1945.

Consolidated-Vultee Aircraft Company, *Model B-32: Erection & Maintenance Manual: Communications Equipment,* Ft. Worth, TX, 1945.

Consolidated-Vultee Aircraft Company, *Model B-32: Erection & Maintenance Manual: Cooling System,* Ft. Worth, TX, 1945.

Consolidated-Vultee Aircraft Company, *Model B-32: Erection & Maintenance Manual: De-icer &b Anti-icer System,* Ft. Worth, TX, 1945.

Consolidated-Vultee Aircraft Company, *Model B-32: Erection & Maintenance Manual: Engine Accessories,* Ft. Worth, TX, 1945.

Consolidated-Vultee Aircraft Company, *Model B-32: Erection & Maintenance Manual: Fire Extinguisher,* Ft. Worth, TX, 1945.

Consolidated-Vultee Aircraft Company, *Model B-32: Erection & Maintenance Manual: Fuselage Equipment,* Ft. Worth, TX, 1945.

Consolidated-Vultee Aircraft Company, *Model B-32: Erection & Maintenance Manual: Gunnery Equipment,* Ft. Worth, TX, 1945.

Consolidated-Vultee Aircraft Company, *Model B-32: Erection & Maintenance Manual: Heating & Ventilating System,* Ft. Worth, TX, 1945.

Consolidated-Vultee Aircraft Company, *Model B-32: Erection & Maintenance Manual: Major Components*, Ft. Worth, TX, 1945.

Consolidated-Vultee Aircraft Company, *Model B-32: Erection & Maintenance Manual: Oil System*, Ft. Worth, TX, 1945.

Consolidated-Vultee Aircraft Company, *Model B-32: Erection & Maintenance Manual: Oxygen System*, Ft. Worth, TX, 1945.

Consolidated-Vultee Aircraft Company, *Model B-32: Erection & Maintenance Manual: Photographic Equipment*, Ft. Worth, TX, 1945.

Consolidated-Vultee Aircraft Company, *Model B-32: Erection & Maintenance Manual: Power Plant*, Ft. Worth, TX, 1945.

Consolidated-Vultee Aircraft Company, *Model B-32: Erection & Maintenance Manual: Power Plant Controls*, Ft. Worth, TX, 1945.

Consolidated-Vultee Aircraft Company, *Model B-32: Erection & Maintenance Manual: Propellers*, Ft. Worth, TX, 1945.

Consolidated-Vultee Aircraft Company, *Model B-32: Erection & Maintenance Manual: Starting System*, Ft. Worth, TX, 1945.

USAAF, *Airplane Commander's Training Manual for the B-32 Dominator*, AAF Manual 51-126-7, 15 July 1945.

USAAF, *Pilot's Operating Manual: B-32 AN01-5EQ-1, 5*, USAAF, 20 July 1944.

USAAF, *Pilot's Operating Manual: B-32 AN01-5EQ-1, 5*, USAAF, 5 March 1945.

USAAF, *Pilot's Operating Manual: B-32 AN01-5EQ-1, 5*, USAAF, 10 May 1945.

Letters, Memos, and Reports

Arnold. Gen. H.H., Air Staff Minutes, 29 March 1945.

Armament Laboratory, "Large Bomb Installation on the B-32 Aircraft," Order No. B4-5-1, 21 April 1945.

Armament Laboratory, "Pull-Up Hoist for the B-32 Aircraft," 16 June 1945.

Blackburn, John, Letter to *Air Force Magazine*, January 1981.

Britt, Maj. Henry, Narrative Report of the Demonstration Mission of March 1945, 24 March 1945.

Britt, Maj. Henry, "The Britt Report," August 1945.

Carlson, Petrus, Memo, May 14, 1943 to T.P. Hall, "Investigation of possible operation of flap controls by possible fouling of the interphone cords or any object falling on the levers of the pilot's side and co-pilot's side."

Cook, Col. Frank, Report: "Combat Test of the B-32 Airplane," to Commanding General, V Bomber Command, APO 710, 17 July 1945.

Cook, Brig.Gen. Orval, Letter: "Functional and Tactical Tests of the B-32," to Brig.Gen. E.L. Eubank, 15 August 1944.

Consolidated-Vultee, "Flight Engineer's Report on Flight Number Six, B-32," R.T. LeVine, 30 August 1944.

Crabb. Brig.Gen. Jarred, Letter to Lt.Col. Selmon Wells, "Combat Test of the B-32 Airplane," 1 June 1945.

Crabb, Brig.Gen. Jarred, Congratulatory Message to Lt.Col. Selmon Wells, 16 June 1945.

5th Air Force Bomber Command Combat Narrative, June 1945.

McElroy, Lt.Col. Stephen, "Report on Special Project 98269S," 2 July 1945.

Gardner, Brig.Gen. Grandison, "Comparative Evaluation of the B-29 and B-32 Airplanes, 26 May 1945.

Gross, Brig.Gen. M.E., Memo, 29 August 1944. "Inspection of the Consolidated-Vultee Aircraft Corporation, Fort Worth, TX," 12 June 1945.

Klein, Maj. J.L., Letter to *Air Force Magazine*, January 1981.

LeVine, R.T., Personal Aero Journal: 14 June 1945 to 13 September 1945.

McKee, Brig.Gen. William, Memo "Comparison of the B-29 and B-32 Airplanes," 30 May 1945.

Mattison, Capt. and Maj. Little, Entry to "B-32 Aircraft," 19 March 1945.

McElroy, Col. Stephen, Letter to Col. Dale Smith, Headquarters of the OC&R. 18 June 1945.

OC&R, Memo: "Production and Use of the B-32 Airplane," 10 August 1945.

Peterson, Col. L.O., "Report on Special Project 982695," 15 June 1945.

Peterson, Col. L.O., Memo: "Utilization of B-32 Airplanes assigned to the PGC," 30 April 1945.

Phillips, Brig.Gen. John, "B-32 Inspection at Fort Worth, Texas," 7 May 1945.

Proving Ground Command, Final Report: "Operational Suitability of Bombing Equipment in the B-32," 6 July 1945.

Roberts, Col. Jack, Memo to Brig.Gen. C.B. McDaniel, 11 February 1945.

Roberts, Col. Jack, Memo to Col. L.O. Peterson, 30 April 1945.

Rogers, D.T. Kelly, W.S. Crockrell, T.P. Hall, Consolidated-Vultee Aircraft Corp., San Diego, CA, 14 May 1943, Declassified 16 September 1958.

Smith, Col. D.C., Telephone conversation of 25 May 1945.

Smith, Brig.Gen. F.H., Memo, 16 December 1944.

Strickland, Brig.Gen. A.C., Letter "B-29 vs. B-32 Airplanes," 26 May 1945.

Tarase, Michael, Letters to the Editor, *Air Force Magazine*, Nov. 1980.

Whitener, 1Lt. Jack, Letter, 28 June 1945.

Williams, Maj. J.C.E., Memo to Col. J.O. Guthrie, "B-32 Defensive Armament," 11 December 1943.

Wilson, Brig.Gen. Donald, Memo to CAS, 14 December 1944.

Wolfe, Maj.Gen. Kenneth, Letter "Comparison of the B-29 and B-32 Aircraft," 28 May 1945.

"XB-32 No.1 Airplane Accumulated Data and Summary of Accident, H.A. Sutton, R.R.

Personnel Narratives

Chana, William, Correspondence to David Dembeck and author, 1979-1981.

Chana, William, Correspondence and Telephone, 2004-05.

Erickson, Beryl, Telephone and Correspondence, 2004-05

James, Cal, Telephone, 2004.

Kirk, Robert, Telephone and Correspondence, 2004-05.

LeVine, R.T, Letters to David Dembeck and author, 1979, 1981.

LeVine, R.T, Correspondence, 2004-05.

Maurer, Erland, Memoirs.

Web Articles

Aviation Enthusiast: *www.aero-web.org*, "Consolidated B-32 Dominator."

Baugher, Joe: *www.jbaugher.com*, "Consolidated B-32 Dominator."

www.Cowtown.net: "Why Not Tulsa?," History of Convair in Texas.

Chilcoat, Rob: *www.geocities.com/sgtroc462/*, "Kingman Army Air Field & WAA Storage Depot 41."

Fast, Howard: *www.trussel.com* "They Remember Girdler,"

Flight Manuals: *www.eflightmanuals.com*, B-32 Flight Manual (description).

Mohave Museum of History and Arts: *www.ctaz.com*, "Kingman Army Air Field."

Military Aircraft: *www.military.cz*, America's WWI Aircraft: "Convair B-32 Dominator."

www.PBS.org: "Brother Can You Spare a Billion?: The Story of Jesse H. Jones."

Truman Library: *www.trumanlibrary.org* , "Gen. Jess Larson Oral History Interview."

USAF biographies: *www.af.mil/bios*, Gen. Thomas Gerrity.

USAF biographies: *www.af.mil/bios*, Brig.Gen. Stephen McElroy

US Warplanes: *www.uswarplanes.net*, "Consolidated-Vultee B-32 Dominator."

Walnut Ridge Army Flying School Museum: *www.walnutridge-aaf.com*, "Walnut Ridge Army Air Field."

Index

(Italics indicates photo or drawing of preceding subject)